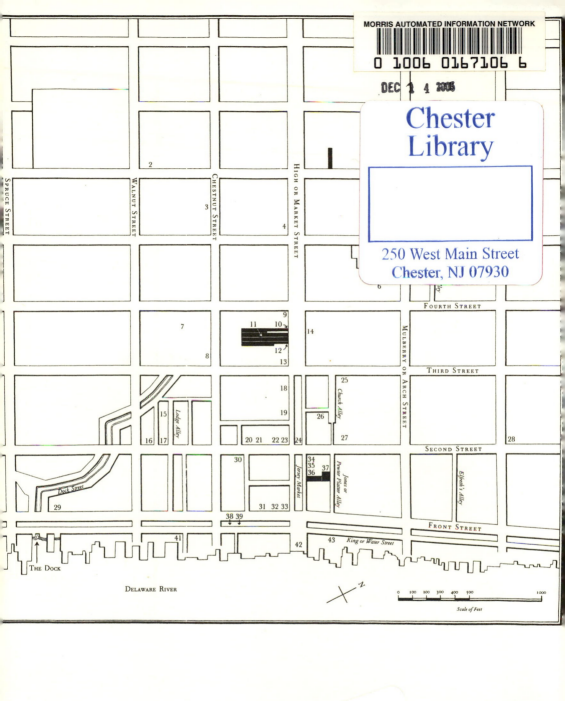

SPRUCE STREET

WALNUT STREET

CHESTNUT STREET

HIGH OR MARKET STREET

MULBERRY OR ARCH STREET

2

3

4

6

FOURTH STREET

7

9

11   10

12

13

14

8

THIRD STREET

18

25

Church Alley

19

26

15   Lodge Alley

27

28

SECOND STREET

16   17

20 21   22 23   24

30

34
35
36   37

Jersey Market

Jones or Pewter Platter Alley

Elfreth's Alley

31   32 33

29

Dock Street

38 39

FRONT STREET

41

42

43   King or Water Street

THE DOCK

DELAWARE RIVER

N

0   100   200   300   400   500   1000

Scale of Feet

The Life of Benjamin Franklin VOLUME TWO

The Life of
Benjamin Franklin

VOLUME TWO

～

Printer and Publisher
1730–1747

J. A. Leo Lemay

PENN

University of Pennsylvania Press
Philadelphia

10   9   8   7   6   5   4   3   2   1

Published by
University of Pennsylvania Press
Philadelphia, Pennsylvania 19104-4112

Library of Congress Cataloging-in-Publication Data

Lemay, J. A. Leo (Joseph A. Leo), 1935–
     The life of Benjamin Franklin / J. A. Leo Lemay.
          p.   cm.
     Includes bibliographical references and index.
     Contents: v. 1. Journalist, 1706–1730—v. 2. Printer and publisher, 1730–1747
     ISBN 0-8122-3854-0 (v. 1 : acid-free paper).—ISBN 0-8122-3855-9 (v. 2 : acid-free
     paper)
     1. Franklin, Benjamin, 1706–1790.   2. Statesmen—United States—Biography.
3. Scientists—United States—Biography.   4. Inventors—United States—Biography. 5.
Printers—United States—Biography.   I. Title.
E302.6.F8L424   2005
973.3'92—dc22
[B]

                                                                              2004063130

Frontispiece: Benjamin Franklin (1745 or 1746) by Robert Feke. Franklin's older brother
John (1690–1756) commissioned the first portrait of Franklin, and he displayed it as a
companion piece to his own portrait in his Boston home. Franklin probably chose how
to present himself. His wig is brown, comparatively short and simple, and the coat and
pants are plain. A gentleman or a professional man would typically be portrayed wearing
a more elaborate, longer, white wig and a more ornamental jacket. The portrait suggests
that the subject is a successful tradesman, a member of the "middling sort." Courtesy,
Harvard University Portrait Collections, bequest of Dr. John Collins Warren, 1856.

Endpapers: Map of Franklin's Philadelphia, with key places of interest indicated.
Reprinted from *The Papers of Benjamin Franklin*, ed. Leonard W. Labaree et al. (New
Haven, Conn.: Yale University Press, 1959–), vol. 2, facing p. 456. Courtesy, Ellen Cohn.

The biography as a whole is dedicated to
Ann C. Lemay, John C. Lemay, Lee C. Lemay, and Kate C. Lemay.

This volume is dedicated to a group of friends who were members of the Natural
History Society of Maryland, 1947–57, especially Romeo Mansueti, John E.
Cooper, Jack Delaney, Henry C. Eichhorn, Jr., Edmund B. Fladung, Joseph
Gentile, John D. Glaser, Harold D. Levy, Anthony G. Marsiglia, Carl Pfeiffer,
James B. Toland, and Manfred Wasserman.

Contents

Appendices

Illustrations

Preface

VOLUME 2 TAKES FRANKLIN from his marriage in 1730 to his retirement as a printer at the very beginning of 1748, a few days after his forty-second birthday. William, Franklin's illegitimate son, was born in 1728 or 1729, and the mystery of his unknown mother is discussed in connection with Franklin's courtship and marriage. On 1 September 1730, Franklin and Deborah Read Rogers joined together in a common-law marriage because her husband, John Rogers, might still have been alive. They took William into their home and brought him up as their son. While Franklin printed on the second floor, Deborah managed the shop on the first, which at first sold legal forms, stationery, and common books, including almanacs, spellers, and Bibles. Gradually, the shop expanded and became a bookstore, stationery shop, and something akin to a general store. On 20 October 1732, Francis Folger Franklin was born, only to die of smallpox at age four. Eleven years after the birth of Francis, Franklin and Deborah had another child, Sarah, on 31 August 1743. By this time, Deborah had help with the house and with Sarah, and she continued to assist Franklin with the shop and his other enterprises. Deborah and the children attended Philadelphia's Anglican Christ Church, where both Francis and Sarah were baptized and where Francis was buried.

Admitted a Freemason in January 1731, Franklin attended his first meeting of St. John's Lodge in February. Three years later, on St. John's Day, 24 June 1734, the young printer was elected grand master, a sign of the local success he was enjoying, partly because of his printing business, especially the *Pennsylvania Gazette*, and partly because of his public-spirited project, the Library Company. On 1 July 1731, Franklin had drafted an "Instrument of Association" for the Library Company of Philadelphia, America's first subscription library. He served as its executive officer, acted for a time as its librarian and for years as its secretary, contributed books to it, printed its first extant catalogue (1741) for free, and nurtured it throughout his life.

To give one indication of the new material in the volume, one might take the Library Company chapter. All Franklin biographers mention the Library Company, but its annual elections have never been discussed. My hypotheses are open to question, but I give evidence that Franklin acted as the CEO from its founding in 1731 to the election of 1740 when he evidently did not win or tie for the most votes. Why? I give several reasons to account for the failure and maintain that he had recovered his popularity by 1746 when he again was acting as the president of the Library Company trustees.

In the fall of 1731, Franklin sponsored his journeyman Thomas Whitmarsh as his printing partner in Charleston, South Carolina. The act was revolutionary in the closed circuit of colonial American printers. Previous patrons of independent printers had been family members, who helped their sons or close relatives start printing businesses. Franklin's system of partnerships was generous—and, he hoped, would be profitable. He gradually established more than half a dozen printing partnerships.

By 1732 the indefatigable Franklin had taught himself to read, write, and translate German fluently. He gradually studied French, Spanish, Italian, and Latin (though he probably had a good knowledge of it earlier), attaining a reading knowledge of them all. In the fall of 1732, finding that his rival Andrew Bradford had arranged to print all the local almanacs, Franklin started his own, *Poor Richard*, predicting in the preface the death of Titan Leeds, the best-known almanac maker of the Middle Colonies. *Poor Richard* instantly became famous and within a decade sold almost ten thousand copies annually. The prefaces were more entertaining, the rustic, humble, naive astrologer persona more engaging, the proverbs (often revised by Franklin) more memorable; and the contents more valuable than those of other almanacs. *Poor Richard* and the *Pennsylvania Gazette* became the mainstays of Franklin's successful publishing business. Even after he retired from printing he continued to supply the copy for *Poor Richard* until 1757, when he wrote the preface (later called "The Way to Wealth") for *Poor Richard Improved . . . 1758* during his voyage to England.

In the spring of 1731, Franklin devised a scheme of thirteen useful virtues and a chart recording the violations that he recorded in part 2 of the *Autobiography*. Franklin's virtues were intended to correct his particular faults. Two were directed at his tendency to be overweight and to prattle, pun, and joke too often (A 68). He included the list and the chart in the *Autobiography* because he thought the method could be valuable for others. Franklin commonsensically concluded that though he fell far short of the ideal envisioned, "I was by the Endeavour made a better and a happier Man than I otherwise should have been" (A 73).

Part 2 of this volume, covering the years 1736–47, begins with Franklin's election as clerk of the Pennsylvania Assembly on 15 October 1736. Besides taking the minutes, the clerk was the legislature's historian and record keeper. The position allowed him to keep up his interest "among the Members, which secur'd to me the Business of Printing the Votes, Laws, Paper Money, and other occasional Jobs for the Public, that on the whole were very profitable." On 5 October 1737 he was appointed postmaster of Philadelphia. That office also helped his printing business. "Tho' the Salary was small," the postmastership "facilitated the Correspondence that improv'd my Newspaper, increas'd the Number demanded, as well as the Advertisements to be inserted, so that it came to afford me a very considerable Income." During these years, Franklin expanded his wholesale paper business and bookselling. He encouraged several papermakers, collected rags for them, and gradually became the largest whole-sale paper merchant in the colonies. In their shops, almost every printer sold almanacs, spellers, and a few other common books, but Franklin gradually added more and more books until he became Philadelphia's largest dealer in books, including used and rare books.

The civic-minded Franklin proposed a fire protection society in the Junto, publicized the necessity of being prepared to fight fires in the 4 February 1734/5 *Pennsylvania Gazette*, and organized the Union Fire Company, Philadelphia's first, on 7 December 1736. In the Junto about 1735 he suggested reforming the night watch and hiring regular watchmen, but this reform was not adopted until 9 February 1751. In addition to public-spirited projects, Franklin devoted considerable time to technical improvements and to science ("natural philoso-phy" was its eighteenth-century name). To hinder counterfeiting paper cur-rency, he devised a new printing technique (reproducing images of plant leaves) and used it on the New Jersey paper currency of 1736.

During the winter of 1737–38, Franklin attempted to design a more efficient stove, and by the winter of 1740–41, he had created the Pennsylvania fireplace. At the time it was the most efficient in the world, and in 1744 he wrote a pam-phlet to popularize it. It not only made rooms warmer than earlier fireplaces but it was less expensive and conserved wood: "My common Room, I know, is made twice as warm as it used to be, with a quarter of the Wood I formerly consum'd." On 21 October 1743, Franklin intended to observe an eclipse of the moon but a hurricane prevented it. Reprinting news of the eclipse, he found Boston newspapers reported it as well as the hurricane that struck there later. That news led him to theorize that though the winds in "all our great Storms" blew from the north, the storms themselves moved up from the south. He did not publish the theory at the time but waited until he had confirmed it by repeated observations. Fascinated by the whirling winds in tornadoes, he ana-lyzed the nature of whirlwinds and waterspouts, correctly theorizing that they had vacuums at the center and ingeniously comparing their motion to the circu-lar motion of water going down a drain.

Some projects failed. Franklin started America's first German-language newspaper, *Philadelphische Zeitung* on 6 May 1732, which soon languished. In partnership with Johann Böhm, he published the *Philadelphier Teutsche Fama* in 1749 and 1750, but Böhm died in July 1751. The next month Franklin started America's first bilingual newspaper, *Hoch Teutsche und Englische Zeitung*, which was discontinued after thirteen issues. He projected the first American magazine in 1740, but his would-be editor, John Webbe, took the idea to his printing rival Andrew Bradford, and they produced the *American Magazine* three days before Franklin's *General Magazine* appeared. The times were premature for any Amer-ican magazine, however, and both folded. He attempted to have the authorities clean up the environment—the dock area in Philadelphia was a public nui-sance—but he succeeded only in making a number of enemies.

A religious Great Awakening came to Philadelphia with the arrival of the Reverend George Whitefield on 2 November 1739. "It was wonderful to see the Change soon made in the Manners of our Inhabitants; from being thoughtless or indifferent about Religion, it seem'd as if all the World were growing Religious; so that one could not walk thro' the Town in an Evening without hearing Psalms sung in different Families of every Street" (A 87). Though theologically worlds apart, Franklin and Whitefield became good friends, mainly because each admired the other's attempts to do good.

On 17 March 1742 Franklin organized and publicized a project to sponsor the exploring trips of botanist John Bartram throughout the colonies and the frontiers to collect American plants, but the funds raised were insufficient. The following year Franklin wrote *A Proposal for Promoting Useful Knowledge*, the founding document of the precursor of America's first scientific society, the American Philosophical Society, but this early attempt did not succeed.

The record of Franklin's life during 1730–47 was one of entrepreneurship in business and in public-spirited projects. Throughout the entire period he wrote prodigiously. Essays, hoaxes, satires, amusing skits, hundreds of news reports and editorial comments, amusing prefaces to *Poor Richard*, original sayings, revised proverbs, and other writings poured from his pen. His family life was happy: he and Deborah loved and cared for one another. Though they suffered the tragedy of the death of their son Francis in 1736, they had the good fortune to have a daughter, Sarah, in 1743. She was five and William was approximately twenty in 1748, when Franklin formed a partnership with his foreman, David Hall, and retired from printing and bookselling.

Franklin had begun experimenting with electricity in 1746 and hoped to have more leisure for scientific pursuits after he retired, but he continued to serve as postmaster and as a wholesale paper merchant. Though many of his business and public projects had succeeded, many had not. His effort to find more time for his scientific research was frustrated, for just at the time he retired, he became caught up in a military crisis.

The noblest question in the world is *What Good may I do in it?*

—*Poor Richard*, December 1737

Others who having scarce a Coat in the World besides that on their Backs,
will venture that, and their Limbs, in saving of Goods surrounded with Fire,
and in rending off flaming Shingles. They do it not for Sake of Reward of
Money or Fame: There is no Provision of either made for them.
But they have a Reward in themselves, and they love one another.

—"Brave Men at Fires," 20 December 1733

PART I

A New Life, Age 24 to 30
(1730–1736)

ONE

Personal and Business Life

I was not to expect Money with a Wife unless with such a one, as I should not otherwise think agreable.—A 70

Rejected

What was wrong with Benjamin Franklin? Philadelphia's eligible young women refused his courtship overtures in 1728, 1729, and early 1730. His failure makes no sense. The evidence suggests that he did not court above his artisan "class." No gossip at the time or later and no correspondence mention Franklin's courtships. Had he expressed interest in one of Philadelphia's fashionable young ladies—like a daughter of James Logan, Andrew Hamilton, Governor Patrick Gordon, or a Pemberton or Norris, records of his presumption would probably exist in the voluminous papers of the Logan, Norris, or Pemberton families—or in the backbiting comments of later enemies. The only person other than Deborah whom we know he courted was a relation of Thomas Godfrey's wife. Godfrey was a genius, but he was a glass-maker, an artisan like Franklin. Though the identities of his wife and her relations are unknown, they were probably artisans also. Franklin reported that he made "Overtures of Acquaintance" to several young women—only to be discouraged by them or their families. His sister Sarah (Franklin) Davenport heard of his courting and wrote him on 15 May 1730 that rumor said he was about to marry, but Franklin replied in June that it was not so.

Dowries were normal, but Franklin found, "I was not to expect Money with a Wife unless with such a one, as I should not otherwise think agreable." Since he was an eligible bachelor, his difficulties are surprising. He was healthy, hardworking, intelligent, honest, attractive, charming, friendly, and highly respected. He was a promising, suitable young bachelor. Franklin attempted to explain away the courting difficulties he experienced: "the Business of a Printer" was "generally thought a poor one" (A 70). Was it? To be sure, Samuel Keimer had failed in 1729 and gone to Barbados, and David Harry, who bought his press and types, failed in 1730 and followed Keimer there. But printer Andrew Bradford was successful. Three years earlier (3 October 1727), he had been elected a Philadelphia Common Councilman—a mark of achievement and success.

Despite his debts in 1729 and early 1730, as well as an unpromising partner (until 14 July 1730), Franklin had already achieved considerable success. He had won the profitable job as printer of Pennsylvania's legislative minutes and its laws. He had edited and owned the *Pennsylvania Gazette* since the fall of 1729—a newspaper that had by mid-1730 become a challenge to Bradford's *American Weekly Mercury*. His future should have seemed bright to prospective brides and prospective in-laws. Why did it not? When telling of his courtships in the *Autobiography*, Franklin concealed the reason for his rejections. He was most likely rejected because he had an illegitimate son, born probably in 1728, for whom he was caring. The existence of an illegitimate son and Franklin's expectation that his future wife would help raise him explain why Franklin was not considered a highly eligible young bachelor.

Mystery: The Date of William's Birth

No one knows when William Franklin was born. Franklin and his son, William, both repeatedly implied that William was born about 1731. Biographical accounts usually give 1731 as William's date of birth.[1] Franklin said William was "now 19 Years of Age" in a letter to his mother, Abiah, on 12 April 1750. Franklin probably meant to suggest to his mother that William was his and Deborah's legitimate son. William kept up the subterfuge to his death, when he was reported to be eighty-two, thus fixing the year of his birth at 1731. Carl Van Doren accepted the date of 1730 or early 1731.[2] In 1959, the editors of *The Papers of Benjamin Franklin* assigned his birth as "c. 1731" (1:lxii). By 1961, however, the editors noted that William Franklin received an ensign's commission on 9 June 1746 in the Pennsylvania troops. Had he been born in 1731, he would have been fifteen in 1746, which, they said, was "unusually young for an officer, even in eighteenth-century America." Therefore, the editors revised their estimate, suggesting that William was born about 1729 (3:474n.).

William Franklin must have secured his father's permission to join Captain John Diemer's company in 1746; otherwise he could not have served as an ensign. It seems to me unlikely that Franklin would have given William permission unless he were about eighteen. He returned alone to Philadelphia in May 1747 to round up deserters from the Pennsylvania forces in order to bring them back to duty at Albany. The revised estimate of the editors of the *Papers* agrees with the major nineteenth-century Franklin biographer, James Parton, who thought William was born about 1729.[3] I believe he was born around 1728.[4] That would make him about eighteen when Franklin allowed him to join Captain Diemar and about nineteen when he returned to Philadelphia in 1747 to bring back deserters.

Who Was William's Mother?

A few Franklinists, including Carl Van Doren, have thought that Deborah Read was the mother of William Franklin.[5] Contemporary eighteenth-century gossips generally did not care or did not know that William was illegitimate until 1762, when he became royal governor of New Jersey. That caused a flurry of bitter comments from disappointed office seekers, from enemies of Benjamin Franklin, from those amused at the hypocrisy of the first two groups, and from persons who considered themselves morally superior.[6] The earliest known reference to William Franklin's illegitimacy occurred in Provost William Smith's attack on him in the *Pennsylvania Journal* on 6 May 1756: "The whole Circumstances of his [William Franklin's] Life render him too despicable for Notice." After the spate of spiteful notices in 1762, the next known reference to William's illegitimacy appeared in a pamphlet published during the 1764 election campaign. In the pamphlet, *What Is Sauce for the Goose Is Also Sauce for a Gander* (prior to October 1764), Hugh Williamson charged that William Franklin's mother was a former prostitute named Barbara, who had been exploited all her life by the Franklins as a servant. (Had the charge any truth, others would have come forward with confirmation.) Williamson also claimed she had recently died and had been buried in a pauper's grave.

Though the mid-nineteenth-century biographer James Parton reported that William was illegitimate and that he was born about 1729, he did not speculate about the identity of William's mother. Jared Sparks, who edited Franklin's writings in ten volumes from 1836 to 1840, was interested in the question. Edward D. Ingraham wrote to Sparks on 22 March 1838: "Has Mr. W. B. Reed sent you word who Governor Franklin's mother was? If not, I must do it for him as soon as he gets the information, which he is to have very soon. My old mother knew . . . never would tell me."[7] Evidently neither Parton nor Sparks, both of whom knew persons who knew Franklin, ever learned the identity of William Franklin's mother.

Deborah Read was not his mother. According to her great-granddaughter, Deborah (Read) Franklin opposed William Franklin's "being a member of the household. But the tenderness of her husband towards herself at last overcame her objections, and her only child, Sarah, . . . was brought up to call him 'brother.'"[8] The 1755 diary of Daniel Fisher confirms Deborah's opposition to William. Fisher wrote that Deborah imagined Franklin sometimes favored William over Sarah, and she occasionally behaved like a jealous stepmother to William, even cursing him to strangers.[9]

Contemporaries of Franklin and his son William wondered about William's mother's identity. Replying to a question from a London acquaintance, George Roberts (the son of Franklin's close friend Hugh Roberts) wrote on 9 October 1763: "'Tis generally known here his Birth is illegitimate and his mother not in good Circumstances, but the Report of her begging Bread in the Streets of this City is without the least foundation in Truth. I understand some small provision is made by him for her, but her being none of the most agreeable Women prevents particular Notice being shown, or the Father and Son acknowledging any Connection with her."[10] Perhaps George Roberts wanted to seem knowledgeable and gave what he thought was a logical reply to the inquiry. He did not identify the mother, and his statement seems vague. The Maryland Loyalist

Reverend Bennet Allen, an infamous slanderer, wrote a sketch of Franklin's life in the London *Morning Post* on 1 June 1779, charging that Franklin had William "by an oyster wench in Philadelphia, whom he left to die in the streets of disease and hunger."

As a port city with numerous transient sailors, Philadelphia naturally had a seamy side. Though the young Franklin, in Silence Dogood No. 13, gave a glimpse of Boston's nightlife, complete with "*Tarpolins* and their Doxies" and a bevy of prostitutes, he wrote little on the subject of Philadelphia's vice. In a 1731 piece against Philadelphia's fairs, he mentioned that they were a rendezvous for prostitutes; and on 3 January 1744/5, as a grand jury member, he listed ten "Disorderly Houses" in Philadelphia, some of them in the section of south Philadelphia near the water called "Hell-Town." He said in the *Autobiography* that the inn at "the Sign of the Three Mariners" was "not a reputable House" (A 25). Franklin, like the young Quaker who advised him to avoid the Three Mariners, must quickly have learned which taverns were reputable and which unsavory. Because of Franklin's account of his early amours, it is natural to suspect that his child resulted from that "hard-to-be-govern'd Passion of Youth," which, as Franklin confessed, "had hurried me frequently into Intrigues with low Women that fell in my Way, which were attended with Some Expense and great Inconvenience, besides a continual Risk to my Health by a Distemper which of all Things I dreaded, tho' by great good Luck I escaped it" (A 70). William Franklin's best recent biographer wrote in 1990, "Historians today lean toward the theory that William's mother was one of the 'low women' whose company Franklin admitted frequenting in the period when he was casting about for a wife."[11]

If however, William resulted from an affair with a prostitute or a "low" woman who was having affairs, how could Franklin have been certain of the infant's paternity? He could not.[12] Unless the mother died in childbirth, she, like Franklin, kept William's birth a secret all her life. It's possible but unlikely that a poor, disagreeable woman (George Roberts's description of the mother) would keep such a secret. After all, once Franklin became famous and his son became governor, would such a woman have remained quiet about her role? Franklin scholar Professor Carla Mulford has suggested that the mother may have been a woman of higher station than Franklin. That might explain how Franklin could be relatively certain that William was his son. I suspect she was the wife of one of Franklin's friends who was away. (In the 18th century, merchants and others who journeyed abroad were often away for a year or more at a time.) Either possibility would explain why Franklin, rather than the mother with Franklin's financial help, took the infant and reared him. These possibilities also might account for the reason that the identity of William's mother was never revealed. Had the mother been a poor woman of the town whom Franklin occasionally helped, her identity would have been known, and Franklin's acquaintances would have identified her. If, however, the revelation of William's parentage would have "ruined" the mother, then Franklin and she both had a good reason for keeping the secret. There is no indication that William ever knew who his mother was.

Poor Richard said, "Three may keep a secret, if two of them are dead."

MARRIED

Illegitimate children were commonly brought up by their mothers; William Franklin was the exception. Historians have considered the plight of unmarried mothers, noting that infants born out of wedlock were not only a financial burden but also ruined any hope for a good marriage: "Impoverished females faced serious obstacles to good marriages. Without dowries or resources, their chances of marrying above their station were virtually nonexistent. . . . Once identified as the mother of an illegitimate child, a woman's chance of marrying respectably diminished ever more."[13] A father bringing up an illegitimate child faced similarly diminished prospects of marriage.

The infant made Franklin's dating difficult. Since Franklin and Deborah brought him up as their own son, Franklin evidently intended for whomever he married to act as William's mother. Franklin's intention to keep and raise William explains why Franklin "was not to expect Money with a Wife unless with such a one, as I should not otherwise think agreable" (A 70). The reason Franklin gave in the *Autobiography*—the supposedly poor business of printing—was a cover-up. Naturally Franklin did not insult his son by calling him an erratum. But William Franklin's birth and parentage are surely among the most important events of Franklin's life—and they are unmentioned in the *Autobiography*.

Though most eligible young women might have scorned Franklin, that was not the case with his former fiancée, Deborah Read Rogers. "A friendly Correspondence as Neighbors and old Acquaintances, had continued between me and" Deborah's mother's "Family who all had a Regard for me from the time of my first Lodging in their House. I was often invited there and consulted in their Affairs, wherein I sometimes was of Service. I pitied poor Miss Read's unfortunate Situation, who was generally dejected, seldom cheerful, and avoided Company." For the second time in the *Autobiography*, Franklin assumed the blame for Deborah's marriage, never mentioning the briefness of the time that elapsed between his sailing from Philadelphia for London and her marriage. "Our mutual Affection was revived, but there were now great Objections to our Union." Her earlier marriage was "indeed look'd upon as invalid" since John Rogers was believed to have a former wife living in England. Franklin emphasized this interpretation in the *Autobiography* by calling Deborah, in the quotation above, "Miss Read." Though Rogers was now believed to have died, it was not certain. If he had died, "he had left many Debts which his Successor might be call'd upon to pay. We ventured however, over all these Difficulties, and I took her to Wife Sept. 1, 1730" (A 71).

Before bureaucracies kept track of every individual's life, many people faced situations similar to that of Deborah Read and Franklin. Her husband, John Rogers, was rumored to have been married before and now was rumored to have died, but if Deborah married, and if Rogers were alive and had not married previously, then she would be a bigamist. Another consideration was that if Franklin married Deborah, John Rogers's creditors might try to sue Franklin for his debts. (Rogers absconded in debt, stealing a slave when he fled in December 1727.) Since an official marriage was impossible, Franklin and Deborah invited their friends and their families to a ceremony on Tuesday, 1 September 1730, and announced that for the future, they would live together as wife and husband. "Ledger A&B," which Franklin began keeping on 4 July 1730, contains the memorandum "D Read came into the House Sept 23."[14] If they joined together on 1 September, one wonders why she did not move in with him then, instead of waiting for more than three weeks. One possible reason is that the house was not ready.

Common-law marriages were not rare in colonial America. Everyone accepted the Franklins' status as a married couple, and not even Franklin's later bitter enemies aspersed him because of his common-law marriage. The Franklins' ritual was common, unlike the ceremony Franklin noticed in the *Gazette* the following year: "a Widow of this Town was married in her Shift, without any other Apparel; upon a Supposition that such a Procedure would secure her Husband in the Law from being sued for any Debts of his Predecessor" (27 February 1731). Years later in the *Autobiography*, Franklin assessed his marriage: "None of the Inconveniencies happened that we had apprehended." That is, John Rogers never appeared, and his creditors never tried to sue Franklin.

Presumably Franklin worked on the morning of his marriage, for several entries in the accounts are recorded under 1 September. The account books contain no entries for the next two days, but the *Pennsylvania Gazette* appeared as usual on Thursday, 3 September, so if Franklin took off any time after the unofficial ceremony on Tuesday afternoon, it was only that afternoon and the following day. Deborah was probably chagrined when her sister Frances borrowed five shillings from Franklin on the day of the marriage. Perhaps Deborah spoke to her sister about it. Though Frances's husband, John Croker, often appears in the accounts, that was the only time that Frances Croker ever did.

Deborah had neither Franklin's ambition nor his intellectual gifts, but she was handsome, hardworking, and loyal. She had her own set of old friends, including Debby Norris, the daughter of Isaac Norris I and sister of the Speaker Isaac Norris II. She had been an early playmate and remained a close friend till death. Though Debby Norris was among the city's gentry, she probably attended the Franklins' ceremony on 1 September 1730, and Deborah Franklin attended her funeral on 18 May 1767. In the *Autobiography* Franklin praised Deborah: "she prov'd a good and faithful Helpmate, assisted me much by attending the Shop, we throve together, and have ever mutually endeavour'd to make each other happy.—Thus I corrected that great *Erratum* as well as I could." Here

Franklin again exonerated Deborah from marrying John Rogers with another reference to his "great *Erratum*" in writing her a letter saying he could not soon return to Pennsylvania (A 71).

Deborah was "as much dispos'd to Industry and Frugality as myself.[15] She assisted me cheerfully in my Business, folding and stitching Pamphlets, tending Shop, purchasing old Linen Rags for the Paper makers, etc., etc." (A 76). The accounts show that "Debby," as Franklin called his wife, commonly kept the shop while Franklin printed upstairs. The shop began as a stationery store but gradually added books, clothing, food, and some hardware. In 1736 Deborah was probably responsible for adding materials for dressmakers and tailors. Deborah kept a record of her credit sales, and it confirms Franklin's appreciation. She generally managed the shop while Franklin printed upstairs, and the shop book entries are primarily in her hand. Franklin wrote a wedding anniversary song for her that said: "Her compassionate Breast feels for all the distress'd," and the accounts support it: she gave credit to a person identified only as "my madman" several times.[16] She also helped by maintaining a household in which one or two persons often roomed and boarded with the Franklins.

Deborah enjoyed entertaining and was known as a good cook. According to Franklin's song, she "chearfully spends, and smiles on the Friends / I've the Pleasure to entertain." Franklin reported from the frontier on 25 January 1756 that her roast beef and veal were "the best that ever were." During the period after Franklin's retirement as a printer, Deborah was the leader of a group of Philadelphia ladies, turning up often in the diary of Charlotte Brown, a key administrator of the hospital maintained by the British forces in America, 1754–56.[17] During Franklin's years abroad, Deborah frequently entertained their old friends. She reported to Franklin on 3 November 1765 that when she had the contractor Samuel Rhoads and his family for tea, "we had the bested Buckwheat Kakes that ever I maid. Thay sed I had ought dun [outdone] my one ought doings."[18]

Deborah identified with and loved her husband, and he seems rarely to have been disappointed in his marriage or in her abilities and character. While Franklin was in England, enemies accused him of supporting the stamp duties and threatened their home on 16 September 1765. Deborah sent away their daughter Sarah, but she herself remained, ready to face the mob and defend their home. Franklin revealed on numerous times that he was proud of her. She was loyal and faithful. From Franklin's account in the *Autobiography*, the marriage was happy. But one bit of hitherto unremarked contemporary evidence suggests that they might have initially had trouble adjusting to marriage.

Rules and Maxims for Promoting Matrimonial Happiness

Just over a month after Franklin and Deborah joined in common-law marriage, he published on 8 October 1730 "Rules and Maxims for promoting Matrimonial Happiness. Address'd to all Widows, Wives, and Spinsters." One cannot help but suspect that Franklin wrote it for Deborah—and for himself. He began by celebrating the "happy State of Matrimony" but added, "Notwithstanding, such is the Perverseness of human Nature . . . that by the Folly and Ill-behaviour of those who enter into it, this is very often made a State of the most exquisite Wretchedness and Misery." The "virtuous of both Sexes, by the Prudence of their Conduct," should attempt to restore the institution of matrimony "to the Honour and Esteem it merits, by endeavouring to make each other as happy as they can" (W 152).

Franklin said that he was addressing women, "not that I suppose their Sex more faulty than the other . . . for I assure them, upon my Honour, I believe the quite contrary," but because "I esteem them better disposed to receive and practice it, and therefore am willing to begin, where I may promise myself the best Success." He rounded off the introduction with a punning risqué proverb: "Besides, if there is any Truth in Proverbs, *Good Wives* usually make *Good Husbands*." He used the more common form of the proverb in *Poor Richard* for 1736: "*Good wives and good plantations are made by good husbands.*" The first rule for promoting matrimonial happiness was fundamental: "The likeliest Way, either to obtain a *good Husband*, or to keep one *so*, is to be *Good* yourself." The third was: "Avoid, both before and after Marriage, all Thoughts of *managing* your Husband. Never endeavour to deceive or impose on his Understanding: nor give him *Uneasiness* (as some do very foolishly) to *try* his Temper; but treat him always beforehand with *Sincerity*, and afterwards with *Affection* and *Respect*" (W 153).

Franklin revealed the common sense that characterized his assessment of the world: "4. Be not over sanguine before Marriage, nor promise your self Felicity without Alloy, for that's impossible to be attain'd in this present State of Things. Consider beforehand, that the Person you are going to spend your Days with, is a Man, and not an Angel; and if, when you come together, you discover any Thing in his Humour or Behaviour that is not altogether so agreeable as you expected, *pass it over as a humane Frailty*." The married state could not preclude the normal causes of unhappiness between persons, and each partner should try to help the other (W 153).

Some rules seem to anticipate Franklin's "Art of Virtue" (i.e., part 2 of the *Autobiography* giving Franklin's supposed plan for moral perfection): "6. Resolve every Morning to be good-natur'd and CHEERFUL that Day: and if any Accident should happen to break that Resolution, suffer it not to put you out of Temper with every Thing besides, and especially with your Husband." He also asked that the couple find satisfaction in helping one another: "8. Be assured, a Woman's Power, as well as Happiness, has no other Foundation but her Husband's Esteem and Love, which consequently it is her undoubted Interest by all Means possible to preserve and increase. Do you, therefore, study his Temper, and command your own; enjoy his Satisfaction with him, share and sooth his Cares, and with the utmost Diligence conceal his Infirmities" (W 153–54).

The list also revealed the economic practicality that Franklin tried (especially early in life, when it was the more necessary) to follow: "13. Have you any Concern for your own Ease, or for your Husband's esteem? then, have a due Regard to his Income and Circumstances in all your Expenses and Desires: For if Necessity should follow, you run the greatest Hazard of being deprived of both." The "Hazard" referred to imprisonment for debt—a common punishment in the eighteenth century. Eight months later, Franklin dramatized the dangers of violating the thirteenth rule in his Anthony Afterwit skit on 10 July 1732. The last rule stressed the self-examination that was part of the New England Puritan inheritance—and that he included in his chart of a day's activities ("daily Examination") in "The Art of Virtue" (A 81): "14. Let not many Days pass together without a serious Examination how you have behaved as a Wife, and if upon Reflection you find your self guilty of any Foibles or Omissions, the best Atonement is, to be exactly careful of your future Conduct."

Finally, because the rules were one-sided, he recurred to the opening—they were as necessary for husbands as for wives: "I am fully persuaded, that a strict Adherence to the foregoing Rules would equally advance the Honour of Matrimony, and the *Glory* of the Fair Sex: And since the greatest Part of them, with a very little Alteration, are as proper for Husbands as for Wives to practice, I recommend them accordingly to their Consideration, and hope, in a short time, to receive Acknowledgments from *married Persons* of both Sexes for the Benefit they receive thereby" (W 154–55). If he wrote the rules for Deborah, he nevertheless knew that they were as important for him as for her. The conclusion contained a typical ironic quip. He knew that people would not follow the rules—and that no one would thank him for them.

Apology for Printers

In May 1731, Franklin brought on himself a maelstrom of criticism. He printed a handbill advertising that a ship would sail for Barbados in a few days and requesting that passengers or freight should come and discuss terms with the captain. Franklin printed dozens of such separate advertisements every month. But this time, perhaps to gain more attention for it, perhaps as a joke, or perhaps to express his irreverence, he and the captain added, "N.B. *No Sea Hens nor Black Gowns will be admitted on any Terms.*" The quip backfired. Most persons in the seaport town of Philadelphia knew that sea hens were noisy, disagreeable birds (and slang for prostitutes)[19] while black gowns of course were ministers. Coupling the two made the insult to the clergy worse. Naturally Philadelphia's ministers were furious with the ship captain and with Franklin. But the captain sailed off to Barbados and Franklin faced the criticism.

Franklin apologized on the front page of the *Gazette* on 10 June 1731. "Being frequently censur'd and condemn'd by different Persons for printing Things which they say ought not to be printed, I have sometimes thought it might be necessary to make a standing Apology for my self, and publish it once a Year, to be read upon all Occasions of that Nature. Much Business has hitherto hindered the execution of this Design; but having very lately given extraordinary Offence by printing an Advertisement with a certain N.B. at the End of it, I find an Apology more particularly requisite at this Juncture, tho' it happens when I have not yet Leisure to write such a thing in the proper Form, and can only in a loose manner throw those Considerations together which should have been the Substance of it." Franklin's introduction undercut the sincerity of the apology. Printers were so often criticized that he needed a "standing apology" that could be "read on all Occasions."

Establishing the ethos of his persona, Franklin portrayed himself as a humble, hardworking printer without leisure to write, even in his own defense. His apology contained six parts: the above introduction; ten general considerations defending the freedom of the press; a brief discussion of the offending advertisement; twelve reasons for printing it; a fable; and a conclusion. The ten general considerations are all related in a serious, high-minded tone. The first was "That the Opinions of Men are almost as various as their Faces; an Observation general enough to become a common Proverb, *So many Men so many Minds*" (1:194).

Since "Printing has chiefly to do with Mens Opinions," the "peculiar Unhappiness" of printing as a profession is that scarcely anything can be published "which shall not probably give Offence to some," whereas a "Merchant may buy and sell with Jews, Turks, Hereticks, and Infidels of all sorts, and get Money by every one of them, without giving Offence to the most orthodox, of any sort; or suffering the least Censure or Ill-will on the Account from any Man whatever." Franklin said that for "anyone to expect to be pleased with every thing that is printed was as unreasonable as to think that nobody ought to be pleased but themselves." In a sentence echoing the thesis of Milton's *Areopagitica* (1644), Franklin wrote: "Printers are educated in the belief that when men differ in opinion, both sides ought equally to have the advantage of being heard by the public; and that when Truth and Error have fair Play, the former is always an overmatch for the latter." One may well question whether most printers really thought so. Franklin, however, no doubt had read the *Areopagitica* and probably did idealistically want to subscribe to the belief. He claimed, "Hence they chearfully serve all contending Writers that pay them well, without regarding on which side they are of the Question in Dispute" (1:194–95).

Printers, Franklin asserted, are employed in serving all parties, so they learn to care little about the right or wrong opinions in what they print. "They print things full of Spleen and Animosity, with the utmost Calmness and Indifference, and without the least Ill-will to the Persons reflected on; who nevertheless unjustly think the Printer as much their Enemy as the Author, and join both together in their Resentment." Printers do not approve of everything they print, for they print opposite and contradictory opinions. Some persons unreasonably say "*That Printers ought not to print any Thing but what they approve*," but if all printers did so, there would be an end to free writing, "and the World would afterwards have nothing to read but what happen'd to be the Opinions of Printers" (1:195).

Franklin added an ironic touch concerning human nature: "if all Printers were determin'd not to print any thing till they were sure it would offend no body, there would be very little printed. If they sometimes print vicious or silly things . . . it may not be because they approve such things themselves, but because the People are so viciously and corruptly educated that good things are not encouraged." In a last general consideration, Franklin said that he and other printers continually discouraged reproducing numerous bad things: "I my self have constantly refused to print any thing that might countenance Vice, or promote Immorality; tho' by complying in such Cases with the corrupt Taste of the Majority, I might have got much Money." He refused to print pieces that would do "real Injury to any Person," no matter how much money he could have made by printing them and no matter how much "Ill-will" he received by his refusal. "In this Manner I have made my self many Enemies, and the constant Fatigue of denying is almost insupportable. But the Publick being unacquainted with all this, whenever the poor Printer happens either through Ignorance or much Persuasion, to do any thing that is generally thought worthy of Blame, he meets with no more Friendship or Favour on the above Account, than if there were no Merit in't at all" (1:195–96).

Lewis P. Simpson wrote that Franklin's "Apology for Printers" was both practical and symbolic, "an announcement of a clear differentiation of the Third Realm in Colonial American history. From this point on, a colonial press— although it was always affected by governmental censorship—would provide for the localization of the politics of literacy in America." American political literature of the eighteenth century reflected the beliefs of the Commonwealth men of England and transformed their ideals into more popular and more democratic forms, first in the newspapers and pamphlets of colonial America, and then in the forms of government during and after the American Revolution. Walter Isaacson, a leading journalist of our time, believed that the "Apology" is among "the best and most forceful defenses of a free press.[20]

Finally taking up the offending advertisement, Franklin tried to depreciate the deliberate insult and to portray himself as an unwitting accomplice. "I come now to the particular Case of the *N.B.* above mentioned, about which there has been more Clamour against me, than ever before on any other Account. In the Hurry of other Business an Advertisement was brought to me to be printed; it signified that such a Ship lying at such a Wharff, would sail for Barbadoes in such a Time, and that Freighters and Passengers might agree with the Captain at such a Place; so far is what's common: But at the Bottom this odd Thing was added, N.B. *No Sea Hens nor Black Gowns will be admitted on any Terms.* I printed it, and receiv'd my Money; and the Advertisement was stuck up round the Town as usual. I had not so much Curiosity at that time as to enquire the

Meaning of it, nor did I in the least imagine it would give so much Offence" (1:197).

Several persons were angry with Franklin for printing the bill. They said he had too much sense not to know what the words implied. They claimed that if they were printers they would not have printed it, despite the payment. They said that the advertisement showed Franklin's abundant malice against religion and the clergy. They therefore declared that they would not subscribe to the *Gazette,* nor have any dealings with Franklin and would try to warn others not to give him any business. "All this," wrote Franklin, "is very hard!" (1:197).

Franklin then directly apologized, but he treated the insult to the clergy as if it were not very serious. "I believe it had been better if I had refused to print the said Advertisement. However, 'tis done and cannot be revok'd. I have only the following few Particulars to offer, some of them in my Behalf, by way of Mitigation, and some not much to the Purpose; but I desire none of them may be read when the Reader is not in a very good Humour." He changed from a serious and formal tone in the ten general defenses above to collegial amusement in the twelve particular justifications.

He began with two evident falsehoods. "1. That I really did it without the least Malice, and imagin'd the *N.B.* was plac'd there only to make the Advertisement star'd at, and more generally read." (He often satirized the clergy, however, and it seems impossible to imagine that he did not recognize the *N.B.* as a criticism.) "2. That I never saw the Word *Sea-Hens* before in my Life; nor have I yet ask'd the meaning of it." But the word was well-known to seamen and others who lived by the ocean. Franklin, a verbal genius, must have known it. He then tried to limit the "black gowns" satirized to Anglican ministers; of course, it referred at least to all the clergy who wore black gowns and, actually, to ministers in general. He also attempted to discount the seriousness of the insult. "And tho' I had certainly known that *Black Gowns* in that Place signified the Clergy of the Church of England, yet I have that confidence in the generous good Temper of such of them as I know, as to be well satisfied such a trifling mention of their Habit gives them no Disturbance" (1:197–98). Franklin claimed in his third defense that the clergy in Pennsylvania and the surrounding area were his customers and some "my very good Friends; and I must be very malicious indeed, or very stupid, to print this thing for a small Profit, if I had thought it would have given them just Cause of Offence." Here he echoed James Franklin in the 4 December 1721 *New-England Courant,* wherein his older brother had said that a number of ministers subscribed to the *Courant,* something they would not do if he were really prejudiced against them.

In the fourth numbered defense, Franklin could not help but use *occultatio* to deride the clergy. He was foolish and amazingly bold in satirizing clergy while ostensibly apologizing. The attack showed that the twenty-six-year-old printer was still the saucy iconoclast of Boston and London—without discretion and without emotional maturity: "That if I have much Malice against the Clergy, and withal much Sense; 'tis strange I never write or talk against the Clergy my self. Some have observed that 'tis a fruitful Topic, and the easiest to be witty upon of all others. I can print any thing I write at less Charge than others; yet I appeal to the Publick that I am never guilty this way, and to all my Acquaintance as to my Conversation" (1:198).

The next three reasons were without substance. "5. That if a Man of Sense had Malice enough to desire to injure the Clergy, this is the foolishest Thing he could possibly contrive for that Purpose. 6. That I got Five Shillings by it. 7. That none who are angry with me would have given me so much to let it alone." After several more excuses, he indirectly asked to be forgiven because he was young and impulsive, and he simultaneously claimed that he had offended less than any previous Pennsylvania printer. In fact, he had already repeatedly given offense to numerous persons, though (thanks perhaps to his patron, Speaker Andrew Hamilton) he had not been prosecuted by the government. His final defense claimed that he had printed more than a thousand advertisements that caused no offense, "and this being the first Offence, I have the more Reason to expect Forgiveness" (1:198–99).

Franklin added the jest book fable of the farmer, his son, and the ass going to town.[21] When the farmer rode the ass, a passerby called out that he was selfish to make the boy walk. They both rode the ass, and the next passerby criticized them for overworking the animal. When the son rode the ass, another person on the road called out that the boy had no respect for his aged father. Then the two walked beside the ass, and a company on the road said they were fools for not riding the ass. Consequently, they resolved to throw the ass over the next bridge. Franklin drew a moral: "Had the old Man been seen acting this last Resolution, he would probably have been call'd a Fool for troubling himself about the different Opinions of all that were pleas'd to find Fault with him: Therefore, tho' I have a Temper almost as complying as his, I intend not to imitate him in this last Particular. I consider the Variety of Humours among Men, and despair of pleasing every Body; yet I shall not therefore leave off Printing. I shall continue my Business. I shall not burn my Press and melt my Letters" (1:199).

It was a strange apology. From a serious, even lofty, defense of the freedom of the press, Franklin went on to satirize ministers even while apologizing for doing so. He concluded by resolving to continue in his own way. And why would he not? Though he had probably lost a few subscribers, the *Pennsylvania Gazette* was doing better all the time, and so was his business. He apologized—after a fashion.

SAWDUST PUDDING

Robert Vaux, the grandson of Franklin's good friend Hugh Roberts, recorded the following anecdote. Though probably apocryphal, it illustrates an aspect of the young Franklin's reputation:

My grandfather & Philip Sing & Luke Morris & some other members of the Junto felt a deep interest in Franklin's success, having many complaints of his tone [in the *Pennsylvania Gazette*], met one day to consider the propriety of advising him to greater moderation. The consultation resulted in the selection of two of them to call on the Editor, & administer a caution on this head. They found Franklin with his sleeves rolled up busy at his press, & on mentioning the purpose of their visit he excused himself from want of time then to hear them, but named an early evening when they, & their constituents should take supper with him, & talk over the matter at leisure. On the appointed night they assembled at his house & some time was spent in communicating their opinions. At length, Franklin's wife made her appearance; she set out a table, covered it with a course tow cloth—placed a trencher & spoon, & a penny porringer for each guest, & having deposited on one end of the board a large pudding, & on the other a stone pitcher filled with water she retired. The Philosopher begged his friends to be seated. To each he served a slice of pudding with some water, & bid them to enjoy themselves. He supplied himself largely and ate heartily, occasionally saying, "Come gentlemen help yourselves we have another pudding in the pot." But his friends tasted, and endeavored in vain to eat their fare.

Finally they looked toward him and were about to leave when Franklin rose and said, "I am happy to have had your Company & to listen to your suggestions—some of you have been my benefactors—your advice is well meant I know, but I do not think with you on this particular subject. You see upon what humble food I can live, & he who can subsist upon saw dust pudding [a name sometimes used for wheat-bran pudding][22] & water, as can Benjamin Franklin, needs not the patronage of any one." Hereupon they parted cordially shaking hands and never more interfered with the intrepid editor.

Isaiah Thomas, the first historian of American printing, recorded a similar anecdote. Though Thomas knew persons who had known Franklin, this anecdote also seems apocryphal. Shortly after Franklin undertook the *Pennsylvania Gazette*, a person brought him a piece to publish in the paper. Franklin looked at it briefly and asked him to return the following day. When he came the next day, Franklin told him, "I have perused your piece, and find it to be scurrilous and defamatory. To determine whether I should publish it or not, I went home in the evening, purchased a twopenny loaf at the baker's, and with water from the pump made my supper; I then wrapped myself up in my great-coat, and laid down on the floor and slept till morning, when, on another loaf and a mug of water, I made my breakfast. From this regimen I feel no inconvenience whatever. Finding I can live in this manner, I have formed a determination never to prostitute my press to the purposes of corruption, and abuse of this kind, for the sake of gaining a more comfortable subsistence."[23]

ESTABLISHED CITIZEN

When did Franklin first vote? As suggested earlier (Volume 1, Chapter 15), he may have done so in 1730, but he surely had by 1 October 1731. He was twenty-five years old, married, and owned his own business, including a thriving newspaper. He was the colony's printer, a member of the Freemasons since February (and a junior warden since June), and the projector (in July 1731) of the Library Company of Philadelphia. He had become a solid citizen and was expected to vote. He was probably first invited to the annual mayor's feast on Tuesday, 5 October 1731. The former mayor, Thomas Griffiths, "made a very splendid Entertainment, at which were present His Honour our Governor, several Gentlemen of the Council, and most of the Gentlemen of this City." Though Franklin was an artisan rather than a gentleman, his ability to write pamphlets (*A Modest Enquiry into the Nature and Necessity of a Paper Currency*), editorials, and newspaper essays made him one of Philadelphia's most important young men.

Three years later, his election as grand master of the Pennsylvania Freemasons certified him as an enterprising and promising young man. As grand master, he gave his own public entertainment on Monday, 24 June 1734, providing "a very elegant Entertainment attended by the Proprietor, the Governor, and several other Persons of Distinction." His feast, however, was not to be compared to the sumptuous celebration given two years later by his fellow Freemason, William Allen, when leaving the office of mayor. Franklin reported in the 20 September 1736 paper: "Thursday last William Allen, Esq; Mayor of this City for the Year past, made a Feast for his Citizens at the Statehouse, to which all the Strangers in Town of Note were also invited. Those who are Judges of such Things, say, That considering the Delicacy of the Viands, the Variety and Excellency of the Wines, the great Number of Guests, and yet the Easiness and Order with which the whole was conducted, it was the most grand and the most elegant Entertainment that has been made in these Parts of America." By that date, Philadelphia's leading citizens expected Franklin's presence.

LANGUAGES

Though Franklin wrote in the *Autobiography* that he began to study languages in 1733, he actually started several years earlier, perhaps even before he left Boston. The account in the *Autobiography* describes his learning to read the modern romance languages French, Italian, and Spanish before Latin, which was then easy to learn. Franklin omits German. It would not help in learning Latin, and listing it in addition to several Romance languages might have made his accomplishments seem quite extraordinary, and Franklin consistently understated his achievements.

He learned German because so many Pennsylvanians were German (locally called "Pennsylvania Dutch") and the language would be useful to him in his personal and business life. He published two books in German in 1730. He probably knew German by then and set Conrad Beissel's books in type. Before 1732, he read German fluently. He translated a letter by some German Palatines who had been mistreated by the ship captain and crew bringing them to America, but did not immediately publish it because he awaited proof that the charges of brutality and starvation were true. Meanwhile, Andrew Bradford secured a copy of Franklin's translation and printed it in the 8 February 1731/2 *American Weekly Mercury*—scooping Franklin with his own work! Irritated, Franklin retranslated the piece, making it "more agreeable to the rude Simplicity of Language and Incoherence of Narrative in the Original." He published it in the *Pennsylvania Gazette* on 15 February 1731/2, along with an account of Bradford's plagiarism (though Franklin did not call it that).

On 6 May 1732, Franklin started America's first German-language newspaper, *Philadelphische Zeitung*. Though Louis Timothée, rather than Franklin, edited it and set in type, Franklin no doubt reviewed its contents. Like many of his ventures, the paper failed. At various later times he again attempted to bring out German newspapers. He printed hundreds of German advertisements separately and often in the *Pennsylvania Gazette*. Franklin no doubt translated some of them into German, as he did the 1755 advertisement (discussed in Volume 3) for General Braddock's wagons. Franklin printed a German pamphlet or book about every other year, but in 1742 he brought out an extraordinary sixteen German imprints. On 14 September 1752 he asked Cadwallader Colden to send him the German translation of Colden's *Explication of the First Causes of Action in Matter*, saying that he would "peruse and return it." He frequently used the German language from 1732 until he left Pennsylvania in 1757. Since he rarely used it thereafter, he had lost his fluency in reading German by 1781 (35:549).

Franklin began studying French about 1730. Two years later, he translated a short French tale to prove his thesis that "Men are Naturally Benevolent as Well as Selfish" (30 November 1732). On 5 July 1733 he wrote an essay on the advantages of "A Scolding Wife" in the *Gazette*, containing a translation of a French poem by Jean Passerat (1534–1602). The editors of the *Papers* identified the source as Abel Boyer, *The Compleat French-Master, for Ladies and Gentlemen* (1729). Boyer, then, was among the texts Franklin studied to learn French. His copy of Andrew Michael Ramsay's *Les voyages de Cyrus* (London, 1727), signed in an early hand, is in the Library Company.[24] So too are copies of Bergerac's *Histoire comique* (Lyon, 1672) and Jean-Baptiste Labat's four-volume *Voyage du chevalier des marchais en Guinée* (Amsterdam, 1731), plus many from his time in France.[25] As part of the propaganda for the Associator militia on 5 December 1747 Franklin translated from French the story of atrocities that the French and Spanish had committed at Portobello. His linguistic ability was well-known to members of the Pennsylvania Assembly. On 14 February 1754, they considered Governor James Hamilton's report that Major George Washington had visited the fort built on the Ohio by the French and that its commandant had declared that "his Orders from the King of *France* are to build more Forts, take Possession of all the Country, and oppose all who shall resist, *English* as well as *Indians*." The report included a letter of 15 December 1753 by the commandant at Fort Le Boeuf, which Franklin translated for his assembly colleagues (4:160).

Franklin read and conversed in French during his two trips to France (28 August–8 October 1767 and 14 July–23 August 1769) and, of course, throughout his mission to France (1777–85). During this last French stay, he wrote numerous letters and literary works, including bagatelles, in French, though he had his French friends correct them, especially in the first few years. We know that he spoke conversational French by 1769, for he and his traveling companion, Dr. John Pringle, were presented at court on 9 September 1769, when Louis XV talked with Franklin during dinner.

After learning French, Franklin studied Italian. He wrote in the *Autobiography* that a friend (possibly David Martin, who became rector of the Philadelphia Academy) was also studying Italian, and the two frequently played chess. Finding that it "took up too much of the Time I had to spare for Study, I at length refus'd to play anymore, unless on this Condition, that the Victor in every Game, should have a Right to impose a Task, either in Parts of the Grammar to be got by heart, or in Translation, etc., which Tasks the Vanquish'd was to perform upon Honor before our next Meeting. As we play'd pretty equally we thus beat one another into that Language" (A 82).

Various bits of evidence confirm Franklin's knowledge of Italian. On 19 May 1749 he thanked James Logan for loaning him both Alessandro Marchetti's Italian translation of Lucretius and Gregorio Leti's *Vita di Sisto V., Pontefice Romano*. He evidently read Machiavelli in Italian (one of the few foreign-language books in the 1741 Library Company *Catalogue*, p. 15). The best evidence for his knowledge of Italian is his correspondence with the Italian scientist Giambatista Beccaria. On 29 May 1766 Franklin wrote Beccaria that he read Italian though he did not write it: "We can therefore correspond with greater facility, if it pleases you, each of us writing in his own language." They frequently corresponded in this manner until Beccaria's death in 1781. Luigi Pio, chargé d'affaires of the Kingdom of Naples in Paris, wrote Gaetano Filangieri on 11 September 1781 that "Mr. Franklin reads Italian rather slowly, but he understands it perfectly well." And Franklin wrote in Italian to correspondents who did not read English. His written Italian was "far from perfect, but he was able to express his thoughts with sufficient clarity."[26]

After learning French and Italian, Franklin turned to Spanish, noting that "with a little Pains-taking [I] acquir'd as much of the Spanish as to read their Books also" (A 97). Franklin probably read *Don Quixote* in Spanish (the Library Company bought a copy before 1741 [*Catalogue*, p. 52]). When Philadelphia's most successful privateer, Captain John Sibbald, seized the ship "*La Nostra Senora de Soledad*, alias *The Prince of Austria*," Franklin reported its capture (6 October 1743) and evidently translated the papers found on the ship, which appeared in the next week's *Gazette*. His Rhode Island friend Catharine Ray knew he read Spanish and sent him a courtship letter addressed to her from

Laureano Donado de el Castillo. He translated it and returned it to her with his letter of 11 September 1755. Years later, writing "I read Spanish a little," he requested on 27 January 1781 that William Carmichael, who was in Madrid, send him the Spanish newspapers and "any new Pamphlets that are curious." When Carmichael quoted a Spanish proverb, Franklin translated and wrote a reply to it on 12 April 1781.[27]

Franklin had occasion to use several modern languages and recommended that they be taught before Latin: "I have already mention'd that I had only one Years Instruction in a Latin School, and that when very young, after which I neglected that Language entirely.—But when I had attained an Acquaintance with the French, Italian and Spanish, I was surpriz'd to find, on looking over a Latin Testament, that I understood so much more of that Language than I had imagined; which encouraged me to apply my self again to the Study of it, and I met with the more Success, as those preceding Languages had greatly smooth'd my Way" (A 97–98). I suspect that he had studied Latin on his own even before he left Boston and that he exaggerated his early ignorance of Latin in order to urge that persons begin with the study of modern languages and then go on, if they wished, to classical Latin. Latin quotations, especially mottos, occur frequently in Franklin's writing throughout his life. He even seems to have created some original ones for the Association flags in 1748,[28] and he often translated bits of Latin into English during the 1730s. Playing on the saying that poets are born, not made, he concocted a self-satirical joke in Latin (20 October 1737) that almanac makers were born not fit, "*almanackorum scriptor nascitur not fit*" (W 272). Knowing that his neighbor James Read avidly read Thomas à Kempis, Franklin punned in Latin on a passage in à Kempis in a letter to Read on 17 August 1745.[29] The classical scholar Richard M. Gummere suspected that "Franklin was much more at home in Latin than has been supposed."[30]

There can be no doubt that Franklin read Latin fluently when he was older. He cited Sallust's *Bellum Catilinae* in *Plain Truth* (1747), both on the title page and in the woodcut, and he provided a translation (3:204). He said of the Greek Orthodox priest Samuel Dömjen, whom he knew in 1748, that he "spoke and wrote Latin very readily and correctly" (5:522). Perhaps most telling are Franklin's corrections of Giambatista Beccaria's Latin treatise on electricity (29 May 1766). Perhaps, though, there was some truth to his statement that he again studied Latin after learning several modern Romance languages. He mentioned to Dr. Benjamin Rush on 12 June 1789 that after learning French, Italian, and Spanish he learned Latin, which he "acquired with great ease."

SECOND VISIT TO NEW ENGLAND, 1733

In 1733 Franklin made his second visit to New England. He had previously returned at age eighteen, in 1724, with Governor Keith's letter of recommendation, to ask his father to sponsor him in business. In June 1730 he wrote that he intended to visit Boston the following spring, but he was evidently too busy. In early September 1733, the twenty-seven-year-old returned as a successful young businessman. He recalled that he had "become more easy in my Circumstances" and so made the journey "to visit my Relations, which I could not sooner well afford" (A 98). Another reason for visiting was business. He was already exchanging newspapers with all the editors in New York and Boston. His accounts reveal he had established business relations with the Boston printer Thomas Fleet, formerly one of the Couranteers, and with the newspaper editor and postmaster Ellis Huske, but a personal visit would help promote further contacts. By 1733 Franklin must have been employing at least two journeymen printers. Their names are unknown, but Franklin left one in charge. That person, as we shall see, proved inadequate.

Franklin probably traveled overland to Boston, visiting the New York printers and booksellers on his way. The traveling salesman must have carried sample publications with him, such as copies of his first *Poor Richard* (1732), Isaac Watts's slow-selling *Psalms* (1729), which he no doubt hoped would do better in the Boston market, and *The Honour of the Gout* (1732). In Boston, he presumably stayed with his parents. They would have had at least one festive family dinner for him—just as they had done years before when the wayward sailor son, Josiah, Jr., briefly visited. Franklin surely spent time with his sisters Jane Mecom, Elizabeth Douse, and Mary Homes, and his brothers Peter Franklin, a shipmaster, and John, a tallow-chandler and entrepreneur. Franklin arranged to sell some of John's "Superfine Crown Soap" (advertised in the *Pennsylvania Gazette* on 16 November). He no doubt called on all the Boston printers and booksellers, learning of their latest ventures and enjoying the company of persons with whom he was now doing business like Thomas Fleet.

A standard Boston tourist attraction for intellectuals was a visit to the studio of the artist John Smibert (1688–1751). The ever-curious Franklin probably saw Smibert on one or more of his Boston trips, if not in 1733 then in 1743 or 1746. Franklin may have visited the Boston Freemasons, though there is no record of his doing so at this time. And surely he looked up some old childhood acquaintances, like schoolmates from the South Grammar School, perhaps Dr. William Clark, Joseph Green, Jeremiah Gridley, and Edmund Quincy, and those who had been involved in the *New-England Courant*'s wars: Nathaniel Gardner, the Reverend Mather Byles, the Harvard scientist Isaac Greenwood (whom he had seen in London in 1725 and 1726), and the Reverend Samuel Mather. He would have heard anecdotes about the wit of the Reverend Mather Byles and about Byles's poetic nemesis, Joseph Green, and perhaps been given copies of some writings by Gridley, Byles, and Green. The talented former Couranteer, Nathaniel Gardner (1692–1770), had presumably stopped writing for the public.

On the way back to Philadelphia, in October 1733, Franklin visited his brother James in Newport, Rhode Island. He and James had been doing business together for at least the previous two years. Franklin had advertised James Franklin's edition of Robert Barclay's *Apology for the True Christian Divinity*

(1729), both in the *Gazette* on 21 December 1731 and at the end of his edition of Alexander Arscott's *Some Considerations Relating to . . . the Christian Religion* (1732). Franklin's accounts show he sold numerous Barclays. James had recently initiated a friendly literary exchange: he recognized his brother's style in the Anthony Afterwit essay (10 July 1732); realized that Franklin probably remembered Abigail Afterwit (one of James Franklin's pseudonyms) from the *New-England Courant* (29 January 1722); reprinted the Anthony Afterwit essay in the *Rhode Island Gazette* (25 January 1733); and replied to it in the same paper as Patience Teacraft. Franklin joined in the intercolonial fun and reprinted Patience Teacraft in the 31 May 1733 *Pennsylvania Gazette*. James Franklin's essay, describing a faithful wife who reclaims her drunken husband by making him a devotee of the tea table, is not as dramatic or as interesting as Franklin's Anthony Afterwit, but the exchange reveals that in addition to financial dealings, the two brothers established friendly relations at least six months before Franklin visited Newport in early October 1733.

Franklin recalled in the *Autobiography*: "Our former Differences were forgotten, and our Meeting was very cordial and affectionate. He was fast declining in his Health, and requested of me that in case of his Death which he apprehended not far distant, I would take home his Son, then but 10 Years of Age, and bring him up to the Printing Business." James was right. He died less than two years later on 4 February 1734/5, his thirty-eighth birthday. James, Jr., was actually three years old in 1733 and not quite five when his father died. Franklin continued, "This I accordingly perform'd, sending him a few Years to School before I took him into the Office. His Mother carry'd on the Business till he was grown up, when I assisted him with an Assortment of new Types, those of his Father being in a Manner worn out.—Thus it was that I made my Brother ample Amends for the Service I had depriv'd him of by leaving him so early" (A 83). Franklin not only educated and brought up young James, but he also assisted Anne Franklin, his brother's widow, by supplying her gratis with his imprints every year (especially with hundreds of the annual *Poor Richard* almanacs).

Rival Philadelphia printer Andrew Bradford criticized Franklin while he was away. On 4 October, Bradford wrote in the *Mercury* that "great Complaint is made among the People in *New-Jersey*, for want of the Acts of Assembly which were passed at *Burlington* the last sitting of the Assembly." Bradford claimed that many persons blamed him, supposing he was at fault in not printing the New Jersey laws. But neither he nor his "father *William Bradford* in *New-York*" had been given the contract. Bradford did not name Franklin, but his point was obvious: Franklin was at fault. Perhaps the slow publication of the New Jersey journals and laws was not really a cause for concern, but something was amiss in Franklin's shop. We do not know why, but the 4 October 1733 *Pennsylvania Gazette* failed to appear. Evidently the job of running the press and editing the newspaper was too much for the journeyman Franklin left in charge. Franklin was needed at home. He arrived back on 13 October, and naturally the *Gazette* subsequently appeared on time.

FAMILY AND CHURCH

To what church did Franklin belong? He was raised a New England Puritan, and in Philadelphia he sporadically attended its closest counterpart, the Presbyterian church. He wrote, "Tho' I seldom attended any Public Worship, I had still an Opinion of its Propriety, and of its Utility when rightly conducted, and I regularly paid my annual Subscription for the Support of the only Presbyterian Minister or Meeting we had in Philadelphia." The Reverend Jedediah Andrews (1674–1747) occasionally called on Franklin and urged him to attend church. Franklin "was now and then prevail'd on to do so, once for five Sundays successively." (Franklin's attendance for five successive Sundays presumably set a personal record.) Not only did Franklin want Sundays for his "Course of Study," but he found Andrews boring and disputatious: "his Discourses were chiefly either polemic Arguments, or Explications of the peculiar Doctrines of our Sect, and were all to me very dry, uninteresting and unedifying, since not a single moral Principle was inculcated or enforc'd, their Aim seeming to be rather to make us Presbyterians than good Citizens." At length Andrews "took for his Text that Verse of the 4th Chapter of Philippians, *Finally, Brethren, Whatsoever Things are true, honest, just, pure, lovely, or of good report, if there be any virtue, or any praise, think on these Things*; and I imagin'd in a Sermon on such a Text, we could not miss of having some Morality: But he confin'd himself to five Points only as meant by the Apostle, viz. 1. Keeping holy the Sabbath Day. 2. Being diligent in Reading the Holy Scriptures. 3. Attending duly the Publick Worship. 4. Partaking of the Sacrament. 5. Paying a due Respect to God's Ministers.—These might be all good Things, but as they were not the kind of good Things that I expected from that Text, I despaired of ever meeting with them from any other, was disgusted, and attended his Preaching no more" (A 77–78). Franklin returned briefly to the Presbyterian church when Samuel Hemphill preached there in late 1734 and early 1735, but after the Hemphill affair in 1735 (Chapter 10), Franklin presumably never returned, though he contributed financial support to the church and its minister.

Deborah had been raised an Anglican and continued to attend Christ Church after she and Franklin joined together in 1730. Franklin must have been paying for a seat for Deborah, and once William started attending for two seats. William was presumably never baptized. Perhaps Franklin's ambivalence concerning church membership was the reason, or perhaps William's baptism would have raised questions about the identity of his mother. Deborah and Benjamin Franklin celebrated the birth of their son Francis Folger Franklin on 20 October 1732. His middle name reveals Franklin's devotion to his mother and to her parents. A sickly child, Francis was finally baptized in Christ Church eleven months later, on 16 September 1733, while Franklin was visiting New

England. Franklin had probably agreed to the baptism before leaving Philadelphia, but Deborah could be strong-minded and may have decided that they had waited long enough and proceeded on her own. As we will see, the decision had far-reaching consequences. After Francis died at age four on 21 November 1736, he was buried at Christ Church.

Rumor held that Francis died of smallpox after being inoculated. Franklin defended inoculation by publishing a notice in the 30 December 1736 *Gazette* that his son had died of smallpox "in the common way of Infection." He added that the rumor probably originated because he was known to believe that "Inoculation was a safe and beneficial Practice." He had intended to have the child inoculated as soon as he recovered from a flux with which he had been long afflicted. But, alas, smallpox took him before his recovery. The death of Francis Folger was a tragedy for Deborah and Franklin. Franklin wrote his epitaph, "FRANCIS F. / Son of Benjamin & Deborah / FRANKLIN / Deceased Nov. 21, 1736 / aged 4 Years, 1 Mon. & 1 Day. / The DELIGHT of all that knew him." Soon after his death, Franklin had "Franky's" portrait painted—the first portrait of any member of the Franklin family. Charles Coleman Sellers, the historian of Franklin's portraits, speculated that a neighbor who was an artist, Samuel Johnson, did the painting. Sellers also thought that since the face looked like Franklin's, the printer probably posed for it. The family resemblance continued, for Deborah wrote Franklin on 13 June 1770 that everyone thought that the picture of Francis could have been drawn from their grandson Benjamin Franklin Bache.[31] Though we have no record of how much Franklin paid for the portrait, it was unusual for an artisan to have a child's portrait painted. It was also, to some degree, an extravagance. The portrait testifies to the Franklins' love for their promising child. More than thirty years later (13 January 1772), Franklin wrote that he had seldom seen "Franky" equaled in all respects and that he could never think of him without a sigh.

Although Franklin was gradually identified with Christ Church, he donated money to each church that appealed to him, including (30 April 1788) Philadelphia's synagogue. (Nazi propaganda in the 1930s, often since repeated, held that Franklin was anti-Semitic. The charge is fraudulent.)[32] When Deborah's prayer book was stolen, Franklin ran an advertisement on 30 June 1737: "Taken out of a Pew in the Church some Months since, a Common Prayer Book, bound in Red, gilt, and letter'd DF on each Corner. The Person who took It, is desir'd to open it and read the *Eighth* Commandment, and afterwards return it into the same Pew again; upon which no further Notice will be taken." The advertisement was repeated on 14 and 21 July, suggesting that if the book were returned, it was not done quickly. Franklin contributed to a fund for refurbishing Christ Church (7 May 1739). Deborah and Franklin's second child, Sarah, was baptized there on 27 October 1743. Despite his numerous associations with the Anglican church, Franklin seems never to have become a member.

When Franklin left for England in 1764, Sarah Franklin expressed a desire to leave Christ Church because the Reverend William Smith, Franklin's political enemy, occasionally preached there. Franklin wrote her, "Go constantly to Church whoever preaches. The Acts of Devotion in the common Prayer Book are your principal Business there; and if properly attended to, will do more towards mending the Heart than Sermons generally can do. For they were composed by Men of much greater Piety and Wisdom, than our common Composers of Sermons can pretend to be. And therefore I wish you wou'd never miss the Prayer Days. Yet I do not mean that you shou'd despise Sermons even of the Preachers you dislike, for the Discourse is often much better than the Man, as sweet and clear Waters come to us thro' very dirty Earth" (8 November 1764). What a comparison! Notice that Franklin viciously condemned Smith while recommending that Sarah go to hear him. Calling Christ Church "our Church" seems as close as Franklin ever came to identifying with it, despite his sustained financial contributions.

The earliest surviving pew books show that Franklin subscribed for three seats from before 1760 (seats for Deborah, William, and Sarah) until his son-in-law started paying for half of the three. (By the time Sarah married Richard Bache, William Franklin was governor of New Jersey and living and attending church there.) Franklin contributed to a fund to purchase a bell and erect a steeple for Christ Church (18 March 1751) and was appointed by the vestry as a manager of a fund for finishing the steeple and purchasing a set of bells (30 October 1752 and 22 February 1753). Sarah married Richard Bache in Christ Church on 29 October 1767,[33] and of course the Bache children were baptized there. When Deborah died, she was buried beside Francis, and Franklin later arranged to be buried beside them. Before the death of Francis, Deborah and Franklin had probably not decided where they would be buried. But once their beloved son Francis was interred in the Christ Church burial ground, it meant that Deborah and Franklin would be also. Perhaps Franklin purchased a plot large enough to accommodate Deborah and himself next to their son when he died in 1736.

Franklin was rarely criticized for not officially adhering to some religion, though many persons commented on it. John Adams believed that Franklin was regarded by various denominations as being nearly of their persuasion: "The Catholics thought him almost a Catholic. The Church of England claimed him as one of them. The Presbyterians thought him half a Presbyterian, and the Friends believed him a wet Quaker."[34] He was chosen a trustee of George Whitefield's "New Building" in the late 1740s because he belonged to "no Sect at all" (A 118).

When William was about six, Franklin advertised in the *Gazette* on 26 December 1734 for a tutor: "Any Person who has a Servant to dispose of that is a Scholar, and can teach Children Reading, Writing, and Arithmetick, may hear of a Purchaser by enquiring of the Printer hereof." Franklin evidently meant to hire a tutor for William. He was brought up to be a gentleman.

WHITMARSH

Franklin and his then-partner Hugh Meredith hired Thomas Whitmarsh, a journeyman printer whom Franklin had known in London, sometime before April 1730. Four months later on 25 August, Franklin "Paid Mr. Whitmarsh since we reckoned in April past, 8.15 & 1/2." Franklin normally settled accounts with his employees every six months (Franklin probably kept an account with his workmen in a ledger that does not survive). Thus April may have marked the sixth month that Franklin and Meredith had employed Whitmarsh. Six months later on 26 October 1730 (after Franklin and Meredith ended their partnership), Franklin paid Whitmarsh £25 for the balance of what he owed him for the previous six months. In May 1731, the South Carolina Assembly offered £1,000 in its currency (about £175 sterling) for a printer who would settle in Charleston, the money to be repaid by work done for the colony. The offer tempted several printers and probably made Franklin think of sponsoring a partner. No doubt on Franklin's recommendation, Whitmarsh became a Freemason, a member of St. John's Lodge, Philadelphia, on 5 July 1731. If Franklin and Whitmarsh knew by that time that he was going to leave shortly, they may have thought that being a Mason might help Whitmarsh in South Carolina, though no Masonic group is known to have existed there at that time.

Franklin and Whitmarsh entered into partnership on 13 September 1731. Franklin's partnerships generally had similar terms (the starting partnership with Hugh Meredith and his retiring partnership with David Hall are exceptions). The partnership was to last six years. Franklin agreed to furnish the printing press, its appurtenances, and four hundredweight of letters, and to ship it to the place of business. Whitmarsh would do the printing or have it performed at his expense. All charges for paper, ink, oil, and other necessaries, together with the charge of all common repairs of the press and rent, would be divided into three equal parts: two parts to be paid by Whitmarsh and one part by Franklin. (Evidently Franklin wanted his partners to be conservative in their outlay.) All money received by Whitmarsh for printing would be divided into three equal parts, with Whitmarsh receiving two parts and Franklin one. (Thus Franklin tried to promote entrepreneurial gambling by his partners.) Whitmarsh would keep accounts of all work and all receipts and disbursements related to printing, with the dates, and submit them whenever required. The accounts would be settled once a year or more often if either partner required it. Franklin settled his accounts every six months, so the twelve-month period was evidently an attempt to accommodate the partner.

During the term of partnership, Whitmarsh could not work with any other printing materials than those belonging to Franklin, nor follow any other business but printing, occasional merchandise excepted. These conditions showed common sense. If the printer became successful with Franklin's materials—and then financed himself, or was financed by others with non-Franklin materials—

the partner could thereafter pay Franklin nothing. Losses by bad debts would be divided by both parties in the same proportion as the money would have been divided if it had been received. Neither party would reap any benefit or advantage by surviving if the other party should die. If Whitmarsh should die, his executors would give the press, types, and other equipment to Franklin. If Franklin should die, the share of money, plus press equipment belonging to him would be due his heirs, provided the heirs of Franklin performed all parts of the agreement with Whitmarsh. At the expiration of six years, Whitmarsh had the right to purchase the press and types, if so disposed, allowing a reasonable abatement for wear and tear. If Whitmarsh did not care to purchase them, he would return them to Philadelphia at his own expense.

The printing house and materials for Whitmarsh cost Franklin £80 sterling. He recorded on 28 October that Whitmarsh had arrived at Charleston on 29 September and that their partnership there began on 1 October. Three printers, however, flocked to Charleston: Thomas Whitmarsh; Eleazer Phillips, Jr., from Boston; and George Webb, presumably the apprentice whom Franklin had trained for Keimer. Each brought a press, types, and other materials necessary for printing. On 18 November, Webb and Whitmarsh petitioned the South Carolina legislature; the following day their petitions were ordered to lie upon the table. Webb printed one tract and vanished from the records. Whitmarsh and Phillips each started a newspaper: Whitmarsh initiated the *South Carolina Gazette* on 8 January 1731/2, and Phillips began the *South Carolina Weekly Journal*; no copy of the latter survives.

Whitmarsh again petitioned the legislature on 27 January 1731/2; Phillips did so on 2 February. A member of the South Carolina Assembly, Othniel Beale, had directly invited Phillips to come to Charleston, and the legislature felt responsible to the Boston printer. On 3 February the House voted to award Phillips the funds. That afternoon, however, the council said that Whitmarsh had better materials and should receive the bonus. But at a meeting the next day, the legislature (both House and council) agreed to give the bounty to Phillips, appointing him printer. Whitmarsh, however, applied again, and on 16 February the legislature awarded Whitmarsh £200 in South Carolina currency. Then Phillips died on 10 July 1732. His father came to settle his estate and was awarded £500 on 15 December 1732. With the death of Phillips, Whitmarsh became South Carolina's printer.[35]

Naturally Franklin sent his partner copies of his own imprints. Under the date 30 October 1731, he sent Whitmarsh three of his recent publications via Captain Benjamin Haskins, who cleared out on 27 November (i.e., the 27 November *Gazette* reported that Haskins had sailed sometime during the preceding week): 200 copies of Godfrey's almanacs, half of them bound and half in sheets; three dozen of Watts's *Psalms* unbound; and 50 copies of Joseph Morgan's *Nature of Riches*. All were advertised in the *South Carolina Gazette* on 8 January 1731/2. According to Franklin's accounts, he continued to send Whitmarsh copies of his publications until 1733. The last issue of Whitmarsh's *South Carolina Gazette* appeared on 8 September 1733. Whitmarsh probably died on 19 or 20 September; he was buried in Charleston's St. Philip's Parish on 22 September.[36]

PARTNERS

There were many successful printers in colonial America before Franklin, but none ever sponsored as independent printers anyone other than family members—sons, nephews, or grandsons. During his Philadelphia career, Franklin sponsored a series of young journeymen as his printing partners. Throughout his life, he attempted to help young persons starting in business. We have noted that he reprinted a *New-England Courant* essay on helping young business persons and that the thirteenth Junto question was, "Do you know of any deserving young beginner lately set up, whom it lies in the power of the Junto any way to encourage?" Since all the Junto members were at the time themselves "young beginner[s]," their attempt to be patrons is surprising.[37] Franklin mentioned in the *Autobiography* that a favor done him by a friend when he began his business "made me often more ready than perhaps I should otherwise have been to assist young Beginners" (A 60). Helping novices remained a concern throughout Franklin's life, and he continued doing so even after death by his bequests for loans to young artisans in Philadelphia and Boston. Since Franklin was not financially secure in 1731, sponsoring a partner in the printing business was a major gamble. It was a good example of his practical idealism. Though he was helping a younger person, he hoped that both the partner and he would ultimately make money. Some partnerships succeeded; some did not.

Scholars have suggested that Franklin formed partnerships to keep the printers he had trained from competing with him in Philadelphia.[38] But the persons he sponsored did not have the capital to set up an independent press, in Philadelphia or elsewhere. Further, it would have been foolish to set up in opposition to Franklin, who, until his retirement in 1748, was the most entrepreneurial and successful printer of colonial America. Naturally Franklin hoped to make money by the partnerships, but in the fall of 1731 sponsoring a printer must have taken all the spare funds Franklin had. Indeed, when he invested in Whitmarsh, Franklin no doubt put off repaying part of the money that he had borrowed to buy out Hugh Meredith. And where did he suddenly come up with a press and types to send to South Carolina with Whitmarsh? It would normally have required about six months to obtain them from London. Franklin must have ordered them for his own expanding business and then decided to use them for a partnership. The venture was not only a compliment to Franklin's willingness to gamble, it was also a tribute to his faith in people in general—and Whitmarsh in particular. In the eighteenth century (and to some degree even in the present), those who have achieved a superior financial or social position sometimes consider themselves innately superior to others and consequently are jealous of their assumed difference. Franklin, however, proud as he was, did not believe himself innately better than others. He wanted to help others who were deserving to attain a position similar to his own. In sponsoring Whitmarsh and other printing partners, Franklin was unique. He was also a good judge of people, and, except for his relatives, sponsored only those in whom he had confidence. One of his partners, James Parker, tried to imitate his example twice—with disastrous results, for both persons proved to be dishonest.[39]

Louis Timothee

Louis Timothée (who changed his name to Lewis Timothy in South Carolina) came to Philadelphia in the fall of 1731 and advertised on 14 October that he kept a "publick *French School*." On 8 April and 6 October 1732, Franklin noted that he had settled accounts with Timothée. Therefore Timothée evidently went to work for Franklin as a journeyman printer in October 1731. Timothée joined the Library Company on 25 March 1732. When the first Library Company books arrived, they were taken to the house he was renting from Robert Grace in Jones Alley. Timothée agreed to be librarian on 14 November 1732. The contract with the Library Company directors required him to keep attendance in the library room on Wednesdays from two to three and on Saturdays from ten till four. At the end of three months he would receive three pounds and whatever further allowance should be thought reasonable. On 6 May 1732, Saturday, Franklin published America's first German-language newspaper, the *Philadelphische Zeitung*, with Timothée as its editor. A second number appeared on 24 June, but the paper evidently failed with that issue.

Franklin probably learned of Whitmarsh's death about the end of October 1733. With the position of printer for South Carolina again open, Franklin must have asked Timothée if he was interested. Timothée wanted to try business on his own, and so Franklin, recalling the competition that Whitmarsh had faced for the semi-sinecure position as printer, suggested that Timothée leave immediately for Charleston. He evidently sailed for South Carolina with either Captain Hugh Percy on the ship *Samuel* (cleared, 25 October *Gazette*) or Captain John Goodwin on the ship *Lydia* (entered out, 1 November *Gazette*). Timothée left abruptly, without taking the time to have the partnership with Franklin drawn up and signed—but Timothée left his power of attorney with his wife, Elizabeth. On 26 November, Franklin signed a partnership agreement with Elizabeth Timothée for her husband, Louis Timothée, to succeed Whitmarsh in South Carolina. The agreement mentioned that Timothée is "now bound on a Voyage to Charlestown in South Carolina." Franklin settled his accounts with Timothée on 26 March 1734, when Mrs. Timothée departed for South Carolina. I assume that she (rather than her husband) took their children and that the six-year-old daughter, Elizabeth, carried the Bible (later a family heirloom, treasured for its associations) given her by Deborah Franklin.[40]

In Charleston on 2 February 1733/4, Timothy resumed publication of the *South Carolina Gazette*. As with Whitmarsh, Franklin sent Timothy copies of his publications. Since Franklin's Philadelphia sales paid for the expenses of printing the materials, he regarded the sales by others as "so much clear Gain" (to Strahan, 31 July 1744). In addition to his other imprints, the accounts show that every fall Franklin sent Timothy three to five hundred *Poor Richard*s. The record of the imprints Franklin actually shipped is incomplete, for in addition to those in the accounts, Timothy advertised several others in the *South Carolina Gazette*: *The Constitutions of the Free Masons* and *The Shorter Catechism* (both 27 July 1734), and all three of Franklin's 1735 Hemphill pamphlets (3 January 1735/6).[41] Timothy died in an otherwise unnamed "unhappy Accident" about 27 December 1738 and was buried on 30 December.[42] (Falling from a horse was the most common "unhappy Accident" in colonial times.)

Elizabeth Timothy

Timothy's widow, Elizabeth (d. 1757), began publishing the *South Carolina Gazette* with the 4 January 1738/9 issue. Though Franklin did not mention the partnership with Whitmarsh in the *Autobiography*, he did briefly discuss Timothy in order to introduce a comment on women's education:

> In 1733, I sent one of my Journeymen to Charleston South Carolina where a Printer was wanting. I furnish'd him with a Press and Letters, on an Agreement of Partnership, by which I was to receive One Third of the Profits of the Business, paying One Third of the Expence. He was a Man of Learning and honest, but ignorant in Matters of Account; and tho' he sometimes made me Remittances, I could get no Account from him, nor any satisfactory State of our Partnership while he lived. On his Decease, the Business was continued by his Widow, who being born and bred in Holland, where as I have been inform'd the Knowledge of Accompts makes a Part of Female Education, she not only sent me as clear a State as she could find of the Transactions past, but continu'd to account with the greatest Regularity and Exactitude every Quarter afterwards; and manag'd the Business with such Success that she not only brought up reputably a Family of Children, but at the Expiration of the Term was able to purchase of me the Printing-House and establish her Son in it. (A 95–96)

Despite Franklin's extended praise for her accounting, Elizabeth Timothy had only one year left in the printing partnership after her husband's death, though she continued doing business with Franklin for another decade. His praise of Elizabeth Timothy seems like another illustration of Franklin's readiness to identify with and to appreciate the talents of independent women. Later he recommended to his daughter, Sarah, that she "acquire those useful Accomplishments Arithmetick, and Bookkeeping" (8 November 1764). Elizabeth Timothy advertised *Poor Richard* and other Franklin imprints in the *South Carolina Gazette*. On 5 June 1746, Franklin sent her "sundry books" to the amount of £12.18.0. Her 23 June advertisement identified them: "Confessions of Faith with Notes at large" (Westminster Confession); Richardson's *Pamela*; James Logan's

Cato on Old Age; *Familiar Instructor*; Watts's *Divine Songs*; Watts's *Psalms and Hymns*; Joseph Allein's *Alarm to Unconverted Sinners*; Dr. Armstrong's *Poems on Health*; Dr. Thomas Cadwalader's *Essays on the Dry Gripes*; and Franklin's *Reflections on Courtship and Marriage*. Franklin sent her another shipment of books on 11 March 1746/7. This time he enumerated them by short title: "6 Conf'ns [the Westminster *Confession of Faith*]; 6 Refl'ns [*Reflections on Courtship and Marriage*]; 6 Health [Armstrong's *On Health; a Poem*]; a doz Watts's Psalter; 2 doz Scotch Psalter." She advertised all these (18 October 1746), plus the others from her 23 June advertisement.

As long as he remained a printer, Franklin did business with Elizabeth Timothy, who left Charleston about the time that Franklin retired as a printer (1748).[43] Her eldest son, however, Peter Timothy (1725?–1782), continued to deal with the partnership of Franklin and Hall. He advertised Franklin and Hall's printing of Richard Peters's *Sermon on Education* along with Franklin's *Reflections on Courtship and Marriage* on 20 November 1752. He bought paper and other supplies from Franklin until the Philadelphian gave up his specialized mercantile business in paper and left for England in 1757. As postmaster general, Franklin named him Charleston's postmaster in 1756. Franklin's official connections with Peter Timothy ceased in 1764 when a separate postal division was created out of the southernmost colonies and the Bahamas. But five years later, Peter Timothy honored the longstanding family connection by naming a son Benjamin Franklin Timothy (1771–1807).[44]

IMPROVING FINANCES

Franklin told an anecdote about his and Deborah's first mark of prosperity in the *Autobiography*: "We kept no idle Servants, our Table was plain & simple, our Furniture of the cheapest. For instance my Breakfast was a long time Bread & Milk, (no Tea.) And I ate it out of a two penny earthen Porringer with a Pewter Spoon. But mark how Luxury will enter Families, and make a Progress, in Spite of Principle. Being Called one Morning to Breakfast, I found it in a China Bowl with a Spoon of Silver. They had been bought for me without my Knowledge by my Wife, and had cost her the enormous Sum of three and twenty Shillings, for which she had no other Excuse or Apology to make, but that she thought *her* Husband deserv'd a Silver Spoon & China Bowl as well as any of his Neighbours." Without directly saying so, Franklin suggested that Deborah's pride and her wanting "to keep up with the neighbors" was responsible for the first step on the road to gentility. "This was the first Appearance of Plate & China in our House, which afterwards in a Course of Years as our Wealth encreas'd, augmented gradually to several Hundred Pounds in Value" (A 76).

The accounts reinforce Franklin's statement. He noted on 20 September 1731 buying "chairs" (the number not specified) for six shillings. At that price, even two chairs had to be "of the cheapest." The Franklins were in much better financial condition four years later. On 27 July 1735, the Franklins bought new materials for four beds. They bought four large mattresses: one for 25 shillings, one for 19 shillings, and two for 18 shillings apiece. They also bought a large bolster for 20 shillings and 3 more bolsters for 15 shillings each; and they bought 3 pillows for 6 shillings each. The material for the beds (evidently excluding the frames) cost 163 shillings (£8 and 3 shillings), whereas the "chairs" in 1731 cost the same as one pillow in 1735.

As we have seen, one indication of the Franklins' improving financial situation was a portrait of their son Francis Folger Franklin. No doubt Franklin correctly recalled that they "kept no idle Servants," but they did have a maid by 1736. On April 24, S (or J?) Warner charged Franklin five shillings for making a pair of shoes for "the maid." The Franklins' son "Franky" was then four years old, and it may be that Deborah had had help since his birth in 1732. As we shall see, the maids continued after their son's death. Franklin indulged his son William not only with a good education but also with that common mark of status, a horse. In colonial America, tradesmen rarely owned a horse. Franklin himself did not until later, but he purchased a small horse for William when the boy was about eight years old. On 18 April 1736, John Biddle charged him 10 shillings and 10 pence for feeding and stabling a horse. We can be fairly certain that the charge was not for a rented horse because five days earlier (13 April), Franklin paid 1 shilling and 6 pence to have a saddle stuffed and altered. In these early years of their marriage, the main indication of the Franklins' improving finances appeared in the accounts concerning the children, William and Francis.

BUSINESS

Few colonial printers took chances on what they published. With the exception of legal forms and almanacs, they set in type only those imprints for which they were paid. As we have seen (Volume 1, Chapter 15), Franklin printed numerous forms, handbills, and advertisements—all together, such items were called job printing.[45] Through the help of scrivener Joseph Breintnall, Franklin stocked the most correct legal forms. Printers also generally stocked the common stationery items: blank and lined paper, pencils, pens, ink, and other writing supplies. The handbills, sermons, pamphlets, religious works, and broadsides issued by most printers were paid for by the advertisers, authors, or booksellers. Franklin's competitor Andrew Bradford was typical. During the years 1729–36 Bradford printed little at his own risk except almanacs and his newspaper, the *American Weekly Mercury*. Bradford did print *A New Version of the Psalms* (1733), but in a rare example of cooperation between rivals, he undertook it jointly with Franklin. A four-page pamphlet in favor of Pennsylvania's Court of Chancery (1736) may have been a gamble by Bradford, but he was probably paid for it. During the same eight-year period, when Bradford seemingly printed no books, pamphlets, or broadsides on his own, Franklin printed at least seventeen.

In addition, like Bradford, Franklin also gambled on almanacs and a news-

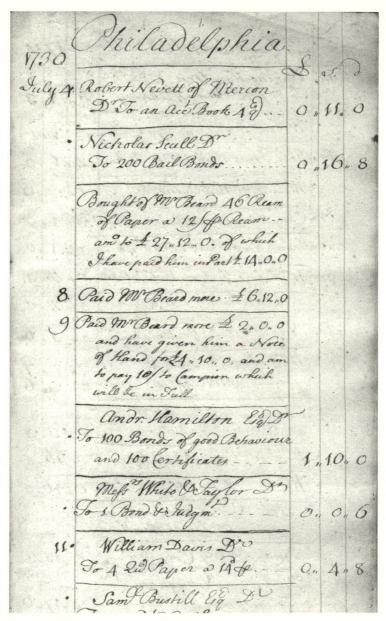

Figure 1. Page 1 of Ledger A&B, Franklin's earliest surviving account book. Ledger A&B contains entries from 1730 to 1738. It primarily records items that others bought from Franklin on credit. Here, on the top of the first page of the ledger, the accounts showing Franklin's debt for paper purchased from the merchant John Beard is an exception. The entries are typical of the materials in the account books. Stationery and ledgers were normally carried by printers ("Robert Nevett of Mercon D[ebto]r To an Acc[oun]t Book"). Legal forms and advertisements were staples of Franklin's business ("Nicholas Scull D[ebto]r to 200 Bail Bonds . . . Andr[ew] Hamilton Esqr. D[ebto]r To 100 Bonds of good Behaviour and 100 Certificates"). The accounts document Franklin's business and life in colonial Philadelphia. Courtesy, American Philosophical Society, Philadelphia.

paper. Even as a starting printer, Franklin ventured to publish a 36-page pamphlet titled *A Modest Enquiry into . . . Paper Currency* (1729), and in the same year, he and Meredith brought out an edition of Isaac Watts's *Psalms of David*, a book of 342 pages, though in a small format. The Watts was a failure, selling slowly over a number of years. In 1730, Franklin made use of Meredith's Welsh background by printing two Welsh ballads and a religious work, *Y Dull o Fedyddio, a dwfr*, of which the single surviving incomplete copy contains 75 pages. In 1731 he printed *The Lady Errant Inchanted: A Poem*, but since no copy exists, we do not know if this was only a broadside ballad or a short pamphlet. In 1732 he undertook a humorous book of 72 pages, *The Honour of the Gout*, which sold slowly (it influenced his 1780 bagatelle, *Dialogue between the Gout and Mr. Franklin*).

In 1733, besides the edition of the psalms with Bradford, he may have brought out at his own expense James Logan's three-page *Latter Part of the Charge to the Grand Inquest*. In 1734, Franklin gambled on at least three imprints: a 94-page book, *The Constitutions of the Free-Masons*, containing a Masonic song not in the English edition; a 56-page health guide, *Every Man His Own Doctor*, to which he added a warning that the herb ipecacuanha was stronger in Pennsylvania than the one found in Virginia; and a brief pamphlet (no copy is known), *The Indian Tale, Interpreted and Told in English Verse*, which sold for six pence. Perhaps he published at his own risk *The Poor Orphan's Legacy*, a 40-page collection of traditional religious material. In 1735 Franklin gambled on *The Gentleman's Pocket Farrier*, an often reprinted title that contained useful information, especially about the care and keeping of domestic animals. It was the kind of publication to which Franklin probably added material, but no copy of his edition is known. He also brought out James Logan's translation of *Cato's Moral Distichs*, a beautifully printed pamphlet of 24 pages. Further, he wrote and published at his own risk three pamphlets defending Samuel Hemphill, at least the first of which, *Some Observations on the Proceedings against the Reverend Mr. Hemphill*, sold well and had two editions. In 1736 he issued a captivity narrative, Jonathan Dickinson's *God's Protecting Providence*, and though no copy of it survives, we know that it was a sizable book. That same year, he brought out another edition of the medical guide, *Every Man His Own Doctor*.

By 1736, Franklin had emerged as colonial America's most venturesome printer. The actual printing of words, however, was only one part of a printer's business. One needed the words to print. Without his own writing, Franklin would have printed far less, and what he printed would have been less enjoyable and less marketable. Franklin was the most productive writer among colonial American printers. Just as he wrote often for the *Pennsylvania Gazette*, he also wrote frequently for his other publications, *Poor Richard* being the best-known. Further, his own writings such as the paper currency pamphlet and the vindication of Samuel Hemphill were his most popular nonperiodical imprints.

The accounts show that Deborah usually ran the shop. The normal day-by-day entries for items purchased on credit are usually in her hand. Franklin later took her chronological entries and arranged them under the names of the purchasers, sometimes recording the date that he entered the account in his ledger rather than the date of the sale. The Franklins gradually expanded the stock sold in the shop. It changed from a stationery store selling legal forms and the commonest books, such as almanacs, spellers, readers, and Bibles, to something like today's convenience stores, stocking a number of the most commonly used foods, clothing, and occasionally hardware. When Franklin took items in barter, he usually sold them in the store. He occasionally purchased a large quantity of some item at a bargain price, then advertised it in the *Pennsylvania Gazette*, and sold it in the shop. Therefore the goods in the shop were not always expanding, but they were continually changing, with the staples being the typical items in a stationery store.

Franklin gradually enlarged the stock of books. On 21 March 1733/4, he advertised a considerable number of books, including the "Whig Bible," Henry Care's *English Liberties*, which printed the Magna Carta and other fundamental documents concerning the rights of the individual. Before 1736, Franklin had become a bookdealer, stocking not only copies of his own and his partners' books but also those published by other American printers. He also began to buy and sell secondhand and rare books.

Printers consumed enormous amounts of paper and ink. Here, too, Franklin was enterprising. Lampblack (i.e., carbon soot, usually produced by burning oil) was an essential ingredient for making ink. Franklin's rival, Andrew Bradford, owned a lampblack house and occasionally advertised lampblack (e.g., 5 March 1728). Franklin purchased a lampblack house on 21 March 1733 and began advertising lampblack on 19 April. Though Franklin had been making and advertising various inks since 23 June 1730, he began experimenting with ink in quantity only after buying the lampblack house. On 17 June 1731, Franklin recorded his trials of "Benjy. Franklin's Ink," "Joseph Breintnal's Ink," "Ink of a very different Sort," "Persian Ink, made by James Austin," "Japan Ink," and "B Franklin's New Ink." He advertised most of these in 1733, and his first advertisement for ink powder appeared on 4 July 1734. Linseed oil was another ingredient for making ink, and Franklin advertised "Choice Linseed Oyl" on 13 April 1738.

Paper was the most expensive continuing supply used by a printer. American papermakers were few, and Andrew Bradford had established relations with the only ones in the Philadelphia area long before Franklin started printing there. But Franklin made inroads on Bradford's monopoly. Franklin began doing business with the Dewees family of papermakers by 1 December 1733 and with Thomas Willcox by 13 March 1735. Franklin's first advertisement for rags, the essential ingredient for good paper, appeared on 11 April 1734: "Ready Money for old Rags, may be had of the Printer hereof." Since cash ("ready money") was in short supply, Franklin's advertisement appealed. The accounts reveal that buying the rags was another of the many chores that Deborah often undertook. The Franklins became the primary source for rags for these paper-makers during the mid-1730s, and by the late 1730s, Franklin bought most of their paper, much of it for resale. As we saw in Volume 1, he had difficulty paying the merchant John Beard for the paper he bought in 1730, but by 1740 Franklin had become Philadelphia's major wholesale paper merchant.

Though Franklin's business was growing during these years, his journeymen printers and apprentices remain largely unknown, except for Thomas Whit-marsh and Lewis Timothy, whom he sponsored as his partners. Stephen Potts, fellow Junto member and bookbinder, turns up in the accounts more than any other person. He lived and boarded with the Franklins, bound books for Frank-lin, and worked as a pressman. He also bound books for others, perhaps paying Franklin a small fee for keeping the accounts and for recommending him. Wil-liam Jones rented a room from Franklin in the fall of 1730 and may have been a journeyman printer working for him. Joseph Rose, son of the poet and printer Aquila Rose, served as an apprentice with Franklin from 1730 until 1739. In the spring of 1733, Franklin hired James Parker as a journeyman printer before seeing the *New York Gazette* advertisement (17 May 1733) for Parker as a runaway apprentice. Franklin encouraged him to return to New York and serve out his apprenticeship. After his apprenticeship, Parker rejoined Franklin as a journey-man, lived at his house, and later became Franklin's partner. By 1735, Franklin must have purchased a second press, for the amount of printing he was doing had become greater than what a single press could handle.

Perhaps the most profitable single job for a colonial printer was printing the government's paper money. As we have seen, Samuel Keimer rehired Franklin in late October 1727 in order to have someone who could print the New Jersey paper currency. After Franklin started his own business, the first currency he printed was the Delaware issue of £12,000 (1729). He brought out Pennsylvania's issue of £40,000 (1731), charging £114.13.5 (1 July 1731). He printed Delaware's issue of £12,000 (1 March 1734/5), charging £61.10.0 (9 April 1735). Using his own newly devised nature printing technique (see Chapter 18), he printed the New Jersey issue of £50,000 in 1736, charging £160 (21 June 1736). He remarked in the *Autobiography* that he made good friends with a number of people in Burling-ton, New Jersey, when he was there with Keimer from late February to May 1728. He no doubt widened his circle of New Jersey friends when he returned there in 1736, and, as we will see, the New Jersey Assembly voted him printer of its votes and laws in 1740. The fact that he took a press and types to Burlington in 1736 proves that he had at least two presses by then (22 July 1736), for the *Pennsylvania Gazette* continued to appear in Philadelphia while he was printing in New Jersey.

To improve the appearance of the *Pennsylvania Gazette*, Franklin ordered a supply of factotems (initial ornamental letters) in late 1730 and used the first one on 11 March 1731. Advertising cuts first appeared in 1734: a small block cut showing a large ship under sail appeared on 30 May; and a cut of a sloop appeared on 12 September. A new typeface (long primer, black letter) appeared in an advertisement on 31 October 1734. The *Gazette* advertisements first took more than two full pages on 29 August 1734. From 1730 to 1736, Franklin's printing business increased every year. By 1736, at age thirty, he was a prominent Philadelphia citizen and a successful printer.

Except for the tragedy of Francis's death, Franklin's family life was happy. Deborah proved to be a good friend as well as a willing partner. William was a bright and promising child. Franklin's social life was enjoyable and the number of his friends was growing. At the same time, he was striving intellectually and morally to improve himself, as we shall see.

TWO

The Art of Virtue

The Morning Question? What Good shall I do this Day? . . . Evening Question,
What Good have I done today?—A 83

MEMBERS OF THE REPUBLIC OF LETTERS—that eighteenth-century unorganized international circle of learned persons who constituted the writers and thinkers of Western countries—wrote often on ethics, virtue, and religion. How to conduct one's life? The question began with manners, a major subject of such popular writings as the *Spectator* and *Tatler* essays, but the question involved attitudes, beliefs, and actions. These, too, were subjects of popular essays. Literati like Pierre Bayle, Voltaire, and Montesquieu in France; Lord Shaftesbury, Bernard de Mandeville, and Jonathan Swift in England; Francis Hutcheson, David Hume, and Lord Kames in Scotland; and numerous others wrote on ethics, virtue, and religion. Franklin was America's preeminent member of the Republic of Letters. Amazingly, he was always careless concerning his contributions. He engaged in the great intellectual quarrels of the day mainly by publishing anonymous or pseudonymous essays in his newspaper, the *Pennsylvania Gazette*. Such essays on the conduct of life as "On Constancy," "On a Pertinacious Obstinacy in Opinion," and "On Simplicity" were written for a local audience and then quickly forgotten.

Franklin contributed to the major questions of eighteenth-century moral philosophy. Are humans naturally altruistic or selfish? What constitutes "A Man of Sense"? Is "Self-Denial the Essence of Virtue"? The persons who posed and argued such questions in Great Britain never had an opportunity to read his writings. Two of his religious parodies, "A Meditation on a Quart Mugg" and "A Parody and Reply to a Religious Meditation," imitated and surpassed Jonathan Swift's burlesques of lugubrious religious essays—but few local readers would have recognized that Franklin was challenging—and trying to surpass—Swift. When he presented the bleakest essay of his early life, "The Death of Infants," few readers realized that he was undercutting the normal bases of religious and moral philosophy.

Had Franklin cared to, he could have gathered these essays together and published them as a long pamphlet, sending copies abroad, where they would have been noticed and would have entered into the ongoing debates on moral philosophy. He did not. He seems to have been satisfied with entering into the debate for himself—as if he were exploring what he thought about the questions. He did, however, repeat one early writing on moral philosophy later, for he thought that it might be useful to others. He made it the major subject of part 2 of his *Autobiography*.

In 1731, Franklin decided to try to impose discipline on his life. He knew numerous schemes for self-discipline, including ones by Aristotle, Francis Bacon, Descartes, Hobbes, Locke, Lord Shaftesbury, Francis Hutcheson, and William Wollaston.[1] Bacon was probably the most important influence. But Franklin's plan was original, tailored to his particular faults. It was not meant for everybody. High-strung, thin people would have little reason to resolve, "Eat not to Dulness." That was a restraint that Franklin, who was inclined to be overweight, should practice. Nor would introverts have occasion to practice "Silence," Franklin's second virtue. Only gregarious persons like the young Franklin, who tended to prattle, pun, and joke too much ("which only made me acceptable to trifling Company" [A 80]), would want to cultivate silence. Though the list was tailored to his personal faults, Franklin held hope for its influence—because of the method, not the actual virtues chosen. The technique had five parts: first, wanting to change oneself and resolving to do so; second, conducting a scrupulous self-examination (one of the many characteristics of Puritanism that influenced Franklin); third, compiling a list of rules to correct one's particular faults; fourth, focusing on one rule or virtue at a time; and fifth, making a daily self-examination to record one's lapses. In the last, Franklin was again (as he had been in founding the Junto) influenced by Cotton Mather's *Bonifacius*: "Frequent self-examination, is the duty and the prudence, of all that would *know themselves*, or would not *lose themselves*. The great intention of self-examination is, to find out the points wherein we are to *amend our ways*."[2]

Franklin presented his youthful project for attaining "moral Perfection," complete with a list of thirteen virtues and a chart showing the hours of a typical day (A 78–91), in part 2 of the *Autobiography*, written in 1784. But the original project, I believe, dates from 1731. Franklin wrote that his first "little Book" became worn out and "full of Holes" (A 86). In the early nineteenth century, his grandson William Temple Franklin reported that he had a copy of the "little Book" containing the plan, dated 1 July 1733, and said that he had a copy of a later version written on "the Ivory Leaves of a Memorandum Book,"[3] thereby implying that the one dated 1 July 1733 was the original. Benjamin Franklin, however, said that each proposed member of the "Society of the *Free and Easy*" should have exercised himself with the "Thirteen Weeks Examination and Practice of the Virtues as in the before-mention'd Model" (A 92). Since the plan for the society was dated 9 May 1731, Franklin must have devised a version of what he later called his "Art of Virtue" before then. A minor supporting reason for accepting a date of the early spring of 1731 is that although the *Autobiography* has topical sections, it is mainly chronological, and Franklin discussed the project and his little book just before the 9 May 1731 observations (A 91).

Another minor reason to think that Franklin had his plan for virtue in mind in 1731 is that he reprinted Addison's *Spectator* No. 447 in the *Pennsylvania Gazette* on 24 June 1731. Addison's thesis was "Custom is a second Nature." Franklin agreed that custom, "if rightly observed, may lead us into very useful Rules of Life." Addison claimed that custom had a "wonderful Efficacy in making every thing pleasant to us." He cited Pythagoras: "Pitch upon that Course of Life which is the most Excellent, and Custom will render it the most Delightful." Impressed with the advice, Franklin later quoted it in *Poor Richard*: "It was wise counsel given to a young man, *Pitch upon that course of life which is most excellent, and Custom will make it the most delightful*. But many pitch on no course of life at all, nor form any scheme of living, by which to attain any valuable end; but wander perpetually from one thing to another" (June 1749).

To Lord Kames

Franklin described the method and purpose of "The Art of Virtue" in a letter to his friend Lord Kames, the Scotch philosopher, on 3 May 1760: "Many People lead bad Lives that would gladly lead good ones, but know not *how* to make the Change. They have frequently *resolv'd* and *endeavour'd* it; but in vain, because their Endeavours have not been properly conducted. To exhort People to be good, to be just, to be temperate, &c. without *shewing* them *how* they shall *become* so, seems like the ineffectual Charity mention'd by the Apostle, which consisted in saying to the Hungry, the Cold, and the Naked, *be ye fed, be ye warmed, be ye clothed*, without shewing them how they should get Food, Fire or Clothing." He repeated the sentiments in the *Autobiography* (A 88–89). Franklin's criticism of former writers echoed Francis Bacon, though he differed because Bacon and most Christian ethical writers believed it necessary to reform the heart and the will before one could reform one's actions.

One could and should, Franklin argued, try to control one's actions. Franklin wrote Kames: "Most People have naturally *some* Virtues, but none have naturally *all* the Virtues. To *acquire* those that are wanting, and *secure* what we acquire as well as those we have naturally, is the Subject of *an Art*. It is as properly an Art, as Painting, Navigation, or Architecture. If a Man would become a Painter, Navigator, or Architect, it is not enough that he is *advised* to be one, that he is *convinc'd* by the Arguments of his Adviser that it would be for his Advantage to be one, and that he *resolves* to be one, but he must also be taught the Principles of the Art, be shewn all the Methods of Working, and how to acquire the *Habits* of using properly all the Instruments; and thus regularly and gradually he arrives by Practice at some Perfection in the Art."

If the person trying to regulate his life does not proceed regularly and gradually, he will probably "meet with Difficulties that discourage him" and abandon the pursuit. "My *Art of Virtue* has also its Instruments, and teaches the Manner of Using them." Some persons might not need a method. "Christians are directed to have *Faith in Christ*, as the effectual Means of obtaining the Change they desire." If such faith were strong enough, it would be effectual. "A full Opinion that a Teacher is infinitely wise, good, and powerful, and that he will certainly reward and punish the Obedient and Disobedient, must give great Weight to his Precepts, and make them much more attended to by his Disciples." Some men, however, have not faith. Others have it "in so weak a Degree, that it does not produce the Effect." For the latter two categories, the plan would be useful. "Our *Art of Virtue* may therefore be of great Service to those who have not Faith, and come in Aid of the weak Faith of others." Even if one had little need of the "Art of Virtue," one "may be more or less benefited by it. It is, in short, to be adapted for universal Use." He confessed to Lord Kames that what he had been writing "will seem to savour of great Presumption." Franklin concluded by hoping for the benefit of Kames's suggestions and corrections when he finished the piece. However, he never sent it to Kames, who died in 1782, two years before Franklin wrote part 2 of the *Autobiography*.

MORAL PERFECTION

When he introduced "The Art of Virtue" in the *Autobiography*, Franklin exaggerated the presumption of the undertaking.[4] He posed as a naïf—a common eighteenth-century literary strategy. His naïf was a speaker so blinded by reason (like Jonathan Swift's narrator in *A Modest Proposal*) that he ignored obvious considerations. The tactic of the naïf made the reader feel superior—until the speaker turned the tables. Franklin began, "It was about this time that I conceiv'd the bold and arduous Project of arriving at moral Perfection. I wish'd to live without committing any Fault at any time; I would conquer all that either Natural Inclination, Custom, or Company might lead me into. As I knew, or thought I knew, what was right and wrong, I did not see why I might not *always* do the one and avoid the other." Every reader knows that the undertaking is impossible and regards the speaker as a fool. When Franklin confessed, "But I soon found I had undertaken a Task of more Difficulty than I had imagined," the reader is justified. The audience silently says, "You dunce! The task is impossible in its nature."

But Franklin continued relentlessly, explaining why he failed—not seeming to realize that the undertaking was futile: "While my *Attention was taken up* in guarding against one Fault, I was often surpriz'd by another. Habit took the Advantage of Inattention. Inclination was sometimes too strong for Reason." Yes, that's true, the reader unwillingly concedes. Then Franklin suppplied a reasonable and indeed logical deduction: "I concluded at length, that the mere speculative Conviction that it was our Interest to be compleatly virtuous, was not sufficient to prevent our Slipping, and that the contrary Habits must be broken and good Ones acquired and established, before we can have any Dependance on a steady uniform Rectitude of Conduct" (A 78). Again, the reader grudgingly concedes.

Franklin explained that though his scheme was not wholly without religion, it did not contain the distinguishing tenets of any particular sect. Believing that his method might be serviceable to persons of any religion, he excluded everything that should prejudice anyone against it. "I purposed writing a little Comment on each Virtue, in which I would have shown the Advantages of possessing it, and the Mischiefs attending its opposite Vice; and I should have called my Book the ART *of Virtue*, because it would have shown the *Means* and *Manner* of obtaining Virtue" (A 88–89). Franklin made the projected "Art of Virtue" part 2 of the *Autobiography*. He gave the thesis that he had meant to include in "The Art of Virtue": "It was my Design to explain and enforce this Doctrine, that vicious Actions are not hurtful because they are forbidden, but forbidden because they are hurtful, the Nature of Man alone consider'd: That it was therefore every ones Interest to be virtuous, who wish'd to be happy even in this World" (A 89). With one stroke, Franklin removed God, theology, and absolutes from ethics. He added a practical argument for morality: "there being always in the World a Number of rich Merchants, Nobility, States and Princes, who have need of honest Instruments for the Management of their Affairs, and such being so rare, no Qualities were so likely to make a poor Man's Fortune as those of Probity and Integrity" (A 89). Franklin here anticipates that aspect of virtue that Tocqueville found characteristically American: "In the United States there is hardly any talk of the beauty of virtue. But they maintain that virtue is useful and prove it every day."[5]

The argument that the Christian ethics are good for people, whether founded on supernatural doctrine or not, often occurs in Franklin's writing. Describing his early beliefs in the *Autobiography*, Franklin wrote: "Revelation had indeed no weight with me as such; but I entertain'd an Opinion, that tho' certain Actions might not be bad *because* they were forbidden by it, or good *because* it commanded them; yet probably those Actions might be forbidden *because* they were bad for us, or commanded *because* they were beneficial to us, in their own Natures, all the Circumstances of things considered" (A 59). He also separated religion from virtue in *Poor Richard*: "Sin is not hurtful because it is forbidden but it is forbidden because it's hurtful. Nor is a Duty beneficial because it is commanded, but it is commanded, because it's beneficial" (October-November 1739). And, as we will see, he expressed a similar belief in writing on the Hemphill controversy (Chapter 10). Franklin's thought was anticipated by Luis Molina, whom he may echo. He also knew Montaigne's version of the idea: "Though I would not follow the right way because it is right, I should however follow it for having experimentally found, that at the end of the reckoning tis commonly the most happy, and of greatest utility."[6]

The caricature of sheer reason that was Franklin's persona in this opening section said: "In the various Enumerations of the moral Virtues I had met with in my Reading, I found the Catalogue more or less numerous, as different Writers included more or fewer Ideas under the same Name. Temperance, for Example, was by some confin'd to Eating and Drinking, while by others it was extended to mean the moderating every other Pleasure, Appetite, Inclination or Passion, bodily or mental, even to our Avarice and Ambition." For the sake of clarity, Franklin resolved to use more categories of virtues with fewer meanings, rather than a few virtues with more meanings. "I included under Thirteen Names of Virtues all that at that time occurr'd to me as necessary or desirable, and annex'd to each a short Precept, which fully express'd the Extent I gave to its Meaning" (A 78–79).

The Virtues

Franklin's list of thirteen virtues was not concerned with ultimate values but instead with ways to correct his personal faults and to improve his situation as a young person in debt. The traditional virtues were the four cardinal ones from the classical tradition—wisdom, courage, temperance, and justice—and the three Christian ones of faith, hope, and charity. Christian writers stressed that love for God and for other humans was the fundamental principle underlying the three theological virtues. Franklin's basic principle, which is only indirectly expressed in the list of virtues, had some similarity to the Christian one. He wrote that true merit or virtue consisted in "*an inclination* join'd with an *Ability* to serve Mankind, one's Country, Friends and Family" (3:419). That is not dissimilar to the injunction to love one another. Shaftesbury, an important influence in Franklin's youth, called "public spirit" a principal virtue, and Franklin occasionally used that term.[7] Though many of his thirteen virtues were traditional ones, others were specific to a modern, time-oriented, capitalistic society, the society in which he lived. When we think of capitalistic values, we often assume that selfish interest is a fundamental component. To Franklin, public spirit was more important than self-interest.

Franklin enumerated the following thirteen virtues: 1. TEMPERANCE. His precept for this classical virtue was simple: "Eat not to Dulness. Drink not to Elevation." Since Franklin became stout as he grew older, he probably did try to diet. 2. SILENCE. Franklin said this unusual (seemingly monastic) virtue was intended to change his habit of "Prattling, Punning and Joking." In 1725, his fellow London printers regarded him as a "jocular verbal Satyrist" (A 47). He resolved, "Speak not but what may benefit others or your self. Avoid trifling Conversation." 3. ORDER. This quality is peculiar to modern, time-oriented society, concerned with efficiency.[8] "Let all your Things have their Places. Let each Part of your Business have its Time" (A 79). 4. RESOLUTION. His precept for resolution was "Resolve to perform what you ought. Perform without fail what you resolve." As defined, *resolution* has qualities of the classical virtue of justice and is similar to perseverance. His 4 April 1734 essay on constancy had as its thesis, "Without Steadiness or Perseverance no Virtue can long subsist."[9]

A seemingly practical, capitalistic-oriented virtue was #5: FRUGALITY. But Franklin's definition of what he meant by frugality was unselfish and humanitarian: "Make no Expense but to do good to others or yourself: i.e. Waste noth-

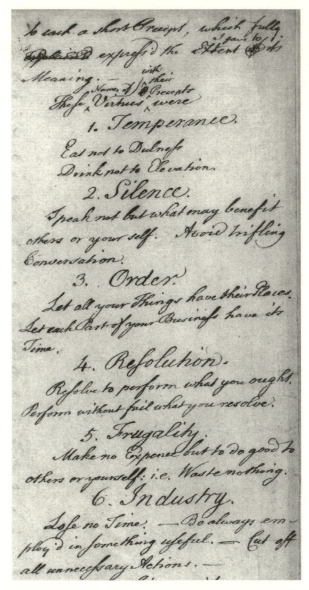

Figure 2. *The first six "Virtues" enumerated in Franklin's scheme for self-discipline, from manuscript page 95 of the* Autobiography. *Part 2 of the* Autobiography, *which contains Franklin's "Art of Virtue," was written in France in 1784, but he originally created the scheme much earlier, probably in the spring of 1731.*

The definition of #5, "Frugality," may hardly seem to describe frugality, for it indirectly says that one should spend money doing good to others (the Christian virtue of charity) or oneself.

Franklin's revisions may be of interest: At the top of the page, he cancelled "explained" and substituted "expressed." After "Extent," he cancelled "of" and inserted "I gave to." After writing "These Virtues were," he inserted "Names of" before "Virtues" and after "Virtues" he inserted "& Precepts," then cancelled the "&" and inserted above it "with their." Courtesy, Huntington Library, San Marino, California.

ing." "To do good to others" contradicts the supposedly selfish capitalistic implications of frugality. Instead, it is allied with the Christian doctrine of loving one's fellow human being. It reveals the generous philanthropy that Franklin, even as a young man, practiced. Frugality was one of the qualities that Franklin had resolved upon in his "Plan of Conduct" formulated at sea in 1726. Now, about six years later, he had finally cleared himself from the debt he was under at that time and from those he had incurred since. 6. INDUSTRY. Though the quality suggests a time-and-machine-oriented value pointing to success in a modern society, industry was a valuable discipline in farming and all other endeavors. "Lose no Time.—Be always employ'd in something useful.—Cut off all unnecessary Actions."

7. SINCERITY. Sincerity is allied to both the classical and Christian traditions of truth. He had included it in his "Plan of Conduct" with what seems to be a surprising praise for such a simple virtue: "aim at sincerity in every word and action—the most amiable excellence in a rational being" (1:100). In metaphysical and theological investigation, Franklin thought that "Sincerity is the Touchstone." Assuming that God would ultimately judge us, then it was "sincerity that will decide our future Condition" (2:79). Franklin explained in a Hemphill tract of 1735: "The Justness of our Reasonings, in all Instances, we cannot absolutely answer for; but we can know whether we be sincere in our Enquiries and Searches after, or Love for any Truth, whereby we suppose God's Glory, and the Good of our Fellow-Creatures may be promoted" (2:79). Sincerity also appealed strongly to him because he was so conscious of the dichotomy between appearance and reality. As Poor Richard said, "What you would seem to be, be really" (March 1744).

Franklin knew, however, that to live in a civilized society, it was necessary to use cant and deceit. He had included sincerity as one of Cato's virtues in Busy-Body No. 3, and then discussed excessive politeness in the sketch of "Patience" in Busy-Body No. 4. Normal politeness required cant. One greets an acquaintance with "How are you?" If experience proves that some hypochondriac among your friends takes the question literally and tells you about his aches, pains, and doctors' diagnoses of his various conditions, you soon learn not to ask him the normal greeting. Franklin appreciated that we all use deceit constantly—and almost always for the benefit of others. His resolution was to use no *hurtful* deceit. "What a beautiful baby!" "What a lovely dress!" "How attractive your new hairstyle looks!" "Have a nice day!" Franklin knew that living is made more pleasant and graceful by the common cant of polite deceit. Franklin's precept on Sincerity was, "Use no hurtful Deceit. Think innocently and justly; and, if you speak; speak accordingly." His definition was cosmopolitan, but the virtue itself also had philosophical and theological implications.

8. JUSTICE, an old classical ideal. Franklin gave it a wide meaning: "Wrong none, by doing Injuries or omitting the Benefits that are your Duty." 9. MODERATION. Franklin's precept began with the traditional classical advice—to

avoid extremes—but then he revealed what he evidently considered a personal failing. He strongly resented injuries to himself, thought that he was probably too sensitive concerning them, and feared that he was tempted to return them more than "they deserve." The virtue spoke directly to what he considered a personal failing. "Avoid Extremes. Forbear resenting Injuries so much as you think they deserve" (A 79).

10. CLEANLINESS. Though physical and spiritual purity are often allied (as in Henry David Thoreau, or in the proverb "Cleanliness is next to godliness"), Franklin's precept is that of fastidious bourgeois modernism: "Tolerate no Uncleanness in Body, Cloaths or Habitation." 11. TRANQUILITY, which Thomas Jefferson ironically if astutely defined as the "*summum bonum* of age,"[10] became in Franklin a normally calm personality. Most commentators on Franklin's personality, including Melville, Carl Becker, and Carl Van Doren, have stressed his tranquility.[11] Though I find multitudinous evidence of his passion, I also see proof of his deliberate and increasing control, perhaps best evidenced by his unchanging countenance and demeanor during the castigation by Alexander Wedderburn in a room at Whitehall called the Cockpit on 29 January 1774. The gloss accompanying tranquility read, "Be not disturbed at Trifles, or at Accidents common or unavoidable."

12. CHASTITY, a Christian virtue that Franklin "frequently" violated as a youth (A 70). But no instances of Franklin's having extramarital sexual affairs after taking Deborah to wife are known. "Rarely use Venery but for Health or Offspring; Never to Dulness, Weakness, or the Injury of your own or another's Peace or Reputation." In this virtue, as in the general philosophy underlying the rules, Franklin was probably influenced by Epicureanism, particularly *De rerum natura*. Franklin's use of the uncommon word *venery* may echo Lucretius's use of "Venus" and "Veneris."[12] The final virtue, #13, HUMILITY, is another Christian one. "Imitate Jesus and Socrates." Franklin was being somewhat ironic in saying that to be humble, one should imitate the two most famous men of Western civilization, though he also had in mind their methods of teaching and of making their points—by anecdotes, parables, and by questioning—as well as the goodness of their characters. Franklin also would have viewed his ironic joke comparing himself to Jesus and Socrates as typical of the vanity people commonly betrayed. It was delicious self-satire, perhaps all the more so because the injunction to imitate Jesus was and is a Christian commonplace.

In sum, four of Franklin's thirteen virtues were rooted in the classical tradition: temperance, resolution, justice, and moderation (nos. 1, 4, 8, and 9). Four were characteristic of the Christian tradition: silence, sincerity, chastity, and humility (nos. 2, 7, 12, and 13). Three bespoke a modern, time-oriented, capitalistic society: order, frugality, and industry (nos. 3, 5, and 6). And two may seem to be outside of the traditional categories: cleanliness and tranquility (nos. 10 and 11).

Such categorization, however, does not quite do justice to the specific meanings that Franklin gave the virtues. Categorized as classical, justice (no. 8) emphasizes duty, which frequently appears in Christian writings. Grouped with the Christian virtues, silence (no. 2) is also, in his definition, a modern, capitalistic virtue. Another Christian one, sincerity (no. 7), can also be considered classical. A third Christian one, chastity (no. 12) is stressed in the Epicurean tradition. One placed in the seemingly capitalistic category, frugality (no. 5) is, in Franklin's definition, a version of the fundamental Christian doctrine to love one another. And finally, though tranquility (no. 11) speaks directly to an aspect of personality and psychology, it is allied with the classical virtue of moderation, just as cleanliness (no. 10) can be considered either a spiritual or a modern value.

PRIDE

Franklin wrote that his list of virtues at first contained only twelve but that a Quaker friend told him he was generally thought proud and convinced him by citing several instances.[13] That seems unlikely. Early in the *Autobiography*, Franklin said that when he was a boy, he met with an example of the Socratic method and "adopted it, dropt my abrupt Contradiction, and positive Argumentation, and put on the humble Enquirer and Doubter" (A 15). He dwelt at length on the "great Advantage" of the habit (A 15–16). Perhaps a Quaker friend in Philadelphia did indeed speak to him about his pride, but throughout his life Franklin urged that persons should be diffident in expressing opinions and in arguments. The authors of the Port Royal *Logic*,[14] which he cited as among the books that most influenced him, stressed the same point. He meant to include humility in his "Art of Virtue," and it was probably in his original list. By pretending that humility was an afterthought put in at a friend's request, he made the virtue more dramatic and memorable. The supposed request also gave him another opportunity to undercut himself—a consummate literary skill especially necessary for an autobiographer, though one that few possess.

Franklin ironically confessed, "I cannot boast of much Success in acquiring the *Reality* of this Virtue; but I had a good deal with regard to the *Appearance* of it" (A 90). And so he again recommended avoiding positive assertions and all words that suggested a fixed opinion. The result was an "Advantage." He specified: "The Conversations I engag'd in went on more pleasantly. The modest way in which I propos'd my Opinions, procur'd them a readier Reception and less Contradiction; I had less Mortification when I was found to be in the wrong, and I more easily prevail'd with others to give up their Mistakes and join with me when I happen'd to be in the right."

He then gave the perceptive reader an ironic, dogmatic, self-parodying example of his vanity in appearing to be humble: "And this Mode, which I at first put on, with some violence to natural Inclination, became at length so easy and so habitual to me, that perhaps for these Fifty Years past no one has ever heard a dogmatical Expression escape me" (A 90).

He concluded part 2 of the *Autobiography* in 1784 with a paragraph that again directly confronted vanity and ended with a paradox (which the previous paragraph had neatly proven): "In reality there is perhaps no one of our natural Passions so hard to subdue as *Pride*. Disguise it, struggle with it, beat it down, stifle it, mortify it as much as one pleases, it is still alive, and will every now and then peep out and show itself. You will see it perhaps often in this History. For even if I could conceive that I had compleatly overcome it, I should probably be proud of my Humility" (A 90–91).

He could not be sure that he would ever be able to return to the *Autobiography* and so, when he concluded part 1 in 1771, part 2 in 1784, and part 3 in 1788, he tried to give the work, as it existed at those times, a sense of closure.[15] In the final paragraph of part 2, Franklin stepped back from his ordinary perspective, the factual, limited viewpoint of everyday experience, to one more philosophical and distanced. The first two sentences deal with "our natural passions," that is, the general passions of humankind, and the point of view is that of a demigod, someone scornful of the struggles of humanity. Then Franklin turns the table on himself and makes the reader the demigod—one who will see the author Franklin inadvertently revealing his own vanity. In the final sentence he drives home the point that vanity is an innate human quality by making a witticism ostensibly against himself, but one that really recurs to an Olympian perspective that views his own actions, as well as humanity's in general, with irony—and some scorn.[16]

Although the prevailing structure of the *Autobiography* is that of simple sequential chronological progress, the conclusion of part 2 has cyclic suggestions. The topic of vanity or pride recalls the beginning of the *Autobiography*, in particular the conclusion of the first paragraph, where Franklin gave as one reason for writing the book that it would gratify his "own vanity." That echo of the earlier passage on vanity, which also splendidly achieved an Olympian perspective by regarding vanity as one of the "Comforts of Life" (A 2), suitably concludes part 2's discussion of Franklin's character.

Franklin had begun the book with an account of the characters of his ancestors. (Of his father he wrote, "I think you may like to know something of his Person & Character" [A 8].) Thus there is a touch of the cyclic round of human life, with various generations striving and failing to escape from the imprisoning effects of their mortality, humanity, and vanity. Although only implicit in part 2 and in several other passages of the *Autobiography*, the interrelation of vanity, human limitation, and cyclic repetition was explicit in Franklin's great bagatelle of six years earlier, "The Ephemera."[17]

The diction at the end of part 2 also suggests a cyclic structure, a return to the book's opening. The direct address to *You* in the sentence "You will see it perhaps often in this History" recalls the opening. *You* of course is the reader. But the opening established the primary supposed reader as Franklin's son William. William Franklin, not the reader, has been the referent for *you* throughout part 1. Franklin's disclaimer about the audience of the *Autobiography* at the end of part 1 (his statement that the latter parts were "intended for the publick" rather than for his son [A 72]), was not added to the manuscript until 1788. Part 2, therefore, at the time Franklin finished it in 1784, still pretended that the primary referent for *You* was William Franklin. Thus the word *You* recalled the opening salutation of the *Autobiography*, "Dear Son," as well as the many references to "you" early in the narrative. Even after Franklin's 1788 addition distanced the reference to *you* from his son to the actual reader, the reference nevertheless recalled the opening.

With these echoes of the opening of the *Autobiography* to jog the reader's memory, the *Autobiography* achieves a finished form, for it has told the story of Franklin's formative years and described the means or method whereby Franklin was able to achieve whatever he had accomplished in life. Thus it recurred back to the opening thematically, by fulfilling his hope in the beginning to present "the conducing means I made use of" (A 1) and by, in the telling of the story, "living" his "Life over again" (A 2). With these various echoes of the *Autobiography*'s opening, the cycle returns from the conclusion of part 2 to the beginning of part 1 and returns again to the conclusion in a constantly turning wheel. Structurally and thematically, the ending of part 2 is aesthetically satisfying.

When finishing part 2, the reader reflects with satisfaction on the last line's clever paradox: "For even if I could conceive that I had compleatly overcome it [pride], I should probably be proud of my Humility." At the same time, the reader acknowledges its truth. In the context of the *Autobiography*, the ostensible paradox recalled Franklin's story of the English lady who lived like a nun in a garret in Duke Street, London, where he lodged in 1726. A priest visited her daily to hear her confession. "I have ask'd her, says my Landlady, how she, as she liv'd, could possibly find so much Employment for a Confessor? O, says she, it is impossible to avoid *vain Thoughts*" (A 48–49).

The Reverend Jonathan Edwards similarly testified, "Pride . . . is the most hidden, secret, and deceitful of all lusts, and often creeps insensibly into the midst of religion; even, sometimes, under the disguise of humility itself."[18] Franklin wrote in *Poor Richard* for August 1749: "Pride is said to be the *last* vice the good man gets clear of, 'Tis a meer *Proteus*, and disguises itself under all manner of appearances, putting on sometimes even the mark of *humility*. If some are proud of neatness and propriety of dress; others are equally so of despising it, and acting the perpetual sloven." The nineteen-year-old Franklin had mentioned in his *Dissertation on Liberty and Necessity* that many persons take "Pride in being thought humble" (1:68). Pride, thought Franklin when taking an Olympian posture, was a necessary part of being human.

METHOD

Franklin planned the order of the virtues so that the early ones would facilitate acquiring the later: "I judg'd it would be well not to distract my Attention by attempting the whole at once, but to fix it on one of them at a time, and when I should be Master of that, then to proceed to another, and so on till I should have gone thro' the thirteen. And as the previous Acquisition of some might facilitate the Acquisition of certain others, I arrang'd them with that View as they stand above. *Temperance* first, as it tends to procure that Coolness and Clearness of Head, which is so necessary where constant Vigilance was to be kept up, and Guard maintained, against the unremitting Attraction of ancient Habits, and the Force of perpetual Temptations." If he acquired some degree of temperance, Franklin thought that silence would be easier. He wanted "to gain Knowledge at the same time that I improv'd in Virtue." Since in conversation, knowledge "was obtain'd rather by the Use of the Ears than of the Tongue," and since he wanted "to break a Habit I was getting into of Prattling, Punning and Joking, which only made me acceptable to trifling Company, I gave *Silence* the second Place" (A 80).

Next came *order*, which Franklin "expected would allow me more Time for attending to my Project and my Studies; RESOLUTION, once become habitual, would keep me firm in my Endeavours to obtain all the subsequent Virtues; *Frugality* and *Industry*, by freeing me from my remaining Debt, and producing Affluence and Independence would make more easy the Practice of *Sincerity* and *Justice*, &c. &c." (A 80–81).

Frugality and *industry* were not virtues in themselves but instruments, means to an end.[19] By them Franklin hoped to avoid poverty, necessity, and dependence—all of which made virtues like *sincerity* and *justice* difficult. When Franklin drafted his scheme of virtues in 1731, his would-be patron, Governor William Keith, was in debtor's prison. Franklin had foolishly spent the money Samuel Vernon had asked him to receive—and was for several years thereafter subject to imprisonment if Vernon had pressed him; debt was a crime in the eighteenth century. Industry and frugality led to "the early Easiness of his Circumstances, and Acquisition of his Fortune, with all that Knowledge which enabled him to be an useful Citizen, and obtain'd for him some Degree of Reputation among the Learned" (A 88).

Franklin believed that daily review of his conduct "would be necessary" and so "contriv'd the following Method": He made a little book in which he allotted a page for each virtue. "I rul'd each Page with red Ink, so as to have seven Columns, one for each Day of the Week, marking each Column with a Letter for the Day. I cross'd these Columns with thirteen red Lines, marking the Beginning of each Line with the first Letter of one of the Virtues, on which Line and in its proper Column I might mark by a little black Spot every Fault I found upon Examination to have been committed respecting that Virtue upon that Day" (A 80–81). In the little book, Franklin scrupulously recorded his behavior—and thereby provided a model of self-examination. He focused for a week at a time on a particular virtue. "Thus in the first Week my great Guard was to avoid every the least Offence against Temperance, leaving the other Virtues to their ordinary Chance, only marking every Evening the Faults of the Day. Thus if in the first Week I could keep my first Line marked T clear of Spots, I suppos'd the Habit of that Virtue so much strengthen'd and its opposite weaken'd, that I might venture extending my Attention to include the next, and for the following Week keep both Lines clear of Spots. Proceeding thus to the last, I could go thro' a Course compleat in Thirteen Weeks, and four Courses in a Year" (A 82).

Franklin compared his faults to weeds. "And like him who having a Garden to weed, does not attempt to eradicate all the bad Herbs at once, which would exceed his Reach and his Strength, but works on one of the Beds at a time, and having accomplish'd the first proceeds to a Second; so I should have, (I hoped) the encouraging Pleasure of seeing on my Pages the Progress I made in Virtue, by clearing successively my Lines of their Spots, till in the End by a Number of Courses, I should be happy in viewing a clean Book after a thirteen Weeks daily Examination" (A 82). He then recited the same existential motto from Addison's *Cato* that he had employed in his 1728 "Articles of Belief," added another from Cicero saying that virtue alone could make a happy life, and composed his own "little Prayer": "*Powerful Goodness! bountiful Father! merciful Guide! Increase in me that Wisdom which discovers my truest Interests; Strengthen my Resolutions to perform what that Wisdom dictates. Accept my kind Offices to thy other Children, as the only Return in my Power for thy continual Favours to me*" (A 83). The last sentence was one that Franklin echoed numerous times throughout his life: "*Doing Good to Men* is the *only Service of God* in our Power" (3:419).

Giving the scheme of discipline visual impact, Franklin drew a chart for the business of a normal day. He rose at five, washed, said his prayer, organized the day's business, and resolved to abide by that week's particular virtue. He asked himself, "What Good shall I do this Day?" He studied for two hours, had breakfast, and then worked from 8 to 12, ate lunch and studied for an hour to 2, then worked until 6. He devoted 6 to 10 p.m. to dinner, music, diversion, and conversation. And at bedtime, he examined his conduct in accordance with his own rules and then asked himself, "What Good have I done to day?" At 10, bed. Even in the 1730s, it is unlikely that he always carried out the plan, but he probably often did.

Still playing the naïf in recounting the project, he said, "I was surpriz'd to find myself so much fuller of Faults than I had imagined," and then he slipped in a note that would upset the condescending reader: "but I had the Satisfaction of seeing them diminish. To avoid the Trouble of renewing now and then my little Book, which by scraping out the Marks on the Paper of old Faults to make room for new Ones in a new Course, became full of Holes: I transferr'd my Tables and Precepts to the Ivory Leaves of a Memorandum Book, on which the Lines were drawn with red Ink that made a durable Stain, and on those Lines I mark'd my Faults with a black Lead Pencil, which Marks I could easily wipe out with a wet Sponge" (A 86).

The last words accomplished Franklin's rhetorical purpose: they turned the

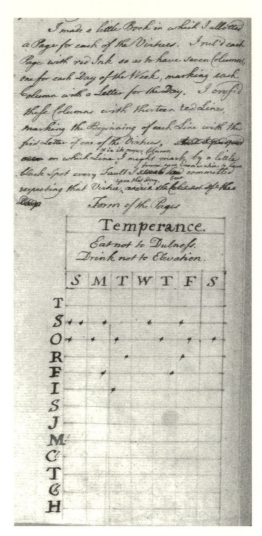

Figure 3. Infractions of Franklin's scheme of thirteen virtues, from manuscript page 97 of the Autobiography. *In the manuscript, he did not bother to put in dots after the sixth virtue. Had he printed the* Autobiography, *he probably would have marked some failings in all the other virtues. He did keep the line "T" for "Temperance" clear (it was the week when he was particularly concentrating on temperance), and he marked six failings for "Order." Commenting on the virtues, Franklin said he "found myself incorrigible with respect to Order" (A 87). Actually, Franklin seems to have been extraordinarily conscious of the possible benefits of systematic approaches and particularly good at devising methods for more efficiently managing time and life. Perhaps only Franklin would have judged himself "incorrigible with respect to Order."*

Notes on the revisions: after "Virtue," Franklin changed the period to a comma and crossed out "And I purpos'd over." After "Line," he inserted "& in its proper Column." After "Fault I," he cancelled "should had" and inserted "found upon Examination to have" with "been" added below the line. After "Virtue" he originally wrote "and in the Column of the Day" then cancelled it and inserted "upon that day." Courtesy, Huntington Library, San Marino, California.

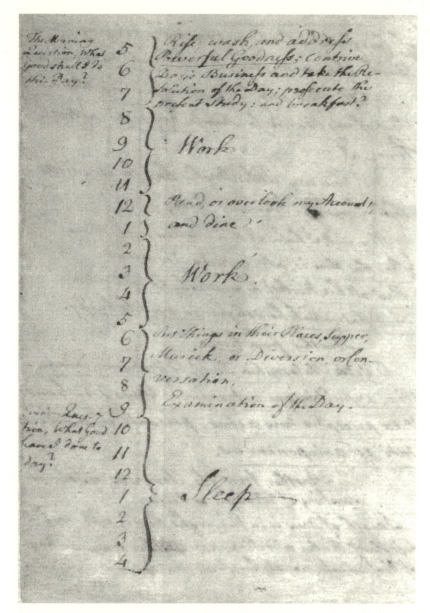

Figure 4. Franklin's chart showing how he tried to spend the time in a typical working day, from manuscript page 99 of his Autobiography. It may seem surprising that Franklin set aside three hours in the morning and two at lunch, and only eight hours a day for work. He spent, however, two hours or more in the morning prosecuting "the present Study" and an hour or so at lunch generally in reading, which was probably serious reading that was part of "the present Study." The unremitting three hours of study, the concluding "Examination of the Day," and the morning and evening questions, "What Good . . . ," are the distinctive Franklin traits. When he was young, many days called for longer hours of work, and when he was older, meetings and other obligations interfered with the schedule, but he thought it good to have a plan and a routine even if one could not always follow it. Courtesy, Huntington Library, San Marino, California.

tables on the reader. Anyone who has not attempted to reform his vices retains all his faults. Such a reader would be, metaphorically, a dirty, tattered, worn-out, cheap paper book, full of holes; the shape-shifter Franklin, however, has transformed himself from a set of worn paper sheets into a beautiful memorandum book of lovely parchment leaves with red lines. "After a while I went thro' one Course only in a Year, and afterwards only one in several Years; till at length I omitted them entirely, being employ'd in Voyages and Business abroad with a Multiplicity of Affairs, that interfered, but I always carried my little Book with me."

Franklin failed to master "order." It "cost me so much painful Attention and my Faults in it vex'd me so much, and I made so little Progress in Amendment, and had such frequent Relapses, that I was almost ready to give up the Attempt, and content my self with a faulty Character in that respect" (A 86). Actually, Franklin had extraordinary organizational ability and imposed systems upon various aspects of his life and his business. One might suspect that it was his exceptional desire to be efficient that made him believe he failed in "order."

Franklin then told a parable about persons who gave up when they found that the effort was hard:

> Like the Man who in buying an Ax of a Smith my Neighbour, desired to have the whole of its Surface as bright as the Edge; the Smith consented to grind it bright for him if he would turn the Wheel. He turn'd while the Smith press'd the broad Face of the Ax hard and heavily on the Stone, which made the Turning of it very fatiguing. The Man came every now and then from the Wheel to see how the Work went on; and at length would take his Ax as it was without farther Grinding. No, says the Smith, Turn on, turn on; we shall have it bright by and by; as yet 'tis only speckled. Yes, says the Man; but—*I think I like a speckled Ax best.*—And I believe this may have been the Case with many who having for want of some such Means as I employ'd found the Difficulty of obtaining good, and breaking bad Habits, in other Points of Vice and Virtue, have given up the Struggle, and concluded that *a speckled Ax was best.* (A 86–87)

It would be hard work to try to control one's life and to live up to one's dream, but Franklin's moral was not to be satisfied with a "speckled Ax." In a minor undercurrent, the anecdote satirizes mankind's self-deceiving reason, which "enables one to find or make a Reason for every thing one has a mind to do" (A 35).[20]

Abandoning his simpleton persona, Franklin concluded the discussion with a cynical remark concerning human nature—a twist revealing the skeptical pessimist underlying the persona's supposed belief in human perfectability. Franklin abandoned the attempt to achieve "a perfect Character" because it might be attended with "the Inconvenience of being envied and hated; . . . a benevolent Man should allow a few Faults in himself, to keep his Friends in Countenance" (A 87).

He next adopted a practical, commonsensical persona: "But on the whole, tho' I never arrived at the Perfection I had been so ambitious of obtaining, but fell far short of it, yet I was by the Endeavour made a better and a happier Man than I otherwise should have been, if I had not attempted it; As those who aim at perfect Writing by imitating the engraved Copies, tho' they never reach the wish'd for Excellence of those Copies, their Hand is mended by the Endeavour, and is tolerable while it continues fair and legible" (A 87). Franklin's fellow members of the Republic of Letters recognized that the passage on the virtues echoed and amplified Francis Bacon and that the last comparison specifically did so: "In the handling of this science [the conduct of life], the writers seem to me to have done as if a man who, professing to teach the art of writing, had exhibited only fair copies of letters, single and joined, without giving any direction for the carriage of the pen and framing of the characters."[21] Franklin's "little Book" and its parchment successor traced the improvement of character through practice, with little expectation of achieving a flawless "engraved" copy.

THEORY OF BEHAVIOR

The implicit theory of behavior in Franklin's *Autobiography* refuted two common views of life. Examining his own life and especially the causes for his behavior, Franklin gave first place to the attempt to change himself through discipline and the gradual formation of habits. One's own resolve and discipline rarely were considered key factors in explaining one's life. Religious autobiographers he had read, like St. Augustine in the *Confessions* and John Bunyan in *Grace Abounding to the Chief of Sinners*, and the numerous Puritan spiritual autobiographies he heard in the New England Puritan churches, all emphasized the necessity of a conversion or a rebirth experience. In them, the sinner was changed into a saint by a moment of rapture and the coming of God's grace. Franklin, however, tried to mold habits, not basic nature. There is no dramatic turning point in his *Autobiography*, only gradual efforts to change and improve.

Franklin adopted part of the method that he applied to virtue from New England Puritanism. For New England Congregationalists, the fundamental experience was the new birth, a specific moment of spiritual crisis, resulting in the conversion experience. Reverend William Perkins (1558–1602), a major theorist of the Puritan covenant of grace, wrote that man was born in sin but that those who experienced an effectual calling or new birth could be expected to proceed through justification, sanctification, and, after death, glorification. He described sanctification as a gradual increase in holiness and righteousness that allowed the visible saint to observe the Ten Commandments and a religious way of life with ever-increasing ease.[22]

Franklin omitted spiritual rebirth, justification, and glorification, but he retained a method that had some similarity to the stage of sanctification. Franklin devised a systematic approach to virtue that emphasized a gradual, bit-by-bit approach toward improvement.

Another common tradition, characteristic of confessions (and biographies) of criminals and their dying speeches, purported that human beings were created by heredity and environment. In these popular works, bad companions, drinking, and gaming had created the miserable lives of the criminals. Analyzing autobiography as a genre, the literary historian Bianca Theisen noted that earlier autobiographers attributed cause to divine providence or to pure chance, but late eighteenth-century writers often replaced transcendental explanations of character with immanent ones, typically holding family background and environment all-important and blaming poverty or a proletariat background for their difficulties.[23]

Franklin contradicted both explanations for character. He stressed that self-discipline, applied to one's own habits, could create one's character.[24] As we will see, he did so in the Hemphill controversy as well as in his *Autobiography*. Numerous persons before Franklin had stressed the importance of self-discipline and habits, from Aristotle and Pythagoras to Addison. Pascal also stressed that custom and habits created persons: "What are our Natural Principles, but our Principles of Custom?"[25] Franklin believed Pascal was right. Franklin came from a bourgeois family: his father was a soap-and-candle maker, and his mother was formerly a servant. Through hard work and good character, they became respectable members of the community, though they remained without wealth or social position. Franklin's personal condition in 1731 when he formed his "Art of Virtue" was little different from that of his parents, but he believed that he could, with good health and hard work, change his habits and himself. Describing his motivations in 1784, when he was among the most famous persons in the world, he believed that the deliberate effort had, to some degree, succeeded. Though no one knew better than Franklin the importance of chance (i.e., luck) in one's life, what one could do was try.

Franklin gathered together the causes underlying his moral condition in a passage evaluating the "State of my Mind" when he first formed the "Art of Virtue." He had "a tolerable Character to begin the World with" because of his family and environment. But after he ran away from Boston, he appreciated that "thro' this dangerous Time of Youth and the hazardous Situations I was sometimes in among Strangers," he could no longer count on "the Eye and Advice of my Father." He had, however, become convinced that "*Truth, Sincerity and Integrity* . . . were of the utmost Importance to the Felicity of Life, and I form'd written Resolutions . . . to practise them ever while I lived." Only one of these three virtues, *sincerity*, is found in the list of his thirteen virtues. *Truth* (definitely) and *integrity* (hopefully) are absolutes or ends rather than disciplines or means, and thus are not present.

Attempting to account for the causes that enabled him to preserve a decent moral status, Franklin gave possible reasons. His "Persuasion" of the excellence of the New Testament morality, together with his resolve to use truth, sincerity, and integrity with others, "with the kind hand of Providence, or some guardian

Angel, or accidental favorable Circumstances and Situations, or all together, preserved" his "tolerable character." The range covers the possible bases: perhaps his education in New Testament morality, or perhaps God Himself, or some subsidiary divine being, or mere chance, or his family, or his environment, or some combination of them all was responsible. One suspects, however, that he thought the primary cause was his effort to discipline and to create himself, particularly to use truth, sincerity, and integrity in his dealings with others. The means to achieve his desired ends was self-discipline, especially as spelled out in the thirteen virtues he practiced, beginning in 1731.

RECEPTION

Franklin's "Art of Virtue" became part 2 of the *Autobiography*, the most famous and infamous section of the world's most popular autobiography. Many persons, including President Jimmy Carter and Nobel Prize winner Chen Ning Yang, have testified to the importance of the *Autobiography* in their lives.[26] Commenting on Franklin's "little Book" containing the plan of conduct, Franklin's French disciple Pierre Cabanis exclaimed that he had seen it: "We have held this precious booklet in our hands. Here was, in a way, the chronological story of Franklin's soul and character."[27] Others have declaimed against the plan. The best-known criticism of Franklin is D. H. Lawrence's chapter "Benjamin Franklin" in *Studies in Classic American Literature* (1923). As others have pointed out, Lawrence failed to perceive that Franklin deliberately presented himself as a naïf and that Franklin himself was the first and most successful burlesquer of the supposed naïf's attempt to attain moral perfection.[28] Lawrence particularly objected to Franklin's leaving out the cultivation of the soul. "The Perfectibility of Man! Ah heaven, what a dreary theme! The perfectibility of the Ford car! The perfectibility of which man? I am many men. Which of them are you going to perfect? I am not a mechanical contrivance. . . . It's a queer thing is a man's soul. It is the whole of him. Which means it is the unknown him, as well as the known. It seems to me just funny, professors and Benjamins fixing the functions of the soul. Why, the soul of man is a vast forest, and all Benjamin intended was a neat back garden. And we've all got to fit into his kitchen garden scheme of things. Hail Columbia."[29]

Franklin's list of virtues represented a regimen or discipline created in order to exercise greater control over himself, including both his appetites and his behavior. D. H. Lawrence assumed that the passions were divinely inspired. The appetites, especially lust, came directly from "the gods." Lawrence wanted to be at the mercy of these passions or gods, and Franklin wanted to control them for his own sake and for the sake of others. In comparison to Franklin, Lawrence's philosophy of virtue seems simple, mystical, repetitious, and old-fashioned. He appeals to the inner gods, whereas Franklin appeals to the complex realities of human frailties and of existence in a democratic society. Franklin's precepts demonstrate greater practicality, sophistication, and complexity than Lawrence's. Lawrence finally seems quite satisfied and indeed rather pleased with himself—in short, he seems smug and provincial, whereas Franklin is amused by his own vanities and his all-too-human presumption.

By the "gods" and the "Holy Ghost," Lawrence means the spiritual depths of persons. He objects to what he sees as the categorization of virtues, assuming that defining and sorting various virtues somehow violates the integrity of the human being or the soul. Franklin separates the virtues for the same reason that an eighteenth-century printer breaks down the galley after using it—so that he can conveniently and easily get at the letters of the alphabet and use them again. Only someone who fears not being "whole" could think that anatomizing virtues destroys the soul's wholeness. In 1925 the very first critic of D. H. Lawrence, the American philosopher Herbert Schneider, pointed out that Franklin was basically concerned with an ethic of means and Lawrence with an ethic of ends. From a different point of view, the English critic and novelist V. S. Pritchett criticized Lawrence in 1941: "Being a romantic, Lawrence imagined that Franklin's devotion to Use, Method and Order indicated the dreary objectives of his genius. They were its starting point, its immense stimulus."[30]

Lawrence never realized that the criticism he made of Franklin was philosophically naive. Schneider pointed out that moral distinctions have no basis in the absolute but must be relative to a human point of view.[31] Franklin, who knew numerous systems of morality, appreciated and echoed different ones. He deliberately did not found his virtues on religion or on an ethics of ends. Since religious beliefs differed and since he, at times, believed in none of the great religions of the world, he separated virtues from religion. Thereby he influenced some persons whom he otherwise would not have reached, including, in late nineteenth-century Japan, the Meiji Empress (later the Empress Dowager Shō-ken). Franklin inspired her to create her own distinctive list of virtues.[32]

In rewriting Franklin's virtues, Lawrence fulfilled Franklin's purpose. Franklin did not intend for his virtues to be blindly adopted. He expected other persons to have other faults, other virtues, and other agendas. He hoped that "some of" his methods might be useful to others (A 1). As the historian of ideas Ralph Lerner has shown,[33] Franklin challenged his readers to give their own opinions and to live their own, quite different lives. He wanted others to define their own goals. He hoped to motivate them to work for their own purposes. And he intended to show them how to use self-discipline to gain their desired ends. Lawrence's criticism of Franklin is, in fact, one of the numerous instances proving that Franklin succeeded in his basic effort. Despite his diatribe against Franklin and America, Lawrence did what Franklin wanted his readers to do—examine themselves and create their own schemes for their own ends. Since Lawrence, writing in the chaos of World War I, attacked America and American civilization as much as Franklin, his choice of Franklin as the essential American is a backhanded compliment.[34]

PERSONAL AND PUBLIC REFORMATION

In the spring of 1731, Franklin considered establishing "*a great and extensive Project.*" On 9 May, he made a series of observations:

> That the great Affairs of the World, the Wars, Revolutions, etc. are carried on and effected by Parties.—That the View of these Parties is their present general Interest, or what they take to be such.—That the different Views of these different Parties, occasion all Confusion. That while a Party is carrying on a general Design, each Man has his particular private Interest in View. That as soon as a Party has gain'd its general Point, each Member becomes intent upon his particular Interest, which thwarting others, breaks that Party into Divisions, and occasions more Confusion. That few in Public Affairs act from a mere View of the Good of their Country, whatever they may pretend; and tho' their Actings bring real Good to their Country, yet Men primarily consider'd that their own and their Country's Interest was united, and did not act from a Principle of Benevolence. That fewer still in public Affairs act with a View to the Good of Mankind. (1:193)

Revolving these ideas in his mind, Franklin thought that there was an occasion for raising a united party for virtue by forming the virtuous men of all nations into a society to be governed by good and wise rules. He wrote that whoever attempted to form such a society, if he was well qualified, could not fail of pleasing God and of meeting with success (1:192). Commenting on the project in the *Autobiography*, Franklin said he had intended to undertake the project "when my Circumstances should afford me the necessary Leisure." Until then, "I put down from time to time on Pieces of Paper such Thoughts as occur'd to me respecting it. Most of these are lost; but I find one purporting to be the Substance of an intended Creed, containing as I thought the Essentials of every known Religion, and being free of every thing that might shock the Professors of any Religion. It is express'd in these Words, viz. That there is one God who made all things. That he governs the World by his Providence. That he ought to be worshiped by Adoration, Prayer and Thanksgiving. But that the most acceptable Service of God is doing Good to Man. That the Soul is immortal. And that God will certainly reward Virtue and punish Vice either here or hereafter" (A 92).

Franklin wrote this version of his deistic creed in August 1788 while composing part 3 of the *Autobiography*, but a similar document from approximately 1731 exists that appears to be what he had in mind. Titled "Doct. to be prea[che]d," the 1731 version says: "That there is one God Father of the Universe. He [is] infinitely good, Powerful and wise. That he is omnipresent. That he ought to be worshiped, by Adoration Prayer and Thanksgiving both in publick and private. That he loves such of his Creatures as love and do good to others: and will reward them either in this World or hereafter. That Men's

Minds do not die with their Bodies, but are made more happy or miserable after this Life according to their Actions. That Virtuous Men ought to league together to strengthen the Interest of Virtue, in the World: and so strengthen themselves in Virtue. That Knowledge and Learning is to be cultivated, and Ignorance dissipated. That none but the Virtuous are wise. That Man's Perfection is in Virtue" (1:213).

The 1731 version is more obviously a platform for a "united party of virtue" than is the deistic creed of 1788, but both are essentially public documents, containing statements that Franklin elsewhere burlesqued—though at times he no doubt wanted to believe in them. The "united party of virtue" had similarities to the Junto. Though more concerned with tolerance and less with eschatology than the "united party," the Junto was also a secret society and the founding group for other juntos. It, too, advanced the practical concerns of its members. Franklin described the projected "united party of virtue" in the *Autobiography*:

> My Ideas at that time were, that the Sect should be begun and spread at first among young and single Men only; that each Person to be initiated should not only declare his Assent to such Creed, but should have exercis'd himself with the Thirteen Weeks Examination and Practice of the Virtues as in the before-mention'd Model; that the Existence of such a Society should be kept a Secret till it was become considerable, to prevent Solicitations for the Admission of improper Persons; but that the Members should each of them search among his Acquaintance for ingenuous well-disposed Youths, to whom with prudent Caution the Scheme should be gradually communicated: That the Members should engage to afford their Advice, Assistance and Support to each other in promoting one another's Interest, Business and Advancement in Life. (A 92–93)

Franklin intended to call the organization the "Society of the *Free and Easy*." He explained its name: "Free, as being by the general Practice and Habit of the Virtues, free from the Dominion of Vice, and particularly by the Practice of Industry and Frugality, free from Debt, which exposes a Man to Confinement and a Species of Slavery to his Creditors." He enlisted two young men in the society "who adopted it with some Enthusiasm" (A 93).

Franklin, however, could not then undertake organizing the society because of his "narrow Circumstances, and the Necessity I was under of sticking close to my Business." Later, when he had the financial resources, his "multifarious Occupations public and private induc'd me to continue postponing, so that it has been omitted till I have no longer Strength or Activity left sufficient for such an Enterprize." He still thought, however, that it was "a practicable Scheme, and might have been very useful."

A last sentence concerning the plan stated a fundamental ingredient of the American Dream, a belief in the possibility of the individual's importance and of a person's making an extraordinary contribution: "And I was not discourag'd by the seeming Magnitude of the Undertaking, as I have always thought that one Man of tolerable Abilities may work great Changes, and accomplish great Affairs among Mankind, if he first forms a good Plan, and, cutting off all Amusements or other Employments that would divert his Attention, makes the Execution of that same Plan his sole Study and Business" (A 93). Franklin's statement of the philosophy of individualism, a necessary belief for any extraordinary accomplishment, has nevertheless something chilling and almost inhuman ("cutting off all Amusements") in its obsessive determination.

"On Constancy"

While a young printer, Franklin contributed two essays to the *Pennsylvania Gazette* that embodied aspects of the ethical advice he later condensed in the *Autobiography*. In the list of virtues, resolution (no. 4) shared meanings with constancy and perseverance, which were qualities necessary in forming his "Party of Virtue." Franklin mentioned constancy as a virtue elsewhere. He wrote Jane Mecom and her husband on 30 November 1752 that if their son Benjamin did not develop "some share of steadiness and perseverance, he can succeed no where." Franklin claimed that his own "Giddiness and Inconstancy" were to blame for Deborah's disastrous marriage to John Rogers (A 71).

"On Constancy" appeared in the *Pennsylvania Gazette* on 4 April 1734. After an epigraph from Lucan's *Pharsalia* (repeated later in *Poor Richard* for 1756), Franklin opened: "When I have sometimes observ'd Men of Wit and Learning, in Spite of their excellent natural and acquir'd Qualifications, fail of obtaining that Regard and Esteem with Mankind, which their Inferiors in point of Understanding frequently arrive at, I have, upon a slight Reflection, been apt to think, that it was owing to the ill Judgment, Malice, or Envy of their Acquaintance: But of late two or three flagrant Instances of this kind have put me upon thinking and deliberating more maturely, and I find within the Compass of my Observation the greatest part of those fine Men have been ruined for want of *CONSTANCY*, a Virtue never too highly priz'd, and whose true Worth is by few rightly understood" (W 225).

Franklin condemned "wavering and inconstant" persons who go through life "with no Enterprize" and adhere "to no Purpose": "Without Steadiness or Perseverance no Virtue can long subsist; and however honest and well-meaning a Man's Principles may be, the Want of this is sufficient to render them ineffectual, and useless to himself or others." Even friendship depended on constancy, for "malicious Misrepresentations frequently" disturb it and "never fail of Success where a mutual Esteem is not founded upon the solid Basis of Constancy and Virtue." A fickle person is "too inconsiderable to be fear'd as a Foe, or caress'd as a Friend" (W 225–26).

Having advanced the thesis, Franklin introduced the proof. All eminently famous persons in history were "distinguish'd" by constancy. A person who has no end in view, no design to pursue, is, Franklin claimed, like an irresolute master of a ship at sea that can fix upon no one port to steer her to, and consequently can call not one wind favorable to his wishes. Franklin cited the actions of famous persons to prove his point, beginning with Cato: "'Tis by his firm and unshaken Adherence to his Country's Cause, his constant Bravery in her Defence, and his burying himself but in her Ruins, that the rigid and severe *Cato* shines thro' those admirable Lines of *Lucan*, of which my Motto is a part, superior to the learn'd and eloquent *Cicero*, the great and majestick *Pompey*, or the mighty and invincible *Caesar* himself" (W 226).

After praising the "extraordinary Constancy of *Charles XII. of Sweden*," Franklin contrasted the characters of King Charles II and Cromwell. Of Charles II, he wrote, "his Inconstancy and Indolence laid him open to every trifling Project, every self-interested Scheme, that an avaritious or revengeful Minister or Mistress could suggest to him." Therefore, many persons have thought that Charles II "acted thro'out his whole Reign upon no Principles and Maxims, and had no one Design in View." In contrast, Franklin commended the "constant and resolute Carriage" of Cromwell. "'Twas this, and this alone, which rais'd him so far above the Malice of his Enemies, or the Expectation of his Friends; and gain'd him that high Character from a judicious Historian, *That never Man chose his Party with more Judgment, and executed his Designs with more Constancy and Vigour*" (W 226–27).

OBSTINACY IN OPINION

A topic that occurs frequently in the *Autobiography* is that of having an open mind: "If you wish Information and Improvement from the Knowledge of others and yet at the same time express your self as firmly fix'd in your present Opinions, modest sensible Men, who do not love Disputation, will probably leave you undisturb'd in the Possession of your Error" (A 16). Franklin's essay on the subject, signed with the pseudonym "Veridicus" (truthful), appeared in the 27 March 1735 *Gazette*. It opened: "As a *pertinacious Obstinacy* in Opinion, and confident *Self-Sufficiency*, is possibly one of the greatest Vices, as well as Weaknesses, that the human Mind is capable of; so on the contrary a Readiness to give up a *loved Opinion*; upon due Conviction, is as great a Glory, as well as Happiness, as we are here capable of attaining." Since the opinion might seem to be irreligious, Franklin gave it a biblical attestation (Proverbs 14:16): "For as *Solomon* justly observes, a *wise Man* feareth; he, conscious of his own Imperfections, and sensible of the numberless Mistakes and Errors we are here subject and liable to, submits to the Dictates of Truth and Wisdom, where-ever he finds them, and thereby avoids the Evil, and attains the Glory. But the *Fool*, the self-sufficient Man, who proudly arrogates all Knowledge and Science to himself, rageth at Contradiction, and will not suffer his Knowledge to be questioned; what wonder is it then, if he *fall into Evil* when he is thus *confident*?" (W 253).

Veridicus/Franklin maintained that "a love of Truth and Goodness is not more essential to an honest Man than a Readiness to change his Mind and Practice, upon Conviction that he is in the wrong: And indeed, these two are inseparably connected in our present fallible Condition" (W 253–54). Franklin elsewhere wrote: "In the present weak State of humane Nature, surrounded as we are on all sides with Ignorance and Error, it little becomes poor fallible Man to be positive and dogmatical in his Opinions" (2:33). Recurring to the concept of the Great Chain of Being (which Franklin used in his "Articles of Belief and Acts of Religion" [20 November 1728]), Veridicus suggested that "those who are arrived at a better State, may get clear of all their Mistakes, as well as their ill Habits immediately, and yet be capable of an endless Improvement in Knowledge, by having their Minds extended still to discover further Objects and new Relations of Things which they had no Notions of before" (W 254).

The skeptical Franklin wrote: "*Prevailing Opinions* insensibly gain the Possession of our Minds, and have commonly the Advantage of being Firstcomers: and yet are very often no better than *prevailing Falshoods*, directly the Reverse of Truth." He observed: "A Man can hardly forbear wishing those Things to be true and right, which he apprehends would be for his Conveniency to find so: And many Perswasions, when they are looked into, plainly appear to have no better a Foundation." If we are not willing to change our minds, "*Reason* would be given us in vain, *Study* and *Converse* wou'd be useless and unprofitable Things." Only those who are willing to change their minds have the chance "to come at the Knowledge of Truth." As Ralph Waldo Emerson later wrote in "Self-Reliance," "A foolish consistency is the hobgoblin of little minds." Franklin continued that though we should not "change our Opinion upon every slight Appearance, or give it up to the Authority of others," we should always have "a regard for Truth, superiour to every other Consideration" (W 255). Franklin's passionate tone and idealism in the conclusion of the essay are surprising. Perhaps he was writing in part about religious beliefs. At the time, he was attending the sermons of the Reverend Samuel Hemphill. Within a few weeks, Franklin exposed himself to ridicule and opprobrium by defending the liberal positions expressed by Hemphill.

SIMPLICITY

Eighteenth-century writers typically scorned the common man and the speech of peasants. Franklin differed. He created what I have called an American aesthetic. Among Franklin's sources, Addison comes closest to his position. He wrote in the *Spectator*: "I know nothing which more shews the essential and inherent Perfection of Simplicity of Thought, above that which I call the Gothick Manner in Writing, than this, that the first pleases all Kinds of Palates, and the latter only such as have formed to themselves a wrong artificial Taste."[35] Other early eighteenth-century critics took Addison to task for his cultural primitivism. John Dennis's opinions typified eighteenth-century thought: "The *Spectator* would make us believe that all People are Judges of Simplicity of Thought, and that the Rabble are better Judges of it, than they who have had a generous Education. . . . as if Men of Education in *Great Britain* were more ignorant than the Rabble."[36] David Hume, who knew Addison's writing on the subject but not Franklin's, tried to adjudicate between the positions of Addison and Dennis. In his 1742 essay "Of Simplicity and Refinement in Writing," Hume argued for a "just medium" between simplicity and refinement and directly condemned the language and "observations of a peasant."[37] Scorn for the common people and their language was the reason that many eighteenth-century literati condescended to proverbs, but Franklin admired and used them.

The opening sentence of Franklin's *Pennsylvania Gazette* essay "On Simplicity" (13 April 1732) has a subversive element: "There is in Humane Nature a certain charming Quality, innate and original to it, which is called SIMPLICITY." The diction "innate and original" recalled and contradicted Locke's refutation of "innate ideas." If simplicity is innate and original, then it must be found in infants. That suggestion is not made by any other eighteenth-century moral philosopher.[38] Indeed, as Franklin's essay progresses, simplicity comes to be identified with goodness (and perhaps, at first, partially with innocence) and the opposite of evil. If it is innate and original in mankind, then mankind is not born in a state of original sin. Though he did not believe in Adam's sin, neither did Franklin hold that mankind was necessarily good. Some men, like some states, were not.

Franklin subtly satirized Mandeville, whose praise of luxury in *A Fable of the Bees* contrasted primitive simplicity with contemporary artifice. Franklin wrote: "In latter Ages, this [simplicity] has been almost universally exploded, and banished from amongst Men, as the Characteristic of Folly; whilst *Cunning* and *Artifice* have prevailed in its stead, and with equal Justice been dignified with the Titles of Wisdom and Understanding. But I believe the juster Account of the Matter is, that Simplicity is the homespun Dress of Honesty, and Chicanery and Craft are the Tinsel Habits and the false Elegance which are worn to cover the Deformity of Vice and Knavery" (W 181). Franklin contributed to the eighteenth-century debate over luxury and simplicity, uniquely opposing Mandeville by praising "homespun Dress." The adjective is characteristic of Franklin. He frequently used *homespun* to give praise and twice made it his pseudonym.[39] The word itself anticipates Franklin's stand toward importation during the pre-Revolutionary period and complements his egalitarian attitudes. It was a patriotic gesture, a celebration of Americanism (in which Franklin had been preceded by numerous persons, including the Virginia historian Robert Beverley, who used furniture made on his plantation rather than the imported English goods favored by his contemporaries),[40] and at the same time *homespun* celebrates the common person, the ordinary American.

The second paragraph associated the "first Ages of the World" with simplicity. The opinion reflects Addison, Shaftesbury, and other writers on simplicity.[41] Franklin believed the growth of "cunning," "luxury," and "ambition" were all antithetical to simplicity, thereby again attacking Mandeville's praise of consumption and luxury. Franklin next linked the prose style of the classics with the actions and manners of the "old Greeks and Romans" and claimed that the classics reflect the "original Simplicity of Mind [that] has gradually been worn off."[42] Franklin contradicted the common beliefs when he praised the talk of farmers: "To prove the natural Charm and Beauty there is in this Simplicity, we need only, at this Day, as false as the World is grown, retire but far enough from great Cities, the Scenes of all worldly Business and Action; and, I believe; the most cunning Man will be obliged to own, the high and sincere Pleasure there is in conversing from the Heart, and without Design. What Relief do we find in the simple and unaffected Dialogues of uncorrupted Peasants, after the tiresome Grimace of the Town!" (W 182).

Franklin exceeded Addison and other previous writers in his appreciation of the picturesque expressions of farmers and artisans. Not until the preface to the *Lyrical Ballads* do we find as great an aesthetic appreciation of the colloquial. The literary historian Raymond D. Havens said that the eighteenth-century writers on simplicity widely admired "an elegant simplicity unknown to real shepherds or farmers." Wordsworth, however, contradicted them. He believed passionately "in a 'seemly plainness,' 'simple manners,' 'simplicity of life,' and 'an entire simplicity of mind.'"[43] Franklin's basic egalitarian philosophy influenced his aesthetic attitudes and thereby anticipated, in his appreciation of a democratic aesthetic, the opinions of Wordsworth.[44] (Franklin's style, of course, was more colloquial than Wordsworth's.) Franklin wrote that one needn't go to the country to find simplicity, for "the Men of the truest Genius and highest Characters in the Conduct of the World, (as few of them as rise in any Age) are observed to possess this Quality in the highest Degree." Similarly, Addison found that "The old *English* Plainness and Sincerity, that generous Integrity of Nature, and Honesty of Disposition . . . always argues true Greatness of Mind, and is usually accompany'd with undaunted Courage and Resolution" (*Spectator* 1:430).

Franklin called simplicity "natural" and "the highest Beauty of Nature." He added that "all that is excellent in Arts which Men have invented is either to demonstrate this native Simplicity and Truth in Nature, or to teach us to transcribe and copy in every Thing from it" (W 183). In *Poor Richard* for 1756 he wrote, "By the Word *Simplicity*, is not always meant *Folly* or *Ignorance*; but often, pure and upright Nature, free from Artifice, Craft or deceitful Ornament" (6:328). Besides being a desired aesthetic ideal, the natural was the foundation for virtue. Near the end of "On Simplicity," he said, "Simplicity of Speech and Manners is the highest Happiness as well as the greatest Ornament of Life; whereas nothing is so tiresome to one's self, as well as so odious to others, as Disguise and Affectation. Who was ever cunning enough to conceal his being so?" He observed, "Wisdom and Virtue are the same Thing, as Knavery and Cunning are generally so too." Franklin's logic rests on the identification of cunning as the opposite of simplicity and on the association of simplicity with wisdom and virtue—associations advanced throughout the essay. He added a

Franklinian remark on appearance and reality: "for the future, we shall resolve to be what we would seem, which is the only sure way not to be afraid to seem what we really are" (W 183). The thought anticipated Poor Richard's advice: "What you would seem to be, be really" (2:396, 8:131).[45]

Contrasting men of cunning with those of the "highest Characters," Franklin wrote: "Cunning, says my Lord *Bacon*, is a sinister or crooked Wisdom, and Dissimulation but a faint kind of Policy; for it asks a strong Wit and a strong Heart, to know when to tell Truth and to do it; therefore they are the weaker sort of Politicians, that are the greatest Dissemblers" (W 182). Though Franklin had read Francis Bacon as a youth and echoed him and praised him in *Poor Richard*, and though he alludes to two of Bacon's essays here, he also knew that Mandeville had quoted Bacon on cunning.[46] Perhaps he was echoing Bacon through Mandeville.

Franklin condemned cunning with a backwoods metaphor. He knew the Indian practice of hunting in pairs and in groups. "A cunning Man is obliged to hunt his Game alone, and to live in the dark; he is uncapable of Counsel and Advice, for his dishonest Purpose dies upon Discovery" (W 182). As Franklin wrote in *Poor Richard* in January 1744: "He that drinks his Cyder alone, let him catch his horse alone." Franklin wrote a version of a sententia that he often used later: "None but Fools are Knaves, for wise Men cannot help being honest." His son William Franklin recalled on 26 May 1808 that one of his father's favorite sayings was, "All Knaves were Fools; for if they were not Fools they would not be Knaves."[47]

The brief penultimate paragraph distinguished between quaint habits and simplicity: "The Plainness and Integrity of Mind, which is here recommended, is very little concerned in any Quaintness of Habit, or Oddness of Behaviour: Nor is it at all of Importance to Vertue and Simplicity, that great care is taken to appear unfashionable." Strangeness of dress and peculiar actions are their own gross affectations. Franklin stated that he well knew that "the Word *Cunning* did in the ancient Sense of it imply Knowledge." But it now commonly signified "the little Subtlety of base Minds, who are incapable of great and honest Actions." Against such persons, Franklin concluded, the best defense was "the Integrity of a wise Man, and the Wisdom of an honest one" (W 184).

Franklin's essay on "Simplicity" reflects his egalitarianism, his hopeful belief that most people are basically good, and his extensive reading of moral philosophy.

Moral Philosophy: Three Essays

Franklin wrote often on moral philosophy, which I arbitrarily distinguish from social satire and from theology as essays having a serious, straightforward manner and devoted to ethical subjects (as opposed to more ostensibly religious ones). Moral philosophy was debated by such predecessors and contemporaries as Francis Bacon, Thomas Hobbes, John Locke, the third earl of Shaftesbury,

Bernard de Mandeville, Joseph Addison, Francis Hutcheson, and, slightly later, David Hume and the Scotch philosophers. Franklin wrote four such essays in the 1730s. He recalled giving two of them in the Junto before printing them in the *Pennsylvania Gazette* in the beginning of 1735. Two earlier ones, "On Simplicity" and "Men Are Naturally Benevolent as Well as Selfish," were also probably first delivered as Junto talks.

The Nature of Human Beings

"Y. Z." (Franklin's pseudonym) wrote (30 November 1732) on the basic nature of mankind, maintaining that "Men are Naturally Benevolent as Well as Selfish." Y. Z. opened by paraphrasing the opinions of Hobbes, Locke, and Mandeville: "Sir, It is the Opinion of some People, that Man is a Creature altogether selfish, and that all our Actions have at Bottom a View to private Interest; If we do good to others, it is, say they, because there is a certain Pleasure attending virtuous Actions." Mandeville had written: "the Reward of a Virtuous Action, which is the Satisfaction that ensues upon it, consists in a certain Pleasure he procures to himself by Contemplating on his own Worth."[48] Franklin argued against the belief: "But how Pleasure comes to attend a virtuous Action, these Philosophers are puzzled to shew, without contradicting their first Principles, and acknowledging that Men are *naturally* benevolent as well as selfish. For whence can arise the Pleasure you feel after having done a good-natured Thing, if not hence, that you had *before* strong humane and kind inclinations in your Nature, which are by such Actions in some Measure gratified?" (W 200–201). Franklin's argument resembles Francis Hutcheson's in *An Inquiry into the Original of Our Ideas of Beauty and Virtue* (1725), but Hutcheson attributed a moral sense (sometimes called a self-approving joy) to a divine origin. Hutcheson's opponents, including Mandeville, mocked his attempt to express the moral sense by a mathematical formula.[49] Franklin ignored both mathematics and the divine in his consideration.

The second paragraph used Shaftesbury to oppose the Hobbes-Mandeville position: "a late ingenious Author, enquiring why we approve and disapprove of Actions done many Ages since, which can no way be suppos'd to affect our present Interest, conceives that we have a certain internal *Moral Sense*, which tastes the Beauty of a rational benevolent Action, and the Deformity of an ill-natured cruel one." Continuing to echo Shaftesbury,[50] Franklin said that "the Fact is certain, that we do approve and disapprove of Actions which cannot in the least influence our present Affairs. How could this happen, if we did not in contemplating such Actions, find something agreeable or disagreeable to our natural Inclinations as Men, that is, to our benevolent Inclinations?" (W 201).

To prove his point, Y. Z./Franklin translated a "short Story" from the French, "for the Pleasure of your Readers, who will therein find wherewith to exercise their *moral Sense* of Tasting, if such a Sense they have." The affecting story concerned a hard-hearted creditor who was finally touched by the great love of a son for his father (the debtor). Consequently, the creditor gave his daughter to the debtor's son, and the sentimental story ended happily. Y. Z. showed the story to a friend, who commented, "That he knew not whose Happiness was most to be envy'd, his whose Affairs were so happily retriev'd, or his who had the Opportunity of giving so much Pleasure to others." The speaker concluded, "I believe my benevolent Friend spoke his real Sentiments. I see Virtue in all those who were concern'd in the Story, yet I know not whether their Virtue is more worthy of Admiration than his [Y. Z.'s friend]" (W 201, 203).

In this early self-reflective example of reader-response criticism, Franklin used the readers' emotions in reading the story to convince them of the innate benevolence of humans. Like many of Franklin's texts, the story takes the reader through various emotional turns. Franklin then asks the reader to confirm the emotions he has experienced. In writing the essay, Franklin put within the framework of contemporary moral philosophy a position that he had proven in describing the reactions of audiences at executions. He had done the same when reporting (29 January 1729) the trial and, at the last moment, the reprieve of James Prouse and James Mitchel. The readers, just like the audience present for the execution, were filled with relief and joy at the unexpected turn. In the essay "Men Are Naturally Benevolent as Well as Selfish," as well as in various news reports, Franklin anticipated David Hume's position in *A Treatise of Human Nature* (1739) on virtue being partly founded on sympathy and Hume's means of proving it by experimental philosophy.[51]

On the other hand, in a letter of 2 October 1781, Franklin seemed to change his mind and to agree with Mandeville in opposition to Hutcheson and Shaftesbury. Some of Dr. Jan Ingenhousz's scientific experiments had been criticized, and Franklin, in comforting the Dutch scientist, seemed to speak autobiographically about the jealous reactions of others. Franklin concluded his solace with the words: "whatever some may think & say, it is worth while to do Men Good, for the Self Satisfaction one has in the Reflection." In the context of the letter (and perhaps of the actuality of Ingenhousz's recent experience), humans were competitive, nasty, and jealous. That did not, however, mean that all humans were—or even that most were. But Franklin was agreeing that in some circumstances the only reward for doing good was the Mandevillean "Self Satisfaction one has in the Reflection."

A Man of Sense

In his *Autobiography*, Franklin mentioned that he had written two Junto essays that he afterward published in the *Gazette*. One was "a Socratic Dialogue tending to prove, that, whatever might be his Parts and Abilities, a vicious Man could not properly be called a Man of Sense" (A 94). Alfred Owen Aldridge has shown that it is one of four essays in the *Gazette* advocating Shaftesburian positions.[52] (Two were reprinted from the *London Journal*, and the other two were by Franklin.) In effect, his "Socratic Dialogue" maintained the thesis that he had stated in his note for the "Doct. to be preached" for the "Society of the Free and Easy": "None but the Virtuous are wise." Like a number of his essays, this one was not simply a contribution to the moral philosophy of the eighteenth century but an exploration of personal values. Most people accept the standards of their society. Franklin did, too, though not without questioning. The pseudonymous *Gazette* author "A. A." (Franklin) on 11 February 1734/5 reported that he heard the following conversation "near the Meeting-House Corner." For those who knew Philadelphia, that would identify the place as near Second and Market Streets. Imitating Plato, Franklin called one conversationalist Socrates and the other Crito.

Crito remarked that a well-dressed gentleman who just passed by was "a *Man of Sense*, but not very honest." Socrates claimed to be at a "Loss to know whether a Man who *is not honest* can deserve" the appellation of a man of sense. Crito said yes, "many vicious Men . . . are nevertheless Men of very good Sense." Thereupon, Socrates began a series of questions.

Are you of opinion "that a Man of Knowledge is a *Man of Sense*"? Yes. S: "Is the Knowledge of Push-pin, or of the Game at Ninepins, or of Cards and Dice, or even of Musick and Dancing, sufficient to constitute the Character of a Man of Sense?"

No, "many silly People . . . understand these Things tolerably well." Socrates asked if the knowledge of languages, or logic or rhetoric, or mathematics, or astronomy, or natural philosophy give a right to the title of a "Man of Sense."

Crito: "At first Sight I should have thought they might: But upon Recollection I must own I have known some Men, Masters of those Sciences, who, in the Management of their Affairs, and *Conduct of their Lives*, have acted very weakly . . . and therefore I cannot find in my Heart to allow 'em the Character of *Men of Sense*" (2:16).

Socrates summed up: "It seems then, that no Knowledge will serve to give this Character, but the Knowledge of our *true Interest* . . . in order to arrive at our main End in View, HAPPINESS." With this statement, Franklin put a familiar thought into a different perspective: Pascal had said that "all Men desire to be happy, that's for certain"; Locke said "all desire happiness" and used the phrase the "pursuit of happiness."[53] Franklin now claimed that our main end in view was happiness and that it was in our self-interest to be virtuous, because virtue alone would make us happy.

Crito granted that the knowledge of our true interest is essential, but he added that some vicious Men "*know* their true Interest, and are therefore *Men of Sense*, but are nevertheless vicious and dishonest Men, as appears from the whole Tenour of their Conduct in Life" (2:16–17).

Thereupon Socrates began another series of questions. "Can Vice consist with any Man's true Interest, or contribute to his Happiness?"

"No certainly; for in Proportion as a Man is vicious he loses the Favour of

God and Man, and brings upon himself many Inconveniences, the least of which is capable of marring and demolishing his Happiness."

Socrates asked how vicious men could have the knowledge of virtue if they act contrary to it. Crito replied, by their talk about virtue. Socrates asked if the knowledge of the terms and expressions concerning shoemaking constituted a shoemaker; or is it knowing how to "go about it and do it?" Crito conceded. Socrates asked if one who could only talk well "about Shoemaking, were to be set to work, would he not presently discover his Ignorance in that Art?" Crito agreed.

Socrates then turned directly to the question: "Can the Man who is only able to talk justly of Virtue and Vice . . . but notwithstanding his talking thus, continues in those Vices; can such a Man deserve the Character of a Temperate and Chaste Man? Or does not that Man rather deserve it, who having *a thorough Sense* that what the other has said is true, *knows* also *how* to resist the Temptation to those Vices, and embrace Virtue with a hearty and steady Affection?" (2:17–18). Acknowledging the point, Crito added: "And since Virtue is really the true Interest of all Men; and some of those who talk well of it, do not put it in Practice, I am now inclined to believe they speak only by rote." Since the talk of virtue has never entered "or made any Impression on their Hearts," it has "no Influence on the Conduct of their Lives."

Socrates concluded: "Vicious Men, then, do not appear to have that Knowledge which constitutes *the Man of Sense.*"

Though Crito granted that "they do not deserve the Name," he then objected, "I am afraid, that instead of *defining* a Man of Sense we have now entirely *annihilated* him: For if the Knowledge of his true Interest in all Parts of the Conduct of Life, and a constant Course of Practice agreeable to it, are essential to his Character, I do not know where we shall find him." Socrates replied: "There seems no necessity that to be a Man of Sense, he should never make a Slip in the Path of Virtue, or in Point of Morality; provided he is sensible of his Failing and diligently applys himself to rectify what is done amiss, and to prevent the like for the future" (2:18). Crito made one more objection: "'twill look hard, that all other Arts and Sciences put together, and possess'd by one Man in the greatest Perfection, are not able to dignify him with the Title of a *Man of Sense*, unless he be also a Man of Virtue." Socrates asked if a man of sense would spend all his time learning sciences of no use. No, Crito conceded. Socrates said the most useful science was "the Science of Virtue." Crito admitted it.

Socrates concluded: "It seems to follow then, that the vicious Man, tho' Master of many Sciences, must needs be an ignorant and foolish Man; for being, as he is vicious, of consequence unhappy, either he has acquired only the useless Sciences, or having acquired such as might be useful, he knows not how to make them contribute to his Happiness; and tho' he may have every other Science, he is ignorant that the SCIENCE OF VIRTUE is of more worth, and of more consequence to his Happiness than all the rest put together. And since he is ignorant of what *principally* concerns him, tho' it has been told him a thousand Times from Parents, Press, and Pulpit, the Vicious Man, however learned, cannot be a *Man of Sense*, but is a Fool, a Dunce, and a Blockhead" (2:18–19). The vituperation of the last sentence is un-Socratic but not atypical of the young Franklin.

Having affirmed an idealistic stance, Franklin gave way in the conclusion to a condemnation of the way many people lived their lives. Franklin's "man of Sense" dialogue alludes to Plato's *Crito*, wherein Crito offers the condemned Socrates a chance to escape imminent death. Being a man of reason and honor, however, Socrates does not seize the opportunity to escape, but remains in jail and thereby chooses death. Franklin intended to suggest the high stakes of the "Man of Sense" essay by using Socrates and Crito as his speakers—virtue is the most important principle in life—more important than life itself.

"*Self-Denial* Is Not the *Essence of Virtue*"

Shaftesbury, in his *Characteristics*, presented virtue as a natural, good affection. But some men attained virtue only by the most heroic efforts over vicious and evil inclinations. Other virtuous men did not have to struggle especially hard against evil.[54] In *The Fable of the Bees*, Bernard Mandeville limited virtue to those who had to struggle against evil. "The Generality of Moralists and Philosophers have" said "that there could be no Virtue without Self-denial; but a late Author, who is now much read by Men of Sense, is of a contrary Opinion, and imagines that Men without any Trouble or Violence upon themselves may be naturally Virtuous." Mandeville restricted virtue to those acts done "contrary to the impulse of Nature."[55]

Writing in the *Pennsylvania Gazette* on 18 February 1734/5, Franklin contradicted Mandeville. In his anonymous essay "Self-Denial *Is Not the* Essence of Virtue," Franklin said, "it is commonly asserted, that without *Self-Denial* there is no Virtue, and that the greater the *Self-Denial* the greater the Virtue." He called for a discrimination: "If it were said, that he who cannot deny himself in any Thing he inclines to, tho' he knows it will be to his Hurt, has not the Virtue of *Resolution* or *Fortitude*, it would be intelligible enough; but as it stands it seems obscure or erroneous" (2:19).

Franklin questioned: "If a Man has no inclination to *wrong* People in his Dealings, if he feels no Temptation to it, and therefore never does it; can it be said that he is not a just Man? If he is a just Man, has he not the Virtue of Justice?" The answer demanded is "yes." Franklin probably did not employ the dialogue form because whoever defended the opposite position would have been a mere strawman. Franklin next asked whether a person who has no temptation to "idle Diversions" and therefore never relaxes his "Application to Business" is not an "Industrious Man. Or has he not the Virtue of Industry?" Using reasoning similar to that in the *Autobiography* concerning the acquisition of virtues, he claimed that the more we "strive against the Temptation to any Vice, and practise the contrary Virtue, the weaker will that Temptation be" until finally it "entirely vanishes." He rounded out the argument: "Does it follow from thence, that in our Endeavours to overcome Vice, we grow continually less and less Virtuous; till at length we have no Virtue at all?" (2:19–20). The idea that a perfect person would have no virtue at all was a reductio ad absurdum of Mandeville's position.

Three Religious Essays and Parodies

"A Meditation on a Quart Mugg"

Franklin's mock "Meditation on a Quart Mugg" appeared in the *Pennsylvania Gazette* on 19 July 1733. It imitated Jonathan Swift's "Meditation upon a Broom-Stick: According to the Style and Manner of the Honourable Robert Boyle's Meditations." Like Swift, Franklin parodied the woeful persona and glum message of the typical religious meditation.[56] Franklin had an additional, underlying subject. As the principle of universal benevolence was becoming common in British moral philosophy, "irresistible compassion" and sentimentality were increasingly prevalent in English literature.[57] Franklin had demonstrated that mankind was by nature sympathetic to the distresses of others (e.g., in his crime reporting on Prouse and Mitchel). As a teenager he even became a vegetarian partially because of sympathy with all animals, including fish. As we have seen, he mocked himself when he found a reason to eat cod: "So convenient a thing it is to be a *reasonable Creature*, since it enables one to find or make a Reason for every thing one has a mind to do" (A 35).

In the meditation, the quart mug becomes a symbol for those persons, criminals and slaves especially, whose predicaments were causing waves of sentiment in popular English literature. Franklin had already written on convicts and was the first person in American literature to use the persona of an African American, but, typically, he also burlesqued his own positions. The "Meditation on a Quart Mugg" is a reductio ad absurdum of the waves of sentiment growing ever more popular in British moral philosophy. Franklin thought that without some commonsense standards of judgment, one might well sympathize with such self-pitying rogues as Samuel Keimer, whose lachrymose writings, like sentimentality itself, are a minor object of Franklin's satire. As Huck Finn observed one hundred and fifty years later, "rapscallions and dead beats is the kind [of persons that] . . . good people takes the most interest in."[58] Franklin lampooned such attitudes. Though no Calvinist, he found ample evidence for the existence of evil and for man's inhumanity to man. He wrote James Logan that humans existed more in a state of war than a state of love; Hobbes seemed closer to the truth than Locke (2:184–85).

In choosing the quart mug as a subject, Franklin was influenced by Thomas Sheridan's fable on the origin of mankind. Sheridan and Swift collaborated on *The Intelligencer*, where, in No. 14, Sheridan suggested that Prometheus made mankind from pottery. The *Maryland Gazette* reprinted the essay on 4 March 1728/9 and Franklin subsequently did so in the *Pennsylvania Gazette* on 27 May 1731. Franklin was also influenced by a minor subgenre of poetry concerning drunks who were transformed into liquor containers. The Reverend Mather Byles, a childhood acquaintance, wrote "Bug Barret Transformed into a Brandy Bottle," and another poem, an eighteenth-century broadside ("Sold by Jas. Lumsden, Engraver, Glasgow"), begins, "Dear Sir, this Brown Jug that now foams with raild Ale / Was once Toby Filpot a thirsty Old Soul." A similar poem, titled "Toby Reduc'd; or The Brown Jug," by Francis Fawkes appeared in the *New York Gazette* on 4 September 1760. The English jugs of pottery with comic human figures called "Toby Jugs" were probably too late to have influenced Franklin, but he might well have seen their German prototypes in Pennsylvania.[59] He certainly knew the biblical comparisons of mankind to clay and of God to a potter (e.g., Job 10:9, 13:12, 33:6); one locus classicus is Isaiah 64:8: "we are the clay, and thou our potter." On another level, the piece belongs with his frequent writings on temperance, condemning the universe of bars and drinking.

Franklin began on a dolorous religious note: "Wretched, miserable, and unhappy Mug! I pity thy luckless Lot, I commiserate thy Misfortunes, thy Griefs fill me with Compassion, and because of thee are Tears made frequently to burst from my Eyes." Franklin's subject, the quart mug, is even more innately ironic than Swift's broomstick, for the juxtaposition of drinking (a quart mug suggests taverns and booze) and holiness is antithetical. The ironic juxtaposition anticipated Franklin's joke in the *Autobiography*: When the Reverend Charles Beatty complained to Colonel Franklin that the soldiers were not faithfully attending his "Prayers and Exhortations," Franklin suggested that Beatty serve as "Steward of the Rum" and "deal it out" immediately after prayers. "Never," Franklin commented, "were Prayers more generally and more punctually attended" (A 148).

"How often have I seen him compell'd to hold up his Handle at the Bar, for no other Crime than that of being empty; then snatch'd away by a surly Officer, and plung'd suddenly into a Tub of cold Water: Sad Spectacle, and Emblem of human Penury, oppress'd by arbitrary Power!" Franklin punned on *bar*; the mug in this sentence has become an oppressed victim at a criminal court, roughly handled by a "surly Officer." Of course, the comparisons do not make good sense ("penury" might suggest a double standard in the way the law handles the rich versus. the poor), but the confused nonsense of such similes and analogies is part of Franklin's parody. "How often have I seen it obliged to undergo the Indignities of a dirty Wench; to have melting Candles dropt on its naked Sides, and sometimes in its Mouth, to risque being broken into a thousand Pieces, for Actions which itself was not guilty of!" (W 217). The personification of the innocent mug, with its poor naked sides and mouth, is absurd, though characteristic of the religious meditation and the minor poetic "Toby" genre mentioned above.

After a series of four "How often" beginnings, Franklin changed to an out-cry: "Alas! what Power, or Place, is provided, where this poor Mug, this unpitied Slave, can have Redress of his Wrongs and Sufferings?" The mug has been trans-formed from an innocent person tried and convicted as a criminal to a wronged slave. "If he prove of a large size, his Owner curses him, and says he will devour more than he'll earn: If his Size be small, those whom his Master appoints him to serve will curse him as much, and perhaps threaten him with the Inquisition of the Standard." Then followed another apostrophe to the "Poor Mug." As the skit continued, its fictive world became increasingly a dirty, smelly bar. "Hast thou been industriously serving thy Employers with Tiff or Punch, and instantly they dispatch thee for Cyder, then must thou be abused for smelling of Rum. Hast thou been steaming their Noses gratefully, with mull'd Cyder or butter'd Ale, and then offerest to refresh their Palates with the best of Beer, they will curse thee for thy Greasiness" (W 217–18). Near the conclusion, the mug is "broken to Pieces, and cast away." But the "avaritious Owner" grieved not for it, "but for the Shilling with which he purchased thee!"

The idea of original sin may also be an underlying subject: "If thy Bottom-Part should chance to survive, it may be preserv'd to hold Bits of Candles, or Blacking for Shoes, or Salve for kibed Heels; but all thy other Members will be for ever buried in some miry Hole; or less carefully disposed of, so that little Children, who have not yet arrived to Acts of Cruelty, may gather them up to furnish out their Baby-Houses." Perhaps alluding to Locke on education and on innate ideas, Franklin suggested that "little children" are naturally kind and loving but that experience with the world gradually brought them to "Acts of Cruelty." He implied that mankind was not born in original sin.

Franklin concluded by continuing with the probable end of mugs: "Or, being cast upon the Dunghill, they will therewith be carted into Meadow Grounds; where, being spread abroad and discovered, they must be thrown to the Heap of Stones, Bones, and Rubbish; or being left until the Mower finds them with his Scythe, they will with bitter Curses be tossed over the Hedge; and so serve for unlucky Boys to throw at Birds and Dogs; until by Length of Time and numerous Casualties, they shall be press'd into their Mother Earth, and be converted to their original Principles" (W 218). The mug ends not in a reunion with God or an afterlife that recompenses the mug/person for the miseries en-dured on earth, but it suffers an entirely materialistic dissolution. This is the Epicurean position, perhaps again reflecting Lucretius. Though Jonathan Swift concluded with the destruction of the broomstick, he does not dwell on the nihilistic materialism of the broomstick's eradication. Franklin seemingly de-parted from religious burlesque in the conclusion, but the final nihilism makes the satire of spirituality more biting.

"The Death of Infants"

Deists and other eighteenth-century writers often compared God to an exquisite clockmaker who, having contrived the world as an ingenious mechanism, needed only occasionally to wind it up in order for it to go on functioning beautifully. Franklin used the comparison in *A Dissertation on Liberty and Necessity* (1725; 1:62); and he used the physico-theology argument upon which the clockmaker analogy was based in both "Articles of Belief" (1728; 1:104) and "On the Providence of God in the Government of the World" (1730; 1:265). Franklin knew the analogy from many sources, including John Ray's *Wisdom of God Manifested in the Works of the Creation* (1691), which he quoted in "Articles of Belief."

Franklin applied his genius for explaining and simplifying complex matters to the doctrine of the argument from design. The God-as-clockmaker analogy held that just as the design of a clock proved that it was created by an intelligence, so the awesomely beautiful intricacy of a human being (the microcosm) or of the universe (the macrocosm) revealed that they must have been created by a superior intelligence. But Franklin burlesqued the teleological argument in "The Death of Infants" without using philosophical language. He had two reasons for avoiding technical diction. First, it would have made his essay less suited for most readers of the *Pennsylvania Gazette*. Second, he could be more daring in his criticisms of the argument from design and of providence using colloquial phrasing than he could using philosophical diction. Had he verbalized the theological argument, he might have been accused of blasphemy. Modern scholars of eighteenth-century thought cite David Hume's posthumously published *Dialogues* (1779) and Immanuel Kant's *Critique of Judgement* (1790) as the first writings to criticize "the notion that teleology in nature is analogous to the teleology of a mechanical artifact."[60] Franklin's critique is half a century earlier and perhaps more devastating.

Franklin's anonymous essay on "The Death of Infants" appeared in the *Pennsylvania Gazette*, 20 June 1734. The author quoted William Petty's *Political Arithmetick*, "that one half of Mankind, which are born into this World, die, before they arrive to the age of Sixteen, and that an half of the remaining part never measure out the short Term of Thirty Years." Franklin noted that bills of mortality and almost any cemetery bore out the truth of Petty's observations. He said, "Many Arguments, to prove a *Future State*, have been drawn from the unequal Lot of good and bad Men upon Earth, but no one seems to carry a greater Degree of Probability in it, than the foregoing Observation."[61] Franklin thus tried to make the essay seem to have a religious purpose. As he knew, Blaise Pascal, John Locke, and William Wollaston were among those who claimed that the justice of God demanded that an afterlife exist to right the wrongs in this world. Franklin continued with a paraphrase of Luke 16:19–21: "To see Virtue languish and repine, to see Vice prosperous and triumphant, to see a *Dives*

faring deliciously every Day, and rioting in all the Excess of Luxury and Wan-
tonness; to see a *Lazarus* poor, hungry, naked, and full of Sores, lying at his
Door, and denied even the Crumbs that fall from his Table, the Portion of his
Dogs, which Dogs are more charitable, more human than their Master: Such a
View, I confess, raises in us a violent Presumption that there is another State of
Retribution, where the Just and the Unjust will be equally punished or rewarded
by an impartial Judge" (W 228).

Franklin voiced another standard religious argument. "When we reflect on
the vast Numbers of Infants, that just struggle into Life, then weep and die, and
at the same time consider, that it can be in no wise consistent with the Justice
and Wisdom of an infinite Being, to create to no end, we may very reasonably
conclude, that those animated Machines, those *Men* in *miniature*, who know no
Difference between Good and Evil, who are incapable of any good Offices
towards their Fellow-Creatures, or of serving their Maker, were made for good
and wise Designs and Purposes, which Purposes, and Designs transcend all the
Limits of our Ideas and all our present Capacities to conceive" (W 228–29).

Having approached a fideistic position, Franklin then introduced his subversive argument. He brought up the God-as-clockmaker analogy—but he derided
it and indirectly mocked the previous two religious assertions: "Should an able
and expert Artificer employ all his Time and his Skill in contriving and framing
an exquisite Piece of *Clock-work*, which, when he had brought it to the utmost
Perfection Wit and Art were capable of, and just set it a-going, he should suddenly dash it to pieces; would not every wise Man naturally infer, that his intense
Application had disturb'd his Brain and impair'd his Reason?" (W 229).

The answer to Franklin's rhetorical question is yes. If there is a God, he must
be mad.

Franklin returned to an extended description of the incredible complexity
and beauty of an infant as a "curious Engine of Divine Workmanship." He had
previously compared man to a machine or to an engine in *A Dissertation* (1:62–
64), reflecting Descartes's definition of animals as automatons and the medical
advances of the past century, as well as anticipating Julien Offray de La Mettrie's
L'Homme machine (1747).[62] In "The Death of Infants," he celebrated humans as
complex microcosms, seemingly to prove that God created them as well as the
universe. "What a rich and artful Structure of Flesh upon the solid and well
compacted Foundation of Bones! What curious Joints and Hinges, on which
the Limbs are moved to and fro! What an inconceivable Variety of Nerves,
Veins, Arteries, Fibres and little invisible parts are found in every Member! What
various Fluids, Blood and Juices run thro' and agitate the innumerable slender
Tubes, the hollow Strings and Strainers of the Body! What millions of folding
Doors are fixed within, to stop those red or transparent Rivulets in their course,
either to prevent their Return backwards, or else as a Means to swell the Muscles
and move the Limbs! What endless contrivances to secure Life, to nourish Nature, and to propagate the same to future Animals!" (W 229). Pascal was among

the authors Franklin knew who had written on the complex workings of the body, of the macrocosm and microcosm. He said that a nit (a young louse) examined under a microscope would show "Legs with Joynts, Veins in these Legs, Blood in those Veins, Humors in this Blood, Drops in these Humours, Vapors in those Drops."[63]

After his sustained appreciation of the intricate mechanism of the bodies of infants, Franklin recurred to their deaths: "Can we now imagine after such a Survey, that so wise, so good and merciful a Creator should produce *Myriads* of such exquisite Machines to no other End or Purpose, but to be deposited in the dark Chambers of the Grave, where each of the Dead lie in their cold Mansions, in Beds of Darkness and Dust." Franklin arouses the reader's horror by dwelling on death: "The Shadows of a long Evening are stretch'd over them, the Curtains of a deep Midnight are drawn around them, *The Worm lies under them, and the Worm covers them*." He rejects the idea of death: "No! the Notion of Annihilation has in it something so shocking and absurd, Reason should despise it; rather let us believe, that when they drop this earthly Vehicle they assume an Aetherial one, and become the Inhabitants of some more glorious Region" (W 229).

Franklin also indulged his imagination concerning the future of infants, using the belief in plenitude that characterized his 1728 "Articles of Belief." May not infants "help to people that infinite Number of *Starry* and *Planetary* Worlds that roll above us; may they not become our better *Genii*, our Guardian Angels, watch round our Bed and our Couch, direct our wandring Paths thro' the Maze and Labyrinth of Life, and at length conduct us safe, even us, who were the Instruments of their passing thro' this *Valley* of Sorrow and Death, to a Land of Peace and the Mountains of *Paradise*?" Franklin's shift from the microcosm to the macrocosm was not uncommon. Immediately after describing the nit, Pascal, in a similar manner, turned to the universe: "an infinite numer of Worlds, every one of which having their Sun, Planets, Earth, in the same Proportion the visible World has" (146).

The author of "The Death of Infants" said he was "led into this Train of thinking by the Death of a desirable Child, whose Beauty is now turning a-pace into Corruption, and all the Loveliness of its Countenance fled for ever" (W 229–30). Perhaps so, but his own sickly child, Francis, was then two years old. One wonders if Franklin wrote the essay during the child's illness.

Though it was unlikely that Franklin's condemnation of the nature of God would do anyone any good, he nevertheless attempted to make the essay useful. "If the foregoing Reflections should urge any one forward in the Paths of Vertue, or yield any Consolation to those in the like Circumstances, and help to divert the Stream of their Sorrow into a better Channel, I shall hope my Thoughts have been employ'd to good Purpose." In concluding, Franklin turned to the fragility of life.

Though his parodies of religious meditations burlesqued their gloominess, Franklin now indulged in melancholy. He probably reflected Nahum Tate's version of Juvenal's fifteenth satire (which Dryden published in his 1697 edition of Juvenal). Tate wrote: "Compassion proper to mankind appears; Which Nature witness'd, when she let us tears." Franklin revised the wording: "When Nature gave us Tears, she gave us leave to weep." Reinforcing the thought and making one last attempt to make the essay seem Christian, Franklin cited John 11:33, 35. "When *Lazarus* died, *Jesus* groaned and wept" (W 230).

Nearly half a century later, Franklin had similar thoughts. He declared to James Hutton on 7 July 1782 the impossibility of reconciling the evil that happened on earth with any reasonable scheme of justice. The lack of justice in this life made Franklin more and more "convinc'd of a future State, in which all that here appears to be wrong shall be set right, all that is crooked made straight." Perhaps showing greater maturity in 1782, Franklin ignored his youthful position on God's responsibility for the miseries of life. But in this 1734 essay on the death of infants, Franklin concluded with an ironic epitaph, reversing the object of pity. Whereas he had been lamenting the death of infants and the brevity of their lives, Franklin suddenly shifted and celebrated an early death as a blessing—not primarily because (in the Christian tradition) the infant is joined to Christ; but because the infant has escaped life's further miseries:

> Read this and weep—but not for me;
> Lament thy longer Misery:
> My Life was short, my Grief the less;
> Blame not my Haste to Happiness! (W 230)

One recalls that Franklin seemed to regret recovering from his severe sickness at age twenty-one because he would have "all that disagreable Work to do" (A 52). He also echoed this pessimistic view of existence in a letter to Jane Mecom on 10 July 1764, comforting her on her daughter's death. After several conventional consolations, he concluded with an acrid reflection on existence: "Our only Comfort under such Afflictions is, that God knows what is best for us, and can bring Good out of what appears Evil. She is doubtless happy: which none of us are in this life." Since he was normally extraordinarily sensitive to the feelings of others, it is surprising that he revealed his bleak pessimism to his favorite sister on such an occasion. The letter to Jane reaffirmed the view of God as a mad clockmaker—a deity who created humans to live in a world of misery. The thought is akin to Franklin's bleakest fictive worlds, such as the supposed news report of 15 February 1731/2 of a man disordered in his senses who bit off his wife's tongue and threw it into a fire saying, "*Let this be for a Burnt-Offering,*" or the Revolutionary War satire of early 1777, "The Sale of the Hessians," or the supposed piece of "West India News," which he sent to Joseph Priestley on 7 June 1782.

Franklin may have believed that his thoughts in the essay on the death of infants were true, but, like deism itself, he may have thought they were "not very useful" (A 58) to himself or to others. Six weeks later, he reversed his position when writing a parody of a religious meditation.

Parody and Reply to a Religious Meditation

In the front page of the 1 August 1734 *Gazette*, Franklin published a "Meditation on the Vanity and Brevity of Human Life" from *A Select Manual of Divine Meditation and Prayers* by the Reverend Joshua Smith. He had seen it in the *London Magazine* (April 1734) and in the *Boston Gazette* (11 July 1734), thought it ridiculous, and reprinted it in order to burlesque it the following week (8 August). He wrote two parodies, prefaced with an editorial disclaimer. "By being too nice in the Choice of the little Pieces sent me by my Correspondents to be printed, I had almost discouraged them from writing to me any more. For the Time to come, and that my Paper may become still more generally agreeable, I have resolved not to regard my own Humour so much in what I print; and thereupon I give my Readers the two following Letters." Though every Franklin skit is not prefaced by an editorial disclaimer, every *Gazette* editorial disclaimer prefaces a Franklin squib.

The first letter travestied the meditation. Bishop Edmund Gibson and other religious figures thought ridicule was unfair, but the third earl of Shaftesbury, in *Sensus Communis; an Essay of the Freedom of Wit and Humour* (1709), which became section 2 of his *Characteristics* (1711), defended ridicule as a test of truth.[64] Franklin agreed with Shaftesbury. The speaker in Franklin's first rejoinder was a comparative optimist: "Mr. Franklin, You gave us in your last a melancholy Account of Human Life, in the Meditation upon that Subject. The gloomy and splenetick Part of your Readers like it much; but as for me, I do not love to see the dark Side of Things; and besides, I do not think such Reflections upon Life altogether just. The World is a very good World, and if we behave our selves well, we shall doubtless do very well in it." The speaker reflected Franklin's deliberate attempts to be positive about life. He wrote his sister Jane, "Take one thing with another, and the World is a pretty good sort of a World; and 'tis our Duty to make the best of it and be thankful" (13:188). The speaker wittily continued, "I never thought even *Job* in the right, when he repin'd that the Days of a Man are *few* and *full of Trouble*; for certainly both these Things cannot be together just Causes of Complaint; if our Days are full of Trouble, the fewer of 'em the better."

Though Franklin repeats the closing thought (the shorter the life, the less the grief) from "The Death of Infants," the witty, light tone contradicts the high seriousness and pessimism of the earlier essay. The speaker is optimistic, not because life consists of unalloyed joy, but because he does "not love to see the dark Side of Things." Life is better if one focuses on the positive. It is healthier and better if one makes the best of it.

Franklin claimed the author of the meditation complained "weakly, and without the least shadow of Reason . . . That he cannot be alive now, and ten

Years ago, and ten Years hence, at the same time." Franklin proposed to compare the minister's "elegant Expressions" to a "Child who laments that he cannot eat his Cake and have his Cake" (W 231).

Joshua Smith:	*Franklin*
All the few days we live are full of Vanity; and our choicest Pleasures sprinkled with bitterness.	All the few Cakes we have are puffed up with Yeast; and the nicest Gingerbread is spotted with Flyshits!
The time that's past is vanish'd like a dream; and that which is to come is not yet at all.	The Cakes that we have eaten are no more to be seen; and those which are to come are not yet baked.
The present we are in stays but for a moment, and then flies away, and returns no more.	The present Mouthful is chewed but a little while, and then is swallowed down, and comes up no more. *[Wonderful humor! The reader cannot help but be jolted into the thought—who would want it to come up!]*
Already we are dead to the years we have liv'd; and shall never live them over again.	Already we have digested the Cakes we have eaten, and shall never eat them over again.
But the longer we live, the shorter is our life; and in the end we become a little lump of clay.	And the more we eat, the less is the Piece remaining; and in the end the whole will become Sir-reverence!

Thus Franklin ends the cake analogy on an excremental note.

Franklin returned to the persona of an optimist who accepts life: "I am for taking *Solomon's* Advice, *eating Bread with Joy, and drinking Wine with a merry Heart.* Let us rejoice and bless God, that we are neither Oysters, Hogs, nor Dray-Horses; and not stand repining that He has not made us Angels; lest we be found unworthy of that share of Happiness He has thought fit to allow us" (W 231–32). Life should be enjoyed and celebrated.

Franklin's other reply did not lampoon Smith but instead focused on the pleasures and happiness in life. Like Smith, Franklin wrote a synopsis of the progress of an individual's life, but he changed the constant lament to pleasure:

Most happy are we, the sons of men, above all other creatures, who are born to behold the glorious rays of the sun, and to enjoy the pleasant fruits of the earth. With what pleasure did our parents first receive us, first to hear us cry, then to see us smile, and afterwards to behold us growing up and thriving in the world. By their good examples and vertuous education, they put us in the right path to happiness, as all good parents do; Then we, by making a right use of that share of reason with which God hath endued us, spend our days in gaining and enjoying the blessings of life, which are innumerable. If we meet with crosses and disappointments, they are but as sowr sauce to the sweet meats we enjoy, and the one hath not a right relish without the other. As time passes away, it carries our past pains with it, and returns no more; and the longer we live the fewer misfortunes we have to go through. If death takes us off the height of our prosperity, it takes us from the pains which may ensue. And a great blessing attends old age, for by that we are naturally wean'd from the pleasures of youth, and a more solid pleasure takes place, the thoughts of our having so far escaped all the hazards that attend mankind, and a contemplation on all our former good actions. And if we have done all the good we could, we have done all that we ought, and death is no terror to a good man. And after we are far declined, with hearty praises and thanks we recommend our soul to God, the eternal Being from whom we received it. Then comes the grave, and the sweet sleep of death, pleasant as a bed to a weary traveler after a long journey. (W 232–33)

Professor Alfred Owen Aldridge pointed out that the reply was similar to a number of optimistic passages in Franklin's earlier and later writings.[65] A bagatelle close in sentiment to this optimistic message is "The Handsome and Deformed Leg" (1780). In it, as in this piece, Franklin tried to be optimistic and to show the foolishness of being pessimistic. Regarding the essential nature of human beings, however, he himself was pessimistic.[66]

CONCLUSION

Though Franklin is often said to be the most modern of his contemporaries, in these moral essays he seems as distant from the present as Addison or Steele. Today, the largest bookstores contain nothing titled "How to obtain Virtue," but they have books on how to fix the house, dozens on how to make money, and scores on how to cook—right beside the scores on how to lose weight. Franklin said that virtue was an art, but for today's readers, it is a lost art—and a boring one. A few persons study eighteenth-century moral philosophy, but with rare exceptions, they do not read any Americans.

Franklin did not identify Hobbes, Locke, Shaftesbury, Mandeville, Hutcheson, or the other moral philosophers he agreed or disagreed with. Had he cited them, the essays may have been more highly regarded at the time and subsequently. Clearly, he was content to have his say, knowing that few readers of the *Pennsylvania Gazette* would recognize or appreciate the stakes for which he played. It was almost as if he wrote the essays entirely for his own intellectual satisfaction; their only practical purpose for him was as newspaper filler. One thinks of Edward Taylor writing his poetry in the frontier town of Westfield, Massachusetts, or of Jonathan Edwards writing his abstract theological treatises in Saybrook, Massachusetts. Though Franklin's situation as a printer in a large town was completely different, he seems to have cared as little for the effect and fame of his writings as if he were writing only for himself in the wilderness.

No colonial American layman wrote as much on religion, ethics, and values as Franklin. Indeed, few ministers did. His great contemporary Edwards took up some of the same questions—and answered them brilliantly. Edwards, however, seemed in some ways a throwback to a time when everyone believed that God immediately caused every action. But perhaps Franklin was even more of a throwback, for he not infrequently seems to hold Epicurean positions and to echo the thoughts of Lucretius. What is one to make of Franklin's different opinions in the various questions of human behavior, ethics, and philosophy? He often contradicts himself, sometimes advocating the essential goodness of mankind, at others, the evil nature of mankind. Sometimes he ridicules sentiment and yet he finds human sympathy a noble quality. He seems to be fundamentally pessimistic, yet he inculcated optimism and behaved as if he believed in it. He criticized God as a madman, yet he wrote and practiced a private religious liturgy worshiping God. He did more to change the world he lived in than any of his contemporaries, yet he thought that the existing world was a "pretty good sort of world." Franklin seems to see the complexity of the issues. As the thesis of an essay above states, "Men are naturally benevolent as well as selfish"; it depends on the circumstances and the person. Franklin is contradicting the thesis that humans are "altogether selfish," but he does not find them altogether benevolent. He is content to say that both positions are true. Elsewhere, contrary positions each have some truth. He wrote James Logan concerning the opposition of Hobbes and Locke, "the Truth perhaps lies between both Extremes." Sometimes he appears to be a being from another universe who can—and occasionally does—deride the philosophical foundations of earthlings, including, of course, himself. Perhaps most surprising, he seems not uncomfortable ridiculing the normal certainties—and ridiculing himself.

THREE

Freemason

Monday last, a Grand Lodge of the Ancient and Honourable Society of Free and Accepted Masons in this Province, was held at the Tun Tavern in Water-Street, when Benjamin Franklin being elected Grand Master for the Year ensuing, appointed Mr. John Crap, to be his Deputy; and James Hamilton, Esq; and Thomas Hopkinson, Gent. were chosen Wardens. After which, the Governor, and several other Persons of Distinction honour'd the Society with their Presence.
—Pennsylvania Gazette, *27 June 1734*

IN 1725 AND 1726, Franklin read about Masonic meetings in the London papers. He probably met John Theophilus Desagulier, a founder of English Freemasonry, through a fellow Bostonian, Isaac Greenwood, who was Desagulier's assistant as experimenter at the Royal Society. When a group of Pennsylvanians started a Masonic lodge in 1730, Franklin evidently thought he would like to join, but he was not asked. He thereupon gently coerced the members into electing him. After spotting a piece ridiculing Masonry in the London *Daily Journal* of 15 August 1730, he revised and reprinted it in the *Pennsylvania Gazette* on 8 December. Franklin probably published the good-natured satire on the Freemasons in order to call attention to himself and his possible influence on public opinion. Such calculated behavior paralleled the way that, in his own opinion, he first gained subscribers to the *Gazette*. He wrote in the *Autobiography* that his remarks on the controversy between Governor Burnet and the Massachusetts Assembly "struck the principal People, occasion'd the Paper and the Manager of it to be much talk'd of, and in a few Weeks brought them all to be our Subscribers." Not only did he use the newspaper for desired personal ends (in this case, gaining subscribers), but he was also aware of the implied threat of a publisher's influence. He commented that the leading citizens, "seeing a News Paper now in the hands of one who could also handle a Pen, thought it convenient to oblige and encourage me" (A 64). Presumably he thought that if he published the satire, the Masons would realize that he was someone whose friendship should be cultivated.

THE SATIRE

Franklin's introductory note said that "The Mystery of *Free-Masonry*" was reprinted from a London paper. Actually, he thoroughly revised the article. The

Gazette essay began: "As there are several Lodges of FREE-MASONS erected in this Province, and People have lately been much amus'd with Conjectures concerning them; we think the following Account of Free-Masonry from London, will not be unacceptable to our Readers."

A comparison of the London essay with Franklin's version demonstrates his literary artistry—and his concern with the *Gazette*'s layout. The *Daily Journal* version opened: "The Grand Whimsy of Masonry has been long the Subject of Amusement to diverse Persons, who have wonder'd, that among so many idle People as have been admitted into that Society, many of whom are not noted for eminent Virtues, or the Gift of Taciturnity, the boasted Secret has never been, thro' Inadvertence, or the Power of Liquor, divulg'd."[1] Franklin revised the rambling sentence, dropping the references to "idle People" and "not noted for eminent Virtues" because the phrases logically had little to do with the discovery of Masonic secrets. He wrote: "The World has long admir'd, that in such a numerous Company, many of them not remarkable for Taciturnity, there has been no one found, that in his Cups or in any other Circumstance, would discover their Mysteries."

After a long, wordy paragraph, the London essay continued, "At last, the Death of a Brother, who for his own Remembrance and Observation, had seem'd to have committed to Writing, the Form and Manner of his Admission, which he kept among his choicest and most private Papers, and in the most secret Part of his Cabinet, has given us a Light into the mysterious Part of Entrance, and into their puerile Signs and Wonders." Franklin divided the rambling sentence into two short ones, dropped vague and unnecessary words ("and Observation"), substituted less insulting expressions ("secret" for "puerile"), and omitted inappropriate diction ("had seem'd"). Franklin wrote: "By the Death of a Gentleman who was one of the Brotherhood of FREE-MASONS, there has lately happen'd a discovery of abundance of their secret Signs and Wonders, with the mysterious Manner of their Admission into that Fraternity. The following is a true Copy of a Manuscript which the Deceased had written for the Benefit of his own private Remembrance, and which was found conceal'd among his choicest Papers in the most hidden Part of his Cabinet."

Franklin inserted an original sentence: "But the whole appears so childish and ridiculous, that this is probably the Case, THEIR GRAND Secret is *That they have no Secret at all*; and when once a Man is enter'd, he finds himself oblig'd, *se defendendo*, to carry on the Jest with as solemn a Face as the rest." Though Franklin here wrote a lengthy compound, complex sentence, the syntax is clear. I might also comment on his use of accidentals. Though only nouns were usually capitalized in the eighteenth century, Franklin capitalized the first two words of "Their Grand Secret" for emphasis—and italicized the following clause for the same purpose.

The London version proceeded, "I shall not pretend to use many Words to bespeak your Readers Belief of the Genuineness of this MS. only referring him

The Pennfylvania Gazette.

Containing the frefheft Advices Foreign and Domeftick.

From Thurfday, December 3. to Tuefday, December 8. 1730.

As there are feveral Lodges of FREE-MASONS erected in this Province, and People have lately been much amus'd with Conjectures concerning them; we think the following Account of Free-Mafonry from London, will not be unacceptable to our Readers.

LONDON, Auguft 12.

BY the Death of a Gentleman who was one of the Brotherhood of FREE-MASONS, there has lately happen'd a Difcovery of abundance of their fecret Signs and Wonders, with the myfterious Manner of their Admiffion into that Fraternity. The following is a true Copy of a Manufcript which the Deceafed had written for the Benefit of his own private Remembrance, and which was found conceal'd among his choiceft Papers in the moft hidden Part of his Cabinet. The World has long admir'd, that in fuch a numerous Company, many of them not remarkable for Taciturnity, there has been no one found, that in his Cups, or in any other Circumftance, would difcover their Myfteries: But the whole appears fo childish and ridiculous, that this is probably the Cafe, Their Grand Secret is, That they have no Secret at all; and when once a Man is enter'd, he finds himfelf oblig'd, fe defendendo, to carry on the Jeft with as folemn a Face as the reft. We fhall not ufe many Words to perfuade the Publick that the following Piece is genuine; it carries all the Marks of Truth in itfelf: We would only refer the Reader to the Conduct of the Brotherhood upon this Occafion; it they ridicule it, or look very grave upon it, or if they are very angry and endeavour to decry it, he may be fatisfied it is the real Truth.

The Myftery of Free-Mafonry.

Queftion, ARE you a Mafon? Anfwer, I am. Q. How fhall I know you are a Mafon? A. By Signs, Tokens, and Points of my Entrance. Q. How was you made? A. Neither naked nor cloathed, ftanding or lying, but in due Form. Q. Give me a Sign? A. Every Square is a Sign; but the moft folemn is the Right Hand upon the Left Breaft, the Arm hanging down, a little extended from the Body. Q. Give me a Letter? A. B, O, A, Z. [When this Queftion is afk'd, you are to give the Letter B. The Querift will fay O. you A. he Z.] Q. Give me another? A. J, A, C, H, I, N. [Alternately as Boaz, N. B. Boaz and Jachin were two Pillars in Solomon's Porch. 1 Kings vii. 21.] Q. To what Lodge do you belong? A. To the holy Lodge of St. John. Q. How is it feated? A. Eaft and Weft as all other Temples are. Q. Where was you enter'd? A. In a juft and perfect Lodge. Q. What makes a juft and perfect Lodge? A. A Mafter, two Wardens, and four Fellows, with Square, Compafs and Common Gudge. [N. B. One of them muft be a Working Mafon.] Q. Where was you made? A. In the Valley of Jehofaphat, behind a Rufh Bufh, where a Dog was never heard to Bark, nor a Cock to Crow, or elfewhere. Q. Where was the firft Lodge kept? A. In Solomon's Porch; the Pillars were called Jachin and Boaz. Q. How many Orders be there in Architecture? A. There be five, Tufcan, Doric, Ionic, Corinthian, and Compofite or Roman Orders. Q. How many Points be there in the Fellowfhip? A. There be Five, 1. Foot to Foot. 2. Knee to Knee. 3. Hand to Hand. 4. Heart to Heart. 5. Ear to Ear. Q. How do Mafons take their Place in Work? A. The Mafter's Place Eaft, the Warden's Eaft, and the Fellows the Eaftern Paffage. Q. How many precious Jewels be there in Mafonry? A. Three; the Mafter, Wardens and Fellows. Q. Whence comes the Pattern of an Arch? A. From the

Rainbow. Q. Is there a Key for your Lodge? A. Yes there is. Q. Where is it kept? A. In an Ivory Box, between my Tongue and my Teeth: Or, under the Lap of my Liver, where the Secrets of my Heart are. Q. Is there a Chain to your Key? A. Yes there is. Q. How long is it? A. As long as from my Tongue to my Heart. Q. Where does the Key of the Working Lodge lie? A. It lies upon the Right Hand from the Door two Feet and a Half, under a green Turf, or under a fquare Afhler. Q. Where does the Mafter Mafon fet his Mark upon the Work? A. Upon the South Eaft Corner. Q. Have you been in the Kitchin? [N. B. You fhall know an enter'd Apprentice by this Queftion] A. Yes, I have. Q. Did you ever Dine in the Hall? [A Brother Mafon by this Queftion] Yes, I did. Q. How old are you? A. Under 5, or under 7. Which you will. [N. B. When you are firft made a Mafon, you are only enter'd Apprentice; and till you are made a Mafter, or, as they call it, pafs'd the Mafter's Part, you are only an enter'd Apprentice, and confequently muft anfwer under 7. for if you fay above, they will expect the Mafter's Word and Signs. Note, There is not one Mafon in a Hundred that will be at the Expence to pafs the Mafter's Part, unlefs it be for Intereft.] Q. How was you admitted? [N. B. Some will afk, what was that Form, after the third Queftion and Anfwer above] A. When I came to the firft Door, a Man with a drawn Sword afked me, If I had any Weapons? I anfwer'd, No. Upon which he let me pafs by him into a dark Entry; there two Wardens took me under each Arm, and conducted me from Darknefs into Light, paffing thro' two Rows of the Brotherhood, who ftood mute, to the upper End of the Room, from whence the Mafter went down the Outfide of one of the Rows, and touching a young Brother on the Shoulder, faid, Who have we here? To which he anfwer'd, A Gentleman who defires to be admitted a Member of the Society. Upon which he came up again, and afked me, If I came there thro' my own Defire, or at the Requeft or Defire of another? I faid, My own. He then told me, If I would become a Brother of their Society, I muft take the Oath adminiftred on that Occafion. To which affenting, a Square was laid on the Ground, in which they made me kneel bare-knee'd, and giving a Compafs into my Right Hand, I fet the Point to my left Breaft, and my left Arm hanging down. The Words of the Oath I can't Remember, but the Purport was as follows:

I Solemnly Proteft and Swear, in the Prefence of Almighty God, and this Society, that I will not, by Word of Mouth or Signs, difcover any Secrets which fhall be communicated to me this Night, or at any Time hereafter: That I will not write, carve, engrave, or caufe to be written, carved or engraven the fame, either upon Paper, Copper, Brafs, Wood or Stone, or any Moveable or Immoveable, or any other Way difcover the fame, to any but a Brother or Fellow Craft, under no lefs Penalty than having my Heart pluck'd thro' the Pap of my left Breaft, my Tongue by the Roots from the Roof of my Mouth, my Body to be burnt, and my Afhes to be fcattered abroad in the Wind, whereby I may be loft to the Remembrance of a Brother.

After which I was cloathed. [N. B. The Cloathing is putting on the Apron and Gloves.] Q. How was the Mafter cloathed? A. In a Yellow Jacket and blue pair of Breeches. [N. B. The Mafter is not otherwife cloathed than common; The Queftion and Anfwer are only Emblematical; the yellow Jacket, the Compafes, and the blue Breeches, the Steel Points.] Q. What was you doing while the Oath was tendering? A. I was kneeling bare knee'd betwixt the Bible and the Square, taking the folemn Oath of a Mafon. [Note, There is a Bible put in the Right Hand, and the Square under the Right Elbow.

FOREIGN

Figure 5. Blackmailing the Masons? "The Mystery of Free-Masonry," Pennsylvania Gazette, 8 December 1730. Franklin thoroughly revised this essay from a London paper before publishing it in the Gazette. Perhaps he meant to suggest to the Philadelphia St. John's Lodge of Freemasons that he could be a valuable friend or a formidable enemy. The next month the lodge invited him to join, and he became a member in February 1730/1. Courtesy, Library Company of Philadelphia.

to the Observation of the Conduct of the Fraternity on this Occasion, who will be sure to be either very *angry*, or very *silent*, or very *zealous* to decry it, if it be really what I in myself have abundant Reason to be satisfied it is." Franklin revised the rambling syntax into shorter, clearer units. He improved the logic by connecting the London writer's "very *angry*" with the similar "very *zealous* to decry it," substituted "*very grave*" for the less graphic "very *silent*," added another possible reaction ("*ridicule*") to make a reply more impossible, omitted the awkward references to "Readers" and "him," and ended his sentence with a point: "We shall not use many Words to persuade the Publick that the following Piece is genuine; it carries all the Marks of Truth in itself: We would only refer the Reader to the Conduct of the Brotherhood upon this Occasion; if they *ridicule* it, or look *very grave* upon it, or if they are *very angry* and endeavour to *decry* it, he may be satisfied it is the *real Truth*." Franklin's preface, though based on the London introduction, has the clarity, brevity, and witty, satirical turns characteristic of his writing—and ends well. The London version trails on, finally stopping after another rambling sentence.

After the prefatory paragraph, Franklin reprinted the piece as supposedly found in the London *Daily Journal*. The preface and the account exactly fill the *Pennsylvania Gazette*'s front page. To take up no more space, Franklin printed the dialogue without paragraph divisions, indenting only the supposed Masonic initiation oath pledging secrecy. Examining the *Pennsylvania Gazette*'s layout, one can see that Franklin rewrote the introduction partly to make the whole piece fit within the front page. For the introduction, he wanted approximately three inches in type—about 280 words. The lengthy, boring London introduction would have taken about fifteen inches. It wasn't worth fifteen inches.

The Philadelphia Freemasons got the underlying message and voted, at their next meeting, to admit Franklin. Subsequently and perhaps consequently, on 13 May 1731 he printed a brief favorable article concerning Freemasons, taken from "Chambers's *Universal Dictionary of all Arts and Sciences*."

FRANKLIN'S LODGE

Though Freemasonry in Europe was associated with radical Enlightenment thought, the American Masonic lodges were generally benevolent male social clubs, whose members pledged to study and increase their skills, to help one another, and to be kind to everyone. Philadelphia's 1730 Freemasons were typical of the American lodges. They had no intellectual members except the rich merchant William Allen until they elected Franklin, and they had no radical members before him. The St. John's Lodge of Freemasons voted to admit Franklin on Monday, 4 January 1730/1.[2] He joined at the next meeting, Monday, 1 February.[3] St. John's Lodge had been founded only the year before, perhaps on St. John's Day, 24 June 1730.[4]

The nine known members who elected Franklin to St. John's Lodge included four bricklayers (Thomas Bode, Thomas Hart, Samuel Nicholas, and Christopher Thompson), a farmer (also named Thomas Hart), an attorney (John Emerson), two persons whose occupations are uncertain (William Button, who was probably a ship captain, and William Pringle), and a successful young merchant (William Allen). Of the bricklayers, at least one, Christopher Thompson, became a builder and an entrepreneur. He later sold Franklin a house on Arch Street between Fourth and Fifth Streets (P 2:311, 18:262–63).

The lodge admitted four other persons during the year (concluding on St. John the Baptist Day, 24 June 1731): John Hobart, proprietor of the Sun Tavern on Water Street where the lodge met until Hobart moved in 1733; Mark Joyce, merchant; Henry Pratt, who was admitted on the same date as Franklin and who later became a member of the Library Company; and Thomas Redman (d. 1748), bricklayer. Thus, with a few exceptions, the Freemasons' lodge that Franklin joined was composed of young artisans.[5]

In addition to meeting on the first Monday of every month, the lodge met on 24 June, St. John the Baptist Day. A surviving account book of St. John's Lodge contains records from 24 June 1731 to 24 June 1734, with summary accounts going forward to 24 June 1738. The original £3 initiation fee increased to £5 in June 1734. Members paid monthly dues of six pence and were fined a shilling for missing a meeting. Since the account book lists the dates of the meetings for the first three years, as well as the money paid, one can deduce the members' dates of attendance.

A report of the "Stock of St. John's Lodge, 1731," allows us to piece together the officers chosen on Thursday, 24 June 1731. The same persons may well have been in office when Franklin was elected to membership that preceding January. William Allen (1704–1780), later chief justice of Pennsylvania, was grand master on 24 June 1731 (that was probably the day he was elected), and William Pringle, deputy. But in that account, William Button is called "Late Master." He does not elsewhere appear except in the account of the "Stock of St. John's Lodge, 1731," which noted that he has "Sailed to Newfoundland." Button, then, was probably the first grand master. Thomas Hart (d. 1749), bricklayer, is mentioned on 5 July 1731 as "Late warden." Thomas Bode (1700?–1781), bricklayer, was secretary/treasurer. These were presumably the officers when Franklin was elected in January 1731.

Franklin regularly attended the Masonic meetings. He was present at the Sun Tavern for every Monday monthly meeting in 1731 from February through December except Monday, 1 November, when he paid a shilling for his absence. Perhaps he missed the 1 November meeting in order to help his mother-in-law, Sarah Read, move; she had been renting a shop from him on 139 Market Street, but after she gave it up on 1 November, Franklin promptly rented it to the bookbinder Stephen Potts.[6] He was at the annual meeting on St. John the Baptist Day, Thursday, 24 June.[7] Sometime after 9 September 1731, when Thomas Whitmarsh left for South Carolina to become Franklin's partner there, Franklin printed one hundred blanks for the Masons at a charge of five shillings. Masonic historian Julius F. Sachse suggested that these were petitions for initiation and membership.[8]

In 1732 Franklin missed three of the thirteen meetings: he was absent on 6 March, 1 May, and 6 November.[9] Since Francis Folger Franklin was born on 20 October and was a sickly infant, perhaps Franklin stayed home with his sick baby that early 6 November evening. On 5 June, he presented his draft for the by-laws of St. John's Lodge, recommending that the lodge buy books of architecture and mathematical instruments. His recommendation that no fines be collected for absences was not adopted. On the same date, the lodge agreed to spend "the present Cash [for] . . . the best Books of Architecture, suitable Mathematical Instruments, etc." (1:232).

WARDEN

The *Pennsylvania Gazette* for Monday, 26 June 1732, reported the annual election: "Saturday last, being St. John's Day, a Grand Lodge of the ancient and honourable Society of Free and Accepted Masons, was held at the Sun Tavern in Water-street, when, after a handsome Entertainment, the worshipful W. Allen, Esq; was unanimously chosen *Grand Master* of this Province, for the Year ensuing; who was pleased to appoint Mr. William Pringle Deputy Master. Wardens chosen for the ensuing Year, were Thomas Boude and Benj. Franklin." For the first time, Franklin published his name in the *Pennsylvania Gazette* in some way other than merely as a printer. By June 1733, the meeting place changed to Thomas Mullen's Tun Tavern, also on Water Street (at the corner of Tun Alley, the first alley south of Chestnut Street).[10] Franklin missed three of thirteen Masonic meetings during 1733: 2 April and 3 and 29 September (the lodge met on Saturday, 29 September, since Monday, 1 October, was Election Day). He missed the September meetings because he was visiting Boston. Since St. John the Baptist Day fell on Sunday in 1733, the lodge postponed its meeting for a day to Monday, June 25. The retiring grand master, William Allen, probably initiated the practice of inviting distinguished guests to attend the annual Masonic feast. The 28 June *Gazette* reported, "A very Elegant Entertainment was provided upon the Occasion, at which the Proprietor, the Governor, the Mayor of this City, and several other Persons of Distinction honour'd the Society with their Presence." The lodge elected Humphrey Murray, Esq., grand master; he appointed Thomas Hart his deputy. Peter Cuff and James Bingham were chosen wardens.

Beginning in 1734, the records in Liber B of St. John's Lodge are not as full. Franklin appears in only four places. He attended meetings on 7 January, 4 February, and 4 March. There are no entries for April and May, but I suspect that Franklin attended the meetings on the first Monday of those two months. The secretary/treasurer was beginning to record only the members' absences. That would have been easier and would have contained the same information.

The last entry in Franklin's 1734 account, for 3 June, charged him a shilling for missing that meeting.

Franklin reprinted James Anderson's *Constitutions of the Free Masons* and advertised it on 26 May 1734. The London edition was out of print. A number of Masonic lodges and individuals in the colonies wanted to purchase Anderson's *Constitutions*, the fundamental work on Freemasonry. Franklin's printing accounts for 1734 show that the book was ready by 13 May, when Thomas Hopkinson and Thomas Penn had copies bound, the latter in gilt. According to an undated entry (May 1734?), Franklin sent twenty-five *Constitutions* to his partner Lewis Timothy in Charleston, South Carolina, and seventy to Thomas Fleet in Boston. When Timothy returned six copies in August, Franklin immediately sent them on to his brother James Franklin in Newport. Besides the lodges in Boston, Charleston, Philadelphia, and possibly Newport, there must have been a Masonic lodge in Lancaster, Pennsylvania, for on 31 August Franklin charged John Catharwood of Lancaster County for three copies and recorded sending eight to Lancaster. Philadelphia's Masonic lodge itself bought two copies "finely gilded" in September. Finally, on 8 October, Philip Syng put on his account a copy bound with gold and silver seams.

GRAND MASTER

On St. John's Day, Monday, 24 June 1734, Franklin was elected grand master. He may have reprinted the *Constitutions* shortly before the election partly to call attention to himself as a candidate but no doubt the main reason was simply that they were needed and would sell. On Thursday, 27 June, he published a news notice of the meeting, one of the few times he called favorable attention to himself in his own paper: "Monday last, a Grand Lodge of the Ancient and Honourable Society of Free and Accepted Masons in this Province, was held at the Tun Tavern in Water-Street, when Benjamin Franklin being elected Grand Master for the Year ensuing, appointed Mr. John Crap, to be his Deputy; and James Hamilton, Esq; and Thomas Hopkinson, Gent. were chosen Wardens. After which, the Governor, and several other Persons of Distinction honour'd the Society with their Presence." The Masonic celebration marked Franklin's first public recognition as a rising tradesman. It contrasts markedly with the way he portrayed himself as a young businessman, presumably about 1730 or shortly thereafter, in the *Autobiography*: "In order to secure my Credit and Character as a Tradesman, I took care not only to be in *Reality* Industrious and frugal, but to avoid all *Appearances* of the Contrary. I drest plainly; I was seen at no Places of idle Diversion; I never went out a-fishing or shooting; a Book, indeed, sometimes debauch'd me from my Work; but that was seldom, snug, and gave no Scandal: and to show that I was not above my Business, I sometimes brought home the Paper I purchas'd at the Stores, thro' the Streets on a Wheelbarrow" (A 68). By 1734, the twenty-eight-year-old printer for the Pennsylvania legislature and editor of the *Pennsylvania Gazette* was becoming a prominent Philadelphian.

On 28 August 1734, Franklin printed one thousand tickets for the Freemasons, charging £4. Julius F. Sachse, who recalled seeing one of them, said that they were "engraved notices, to be sent out for the Quarterly Communications."[11] The supply evidently lasted until October 1736, when Franklin printed another eleven hundred tickets, charging £4.11.8.[12] From June 1734 to 24 June 1738, the Freemasons' book of minutes, Liber B, only recorded on every 24 June the payment of dues. In June 1735 through 1738, Franklin paid 6s. each year for membership. That might incorrectly suggest that Franklin missed no meetings during those years. Though some members had perfect attendance during the previous years when Franklin missed several meetings and though the record shows other members paying fines for missing meetings, it is impossible that Franklin never missed a meeting during these four years. He was ill for an extended period in 1735 and must have missed several meetings then. After 1733, the surviving records evidently provide no evidence regarding Franklin's presence at the lodge's meetings.

When Franklin visited Boston in September 1733 he met the merchant Henry Price, who had been appointed grand master of New England in April 1738. Price promised to visit Philadelphia the following fall. In 1734 he was appointed grand master of all British North America. After becoming ill, he wrote Franklin on 23 October 1734 that he would not be able to visit. Franklin replied on 28 November with both a personal letter and a letter from the Grand Lodge of Pennsylvania, signed by him as grand master, asking that Price give a deputation or charter to the Philadelphia Grand Lodge. Price probably did so, but no such document survives. On 24 February 1734/5, however, the *Boston Gazette* printed the following:

> On Friday last [21 February] was held a Grand Lodge of that Ancient and Honourable Society of Free and Accepted Masons, at the Bunch of Grapes Tavern in King Street, where Mr. Henry Price, Grand Master of His Majesty's Dominions in North America, Nominated and Appointed his Grand Officers for the year ensuing viz. Andrew Belcher, Esq., Deputy Grand Master; Mr. James Gordon and Mr. Frederick Hamilton, Grand Wardens for this Province; and Mr. Benjamin Franklin, Provincial Grand Master for the Province of Pennsylvania.

The first mention of Benjamin Franklin other than as a printer outside of Philadelphia, the notice was reprinted in the *American Weekly Mercury* on 27 March 1735. The Masonic news item inaugurated his American (as opposed to a local Pennsylvania) reputation. The *Pennsylvania Gazette* for 3 July 1735 and 8 July 1736 announced the results of the annual election: Franklin was succeeded as grand master by James Hamilton in 1735, who was then succeeded by Thomas Hopkinson in 1736.

FELLOW FREEMASONS

The surviving Masonic account book discloses Franklin's influence on his friends and on St. John's Lodge. In addition to the twelve early members already mentioned, the manuscript records that thirty-eight additional persons became lodge members before 26 June 1738. Franklin evidently suggested a number of his friends and associates for membership. The only Mason when he joined who became a frequent associate in the future was William Allen, later a member and director of the Library Company, a subscriber and trustee of the Academy of Philadelphia, a manager of the Pennsylvania Hospital, and a sponsor when Franklin applied for the position of postmaster general of the colonies. Gradually, however, as a Proprietary Party leader, Allen became Franklin's enemy in the mid-1750s.

Another nine persons, associated with Franklin in various ways, became members of St. John's Lodge. Thomas Whitmarsh (d. 1733), who was working as a journeyman printer for Franklin, was charged an entrance fee on 5 July 1731, a month before Franklin sponsored him as his first printing partner (1:205). Thomas Hopkinson (1709–51), lawyer, a Junto and Library Company member, a fellow experimenter in electricity, as well as a trustee of the Academy of Philadelphia, paid his entrance fee on 5 November 1732. James Hamilton (1710?–1783), lawyer, Library Company member, trustee of the Academy of Philadelphia, governor of Pennsylvania, and son of Franklin's patron Andrew Hamilton, was charged an entrance fee during April 1734. Thomas Bond (1712–84), Franklin's "particular friend," a member of the Library Company, later a principal founder of the Pennsylvania Hospital, and a member of the first American Philosophical Society, was charged an entrance fee on 3 June 1734. Joseph Breintnall (d. 1746), scrivener, a member of the Junto as well as secretary of the Library Company, paid the entrance fee on 5 August 1734. Dr. Thomas Cadwalader, a Library Company director and member of the original American Philosophical Society, paid on 6 June 1737. And John Jones, an original Library Company director, was charged an entrance fee on 6 June 1737.

By 1740 the Philadelphia St. John's Lodge had gradually changed. Almost all the earliest members had been artisans, but most members elected after 1732, including those just mentioned, were merchants or professional men.[13] A similar transformation, as we will see, was happening to the membership of the Library Company. At the same time, a number of the early members of the St. John's Lodge were going through the same process, with the former young artisans becoming successful practitioners of their crafts.

Perhaps the Masons supplied Franklin with one or two persons who were later important in his life, but we can be certain that the nine above were Franklin's friends before joining the lodge. No doubt a few of the other twenty-nine persons who joined the Masons between 1731 and 1738 were also previously Franklin's friends, but they remain comparatively unknown in the life of Franklin. Those just listed, however, were, with William Allen and Benjamin Franklin, major creators of the political, intellectual, literary, and cultural life of colonial Philadelphia. The Junto was probably more important than the Masons in Franklin's personal life, for the Junto was his primary philosophical and civic discussion group. It met more frequently and required its members to prepare for the meetings by reading on assigned topics, and it carried out, as we have seen, various programs for civic improvement. On the other hand, the Masons comprised a national and international organization, providing Franklin easy access to a circle of like-minded benevolent persons in other colonies and, in later years, in England and Europe.

LATER DISCUSSIONS

Several episodes concerning Franklin and Freemasonry will be discussed later in this volume and in Volume 3. Franklin remained active in the Pennsylvania Freemasons from 1731 until 1757, attending the opening ceremonies of the Phila-delphia's Grand Lodge on St. John the Baptist's Day, 24 June 1755. He attended Masonic meetings when visiting Boston (e.g., 25 May and 8 June 1743; 11 October 1754) and probably other colonial cities. Later, when in Great Britain and Eu-rope, he occasionally attended Masonic meetings. His involvement in French Masonic activities will be discussed in Volume 6. After Franklin left for England in 1757, the Masonic group called the "Ancients" gradually came to dominate the "Moderns" in Philadelphia. The group to which Franklin belonged (the "Moderns," the only organized group in 1730) dwindled after the rival group founded a new Grand Lodge in London in 1751. Franklin seems not to have attended any functions as a Freemason during his Philadelphia stays in 1762–64 or in 1775–77. By the time he returned to Philadelphia in 1785, the only active Philadelphia Masons had become identified with the "Ancients."[14] Franklin's lodge had been superseded. The Masons were not officially represented at his funeral in 1790.

FOUR

The Library Company of Philadelphia

These Libraries have improv'd the general Conversation of the Americans, made the common Tradesmen and Farmers as intelligent as most Gentlemen from other Countries, and perhaps . . . contributed in some degree to the Stand so generally made throughout the Colonies in Defence of their Privileges.—A 72

FRANKLIN SPENT MORE TIME AND CARE on the Library Company than any other civic project. He founded it, attended its meetings faithfully as a director from 1731 to 1757, acted as the librarian in 1733 and 1734, served as the secretary from 1746 to 1757, became its book agent in London from 1757 to 1762, served again as a director from 1762 to 1764 and again as its London book agent from 1765 to 1775. No other project involved so much of his time and energy for so long, and no project pleased him more to write about in the *Autobiography*. Franklin loved books. The friends he formed in Philadelphia at age seventeen were "Lovers of Reading" (A 27). Returning from Boston in 1724, he brought back his early book collection. When the ship stopped in New York, the captain told New York's governor William Burnet about the young man with the large library. Burnet, son of the author Bishop Gilbert Burnet, knew the English literary world intimately. He asked Franklin to call, "treated me with great Civility, show'd me his Library, which was a very large one, and we had a good deal of Conversation about Books and Authors" (A 33). In London (1725), Franklin lived next door to the bookseller John Wilcox, who "had an immense Collection of second-hand Books," which Franklin arranged to borrow "on certain reasonable Terms. . . . This I esteem'd a great Advantage, and I made as much Use of it as I could" (A 43).

Back in Philadelphia, Franklin keenly missed the Boston and London bookstores. "There was not a good Bookseller's Shop in any of the Colonies to the Southward of Boston. In New York and Philadelphia the Printers were indeed Stationers, they sold only Paper, etc., Almanacks, Ballads, and a few common School Books. Those who lov'd Reading were oblig'd to send for their Books from England" (A 73). Since the Junto members all owned books, Franklin proposed about 1729 that they combine together the books they could best spare. By then, the Junto had stopped meeting at Nicholas Scull's Indian Head Tavern and had rented a room at Robert Grace's house (site of the present 131 Market Street). Franklin reasoned that "since our Books were often referr'd to in our

Disquisitions . . . it might be convenient to us to have them all together where we met, that upon Occasion they might be consulted." Franklin also reasoned that by "clubbing our Books to a common Library, we should, while we lik'd to keep them together, have each of us the Advantage of using the Books of all the other Members, which would be nearly as beneficial as if each owned the whole" (A 71). By uniting with others in a common cause, one could accomplish more than one could possibly do alone.

The members liked the proposal, "and we fill'd one End of the Room with such Books as we could best spare." Franklin was disappointed, however, for "the Number was not so great as we expected." And though the Junto members used the books in their discussions and though they benefitted from borrowing them, a few disappeared and others were hard-used and damaged. The experiment failed. Franklin reported, "some Inconveniences occurring for want of due Care of them, the Collection after about a Year was separated, and each took his Books home again" (A 72).

ORGANIZED

The failure inspired Franklin. How could he establish a book collection that would not have the "inconvenience" of the owner's disgust at finding his books missing or misused? He probably proposed the subscription library to the Junto in the spring of 1731. Each subscriber would pay forty shillings to join the library and ten shillings a year as an annual contribution for buying more books. The Junto members evidently agreed. "I drew a Sketch of the Plan and Rules that would be necessary, and got a skilful Conveyancer Mr. Charles Brockden to put the Whole in Form of Articles of Agreement to be subscribed." The subscribers would annually elect ten directors and a treasurer, and the directors would elect a secretary. The "Instrument of Association" for the Library Company of Philadelphia was dated 1 July 1731. Franklin recalled nearly fifty years later that "when we were about to sign the above-mentioned Articles, which were to be binding on us, our Heirs, etc. for fifty Years, Mr. Brockden, the Scrivener, said to us, 'You are young Men, but it is scarce probable that any of you will live to see the Expiration of the Term fix'd in this Instrument.'" Franklin happily noted, "A Number of us, however, are yet living" (A 74).

As a printer, Franklin worked with iconology in watermarks, on paper currency, and coats of arms for bookplates and other purposes. He displayed his own creative iconographic talent in designing a seal for the Library Company: "two books open, each encompass'd with glory, or beams of light, between which water streaming from above into an urn below, thence issues at many vents into lesser urns, and motto circumscribing the whole, *Communiter bona profundere deum est.*"[1] He also no doubt wrote the motto: "To pour forth benefits for the common good is divine." He used the motto in the 1741 *Catalogue* of the Library Company, in the book labels of the company, and in his introduction to a plan for benefitting the New Zealand natives on 29 August 1771. Philip

Syng, goldsmith and a Junto member, made the original die, which is extant at the Library Company.

According to the Library Company's articles of association, Franklin named the ten directors, the treasurer, and the secretary. They would serve until a meeting of the subscribers, which would take place on the first Monday in May, when the officers for the following year were to be elected. Thereafter, annual elections would be held. Franklin appointed as the first directors Thomas Hopkinson, William Parsons, Philip Syng, Thomas Godfrey, Anthony Nicholas, Thomas Cadwalader, John Jones, Jr., Robert Grace, Isaac Penington, and himself. In addition, he appointed William Coleman, Jr., treasurer, and Joseph Breintnall, secretary. Parsons, Godfrey, Grace, Coleman, Breintnall, and Franklin had been original Junto members. Hopkinson, Syng, and Nicholas had probably become Junto members before 1731. Altogether, at least nine of the first appointed twelve officers belonged to the Junto; the three exceptions were Cadwalader, Jones, and Penington. Dr. Thomas Cadwalader (1707–79) was later a member of the American Philosophical Society; John Jones, Jr., was a Quaker shoemaker who became a Freemason in 1737; and Isaac Penington (1700–1742), farmer, became a justice and sheriff of Bucks County. All were young men; most were artisans. The wealthiest were probably the merchants William Parsons and Robert Grace. The two professional men were Hopkinson, a lawyer, and Cadwalader.

The articles of association specified that each member after the first fifty must be approved by the directors, sign the articles, and pay the subscription. Admitting new members and selecting new books were the directors' ordinary duties. Franklin interjected a comment on vanity and psychology into his reminiscence about organizing the Library Company: "The Objections and Reluctances I met with in Soliciting the Subscriptions, made me soon feel the Impropriety of presenting one's self as the Proposer of any useful Project that might be suppos'd to raise one's Reputation in the smallest degree above that of one's Neighbours, when one has need of their Assistance to accomplish that Project." Franklin soon learned how to avoid this difficulty. He presented himself merely as a spokesperson: "I therefore put my self as much as I could out of sight, and stated it as a Scheme of *a Number of Friends* [Franklin punned], who had requested me to go about and propose it to such as they thought Lovers of Reading. In this way my Affair went on more smoothly, and I ever after practis'd it on such Occasions; and from my frequent Successes, can heartily recommend it. The present little Sacrifice of your Vanity will afterwards be amply repaid. If it remains a while uncertain to whom the Merit belongs, someone more vain than yourself will be encourag'd to claim it, and then even Envy will be dispos'd to do you Justice, by plucking those assum'd Feathers, and restoring them to their right Owner" (A 74–75).

Franklin invested hundreds of hours annually in the fledgling institution. "So few were the Readers at that time in Philadelphia, and the Majority of us so

Figure 6. The Library Company seal, drawn by Nian-Sheng Huang from the impression made by Philip Syng's die. Franklin created numerous original emblems, but the Library Company's seal was perhaps his earliest. Franklin described the design as "two books open, each encompass'd with glory, or beams of light, between which water streaming from above into an urn below, thence issues at many vents into lesser urns, with a motto circumscribing the whole, Communiter bona profundere deum est." The motto may be translated: "To pour forth benefits for the common good is divine."

Franklin's design is intriguing. Books often represent knowledge and the traditions of culture. Being "encompass'd with glory" usually represented divinity, and "beams of light" (if they can be distinguished from "glory") may also (like books) suggest enlightenment and knowledge. Water is an archetypal symbol of fertility and in this context implies ever-increasing knowledge. The passing from one urn into many emphasizes the theme of fecundity, the continual enrichment of knowledge and tradition through books. The motto "Communiter bona profundere deum est" reinforces the suggestions of divinity and fecundity and emphasizes that learning and knowledge are for the common good of humanity and that to multiply them is to imitate the divine. The original die made by Philip Syng sometime before 24 April 1732 is at the Library Company. The impression of Syng's die is courtesy of the Library Company of Philadelphia.

poor, that I was not able with great Industry to find more than Fifty Persons, mostly young Tradesmen, willing to pay down for this purpose Forty shillings each, and Ten Shillings per Annum" (A 74). But by Monday, 8 November 1731, he had come up with fifty subscribers and notified Joseph Breintnall, secretary. Breintnall thereupon called the first meeting of the Library Company directors for 5 p.m. at Nicholas Scull's Bear Tavern. Treasurer William Coleman gave his bond then. Franklin proposed that the treasurer should attend one evening later in the week at Scull's to begin receiving the subscriptions, and that one-third or more of the subscribers should be notified to bring in their money. Further, the treasurer should attend at Scull's another evening to receive the subscribers who lived out of town or were not as likely to have their money ready. At that first meeting, Franklin and the other directors optimistically expected that they could soon send off a book order to England, but they found that funds came in slower than pledges—and some persons who had pledged changed their minds. Franklin probably printed the "Subscription Receipts" for the Library Company the following day, Tuesday, 9 November.

Early Members

Treasurer William Coleman was to be at Nicholas Scull's Bear Tavern on the following Thursday, 11 November, from six till nine to receive subscriptions. The messenger, however, mistakenly told the subscribers 10 November. The treasurer and the secretary learned of the mistake and attended at Scull's that evening, when ten persons paid their forty shillings: Robert Grace (share no. 1), Thomas Hopkinson (share no. 2),[2] Benjamin Franklin (share no. 3), John Jones, Jr. (4), Joseph Breintnall (5), Anthony Nicholas (6), Thomas Godfrey (7), Joseph Stretch (8), Philip Syng, Jr. (9), and John Sober (10). Thomas Cadwalader (11) had paid but had not signed the oath before leaving the province.[3] It was a disappointing turnout: all but John Sober and the hatter Joseph Stretch, who later became a Pennsylvania assemblyman, were officers. The library now had eleven paid-up members.

Twelve more persons paid the following night: Joseph Wharton (share no. 12); Nicholas Reddish (13); Richard Standley (14); Samuel Hale (15); merchant David Bush (16); Francis Richardson (17); John Nicholas (18); John Roberts (19); Charles Read, Jr. (20); Evan Morgan (21); Thomas Edwards (22); and Alexander Paxton (23). Though the minutes record that John Tomkins sent in his subscription by a proxy on 11 November, he did not take the oath until 14 November 1733, so his share (no. 56) was dated then. Including Tomkins, the Library Company now had twenty-four members—less than half of those who had promised to join.

Franklin notified the remaining library subscribers to come to Owen Owens's tavern to pay their subscription on Monday, 29 November. Only one additional member came, Rees Lloyd (share no. 24). On 13 December, Monday, the directors met at Nicholas Scull's. Franklin said he would ask Charles Brockden what he would charge for drawing up an instrument of partnership in the Library Company and whether he would accept a certificate instead of cash toward it. The next day Benjamin Eastburn (share no. 25) paid his subscription. The directors met on 8 January, 10 January (the time of the regular monthly meeting but only six persons turned up, "the weather being exceeding cold"), and 20 March, when Franklin agreed to print a short note to send to all delinquent subscribers. They were asked "to appear without Fail, either to pay or relinquish; that it may then be known who are, and who are not concerned" (1:230).

The directors met at Scull's that following Saturday night, 25 March, to receive subscriptions. New shareholders were: Josiah Rolfe (share no. 26); Thomas Potts, Jr (27); Jacob Duché (28); William Maugridge (29); Nicholas Cassell (30); James Fox (31), who sold his share to Edward Evans on 11 December 1732; Benjamin Paschall (32); Thomas Green (33); William Parsons (34); and Louis Timothée (35), who sold his share to Joshua Richey on 28 January 1734. Ephraim Andrews and Isaac Brown relinquished their shares. Later in 1732, but before the election on 1 May, Nicholas Scull (share no. 36), an original Junto member, paid his subscription; so did Henry Pratt (share no. 37); Isaac Penington (38), who sold his share to Anthony Benezet on 17 August 1734; and Hugh Roberts (39), another Junto member and good friend of Franklin. These were the founding members of the Library Company.

At a directors' meeting on 29 March 1732, Thomas Godfrey reported that James Logan had "let him know he had heard of their Design and approved of it and would willingly give his Advice in the Choice of the Books. Upon this Information he was desired to return the Thanks of the Committee to Mr. Logan for his generous offer—And the Committee esteeming Mr. Logan to be a Gentleman of universal Learning, and the best Judge of Books in these Parts, ordered that Thomas Godfrey should wait on him and request him to favour them with a Catalogue of suitable Books against tomorrow Evening." The next day Godfrey and Franklin called on Logan at Stenton and stayed with him until late. By the time they returned, the directors waiting at Scull's had adjourned until the next evening. That night, Friday, 31 March 1732, they revised the list supplied by Logan[4] and gave it to Thomas Hopkinson (who was about to leave for London), together with Robert Grace's note for £45 drawn on the London merchant Peter Collinson. The exchange marked Franklin's first known connection (albeit an indirect one) with Collinson, who gradually became a close friend.

The amount of the bill, £45, might suggest that only 25 persons had subscribed and that only £50 pounds had been raised, but the subscriptions were in Pennsylvania currency, and the £45 note was in sterling. Since £1 sterling was worth approximately £1.6 in Pennsylvania currency, the bill represented over £72 in Pennsylvania currency, or the initial subscription for more than 36 persons. In fact, Treasurer Coleman paid £74.5 Pennsylvania currency for Grace's £45 sterling note. Charges for insurance and shipping were additional, so the initial cost for the books would have required subscriptions from more than forty persons. Furthermore, most if not all of the 56 titles in 141 volumes (including two titles that Peter Collinson generously donated) arrived unbound; that was common, since many persons preferred to have their own binding. The directors had resolved on 8 January 1731/2 to have the books covered with sheathing paper and arranged to pay the bookbinder Stephen Potts, who was currently living and boarding with Franklin, for it.

Charles Brockden presented the Library Company with the instrument he drew for them, and for his work the directors on 24 April 1732 voted him a present of his payment as a subscriber and also sixteen years freedom of the company—that is, he was excused from paying the yearly payment during that time. (In the list of subscribers, his share, no. 54, is dated the following year.) Their attention having been called to the extraordinary services performed by some members, the directors asked Joseph Breintnall, Philip Syng, and Benjamin Franklin to present charges for their time and efforts. All three "generously declined," but the directors, "other than the said B. Franklin and Philip Syng in their own Cases," insisted they accept the following: "Vizt, Joseph Breintnall for his Time Trouble and Expence as Clerk to Mr. Brockden, in taking down the rough Draught of the Library Instrument and engrossing it, Six Years Freedom of the Company, Philip Syng for making and engraving the Company's Seal, two Years like Freedom of the Company, and B. Franklin for printing Certificates Advertisement &c. two Years Freedom also." Since the annual dues were ten shillings, Franklin and Syng were each paid twenty shillings for their extra work.

ELECTION, 1732

On Monday, 1 May 1732, Franklin missed the monthly Freemasons' meeting (paying a shilling for his absence) in order to attend Nicholas Scull's tavern for the Library Company's first election. The subscribers chose the following directors: Franklin, William Parsons, Thomas Godfrey, Anthony Nicholas, Robert Grace, John Jones, Jr., John Nicholas, Hugh Roberts, Henry Pratt, and William Maugridge. William Coleman was elected treasurer, and the directors appointed Breintnall secretary. Since Franklin was listed first, he probably had the most votes (or tied for the most) and acted as the executive officer. Philip Syng asked not to be elected a director that year, Thomas Hopkinson and Dr. Thomas Cadwalader were both in England, and Isaac Penington, the Bucks County farmer, lived too far away to attend. Two of the four new directors, Maugridge and Roberts, were Junto members. Hugh Roberts subscribed on 1 May (evidently just before being elected a director) and paid his subscription a week later on 8 May. The silversmith Henry Pratt and the carpenter John Nicholas were the other new directors. During the 1732–33 year, Franklin evidently attended every directors' meeting, though two meetings did not record attendance.

BOOKS

At the end of October 1732, the ship *Molly*, Captain Samuel Cornock from London, brought the Library Company's first order of books, together with a catalogue and notes by Thomas Hopkinson.[5] He informed the directors that Peter Collinson had been of great assistance and had donated two titles: *A View of Sir Isaac Newton's Philosophy* (London: S. Palmer, 1728) by Franklin's former London acquaintance Henry Pemberton, and Philip Miller's *Gardeners Dictionary* (London, 1731). The boxes of books were taken to Grace's house in Jones Alley, now Pewter Platter Alley, behind 47 Market Street. The most expensive volumes were the eight folios: Andrea Palladio's two-volume *Architecture* (London: Darby, 1721); the two-volume *Works of Tacitus*, translated by Thomas Gordon (London: Woodward and Peele, 1728–31); *The Historical and Chronological Theatre of Christopher Helvicus* (London: M. Flesher, 1687); Thomas Wood, *An Institute of the Laws of England* (London: Nutt and Gosling, 1728); Algernon Sydney, *Discourses Concerning Government* (London: Darby, 1704); Samuel Puffendorf, *Of the Law of Nature and Nations* (London: Walthoe, 1729); Nathaniel Bailey, *Dictionarius Britannicum: Or a More Compleat Universal Etymological English Dictionary Than Any Extant* (London: T. Cox, 1730); and Thomas Stanley, *The History of Philosophy* (London: Battersby et al., 1701).

The Library Company purchased far less theology than most eighteenth-century libraries and more science and literature.[6] Although James Logan was probably responsible for a number of titles in the first order, especially those in the classics (in the best English translations), the following seem to show Franklin's influence: eight volumes of *Plutarch's Lives* (London: Tonson, 1727); Xenophon's *Memorable Things of Socrates* (London: J. Batley, 1722); Daniel Defoe's two-volume *Complete Tradesman* (London: Rivington, 1732); four volumes of the Port Royal *Moral Essays* (London: Parker, 1724); eight volumes of Addison and Steele's *Spectator* (London: Tonson, 1726); four volumes of Steele's *Tatler: i.e., The Lucubrations of Isaac Bickerstaff* (London: Nutt, 1728); two volumes of Steele's *Guardian* (London, 1729); three volumes of Addison's *Miscellaneous Works* (London: Tonson, 1726); James Greenwood's *Essay Towards a Practical English Grammar* (London: Bettesworth, 1729); and John Brightland [i.e., Charles Gildon], *A Grammar of the English Tongue* (London: Roberts, 1721). Franklin had read most of these but evidently thought they should be in the Library Company. Of the nine titles ordered but not secured in the first purchase, I suspect Franklin was responsible for John Trenchard and Thomas Gordon, *Cato's Letters* (4 volumes); and for Pierre Bayle's *Critical Dictionary* (five volumes). Both were supplied later. So the subscribers could know what books the Library Company had, Franklin printed a broadside short title list (not extant).

For his own satisfaction, Franklin made a subject breakdown of the first books. He divided them into the following categories: History, Architecture,

Mathematics, Morality, Geography, Physick, Anatomy, Natural Philosophy, Botany, Politicks, "*The Compleat Tradesman*" (no category), Animals, Chronology, Logics, Philology, "Wood's *Institutes*" (no category), and catalogues. "History" had the most titles with nine; "Morality" was second with seven, and "Philology" was third with six (counting "Homer's *Iliad* & *Odyssey*" as one title). The titles he listed under "Morality" were "Spectators, Guardians, Tatlers, Puffendorf's *Law of Nature* &c, Addison's *Works* in 12mo, *Memorable Things of Socrates*, and the *Turkish Spy*."

Collinson's generosity demanded an acknowledgment. Though Joseph Breintnall as secretary signed the letter to him of 7 November 1732, the minutes show that Franklin wrote it. The concluding paragraph said, "Every Encouragement to an Infant Design, by Men of Merit and Consideration, gives new Spirit to the Undertakers, strengthens the Hands of all concern'd, and greatly tends to secure and establish their Work; Hence, as well as from the noble Knowledge communicated in the Books you have given us, will arise the lasting Obligation we shall find ourselves under to Mr. Collinson. We wish you every kind of Happiness and Prosperity, and particularly that you may never want Power nor Opportunity of enjoying that greatest of Pleasures to a benevolent Mind, the giving Pleasure to others."

On 14 November 1732 the directors met for the first time in "the Library Room." What satisfaction they must have felt with their small but valuable treasure trove of useful books. The first order of business was finding a librarian. The logical person was Louis Timothée. He was renting Robert Grace's house, where the Junto met—and where the Library Company's books were now installed. Timothée agreed to keep attendance in the library room on Wednesdays from two to three and on Saturdays from ten till four. At the end of three months, he would be paid three pounds plus whatever further allowance should be thought reasonable. Excepting James Logan, only Library Company members could borrow the books. Each book or set of books had the length of time for which it could be borrowed marked in it. Members could borrow only one book or set at a time and had to sign a promissory note for its return "undefaced." If the book was not returned in good condition, they were required to pay double its value.

The prime mover in the Library Company, Franklin, donated occasional gifts of printing and books to it. At the 11 December 1732 meeting, the directors asked Franklin his charge for printing a short title catalogue. He replied that he designed the catalogues as presents. Unfortunately, no copy of this broadside catalogue survives, but Edwin Wolf 2nd, has reconstructed its probable contents and suggested that Franklin used the Library Company's motto on the broadside.[7] Two months later on 19 February 1733, Franklin presented six books to the Library Company: Languet du Fresnoy, *A New Method of Studying History Geography and Chronology* (2 volumes, 1730); [John Locke,] *Two Treatises on Government* (1698); *A Collection of Several Pieces of Mr. John Locke* (1720; it included Locke's "Rules of a Society which met once a Week for the Improvement of useful knowledge," a model for the Junto); *Essays of Michael de Montaigne, v. 1 & 3* (1685); *Burgersdicius's Logic* (1697); and *Logic, or The Art of Thinking by Messers Port Royal* (1717). The last had been one of his childhood books, mentioned in the *Autobiography* (A 15) and bears his early signature (illustrated in Volume 1, Figure 5.)

A stranger offered to sell Amedée Francois Frezier's *Voyage to the South Sea and along the Coasts of Chile and Peru* to the library, and the directors made this first additional purchase on 3 March 1732/3. At the 12 March meeting the new member William Rawle, who operated a ferry to New Jersey, presented Edmund Spenser's six-volume *Works*, which included *The Faerie Queen*.

The membership receipt (share no. 44) dated 20 January 1732/3 of the pacifist Quaker James Morris, a Philadelphia County assemblyman from 1739 to 1749, is the earliest one extant. Printed by Franklin, the receipt is signed by William Coleman as treasurer. In the book of shares, Morris's share was recorded on 14 December 1732. After the initial members joined, there were three stages in the admission process: first, the members voted to allow a person to join (that action was generally recorded in the minutes); second, the nominee paid the fee; and third, he signed the articles. Not infrequently, after a candidate was admitted, months passed before he paid (which could be done by sending in the money) and then subscribed (which had to be done in person).

ROUTINES

The directors began meeting in 1731 at Nicholas Scull's Bear Tavern on the southwest corner of Market and Third Streets. After the books arrived, they were put in the "Library Room" in the house that Louis Timothée was renting from Robert Grace. The directors met there, from 14 November 1732 until 8 April 1734, when they began meeting at John Roberts's coffeehouse, located "in High Street near the Market."[8] In early April 1739, Roberts moved to Second Street. He died later that year, but the directors continued to meet at the Widow Roberts's coffeehouse until 1745. That year Breintnall opened a tavern, the Hen and Chickens, on Fourth Street between Market and Chestnut, and the directors met there. After his death on 16 March 1746, they continued to meet at the Widow Breintnall's.

On Monday, 7 May 1733, the subscribers were asked to bring in their first annual payment of ten shillings "at the House of Mr. Louis Timothée, where the Library is kept, in the Ally next the Boar's-Head Tavern, at Two in the Afternoon." They then had their second election. The directors chosen were Franklin; Junto members William Parsons, Thomas Hopkinson, Hugh Roberts, Thomas Godfrey, and Robert Grace; tavern-keeper Henry Pratt, who had been elected a member of St. John's Masonic Lodge with Franklin; Dr. Thomas Cadwalader, whose *Essay on the West-India Dry-Gripes* Franklin printed in 1745; William Rawle; and the cordwainer John Jones, Jr., who became a member of

St. John's Lodge in 1737. William Coleman was reelected treasurer, and the directors again chose Joseph Breintnall as secretary. Dr. Thomas Cadwalader and William Rawle replaced Anthony Nicholas and John Nicholas. On 10 December, Anthony Nicholas was elected a director in the room of Robert Grace, who had sailed to Barbados. During the year 1733–34, Franklin attended all but two meetings: visiting New England in the fall of 1733, he was absent on 10 September and 8 October.

No doubt hoping to encourage the chief proprietor to make a contribution to the Library Company, Franklin proposed an address to Thomas Penn, who had come to Pennsylvania the previous August. He prepared the letter with Hopkinson, Coleman, and Breintnall on 15 May 1733. Since Franklin chaired the committee, he presumably wrote the draft. Though some Quaker directors wanted a plainer style, the committee's document was adopted. The fair copy was dated 16 May and signed by Breintnall as secretary. It began by welcoming Thomas Penn to the province and praised Pennsylvania and its inhabitants: "Your Province of Pennsylvania, Sir, happy in its Climate and Situation, and in the Constitution of its Government, is thought to be no less happy in the Native Genius of its People; prone as it is to Industry, and capable of every kind of Improvement." Like the Maryland poet Richard Lewis, Franklin echoed Francis Bacon on the development of civilization:[9] "But when Colonies are in their Infancy, the Refinements of Life, it seems, cannot be much attended to. To encourage Agriculture, promote Trade, and establish good Laws must be the principal Care of the first Founders; while other Arts and Sciences, less immediately necessary, how excellent and useful soever, are left to the Care and Cultivation of Posterity. Hence it is that neither in this, nor in the neighbouring Provinces, has there yet been made any Provision of a publick generous Education." The Library Company was a small beginning. "And when on this Account we address a Son of the great and good, and ever memorable William Penn, we are persuaded than [*sic*] an Endeavour, however small, to propagate Knowledge, and improve the Minds of Men, by rendring useful Science more cheap and easy of Access, will not want his Countenance and Protection." Franklin closed with an apostrophe expressing the *translatio studii* ideal: "May your Philadelphia be the future Athens of America."[10] The Library Company's best-known members—the well-to-do Robert Grace; the founder, Franklin; William Rawle; attorney Thomas Hopkinson, Esq.; and Dr. Thomas Cadwalader—presented the address to Thomas Penn on 24 May. The address and Penn's brief reply appeared in the 31 May *Gazette*.

On 28 May the directors completed a new list of books to order. They agreed to a fine of "One pint of Wine" for absence and set the meeting time at or before 9 p.m. The books arrived by 2 November and Franklin said on 12 November that he would print a new list of all the books. About that time, Timothée left for Charleston as Franklin's printing partner, and Franklin assumed his duties as librarian. At the 10 December 1733 meeting, Franklin mentioned that Timothee had "been serviceable to him, & that he was willing to officiate for him as Librarian until his current Year should be expired." Franklin served as librarian until 11 March 1733/4. The month before, on 11 February, he pointed out that borrowers rarely came on Wednesdays. He proposed, and "a proper Majority of the said Directors" agreed, that the library hours should be on "Saturday & from Four in the Afternoon until Eight. That the Librarians Salary for his Service & finding a Fit Room for the Books shall be at the Rate of Six pounds per Year." The Library Company directors determined on 11 March 1734 that Timothée was owed six pounds for two quarters. Then William Parsons was chosen librarian, and on 14 March the directors took his bond. Parsons served as librarian until 1746. Franklin printed blank promissory notes for the librarian to complete when books were borrowed.

Among the new members in 1733–34 were George Boone (share no. 53), the uncle of Daniel Boone; and Franklin's workman Stephen Potts (55), who sold his share the following year. In 1734–35, the new members were James Hamilton (57), future governor and son of Andrew Hamilton; Franklin's friend William Plumsted (58); Dr. John Bard (60), who was probably Franklin's physician before moving to New York in 1746; Samuel Morris (62), who served as a director from 1742 to 1762; Samuel Norris (64), who also served as a director from 1742 to 1762; and John Mifflin (no. 65), a director from 1746 to 1758. The new members were no longer mainly artisans but doctors, lawyers, merchants, and other members of Philadelphia's middle class.

FORMATIVE YEARS, 1734–40

The Library Company was successful in part because of its stable and dedicated officers. Throughout the seven years 1734–40, Franklin, William Coleman, Thomas Hopkinson, Hugh Roberts, and Philip Syng were directors; and for six of the seven years, Dr. Thomas Cadwalader and William Plumsted were also. In 1734 James Morris was elected treasurer, replacing Coleman, who was elected a director. Throughout these years, Morris served as treasurer and Breintnall continued as secretary. In 1738, with the election of William Allen and Reverend Richard Peters as directors, a majority of the Library Company officials were merchants or professional men. After the annual election of new directors on the first Monday in May, the minutes usually recorded the persons with the most votes sequentially. The report for 1734–35 was an exception, for William Rawle's name appeared first; however, when John Mifflin was admitted to the Library Company on 27 August 1734, Franklin's signature came first, suggesting that he was still the chief executive officer. In 1734–35 (the Library Company year ran from May to May), he missed only one meeting, 21 October 1734.

Franklin's attendance provides information for his biography. In 1735 the printer suffered his second major sickness. Like his 1727 illness and the malady that finally killed him, it was pleurisy. Franklin was sick for "six or seven weeks" during 1735; he reported that illness in his pamphlet *Some Observations on the*

Proceedings against the Rev. Mr. Hemphill (2:38). Though advertised on 12 June, it did not appear until mid-July. Attendance at the directors' meetings, however, reveals that the July recovery was only temporary. Franklin missed the directors' meetings on 12 May, 9 June, 11 August and 8 September 1735, and 12 January 1736. Evidently he was sick from May through September, with a brief period of recovery in July. And perhaps he was not entirely well until February 1736. In 1736–37, Franklin missed only two meetings, 9 August and 13 September 1736, when he was in New Jersey, printing its paper currency. The following year, 1737–38, Franklin attended all the directors' meetings; in 1738–39, he missed only the 12 March 1739 meeting; and in 1739–40, he again attended all the directors' meetings.

After the death of James Merrewether (share no. 71), a shopkeeper whose obituary Franklin wrote, the directors agreed on 10 May 1742 that Elizabeth North, "Niece and Devisee of James Merrewether deceased, be allowed to take out Books, conformable to the Rules of the Company." Elizabeth North was the first woman to belong to the Library Company and was a second cousin of Deborah Franklin.[11] Three years later, she transferred the share to her husband Daniel Benezet on 13 May 1745.

After the younger proprietor John Penn (sometimes called "The American" because he was born in America) arrived from England, the directors requested on 13 October 1734 that Franklin and Coleman draw up an address to him. But Franklin was pressed. On 21 October, Coleman presented "a rough Drought of an Address, in which B. Franklin had not had Leisure to assist, but desired Time either till next Monthly Meeting or if they could complete it sooner then to inform" Breintnall, who would call a meeting. The directors decided at the 9 December meeting that since the address to John Penn had been delayed for so long, they might as well wait till the election in May, when the whole company of subscribers could vote. On 14 April 1734/5, the directors requested Franklin, Coleman, Hopkinson, and Breintnall to prepare the address to John Penn. It was to be presented by James Hamilton, William Plumsted, William Rawle, Thomas Cadwalader, Franklin, Thomas Hopkinson, and Joseph Breintnall. With a few small alterations, the directors approved it. The *Pennsylvania Gazette* of 5 June 1735 explained that "the Proprietors being out of Town, it was not presented till last Week" (31 May). Like the earlier address to Thomas Penn, it celebrated William Penn and the government of Pennsylvania, but it was not so striking as the earlier address. Perhaps Franklin did not write it. He was ill and did not attend the presentation ceremony on 31 May.

Like all librarians, the directors were concerned not only with adding to the collection but keeping track of what was in it, of where on the shelves the books were, and of whether they were currently borrowed. In the two years since Franklin printed the first catalogue, the Library Company's collection had more than doubled, and more books were expected. At the 13 January 1734/5 meeting, the directors asked Franklin to print a new library catalogue. At the February meeting, the directors agreed that he should wait to print the new catalogue until the new books had arrived. Franklin reported that James Logan sent the directors his kind respects and promised a handsome present of books, two folios of which "Mr. Logan had already delivered him." The directors returned their thanks. A group of directors gathered at the library on 18 April 1735 to open the trunk of new books. When Breintnall visited the Library Company on Saturday, 26 April, he found Franklin poring over the new shipment. Shortly after this time Franklin evidently printed a new brief catalogue of the books, but no copy survives. It was probably another short-title list, arranged by the size of the books. A year later on 12 April 1736, Franklin presented his bill for it.

That same day, Parsons charged the Library Company two shillings for moving the books to his home "from Timothee's & Liquor for the Workmen at putting up the Boxes." At the last 1736 meeting, 13 December, the directors asked that "B. Franklin print a number of copies of the company's constitution, that each subscriber may have one, and our friends a few."

A Degree of Success

When Franklin wrote an address to Thomas Penn from the Library Company in 1733 and when the directors composed another in 1734 to John Penn, they hoped that the proprietors would contribute land or money to the endeavor. Several years later the proprietors did. They inquired on 12 December 1737 about the trustees for a Library Company property. The directors named William Allen, Benjamin Franklin, William Plumsted, and James Hamilton. All but Franklin were Proprietary Party members and wealthy Philadelphians. On 1 May 1738, Thomas Penn gave a lot for the building site (until the Library Company had a charter, the lot had legally been given to the four individuals just named), and John Penn, who had sailed for London on 21 September 1735, sent the Library Company an air pump, an expensive scientific machine for removing or compressing air, accompanied by his letter dated London, 31 January 1737/8. The *Pennsylvania Gazette* noted on 4 May: "Monday last the Library Company of this City had their Yearly Meeting, for the Choice of their Officers, paying their Annual Subscription, &c., when they were acquainted, That the Hon. Proprietary Thomas Penn, Esq; had presented the Company with a large and commodious Lot of Ground, whereon to build an House for their Library; and also that the last Ship from London had brought them a valuable Present from the Hon. John Penn, Esq; consisting of an Air Pump, and other curious Instruments of great Use in the Study of Natural Knowledge. Both which Donations were exceedingly agreeable to the Company, not only with respect to their Value, but as they shew a Disposition in our greatest Men to encourage the Design of Promoting useful Learning in Pennsylvania."

With a group of close friends, a celebratory occasion, and a little wine, Franklin no doubt had a major role in what Joseph Breintnall called "a facetious agreeable conversation" on 8 May 1738, when the Library Company directors celebrated the gifts. They gathered at Thomas Mullen's tavern, having invited Mr. Samuel Jenkins, who brought the air pump; proprietor Thomas Penn; Mr. Freame, the proprietor's brother-in-law; the merchant Alexander Forbes; Captain Norris; Robert Grace; the merchant Charles Willing; and James Hamilton. The proprietor Thomas Penn was supposedly engaged (as we will see in Volume 3, he did not approve of the Library Company), but all the other gentlemen, together with all the directors of the Library Company, the treasurer, and the secretary, met for dinner. Before dinner, the directors "ordered that B. Franklin, Hugh Roberts, and Alexander Graydon meet at the Library tomorrow in the Afternoon and inspect the condition of the Books, to see which ones wanted binding and repairing, and to count the whole number belonging to the Library." They also appointed Franklin, William Coleman, and Richard Peters to draw up addresses of thanks to the proprietors.

Though the air pump must have come with a serviceable frame (or else it could not work), on 15 May 1738 the directors asked Franklin, Philip Syng, and Hugh Roberts to "get a Frame & Case made with Glass Lights in the Door to receive & preserve the Air Pump with its Appendages, and to look ornamental in the Library Room." The committee asked the joiner John Harrison to prepare an "ornamental" case for it. The directors adopted a letter thanking John Penn for the air pump (8 August). At the 8 January 1739 meeting, the air pump was brought to the library room. Hopkinson and Syng, two co-experimenters with Franklin on electricity in the late 1740s and early 1750s, evidently became the local experts on the pump. On 7 May 1739 Hopkinson was paid 16 shillings "for Quick Silver, Leather, Bladders, Oil, a Spunge &c for the Air pump"; and the silversmith Syng received 20 shillings "for cementing Air pump Glasses and for two Keys with other necessaries towards making Experiments with the Pump." Harrison finished the elaborate case and was paid £10 on 20 September 1739. It more than fulfilled the directors' hopes for an "ornamental" case. It is the best-known early example of Palladian Revival woodwork made in the colonies.

On 22 May 1738, the directors agreed to meet at 8:30 p.m. through August, then at 8 p.m. through October, and at 7 p.m. from November through May. They learned on 11 September that Dr. Walter Sydserfe of Antigua had donated to the Library Company the money owed him by William Alexander of Maryland. When Alexander was in Philadelphia on 2 October, he renewed the bond, promising to pay £34.6.3 sterling "on or before the 2nd day of April next with interest." On 9 October 1738, the directors requested Franklin and Richard Peters to write a letter of thanks to Dr. Sydserfe. The directors sold the bond to William Allen, but Sydserfe's gift proved difficult to collect. Three years later, Alexander had still not paid. The directors heard on 9 March 1741 that Allen intended shortly to return the bond to the Library Company. At the 11 May meeting, the directors resolved to repay Allen and to put William Alexander's bond into suit. Consequently on 20 May they ordered James Morris, treasurer, to pay Allen £51.13.6, Pennsylvania currency, "in full of his demand against the

Library Company of Philadelphia." The next meeting, 8 June, Franklin sent Alexander's bond to the Annapolis lawyer Daniel Dulany for legal action. On 14 October 1741, William Alexander finally delivered bills of exchange discharging the bond; and thereupon Franklin wrote Dulany to send it back with the costs of the suit. At the 9 November meeting, the directors ordered the treasurer to reimburse Franklin £3.15.10 for having paid Dulany.

When innkeeper John Roberts moved from High (Market) to Second Street in April 1739, the Library Company directors began meeting at his new location. On the occasions when Roberts evidently did not have a separate room available for them, the directors met at David Evans's inn (e.g., 30 April, 28 August, and 29 October 1739) at the Sign of the Crown on the south side of Market Street, two doors below Third Street.

In the minutes, Breintnall added at the end of 1738 a comment on his personal pleasure with the thriving state of the Library Company after its first seven years:

> The Library Affair has hitherto been many ways fortunate. The books sent for to England have always come safe and without Damage; very few of the Books have been lost or carelessly defaced; a good agreement has for the most part subsisted in the Company, and all the Officers have proved faithfull in their several Trusts, as far as hath yet been discovered; the Library has received Benefactions from several Gentlemen and well-wishers; and increases in its Reputation. And not one Subscriber is deceased (that I have heard of) except Joseph Growdon who died the 22nd of May last. I have presumed to make this Note without Direction, because I think it will not be disapproved of, and may prove useful. Another seven years, as successful as the foregoing must shew the Library Company in a very flourishing Condition, and to be more publickly known and esteemed.

During the spate of 1739 June meetings (11, 18, and 21), the Library Company directors decided which books to purchase next. They changed their London bookseller from William Meadows to William Innys on 9 July. Peter Collinson remained their agent and dealt with the booksellers without charging the Library Company for his services. The librarian, William Parsons, demanded on 8 October that the directors raise his salary or take the books from his house and appoint another librarian. The directors valued Parsons but also thought it would be desirable to have a room for the books that was not in someone's home. Franklin promptly petitioned the Pennsylvania Assembly, "praying (for the better Security of their [the Library Company's] Books from Fire) Leave to deposit them in a Room over one of the Offices of the State-House, till such Time as the Publick have Occasion to use the same." On 18 October the House considered the petition and granted permission. At its next meeting, the directors discussed the forthcoming move, including the need for new, sturdier shelves. On 7 April 1740, the Library Company moved from Parsons's home "to the Upper Room of the Westernmost Office in the State House." The State House (Independence Hall) remained the Library Company's location until 1773. After Parsons's ultimatum, in addition to moving the books the directors raised his salary, and he remained librarian for another seven years.

FRANKLIN'S LOSS OF POPULARITY

As the founder, Franklin received or tied for the most votes as a Library Company director until 1740, though by the late 1730s a few others were putting in almost as much time and energy as Franklin. At the ninth annual election on 5 May 1740, held in the library room of the State House, Franklin's popularity waned and he came in fifth. The directors chosen were Hugh Roberts, Thomas Hopkinson, William Coleman, Philip Syng, Franklin, Phineas Bond, Evan Morgan, Samuel Rhoads, Israel Pemberton, and Joseph Stretch. James Morris was reelected treasurer, and the directors continued Breintnall as secretary. Dr. Phineas Bond, the Quaker merchant Israel Pemberton, and Joseph Stretch were new directors; the cooper and merchant Evan Morgan, who became an assemblyman, had previously been a director (1735–37); and Alexander Graydon, William Plumsted, Robert Grace, and William Allen were replaced.

My interpretation of the election return may well be questioned. The only early meeting for which we have the actual vote was for 6 May 1754. On that occasion, five persons tied for the most votes. As secretary, Franklin recorded the voters and the officers elected. The members voting were Dr. Richard Farmer, Franklin, Joseph Stretch, John Mifflin, Michael Hilligas, Daniel Williams, Evan Morgan, Jonathan Evans, William Parsons, Samuel Shoemaker, John Smith, Hugh Roberts, Samuel Rhoads, and William Coleman—a total of fourteen. The directors chosen were Samuel Rhoads, with 14 votes; Joseph Stretch, with 14 votes; Richard Peters, 14; Thomas Cadwalader, 15; Samuel Morris, 15; Evan Morgan, 13; Philip Syng, 14; Amos Strettell, 15; John Mifflin, 15; and Benjamin Franklin, 15. Treasurer William Coleman received 14. Other persons voted for as director included Hugh Roberts, 1 vote (he also received 1 vote as treasurer); Charles Norris, 1; Samuel Sansom, 1; and Thomas Bond, 1. Evidently one member came late, after two directors (Rhoads and Stretch) had been chosen. One hundred forty-eight votes were cast for the 10 directors. If 15 voters had been present throughout the voting, 150 votes should have been cast. Whoever came late voted for only 8 of the 10 directors. If we assume that whoever came late would also have voted for Rhoads and Stretch, then 7 members would have tied for a position as director.

Indirect evidence shows that other elections were close. In the 1738 election, a number of votes must have been cast for directors who did not quite win. That fall, when director William Coleman went on a voyage, the other directors consulted the votes for the past election, found that Samuel Rhoads had the next highest number, and appointed Rhoads a director in Coleman's place (11 December 1738). Further, the 1740 voting, where Franklin came in fifth, elected four new directors (an unusual one-third turnover in leadership), whereas in some years (e.g., 1735 and 1736, and 1742–45), the same directors were continued in office. The Library Company's leadership had a major change in 1740.

Despite the lack of absolute proof, it makes sense that Franklin suffered a loss of popularity with many Library Company members in 1740. There were four good reasons, each of which will be discussed in its context elsewhere, but I will enumerate them here. First, Franklin had recently opposed the Quaker pacifist position in the assembly and organized a petition for a militia (1 January 1740). Pacifist Quakers had reason to oppose him, and most of the Library Company subscribers were Quakers, many of them pacifists. Second, the Proprietary Party had recently censured Franklin (25 January) for not printing in the *Pennsylvania Gazette* the governor's reasons for rejecting a bill. Therefore, strong Proprietary partisans, like Richard Peters, Lyndford Lardner, James Hamilton, and William Allen, probably opposed him. His close friends Thomas Hopkinson and William Parsons, though stalwart Proprietary Party members, were probably exceptions. Third, the "gentlemen" among the Library Company members were angry with Franklin for the newspaper exchange on closing the Dancing Assembly (1 May). And fourth, the tanners (especially Samuel Morris) resented his 1739 attempt to clean up Philadelphia's environment by moving the tanyards from the area around Dock Street. Altogether, a number of Library Company members had reasons in 1740 not to vote for Franklin.

The founder was nevertheless voted a director and attended all the 1740–41 meetings. At the 8 December 1740 meeting, the directors asked him to "get made a Dozen of Sheep skin Covers or Cases for Folio Books to be put on them when they are lent out." At the tenth annual election, 4 May 1741, the directors remained the same as the previous year, but Franklin moved from fifth to second in the listing. At the 1742 election, Franklin was listed first, but at the 1743 election, Thomas Hopkinson was. Thereafter, in all recorded elections to 1757 (by which time Franklin knew he was going to England on Pennsylvania Assembly business), Franklin was listed first. I conclude that Franklin was the executive officer of the Library Company from its founding in 1731 to 1740, and from 1744 to 1757.

The directors agreed on 11 May 1741 to appoint the meeting time at 8:30 p.m. through August, then at 8 p.m. until November, and at 7 p.m. from November until May. William Plumsted, who had recently returned from London, delivered on 8 June 1741 a camera obscura and a double microscope, presents from proprietor John Penn. On 13 July the Library Company directors "Ordered that Wm. Coleman, Benj. Franklin and Thos. Hopkinson be a Committee to write a Letter of Thanks to the Honorable John Penn, Esq." for his gift. These gifts, like his earlier donation of the air pump, showed that John Penn had an interest in science and knew that his Philadelphia friends like Thomas Hopkinson also did. What Penn, along with everyone else, did not know, was the extraordinary scientific ability of Franklin.

THE 1741 *CATALOGUE*

Though the librarian kept a list of the books the Library Company owned, it was convenient for the members to have a copy. The last printed list had appeared in 1735. On 9 June 1740 the Library Company directors asked Franklin to print a new catalogue. Evidently they discovered that the librarian's list of books was either confusing or incomplete. They asked on 11 August that "William Coleman, Hugh Roberts, F. Hopkinson,[12] & Franklin be a Committee to make & complete a Catalogue of the Books belonging to the Library." On 13 April 1741, the directors requested Franklin to print two hundred copies before the election on 4 May. Either he did not have the time to do it by then or the manuscript catalogue was not yet ready because the request was not fulfilled. At the 13 July meeting, Franklin read a paper containing a brief account of the library, which he said he wrote to fill up a blank page at the end of the catalogue he was printing; the other directors approved. It concluded: "a Share which at first was worth but 40s is now valued at 6.10s. But for this small Sum which laid out in Books would go but a little Way, every Member has the use of a Library now worth upwards of £500. Whereby Knowledge is in this City render'd more cheap and easy to be come at, to the great Pleasure and Advantage of the studious Part of the Inhabitants." Perhaps Franklin did not realize that the price of admission was becoming so high that it was excluding the kind of young artisans who, a decade earlier, had organized the library.

By the 10 August directors' meeting, Franklin had printed the 1741 *Catalogue.* As was often the case, he was an innovator. He gave more publication information and longer titles than appeared in most earlier library catalogues. For the times, it was a book man's catalogue. It contained 375 titles, with a single title sometimes representing numerous volumes. The major subjects continued to be history, literature, and science, with fewer volumes in theology and in foreign languages than other colonial American libraries. Though the directors purchased the standard dictionaries and grammars in Latin and modern European languages, as well as a Bible in Latin, they had purchased only four other non-English books: Cervantes' *Don Quixote* in Spanish; Grotius's *De Jure Belli* in Latin; Pascal's *Lettres provinciales* in French; and Plautus's *Comoediae.*[13] (All other non-English books were gifts.) Franklin, "ravished" by Pascal when a boy, was no doubt responsible for its purchase.[14] Since we know he read Cervantes and taught himself to read Spanish, he probably wanted the Library Company to purchase *Don Quixote* (A 97, 134). Though Franklin was one of the best linguists among the early members, he supported the decision to select books in English. He wrote in 1789 that "in the Scheme of the Library I had provided only for English Books."[15]

While printing the *Catalogue,* Franklin annotated several entries. Of John Locke's *Essay Concerning Human Understanding* (2 volumes), he wrote: "Esteemed the best Book of Logick in the World." After the entry for *Spectator* (8 volumes), *Tatler* (4 volumes), and *Guardian* (2 volumes), he added: "Written by some of the most ingenious Men of the Age, for the Promotion of Virtue, Piety and good Manners" (*Catalogue* [1741] 30, 46). Most comments are descriptive, though some are implicitly appreciative: Of *The Practice of Perspective: Or, An Easy Method of Representing Natural Objects According to the Rules of Art*, Franklin noted, "A Work highly necessary for Painters, Engravers, Architects, Embroiderers, &c" (*Catalogue* [1741] 16). The inclusion of "Embroiderers" in that list may be a minor example of Franklin's proto-feminism. Copies of the catalogue were given to every Library Company member, and the directors voted to present a copy to each member of the General Assembly, to Peter Collinson, and to John Penn. Were the gifts to the assembly members in gratitude for allowing the library to use a room in the state house? Was it an attempt to enlist members from the assembly? It seems unlikely that the Library Company directors could hope for any funds from the legislature.

The titles of the books in the Library Company document the Whiggish influences on Franklin as well as on early American political thinking. They reinforce the impressions made by Franklin's quotations from *Cato's Letters* in Silence Dogood and by his references to Algernon Sydney and John Trenchard in the Obadiah Plainman series (1740). Most Whig classics were in the library by 1741. Surprisingly, Henry Care's compilation, *English Liberties*, was not. Franklin advertised copies in the *Gazette* on 21 March and 5 September 1734 (the latter an especially long, descriptive book advertisement); 25 November 1736; and 18 and 22 January 1739. Perhaps so many members owned their own copy that it was not greatly desired.[16] John Locke's *Two Treatises of Government*, and *A Collection of Several Pieces*, both given by Franklin, were there. Locke's *Works* in a folio edition of three volumes (including of course the *Two Treatises*), like *An Essay Concerning Human Understanding* and *An Essay upon Education of Children*, had been purchased by the company. Even the translations from foreign-language histories, including the five titles of René Vertot's histories of other countries, "dealt with revolution and the subversion of established monarchies."[17]

The collection of English literature was among the best in the colonies in 1741. In addition to the major English periodicals, the Library Company owned the works of Joseph Addison, John Arbuthnot, Francis Bacon, William Congreve, Anthony Ashley Cooper (third earl of Shaftesbury), Abraham Cowley, John Dryden, John Gay, Matthew Prior, Nicholas Rowe, Edmund Spenser, Richard Steele, Jonathan Swift, and Edmund Waller, as well as Butler's *Hudibras*. Lesser contemporary litterateurs, like John Pomfret, Richard Blackmore, Samuel Garth, and Henry Needler (to select only those on page 50 of the *Catalogue*) were found throughout the collection. The only colonial American libraries that I am sure contained more belletristic literature were those of the Virginia litterateurs William Byrd of Westover (d. 1744) and John Mercer (d. 1768).

THE CHARTER AND, FINALLY, THE LAND

Thomas Penn's gift of a plot of ground could not be formally presented to the Library Company until it had a charter. The Reverend Richard Peters informed the directors on 21 June 1739 that the proprietors would grant a charter. The directors drafted one on 20 July 1741 and called a special general meeting to consider it on 3 August. One clause provoked dissatisfaction. It said that the members had the power to make laws for the company but that no law would be binding unless notice had been given to all members and unless one-fifth of all members were present. After one-fifth was changed to one-fourth, the draft was approved. The directors drew up a letter of thanks to the proprietors. On 8 March 1742, Israel Pemberton reported that the members who had reservations "now declared themselves satisfied." On 15 March the directors considered minor revisions to the prospective charter. They sent off the charter to Governor George Thomas, who signed it on 25 March. At the next general meeting on 3 May 1742, fifty-three subscribers showed up or sent in their proxies to sign the charter.

Franklin, Hopkinson, and Coleman were named a committee at the 10 May 1742 directors' meeting to draw up an address of thanks to the proprietors. At the next meeting, 14 June, the directors read and approved it. The address was engrossed and signed in July. The sentiments of the concluding paragraph reflect Franklin's opinions: "The Powers and Privileges now granted us will, without Doubt, very much conduce to the Increase and Reputation of the Library; and as valuable Books come to be in more general Use and Esteem, we hope they will have very good Effects on the Minds of the People of this Province, and furnish them with the most useful kind of Knowledge, that which renders Men benevolent and helpful to one another." Surprisingly, the directors also referred to the political controversy between the governor and the Quaker-dominated assembly over appropriations for the war between Great Britain and Spain: "Our unhappy Divisions and Animosities, of late, have too much interrupted that charitable and friendly Intercourse which formerly subsisted among all Societies in this Place; but as all Parties come to understand their true Interest, we hope these Animosities will cease, and that Men of all Denominations will mutually assist in carrying on the publick Affairs in such manner as will most tend to the Peace and Welfare of the Province."

On 9 August 1743, John, Thomas, and Richard Penn acknowledged the thanks of the Library Company. The directors agreed on 14 November that "the Addresses lately sent to the Proprietors, together with their Answer, should be printed, and Evan Morgan was desired to get Copies from the Secretary and deliver them to Mr. Franklin for that Purpose." At the 12 November 1743 meeting, Franklin was asked to have the title to the property on the south side of Chestnut Street transferred from the four individuals (Franklin, Allen, Plumsted, and Hamilton) to the Library Company. Thomas Penn, however, did not make out the official patent for the lot until 12 January 1760, and the Library Company finally received it on 12 April 1762.

STABILITY

At the annual election on 3 May 1742, the subscribers chose Benjamin Franklin, Evan Morgan, Hugh Roberts, Philip Syng, Joseph Stretch, Thomas Hopkinson, Samuel Rhoads, John Jones, Jr., Samuel Morris, and Jacob Duché as directors. William Coleman, the first treasurer (1731–33), returned to the job, replacing James Morris, who had served from 1734 to 1742. The directors reappointed Joseph Breintnall secretary. Jones, Morris, and Duché were new directors, replacing William Coleman, Phineas Bond, and Israel Pemberton. In a remarkable showing of continuity, the same 1742 slate of officers was reelected for the three following years, 1743–45.

At the 1742 annual meeting, in addition to approving the charter, the subscribers passed a series of laws confirming the company's practices. For example, they voted that "no Person shall be admitted a Member, without the Approbation of the Directors, and paying the Value of a Share, of which a Certificate is to be given, and a Record made." A new law specified that the subscribers would have to pay a "Penalty of Five Shillings for every three Months Default of making the annual Payments." At the meeting, the tenth annual payment was made.

Perhaps responding to the Library Company's gift of its catalogues, the assembly ordered Franklin on 13 September 1742 "to deposit one of the new Pennsylvania law books in the Library." Franklin attended all the directors' meetings in 1742–43. The following year, he missed one (13 June 1743) while visiting New England. In 1744–45, Franklin missed the 9 July 1744 meeting. In 1745–46, he attended them all.

The directors noted on 11 October 1742 that some glasses of the air pump had been broken "but no one knew how or why." They appointed Franklin, Thomas Hopkinson, and Samuel Rhoads "to have the Care & Management of the Air pump & what belongs to it, & the keeping the Key of the Press." Franklin presented fossils on 13 December that the botanist John Bartram had collected in the Allegheny Mountains, "in which were Shells, & Impressions of Shell fish." The fossils heightened Franklin's interest in paleontology and the age of the world. Franklin also told the directors that when he was "lately at Stenton, Mr. Logan expressed a Desire of seeing the Company's Charter & their Laws; & the Directors consented the Book should be sent him, belonging to the Library, in which the said Charter & Laws were recorded." At the same meeting, Hopkinson said that he, Franklin, and Rhoads had inspected the air pump and its apparatus and taken an account of its glasses.

On 28 April 1743, Franklin "exhibited his Account (from August 1741) for printing Advertisements, Blank Notices and Notes, and Catalogues, and for Paper, Parchment &c. amounting to £12.12.6." At the same meeting Breintnall presented Peter Collinson's letter of 24 February, in which he "begs a Favour of the Gentlemen of the Library Company that they will admit his Friend John Bartram (of whose Desert he speaks warmly) an honorary Member, without any Expence, and to have a free Access to the Library.—The Directors immediately agreed, that as Mr. Collinson had been a Constant Benefactor to the Company (never charging them with any Commissions, and had presented them with several valuable Books) and as Mr. Bartram was also in their Esteem a deserving Man, he should have free Access to the Library." With this vote, the directors of the Library Company of Philadelphia, who had begun in 1730 as primarily a group of young artisans, assumed the role of patrons of learning and culture. Of course the botanist Bartram had already, through Franklin, presented the Library Company with fossils from his expeditions.

As the gifts of fossils and an air pump show, the Library Company in its early years contained a cabinet of curiosities as well as scientific instruments. Franklin added to the latter by giving a magnifying glass twelve inches in diameter to the library on 9 May 1743.

GIFTS AND BUSINESS

Throughout its history, the Library Company of Philadelphia had benefitted from gifts, beginning with the books that Peter Collinson added to the first order in 1731 (though if one included time, effort, and money spent, Franklin would come first). The greatest eighteenth-century gift of books, however, was James Logan's library. He had decided to leave his great private library to the citizens of Philadelphia. Like Franklin, Logan was a genius who independently studied and mastered various fields. Unlike Franklin, he was a classical scholar and owned the finest private collection of classics in colonial America. He was also a superior student of higher mathematics, annotating and occasionally correcting errors in all three early editions of Newton's *Principia Mathematica*.[18] In the areas of science and the classics, his collection was unrivaled in America before 1750. He drew up a deed of trust on 8 March 1745, appointing Israel Pemberton, Jr., William Allen, Richard Peters, and Benjamin Franklin trustees of his library. It opened as a separate institution in 1760 but became part of the Library Company in 1793. The *Library of James Logan* (1974) by Edwin Wolf 2nd is perhaps the greatest catalogue of any colonial American library.

Though the English merchant and botanist Peter Collinson gave many gifts of considerable value to the Library Company, his most important gift arrived in the fall of 1745. It was a six-pence pamphlet. The price was so little and its importance was at the time judged so negligible that it was not mentioned in the Library Company minutes, nor recorded in the 1746 *Additions*[19] to the Library Company *Catalogue* of 1741. With the pamphlet, Collinson presented a glass tube to the Library Company. These two presents started Franklin, Ebenezer Kinnersley, Thomas Hopkinson, and Philip Syng on their electrical experiments, which will be described in Volume 3.

After the fourteenth annual election on 6 May 1745, Franklin presented his charge of twenty shillings "for printing Notices of the general Meeting for 1744 & 1745 and blank Receipts in those two Years." At the 8 July 1745 meeting, Franklin was asked to get from Breintnall a copy of the 1741 catalogue either "printed or in Manuscript, to help the Directors in a new Choice of Books to be sent for." At the 11 and 14 November meetings, they decided what books to order. When the directors met on 13 January 1745/6, Franklin, Hugh Roberts, and William Coleman "were appointed a Committee to revise the Rules for lending Books &c and report to the next Meeting of the Directors, what Alterations they think necessary to be made in them." On 14 April, the directors asked Franklin "to draw from the Minutes an Account of the Pamphlets that ought to be in the Library." No such account survives.

The meeting venue changed during 1745. The 14 October meeting was the last at the Widow Roberts. Beginning with the 11 November meeting, the directors gathered at Joseph Breintnall's coffee house at the Sign of the Hen and Chickens on Chestnut Street. After Breintnall committed suicide on 16 March 1745/6, Franklin took over as secretary for the next decade. The directors continued meeting at the Widow Breintnall's. At the 5 May 1746 meeting, they "took into Consideration, that Joseph Breintnall, late Secretary, had faithfully served the Company Yearly, without any adequate Recompence for the same, in Gratitude for which, they unanimously voted a Present of £15 to his Widow for the Use of his Family; and that his Son George shall have the free Use of the Books in the Library during Life; but that, during his Minority some Person approved by the Directors sign Notes for him." After the election of 1746, the directors learned that former director Samuel Norris had left the Library Company £20 in his will, the organization's first legacy.

From May 1746 to May 1748, Franklin attended all the recorded meetings (the record only goes through September 1747) except those on 10 November and 8 December 1746 when he was visiting New England. Franklin informed the directors on 5 May 1746 that the Reverend Hugh Jones, who lived nearby in Maryland, had presented a valuable book titled *Reliquiae Bodleianae* and another titled *Catalogue Universalis Libraorum in omni Facultate Linguague insignum & rarissimorum &c.* in two volumes. Joseph Breintnall's widow presented several unique gifts: two manuscript volumes he kept containing records of the weather for the previous several years, a manuscript titled "Remarks on Grafting and Inoculating," and a large collection of nature prints of leaves of plants growing near Philadelphia.[20]

THE 1746 *CATALOGUE*

On 8 July 1745, the Library Company directors requested that Franklin print the charter and a catalogue of the books added since 1741, which would be supplied by librarian William Parsons. Ten months later, on 12 May 1746, the directors again asked Franklin to print the company's charter. Robert Greenway was directed on 14 July 1746 to furnish Franklin "with a Copy of the Charter, for the

Press." Since librarian Parsons still had not compiled the list, John Sober and Lynford Lardner were appointed to compile it. On 13 October, the directors asked that the laws of the company be printed with the charter. Perhaps after the rest of the pamphlet had been set in type, the directors requested on 9 March 1747 that the rules be added. The resulting imprint was *The Charter of the Library Company of Philadelphia* (Philadelphia: Franklin, 1746 [1747]). Franklin charged the Library Company £7.10. for "Catalogues" on 1 January 1746/7.

The 1746 catalogue contained more complete title entries than had the 1741 catalogue. Altogether, 187 new titles appeared, 41 folios, 13 quartos, 106 octavos, and 27 duodecimos, with many titles representing multiple volumes. Added to those in the 1741 catalogue, the Library Company now had 562 titles. Pamphlets were not listed. Franklin annotated four entries: after *An Universal History, from the Earliest Account of Time to the Present* (2nd ed., 7 volumes [London, 1740]), he wrote, "Esteemed a very judicious, elaborate, and learned Collection" (p. 4); of Jonathan Swift's two-volume *Gulliver's Travels* (London, 1726), he said, "Being a severe Satyr and Ridicule upon the Follies, Infirmities, and Vices of particular Nations, and the Human Race" (p. 12); after Sir Joshua Childe, *A Discourse on Trade and Money, with Its Use* (London [n.d.]), he commented, "esteem'd the clearest and best Treatise extant upon those Subjects" (p. 27); of Herodotus, translated by Dr. Littlebury (2nd ed. [London, 1720]), he wrote, "Esteemed one of the first Authors who raised his Stile and Method above common Narration, to the Dignity of History" (p. 13). Surprisingly, the Library Company had two copies of it. The catalogue (p. 27) recorded that Franklin gave the company an incunabulum, the *Magna Charta* (London, 1556).

As usual, the catalogue was arranged by the size of the books. The 41 folios contained a larger proportion of law books than had the 1741 catalogue. The folios concluded with two volumes of bound newspapers: "*The American Mercury*; from its first Publication in 1719, to the Year 1746. 6 v."; and "*The Pennsylvania Gazette*; from its first Publication in the Year 1728, to 1747. 5 v." Both were gifts of Thomas Hopkinson. *The Laws of Pennsylvania* (Philadelphia: Franklin, 1742) was given by the legislature. Franklin would have been especially interested in the revised and enlarged edition of Bayle's ten-volume *Dictionary* (London, 1734).

Franklin was probably responsible for ordering at least four of the thirteen books in quarto: *The Koran or Alcoran of Mohammed* (London, 1734); the three-volume *Philosophical Works of . . . Robert Boyle* (London, 1738); *An Enquiry into the Morals of the Antients* (London, 1737); and *A Course of Experimental Philosophy*, by J. T. Desaguliers (London, 1732).

Of the 106 books in octavo, those with special significance for Franklin included John Pointer, *A Rational Account of the Weather [with] the Cause of an Aurora Borealis* (2nd ed. [1738]); the four-volume *Works of the Hon Robert Boyle* (1699); Benjamin Martin's *New and Compendious System of Opticks* (London, 1740); Père du Halde's four-volume *History of China* (London, 1741); Humphrey

Bland's *Treatise of Military Discipline* (London, 1740), which Franklin excerpted in his *General Magazine* in 1741, and which he partly reprinted as a pamphlet in 1746 and again in 1747; Sir John Floyer's *History of Cold Bathing, Antient and Modern* (London, 1732); Bishop Fleetwood's *Chronicon Pretiosum; or an Account of English Gold and Silver Money* (London, 1745); Henry Baker's *Microscope Made Easy* (London, 1742), and Baker's *Attempt towards a Natural History of the Polype* (London, 1743), which Franklin used in his article on the microscope in *Poor Richard* for 1751. One entry contains three works by James Logan that Franklin printed: M. T. Cicero's *Cato Major* (Philadelphia: Franklin, 1744); *Charge Deliver'd from the Bench to the Grand Inquest* (Philadelphia: Franklin, 1736); and *Cato's Moral Distichs, Englished in Couplets* (Philadelphia: Franklin, 1735).

Among the twenty-seven books in duodecimo there were Joshua Gee's *Trade and Navigation of Great-Britain Consider'd* (London, 1738), which Franklin cited in the 5 January 1731 *Gazette* (it was first published in 1729); and an English translation (hopefully not the "poor one" he read as a boy) of his childhood favorite, Pascal's *Les Provinciales; or the Mystery of Jesuitism* (2nd ed. [London, 1658]). In addition to these volumes, the scientific works and the Americana would especially have appealed to him. Among the latter was an imprint by his South Carolina partner Lewis Timothy, *A True and Historical Narrative of the Colony of Georgia* (Charlestown: Timothy, 1741). One puzzle in the 1746 catalogue is *An Account of the Shipwreck of Robert Barrow, and Others, on the Coast of Florida, and Their Deliverance; by Jonathan Dickenson [sic], One of the Persons Concern'd* (Philadelphia, 1730). This is an edition of Jonathan Dickinson's *God's Protecting Providence* (1699), but no 1730 edition is known. Franklin reprinted it in 1736. No copy of that edition is extant, but the advertisement (1 April 1736 *Gazette*) used the standard title *God's Protecting Providence* and called it "The Second Edition." Had there been a previous "second edition" published in Philadelphia, Franklin would have known it. The date 1730 is probably an error for 1736, and the title in the 1746 *Catalogue* described the exciting contents instead of reproducing the actual title. The entry probably refers to the lost Franklin 1736 imprint.

LATER HISTORY

The Library Company of Philadelphia inspired the founding of similar institutions in Philadelphia, the surrounding area, and other colonies. John Bartram reported to Peter Collinson on 21 June 1743 that another library had started in imitation of the Library Company in Darby, Pennsylvania.[21] In 1747 the Redwood Library in Newport, Rhode Island, and the Union Library Company in Philadelphia were founded. Two more Philadelphia libraries started in 1757, the Association and Amicable Libraries. All these and other colonial American libraries were inspired by the Library Company, and the three additional Philadelphia libraries (the Union, Association, and Amicable) merged with the Library Company in 1769.

When the Philadelphia libraries merged, the Library Company gained an influx of new members. They were welcome because membership in the Library Company had not been increasing. The founding members paid £2 to join and every year thereafter paid ten shillings. To match what the existing members had paid, the price to new members went up by ten shillings every year, reaching £10 in May 1748. The increasing cost of admission meant that fewer persons could afford to join. That was the primary reason that three new libraries started in Philadelphia during these years. By 1765, admission was £20, and no new members had joined in four years. The 1765 directors realized that the high price hindered the company's growth, and they voted to cut the cost of admission in half. Within a few months, the Library Company gained fourteen new members. In the future, as the cost of admission grew, the directors voted further reductions.

Franklin was continuously voted a director from 1731 to the 3 May 1757 election. By then he knew he was going to London during the following year; therefore the election of 1756 was the last time he stood for office. He had been a director for a quarter of a century. For his last year in office (1756–57), the other directors, together with their terms of office, were the following: Philip Syng (24 years as director); Evan Morgan (19 years); Samuel Rhoads (18 years); Samuel Morris and Joseph Stretch (both 15 years); Thomas Cadwalader (12 years); John Mifflin (11 years); and Richard Peters and Amos Strettell (both 7 years). It was William Coleman's eighteenth year as treasurer, Benjamin Franklin's eleventh as secretary, and Robert Greenway's twelfth as librarian. The stability of the directors, secretary, treasurer, and librarian was a major reason for the Library Company's success.

THE LIBRARY COMPANY IN THE *AUTOBIOGRAPHY*

The paper upon which Franklin wrote the holograph manuscript of the *Autobiography* provides evidence concerning his literary intentions and his 1771 feelings about the Library Company.[22] He wrote the manuscript on folio sheets (each folded to make four pages) through manuscript page 84. He was at the end of his stay with Jonathan Shipley, the bishop of St. Asaph, and had to return, probably the next day, to London, where he would not have time to continue writing the story of his life. So he took up a single leaf (one half of a folio sheet, containing only two pages). Evidently he planned to conclude his writing within two pages. (An alternative but unlikely explanation is that he had used up all the full sheets of paper on hand and had only half leaves left.) The last full sheet he had written described his hardships and gradual success as an independent printer in Philadelphia. At the very end of page 84, he introduced the next topic, his marriage to Deborah Read. He probably hoped to deal with it in one page and with the following topic, the Library Company, in one more page. These two topics appear in sequence in the "Outline" for the autobiography (A 203), and they conclude part 1 of the book. It was a logical place to stop writing, not only because his time had run out but also because he had brought his biography through his youth and early manhood, through all his most formative years, and to the point where he was established in life with a wife, a business, and his first public project.

But Franklin was not quite finished when he exhausted the space on manuscript page 86, the end of the half leaf of paper. The concluding sentence was "his was the Mother of all the N American Subscription Libraries now so numerous." He wrote "It" and then took up another leaf (not another full sheet) and finished the sentence: "is become a great thing itself, and continually increasing." He added a dash or flourish—a symbol that he often employed at rhetorical conclusions in his manuscripts.[23] Evidently he intended, if only for a second, to end part 1 of the autobiography there. He was, however, unsatisfied with that closing, and so he added another sentence about the significance of the libraries: "These Libraries have improv'd the general Conversation of the Americans, made the common Tradesmen & Farmers as intelligent as most Gentlemen from other Countries, and perhaps have contributed in some degree to the Stand so generally made throughout the colonies in Defence of their Privileges."

These words conclude part 1. The final sentence opened up the focus and provided a definite sense of an ending. Franklin had shifted his perspective from the nitty-gritty details and particular circumstances (which characterize the usual point of view in the *Autobiography* and are part of the sense of texture and dense Lockean reality the book conveys)[24] to a time-spanning and world-spanning view recalling the Stamp Act and subsequent and ever-growing tensions between America and England. Though the story of his life has only been brought down to his twenty-fifth year, 1731, the references in the final sentence bring the situation down to the present time in which he was writing (1771) and to the great, unresolved, and ever more threatening conflict between Britain and its colonies.

The last sentence was also a fitting closure because of the explicit and implicit attitudes conveyed. Franklin began by implying that Americans have benefitted from the libraries and that the improvement was reflected in their "general conversation." The philosophy underlying the statement implied that the majority of people will "improve" in ideas and learning if they have the opportunity. It conveyed an egalitarian and a positive, even optimistic, view of humanity. Second, he said that the libraries have made the "common Tradesmen & Farmers as intelligent as most Gentlemen from other Countries." The Americanism is anti-aristocratic and egalitarian.

The use of the word *intelligent* is especially interesting, for its primary meaning is not knowledge of books and ideas (listed only third in the unabridged *Oxford English Dictionary*) but instead "having the faculty of understanding."

Franklin, a literary genius sensitive to denotations as well as connotations of words, was asserting that no difference existed between the "common Tradesmen & Farmers" in America and "most Gentlemen" in other countries. The America that Franklin portrayed in the *Autobiography* was comparatively classless. The reality, of course, was different. In America, as in England and Europe, the social structure was hierarchical. Gentlemen sent for laborers and craftsmen (including printers like Franklin) when they had business for them. Ordinary people were automatically supposed to defer to gentlemen (for example, to step off a narrow paved path into the mud when they met). But times were changing, especially in America—and even more so in the imagination of Franklin. Wealth and family had been attacked and discredited as the basis for social distinction. What remained for most thoughtful students of social organization in the eighteenth century was not just acquired ability but a profound difference in the degree of ability. The faculty of intelligence was supposed to distinguish the upper from the lower classes.[25]

Franklin, however, attacked the supposed distinction. There is no difference in ability, in fundamental intelligence, he says, between the "common Tradesmen & Farmers" and "most Gentlemen." Thus he annihilated the basis of social hierarchy as it commonly existed in the Enlightenment—and in the beliefs of almost all of his fellow members of the Third Realm. In a letter to Lord Shelburne, England's prime minister during the peace treaty negotiations in 1782, Franklin's friend Benjamin Vaughan explained his radical attitudes toward class and intellectual differences: Franklin "thinks that the lower people are as we see them, because oppressed; and then their situation in point of manners, becomes the reason for oppressing them." Jefferson's advocacy of a natural "aristoi" in his letter to John Adams of 28 October 1813 was more typical of the members of the Third Realm. Franklin, however, implied that America is the land of democracy and achieved opportunity because the "common" Americans have reached the intellectual level achieved by "most Gentlemen" in England or Europe. Franklin's visionary Republic of Letters was a world more democratic, less elitist, than Hume's or Jefferson's. Franklin's Third Realm became, of course, the wave of the future, though it may perhaps never be entirely fulfilled.[26]

The difference between Americans and the English people reminded him of their political differences and of the Americans' revolutionary stand from the time of the Stamp Act "in Defence of their Privileges" to 1771. The sentence suggested that republican principles are synonymous with knowledge. Learning will naturally convince the student that the rights and liberties (or "Privileges") of the people are fundamental principles that must be defended and upheld. Learning, Franklin implied, will necessarily lead to belief in a democracy.

Thus the conclusion of part 1 achieves the sense of an ending not only by enlarging the perspective from a confined, limited, Lockean reality in place and time to a global perspective, but also by making the final sentence resound with meanings, significance, and implications. Had Franklin never been able to return to the *Autobiography*, part 1 alone would have survived as a consummate work of art.

CONCLUSION

According to Franklin, the Library Company was responsible for major changes in American society and thought: "The Institution soon manifested its Utility, was imitated by other Towns and in other Provinces, the Librarys were augmented by Donations, Reading became fashionable, and our People having no publick Amusements to divert their Attention from Study became better acquainted with Books, and in a few Years were observ'd by Strangers to be better instructed and more intelligent than people of the same Rank generally are in other Countries" (A 74). Franklin's friend Jean Baptiste Le Roy wrote Abbé Claude Fauchet after Franklin's death about the influence of the Library Company, pointing out that similar ones were formed in imitation of it, and concluded that Franklin was "not only . . . the founder, but, as it were, the schoolmaster of American independence."[27]

Franklin believed that the Library Company was a major factor in his own development, affording him "the Means of Improvement by constant Study, for which I set apart an Hour or two each Day." He thereby managed to make up "in some Degree the Loss of the Learned Education my Father once intended for me." Reading and study were his only recreations. He recorded that he "was in debt for my Printing-house, I had a young Family coming on to be educated, and I had to contend with for Business two Printers who were establish'd in the Place before me. My Circumstances however grew daily easier: my original Habits of Frugality continuing." Franklin cited his father's frequent quoting of Solomon: *Seest thou a Man diligent in his Calling, he shall stand before Kings, he shall not stand before mean Men*, thereby attributing the virtue of industry not only to his father but also to the Christian tradition (A 75).

The literary historian Larzer Ziff has called "the *social* advantages that adhere to the possession and reading of books" a prominent theme in the *Autobiography*. He claimed that books were Franklin's "passport to social and thence to commercial and political advancement."[28] I agree, though I would place greater emphasis on the connection that Franklin makes between books, learning, and egalitarianism. The social advantages were a by-product. The availability of books and the possibility of self-education meant that the common man did not automatically have to be satisfied in the roles he found himself by birth and early training. Franklin hoped that education could transform the hierarchical world in which he had been born into one where persons could create themselves. He wrote in his *Autobiography* that the availability of self-education through books made the American "common Tradesmen & Farmers" as intelligent as most Gentlemen from other Countries. He also linked education with a belief in political rights, adding that the availability of books "perhaps . . . contributed in some degree to the Stand so generally made throughout the Colonies in Defence of their Privileges" (A 72).

For Franklin, education would characterize the future American society; until that time, however, the ambitious individual could educate himself. Benjamin Vaughan knew Franklin's oral stories of his self-education, and thus private study was among the themes that Vaughan expected the *Autobiography* to contain. In urging Franklin to go on with it, Vaughan said it would "give a noble rule and example of *self-education*," showing that it was possible by one's own effort for "many a man" to achieve success (A 186).

Like the Junto, Franklin founded the Library Company partly as a means of self-education and partly as a means to spread education among his friends. Unlike the Junto, it was meant to be a useful means of self-education for others in the future. Later, when he wrote of his ideas in starting the Academy of Philadelphia, he recalled that the books in the Library Company were in English and were meant to be useful. Like the Academy of Philadelphia, the Library Company was intended to be an educational institution for the future.

The Library Company of Philadelphia was a manifestation of Franklin's belief in democracy and egalitarianism. Though the leaders of the Library Company gradually changed from the young artisans who founded it in 1730 to include many of Philadelphia's most successful merchants and elite intellectuals, such as William Allen, John Smith (James Logan's son-in-law), and John Dickinson, the early members like Franklin, Philip Syng, and Hugh Roberts had also become wealthier and more established members of society, as had the young founding professionals such as lawyer Thomas Hopkinson and early members Drs. Thomas and Phineas Bond. Thus, the gradual gentrification of the Library Company came both from the addition of Philadelphia's gentry to membership and from the rise in status of its founding "Artificers."

When asked for an inscription for the cornerstone of the 1789 building that would house the Library Company, Franklin chose to emphasize its working-class origins: "Be it remembered, / In honor of the PHILADELPHIAN Youth, / (Then chiefly Artificers) / That in MDCCXXXI / They cheerfully / INSTITUTED the PHILADELPHIA LIBRARY / which tho' small at first, / Is become highly valuable, / And extensively useful." After "cheerfully," the 1789 directors added, "At the Instance of BENJAMIN FRANKLIN / One of their Number." And at the end the directors further added, "And which the Walls of this Edifice / Are now destined to contain and preserve. / The first STONE of whose FOUNDATION / Was here placed / The thirty first Day of AUGUST / An: Dom: MDCCLXXXIX."

The Library Company of Philadelphia remains today a premier collection of more than half a million books, in great part from the eighteenth century, making it a scholarly research library of national and international importance. It continues to be what Franklin wanted it to be—a useful and valuable addition to the culture of Philadelphia and the United States.

FIVE

Man of Letters

There are in the World infinitely more He-Tyrants than She-Ones.—*"Reply to a Piece of Advice" that claimed "every Woman is a Tyrant," 2:22–23*

BETWEEN 1731 AND 1736 Franklin wrote more than twenty essays (not discussed in other chapters) on such varied subjects as consumerism, vanity, writing, shopkeeping, and dramdrinking.[1] The "Casuist" series began in the *Pennsylvania Gazette* on 9 December 1729. By 25 January 1731/2, it had become an inquiry into moral complexity. Franklin abandoned that approach (which probably interested him more than his readers) on 26 June 1732 when he took up a topic now common to tabloid journalism: adultery. He wrote a follow-up piece on 3 July but decided that it was too risqué and suppressed it. About the same time he drafted "The Morals of Chess" but did not publish it until fifty years later when he was in France. In that essay, he justified the time spent playing chess as valuable preparation for the conduct of life. The following winter, imitating *The Tatler*, he printed a piece on "The Box Family" on 11 January 1732/3. He wrote two essays on literary style, the first an appreciation of what constitutes a normally good style (2 August 1733) and the second, on the excesses of amplification (17 June 1736), which satirized legal circumlocutions.

Three related skits on shopkeepers, customers, and wholesalers appeared in late 1730 and expressed Franklin's distaste for the commercial bases of society. Beginning with the common prevarications of shopkeepers (19 November 1730), he moved to the self-justification of a typical shopkeeper, "Betty Diligent," who lies even to herself; and then to the falsehoods of a wholesaler, "Mercator" (3 Dec 1730). Two years later he turned to the spending habits of the ordinary citizen in two social satires of mid-1732. "Anthony Afterwit" (10 July 1732) nearly ruins himself financially trying to please his wife but recovers. Reversing the situation, "Celia Single" (24 July 1732) criticizes "Mr. Gazetteer" (Franklin) and tells of "Mrs. C——ss," who triumphs over her husband's attempts to be frugal. The following year he wrote another social satire, "On Ill-Natur'd Speaking" (12 July 1733).

In his second use of an African American persona (the first was "Dingo" in 1723), Franklin as "Blackamore" wrote "On Molatto Gentlemen" (30 August 1733), criticizing condescending persons. Franklin also reversed the usual war-of-the-sexes diatribe by celebrating a "Scolding Wife" (5 July 1733). At its end, the shape-shifting speaker turned the piece into a satyr's celebration of sensuality. Franklin adopted his frequent proto-feminist attitude in "Reply to a Piece of Advice" (4 March 1734/5). A delightful brief satire featuring different personae, "Advice to a Pretty Creature and Replies" (20 and 27 November 1735), exposes mankind's vanity. Franklin's editorial campaign against excessive drinking concludes the chapter.

PERSONAE

Eighteenth-century periodical writers rarely signed pieces with their own names.[2] Almost all poems, skits, hoaxes, satires, and essays published in the newspapers and magazines were anonymous or pseudonymous. A minor reason was simply the tradition of aristocratic anonymity: as the colonial Virginia poet Robert Bolling noted in a manuscript volume of his own verse, a writer would be "indiscreet . . . in blazoning his Name and abod to he knew not whom."[3] The major reason, however, was that the speaker or persona (i.e., the personality or mask chosen as the author) was an artful aspect of its literary quality. As a boy, Franklin read in the Port Royal *Logic* that "the Air of the Speaker" was even more important in writing and speaking than the argument, for the presentation of self was generally more easily and clearly perceived than logic.[4] Aristotle had also emphasized the significance of the character, the *ethos*, of the speaker.

Franklin was typical in using a variety of masks or speakers for his different literary compositions. That said, his speakers or personae are nevertheless remarkable. First, few other writers had so many different and opposing masks. We have seen that Franklin used different personae in his earliest writings—and the same persona sometimes had different and seemingly opposite characteristics—even in the title of a treatise on paper currency. During the course of a lifetime of writing, Franklin created hundreds of different speakers. He chose them for the specific occasion. He often used a pseudonym, but he also often let the characteristics of an anonymous speaker gradually appear. Among the nearly bewildering quantity of his personae, some are novices, some experts; some are guileless, some shrewd; some revealing, some concealing; some sympathetic humans, some inhuman monsters; some humble, some proud; some gullible, some skeptical; some laymen, some clergy; some uneducated, some learned; some sexually innocent, some satyrs; some rigid, some flexible; some straightforward, some wily shape-shifters. Numerous Franklin personae also appear in his letters. Further, with someone so intelligent and so sophisticated as Franklin, the dazzling number of personae implies a concern for philosophical questions of identity and reality as well as a delight in different voices and play.[5] No one better realized the printed word's possibilities for revealing and concealing than Franklin.

Franklin probably has more feminine personae than any other eighteenth-century essayist. With the exception of the battle-of-the-sexes writings, comparatively few female personae are found in eighteenth-century hoaxes, satires, or essays. Franklin's feminine personae were chosen for literary reasons: they are the best possible speakers for that particular essay or poem or skit. But some feminine personae also reflect his belief in women's equality—and in his intellectual sympathy for and empathy with them. For his day, he was a feminist. He often identified with the weak and oppressed in society. Thus, his masks include not only women and African Americans but also the young, the poor, the weak, and the old. Though he selected each for the purpose of the particular rhetorical context, altogether his various personae testify to his empathy with the disadvantaged in society. Throughout his life he remained sympathetic to those who suffered prejudice, as shown by such writings as "The Speech of Miss Polly Baker," his comments on Judge Foster's defense of impressing seamen, and the bagatelle "A Petition" (1785), concerning society's unfair treatment of one twin sister ("The Left Hand") in favor of another.[6]

Personae also sometimes concealed authorship—which could be useful and even, on occasion, necessary.[7] On several occasions, Franklin delightedly observed responses to his writings made by persons who did not know he was the author. He told in the *Autobiography* of his pleasure in hearing the Couranteers discuss the possible authors of the first Silence Dogood letter. Later, in Philadelphia, in the poetry contest of about 1724 or 1725 with James Ralph, Charles Osborne, and Joseph Watson, Franklin pretended that Ralph's poem was his own. When Osborne praised his rival's poem, Franklin enjoyed Ralph's secret delight in Osborne's praise almost as much as Ralph did. Franklin commented in Busy-Body No. 8 on the elation an author felt upon hearing his writing praised and said that hiding one's identity was "absolutely necessary to this Self-Gratification." In the essay on literary style discussed below he observed: "When the Writer conceals himself, he has the Advantage of hearing the Censure both of Friends and Enemies, express'd with more Impartiality" (1:328). Later he often enjoyed a similar situation. We will see a wonderful example of it when he described the reception of "An Edict by the King of Prussia" (22 September 1773). Franklin thought that persons were more honest when they did not know they were speaking before the author, and he evidently found it fun when he knew a secret.

ESSAYS

"The Morals of Chess"

Chess player Franklin and one or two of his chess opponents were probably criticized in the Junto for wasting their time. "The Morals of Chess" replied, claiming that the game was useful—a preparation for life and an exercise in the disciplines necessary for success. Franklin drafted it about 1732, presumably for presentation in the Junto. The reference to its being written for "a few young friends" (29:753) tends to confirm this hypothesis. Though the editors of *The*

Papers of Benjamin Franklin knew it was written early in Franklin's life (1:270n.), they printed and discussed it with the materials for 1779 (29:750–57), the date usually given for its composition.[8] Franklin added a prefatory paragraph and probably revised the early version when he published it in Passy, France.

Franklin's paragraph on checkers in the 1726 sea journal had similarities (as noted in Volume 1) to "The Morals of Chess." Both games were briefly compared to war, and "courage" was a quality necessary to victory. The basic idea of "The Morals of Chess" was that life is like chess. Like life, it creates an artificial scheme of order, and then, like all games (including life), it plays according to those arbitrary rules. If Franklin had a particular literary work in mind, it may have been Machiavelli, for many of the virtues that Franklin praises are akin to those in *The Prince* and the *Discourses*. He probably read Machiavelli when working for his brother in Boston, for on 6 August and 10 December 1722, the *New England Courant* authors cited the Italian. Further, the *Courant* of 11 September 1721 quoted Machiavelli from *Cato's Letters*. Franklin alluded to Machiavelli in his poem "The Rats and the Cheese" (24 September 1730). His *Works* were in the Library Company *Catalogue* of 1741 (p. 15). Franklin later cited Machiavelli's *The Prince* in the "Canada Pamphlet" (1760).[9] Machiavelli wrote that one "should never lift his thoughts from the exercise of war, and in peace he should exercise it more than in war."[10] Though all the morals that Franklin located in chess were useful in war, they were also useful in peace—as well as throughout life.

"The Morals of Chess" has two parts. First, Franklin gave four virtues chess taught that were useful in life; and second, he addressed improprieties in playing chess. He began with an appreciation of the game's antiquity. He argued that "in its effects on the mind," chess was "not merely *innocent*, but *advantageous*, to the vanquished as well as to the victor" (29:753–54). He did not give the underlying reason for its usefulness that he noted in his early outline. (There, he wrote that just as "Wrestling of Bodies strengthen them," so the wrestling of minds exercises and strengthens them [29:752]). He continued: "The game of Chess is not merely an idle amusement. Several very valuable qualities of the mind, useful in the course of human Life, are to be acquired or strengthened by it, so as to become habits, ready on all occasions." He may partly have been recalling the Port Royal *Logic*, which maintained that "some Advantage" was to be gained "by exercising ourselves in the Solution of knotty Questions," for "The Capacity of the Mind is enlarged and strengthened by Use," though it conceded that it was foolish to waste time on useless affairs, quoting Martial, *Stultum est difficiles habere nugas.*[11]

The first quality that chess taught was "*Foresight*, which looks a little into futurity, and considers the consequences that may attend an action: for it is continually occurring to the player, 'If I move this piece, what will be the advantages of my new situation? What use can my adversary make of it to annoy me?

What other moves can I make to support it, and to defend myself from his attacks?'"

Second came an overall appreciation of one's position: "*Circumspection,* which surveys the whole chess-board, or scene of action, the relations of the several pieces and situations, the dangers they are respectively exposed to, the several possibilities of their aiding each other; the probabilities that the adversary may make this or that move, and attack this or the other piece; and what different means can be used to avoid his stroke, or turn its consequences against him" (29:754).

Third, chess taught caution, for life, like chess, is played by a series of rules. The better one knows the rules (whether they concern technology, law, finance, or virtue), the more likely one's chances of survival—and, perhaps, of winning. The rules constitute an "image of human life, and particularly of war." One must realize the consequences of actions and try to control them. Franklin did not suppose that most persons would be in charge of actual warfare, but combat dramatized the allegory of life that he was making: "If you have incautiously put yourself into a bad and dangerous position, you cannot obtain your enemy's leave to withdraw your troops, and place them more securely; but you must abide all the consequences of your rashness" (29:754).

Last, chess taught players not to be discouraged by the appearance of their affairs. It inculcated the habit of hoping for a favorable change, and that of persevering. Franklin explained, "The game is so full of events, there is such a variety of turns in it, the fortune of it is so subject to sudden vicissitudes, and one so frequently, after long contemplation, discovers the means of extricating one's self from a supposed insurmountable difficulty, that one is encouraged to continue the contest to the last, in hopes of victory by our own skill, or, at least, of getting[12] a *stale mate,* by the negligence of our adversary." Life is full of changes and surprises. Though Franklin repeatedly emphasized that chance and the wheel of fortune may alter one's condition, and therefore one should never be absolutely secure and comfortable, persons should act as if they could control their lives. "And whoever considers, what in chess he often sees instances of, that particular pieces of success are apt to produce *presumption,* and its consequent, inattention, by which more is afterwards lost than was gained by the preceding advantage; while misfortunes produce more care and attention, by which the loss may be recovered, will learn not to be too much discouraged by the present success of his adversary, nor to despair of final good fortune, upon every little check he receives in the pursuit of it" (29:755).

In the second part of "The Morals of Chess," Franklin took up the improprieties among some chess players. In effect, this section concerned manners— the rules for life in civilized society. Since both players wanted "to pass the time agreeably," Franklin advised that "every circumstance, that may increase the pleasure of" chess "should be regarded; and every action or word that is unfair, disrespectful, or that in any way may give uneasiness, should be avoided." Both parties should observe the same regulations. If your adversary takes a long time between moves, "you ought not to hurry him, or express any uneasiness at his delay. You should not sing, nor whistle, nor look at your watch, nor take up a book to read, nor make a tapping with your feet on the floor, or with your fingers on the table, nor do anything that may disturb his attention. For all these things displease. And they do not show your skill in playing, but your craftiness or your rudeness." Franklin recommended not to try to "deceive your adversary, by pretending to have made bad moves, and saying you have now lost the game . . . for this is fraud, and deceit, not skill in the game." If you win, you should not "use any triumphing or insulting expression, nor show too much pleasure; but endeavour to console your adversary, and make him less dissatisfied with himself by every kind and civil expression, that may be used with truth" (29:755–56).

To watch politely while others play, "observe the most perfect silence. For if you give advice, you offend both parties; him, against whom you give it, because it may cause the loss of his game; him, in whose favour you give it, because, though it be good, and he follows it, he loses the pleasure he might have had, if you had permitted him to think till it occurred to himself." After a move or moves or after the game, you should not replace the pieces to show how it might have been played better, "for that displeases, and may occasion disputes or doubts about their true situation." Talking lessens or diverts the players' attention, and is therefore unpleasing: "nor should you give the least hint to either party, by any kind of noise or motion.—If you do, you are unworthy to be a spectator.—If you have a mind to exercise or show your judgments, do it in playing your own game when you have an opportunity, not in criticising or meddling with, or counseling, the play of others" (29:756–57).

The conclusion gave additional rules for behavior, which had general applications for conduct in life. If the game is not to be played simply to win, "then moderate your desire of victory over your adversary, and be pleased with one over yourself. Snatch not eagerly at every advantage offered by his unskilfulness or inattention; but point out to him kindly that by such a move he places or leaves a piece in danger and unsupported; that by another he will put his king in a dangerous situation, &c. By this generous civility . . . you may indeed happen to lose the game to your opponent, but you will win what is better, his esteem, his respect, and his affection; together with the silent approbation and good will of impartial spectators" (29:757).

Biographical evidence suggests that Franklin was sometimes guilty of the "improprieties" he specified. Perhaps he wrote "The Morals of Chess" not only to defend himself from the charge of wasting time playing chess but also to correct his own faults as a player. According to the grandson of his Passy landlord, Le Ray de Chaumont, Franklin impatiently drummed his fingers on the table when his opponents were slow. Chaumont even said that Franklin would change the positions of the pieces if his opponent left the room.[13] Franklin's reputation as rebel against the king of England—and perhaps his attitude concerning the rules of chess—influenced a set of anecdotes about him. His grandson William Temple Franklin reported that when Franklin was playing one night at Passy, his opponent put Franklin's king in check, but Franklin ignored the rules and checked his opponent's king. "Sir," protested his French antagonist, "you cannot do that, and leave your king *in check*." "I see he is in check," said Franklin, "but I shall not defend him. If he was a good king like yours, he would deserve the protection of his subjects; but he is a tyrant and has cost them already more than he is worth:—Take him, if you please; I can do without him, and will fight out the rest of the battle, *en Républicain*—as a Commonwealth's man." Thomas Jefferson told a similar anecdote about Franklin's playing chess with "the old Duchess of Bourbon." And the American artist Frances Wright had still another version, in which Franklin lost his king but continued to play, remarking to his dumbfounded opponent that "the party without a king will win the game."[14]

Perhaps these incidents actually happened, but if so, Franklin knew he had lost and continued playing as a joke or to make a point. Perhaps Franklin was playfully suggesting that the new order demanded new rules—as, of course, it did. Another anecdote, this one true, has Franklin and an opponent starting a chess game while Madame Brillon was bathing behind a screen. In their concentration on chess, they forgot her. She was unwilling to remind them of her predicament and as the water in her bath gradually cooled, the two played on.[15] But maybe Franklin's most famous chess games were those with Mrs. Caroline Howe, sister of Admiral Richard Howe, in December 1774, which were used as a subterfuge for a series of meetings trying to reconcile the American colonies and Great Britain. The game was indeed the game of life.

"The Box Family"

A periodical essay in the 11 January 1732/3 *Pennsylvania Gazette* imitated *Tatler* No. 11 on the family of Staffs. Perhaps Franklin wrote this typical eighteenth-century essay as an exercise in composition. He named the various family members after boxes, finding different characteristics in their names and purposes. "We give the first place to the Females. There are Mistresses, *Saltbox, Knifebox, Candlebox, Ironingbox, Bandbox, and Dustbox*, all tight cleanly Dames, and well respected in their Places; tho' it must be acknowledged that Mrs. *Saltbox*, like some other good Houswives, is apt to be a little loud, somewhat sharp with her Tongue, and commonly reputed a Scold. Madams *Powderbox, Dressingbox*, and *Patchbox* are gay Ladies, and Admirers of fine Company; they don't trouble themselves much with Family Drudgery."

As for the males, "*Cartouch box* is a great Soldier, and has done some Good and much Mischief in his Time, but of late Years has little Business, and 'tis hoped long Peace will oblige him to turn himself to something else." Franklin continued by making comments about Dicebox, Strongbox, Moneybox, Tinderbox, and Tobacco-box. Discussing Sandbox, Franklin anticipated his later essay on lawyers and amplification (17 June 1736). Here he wrote, "*Sandbox* is a Scrivener, a useful Man in his Neighbourhood, but a prodigious Lover of Circumlocution and Tautology: that he may have it in his Power to say the same Things over and over again, he speaks, and immediately eats his Expressions: A Man of Words and not of Deeds, has been always a contemptible Character." Franklin cited the full proverb in a letter to his sister Jane: "A Man of Words and not of Deeds, / Is like a Garden full of Weeds" (16 September 1758). The foolish Sandbox, however, "has the same Opinion of a Man of Deeds who is not a Man of Words."

After characterizing several more boxes, Franklin concluded by joking that a mischievous box received what he deserved, a "box in the ear": "*Saucebox* is a Jackanapes Brother of mine, so much like me, that we have frequently been mistaken for each other. But I shall not allow *Wrongbox*, nor *Box in the Ear*, to be of our Family; especially the latter, who has been a declared Enemy to me from my Infancy, and has given me frequent Insults." After the dateline "Nest-of-Boxes," the piece is signed with a self-satirical pseudonym, "CHATTER-BOX."[16]

"On Literary Style"

"On Literary Style" appeared in the *Pennsylvania Gazette* on 2 August 1733.[17] Franklin observed that most men have "frequent Occasion to communicate their Thoughts to others in *Writing*; if not sometimes publickly as Authors, yet continually in the Management of their private Affairs, both of Business and Friendship." Therefore, "Scarce any Accomplishment" is more necessary than "*Writing well*." Franklin attempted to promote submissions to the *Gazette* by claiming there was "no better Means of learning to write well, than this of attempting to entertain the Public now and then in one of your Papers." Then, in an unexpected turn (for authors hope and expect to hear praise, not censure), he commented on the concealed author's advantage of hearing "the Censure both of Friends and Enemies, express'd with more Impartiality" (1:328).

What was good writing? "I have thought in general, that whoever would write so as not to displease good Judges, should have particular Regard to these three Things, viz. That his Performance be *smooth, clear,* and *short*: For the contrary Qualities are apt to offend, either the Ear, the Understanding, or the Patience." He discussed "smoothness," by which he meant the sound of words, citing Jonathan Swift: "'Tis an Observation of Dr. Swift, that modern Writers injure the Smoothness of our Tongue, by omitting Vowels wherever it is possible, and joining the harshest Consonants together with only an Apostrophe between; thus for *judged*, in it self not the smoothest of Words, they say *judg'd*; for *disturbed, disturb'd,* etc.[18] It may be added to this, says another [Franklin himself?], that by changing *etb* [a typo for *eth*] into *s*, they have shortned one Syllable in a multitude of Words, and have thereby encreased, not only the *Hissing,* too offensive before, but also the great Number of Monosyllables, of which, without great Difficulty, a smooth Sentence cannot be composed." Franklin had in mind such instances as "hath" becoming "has," "loveth," "loves."[19] He continued, "The Smoothness of a Period [i.e., a sentence] is also often Hurt by Parentheses, and therefore the best Writers endeavour to avoid them" (1:329).

Next, clarity: "not only the most expressive, but the plainest Words should be chosen." Writers who use the specialized diction of formal learning render their words "unintelligible to more than half their Countrymen." Without giving the reference, he cited an anecdote from Swift who attributed it to Lucius Cary, Lord Falkland.[20] "If a Man would that his Writings have an Effect on the Generality of Readers, he had better imitate that Gentleman, who would use no Word in his Works that was not well understood by his Cook-maid." He also echoed Swift's warning against too frequently using idiomatic expressions. "They trouble the Language, not only rendring it extreamly difficult to Foreigners, but make the Meaning obscure to a great number of English Readers. Phrases [i.e., idioms], like learned Words, are seldom used without Affection; when, with all true Judges, the simplest Stile is the most beautiful" (1:329). The last opinion was hardly universal (compare the writings of his English contemporary, Dr. Samuel Johnson), though Franklin argued for a simple, even colloquial style in his essay on "Simplicity" and in his appreciation of proverbs.

Franklin proceeded from style (smooth, clear, and short) to organization— the order, sequence, or method of a piece: "But supposing the most proper Words and Expressions chosen, the Performance may yet be weak and obscure, if it has not *Method*. If a Writer would *persuade*, he should proceed gradually from Things already allow'd, to those from which Assent is yet with-held, and make their Connection manifest. If he would *inform*, he must advance regularly from Things known to things unknown, distinctly without Confusion, and the lower he begins the better" (1:329–30). The Port Royal *Logic*, echoing Descartes, stressed this procedure. Franklin used the method when he wrote two lectures on electricity for his neighbor Ebenezer Kinnersley, "in which the Experiments were rang'd in such Order and accompanied with Explanations, in such Method, as that the foregoing should assist in Comprehending the following" (A 153).

Franklin advocated the third characteristic, shortness, by ridiculing its opposite: "*Amplification*, or the Art of saying Little in Much, should only be allowed to Speakers. If they preach, a Discourse of considerable Length is expected from them, upon every Subject they undertake, and perhaps they are not stock'd with naked Thoughts sufficient to furnish it out. If they plead in the Courts, it is of Use to speak abundance, tho' they reason little; for the Ignorant in a Jury, can scarcely believe it possible that a Man can talk so much and so long without being in the Right." Though Franklin thought that amplification was permissible in oral discourse, he found it reprehensible in materials that could be "subjected to the calm leisurely Examination of nice Judgment." In writing, "every Thing that is needless gives Offence" (1:330).

Nearly a century later, Washington Irving wrote that in the tale, every page must contribute something toward the desired end.[21] But Franklin had surpassed him and approached Edgar Allan Poe, who thought that every word should contribute to the effect desired.[22] On the other hand, Franklin said "a Writer should take especial Care . . . that his Brevity doth not hurt his Perspicuity." Since the last word is long and learned, it perfectly embodies Franklin's principal that brevity should not hurt perspicuity. If an author has a special audience in mind, "he must exactly suit his Stile and Manner to the particular Taste of those he proposes for his Readers." He gave as an example the "different Ways of Writing and Expression used by the different Sects of Religion." Everyone, he said, "can readily enough pronounce, that it is improper to use some of these Stiles in common, or to use the common Stile, when we address some of these Sects in particular" (1:330–31).

Franklin gave as a maxim, "*No Piece can properly be called good, and well written, which is void of any Tendency to benefit the Reader, either by improving his Virtue or his Knowledge.*" Of course, Franklin himself often violated the common pose of the *censor morum*. Here, he showed that he especially had in mind humorous writing: "Besides, Pieces meerly humorous, are of all Sorts the hardest to succeed in. If they are not natural, they are stark naught; and there can be no real Humour in an Affectation of Humour." He concluded, "That is best wrote, which is best adapted to the Purpose of the Writer," adding his usual concluding note of self-deprecation: it was "much easier . . . to offer Rules than to practise them" (1:331).

AMPLIFICATION

Franklin also satirized and exemplified verbosity in the 17 June 1736 *Gazette*.[23] "Amplification, or the Art of saying *Little in Much*, seems to be principally studied by the Gentlemen Retainers to the Law. 'Tis highly useful when they are to speak at the Bar; for by its Help, they talk a great while, and appear to say a great deal, when they have really very little to say. But 'tis principally us'd in Deeds and every thing they write. You must abridge their Performances to understand them." Franklin added a homely American comparison to his introduction: "When you find how little there is in a Writing of vast Bulk, you will be as much surpriz'd as a Stranger at the Opening of a *Pumpkin*" (2:146).

After pretending to trace through recent centuries the ever-increasing amount of words to convey an estate, Franklin hypothesized that the recent development of amplification may have been caused by the invention of printing. The new technology "took from the Scribes great Part of their former Employment, put them on the Contrivance of making up by a Multitude of Words, what they wanted in real Business; hence the plain and strong Expression, *shall be his own*, is now swoln into, *shall and may at all Times hereafter forever, and*

so from time to time, freely, quietly and peaceably, have, hold and enjoy, &c."
(2:146).

Franklin asserted that "of all the Writings I have ever seen, for the Multiplicity, Variety, Particularity, and prodigious Flow of Expression, none come up to
the Petition of Dermond O'Folivey, an Attorney of the Kingdom of Ireland."
Perhaps it was an actual petition, but if so, Franklin adopted and added to it.
Consider, for example, the words I have set off in italics: "THAT your Lordship
will be pleased, *and satisfied, and resolved,* to grant, *and give, and deliver, and
bestow,* upon me Mr. Dermond O'Folivey, your before recited, and nominated
Petitioner and Sollicitor-General aforesaid, an Order and Judgment, *and Warrant, and Authority of Preference* to my Lord Kerry, and Mr. Henry Punceby,
Esq; and Justice of the Peace and Quorum, or to any four or five *or more or less,
or either or neither of them, now, and then, and there, and here, and any where,
and every where, and somewhere, and nowhere, to call and bring, and fetch, and
carry, before him, or them, or either of them, or neither, or both, such Party or
Parties as they shall imagine, and conceive, and consider, and suppose, and assent,
and esteem, and think fit, and meet, and necessary, and decent, and convenient,
all, and every, and either, or neither of them, to call, to examine, and call* to a strict
Account" (2:148). Franklin's satirical tour de force belongs in the tradition of
eighteenth-century mock praise, a genre descended in part from Erasmus's *In
Praise of Folly.*[24]

Social Satires: Five Topics

In the early 1730s, Franklin wrote a series of social satires. I distinguish them
from moral philosophy. The latter are generally philosophical discussions of
ethics, serious in subject and tone. Though his social satires may have contributed to eighteenth-century ethical thought, Franklin intended them more as
entertainment than as philosophical contributions. Social satires, like the essays
in moral philosophy, may be instructive; but they are humorous, satiric, or
ironic in tone, rather than serious—except, perhaps, on an underlying level.

Shopkeepers

At the end of 1730, Franklin satirized commerce. The profoundly pessimistic
worldview of lying and conniving by customers, shopkeepers, and wholesale
merchants—in short, by everybody in trade—that emerges from this three-part
series is extraordinary, especially in the eighteenth century, when trade was frequently celebrated.[25] The cynicism characterized, however, some aspects of the
private Franklin. ("He that best understands the World, least likes it"; and
"none of us are [happy] while in this Life" [4:405, 11:253].)[26] Taken together, the
following three essays may shed light on the reason why Franklin, when he fell
seriously ill while working for Thomas Denham as a shopkeeper, resigned himself to death and was rather disappointed to find himself recovering, "regretting
in some degree that I must now sometime or other have all that disagreable

Work to do over again" (A 52). The essays may partially explain why he gave up shopkeeping and returned to printing in 1727. Incidently, they also provide a background for his epithet condemning England and Holland during the Revolution as *shopkeeping* nations (15:78, 24:513; S 8:291), and for his statement that "*Commerce* . . . is generally *Cheating*" (16:109).

The anonymous essay on "Lying Shopkeepers" (19 November) opened with an anecdote: "A Friend of mine was the other Day cheapening some Trifles at a Shopkeepers, and after a few Words, they agreed on a Price; at the lapping up this Purchase, the Mistress of the Shop told him, People were grown very hard, for she actually lost by every thing she sold: How then is it possible, replied my Friend, that you can keep on your Business? Indeed, Sir, answer'd she, I must of Necessity shut my Doors, had I not a very great Trade" (W 158–59). The author said that many shopkeepers "falsely imagine that being *Historical* (the modern Phrase for *Lying*) is much for their Advantage; and some of them have a Saying, *That 'tis a Pity Lying is a Sin, it is so useful in Trade.*" It may have been a saying, but Franklin knew it from John Wise.[27] He claimed, however, that the reason some merchants were wealthy and others bankrupt was that the former became known for their "Truth, Diligence and Probity," whereas the latter became known for imposing "on such Customers as they found had no Skill in their Goods." Saying that example works more than precept, the author cited several anecdotes from classical history of truthfulness being rewarded and lying punished. He concluded with one inconvenience of lying. A liar "must be always on his Guard, for Fear of contradicting, and exposing himself to the Derision of his Hearers" (W 159, 160–61).

Two weeks later, 3 December 1730, Franklin printed two replies on the topic, one supposedly from a shopkeeper and the other from a wholesaler. Betty Diligent, the shopkeeper, thought she was "the Person at whom some Reflections are aimed in one of your late Papers. It is an easy Matter for Gentlemen that can write, to say a great deal upon any Subject, and to censure Faults of which perhaps they are as guilty as other People" (W 161). Franklin pretended that he was among those "Gentlemen that can write," though he knew that only the fiction of print allowed him, a twenty-four-year-old artisan, to enjoy that status. He likewise realized that the new world of print allowed morally ordinary persons to adopt the persona of the *censor morum*—a role supposedly reserved in the past for those few persons above personal criticism. Thus, through the persona of the naive Betty Diligent, who supposed the previous satire was meant for her, Franklin commented on some of the ways that the print culture affected society and at the same time indulged in a bit of self-satire.

Betty Diligent declared that shopkeepers were forced to lie in their own defense, because "of the general Lying practis'd by *Customers. I am sure 'tis very ordinary at that Price; I have bought much better at such a one's Shop for less Money*; are very common Falsities repeated on this Occasion, almost worn threadbare; but some have even the Confidence to aver, *that they have bought cheaper of me*; when I know the Price they mention is less than the Goods cost me. In short, they will tell a hundred Lies to undervalue our Goods, and made our Demands appear extravagant: So that the Blame of all the Lying properly belongs to the Customers." Franklin's self-justifying Betty Diligent anticipated the character of Polly Baker (1747), a person blind to the realities and one who believes her own inflated opinion of herself—a trait Franklin found typical of humanity.

In a companion reply, Mercator, a wholesale export-import merchant, also denounced shopkeepers for lying—but in buying, not selling, their goods: "you have omitted just one half the Story, *viz.* their Lying when they come to the Stores to *buy*. I believe they think Lying full as convenient and beneficial in *buying* their Goods as selling them; for to my Knowledge some of them are most egregiously guilty in this Particular" (W 162). According to Mercator, only he, the self-deceiving wholesale merchant, is free of the deceit that everywhere else characterizes the world of commerce.

Spendthrifts

Anthony Afterwit

In mid-summer 1732, Franklin wrote two essays about wives who spent more money than their husbands could afford.[28] The first, featuring Anthony Afterwit, had a personal application as shown in the discussion of *Poor Richard*'s origin. Could it possibly have had two personal applications? Was Deborah not being as frugal as Franklin thought prudent? Gary E. Baker hypothesized that Franklin wrote the essay just after Deborah bought him a china bowl and a silver spoon[29] at the "enormous Sum of three and twenty Shillings, for which she had no other Excuse or Apology to make, but that she thought *her* Husband deserv'd a Silver Spoon & China Bowl as well as any of his Neighbours" (A 76). In the *Autobiography*, Deborah's only foible (if it may be considered such) is that she was proud of her husband, though perhaps Franklin was gently mocking both her and reasoning itself when she made him the excuse for buying china and silver of which she could be proud.

Anthony Afterwit was "an honest Tradesman" whose "Affairs went on smoothly while a Batchelor," but recently he encountered "some Difficulties." After marrying, he "saw that with Care and Industry we might live tolerably easy, and in Credit with our Neighbours." His wife, however, wanted "to be a *Gentlewoman*." So the "old-fashioned Looking-Glass was one Day broke, as she said, *No Mortal could tell which way.* However, since we could not be without a Glass in the Room, *My Dear*, says she, *we may as well buy a large fashionable One that Mr. Such-a-one has to sell; it will cost but little more than a common Glass, and will be much handsomer and more creditable.* Accordingly the Glass was bought, and hung against the Wall." Then the table was not suitable to the mirror, and then the chairs did not match the table.

Franklin may have been anticipating a saying that he put in *Poor Richard* for June 1751, "'Tis easier to suppress the first Desire, than to satisfy all that follow it," and he almost certainly had this moral and the Anthony Afterwit sketch in mind when he wrote in "The Way to Wealth": "When you have bought one fine Thing you must buy ten more, that your Appearances may be all of a Piece; but Poor Dick says, *'Tis easier to* suppress *the first Desire, than to* satisfy *all that follow it*" (7:347). In the 1732 essay Afterwit continued, "And thus, by Degrees, I found all my old Furniture stow'd up into the Garret, and every thing below alter'd for the better. Had we stopp'd here, we might have done well enough" (1:237–39).

The expenses continued. Next came the tea table "with all its Appurtenances of *China* and *Silver*." The tea table, like keeping a carriage, was a sign of luxury and conspicuous consumption at the time. The wife next claimed to be over-worked and needed a maid, who was hired. Then "it happened frequently, that when I came home at *One*, the Dinner was but just put in the Pot; for, *My Dear thought really it had been but Eleven*: At other Times when I came at the same Hour, *She wondered I would stay so long, for Dinner was ready and had waited for me these two Hours*. These Irregularities, occasioned by mistaking the Time, convinced me, that it was absolutely necessary *to buy a Clock*; which my Spouse observ'd, *was a great Ornament to the Room!*"

Franklin weighed the stakes against the profligate wife, who was not above breaking a mirror or repeatedly inconveniencing her husband in order to get her way. She gradually changed her surroundings from those of the tradesman's wife to those of a gentlewoman. Afterwit reported, "And lastly, to my Grief, she was frequently troubled with some Ailment or other, and nothing did her so much Good as *Riding*; And *these Hackney Horses were such wretched ugly Creatures, that*—I bought a very fine pacing Mare, which cost £20. And hereabouts Affairs have stood for some Months past" (1:239).

Afterwit could not afford the expenses and he was constantly borrowing money, which he could not repay because he had not "Resolution enough" to refuse his wife. Finally he was sued. The trial would be at the next court, and the result was predictable—he must go to debtor's prison. "Last Monday my Dear went over the River, to see a Relation, and stay a Fortnight, because *she could not bear the Heat of the Town*."

Afterwit took action:

I have turn'd away the Maid, Bag and Baggage (for what should we do with a Maid, who have (except my Boy) none but our selves). I have sold the fine Pacing Mare, and bought a good Milch Cow, with £3 of the Money. I have dispos'd of the Tea Table, and put a Spinning Wheel in its Place, which methinks *looks very pretty*: Nine empty Canisters I have stuff'd with Flax; and with some of the Money of the Tea-Furniture, I have bought a Set of Knitting-Needles; for to tell you a Truth, which I would have go no farther, *I begin to want Stockings*.

The stately Clock I have transform'd into an Hour-Glass, by which I gain'd a good round Sum; and one of the Pieces of the old Looking-Glass, squar'd and fram'd, supplies the Place of the Great One, which I have convey'd into a Closet, where it may possibly remain some Years. In short, the Face of Things is quite changed; and I am mightily pleased when I look at my Hour-Glass, *what an Ornament it is to the Room*. I have paid my Debts, and find Money in my Pocket. (1:239–40)

Afterwit's repetition of his wife's phrases adds an ironic and humorous note to the honest tradesman's character.

Though most of his retrenchment was necessary, Afterwit might seem to some readers too severe. So Franklin makes him attempt to keep at least one of his wife's purchases. "I expect my Dame home next Friday, and as your Paper is taken in at the House where she is, I hope the Reading of this will prepare her Mind for the above surprizing Revolutions. If she can conform to this new Scheme of Living, we shall be the happiest Couple perhaps in the Province, and, by the Blessing of God, may soon be in thriving Circumstances." If so, some of his wife's desires may be gratified. "I have reserv'd the great Glass, because I know her Heart is set upon it."

Afterwit demonstrates his resolve in the conclusion: "I will allow her when she comes in, to be taken suddenly ill with the *Headach*, the *Stomach-ach, Fainting-Fits*, or whatever other Disorders she may think more proper; and she may retire to Bed as soon as she pleases: But if I do not find her in perfect Health both of Body and Mind the next Morning, away goes the aforesaid Great Glass, with several other Trinkets I have no Occasion for, to the Vendue that very Day. Which is the irrevocable Resolution of, Sir, Her loving Husband" (1:240).

James Franklin recognized his brother's hand in the Anthony Afterwit essay, recalled that Franklin was probably influenced by Abigail Afterwit (one of James Franklin's pseudonyms) from the *New-England Courant* (29 January 1722), and realized that Franklin used the theme of his Anthony Fallshort essay (26 March 1722) concerning a wife who did not labor and demanded servants, fine food, and sumptuous furnishings. In American literature of the late eighteenth and nineteenth centuries, the extravagant behavior of a wife or a husband became a common subject, perhaps because of the increasing gentrification of American society.[30] The relationship between the two brothers changed as they indulged in an intellectual dialogue and appreciation. James Franklin reprinted the Anthony Afterwit essay in the *Rhode Island Gazette* on 25 January 1733 and replied to it as Patience Teacraft. Franklin joined in the fun and responded by reprinting James Franklin's Patience Teacraft in the 31 May 1733 *Pennsylvania Gazette*. James Franklin's essay, describing a faithful wife who reclaims her drunken husband by making him a devotee of the tea table, is neither as dramatic nor as interesting as Franklin's Anthony Afterwit, but the exchange shows that the brothers had reconciled.

Celia Single

Two weeks after the Anthony Afterwit essay appeared in the *Pennsylvania Gazette*, Celia Single (a.k.a. Franklin) wrote in a "delightful gossipy voice"[31] to the editor (24 July 1732} that some things he published did more harm than good. She herself overheard the following quarrel between her neighbors: "last Wednesday Morning" when visiting Mrs. "C——ss," Mr. "C——ss" had just returned from market where he bought some thread. He said he liked *"mightily those Stockings which I yesterday saw Neighbour Afterwit knitting for her Husband, of Thread of her own Spinning.* (Thus we learn from a following skit that Afterwit's wife has reformed and that they are reconciled.) Mr. C——ss continued, *"Your Maid Mary is a very good Knitter"* and he would like her to knit him some stockings (1:241).

"Mrs. C——ss was just then at the Glass, dressing her Head; and turning about with the Pins in her Mouth, *Lord, Child,* says she, *are you crazy? What Time has Mary to knit? Who must do the Work, I wonder, if you set her to Knitting?* Perhaps, my Dear, *says he,* you have a mind to knit 'em yourself. . . . *I knit Stockins for you,* says she, *not I truly; There are poor Women enough in Town, that can knit; if you please you may employ them."*

"Well, but my Dear, *says he,* you know a penny sav'd is a penny got, a pin a day is a groat a year, every little makes a mickle, and there is neither Sin nor Shame in Knitting a pair of Stockins; why should you express such a mighty Aversion to it?" Franklin here anticipated the prudential sayings he would use in *Poor Richard* (sayings that he believed were good for him and generally for his audience) but in this skit, they are promptly rejected. The husband added, "As to *poor* Women, you know we are not People of Quality, we have no Income to maintain us, but what arises from my Labour and Industry; methinks you should not be at all displeas'd, if you have an Opportunity to get something as well as myself."

"*I wonder,* says she, *how you can propose such a thing to me; did not you always tell me you would maintain me like a Gentlewoman? If I had married Capt.* ———, *he would have scorn'd even to mention Knitting of Stockins"* (1:241–42).

The quarrel became acrimonious, drifted from the subject, and then returned. The husband said: "How long d'ye think I can maintain you at your present Rate of Living? *Pray,* says she, (somewhat fiercely, and dashing the Puff into the Powder-Box) *don't use me after this Manner, for I assure you I won't bear it. This is the Fruit of your poison News-papers; there shall come no more here, I promise you.* Bless us, *says he,* what an unaccountable thing is this! Must a Tradesman's Daughter, and the Wife of a Tradesman, necessarily and instantly be a Gentlewoman? You had no Portion; I am forc'd to work for a Living; if you are too great to do the like, there's the Door, go and live upon your Estate, if you can find it, in short, I don't desire to be troubled w'ye" (1:241–42).

Celia Single closes with an observation about the effect of overhearers upon some arguments: "What Answer she made, I cannot tell; for knowing that a Man and his Wife are apt to quarrel more violently when before Strangers, than when by themselves, I got up and went out hastily: But I understood from Mary, who came to me of an Errand in the Evening, that they dined together pretty peaceably, (the Balls of Thread that had caused the Difference, being thrown into the Kitchen Fire) of which I was very glad to hear" (1:242). Thus Franklin supplies the reader with the information that Mrs. C——ss won the spat. No knitting for her. Franklin also may have meant to joke that Celia Single, being a woman, was "glad to hear" that the wife prevailed.

Celia Single complained about the double standard. "I have several times in your Paper seen severe Reflections upon us Women, for Idleness and Extravagance, but I do not remember to have once seen any such Animadversions upon the Men. If I were dispos'd to be censorious, I could furnish you with Instances enough: I might mention Mr. Billiard, who spends more than he earns, at the Green Table; and would have been in Jail long since, were it not for his industrious Wife." After characterizing other masculine ne'er-do-wells, Celia Single condemned the editor: "And for your part, I would advise you, for the future, to entertain your Readers with something else besides People's Reflections upon one another; for remember, that there are Holes enough to be pick'd in your Coat as well as others; and those that are affronted by the Satyrs you may publish, will not consider so much who *wrote*, as who *printed*" (1:242–43). Thus the "poison of the newspapers" (Franklin's efforts to try to influence people to live within their means and to help one another) is ridiculed. Franklin satirized himself, lampooned his failure, and accepted it. The man of letters, the *censor morum*, the guide to happiness, might influence a few persons—but many would consider his well-meant efforts "poison."

True Gentlemen

Franklin wrote a brief essay on conversation in the 12 July 1733 *Gazette*, condemning "Ill-Natured Speaking." He observed that it was "strange that among Men, who are born for Society and mutual Solace," any should exist "who take Pleasure in speaking disagreeable Things to their Acquaintance: But such there are, I assure you, and I should be glad if a little publick Chastisement might be any Means of reforming them." The short composition thus introduces two opposing theories of human nature. On the one hand, persons are "born for Society and mutual Solace," and on the other, they take pleasure in hurting their acquaintances. Franklin gives a disgusted portrait of the malicious: "They communicate their wonderful Discoveries to others, with an ill-natur'd Satisfaction in their Countenances, *Say such a Thing to such a Man, and you cannot mortify him worse*. They delight (to use their own Phrase) in *touching gall'd Horses* that they may see 'em *wince*. Like Flies, a *sore Place* is a Feast to them." The pessimist Franklin finished by portraying such persons as lower than insects. "Know, ye Wretches, that the meanest Insect, the trifling Musketoe, the filthy Bugg, have, as well as you, the Power of giving Pain to Men; but to be able to give Pleasure to your Fellow Creatures, requires Good-Nature, and a kind and humane Disposition, joined with Talents to which ye seem to have no Pretension" (1:327).

Blackamore

An untitled essay that appeared on 30 August 1733 also had as its subject the true gentleman. Its thesis was that courtesy and respect characterized the gentleman. The epigraph, "Set a Beggar on Horseback, &c," was left incomplete. In the oral culture of the eighteenth century, the proverb was so well-known it did not need to be quoted in full. The remainder of the saying was, "and he'll ride a gallop." Its import was that a beggar on horseback would immediately pretend to be a gentleman on a desperately urgent mission. The beggar would violate normal riding decorum, trample over the feelings and rights of his fellows on the road, and ravage the health of his horse.

The essay began by considering the role of mixed-race people in society. "They are seldom well belov'd either by the Whites or the Blacks. Their Approach toward Whiteness, makes them look back with some kind of Scorn upon the Colour they seem to have left, while the Negroes, who do not think them better than themselves, return their Contempt with Interest: And the Whites, who respect them no Whit the more for the nearer Affinity in Colour, are apt to regard their Behavior as too bold and assuming, and bordering upon Impudence. As they are next to Negroes, and but just above 'em, they are terribly afraid of being thought Negroes, and therefore avoid as much as possible their Company or Commerce: and Whitefolks are as little fond of the Company of *Molattoes*." The seemingly racist opening actually condemned the conduct of all who thought themselves better than others, but the twentieth-century reader is more likely merely to recognize its prejudices than to appreciate its moral. The remarks on race were meant as an analogue to Franklin's comments on class differences. Some persons who gained wealth changed their clothes and behavior, thereby thinking they were "immediately to become *Gentlefolks*." But it was "no easy Thing for a Clown or a Labourer, on a sudden to hit in all respects, the natural and easy Manner of those who have been genteelly educated." Franklin's use of *clown* is surprising, for three years later, Franklin satirized the use of *clown* to mean farmer (*Poor Richard* for 1736), though that usage remained common through the nineteenth century.

Franklin may have written the essay to caution himself. In 1733 he was beginning to rise from a poor tradesman to an important Philadelphia citizen, and the essay may reveal insecurities about his changing status. Though he identified with tradesmen, he had become a key member of the Freemasons (1730), the printer for the Pennsylvania legislature (1730), and the founder of the Library Company of Philadelphia (1731). Perhaps he was warning himself when he wrote, "And 'tis the Curse of Imitation, that it almost always either under-does or over-does" (W 218–19).

The speaker defined the true gentleman as one who "can take a Walk, or drink a Glass, and converse freely, if there be occasion, with honest Men of any Degree below him, without degrading or fearing to degrade himself in the least." The author said that he was "an ordinary Mechanick, and I pray I may always have the Grace to know my self and my Station. As little as I have learnt of the World, whenever I find a Man well dress'd whom I do not know, and observe him mighty cautious how he mixes in Company, or converses, or engages in any kind of equal Affair with such as appear to be his Inferiors; I always judge him, and I generally find him, to be some *new Gentleman*, or rather *half Gentleman*, or *Mungrel*, an unnatural Compound of Earth and *Brass* like the Feet of *Nebuchadnezzar's* Image" (W 219). Franklin then gave a second example of persons who changed their behavior, now using a woman rather than a man. "If in the Way of my Business, I find some young Woman Mistress of a newly fine furnished House, treating me with a kind of Superiority, a distant sort of Freedom, and a high Manner of Condescension that might become a Governor's Lady, I cannot help imagining her to be some poor Girl that is but lately well married: Or if I see something in her very haughty and imperious, I conclude that 'tis not long since she was somebody's Servant Maid" (W 219).

Writing about the nature of a true gentleman in *Spectator* No. 202, Richard Steele said that false gentlemen often fail in regard to their behavior with domestics, expressing their humors with "unnatural Excrescences." In his example of the well-dressed man who is "mighty cautious" about dealing with his supposed "inferiors," Franklin may allude to Steele. Besides referring to Daniel 2:33, 41, Franklin's reference to "unnatural Compound of Earth and *Brass* like the Feet of *Nebuchadnezzar's* Image" may echo Steele's "unnatural Excrescences."

In the essay, Franklin uses race and class to reveal his irritation and contempt for those who considered themselves superior. "With Regard to the Respect shown them by the *true Gentry* and the *no Gentry*, our *half Gentry* are exactly in the Case of the *Mulattoes* abovementioned. They are the Ridicule and Contempt of both sides." Franklin's ordinary mechanic had an acquaintance who "has got a little Money" and now "thrusts himself into Conversation with People of the best Sense and the most polite." He is a laughingstock to them, as well as to those he thinks he has left behind. "At the same time, we below cannot help considering him as a Monkey that climbs a Tree, the higher he goes, the more he shows his Arse" (W 220). The scatological note never appears in the journalistic writings of Addison or Steele, but it is not uncommon in Franklin. It reveals his disgust for those who consider themselves superior. As Poor Richard wrote in the almanac for 1737: "The greatest monarch on the proudest throne, is oblig'd to sit upon his own arse" (2:166).[32] Franklin's true gentleman is an egalitarian.

The concluding signature, "BLACKAMORE," shifts the perspective. Though

Pennſylvania GAZETTE.

Containing the freſheſt Advices Foreign and Domeſtick.

From Auguſt 23. to Auguſt 30. 1733.

Set a Beggar on Horſeback, &c.   Cheſh.

Mr. Gazetteer,

IT is obſerved concerning the Generation of *Molattoes*, that they are ſeldom well be-lov'd either by the Whites or the Blacks. Their Approach towards Whiteneſs, makes them look back with ſome kind of Scorn upon the Colour they ſeem to have left, while the Negroes, who do not think them better than themſelves, return their Contempt with Intereſt: And the Whites, who reſpect them no Whit the more for the nearer Affinity in Colour, are apt to regard their Behaviour as too bold and aſſuming, and bordering upon Impudence. As they are next to Negroes, and but juſt above 'em, they are terribly a-fraid of being thought Negroes, and there-fore avoid as much as poſſible their Company or Commerce: and Whitefolks are as little fond of the Company of *Molattoes*.

When People by their Induſtry or good Fortune, from mean Beginnings find themſelves in Circumſtances a little more eaſy, there is an Ambition ſeizes many of them immediately to become *Gentlefolks*: But 'tis no eaſy Thing for a Clown or a Labourer, on a ſudden to hit in all reſpects, the natural and eaſy Manner of thoſe who have been genteely educated: And 'tis the Curſe of *Imitation*, that it almoſt al-ways either under-does or over-does. The *true Gentleman*, who is well known to be ſuch, can take a Walk, or drink a Glaſs, and converſe freely, if there be occaſion, with honeſt Men of any Degree below him, without degrading or fearing to degrade himſelf in the leaſt. For my Part, I am an ordinary Me-chanick, and I pray I may always have the Grace to know my ſelf and my Station. As little as I have learnt of the World, whenever I find a Man well dreſs'd whom I do not know, and obſerve him mighty cautious how he mixes in Company, or converſes, or engages in any kind of equal Affair with ſuch as appear to be his Inferiors; I always judge him, and I ge-nerally find him, to be ſome *new Gentleman*,

or rather *half Gentleman*, or *Mungrel*, an unna-tural Compound of Earth and *Braſs* like the Feet of *Nebuchadnezzar's* Image. And if in the Way of my Buſineſs, I find ſome young Woman Miſtreſs of a newly fine furniſhed Houſe, treating me with a kind of Superiori-ty, a diſtant ſort of Freedom, and a high Man-ner of Condeſcenſion that might become a Go-vernor's Lady, I cannot help imagining her to be ſome poor Girl that is but lately well married: Or if I ſee ſomething in her very haughty and imperious, I conclude that 'tis not long ſince ſhe was ſomebody's Servant Maid.

With Regard to the Reſpect ſhown them by the *true Gentry* and the *no Gentry*, our *half Gentry* are exactly in the Caſe of the *Molattoes* abovementioned. They are the Ridicule and Contempt of both ſides.

There is my former Acquaintance (but now he cannot ſpeak to me) the lumpiſh ſtupid *Jack Chopſtick*, while he kept in his natural Sphere, which (as that of all heavy Bodies) is the loweſt, the Figure he made among Ac-quaintance of his own Rank was well enough; none of us envy'd him, 'tis true, nor none of us deſpis'd him: But now he has got a little Money, the Caſe is exceedingly alter'd. With-out Experience of Men or Knowledge of Books, or even common Wit, the vain Fool thruſts himſelf into Converſation with People of the beſt Senſe and the moſt polite. All his Abſurdities, which were ſcarcely taken No-tice of among us, ſtand evident among them, and afford them continual Matter of Diverſion. At the ſame time, we below cannot help con-ſidering him as a Monkey that climbs a Tree, the higher he goes, the more he ſhows his Arſe.

To conclude with the Thought I began; there are perhaps *Molattoes* in Religion, in Politicks, in Love, and in ſeveral other Things; but of all ſorts of *Molattoes*, none appear to me ſo monſtrouſly ridiculous as the *Molatto Gentleman*.   I am Tours, &c.

BLACKAMORE.

Figure 7. "Blackamore," the second African American persona in American journalism, Pennsylvania Gazette, *30 August 1733. Franklin's essay on the social classes of colonial America criticized those who condescend to others and prescribed a behavior that he identified with the "true Gentleman." He satirized persons who behave in a patronizing manner when socializing with their "inferiors." In the essay he called himself an "ordi-nary Mechanick," but he surprised the reader at the end by revealing himself to be a "Blackamore." (For the first African American persona in American journalism, see Vol-ume 1, figure 17). The underlying theme celebrated the dignity and worth of every individ-ual. An expert printer and journalist, Franklin wrote the essay to fit the exact size of the front page. Courtesy, Library Company of Philadelphia.*

the essay had been satirizing persons who condescendingly patronized their sup-posed inferiors, the author was ostensibly an ordinary mechanic, though one who could instruct others in polite behavior. The author began with the typical, rather superior voice of the *Spectator,* a version of the *censor morum.* Toward the end, however, the author undercut his supposedly superior position and revealed himself as a mechanic. Finally, in a Franklinesque undercutting of him-self, the speaker proclaimed himself one of the eighteenth-century's "lowest sort," the blackamoor. The pseudonym complemented and even surpassed the essay's egalitarian thesis. It is appropriate that the essay on race and class ends with Franklin using the second African American persona in American jour-nalism.[33]

Battle of the Sexes

"A Scolding Wife"

The battle of the sexes was a frequent subject of poetry and prose in the eigh-teenth century. Franklin enjoyed writing on the topic, often sided with women, and used feminine personae. The speaker who praised "a Scolding Wife" (5 July 1733) is among Franklin's shape-shifters, anticipating aspects of the persona of "Old Mistresses Apologue" (25 June 1745). "A Scolding Wife" opened with a paradox, "'Tis an old Saying and a true one, that *there is no Conveniency without an Inconveniency*: For aught I know, there might be a Saying not less true, tho' more new, *That there is no Inconveniency without a Conveniency.*" The male speaker defended his paradox by celebrating scolding wives: "Rightly consid-er'd," he declared, such a wife was a prize. He spoke both from "Experience" and "a long Course of Observation." Scolds generally have "sound and healthy Constitutions, produce a vigorous Offspring, are active in the Business of the Family, special good Housewives, and very Careful of their Husbands Interest. As to the Noise attending all this, 'tis but a Trifle when a Man is us'd to it, and observes that 'tis only a mere Habit, an Exercise, in which all is well meant, and ought to be well taken."

The speaker further surprised the reader and revealed that he had been thrice married: "For my own Part, I sincerely declare, that the meek whining Complaints of my first Wife, and the silent affected Discontent in the Counte-nance of my second, gave me (either of them) ten Times the Uneasiness that the Clamour of my present dear Spouse is capable of giving. 'Tis my Opinion, in short, that their Freedom of Speech springs from a Sense they have, that they do their Duty in every Part towards their Husbands, and that no Man can say, *Black is* (the white of) *their Eye*" (1:325). Franklin's microcosmic paradox matches the essay's ostensible contradiction.

At the conclusion, Franklin transformed the thrice-married celebrant of scolding wives into a lecherous would-be bigamist. The speaker claimed that his purpose was to recommend two maids "among my Acquaintance . . . [who]

will make Wives of this Sort: And I wish these Hints may be of any Service towards getting them good Husbands." He added that a French poet "could be so calm in the midst of his Wife's Tempest, as to write" a poem on it. He quoted the poem and translated it. Then the celebrant of scolds made another revelation: "The Reader perhaps will hardly believe me, if I tell him that this [a scolding wife] is nothing but *Musick*, and that I think 'tis pity a Man can be allow'd to keep but one Instrument of it in his House at a Time; yet if there were not a Law of this Province prohibiting Poligamy, I should certainly be for marrying the two Girls above-mention'd, in order to compleat my Consort" (1:325–27).

The ending astonishes the reader. What is going on? Is Franklin really a would-be polygamist? Is he merely joking about sex? Or is he suggesting that the human race has more possible strangeness than one may imagine? One recalls Franklin's story in the *Autobiography* of the lady who lived like a nun with his Catholic landlady in London in 1725–26. He found her way of life and belief in Veronica's veil amazing, but he made the anecdote seem like a practical lesson by giving it as an example of how little it costs to live (A 48–49). The story illustrates the triumph of faith over materialism, but Franklin says he uses it to illustrate the practical. Actually, the anecdote is an example of the incredibility of life. One recalls, too, his savage newspaper report on 15 February 1731/2 on the man who bit off part of his wife's tongue and threw it into the fire for a "Burnt-Offering." Life can be stranger than fiction, but Franklin's fiction can sometimes be stranger than life. So, too, the husband amazes the audience when he reveals he would gladly add two more scolds as wives.

"Reply to a Piece of Advice"

A poem in the 18 February 1734/5 *Pennsylvania Gazette* advised a friend not to marry, for women were "a Plague at best." The poem is beneath the level of Franklin's verse, and he no doubt reprinted it in order to answer it. "Reply to a Piece of Advice" appeared in the 4 March 1734/5 *Gazette*. The speaker was an old, thrice-married man but not the same person as the previous persona. According to this speaker, the poem said: "That 'tis mighty silly for a single Man to change his State; for as soon as his Wishes are crown'd, his expected Bliss dissolves into Cares in Bondage, which is a compleat Curse; That only Fools in Life wed, for every Woman is a Tyrant: That he who marries, acts contrary to his Interest, loses his Liberty and his Friends, and will soon perceive himself undone; and that the best of the Sex are no better than a Plague."

The old man (a.k.a. Franklin) charged that the poem's author must have been "some forlorn old Batchelor, or some cast-away Widower, that has got the Knack of drowning all his softer Inclinations in his Bowl or his Bottle." He said, "It is wrong to assert *that tis silly in a single Man to change his State*: For what old Batchelor can die without Regret and Remorse, when he reflects upon his Deathbed, that the inestimable Blessing of Life and Being has been communicated by Father to Son through all Generations from Adam down to him, but in him it stops and is extinguished; and that *the Humane Race divine* would be no more, for any Thing he has done to continue it; he having, like the wicked Servant, *wrapt up and hid his Talent in a Napkin,* (i.e. his Shirt Tail,) while his Neighbours the Good and Faithful Servants, had some of them produced *Five* and some *Ten,* I say such an one shall not only die with Regret, but he may justly fear a severe Punishment" (2:22). Franklin's bawdy touch was all the more surprising for travestying the parable of the talents (Matthew 25:14–30) and St. Jerome's *Letters* (14, section 8).

Franklin's rejoinder continued: "Nor is it true that *as soon as a Man weds, his expected Bliss dissolves into slavish Cares and Bondage.* Every Man that is really a Man is Master of his own Family; and it cannot be *Bondage* to have another submit to one's Government. If there be any Bondage in the Case, 'tis the Woman enters into it, and not the Man." Franklin amended and partially reversed the misogynous statements. He said that the cares are "the most delightful Cares in the World"—bringing up children. The old man compares raising children to planting and gardening, but deems child-rearing more honorable. "As to the Adviser's next Insinuation, that *only Fools wed, and every Woman is a Tyrant*; 'tis a very severe and undutiful Reflection upon his own Father and Mother; and since he is most likely to know best the Affairs of his own Family, I shall not contradict him in that particular, so far as relates to his own Relations." After the insult (which cleverly introduces the most normally appealing example of marriage), the old man/Franklin utterly dissents and declares "that I scarce ever knew a Man who knew how to command in a proper Manner, but his Wife knew as well how to show a becoming Obedience." Then Franklin, reversing the charge, stated, "there are in the World infinitely more He-Tyrants than She-Ones" (2:22–23).

In opposition to the poet being refuted, the old, thrice-married speaker praised marriage: "A Man does not act contrary to his Interest by Marrying; for I and Thousands more know very well that we could never thrive till we were married; and have done well ever since; What we get, the Women save; a Man being fixt in Life minds his Business better and more steadily; and he that cannot thrive married, could never have throve better single; for the Idleness and Negligence of Men is more frequently fatal to Families, than the Extravagance of Women." The speaker claimed, "Nor does a Man *lose his Liberty* but encrease it; for when he has no Wife to take Care of his Affairs at Home, if he carries on any Business there, he cannot go Abroad without a Detriment to that; but having a Wife, that he can confide in, he may with much more Freedom be abroad, and for a longer Time; thus the Business goes on comfortably, and the good Couple relieve one another by turns, like a faithful Pair of Doves."

Franklin followed his own advice. When he visited New England in 1733 and when he made other trips in the future, he left Deborah his power of attorney as well as made her an executrix of his will. "Nor does he *lose Friends* but gain them, by prudently marrying; for there are all the Woman's Relations added to his own, ready to assist and encourage the new-married Couple; and a Man that has a Wife and Children, is sooner trusted in Business, and can have Credit longer and for larger Sums than if he was single, inasmuch as he is look'd upon to be more firmly settled, and under greater Obligations to behave honestly, for his Family's Sake" (2:23–24).

The essayist again cited the poet to whom he was replying: "*The best of the Sex are no better than Plagues.* Very hard again upon his poor Mother, who tho' she might be the best Woman in the World, was, it seems, in her graceless Son's Opinion, no better than a Pestilence." The writer then turns slightly scurrilous, accusing the woman-hater of being impotent. "Certainly this Versifyer never knew what a Woman is! He must be, as I conjectur'd at first, some forlorn old Batchelor. And if I could conjure, I believe I should discover, that his Case is like that of many other old He-Maids I have heard of. Such senseless Advice as this can have no Effect upon them; 'tis nothing like this, that deters them from marrying. But having in some of their first Attempts upon the kinder Sort of the Fair Sex, come off with Shame and Disgrace, they persuade themselves that they are (and perhaps they are) really Impotent: And so durst not marry, for fear of those dishonourable Decorations of the Head, which they think it the inevitable Fate of a Fumbler to wear." The speaker/Franklin cited Aesop's fable "The Fox without a Tail": "Then, like the Fox who could not use his Tail, (but the Fox had really lost it) they set up for *Advisers*, as the Gentleman I have been dealing with; and would fain persuade others, that the Use of their own Tails is more mischievous than beneficial" (2:24). Concluding, Franklin quoted Milton and Thomson on marital bliss.

A news report of 17 April 1735 warned men who abused their wives of the possible reprisal: "We hear from Chester County, that last Week at a Vendue held there, a Man being unreasonably abusive to his Wife upon some trifling Occasion, the Women form'd themselves into a Court, and order'd him to be apprehended by their Officers and brought to Tryal: being found guilty he was condemn'd to be duck'd 3 times in a neighboring Pond, and to have one half cut off, of his Hair and Beard (which it seems he wore at full length) and the Sentence was accordingly executed, to the great Diversion of the Spectators."

Such acts of popular justice were not unusual in the seventeenth and eighteenth centuries. When accompanied by a procession and music made by beating pots and pans, the demonstrations were known as Rough Music, Charivari, or Skimmingtons.[34] But since the notice appeared in the *Pennsylvania Gazette*, where Franklin often printed news-note hoaxes, one wonders, did Franklin make it up? Was it another of Franklin's expressions of a feminist point of view?

Vanity, Vanity

Perhaps Franklin's most delightful social satire of the 1730s was the shortest. The 20 November 1735 *Gazette* contained the following one-sentence letter: "Mr.

Franklin, Pray let the prettiest Creature in this Place know, (by publishing this) That if it was not for her Affectation, she would be absolutely irresistible." The following week, he wrote six supposed replies: "*The little Epistle in our last, has produced no less than six, which follow in the order we receiv'd 'em*" (2:128). The different personae and voices of the replies testify to Franklin's literary artistry.

"Mr. Franklin, I cannot conceive who your Correspondent means by *the prettiest Creature* in this Place; but I can assure either him or her, that she who is truly so, has no Affectation at all." Wonderful! The first vain persona believes she is the most beautiful person in Philadelphia but rejects the charge of affectation.

"Sir, Since your last Week's Paper I have look'd in my Glass a thousand Times, I believe, in one Day; and if it was not for the Charge of Affectation I might, without Partiality, believe myself the Person meant." This second female Narcissus also cannot accept a criticism.

"Mr. Franklin, I must own that several have told me, I am the prettiest Creature in this Place; but I believe I should not have been tax'd with Affectation if I could have thought as well of them as they do of themselves." Another lovely lady cannot find any fault in herself. As *Poor Richard* said, "The Proud hate Pride—in Others" (December 1751).

"Sir, Your Sex calls me pretty; my own affected. Is it from Judgment in the one, or Envy in the other?" The fourth vain persona has separated the compliment from the criticism, attributing them to different sexes and calling all other women jealous.

"Mr. Franklin, They that call me affected are greatly mistaken; for I don't know that I ever refus'd a Kiss to any Body but a Fool." This senseless flirt thinks affectation is limited to not allowing a kiss. Or perhaps Franklin's satire is more subtle, suggesting that she is confusing affectation with affection.

"Friend Benjamin, I am not at all displeased at being charged with Affectation. Thou know'st the vain People call Decency of Behavior by that Name" (2:129). The sixth vain lady is a Quaker who knows she is both the prettiest creature in the place and a model of behavior.

The filler is ostensibly light, delightful satire. Its purpose is to amuse the reader. John Adams said of Franklin, "He had humor that, when he pleased, was delicate and delightful. He had a satire that was good-natured or caustic, Horace or Juvenal, Swift or Rabelais, at his pleasure" (*NCE* 248). "The prettiest creature" is ostensibly good-natured, Horatian satire. But what is the essential subject of the hoax? Vanity and self-delusion. Each respondent believes herself to be the most beautiful woman in Philadelphia, but each rejects or discredits any possible criticism. Despite the light tone, the hoax portrays a series of unremittingly self-deceptive, vain personae—and the authorial voice underlying the satire claims that vanity and self-delusion characterize mankind.

Excessive Drinking

The chapter on Franklin as a journalist (Volume 1, Chapter 18) concluded with a discussion of Franklin as a reformer. He protested against the plight of the poor in Ireland, the wretched condition of persons in prisons, and the censorship of the deists imprisoned for their religious opinions. Earlier, in Silence Dogood No. 12 (10 September 1722), Franklin condemned the evils caused by excessive drinking. Alcoholism was a recurrent topic in the *Gazette*. On 2 April 1730, he mentioned that several persons had died in Philadelphia within the previous two weeks of excessive drinking. He reported on 7 December 1732, "Last Monday Morning a Woman who had been long given to excessive Drinking, was found dead in a Room by her self, upon the Floor. She could not be persuaded to go to Bed the Night before, but would sit up alone, as was her frequent Custom. The Coroners Inquest ascribe her Death to the too great Quantity of Liquor she took at one Time. Her former Husband had many Times put several Sorts of odious Physick into her Drink, in order to give her an Aversion to it, but in vain; for who ever heard of a Sot reclaim'd? If there are any such they are Miracles. People cannot be too cautious of the first Steps that may lead them to be engaged in a Habit the most invincible and the most pernicious of all others."

"On Drunkenness"

Franklin followed up that news article with an essay "On Drunkenness" in the 1 February 1732/3 paper.[35] The writer pretended to be the "nearest" relation to a woman who drank too much but had reformed after reading the 7 December account of the woman's death by drinking. He asked Franklin to write again on the subject and continued with a brief essay: "It is now become the Practice of some otherwise discreet Women, instead of a Draught of Beer and a Toast, or a Hunk of Bread and Cheese, or a wooden Noggin of good Porridge and Bread, as our good old English Custom is, or Milk and Bread boiled, or Tea and Bread and Butter, or Milk-Coffee, etc. They must have their two or three DRAMS in a Morning; by which, as I believe, their Appetite for wholesome Food is taken away, and their Minds stupified, so that they have no longer that prudent Care for their Family, to manage well the Business of their Station, nor that regard for Reputation, which good Women ought to have. And tho' they find their Husband's Affairs every Day going backward thro' their Negligence, and themselves want Necessaries; tho' there be no Bread in the House, and the Children almost barefoot this cold Weather, yet, as if Drinking Rum were part of their Religious Worship, they never fail their constant daily Sacrifice" (W 212–13).

Franklin made the essay more dramatic by having the persona relate a recent experience, complete with dialogue: "Enters one who was once a handsome Woman, but now with bloated Face and swollen Legs, *How do you do, Neigh-*

bour? Indifferent. *Bless me, it's very cold, and I've no Wood at home; but I'll go down to——, and they'll help me to Wood; for they have a penny to spend, and a penny to lend, and a penny to lay up. Come, can't you give us a Dram?* No, I wish I had one. *Come, I've got a Penny.* And I've got but a Penny, if more would save my Life I ha'nt it. *Come then, I've got two pence, and your Penny will fetch half a Pint of Rum; and you shall be two-pence another time.* So away goes the half-pint Bottle. *And you shall find Sugar, and a little Bit of Butter, and that's pure good this cold Weather*" (W 213).

The author then returned to the discursive voice: "I for my part shall never more speak against TEA; let those that like it enjoy it for ever: Tea will not take away their Sense of Shame and of Duty, nor their Fear of Censure: Their Pride in this Particular, may make them careful, and industrious, and frugal in other Respects, that they may have wherewith to support their Rank and Credit in the World. They may still preserve their Modesty, and their natural Affection; But Drunkenness is utterly inconsistent with any one of those Virtues which make Women amiable or valuable to Men" (W 213).

Following the essay, Franklin, in a comparatively uncommon appearance of his own voice as editor, commented that men were generally the greater drunkards. "Altho' it has happened, that of the four unfortunate Wretches, who within these few Weeks have died suddenly in this Country, by excessive Drinking of strong Liquor, two were indeed Women; yet it must be acknowledged, that this Kind of Intemperance is by far more frequent among the Men than among them: And perhaps 'tis owing to the general Moderation of Women in the Use of strong Drink, that the present Race of Englishmen retain any considerable Degree of the Health, Robustness, and Activity of their Ancestors." Alluding to Judges 13:4, Franklin continued: "There are, however, some, it seems, who, directly contrary to the Advice given by the Angel to the Mother of the strongest Man, instead of refraining all Drink that may intoxicate, are determin'd to drink nothing else. Their Fault will be its own Punishment" (W 214).

Franklin next considered the plight of the unborn and the infant: "But what Crimes have their unhappy Offspring committed, that they are condemn'd to bring Misery into the World with them, to be born with the Seeds of many future Diseases in their Constitution" (W 215). He then related the history of alcoholism, believing that it was comparatively modern in English society.

> The Practice of Drinking Drams is so general, and so well establish'd in the World at present, that some People are apt to wonder, and scarce think it possible, when they are told, that Men formerly lived and performed their Labour without it; and that 'tis scarce 50 Years since distill'd Spirits have been commonly used in England. . . . Our Forefathers, 'tis true, have had Beer many Ages; but within the Memory of Men, Temperance in Drinking was so universal amongst them, especially in the inland Country Places, that a good old Man not long since dead with us, could speak it as an extraordinary Thing, *Verily I tell thee,*

> *Friend, I knew a Smith in our Town, who would sometimes go to th' Alehouse,*
> *when he had no other Business there, but to drink!* Observe it was a *Smith*, which
> is allow'd to be a thirsty Trade, *and but one Smith!* I am afraid we have never a
> modern Miracle on the other side to match it; that is to say, *A Smith*, or indeed
> any other Tradesman, *in our Town, who never goes to the Tavern* but when he
> has other Business there *beside Drinking.* (W 214)

Citing the preamble of the act of 1729 condemning the drinking of spirits
and strong waters, Franklin noted that it was not only a few men who condemned excessive drinking but the "united Wisdom of the British Nation, King,
Lords, and Commons in Parliament assembled." He added the opinion of the
physician John Allen, author of *Synopsis Medicinae*, who wrote on alcoholic
beverages in his chapter on poisons. To reinforce the essay, Franklin printed a
news note in the same 1 February 1732/3 *Gazette*: "On the 16th past, one Mary
Sullivan, a Servant Maid in this City, having drank a large Quantity of Rum,
died in a few Hours."

The Murder of a Daughter

A horrifying report about the actions of a drunken couple appeared in the *Gazette* on 24 October 1734.[36] Franklin wrote: "Saturday last, at a Court of Oyer
and Terminer held here, came on the Tryal of a Man and his Wife, who were
indicted for the Murder of a Daughter which he had by a former Wife, (a Girl
of about 14 Years of Age) by turning her out of Doors, and thereby exposing
her to such Hardships, as afterwards produced grievous Sickness and Lameness;
during which, instead of supplying her with Necessaries and due Attendance,
they treated her with the utmost Cruelty and Barbarity, suffering her to lie and
rot in her Nastiness, and when she cried for Bread giving her into her Mouth
with a Iron Ladle, her own Excrements to eat, with a great Number of other
Circumstances of the like Nature, so that she languished and at length died."

Though there was no doubt about the barbarism of the couple's behavior,
the physician testified that the daughter's illness was so fatal that she would have
died in any case. The jury therefore brought in a verdict only of manslaughter.
"A Verdict which the Judge, (in a short but pathetic Speech to the Prisoners
before the Sentence) told them was *extreamly favourable*; and that, as the Relation of their hitherto unheard of Barbarity had in the highest Manner shocked
all that were present; so, if they were not perfectly stupified, the inward Reflection upon their own enormous Crimes, must be more terrible and shocking to
them, than the Punishment they were to undergo: For that they had not only
acted contrary to the particular Laws of all Nations, but had even broken the
Universal Law of Nature; since there are no Creatures known, how savage, wild,
and fierce soever, that have not implanted in them a natural Love and Care of
their tender Offspring, and that will not even hazard Life in its Protection and
Defence" (W 233–34). One wonders if the judge said this or if Franklin added

it. In either case, Franklin knew better, but the claim served the account's propagandistic purposes.

Interrupting the report, Franklin inserted his editorial opinion: "But this is not the only Instance the present Age has afforded, of the incomprehensible Insensibility *Dramdrinking* is capable of producing." He then returned to the court scene, reporting that the husband and wife were both sentenced to be burnt in the hand, which was accordingly executed, but first upon the man. The news story concluded by reporting that the husband offered to take the punishment for his wife and be burnt again (W 234), an apparent irrelevancy that is a master stroke rhetorically, for it demonstrated that the father of the girl, a supposed monster of inhumanity, actually possessed altruistic feelings of love for his wife. The husband's request suggested that if he had been sober, he could not have treated his child as he did. Drunkenness turns even people with humane feelings into monsters unknown to themselves and unrecognizable by their better natures.

On 19 June 1735, Franklin reported the death of Rachel Twells the previous Sunday "by drinking too plentifully of Rum and other strong Liquors. . . . 'Tis said she had drank sixteen Drams of Rum and two Mugs of strong Beer that Day." Two years later, Franklin made an impassioned plea against drunkenness in the paper of 21 July 1737, reporting the death of "JOHN THOMPSON, an aged Man . . . who was very Poor, but very subject to drink Rum; had been drinking Rum the fore-part of the Night till he was Drunk, or very near it; and being got in a Passion with his Wife told her, HE WOULD PACK UP HIS ALL, AND GO TO CAROLINA; and thereupon he took a Bundle of things in a Wallet, or Bag, and went to the Wharf at the lower end of the Town, and by Endeavouring to get into a Cannoe, (a Vessel he had chosen to make his Voyage in,) accidentally slipt off the Wharffe into the Water, and was drowned. He had a Son drowned near the same place, about two Years ago, in the like condition of being drunk with Rum." Despite the consequences of excessive drinking, "People will not be deterred from the immoderate Use of strong Liquors: This certainly bespeaks want of due Conduct in the Use of Things, a Defect too frequent among Mankind, which is, I think, a perfect Blot in that Escutcheon of Reason annexed to the Fabrick of human Bodies."

In his various reports and essays on drinking, Franklin carried on Silence Dogood's crusade against drunkenness. He had called attention to it with a standing query for the Junto: "What unhappy effects of intemperance have you lately observed or heard?" (1:257), with notes made in his commonplace book on temperance (1:263, 271) and with the first ("Temperance") of thirteen virtues in his projected "Art of Virtue." Later, in the *Autobiography*, Franklin continued to crusade against excessive drinking. He testified against the London printers' "detestable Custom" of constantly drinking beer, and he blamed the failures of both his promising early friend John Collins and his first partner, Hugh Meredith, on drinking.

But Franklin, like practically everyone in the eighteenth century, drank beer, cider, and wine. Water was considered unhealthy—especially in Europe. Franklin did not object to drinking, but to excessive drinking. Drinking and singing with convivial friends was a normal part of eighteenth-century life. Meeting with the Freemasons and with the Union Fire Company members in taverns, Franklin often drank socially. Franklin wrote several drinking songs, and he ran up the considerable sum of £10.13.19 for beer at home (6 October 1747). Later, in France, he wrote a spoof of scientific deism and the teleological argument by proving that God made the elbow in the middle of the arm so that men could quaff wine from glasses.[37]

Conclusion

During 1730–36, Franklin became America's most prolific man of letters. He wrote on many of the most widely debated topics of eighteenth-century thought, especially religion, ethics, and social issues. His writings frequently reveal personal concerns that he transformed into public considerations: Was he reflecting his personal distaste for shopkeeping in the essays featuring customers, wholesalers, and shopkeepers? Was he warning himself against his own bad habits in "The Morals of Chess"? Was he cautioning himself about his own changing status in the essay signed Blackamoor? His favorite topic, the vanity of humans, occurs frequently. Two other characteristics often surface. First, some form of self-satire appears frequently in the skits and often concludes them. Second, his personae not infrequently go through surprising transformations: thus the speaker of the essay on true gentlemen begins as a *censor morum* in the tradition of the gentlemen-narrators of the *Spectator* and other English periodicals, then reveals himself to be really a mechanic, and finally discloses his mulatto identity. So, too, the old man who celebrates scolds gradually discloses that he has actually been married thrice, and at the conclusion uncovers his desire to be a bigamist.

Franklin believed that the most worthwhile effort in life was to do good for other people. His commitment to social causes appeared not only in practical ways (the Library Company was his first effort to foster education, and the Union Fire Company embodied civic responsibility) but also in his writing. His use of feminine and African American personae, his editorial comments and news reports against excessive drinking, and even his practical concern with reasonable finances—all are part of his efforts to do good. His prolific writing gave him the practice that he would later use in more public arenas throughout his life. Litterateurs throughout the colonies were beginning to recognize that the editor-printer of the *Pennsylvania Gazette* was a gifted man of letters. No other colonial American journalist approached his ability or productivity as a writer.

SIX

Politics, Religion, and the Rivalry with Bradford

1732

This is the practice at home. This is the practice at home.—Franklin's epigraph, 20 April 1732, satirizing a condescending recent immigrant's constantly telling Americans how things were done in England

OVERVIEW

In 1732, Andrew Bradford's *American Weekly Mercury* was still Philadelphia's dominant newspaper, partly because Bradford as postmaster was thought to have better information and distribution than the upstart Franklin, and partly because the *Mercury* had been the first and only Philadelphia newspaper until three years before. But Franklin and the *Gazette* were gaining customers, and Bradford and the *Mercury* were losing them. Thus Bradford resented Franklin. Bradford also was unhappy with Andrew Hamilton, for the Speaker of the Pennsylvania House of Representatives had replaced him with Franklin as printer of the assembly's *Votes and Proceedings* and other official printings. Consequently, when an author wrote against Hamilton or Franklin, Bradford was not unhappy to print the piece in the *Mercury*.[1]

An extended exchange between the *Mercury* and the *Gazette* began on 8 February 1731/2 and continued, though the subjects gradually changed, for eight months. The author of most of the essays in the *Mercury* was John Webbe (fl.1732–1750), who had recently emigrated to America. A lawyer and planter, Webbe was living on the Eastern Shore in Kent County, Maryland, and practicing law throughout Maryland and in the Philadelphia area. Four years later, from 1 April to 10 June 1736, he wrote a series of essays on government in the *Pennsylvania Gazette*, signed "Z," which his contemporaries criticized as being mainly redactions of John Locke's *Two Treatises of Government* (1690). Franklin asked Webbe in 1740 to edit a magazine (below, Chapter 12), but Webbe found better terms with Andrew Bradford and became the editor of the first magazine published in America. Later, he wrote as "A Planter" in the *Maryland Gazette* of 23 and 30 June 1747, leading to Dr. Alexander Hamilton's satire of him in a literary history of the early *Maryland Gazette*.[2]

Since there were twenty-four essays in the literary war, and since I will deal only with Franklin's writings in detail, a chronological list of the entire exchange may be helpful. I find reasons (many given in the course of the following discussion) to attribute nine of the *Mercury* essays to John Webbe.

Date	American Weekly Mercury	Franklin in the Pennsylvania Gazette
8 February	"Z" (Webbe) on American lawyers	
29 February	"Portius" (Webbe) on irreligion	
23 March	"Portius" (Webbe) on irreligion	
30 March	Anon. (Webbe) on irreligion	"Marcus" burlesques Portius
6 April	Anon. (Webbe) against those who satirize religion	
13 April	Anon. (Webbe) reply to "Marcus"	
20 April		#1: Anon., on English condescension
		#2: "Marcus," brief reply to 13 April
27 April	"Prosit" (Webbe) to "Marcus Porcus" (i.e., to Franklin in the 20 April *Gazette*)	
4 May		"Prosit" travestied
11 May	"Marcus Verus" (Webbe) calls the *Gazette* Prosit a counterfeit	
18 May	"S. H." against witty gentlemen	
25 May		Praising Persius
1 June	#1: Anon. says Persius essay slanders priests	#1: An "Old American" calls the newspaper quarrel senseless
	#2: "Marcus Verus" (Webbe) claims Persius essay echoes Tindal's *Christianity as Old as the Creation*	#2: The Persius author, "On Declamation"
8 June	"Socrates" on immortality, pt. 1	
15 June	"Socrates" on immortality, pt. 2	
31 August	"Civicus" on envy, pt. 1	
7 September	"Civicus" on envy, pt. 2	"On Censure"
12 September		"Alice Addertongue"

ENGLISH CONDESCENSION

On 8 February 1731/2, Z (John Webbe) published an essay in Bradford's *American Weekly Mercury* that condescended to American county court lawyers: "It shall be allow'd that a Practicioner in this Province, out of the City, needs not a Tenth Part of the Reading, Learning and Experience as one in *Great Britain*, and yet may prove a serviceable Man in a Country Court." Insulting American lawyers and justices was standard anti-Americanism, a motif mocked by the Maryland planter and lawyer Ebenezer Cook in *The Sot-Weed Factor* (1708). Franklin must have read Cook's double-edged satire, though perhaps not until its Annapolis editions appeared in 1728 and 1731.³ Like Cook, Franklin was irritated by such attitudes, as his 20 April 1732 essay demonstrated, but he did not reply immediately.

Three weeks later, "Portius" ("Z" under a different pseudonym) assailed politicians in the 29 February *Mercury* and did so again on 23 March. In the latter essay, he wrote that those who attained power often lost their judgment, and "from a dread of *Priestcraft and Spiritual Tyranny* . . . plunged themselves into Irreligion and prophaneness." He claimed that "Men cannot be good Subjects without some Religion." In his last paragraph Portius said, "The unhappy Way to all Revolutions and all Conquests has been paved by *Atheistical Opinions* and *Dissolution of manners*: But what *Application* we should wisely make of these Observations, what Thanks, we owe on this Account to our present *Blasphemers* and revilers of *Establishments*, may at this Time deserve a due Consideration and serious Debate among true *Englishmen* and Lovers of their Country, as well as of their Well-wisher *PORTIUS*." The essay pointed to the deist Andrew Hamilton, Speaker of the Pennsylvania Assembly, and also glanced at Franklin, well-known as both a doubter and a friend of Hamilton.

Portius Burlesqued

Since the 23 March essay insulted Hamilton and Franklin, the printer replied as "Marcus" with a mock religious essay burlesquing Portius (30 March *Pennsylvania Gazette*).⁴ Portius was too simple-minded an author, however, for Franklin to be content merely to attack him, so Marcus/Franklin also wrote what Portius might have said against skepticism. Though Franklin was sometimes a Pyrrhonist, he seemed almost unable not to consider what could be said against any metaphysical position, including radical skepticism. He could not resist the temptation to ridicule Pyrrhonism—even if he often believed in it. As he said in a draft of a letter to his parents on 13 April 1738, he did not think that all the things he believed to be true were true.

A minor underlying purpose in Franklin's 30 March essay was to consider the Port Royalists' attitudes toward skepticism. As I mentioned in discussing the Port Royal *Logic* in Volume 1 (Chapter 3), the Greek Academicians held that "It is certain that there is nothing certain," whereas the Pyrrhonists said that "everything was so uncertain, that it was even uncertain whether there was nothing certain."⁵ Franklin put these sentiments into the mouth of his obtuse narrator Marcus (who was supposedly like Portius): "Scepticism infests almost every Conversation; and one continually meets with People, otherwise seemingly of tolerable Sense, who openly declare, that they know not but as much may be said against any Opinion as for it: Some profess they know only this, That they know nothing; and there are others who assert, that even this cannot certainly be known."

Franklin ridiculed the Port Royalists' dismissal of skepticism by having the simple-minded persona Marcus make the remarks. While doing so, Franklin also employed the verbal mockery that the Port Royalists condemned, thereby disagreeing with their remarks on style as well as content.[6] In addition, perhaps Franklin was satirizing his own skepticism, saying that empiricism refuted it. He knew from Lucretius that the Epicurean philosophy considered empiricism one possible answer to absolute skepticism.[7] Francis Hutcheson and Bishop Berkeley, following the thoughts of John Locke, attempted to use empiricism to reinforce religion. In the future, Hume employed it to reinforce skepticism. In his own empiricism, Franklin seemed sometimes to follow the rationalism and idealism of Hutcheson and Berkeley, and more often to anticipate the skepticism of Hume. Franklin's empiricism differed from both, however, by causing him to gradually abandon abstract philosophical and theological reasoning and increasingly to devote his energies to other topics. These especially included natural philosophy, or what we today call engineering and science, and such developing fields as economics and demography.

Marcus/Franklin next turned to a mock encomium of Portius's essay: "Often have they [the unbelievers] been attack'd with great Strength and Judgment . . . but never so effectually as in the last Weeks Mercury; *Portius* has afforded a Blow that staggers even the stoutest of 'em; and needs only to be well follow'd, to cause their entire Overthrow." So Marcus will "add my Force to his" in "Five Hundred several Propositions . . . each of which shall be clear to the Understanding, convincing to the Judgment, undeniable by the most perverse Sceptic, and against which the least Shadow of an argument can not be raised." Marcus followed his claim with five grotesquely illogical and redundant paragraphs that splendidly parodied Portius's tautologies and weak reasoning. Marcus ended by congratulating himself on his performance and advising the reader to "preserve this Paper carefully" for the "irrefragable Truths" in it that will "hereafter serve as first Principles indisputable, from which to prove and demonstrate Truths more abstruse and remote." The persona's vanity matched his obtuseness.[8]

The same day, 30 March, the *Mercury* carried an anonymous essay (evidently by Portius) with the thesis that "Each National Government found it impossible to keep their People in due Subjection without the help of *Religion*." On 6 April, the *Mercury* author continued his rambling diatribes against those who satirized religion. Toward the end of his essay on religion and government, he paraphrased John Locke and asserted, "All Men are born free: Liberty is a Gift which they receive from God himself; nor can they alienate the same by Consent, tho' possibly they may forfeit it by Crimes. No Man has Power over his own Life, or to dispose of his own Religion, and cannot consequently transfer the Power of either to any body else: Much less can he give away the Lives and Liberties, Religion or acquired Property of his Posterity, who will be born as free as he himself was born, and can never be bound by his wicked and ridiculous Bargain." Since Webbe frequently quoted Locke, the paraprase is another suggestion that the author was Webbe. One might suppose that this confusing writer is arguing against the doctrine of original sin, but he concluded by saying that magistrates who exceeded their commissions should be punished. That charge pointed at Andrew Hamilton, who, as we will see, was sometimes accused by his enemies of improper behavior as a judge.

On 13 April an anonymous *Mercury* author replied to Marcus/Franklin. The *Mercury* writer indirectly identified Marcus as Franklin, who was well-known for punning and humor. His opponent wrote, "I am willing to discover my Ignorance, and want of Skill in Punning, by confessing freely; that I found it hard to understand *Marcus*'s Discourse, in the Gazette of *March* the 30th." The self-appointed censor of Hamilton and Franklin asked Marcus/Franklin to explain what he meant.

Condescending Englishmen Lampooned

On 20 April, Franklin, writing anonymously, defended Marcus (i.e., himself) and lampooned supercilious and condescending Englishmen who constantly instructed Americans.[9] The immediate reference was to Z in the 8 February *Mercury*. Franklin's epigraph, "*This is the Practice at home. This is the Practice at Home*," suggested a redundant whining instruction. (In America before 1765, "home" commonly referred to England, though self-conscious Americans referred to immigrants from Great Britain as "strangers.") The anonymous speaker (Franklin) is an exasperated American who resents the frequent instruction of visiting Englishmen. The American said that Portius's essay on Christianity was "so lamely and wretchedly perform'd, that suspicious People are apt to think they are only Sham Defences, made purposely by the crafty Infidels themselves, thereby artfully to insinuate that the Cause of Christianity is not really capable of better." Thus, the anonymous patriot satirizes Z and Portius while defending both Marcus/Franklin and the *Pennsylvania Gazette* from the possible charge of satirizing religion.

Franklin attacked one *Mercury* scribbler as a plagiarist whose "bad connexion and Arrangment of the parts" characterize his own poor composition, while the borrowed materials are clearly superior. Franklin evidently referred to Webbe and his frequent borrowings from Locke. The American derided his opponent Portius as an Englishman who assumed superiority over "a People, who, living in a remote Corner of the Earth, must of necessity be extreamly weak and ignorant." The Englishman/Portius "believes we can have had no Opportunity to learn good Manners, and therefore is continually instructing us. He thinks we cannot probably have read many good Books, and therefore cannot detect him when he steals whole Paragraphs, and claims Regard as the Author. Nay, he thinks we have scarcely seen the old Jest Books, and therefore ventures to tell of witty Repartees which he has made, and notable Adventures he has been concern'd in, tho' they were in Print before he was born. He as-

Pennſylvania GAZETTE.

Containing the freſheſt Advices Foreign and Domeſtick.

From Thurſday, April 13. to Thurſday, April 20. 1732.

This is the Practice at home. This is the Practice at home.

GOOD CAUSE is often leſs prejudic'd by a ſtrong Attack, than by a weak or fooliſh Defence: It is therefore Matter of Concern to me, to ſee Religion ſupported of late by ſuch weak Advocates, and pitiful Pretenders to Reaſoning. All the Pieces which have been publiſh'd among us for ſome time paſt on that Subject, are ſo lamely and wretchedly perform'd, that ſuſpicious People are apt to think they are only Sham Defences, made purpoſely by the crafty Infidels themſelves, thereby artfully to inſinuate that the Cauſe of Chriſtianity is not really capable of better. When ſuch Performances are ridicul'd, it is far from being a Diſſervice to Religion, and therefore the Paper of *Marcus*, which I ſuppoſe had no other View, is tolerable if not commendable.

There is one of theſe Scribblers, (ambitious of being thought a fine Writer) who ought to be particularly caution'd about his borrowing from others without quoting: This is what is commonly call'd *Plagiariſm*; but every Man that can read is not fit for a Plagiary. He ought to have exquiſite Judgment in the Choice of the Authors he makes bold with, and in the particular Sentiments or Paragraphs he intends to uſe; He ſhould alſo himſelf be abſolutely able to write as well as any of them, (if he would take the Pains;) Otherwiſe, the bad Connexion and Arrangement of the Parts, will manifeſtly ſhow the whole to be Patchwork, and grievouſly offend the judicious Reader. In ſhort, to be a good Plagiary requires a peculiar Genius, lofty, ſtrong, and commanding ; and which, like that for Epic Poetry, riſes ſcarce once in a thouſand Years.

But the Misfortune is, that when one of the travelling C–x–mbs of Europe happens to arrive among us, it is ſome Time before he knows either himſelf or his Company half ſo well as he did at home. During his Voyage hither, he dreams he is going among a People, who, living in a remote Corner of the Earth, muſt of neceſſity be extreamly weak and ignorant; and therefore propoſes to himſelf to ſhine exceſſively, where he ſhall be without a Rival, procuring by his extraordinary Acquirements univerſal Admiration. Suitable to this Prepoſſeſſion is his Conduct for the firſt Year or two. He believes we can have had no Opportunity to learn good Manners, and therefore is continually inſtructing us? He thinks we cannot probably have read many good Books, and therefore cannot detect him when he ſteals whole Paragraphs, and claims Regard as the Author. Nay, he thinks we have ſcarcely ſeen the old Jeſt Books, and therefore ventures to tell us witty Repartees which he has made, and notable Adventures he has been concern'd in, tho' they were in Print before he was born. He aſſumes the Dictator in all Converſations, and decides every Diſpute with Authority, as being lately come from the Sources of Science and Politeneſs. A certain ſagacious Farmer of *my* Acquaintance, once ſhewed me ſome Pigs of Engliſh Breed which he had lately procur'd from the Captain of a London Ship; *Theſe New-comers, ſaid he to me, manifeſt in every Part of their Behaviour, that they think they have more Senſe and Merit than the reſt of my Pigs.* 'Tis poſ-

ſible other People could not diſcern ſuch remarkable Difference in the Deportment of Pigs; but had they been brought from ſome Place near *Weſtminſter-Hall*, who knows but it might have been obvious to every body? There are among us, however, ſome Perſons, who claim a particular Relation to that ſame Hall, yet by their impertinent and ſcurrilous manner of treating thoſe they deſire to contend with, one would think belong more properly to *another*, equally famous for Diſpute and Altercation, but ſituate, lying, and being, quite at the other end of the Town.

Marcus is amazed that his Inconteſtibles ſhould be unintelligible to any body, but eſpecially that a Gentleman of ſuch profound Thought as the Remarker in the laſt Mercury ſhould declare he cannot underſtand them. One would imagine that any Thing might more juſtly be accus'd of Obſcurity, than Principles ſo clear and perſpicuous, big as they are with Truth, and even ready to burſt with Self-evidence. But there are certain Birds, of notable Gravity, whom to much Light rendereth blind.

From the Political State of Great Britain, Lond. Octob. 1731.

THE Aſſembly of the Province of the *Maſſachuſetts-Bay*, in *New-England*, have agreed to allow Mr. *Belcher* their Governor a thouſand Pounds, as a Salary for the Year enſuing, and ſo leave it to the next Aſſembly to allow what Salary they pleaſe for the Year next after; and the Governor having received freſh Inſtructions from *England* has at laſt accepted of this Allowance, but ſtill inſiſts upon having it confirmed to him during the time of his Government purſuant to his firſt Inſtructions: Hovever, by his accepting of a Salary for a Year, it appears that the Government here are reſolved to act the prudent Part they uſually do, and to follow the Inclinations of the People, who while they remain free are to be perſuaded, but not forced or threatned into any Meaſure whatever; and therefore it's hoped that the Affair of fixing a Salary for any long time may be laid aſide, by which the Peace and Quietneſs of that Province will be re-eſtabliſhed.

If we compare this Settlement made upon their Governor only for a Year, with the Settlements that have been made in ſome of our other Provinces upon their Governours for the time of their Government, we may obſerve the different Spirit which actuates the People of different Provinces, and that the ſame Spirit which makes People laviſh in private Life, will make them laviſh of the Publick Money : In *New-England* the People are reputed to be induſtrious and frugal in their Domeſtick Oeconomy, and ſo we may obſerve that the Gentlemen of their Aſſembly are as frugal and cautious of giving away the publick Money, as they are in their own private Concerns ; whereas in ſome of the other Provinces, where the People are reputed to be laviſh and luxurious, we may obſerve ſome of their Aſſemblies loading the People with the Payment of Salaries which they are really not able to comply with; from hence we may look upon it as a Maxim in Politicks, that where a Government has a mind to draw great Sums of Money from the People, they muſt firſt introduce private Luxury and Prodigality among them ; bu[t]

Figure 8. *"Condescending Englishmen Lampooned," Pennsylvania Gazette, 20 April 1732. Franklin's Americanism surfaces in this satire on the frequent instructions by a recent immigrant to America on the way things were done "at home" (England). Franklin prefaced his travesty of Webbe's essays in the* American Weekly Mercury *with the whining, repeated epigraph, "This is the Practice at home. This is the Practice at home." What an irritating bore! The essay itself combines Franklin's satire of Webbe's religious arguments (which had appeared in several previous issues of the* Mercury*) with Franklin's mocking the supercilious foreign visitors who patronized Americans. Courtesy, Library Company of Philadelphia.*

sumes the Dictator in all Conversations, and decides every Dispute with Authority, as being lately come from the Sources of Science and Politeness."

As I have shown in the chapter on Franklin in London (Volume 1), a number
of Americans had earlier chafed at English attitudes concerning America and
Americans. Franklin's ironic technique anticipated Washington Irving's satire in
the preface to *The Sketch Book*. After mentioning the degeneration of all life in
America, Irving wrote: "A great man of Europe, thought I, must therefore be as
superior to a great man of America, as a peak of the Alps to a highland of the
Hudson; and in this idea I was confirmed by observing the comparative importance and swelling magnitude of many English travelers among us; who, I was
assured, were very little people in their own country."

The *Pennsylvania Gazette* spokesman concluded with an anecdote typical of
Franklin's earthy style: "A certain sagacious Farmer of *my* Acquaintance, once
shewed me some Pigs of English Breed which he had lately procur'd from the
Captain of a London Ship; *These new-comers*, said he to me, *manifest in every
Part of their Behaviour, that they think they have more Sense and Merit then the
rest of my Pigs*. 'Tis possible other People could not discern such remarkable
Difference in the Deportment of Pigs; but had they been brought from some
Place near *Westminster-Hall*, who knows but it might have been obvious to
everybody?" The Orwellian *Animal Farm* anecdote reveals Franklin's egalitarian
tendencies, continues an American tradition of rustics besting their "betters,"
and puts down the superior pretensions of the English prigs/pigs.[10]

The same *Gazette*, 20 April, contains a three-sentence reply by Marcus/
Franklin to the 13 April *Mercury*'s questioning his meaning: "Marcus is amazed
that his Incontestibles *should be unintelligible to any body, but especially that a
Gentlemen of such profound Thoughts as the Remarker in the last* Mercury *should
declare he cannot understand them. One would imagine that any Thing might
More justly be accus'd of Obscurity, than Principles so clear and perspicuous, big
as they are with Truth, and even ready to burst with Self-evidence*."

In burlesquing the style of Marcus, Franklin used a technique condemned
by the Port Royalists but one he appreciated not only in Montaigne (whom
the Port Royalists particularly castigated for using burlesque) but also in the
Massachusetts hero of his boyhood, the Reverend John Wise. Marcus concluded: "*But there are certain Birds, of notable Gravity, whom too much Light
rendreth blind*." The last sentence directly counters the "Remarker" with a trope
anticipating Mark Twain's conclusion in "Baker's Blue-jay Yarn": "And they
could all see the point, except an owl that came from Nova Scotia to visit the
Yo Semite, and he took this thing in on his way back. He said he couldn't see
anything funny in it. But then, he was a good deal disappointed about Yo Semite, too."

Adopting a new pseudonym, "Prosit," Webbe replied to the satire bestowed
upon supercilious Englishmen in the next *Mercury* (27 April). His address to
"Marcus Porcus" showed that he recognized that the anonymous American

(Franklin) who told the story of the farmer's pigs was the same person who used the pseudonym "Marcus." He began: "Marcus Porcus, Your flat and insipid Story of the *Farmers Pigs*, would tempt any Reader to imagine you had been bred among them; If this be the Case, you are certainly proof against any Attempts that may be made for instructing you in *good Manners*." Having again demonstrated his superciliousness, Webbe as Prosit degenerated into scurrilous abuse.

PROSIT TRAVESTIED

Franklin further bamboozled Prosit. Printers generally respected the pseudonyms of authors, allowed them to use the same pseudonym repeatedly, and would not print writers who used another's cognomen. Franklin had earlier burlesqued Prosit's content and style under the pseudonym Marcus. Now he decided to travesty Prosit by adopting his pseudonym. The tactic has confused some scholars,[11] but the key is simple: in this exchange, Franklin wrote only in the *Gazette*; his opponents wrote in the *Mercury*. Franklin prefaced the 4 May 1732 article with a six-line poem on vanity (alluding to Prosit's high opinion of himself) and a mock editorial apology: "I do not love to have the Gazette filled with these *Controversies about Religion*, yet I cannot refuse to insert the following Piece, as it appears to be written in his own Vindication, by a Gentleman who has not been very tenderly used in my Papers." Printer Franklin (the author of the preface) pretended not to realize that the following piece signed Prosit (also Franklin) really travestied the *Mercury* Prosit.

Prosit/Franklin opened with the statement that though "the Criticks, (profess'd Enemies to every thing I write)" censured his last performance, he believed that it was "the best Piece" he had ever written. Franklin then undercut Bradford and the *Mercury*. Prosit/Franklin was changing papers "because the Witlings have of late taken much Pains to decry the *Mercury*, and hinder its being so universally read as it ought to be." (How Bradford must have chafed at that!) "The first Thing they cavil at, is my saying *'Tis beneath one to return railing for railing*, &c. These blind Criticks do not perceive the Beauty of this Sentence, wherein I make use of a Figure in Rhetorick by which the Orator seems not to do what he is then doing: By the Help of this Figure, I appear (with the Majority of my Readers) to be a Man of close Reasoning, Modesty, and Moderation. No Affront, I hope, to the Majority of my Readers; for considering the little Time I have been in the Country, it cannot be suppos'd they have gain'd much Knowledge of the polite Arts." The repetition of "the Majority of my Readers" and the contradiction in its application burlesque both the style and logic of Prosit. While paraphrasing and burlesquing him, Franklin ensured Prosit's condemnation because of his condescension to Americans. Franklin also hereby revealed that he thought Z (who condescended to Americans) and the *Mercury* Prosit were the same person.

Franklin travestied the arrogance of Prosit/Webbe. Eighteenth-century schools taught classical rhetoric, and every educated person knew the trope *occultatio*, or emphasizing something by saying that it is being ignored ("the Orator seems not to do what he is then doing"). Further, in Aristotle's *Rhetoric* (and its numerous imitators), one "proof" was the speaker's establishing his own ethos. That Prosit (Franklin) is such a fool as to think the one brief sentence establishes himself a "a Man of close Reasoning, Modesty, and Moderation" is absurd.

Prosit/Franklin then defended a series of mixed metaphors in his last *Mercury* essay, thereby calling attention to the original Prosit's mixed metaphors and poor style. Franklin parodied his opponent's pride: "I must repeat what I have said to several worthy Gentlemen, *I am already employ'd in almost every Cause in the Province, and made such a Speech in Kent [County] Court, as never was made there before.*" Prosit/Franklin concluded by saying that he will write nothing more in the *Mercury* and that if anything appears there which pretends to be by him, *it will be only a Contrivance of my Enemies, to render me more ridiculous.*" "More ridiculous"—it was delicious irony.

In the 11 May *Mercury*, "Marcus Verus"/Webbe said that Prosit in the *Gazette* was a counterfeit, "a pitiful Contrivance of his Enemies, as their last Shift, to throw Dirt upon the *real Author* known by that Name." In choosing Marcus Verus as his pseudonym, Webbe attempted to use and reverse Franklin's strategy. On 18 May, "S. H." in the *Mercury* referred to Franklin's reputation for humor when condemning "Satyrical and Witty Gentlemen, who Pride themselves in being Ludicrous upon every subject." Such writers, he claimed, made no contribution to society.

Persius Praised

The following week, 25 May 1732, Franklin published an essay praising the Latin poet Persius. Though the essay made no reference to the current quarrel between the *Mercury* writers and Franklin, it subtly presented his position concerning the relations of the church and the state. Persius lived during Nero's degenerate reign when, as usual, the official religion supported the state. In satire 2, Persius praised virtue in opposition to the state's religion. Franklin must have known Dryden's translation (the most popular one in the early eighteenth century), but he chose a prose translation, perhaps his own. Satire 2, lines 69–75, as given by Franklin, follow: "Tell me, you who are our Priests, of what use is Gold in our holy Places? even just as much as the little Babies, which bridal Virgins offer to *Venus*. Why, do we not offer to the Gods something, which neither the *Cottas* nor the *Messalas* can present to them, with all their magnificent Charges, piled up with the Flesh of the most exquisite Victims? Let us offer to them, a sincere and generous Heart, deeply imbued with the most lively Sentiments of Justice and Honour. Let us but have this Present to make them, and the meanest Sacrifice shall not fail to draw down upon us the choicest Blessings."

The essayist said that Persius's lines contain "more solid Divinity and purer Morality, than many elaborate Treatises, which in ponderous Volumes, and with great Ostentation, have been ushered into the World by the ill informed Doctors of Theology and Ethicks." The lines, like much deistic propaganda, attacked any official religion and any official support of the clergy.

On 1 June an anonymous *Mercury* writer censured the *Gazette* Persius essay for implying that the Bible was not as morally noble as Persius and for throwing "a slur upon *Priests of all Denominations.*" In Bradford's same paper, Marcus Verus/Webbe appeared again, now claiming that the Persius essay followed the two theses of Matthew Tindal's deistic *Christianity as Old as the Creation* (1730). One purpose was "to vilify the holy Scriptures," and the other was "to magnify the Law of Nature." Such writers, claimed Marcus Verus, "are like the troubled Sea, when it can't rest, thro' the consciousness they have of their *detestable Principles and Practices*; and then what Wonder is it, if they perpetually cast up Mire and Dirt."

THE OLD AMERICAN

In the *Pennsylvania Gazette* of the same date, 1 June 1732, Franklin contributed two essays to the continuing quarrel. The first was addressed "*To both the Printers, with their Readers and Writers.*" The speaker claimed to be an "oldish Man" who has "lived long in this Country" and calls it "my own." The old American has tried to imitate "those worthy Antients, who not only took pleasure in seeing the Improvements and Advances their respective Countries made in Science as well as Safety, but contributed all in their Power towards them." The notices and proclamations that have appeared recently in the papers have assured him "That *Wit* and *bright Geniuses* abound, and are the growing natural Product of this our Young (tho' in the Eyes of a great Part of the World insignificant) Colony." Formerly he occasionally contributed to the paper himself, but both printers have been recently "fully and abundantly supply'd. . . . Yet now this Morning about seven a Clock, smoking my Pipe, not having much Business in Hand, and thinking. . . ." And so Franklin's rambling narrator wrote a brief mock digression on the association of ideas before returning to the subject. "As I was . . . thinking of our News-Papers . . . I began to hope, that altho' I might not live to see it, a little Time would confirm those Proclamations: And considering how small a *Dot* our Globe is, in respect to those innumerable vast Bodies which are in and out of Ken around us . . . why should it be doubted but that the little Part of this *Dott* which lies between us and *California* (perhaps all *terra firma*) may soon be travel'd by some of our Improvers" and great additions to our knowledge brought back from there and from the moon.

From a naive, rambling old American who defers to the recent newspaper writers, Franklin gradually transformed the persona into a satirist. The speaker said that some mysterious writers from afar have appeared in the recent papers: "all that's wanting is our Ability to understand, either *what they mean, or what they say.*" Franklin then satirized himself as well as the other authors in the continuing newspaper quarrel. Their quarrels were irrelevant and boring. "A Word of Caution however, may not be improper to us all, the present Class of Writers, whether foreign or native, to make our Interest one, and join our Force for our common Support; for I have a Whisper, that the honest homespun Coats and leather Jackets are resolved to laugh us down." He concluded by expressing another journalistic fear: that either he will ramble on too long and so have his piece divided "with the Note *To be continued in our next*," or that his piece would begin the newspaper (which it did) and so the knowing reader will skip it and hurry on to the news, "however poor that may be."

Franklin's second essay in the 1 June 1732 *Gazette* was "On Declamation," and he used the same persona who had praised Persius. Franklin said that he had heard several criticisms of his Persius essay, especially of its declamatory style and structure. (He ignored the only published criticisms, which concerned its irreligion and satire of ministers.) He blamed the printer, however, for not noting that the essay was "*To be continued in our next.*" Franklin deliberately contrasted this author with the old American in the same paper who feared his piece might be divided with those words. Perhaps Franklin was showing it was impossible to please everybody (a point made the year before in "Apology for Printers," 10 June 1731), or perhaps he simply found the contrast amusing. After an epigraph from Pope's *Essay on Criticism* on the appropriateness of different styles, a quotation from William Wycherley on "easy Writing," and a commendation of the "*Moral Painter*, described by my Lord Shaftesbury in his Characteristics,"[12] Franklin wrote an appreciation of the declamatory style: "The Business of Declamation, if I understand it, is to agitate the Passions in a Manner proper to subdue the Judgment. For this Reason it quits the Familiar, and assumes the Sublime; it adorns itself with all the Majesty of Dress; it astonishes by the Boldness and Variety of its Figures; it charms the Ear by Periods round and musically turned: it hurries away the Imagination, and hath something divine in its Fury."

Franklin attempted to embody the declamatory style in this essay and to contrast it with an expository style. "The Impressions" that the declamatory style "make upon the Mind, discover its native Excellence and commanding Force. Would you for the purpose, describe the Guilt and Horror of *Nero*'s Court, that Madman, that Monster! Or would you paint the everlasting Charms of Virtue, and Moral Truth her inseparable Companion, still blooming with fresh Delight! Would you do this I say, in such a Manner as to fire your Reader with Indignation against the one, and teach his Heart to pant and heave with strong Desires towards the other: 'Tis not by saying *Nero was an abandoned Tyrant, Vertue is all lovely and divine*, that you can gain your Point." Though the quarrel between the *Mercury* writers and the *Gazette* occasioned the essay, the subject matter demonstrated Franklin's interest in rhetoric and anticipated and complemented his essay "On Literary Style" (2 August 1733).

On the last page of the 1 June *Gazette*, Franklin printed a mock advertisement for a collection of essays by Timothy Scrub including "An Essay upon the Nonsense of the Pulpit" and "An Essay upon the Nonsense of the Bar." In the following week's *Mercury*, 8 June, Bradford wrote that he refused to print a letter addressed to "T. Scrub" because it was "too full of personal Invectives. . . . Most People think that *Scrub*, be who he will, has sufficiently exposed *himself* and the *Publisher of the Gazette*." Bradford did, however, print on 8 and 15 June "An Essay on the Usefulness of the Doctrine of Immortality," which implicitly replied to Franklin's deistic beliefs and to his anti-*Mercury* essays.

ON CENSURE

As the time for the annual election of assembly members drew near (1 October), a *Mercury* writer sent in "An Essay on Envy, Philosophical and Political" (31 August 1732). Near the end, the author wrote: "What but this mean and unmanly Passion has raised and propagated so much *Fury* and *personal Scandal* of late between Gentlemen? *Patriotism* and the *good of Mankind* have been pretended; but, alas! Men are not excited to such present Passions *for the Sake of others* or the *Good of Mankind*: Superficial People may think them excellent Patriots who oppose Men in Power with *loud Clamours* and *Personal Outrage*; but *true Patriotism* is not so common in the World as these People imagine, neither has it those *violent Effects*. But *Envy* and *Self-Interest*, or the *Interest of a Party*, will excite Men to speak *all manner of Evil falsely*, concerning them they are desirous to *supplant*, and are frequently attended with those *violent Symptoms* we have seen so notorious in some late Productions."

Perhaps Franklin thought the author had in mind some of his writings, perhaps Franklin suspected that the essayist alluded to Franklin's replacing Bradford, or perhaps the author's introduction of a favorite topic interested Franklin. He responded on 7 September with "On Censure or Backbiting," which had as its underlying subjects human nature and Providence. Franklin at first assumed the usual pedagogical stance of the writer on moral philosophy, but one with an iconoclastic view—and with common sense. "There is scarce any one Thing so generally spoke against, and at the same time so universally practis'd, as *Censure* or *Backbiting*." All divines and writers on morality have condemned it and all religions have forbidden it. But "I shall in a very fearless impudent Manner take upon me to oppose the universal Vogue of Mankind in all Ages, and say as much in Behalf and Vindication of this decry'd Virtue, as the usual Vacancy in your Paper will admit."

Franklin claimed censure was useful and did "great Good . . . to Society" (W 192). The anonymous speaker gave four of its advantages. First, it "is frequently the Means of preventing powerful, politick, ill-designing Men, from growing too popular" by exposing them or by forcing them "to enter into a Course of true Virtue, without which real Grandeur is not to be attained." Second, fear of censure "assists our otherwise weak Resolutions of living virtuously." It "preserves the Integrity of the Wavering, the Honesty of the Covetous, the Sanctity of some of the Religious, and the Chastity of all Virgins." (The sexual joke is delightful, partially because the progress from "some" to "all.") Third, censure helps "a Man to *the Knowledge of himself,*" for our Friends are not "sincere or rash enough to acquaint us freely with our Faults," though our enemies do so freely behind our backs. "Thanks be to Providence, (that has given every Man a natural Inclination to backbite his Neighbour) we now hear of many Things said *of* us, that we shall never hear said *to* us; (for out of Good-will to us, or Illwill to those that have spoken ill of us, every one is willing enough to tell us how we are censur'd by others,) and we have the Advantage of mending our Manners accordingly" (W 193–94). The implied satire of providence and scorn for the nature of mankind recurred often in Franklin.

Fourth, backbiting "helps exceedingly to a thorough *Knowledge* of *Mankind.*" The observation on human nature (humans are implicitly defined as those animals that enjoy condemning others) echoed Franklin's satire in Busy-Body No. 1. At the end, Franklin wrote a mock encomium on censure: "But it is endless to enumerate every particular Advantage arising from this glorious Virtue! A Virtue, which whoever exerts, must have the largest Share of Publick Spirit and Self-denial, the highest Benevolence and Regard to the Good of others; since in This he entirely sacrifices his own Interest, making not only the Persons he accuses, but all that hear him, his Enemies; for all that deserve Censure (which are by far the greatest Number) hate the Censorious." Franklin continued in a declamatory style for several more sentences before breaking off: "But, dear Reader, . . . I shall offer you at present only one more convincing Argument in its Behalf, *viz.* that you would not have had the Satisfaction of seeing this Discourse so agreeably short as I shall make it, were it not for the just Fear I have of incurring your *Censure,* should I continue" (W 194–95). After ending on a self-satiric note, Franklin resumed the consideration of censure the following week under a female pseudonym.

ALICE ADDERTONGUE

Franklin's persona Alice Addertongue delighted in scandal and described herself as "a young girl of about thirty-five" living with her mother.[13] In this 12 September 1732 *Gazette* essay, Franklin attempted both to prove the truth of his partly mocking defense of censure and to defend women from the usual contemptuous treatment typical in battle-of-the-sexes literature. Franklin's style imitated Alice's breathless conversation and recalled the much put-upon shopkeeper Patience in the fourth Busy-Body:

> I was highly pleased with your last Week's Paper upon SCANDAL, as the un-common Doctrine therein preach'd is agreeable both to my Principles and Practice, and as it was published very seasonably to reprove the Impertinence of a Writer in the foregoing Thursdays *Mercury,* who at the Conclusion of one of his

silly Paragraphs, laments, forsooth, that the *Fair Sex* are so peculiarly guilty of this enormous Crime: Every Blockhead ancient and modern, that could handle a Pen, has I think taken upon him to cant in the same senseless Strain. If to *scandalize* be really a *Crime*, what do these Puppies mean? They describe it, they dress it up in the most odious frightful and detestable Colours, they represent it as the worst of Crimes, and then roundly and charitably charge the whole Race of Womankind with it. Are they not then guilty of what they condemn, at the same time that they condemn it? If they accuse us of any other Crime, they must necessarily *scandalize* while they do it: But to *scandalize* us with being guilty of *Scandal*, is in itself an egregious Absurdity, and can proceed from nothing but the most consummate Impudence in Conjunction with the most profound Stupidity. (1:243–44)

Alice finds it her "Duty as well as Inclination, to exercise my Talent at CENSURE" for the good of Philadelphia. She confesses, however, that she did not begin to censure others until she had been often corrected by her parents for "talking in my own Praise, and being continually told that it was ill Manners." Once she was even "severely whipt for it," and so "the confin'd Stream form'd itself a new Channel, and I began to speak for the future in the Dispraise of others" (1:244–45).

Franklin believed that such was the actual origin of censure, for he later wrote in a letter to Jared Eliot (12 September 1751): "Fondness for ourselves, rather than Malevolence to others, I take to be the general Source of *Censure and Backbiting*." He said to Eliot, "That this is a natural Inclination, appears, in that all Children show it, and say freely, *I am a good Boy; Am I not a good Girl?* and the like; 'till they have been frequently chid, and told their Trumpeter is dead; and that 'tis unbecoming to sound their own Praise, &c." The humorous sketch of Alice had as an undercurrent Franklin's serious attempt to anatomize an aspect of human psychology.

Alice inverted an old proverb: "*Scandal*, like other Virtues, is in part its own Reward, as it gives us the Satisfaction of making our selves appear better than others, or others no better than ourselves." Though her mother had constantly warned her against criticizing others, Alice insisted that scandal was the most enjoyable conversation. "Our Disputes once rose so high, that we parted Tea-Table, and I concluded to entertain my Acquaintance in the Kitchin. The first Day of this Separation we both drank Tea at the same Time, but she with her Visitors in the Parlor. She would not hear of the least Objection to any one's Character, but began a new sort of Discourse in some such queer philosophical Manner as this; *I am mightily pleas'd sometimes*, says she, *when I observe and consider that the World is not so bad as People out of humour imagine it to be. There is something amiable, some good Quality or other in every body*." And she went on to give examples for "near half an Hour." Then she asked her friends for similar examples. Alice "peep'd in at the Door, and never in my Life before saw such a Set of simple vacant Countenances; they looked somehow neither glad, nor sorry, nor angry, nor pleas'd, nor indifferent, nor attentive; but, (excuse the Simile) like so many blue wooden Images of Rie Doe."

Franklin was, in part, deriding himself. In his 1726 "Plan of Conduct" he had made the same resolve as Alice Addertongue's mother: "I resolve to speak ill of no man whatever, not even in a matter of truth; but rather by some means excuse the faults I hear charged upon others, and upon proper occasions speak all the good I know of everybody" (1:100). He found the resolve impractical, if not impossible and, in addition to ridiculing himself, excused himself for attempting to be morally perfect in an imperfect world.

Unlike her mother, Alice "in the Kitchin had already begun a ridiculous Story of Mr. ———'s Intrigue with his Maid, and his Wife's Behaviour upon the Discovery; at some Passages we laugh'd heartily, and one of the gravest of Mama's Company, without making any Answer to her Discourse, got up *to go and see what the Girls were so merry about*: She was follow'd by a Second, and shortly after by a Third, till at last the old Gentlewoman found herself quite alone, and being convinc'd that her Project was impracticable, came her self and finish'd her Tea with us" (1:245–46).

Alice has become the most famous backbiter in Pennsylvania. Not only does she have numerous natural allies, but she has a method "by which I can pump Scandal out of People that are the least enclin'd that way. Shall I discover my Secret? . . . If I have never heard Ill of some Person, I always impute it to defective Intelligence; *for there are none without their Faults, no not one.* If she is a Woman, I take the first Opportunity to let all her Acquaintance know I have heard that one of the handsomest or best Men in Town has said something in Praise either of her Beauty, her Wit, her Virtue, or her good Management. If you know any thing of Humane Nature, you perceive that this naturally introduces a Conversation turning upon all her Failings, past, present, and to come" (1:246).

According to Alice, scandal especially flourished just before the annual election. She commends "every Candidate before some of the opposite Party, listning attentively to what is said of him in answer: (But Commendations in this latter Case are not always necessary, and should be used judiciously;) of late Years I needed only observe what they said of one another freely; and having for the Help of Memory taken Account of all Informations and Accusations received, whoever peruses my Writings after my Death, may happen to think, that during a certain Term, the People of Pennsylvania chose into all their Offices of Honour and Trust, the veriest Knaves, Fools and Rascals in the whole Province." Alice laments that the current year seems to be an exception—thus contradicting the 31 August *Mercury* essay.

Alice owns that she generally adds some more damning circumstances to the stories she hears. For "the worst that is said of us is only half what *might* be said, if all our Faults were seen" (1:248). Alice is writing for the *Gazette* because she has such "an extream Cold that I can scarce speak, and a most terrible

Toothach that I dare hardly open my Mouth." She advises the editor, "if you would make your Paper a Vehicle of Scandal, you would double the Number of your Subscribers." She therefore is sending accounts of "*4 Knavish Tricks, 2 crackt M———ds, 5 Cu—ld-ms, 3 drub'd Wives,* and *4 Henpeck'd Husbands*, all within this Fortnight; which you may, as Articles of News, deliver to the Pub-lick." Franklin, as editor, ironically replied, "*I thank my Correspondent Mrs. Addertongue for her Good-Will; but desire to be excus'd inserting the Articles of News she has sent me; such Things being in Reality* no News at all" (1:248). Editor Franklin reaffirmed Alice's low estimation of human nature.

Conclusion

High points of the warfare with the *Mercury* writers occurred in the 30 March consideration of the Port Royalists; the 20 April satire of English condescension ("This is the practice at home! This is the practice at home!"); the wonderfully confusing essay of 4 May travestying "Prosit"; and the persona and breathless, hurried speech of Alice Addertongue, who objected to women being found "pe-culiarly guilty" of scandal. Though the essays began with a political motivation, they reflected a number of favorite Franklin themes: the limits of logic and skepticism; Americanism; defense of women from criticism; praise of virtue; and satire of both religion and the clergy. The last subjects were those for which he was repeatedly criticized, to which the enemies in the *American Weekly Mer-cury* added their calumny.

While conducting the newspaper war in 1732, Franklin was devoting hun-dreds of hours to founding the Library Company of Philadelphia, writing at least fifteen other pieces,[14] and carrying on a struggling, fledgling business as a printer. The rivalry with Bradford's *American Weekly Mercury* continued until Bradford's death in 1742. Franklin occasionally lampooned the quality of Brad-ford's writing and reporting, and Bradford opposed Franklin's *Gazette* whenever possible, but exchanges as frequent as those in 1732 did not recur.

SEVEN

Poor Richard's *Prefaces*

1733–1747

What a peasecods! cannot I have a little Fault or two, but all the Country must see it in print!—Bridget Saunders in Poor Richard, *1738*

ALMANACS WERE THE STAPLE PRODUCT of a colonial printer. They sold more than all other books and pamphlets combined. Along with such job printings as handbills and forms, they provided the livelihood of most colonial printers. Families with few possessions often owned a Bible and a current almanac. The one printed piece that people purchased annually served eighteenth-century families as a calendar and date book. Sheet almanacs (printed on a single sheet of paper) sold for one pence retail and were little more than the briefest calendars. The larger almanacs (more expensive and thus, to a printer, more profitable) sold for five pence retail and contained a variety of information. They gave the times of sunrise and sunset, the periods of the moon, high and low tides, eclipses, and other such information. They were also handbooks of useful facts, listing court days, dates of fairs, and distances between places on the roads. Like encyclopedias, they carried a list of the kings of England and their reigns, lists of the major monarchs of Europe, and a chronology of important dates since the birth of Christ. They also contained jokes and sayings, thus providing entertainment as well as instruction.

About a year after Franklin and Meredith opened their printing shop, Franklin evidently suggested to their renter, Thomas Godfrey, that he prepare an almanac. Godfrey was Pennsylvania's best mathematician, though Theophilus Grew, James Logan, and Jacob Taylor were close rivals. Godfrey's *Almanac for 1730*, which Franklin and Meredith advertised on 2 October 1729 as "Speedily" to be "Published," was Godfrey's first. In the fall of the following two years, 1730 and 1731, Franklin printed both Godfrey's *Almanac* and John Jerman's *American Almanac*. He could not secure, however, Titan Leeds's *American Almanac*, the best-known one in the Middle Colonies. Only Nathaniel Ames's *Astronomical . . . Almanac* (1725–64) had a greater circulation, but it was popular primarily in New England. Advertising Leeds's almanac in the *Pennsylvania Gazette*, printer David Harry claimed on 2 October 1729 that Leeds's almanac was "far preferable to any yet published in America." It even had the unwelcome distinction of being forged by rival printers. In the fall of 1732, Franklin probably expected to continue printing both Godfrey's and Jerman's almanacs, but Andrew Bradford offered better terms than Franklin and secured the printing of all five Philadelphia almanacs for 1733.

ORIGIN

It may seem surprising that Thomas Godfrey, a fellow Junto member who rented from Franklin and Meredith in 1728 and a person whom Franklin probably encouraged to start compiling almanacs, would take his copy to Bradford, but Godfrey had a reason. In the *Autobiography*, Franklin described his courtship of a girl related to Mrs. Godfrey. (Nothing is known of Mrs. Godfrey's relation, not even her name.) The parents encouraged him with "continual Invitations to Supper, and by leaving us together, till at length it was time to explain." Mrs. Godfrey acted as the go-between for Franklin and the parents, but the parents abruptly refused to meet the young printer's expectations of a customary marriage settlement and forbade him to call again. Franklin thought they cunningly supposed he and the girl were too much in love and "therefore that we should steal a Marriage, which would leave them at Liberty to give or withhold what they pleas'd." Furious at their conniving with his affections, Franklin "went no more," though Mrs. Godfrey later brought him "some more favourable Accounts of their Disposition." The supposed change confirmed Franklin's suspicions, and he "declared absolutely my Resolution to have nothing more to do with that Family." The Godfreys "resented" Franklin's attitude, "we differ'd, and they removed, leaving me the whole House" (A 69–70).

The quarrel probably occurred in the late winter or early spring of 1730 (the Godfreys moved out in mid-April), but Godfrey continued to publish his almanac with Franklin for 1731 and 1732. Franklin's disgust with the manipulations of Mrs. Godfrey's relatives found its last statement in the *Autobiography*, but he described a situation similar to his courtship in his Anthony Afterwit sketch of 10 July 1732, thus publicly embarrassing the Godfreys and the family to all who knew about the courtship.[1] Afterwit/Franklin said that

> when the old Gentleman saw I was pretty well engag'd, and that the Match was too far gone to be easily broke off; he, without any Reason given, grew very angry, forbid me the House, and told his Daughter that if she married me he would not give her a Farthing. However (as he foresaw) we were not to be disappointed in that Manner; but having stole a Wedding, I took her home to my House; where we were not in quite so poor a Condition as the Couple describ'd in the Scotch Song, who had *Neither Pot nor Pan, / But four bare Legs together*; for I had a House tolerably furnished, for an ordinary Man, before. No thanks to Dad, who I understand was very much pleased with his politick Management. And I have since learn'd that there are old Curmudgeons (*so called*) besides him, who have this Trick, to marry their Daughters, and yet keep what they might well spare, till they can keep it no longer. (1:238)

Franklin's case, complete with "a House tolerably furnished," corresponded to that of Anthony Afterwit—except that Franklin did not marry. The indirect attack on the family naturally upset Thomas Godfrey, who retaliated by giving the copy for his 1733 almanac to Andrew Bradford.

Faced with losing an important part of his developing printing business, Franklin, at the last minute, compiled his own almanac. Although almanacs were usually published in late October or early November, Franklin's first *Poor Richard* was not printed until the last week in December. Hurrying to get out the almanac, Franklin made a major printing error. Advertising for the second edition (11 January 1732/3), he revealed, "*A few of the first that were printed had the Months of September and October transpos'd; but that Fault is now rectified.*" The retail price of *Poor Richard* from 1733 to 1747 was, like its rivals, five pence a copy. Franklin's challenge in publishing an unknown almanac was how to get a share of the market and, hopefully, how to get the lion's share away from Titan Leeds. He took the name of his almanac maker, Richard Saunders, from Richard Saunder, whose popular (and serious) English almanac, *Apollo Anglicanus*, appeared from 1684 to 1736 (before 1684, the compiler used the name Richard Saunders), and adapted the title from the most popular humorous English almanac (by William Winstanley) titled *Poor Robin's*.[2] As Franklin knew, his brother James imitated the latter and attributed his *Rhode Island Almanac* (1727–35) to "Poor Robin."[3] "Poor" in the title signaled that an almanac would contain humor.

Franklin advertised the first edition of *Poor Richard* as "Just Published" in the *Pennsylvania Gazette* on Thursday, 28 December. The advertisement began by listing the usual useful contents: "POOR RICHARD: AN ALMANAC containing the Lunations, Eclipses, Planets Motions and Aspects, Weather, Sun and Moon's rising and setting, Highwater, &c." The mathematical parts of the almanac would have been the most time-consuming for Franklin to write. He could do them but by 1738 he employed Theophilus Grew to compile them—and perhaps paid Grew to do the mathematics (time of the tides, etc.) earlier. The long advertisement also claimed that the almanac contained jokes, poetry, sayings, and—buried within the list—a startling astrological prognostication: "besides many pleasant and witty Verses, Jests and Sayings, Author's Motive of Writing, *Prediction of the Death of his friend Mr. Titan Leeds* [emphasis mine], Moon no Cuckold, Batchelor's Folly, Parson's Wine and Baker's Pudding, Short Visits, Kings and Bears, New Fashions, Game for Kisses, Katherine's Love, Different Sentiments, Signs of a Tempest, Death a Fisherman, Conjugal Debate, Men and Melons, H. the Prodigal, Breakfast in Bed, Oyster Lawsuit, &c. by RICHARD SAUNDERS, Philomat." Franklin intended the almanac to be both useful and entertaining.

The heart of the almanac was the twelve pages of calendar, each month having a separate page, with a four- to eight-line poem at the top, notes on the phases of the moon, the time of the rising and setting of the sun, weather predictions, and proverbs and aphorisms scattered throughout the otherwise blank spaces. The proverbs and sententiae, like the prefaces, revealed Franklin's literary genius. The poems at the top of the pages were usually borrowed: Franklin took most of the 1733 poems from *Wits Recreation* (1655), though he lifted three from Dryden's translation of "The First Book of the Georgics."[4]

The *Poor Richard* almanacs through 1748 contained twenty-four pages. The usual contents were:

> p. 1: a title page, which included five estimates of the age of the world, ranging from 7,241 to 5,494, the first according to "the Eastern Greeks" and the last according to the "Jewish Rabbies."
>
> p. 2: an address to the reader (not all almanacs contained a preface, but Franklin's skits were a major reason for the popularity of *Poor Richard*)
>
> p. 3: "The Anatomy of Man's Body as govern'd by the Twelve Constellations" (a standard almanac feature)
>
> p. 4: "Planets Motions for the 1, 8, 15, and 22 days in each Month" (a standard feature)
>
> p. 5: "Explanation of this ALMANAC" (standard)
>
> p. 6: a chronological table of the kings of England (standard)
>
> pp. 7–18: the twelve months (the proverbs appeared interspersed among the astronomical signs and weather predictions)
>
> p. 19: "Of the Eclipses" (standard)
>
> pp. 19–20: "Chronology of Things remarkable"
>
> pp. 21–23: times of the meetings of courts in Pennsylvania and the neighboring colonies
>
> p. 24: "A Catalogue of the principal Kings and Princes in *Europe*, with the time of their births and ages." Finally, "A Description of the Highways and Roads" from Williamsburg to Philadelphia (the "Description" merely gave the mileage between places). Franklin omitted the roads going "Northeastward" through Boston to Norridgewock from the first two almanacs, and when he added them in 1735, he also added the roads going "Southwestward" from Williamsburg to Charleston, South Carolina.[5]

PREDICTION: THE DEATH OF TITAN LEEDS

Franklin used the first preface to startle the reader and to win away purchasers from Titan Leeds's almanac. His model was Jonathan Swift's 1708 satire on the astrologer and almanac maker John Partridge (1644–1715). Swift used as his persona an educated and wealthy gentleman named "Isaac Bickerstaff," who had become an adept in astrology and decided to demonstrate its validity by predictions. Bickerstaff's first forecast concerned Partridge: "I have consulted the Star of his Nativity by my own Rules, and find he will infallibly die upon the 29th of *March* next, about eleven at night, of a raging fever."[6] In addition to Swift's original Bickerstaff-Partridge hoax and the English wit's further satires of Partridge, Franklin knew an American imitation. While Franklin was setting type for the *New-England Courant*, the printer Thomas Fleet wrote a mock prognostication for the 12 February 1721/2 issue, in the persona of "Sidrophel," an "old Starmonger" with "Skill in the Art of Astrology," who predicted the death of the Boston postmaster Philip Musgrave.

Franklin did not employ Swift's persona of the rich, highly educated Bickerstaff with his haughty tone of superiority. Instead, Franklin's persona was similar to the one Swift gave to John Partridge—a poor man who makes almanacs because he has "a Wife to maintain, and no other Way to get my Bread."[7] Partridge may not believe in astrology, but Poor Richard pretends to, though an underlying (and, on occasion, obvious) note of irony emerges. Swift's mock prognostication inspired Franklin, who Americanized and transformed it. Franklin changed the speaker's tone from scorn and superiority to respect and sympathy. He changed the main persona from the rich, superstitious Bickerstaff to the poor, impractical, but brilliant (at least in mathematics and astrology) naïf, Richard Saunders. (Thus Poor Richard bears some relation to the brilliant but impractical mathematician Thomas Godfrey.)

Poor Richard further differed in two key ways from Partridge. First, Partridge's wife existed only as a person whom he supports.[8] Poor Richard's wife, Bridget, emerges as a full character—the dominant person in the marriage, with Poor Richard a henpecked, meek husband. Second, Poor Richard is a man of tender sensibilities, especially considerate of his old friend Titan Leeds. At the same time, Franklin has Poor Richard use the language of astrology, a specialized diction and symbolism that Swift's Bickerstaff ignored. Consequently, Poor Richard seems to be more realistic as an astrologer than Bickerstaff, as well as a greater expert. Swift's Bickerstaff speaks in an impatient, superior, humorless, and severe tone, whereas Franklin's Poor Richard is humble, serious, considerate, and homespun. Franklin changed the level of diction, especially in the early almanacs, from learned to colloquial—except for the specialized language of astrology. Swift's underlying voice is serious and biting; Franklin's is humorous and mocking. Swift wrote to expose astrology and Partridge; Franklin wrote to mock astrology, to entertain, to supply useful information, and, above all, to sell almanacs.[9]

Franklin began the hoax with an appeal to the reader's supposedly superior understanding: "I might in this place attempt to gain thy Favour, by declaring that I write Almanacs with no other View than that of the publick Good; but in this I should not be sincere; and Men are now adays too wise to be deceiv'd by Pretences how specious soever." Franklin proceeded to give a sympathetic portrait of the compiler, Richard Saunders, a poor, naive, superstitious, humble, astrologer, with an outspoken wife: "The plain Truth of the Matter is, I am excessive poor, and my Wife, good Woman, is, I tell her, excessive proud; she cannot bear, she says, to sit spinning in her Shift of Tow, while I do nothing but gaze at the Stars; and has threatned more than once to burn all my Books and

Rattling-Traps (as she calls my Instruments) if I do not make some profitable Use of them for the good of my Family." So, lured by the "considerable share of the Profits" that printer Franklin promised, Poor Richard has turned almanac maker.

Indeed, continued Poor Richard, he would have compiled almanacs many years ago, were his desire for money not "overpower'd by my Regard for my good Friend and Fellow-Student, Mr. Titan Leeds, whose Interest I was extreamly unwilling to hurt." But Poor Richard sadly records that "this Obstacle (I am far from speaking it with Pleasure) is soon to be removed, since inexorable Death, who was never known to respect Merit, has already prepared the mortal Dart, the fatal Sister has already extended her destroying Shears, and that ingenious Man must soon be taken from us." Then he predicts the exact hour, minute, and second of the death of Titan Leeds. "He dies, by my Calculation made at his Request, on Oct. 17. 1733. 3 ho. 29 m. *P.M.* at the very instant of the [symbol for] conjunction of [symbol for] sun and [symbol for] mercury."

Since his friend Titan Leeds will soon die, Poor Richard feels free to become an almanac maker. He requests "a share of the publick Encouragement; which I am the more apt to hope for on this Account, that the Buyer of my Almanac may consider himself, not only as purchasing an useful Utensil, but as performing an Act of Charity, to his poor Friend and Servant R. Saunders." Poor Richard's final characterization in his first almanac occurs on the last page, concluding "A Catalogue of the principal Kings and Princes in Europe, with the Time of their Births and Ages." Franklin appended, "Poor Richard, An American Prince, without Subjects, his Wife being Viceroy over him," and gave his birth as 23 October 1684 and his age as forty-nine.

Poor Richard immediately became a best-seller. A second impression was announced in the 11 January 1732/3 *Pennsylvania Gazette* to be published on "Saturday next" (13 January), and a third impression was announced in the paper of 18 January to be published next Saturday (20 January). The few remaining accounts give no good indication of the sales of the first *Poor Richard*s, but Franklin probably printed one thousand or so of the first edition, and perhaps a similar number of the second impression, and perhaps half as many for the third, all within a month. We know that *Poor Richard* became the best-selling almanac of the Middle Colonies (with strong sales in the South), and that before Franklin retired as a printer in 1748, *Poor Richard* was selling ten thousand copies a year (Λ 93).[10]

LEEDS MUST BE DEAD

Titan Leeds evidently did not know the Swift-Bickerstaff hoax. Indeed, probably only the litterateurs among Franklin's audience did. Instead of pointing out Franklin's source and chuckling about the borrowing, Leeds triumphantly announced in his 1734 almanac that he was alive! He called Poor Richard an impostor, "a Fool and a Lyar." Franklin was ready and waiting. He no doubt had

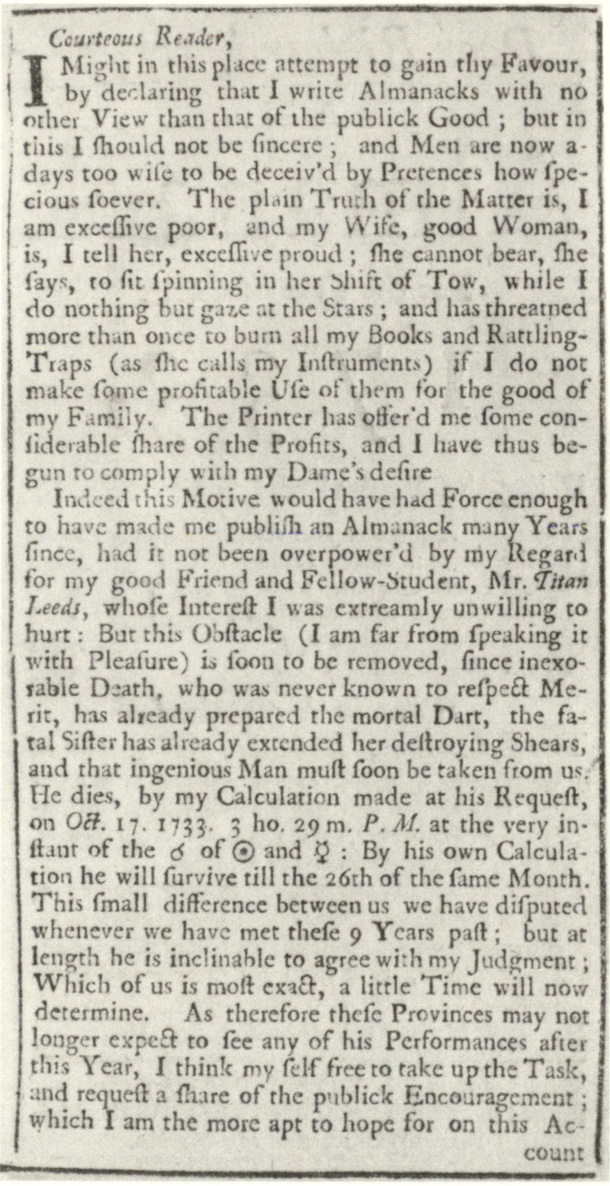

Courteous Reader,

I Might in this place attempt to gain thy Favour, by declaring that I write Almanacks with no other View than that of the publick Good; but in this I should not be sincere; and Men are now adays too wise to be deceiv'd by Pretences how specious soever. The plain Truth of the Matter is, I am excessive poor, and my Wife, good Woman, is, I tell her, excessive proud; she cannot bear, she says, to sit spinning in her Shift of Tow, while I do nothing but gaze at the Stars; and has threatned more than once to burn all my Books and Rattling-Traps (as she calls my Instruments) if I do not make some profitable Use of them for the good of my Family. The Printer has offer'd me some considerable share of the Profits, and I have thus begun to comply with my Dame's desire.

Indeed this Motive would have had Force enough to have made me publish an Almanack many Years since, had it not been overpower'd by my Regard for my good Friend and Fellow-Student, Mr. *Titan Leeds*, whose Interest I was extreamly unwilling to hurt: But this Obstacle (I am far from speaking it with Pleasure) is soon to be removed, since inexorable Death, who was never known to respect Merit, has already prepared the mortal Dart, the fatal Sister has already extended her destroying Shears, and that ingenious Man must soon be taken from us. He dies, by my Calculation made at his Request, on *Oct.* 17. 1733. 3 ho. 29 m. *P. M.* at the very instant of the ☌ of ☉ and ☿: By his own Calculation he will survive till the 26th of the same Month. This small difference between us we have disputed whenever we have met these 9 Years past; but at length he is inclinable to agree with my Judgment; Which of us is most exact, a little Time will now determine. As therefore these Provinces may not longer expect to see any of his Performances after this Year, I think my self free to take up the Task, and request a share of the publick Encouragement; which I am the more apt to hope for on this Account

Figure 9. The preface to Poor Richard *for 1733, predicting the death of the rival almanac maker Titan Leeds. Leeds's almanac was the most popular in the Middle Colonies. In his* Poor Richard *for 1733, Franklin, writing as the astrologer Richard Saunders, predicted the exact hour and minute of the death of Leeds, his supposed friend and fellow student of astrology. Franklin's persona as a poor, humble, henpecked, impractical astrologer, who had refrained for years from starting his own almanac out of consideration for his friend Leeds, was great fun—to everyone but Leeds. The preface made the almanac a sensational success. Some readers would have recognized that Franklin was imitating Jonathan Swift's Bickerstaff hoax and that he was ridiculing astrology, but Titan Leeds was no litterateur and lacked a sense of humor. He triumphantly announced in his following year's almanac that he was alive! Courtesy, Rosenbach Museum and Library, Philadelphia.*

prepared his 1734 almanac, complete with a brief introduction, but held off printing it until Leeds's almanac appeared. Then he revised the preface, adding a reply to Leeds, echoing Swift's strategy with the hapless Partridge. The comparatively small number of persons in Pennsylvania and the neighboring colonies who knew Swift's original would have laughed all the more at the continuing imitation.

Poor Richard began the 1734 preface by emphasizing his poverty, his impracticality, and his dominant wife. He was a pitiable, sympathetic figure who made the public feel superior. He thanked his "Courteous Readers": "Your kind and charitable Assistance last Year, in purchasing so large an Impression of my Almanacs, has made my Circumstances much more easy in the World, and requires my grateful Acknowledgment." The almanac author happily detailed his increasing possessions: "My Wife has been enabled to get a Pot of her own, and is no longer oblig'd to borrow one from a Neighbour; nor have we ever since been without something of our own to put in it." (He may here have echoed the Scottish song, quoted in the Anthony Afterwit sketch, describing the couple who had "Neither Pot nor Pan, / But four bare Legs together"; or he may have been alluding to the scatological saying, "without a pot to piss in or . . .") "She has also got a pair of Shoes, two new Shifts, and a new warm Petticoat; and for my part, I have bought a second-hand Coat, so good, that I am now not asham'd to go to Town or be seen there." Just as most of the goods are for his wife, so the effect is also primarily upon her: "These Things have render'd her Temper so much more pacifick than it us'd to be, that I may say, I have slept more, and more quietly within this last Year, than in the three foregoing Years put together."

Poor Richard then recalled his prediction of the time of Titan Leeds's death and Leeds's slightly different prediction: "At which of these Times he died, or whether he be really yet dead, I cannot at this present Writing positively assure my Readers; forasmuch as a Disorder in my own Family demanded my Presence, and would not permit me as I had intended, to be with him in his last Moments, to receive his last Embrace, to close his Eyes, and do the Duty of a Friend in performing the last Offices to the Departed." Franklin again imitated and changed Swift: a curious person called on Partridge at the time of his predicted death, only to find that he died some four hours earlier.[11] Poor Richard said he did not know whether Leeds died, "for the Stars only show to the Skilful, what will happen in the natural and universal Chain of Causes and Effects," but that Providence can always intervene and "set aside" or postpone "the Course of Nature." Franklin alluded to Samuel Clarke's position in his debate with Leibnitz: God occasionally intervened in the course of nature in order to set things right.[12]

Poor Richard lamented, "(and I cannot speak it without Sorrow) there is the strongest Probability that my dear Friend is *no more*; for there appears in his Name, as I am assured, an Almanac for the Year 1734, in which I am treated in a very gross and unhandsome Manner; in which I am called *a false Predicter, an Ignorant, a conceited Scribler, a Fool, and a Lyar.*" The actual Leeds, said Poor Richard, never used anyone "so indecently and so scurrilously," and his affection for "me was extraordinary." Poor Richard therefore feared that the Leeds almanac was but a contrivance by some publisher (Andrew Bradford, Franklin's rival, published Leeds in 1733 and 1734) to sell almanacs "by the sole Force and Virtue of Mr. Leeds's Name." Poor Richard heaped further praise upon Leeds, concluding, "although it should be so, that, contrary to all Probability, contrary to my Prediction and his own, he might possibly be yet alive, yet my Loss of Honour as a Prognosticator, cannot afford me so much Mortification, as his Life, Health and Safety would give me Joy and Satisfaction." Surely the litterateurs among his audience enjoyed the comparison to Swift's Bickerstaff. Persons like Joseph Breintnall would have appreciated that Franklin's persona is more sympathetic, his language more vernacular, and his narrative more dramatic.

THE HONOR OF ASTROLOGY

Poor Richard opened the 1735 almanac with his thanks to the purchasers, then commented on Leeds's most recent attack. "Whatever may be the Musick of the Spheres, how great soever the Harmony of the Stars, 'tis certain there is no Harmony among the Stargazers; but they are perpetually growling and snarling at one another like strange Curs, or like some Men at their Wives." He has been abused by "Titan Leeds deceas'd, (Titan Leeds when living would not have us'd me so!)" and remonstrated that "tho' I take it patiently, I take it very unkindly." Franklin then gave a series of mock proofs that Leeds "is really defunct and dead." "First because the Stars are seldom disappointed . . . and they fore-show'd his Death at the Time I predicted it. Secondly, 'Twas requisite and necessary he should die punctually at that Time, for the Honour of Astrology, the Art professed both by him and his Father before him."

With the third reason, Franklin again borrowed from Swift, who claimed that numerous gentlemen bought Partridge's almanac for 1709 merely to see "what he said against me; at every Line they read, they would lift up their Eyes, and cry out, betwixt Rage and Laughter, *They were sure no Man* alive *ever writ such damned Stuff as this.*"[13] Franklin echoed Swift: "Thirdly, 'Tis plain to every one that reads his two last Almanacs (for 1734 and 35) that they are not written with that *Life* his Performances use to be written with; the Wit is low and flat, the little Hints dull and spiritless, nothing smart in them but Hudibras's Verses against Astrology at the Heads of the months in the last, which no Astrologer but a *dead one* would have inserted, and no Man *living* would or could write such Stuff as the rest." Franklin followed Swift so closely that we may be sure that he was not simply recalling Swift but rereading him in preparing his reply to Leeds.[14]

Franklin also borrowed his next mock proof from Swift. Swift's Bickerstaff quoted Partridge: "He . . . says, *He is not only* now *alive, but was also alive upon that very 29th of* March, *which I foretold* he *should die on*: By this, he declares his Opinion, that a Man may be alive *now*, who was not alive a Twelve-month ago. And indeed, there lies the Sophistry of his Argument. He dares not assert, he was alive ever since the 29th of *March*, but that he *is now alive, and was so on that Day*: I grant the latter, for he did not die till Night."[15] Swift depended on the past tense "was . . . alive" to prove that Partridge had been dead since that time. Franklin's similar argument was clearer: "But lastly, I shall convince him from his own Words, that he is dead . . . for in his Preface to his Almanac for 1734, he says, 'Saunders adds another Gross Falshood in his Almanac, viz. *that by my own Calculation I shall* survive *until the* 26th *of the said Month October 1733, which is as* untrue *as the former*.' Now if it be, as *Leeds says*, untrue and a *gross Falshood* that he surviv'd till the 26th of October 1733, then it is certainly *true* that he died *before* that Time: And if he died before that Time, he is dead now, to all Intents and Purposes, any thing he may say to the contrary notwithstanding."

Poor Richard concluded by politely threatening to exorcize the walking spirit of the deceased Leeds: "But if some People will walk and be troublesome after Death, it may perhaps be born with a little, because it cannot well be avoided unless one would be at the Pains and Expence of laying them in the *Red Sea*." Poor Richard added that spirits "should not presume too much upon the Liberty allow'd them; I know Confinement must needs be mighty irksome to the free Spirit of an Astronomer, and I am too compassionate to proceed suddenly to Extremities with it; nevertheless, tho' I resolve with Reluctance, I shall not long defer, if it does not speedily learn to treat its living Friends with better Manners." From specific echoes of Swift, Franklin passed into the manner of Defoe, imitating his works that pretended to be stories of the supernatural, like "The Apparition of Mrs. Veal." In folklore, the Red Sea was the place to lay the dead if all else failed. Franklin also knew the belief from at least one literary source, Addison's *The Drummer*.[16]

WHO IS POOR RICHARD?

Though Franklin, writing in the 1736 almanac as Poor Richard, referred to "the great Reputation I gain'd by exactly predicting another Man's Death," he thereafter dropped the imitation of Swift and instead joked about Poor Richard's persona. The almanac writer reported that some persons have said "that I my self was never alive. They say in short, *That there is no such a Man as I am*; and have spread this Notion so thoroughly in the Country, that I have been frequently told it to my Face by those that don't know me." The tender naïf Poor Richard complained, "This is not civil Treatment, to endeavour to deprive me of my very Being, and reduce me to a Non-entity in the Opinion of the publick. But so long as I know my self to walk about, eat, drink and sleep, I am satisfied that *there is really such a Man as I am*, whatever they may say to the contrary."

If he did not exist, "how is it possible I should appear publickly to hundreds of People, as I have done for several Years past, in print?" Though Franklin was joking, an uneasy strain of seriousness underlay the voice. Questions of identity, of reality and appearance, of the multiple personalities that personae allowed the literary artist—these always fascinated Franklin. Such topics appeared repeatedly in his writings and constituted a minor subject of Poor Richard's proverbs.

Poor Richard said he would not have bothered to answer such a ridiculous charge, were it not "for the sake of my Printer, to whom my Enemies are pleased to ascribe my Productions; and who it seems is as unwilling to father my Offspring, as I am to lose the Credit for it." He therefore solemnly declared, "*That what I have written heretofore, and do now write, neither was nor is written by any other Man or Men, Person or Persons whatsoever.*" He concluded with thanking the readers and hoping that they would be pleased.

The play between Franklin and his persona is good fun, and the suggestion that the printer found himself superior to the writing and the character of Poor Richard reveals Franklin's concern with the persona of Poor Richard. Though authorship freed the writer from his known identity and usually made him superior (the *censor morum* was the commonest pose of the eighteenth-century essayist), at the same time it falsified an identity. Franklin was conscious that the Republic of Letters all too easily allowed an author this freedom, which was often abused. As a teenager in Boston, Franklin no doubt thought that Captain Christopher Taylor, a Couranteer who anonymously criticized the morals of other Bostonians, was a knave and a hypocrite. When Franklin adopted the persona of an almanac maker and made the persona sympathetic, he was probably partially ashamed of himself. Was he like the contemporary writer he most admired, Jonathan Swift, or was he instead really like the almanac maker Partridge?

ALMANAC MAKERS

Pretending to be a simple-minded lover of almanacs, Franklin wrote in the 20 October 1737 *Gazette* a burlesque of almanac writers, signed "Philomath." Titled "Upon the Talents Requisite in an Almanac-Writer," the author claimed to be "a great Lover of all Works of Ingenuity, and the Authors of them . . . especially . . . those *Labours of the Learned*, called ALMANACS."

Few persons, if any, considered almanacs to be literature or labors of the learned. They were scorned as a sub-literary genre, like comic books today, and almanac makers were generally despised as believers in an outmoded science, astrology. Philomath, however, said, "As I am a considerable Proficient in this Sort of Learning; and as at this time of the Year, Copies of Almanacs for the next Year usually come to the Press, long before they are wanted: And as I have laid out many a Six-pence among your Customers, the Profit whereof has in a great Measure redounded to you: So I may reasonably hope to be look'd on as a good Customer, and claim a favourable Place in your Paper."

Philomath has "a large Volume in Manuscript . . . on the Important Subject of *Almanac-making*, which I may in time communicate to the Publick; but at present I am willing to oblige them, with only a Taste of my Skill, which (if I have any Title to the Art of Prognostication) will certainly make them long for the whole." Franklin expects the readers to see through his persona and to realize that they are supposed to say, "No! No! Condemn the 'large Volume' to the garbage!" In fact, the humorous style and contents make the readers look forward to the jokes the persona will play. "My present Design, is to give to you and the Publick, *a short Essay*, upon the Talents requisite in *an Almanac-Writer*, by which it will plainly appear, how much the Community is indebted to Men of such *great and uncommon Parts and Sagacity*. An *Almanac-Writer*, Sir, should be born one like a Poet; for as I read among the Works of the learned *Poeta nascitur non fit* [a poet is born, not made]; so it is a Maxim with me, that *Almanackorum scriptor nascitur not fit*."

Had he wanted to be correct, Franklin would have written *Almanacator non nascitur sed fit*.[17] Franklin's mongrel combination of Latin and English is a joke, and the literal meaning is that *an almanac maker is born not fit [for anything]*.

An almanac maker, said Philomath, "*should be descended of a great Family, and bear a Coat of Arms*." The crest asserted his importance and helped the almanacs sell. Franklin again satirized Titan Leeds's almanac, which used a coat of arms. If the author "has the Misfortune to be meanly descended," he can always look in the *Peerage of England* and borrow a device. Franklin thereby implied that Leeds was not entitled to the heraldic arms. "The next Talent requisite in the forming of a *compleat Almanac-Writer*, is a Sort of Gravity, which keeps a due medium between Dulness and Nonsence, and yet has a Mixture of both." People commonly take grave men for wise men. "And to compleat an Almanac-maker, in this particular, he shou'd write Sentences, and throw out Hints, that neither himself, nor any Body else can understand or know the Meaning of. . . . I will give you some Instances of this Way of Writing, which are almost inimitable, such as these, *Leeds, Jan. 23. 1736. Beware, the Design is suspected*. Feb. 23. *The World is bad with somebody*. Mar. 27. *Crimes not remitted*. April 10. *Cully Mully puff appears*. May 21 *The Sword of Satan is drawn*. June 7. *The Cat eat the Candle*." Though the expressions were absurd in themselves, Philomath/Franklin made them more so by supposing that they were connected: "Now, Sir, Why should the Sword of Satan be drawn to kill the Cat on the 21st Day of *May*, when it plainly appears in Print, that the Cat did not eat the Candle till the 7th of *June* following? This Question no Man but an Astrologer can possibly answer." Thus Franklin made gibberish of Leeds's nonsense.

"In the next Place, I lay it down as a certain Maxim or Position, that *an Almanack-Writer shou'd not be a finish'd Poet, but a Piece of one*, and qualify'd to write, what we vulgarly call Doggerel; and that his Poetry shou'd bear a near

Resemblance to his Prose." To emphasize the dreadful quality of Leeds's poetry, Franklin cited Lord Roscommon's translation of Horace on writing, and then quoted some wretched verse from Leeds's almanac of December 1736. "I do not pretend to say, that this is like the Poetry of *Horace*, or Lord *Roscommon*, but it is the Poesy of an Astrologer; it is his own and not borrowed; It is occult and mysterious. It has a due Degree of that Sort of Gravity, which I have mentioned." Franklin proclaimed Leeds a pretentious impostor as an aristocrat and a dunce in both prose and poetry. And yet, there is self-satire in the essay, for Philomath/Franklin, like Leeds, compiled "those *Labours of the Learned*, called ALMANACS."

Accurate Predictions

In 1737 Poor Richard reminded his audience that this was the fifth almanac in which he had foretold "what shall, and what may, and what may not come to pass; in which I have the Pleasure to find that I have given general Satisfaction." A few predictions had failed, but "'tis well known that a small Error, a single wrong Figure overseen in a Calculation, may occasion great Mistakes: But however we Almanac-makers may *miss it* in other Things, I believe it will be generally allow'd *That we always hit the Day of the Month*, and that I suppose is esteem'd one of the most useful Things in an Almanac." The foolish naïf seemed to triumph in knowing what day follows Monday and how many days are found in each month. Franklin also mocked his popularity, for almanacs were primarily useful as calendars.

Poor Richard claimed that if he followed the method of his brother almanac maker John Jerman on weather predictions, and said, "*Snow here or in New England,—Rain here or in South-Carolina*," etc., he would never be detected in his errors, but the predictions would be of no use. "Therefore I always set down positively what Weather my Reader will have, be he where he will at the time." Franklin, if not Poor Richard, made it clear that his weather predictions must be false—for they were the exact same for tidewater Virginia as for the mountains of Pennsylvania. Poor Richard claimed that he only asked the reader "the favourable Allowance of *a day or two before* and *a day or two after* the precise Day against which the Weather is set." But if the prediction failed to come about, "let the Fault be laid upon the Printer, who 'tis very like, may have transpos'd or misplac'd it, perhaps for the Conveniency of putting in his Holidays." Since people insisted on giving him "great part of the Credit of making my Almanacs, 'tis but reasonable he should take some share of the Blame." Poor Richard thanked the public and told "the generous Purchaser of my Labours" that if he "could see how often his *Fi'pence* helps to light up the comfortable Fire, line the Pot, fill the Cup and make glad the Heart of a poor Man and an honest good old Woman, he would not think his Money ill laid out" even if the almanac "were one half blank Paper."

BRIDGET SAUNDERS

The 1738 almanac had a delightful preface, supposedly written by Poor Richard's wife, Bridget Saunders: "My good Man set out last Week for *Potowmack*, to visit an old Stargazer of his Acquaintance, and see about a little Place for us to settle and end our Days on. He left the Copy of his Almanac seal'd up, and bid me send it to the Press. I suspected something, and therefore as soon as he was gone, I open'd it, to see if he had not been flinging some of his old Skitts at me." What a wonderful character Franklin created in a few words! Curious, a little suspicious, bold (at least where her husband is concerned), somewhat dismissive of him and his occupation ("an old Stargazer"), concerned about what others think about her, and a rapid talker full of passion, Bridget nevertheless has the direct, humble, human appeal of her husband in desiring "a little Place for us to settle and end our Days on." Though she appears in her own voice only once, Bridget is a more fully developed and interesting individual than Poor Richard. The best original contribution to the *Poor Richard* prefaces, she is one more example of Franklin's androgynous imagination and his delight in playing roles in the battle of the sexes. She belongs in the gallery of Franklin's best feminine characters, who begin with Silence Dogood and Betty Diligent and later include Polly Baker and Madame Gout.

Franklin awakened the reader's curiosity about what Poor Richard has said about his wife—and then, of course, deliberately suspended the answer. "Just as I thought, so it was. And truly, (for want of somewhat else to say, I suppose) he had put into his Preface, that his Wife *Bridget*—was this, and that, and t'other.—What a peasecods! cannot I have a little Fault or two, but all the Country must see it in print! They have already been told, at one time that I am proud, another time that I am loud, and that I have got a new Petticoat, and abundance of such kind of stuff; and now, forsooth! all the World must know, that *Poor Dick's* Wife has lately taken a fancy to drink a little Tea now and then. A mighty matter, truly, to make a Song of!" Her colloquial diction and the rushed, vernacular rhythms of her syntax are distinctive. The mild "sin" that Poor Richard intended to report—and that she, almost inadvertently, revealed to justify herself—is perfectly in keeping with the attributes that Poor Richard had supplied about his wife in the second almanac. With more money, she had progressed from the necessities of life to its luxuries. Of course she vindicated her action.

"'Tis true; I had a little Tea of a Present from the Printer last Year; and what, must a body throw it away? In short, I thought the Preface was not worth a printing, and so I fairly scratch'd it all out, and I believe you'll like our Almanac never the worse for it." So much for the labors of Poor Richard. She also may be assuming some credit for the past productions of "our" almanac. Bridget Saunders added that she found too much foul weather predicted and so put in some "*fair, pleasant, sunshiny*, &c. for the Good-Women to dry their Clothes in.

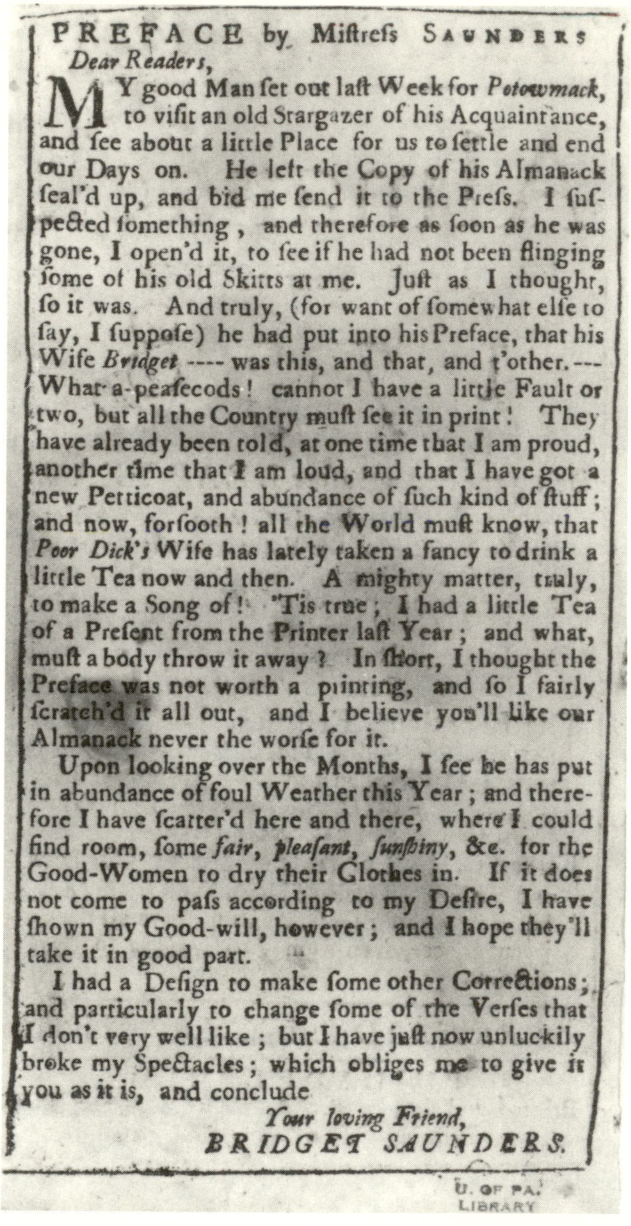

Figure 10. Poor Richard's wife, Bridget, trashes her husband's preface and writes her own in Poor Richard *for 1738. Franklin pretended that Bridget opened the sealed almanac copy, found herself slightly criticized, threw away Poor Richard's preface, and substituted hers. Bridget's colloquial diction ("What a peasecods!"), self-justifying, impatient character ("cannot I have a little fault or two"), her little foibles (tea was a luxury item), the rivalry between the husband and wife (she thought his preface not worth printing), and her goodwill to the reader all create a delightful skit. Bridget Saunders is one of Franklin's many wonderful feminine personae. Like his sayings, Franklin's prefaces are superior to those in other almanacs: the characters of Poor Richard and Bridget are more interesting, and the contents more dramatic and humorous. Courtesy, University of Pennsylvania.*

If it does not come to pass according to my Desire, I have shown my Good-will, however; and I hope they'll take it in good part." She concluded by saying that she meant to revise the poetry, but "just now unluckily broke my Spectacles" and so had to send off the almanac without further changes.

Readers loved it. Did they believe it? No more than we believe the movies we see—but some are better than others. And no almanac preface was ever more entertaining than the one Bridget Saunders wrote. Every year readers bought more *Poor Richards*. Franklin said in his *Autobiography* that it "came to be in such Demand that I reap'd considerable Profit from it, vending annually near ten Thousand" (A 93). It became the second bestselling American almanac (Nathaniel Ames's *Astronomical . . . Almanac* dominated the New England market). Franklin's account books suggest that he printed more copies every year until 1743, when he achieved about 10,000. The later accounts (which are more complete) of his partner David Hall show that slightly more than 10,000 copies were printed annually from 1752 to 1765.[18]

ASTROLOGY

The 1739 almanac ridiculed astrology. For the satire, Franklin made Poor Richard as colloquial as—but more vulgar than—he previously appeared. Poor Richard said that while the reader was "putting Pence in my Pocket, and furnishing my Cottage with Necessaries," he was watching the stars carefully, "that thou mayst be acquainted with their Motions, and told a Tale of their Influences and Effects, which may do thee more good than a Dream of last Year's Snow." Franklin, if not Poor Richard, here undercut the value of the "Influences and Effects" of astrology: "Ignorant Men wonder how we Astrologers foretell the Weather so exactly, unless we deal with the old black Devil. Alas! 'tis as easy as pissing abed. For Instance; The Stargazer peeps at the Heavens thro' a long Glass." If he sees Taurus in motion, "swinging his Tail about, stretching out his Neck, and opening wide his Mouth," he concludes that the bull is "puffing, blowing, and roaring. Distance being consider'd, and Time allow'd for all this to come down, there you have Wind and Thunder." Or he watches Virgo: "she turns her Head round as it were to see if any body observ'd her; then crouching down gently, with her Hands on her Knees, she looks wistfully for a while right forward. He judges rightly what she's about: And having calculated the Distance and allow'd Time for it's Falling, finds that next Spring we shall have a fine *April* shower." The explanations are absurd, and the scatological suggestion that rain is a goddess's urine mirrored Franklin's contempt for astrology.

He continued with a mock panegyric: "O the wonderful Knowledge to be found in the Stars! Even the smallest Things are written there, if you had but Skill to read. When my Brother *J—m-n* erected a Scheme to know which was best for his sick Horse, to sup a new-laid Egg, or a little Broth, he found that the Stars plainly gave their Verdict for Broth, and the Horse having sup'd his Broth;—Now, what do you think became of that Horse? You shall know in my next." Franklin satirized astrology by pretending that it answered the most mundane questions. "J—m-n" referred to John Jerman, author of the *American Almanac*, which Franklin sometimes printed.

For the first time Poor Richard mentioned the proverbs and maxims in the almanac, apologizing that some were light and humorous. Herein, Franklin almost dropped his Poor Richard mask. He said he hoped the clergy would excuse him for "scattering here and there some instructive Hints in Matters of Morality and Religion." On the other hand, he apologized for "trifling now and then, and talking idly." His reason was that "squeamish Stomachs cannot eat without Pickles; which, 'tis true are good for nothing else, but they provoke an Appetite. The Vain Youth that reads my Almanac for the sake of an idle Joke, will perhaps meet with a serious Reflection, that he may ever after be the better for." In fact, these early prefaces contained few of the proverbs concerning industry and economy that he was to gather together and augment in "The Way to Wealth"— the name by which his preface to the 1758 almanac is best-known. He concluded the 1739 almanac by reporting that because the almanac sold well, some people thought he must by now be rich and so should stop calling himself "Poor Richard." But he replied that when he first made an almanac, he agreed with the printer to terms that gave the printer almost all the profit. Poor Richard, however, does not "grudge it him; he is a Man I have a great Regard for, and I wish his Profit ten times greater than it is." So Franklin concluded the preface with a little joke.

At the almanac's end, Franklin imitated Rabelais's Pantagruelian prognostications. Among other subjects, Poor Richard wrote "Of the Diseases this Year":

> This Year the Stone-blind shall see but very little; the Deaf shall hear but poorly; and the Dumb shan't speak very plain. And it's much, if my Dame Bridget talks at all this Year. Whole Flocks, Herds and Droves of Sheep, Swine and Oxen, Cocks and Hens, Ducks and Drakes, Geese and Ganders shall go to Pot; but the Mortality will not be altogether so great among Cats, Dogs and Horses. As for old Age, 'twill be incurable this Year, because of the Years past. And towards the Fall some People will be seiz'd with an unaccountable Inclination to roast and eat their own Ears: Should this be call'd Madness, Doctors? I think not.—But the worst Disease of all will be a certain most horrid, dreadful, malignant, catching, perverse and odious Malady, almost epidemical, insomuch that many shall run Mad upon it; I quake for very Fear when I think on't; for I assure you very few will escape this Disease; which is called by the learned Albumazar, *Lacko'-mony*.

LEEDS'S SECOND DEATH

Titan Leeds died in 1738, and the Bradfords, who had been publishing his almanac, announced his death in the Leeds almanac for 1739, claiming that he had left them materials for the next several years' almanacs. Poor Richard took up the death of Leeds in his 1740 almanac: "You may remember that in my first Almanac, published for the Year 1733, I predicted the Death of my dear Friend *Titan Leeds*, Philomat. to happen that Year on the 17th Day of *October*, 3h. 29m. *P.M.* The good Man, it seems, died accordingly: But *W[illiam]. B[radford].* and *A[ndrew]. B[radford].* have continued to publish Almanacks in his Name ever since; asserting for some Years that he was still living; At length when the Truth could no longer be conceal'd from the World, they confess his Death in their Almanac for 1739, but pretend that he died not till last Year, and that before his Departure he had furnished them with Calculations for 7 Years to come. Ah, *My Friends,* these are poor Shifts and thin Disguises; of which indeed I should have taken little or no Notice, if you had not at the same time accus'd me as a false Predictor; an Aspersion that the more affects me, as my whole Livelyhood depends on a contrary Character."

Poor Richard had not exorcised Titan Leeds's ghost. During the night of 4 October, "towards midnight," as Poor Richard "sat in my little Study writing this Preface, I fell fast asleep" and when he awakened, he found "lying before me the following Letter": "Dear Friend Saunders, My Respect for you continues even in this separate State, and I am griev'd to see the Aspersions thrown on you by the Malevolence of avaricious Publishers of Almanacks, who envy your Success. They say your Prediction of my Death in 1733 was false, and they pretend that I remained alive many Years after. But I do hereby certify, that I did actually die at that time, precisely at the Hour you mention'd, with a Variation only of *5 min. 53. sec.* which must be allow'd to be no great matter in such Cases. And I do farther declare that I furnish'd them with no Calculations of the Planets Motions, &c. seven Years after my Death, as they are pleased to give out: so that the Stuff they publish as an Almanac in my Name is no more mine than 'tis yours." Though Franklin began with a possibly spooky subject, he made the ghost as friendly as Casper. The slightly awkward syntax (unusual for Franklin) in the last sentence is deliberate. Though the ostensible meaning is that the Bradford almanacs are not by Titan Leeds, Franklin joked and said that the materials in his own almanac are not by Poor Richard—but by Franklin and the host of proverb writers from whom Franklin borrowed.

In a flight of fancy that used the technique of the tall tale, the departed spirit of Leeds explained to Poor Richard how he wrote the paper Poor Richard found on his desk: "You must know that no separate Spirits are under any Confinement till after the final Settlement of all Accounts." Until that "final Settlement," spirits wander about, "visit our old Friends, observe their Actions, enter sometimes into their Imaginations, and give them Hints waking or sleeping that may be of Advantage to them." Then Franklin told his microcosmic tall tale, piling on realistic detail to create an extravagantly impossible event: "Finding you asleep, I entred your left Nostril, ascended into your Brain, found out where the Ends of those Nerves were fastned that move your right Hand and Fingers, by the Help of which I am now writing unknown to you; but when you open your Eyes, you will see that the Hand written is mine, tho' wrote with yours."

The spirit of Titan Leeds gave three predictions to convince Poor Richard that he was telling the truth. First, "About the middle of June next, J. J[erma]n, Philomat, shall be openly reconciled to the Church of Rome, and give all his Goods and Chattles to the Chappel." Second, on 7 September, "my old Friend W. B——t shall be sober 9 Hours, to the Astonishment of all his Neighbours," and third, "W[illiam] B[radford] and A[ndrew] B[radford] will publish another Almanac in my Name, in spight of Truth and Common-Sense." Poor Richard said that he believed the letter to be genuine, and that if the reader had any doubts, he should be convinced if the predictions came true (2:246–47).

In his *American Almanac* for 1741, John Jerman protested that Poor Richard's prophecy regarding his conversion to Roman Catholicism was "false and untrue." Franklin, swamped with printing jobs relating to the Great Awakening throughout 1740, did not write a preface for the 1741 *Poor Richard*. Instead he filled the page with a chronology of important dates since the birth of Christ (a standard item in the final pages of the earlier *Poor Richard*s), and filled page three with a list of England's kings.

Jerman a Roman Catholic

In the 1742 *Poor Richard*, Franklin claimed that the success of his almanacs "must be ascrib'd" to the charity of readers, "excited by the open honest declaration I made of my Poverty at my first Appearance." His success has produced imitators, a *Poor Will* and a *Poor Robin*, "and no doubt *Poor John*, &c will follow, and we shall all be *In Name* what some Folks say we are already *in Fact*, A Parcel of *poor Almanac Makers!*" He listed the questions that a successful astrologer was supposedly plagued with:

> The perpetual Teasing of both Neighbours and Strangers, to calculate Nativities, give Judgments on Schemes, erect Figures, discover Thieves, detect Horse-Stealers, describe the Route of Run-aways and stray'd Cattle; the Crowd of Visitors with a 1000 trifling Questions; *Will my Ship return safe? Will my Mare win the Race? Will her next Colt be a Pacer? When will my Wife die? Who shall be my Husband, and HOW LONG first? When is the best time to cut Hair, trim Cocks, or sow Sallad?* These and the like Impertinences I have now neither Taste nor Leisure for. I have had enough of 'em. All that these angry Folks can say, will never provoke me to tell them where I live. I would eat my Nails first.

Since many people bite their nails, the oath was amusing. The catalogue of questions was expertly done, with a surprisingly vicious question, "When will my Wife die?" and a sexual innuendo, "HOW LONG," mixed in with the humdrum.

Franklin returned to his philomath competitors, recalling John Jerman's claim in his 1741 almanac that Poor Richard's prophecy that he would turn

Roman Catholic was "false and untrue." But Poor Richard said that Jerman's 1741 almanac itself confirmed his reconciliation with the Church of Rome. First, Jerman called 1 November "*All Hallows Day*. Reader; does not this smell of Popery? Does it in the least savour of the pure Language of Friends?" As all contemporaries knew, the Friends called Sunday "first day," Monday, "second day," etc., deliberately avoiding the names of pagan gods. Franklin added another mock charge: "But the plainest Thing is; his Adoration of Saints, which he confesses to be his Practice, in these Words, page 4.

> When any Trouble did me befal,
> To my dear *Mary* then I would call:

Did he think the whole World were so stupid as not to take Notice of this? So ignorant as not to know, that all Catholicks pay the highest Regard to the *Virgin-Mary*?" Though Franklin had printed his almanacs for the past two years, Jerman became upset with Franklin's teasing and replied in his almanac for 1743 that because of Franklin's "facetious Way of proving me *no Protestant*" Jerman would not give "the *Printer* of that witty Performance" his almanac "for this Year." Franklin's preface to *Poor Richard* for 1743 was disappointing, giving only directions for making wine. He was probably simply too busy with other printing jobs and an extraordinarily long fall meeting of the Pennsylvania Assembly (14 October–6 November) to write a preface.

HUMAN NATURE

Poor Richard's preface for the 1744 almanac revealed Franklin's own contempt for human vanity rather than Poor Richard's humble, pleasant and humorous persona of the early almanacs. "This is the Twelfth Year that I have in this Way laboured for the Benefit—of Whom?—of the Publick, if you'll be so good-natured as to believe it; if not, e'en take the naked Truth, 'twas for the Benefit of my own dear self; not forgetting in the mean time, our gracious Consort and Dutchess the peaceful, quiet, silent Lady Bridget." Franklin returned to satirizing John Jerman, who in his almanac for 1743 predicted an eclipse on 1 April 1744 that would show "Heat, Difference and Animosities between Persons of the highest Rank and Quality." Poor Richard said there was no truth in the prediction. "And I caution his Readers (they are but few, indeed, and so the Matter's the less) not to give themselves any Trouble about observing this imaginary Great Eclipse. . . . I leave him to settle the Affair with the Buyers of his Almanac as well as he can, who perhaps will not take it very kindly, that he has done what in him lay (by sending them out to gaze at an invisible Eclipse on the first of April) to make *April Fools* of them all." Franklin had begun in 1740 by kidding Jerman in good humor, but here he degenerated into petulant criticism.

THE USE OF ALMANACS

The almanac for 1745 again abandoned the Poor Richard persona and instead gave impersonal directions for identifying planets. The 1746 preface was in verse, giving "slight Sketches of my Dame and me." The poem briefly described the typical chores of the farmer and his wife, then portrayed the moral condition of the couple. The first four lines are by Franklin and the whole poem may be, but it is so typical of the verse in "The Happy Man" and *beatus vir* traditions that it may well be adapted (as are most of the poems in the almanacs) from an earlier model. The preface to *Poor Richard* for 1747 expanded the discussion of the almanac's contents found in the 1739 preface. Franklin said that he hoped the almanac would be profitable to the reader because of the maxims and sayings interspersed throughout the almanacs, "many of them containing *much good Sense* in *very few* Words, and therefore apt to leave *strong* and *lasting* Impressions on the Memory of young Persons." He again apologized for inserting jokes, "since perhaps for their Sake light airy Minds peruse the rest, and so are struck by somewhat of more Weight and Moment." He also confessed again that most of the poetry was borrowed. He concluded by celebrating the deceased Philadelphia almanac maker Jacob Taylor. Franklin said that for forty years Taylor had produced "the most compleat Ephemeris and most accurate calculations that have hitherto appear'd in America. He was an ingenious Mathematician, as well as an expert and skilful Astronomer; and moreover, no mean Philosopher, but what is more than all, He was a Pious and an Honest Man." Franklin had celebrated Taylor in similar terms in the 11 March 1746 *Gazette* obituary where he mentioned Taylor's former position as Pennsylvania's surveyor general. The 1747 almanac was the last one in a twenty-four-page format. The following year, Franklin imitated Jacob Taylor's thirty-six-page almanac, under the title *Poor Richard Improved*.

Conclusion

Poor Richard was one of the four key elements in Franklin's business. The newspaper, the almanac, the position as printer to the legislature, and the willingness to gamble as a printer-publisher-partner all contributed to Franklin's becoming the dominant printer of colonial America. His *Pennsylvania Gazette* made an immediate impact with Franklin's editorial comments on the Massachusetts political scene, and *Poor Richard* made an even greater initial impact with the prediction of Titan Leeds's death.

Today, perhaps the most surprising fact about Poor Richard's almanac is the continuing identification of Franklin with the persona Poor Richard. Franklin used hundreds of personae, but no other one has as frequently been used as synonymous with the actual Franklin. Among the possible reasons are the knowledge that Poor Richard was a mask of Franklin, the popularity of the *Poor Richard* almanac in the colonial period, the appeal of the persona (yet no one calls Franklin Bridget Saunders), the deliberate play in the almanacs between the persona and the publisher, the concern with identity, and the instability of the persona—but none of these possible considerations explains why Franklin has been so often identified with Poor Richard.

Franklin was rarely called Poor Richard in his own lifetime. The tradition started after his death, probably in part because of the popularity of "The Way to Wealth" in the nineteenth and twentieth centuries. Comparatively few people have read the *Poor Richard* almanacs, but many have read "The Way to Wealth." As a result of the popularity of that preface to the 1758 almanac, the idealistic Franklin came to be identified with materialism. At the same time, the self-portrait in the *Autobiography* presents Franklin with a familiarity characteristic of no other famous founder of the United States. The combination of familiarity and materialism created a mythical "Poor Richard" with whom later generations could identify and feel friendly—and could also condescend to.

Poor Richard, the impoverished, impractical, humble astrologer, living in the country (presumably on a small, neglected farm), is an endearing intellectual. His concern with his identity, playfully recorded in prefaces to both the 1736 and 1739 almanacs, reflects Franklin's interest in the relationship among literature, culture, and the Third Realm. Jonathan Swift would have scorned (even more than did his persona, Isaac Bickerstaff) any identification with Partridge, but Franklin invited and played upon the identification with Poor Richard. The shrewd businessman-printer and man of letters, Benjamin Franklin, transformed himself into the naive, simple, henpecked, humble lover of astrology and of learning, Poor Richard. The Third Realm was moving from the world of Milton, Swift, Bayle, Voltaire, and Hume to the poor farmer, in great part because of the "democratic literacy inherent in the technology of print."[19] Franklin's egalitarianism permitted him to express and value this insight while playing the simple role of Poor Richard. That imaginary persona flatters us. Franklin as Poor Richard is more accessible than the fiercely hardworking Franklin who was a dominant figure in the second half of the eighteenth century in science, literature, and statesmanship.

EIGHT

Poor Richard's *Proverbs*

To lengthen thy Life, lessen thy Meals.—June 1733

If you wou'd have Guests merry with your cheer, / Be so your self, or so at least appear.—December 1734

The noblest question in the world is What Good may I do in it?—December 1737

What you would seem to be, be really.—March 1744

9 Men in 10 are suicides.—October 1749

FRANKLIN'S LOVE FOR AND USE OF PROVERBS was partially a deliberate literary and political statement, identifying himself with the common man. He frequently used them in other writings besides *Poor Richard*.[1] His informal and often colloquial prose and his use of proverbs were among the reasons that some later would-be aristocratic Americans scorned him.[2] But his prose style, as I pointed out in concluding the discussion of Franklin as a journalist (Volume 1, Chapter 18), became characteristic of American journalism and American literature. Franklin knew the eighteenth-century theories concerning writing and agreed with Joseph Addison in preferring a simple style, but he outdid Addison by cultivating a colloquial quality, as we have seen in comparing Franklin's first Silence Dogood essay with the *Spectator*.[3] He inserted proverbs and aphorisms in *Poor Richard* wherever space in the monthly calendars allowed. Most almanacs contained proverbs, and those in *Poor Richard* differed only in being superior. However, eighteenth-century genteel men of letters, like Jonathan Swift and John Gay, disdained proverbs. Lord Chesterfield, whose letters to his son are a standard source for eighteenth-century conduct, wrote: "Old sayings and common proverbs . . . are . . . proofs of having kept bad and low company."[4]

In contrast, James Howell observed in his 1659 collection: "Proverbs may be called the truest Franklins or Freeholders of a country; they have no other parent but the People, being Traditional Sayings, Precepts, and Memorandum, handed over as it were from Father to Son, Mother to Daughter, from Nurse to Children time out of mind."[5] Howell's usage of *Franklins* would no doubt have especially appealed to Franklin, who twice in the *Autobiography* cited authorities to prove that the name *Franklin* "was anciently the common name of an order or rank in England" (A 176).

Franklin wrote that he observed *Poor Richard* "was generally read" and that he consequently "consider'd it as a proper Vehicle for conveying Instruction among the common People, who bought scarce any other Books. I therefore filled all the little Spaces that occur'd between the Remarkable Days in the Calendar, with Proverbial Sentences, chiefly such as inculcated Industry and Frugality, as the Means of procuring Wealth and thereby securing Virtue, it being more difficult for a Man in Want to act always honestly, as (to use here one of those Proverbs) *it is hard for an empty Sack to stand upright*" (A 93–94). Though that proverb is among the few repeated in later almanacs (found in slightly different versions in 1740, 1750, and 1758), Franklin incorrectly remembered that the proverbs mainly concerned prudential and economic virtues. In 1739, he more accurately described the almanac proverbs: "Be not thou disturbed, O grave and sober Reader, if among the many serious Sentences in my Book thou findest me trifling now and then, and talking idly. In all the Dishes I have hitherto cook'd for thee, there is solid Meat enough for thy Money. There are Scraps from the Table of Wisdom that will, if well digested, yield strong Nourishment to thy Mind. But squeamish stomachs cannot eat without pickles; which, 'tis true, are good for nothing else, but they provoke an Appetite." Humor and references to sex, as we will see, are frequent in the proverbs.

Most proverbs in *Poor Richard* were quoted from previous collections. He especially relied on James Howell's *Lexicon Tetraglotton* (1659) in the early almanacs (1733–42); Thomas Fuller's *Gnomologia* (1732) in the almanacs 1745–51; and George Herbert's *Outlandish Proverbs* (1640) in those for 1753–54 and 1757.[6] Franklin selected the particular proverbs from among thousands of possibilities because they appealed to him or because he thought they would appeal to, and be good for, his audience. His proverbs are better known than those of other almanac makers partly because he often revised and improved the old sayings. He also created some. Though the subjects were more suitable to his times and to his audience—the early and mid-eighteenth-century farmers of Pennsylvania and the neighboring colonies—than to contemporaries today, most people today will find some of his proverbs striking.

TECHNIQUES OF REVISION

Because Professor Robert H. Newcomb identified the collections of proverbs that Franklin used, he was able to document the specific form of the sayings that Franklin revised. I rely on his identifications of the originals in the following comparisons.[7] Franklin's revisions can be roughly grouped under one or more of the following seven stylistic changes. 1) He often made the language of an old proverb more simple and modern, and, consequently, his versions seem more natural. 2) He sometimes added sentiments that made the proverbs more pointed and/or obvious. 3) He sometimes improved an old saying by making it shorter and more pungent, perhaps because the narrow almanac columns demanded brevity. 4) He made other proverbs more immediate and dramatic. 5) He used balance and antithesis, often employing natural opposites or continuing a metaphor. 6) Special categories of balance and antithesis are rhyme and alliteration. He used them to make some expressions more memorable. 7) He sometimes emphasized possible sexual readings.

Anyone who studies the proverbs will find additional ways that Franklin revised proverbs, but these seven are common. Many revisions use several of the techniques and could have been categorized under more than one heading.

Simplicity

Franklin often made the language seem more natural, as well as simpler. His versions seem modern, while the originals often seem antiquated. He took the saying "Nor the absent is without fault, nor the present without excuse" and changed it to "The absent are never without fault, nor the present without excuse" (July 1736). A revision cited herein, "What maintains one Vice, would bring up two Children" (September 1747), could have just as well have been included in a list of those that he changed in order to attain better balance and antithesis.

Original	Franklin's Revision
"Now that I've a Sheep and an Ass, every body bids me good morrow."	"Now I have a sheep and a cow everybody bids me good morrow" (June 36; Preface 58).
"God restoreth health and the physician hath the thanks."	"God heals and the doctor takes the fee" (November 1736).
"That cheese is wholesomest which comes from a Miser."	"The misers cheese is wholesomest" (February 1737).
"Who will have a handsome Wife let him choose her upon Saturday and not upon Sunday."	"If you want a neat Wife, chuse her on Saturday" (October 1737).
"Go neither to the Physician upon every distemper, nor to the Lawyer upon every brabble, nor to the pot upon every thirst."	"Don't go to the doctor with every distemper, nor to the lawyer with every quarrel, nor to the pot for every thirst" (November 1737).
"When thou receivest a kindness, remember it: when thou restorest one, forget it."	"When befriended, remember it: When you befriend, forget it" (November 1740).
"To err is human, to repent is divine, to persevere is diabolical."	"To err is human, to repent divine, to persist devilish" (November 1742).
"Experience teacheth fools; and he is a great one that will not learn by it."	"Experience keeps a dear school, yet Fools will learn in no other" (December 1743); in the Preface, 1757: "Experience keeps a dear School, but Fools will learn in no other, and scarce in that."
"He that loves Life, and yet wears out Time, squanders away the stuff that Life is made of."	"Dost thou love Life, then do not squander Time, for that's the Stuff Life is made of" (June 1746).

"The maintaining of one vice, costeth more than ten virtues."

"What maintains one Vice, would bring up two Children" (September 1747; Preface 58).

"We may give good Council, but cannot bestow good Conduct."

"We may give Advice, but we cannot give Conduct" (February 1751; Preface 58).

"Praise reproaches, when applied to the undeserving."

"Praise to the undeserving, is severe Satyr" (November 1752).

"Great merit is coy. Coyness has not always its foundation in pride."

"Great merit is coy, as well as great Pride" (August 1752).

"A great Talker may be a man of Sense, but he cannot be one, who will venture to rely on him."

"A great Talker may be no Fool, but he is one that relies on him" (February 1753).

"A discontented man knows not where to sit easy."

"The discontented Man finds no easy Chair" (December 1753).

"A gloved cat can catch no mice."

"The Cat in Gloves catches no Mice" (March 1754; Preface 1758).

Greater Meaning or Clarity

To the original saying, "He is a greater Liar than an epitaph," Franklin added a personification and made the saying stronger. "Here comes *Glib-tongue*: who can out-flatter a Dedication; and lie, like ten Epitaphs" (December 1742). Another saying was simply a cynical observation: "In a corrupted Age the putting the World in order would breed Confusion"; Franklin added an application making it more meaningful: "In a corrupt Age, the putting the World in order would breed Confusion; then e'en mind your own Business" (September 1758).

Original	Franklin's Revision
"Necessity has no law."	"*Necessity* has no Law; I know some Attorneys of the name" (October 1734).
"Men never play the fool more than by endeavouring to be overwise."	"A learned blockhead is a greater blockhead than an ignorant one" (November 1734).
"Hope is the poor man's bread."	"Hope and a Red-Rag, are Baits for Men and Mackrel" (December 1742).
"A small Leak will sink a great Ship."	"Beware of little Expenses, a small Leak will sink a great Ship" (January 1745; Preface 58).
"It is much like a Blacksmith with a white silk Apron."	"What's proper, is becoming: See the Blacksmith with his white Silk Apron" (July 1746).
"The brave and the wise know both how to pity and excuse."	"The Brave and the Wise can both pity and excuse; when Cowards and Fools shew no Mercy" (October 1752).
"What's a Sun-dial in the Shade good for?"	"Hide not your Talents, they for Use were made. What's a Sun-dial in the Shade" (October 1752).

"The morning sun never lasts the day."

"For Age and Want save while you may; No Morning Sun lasts a whole Day" (November 1754; Preface 1758).

Pungency

Franklin shortened "The greatest talkers are the least doers" to "Great Talkers, little Doers" (April 1733). Besides being more pungent, the last revised proverb in the following list has a better antithesis and a better (because more emphatic) ending.

Original	Franklin's Revision
"It is better to have an egg today than an hen to-morrow."	"An Egg today is better than a Hen tomorrow" (September 1734).
"Some crosses, and fits of sickness do well with a strong or proud man."	"After crosses and losses, men grow humbler and wiser" (April 1737).
"Be not lazy; and thou shalt have no occasion to wish."	"Industry need not wish" (October 1739; Preface 1758).
"A Thing well done is twice done."	"Well done, is twice done" (September 1741).
"The Fox who sleeps in the morning hath not his tongue feathered."	"The sleeping Fox catches no poultry. Up! Up! (September 1743), and in "The Way to Wealth" he dropped the "Up! Up!" (1758).
"The Way to be safe, is never to be secure."	"He that's secure is not safe" (August 1748).
"Plain dealing is dead and died without issue."	"Poor Plain dealing! Dead without issue" (September 1750).
"One Man may be more cunning than another, but not more cunning than every body else"	"You may be too cunning for One, but not for All" (September 1750).
"Success has blown up, and undone, many a man."	"Success has ruined many a Man" (December 1752).
"To understand the World, and to like it, are two things not easily reconciled."	"He that best understands the World, least likes it" (June 1753).
"A Man had as good go to Bed to a Razor, as to be intimate with a foolish friend."	"To be intimate with a foolish Friend, is like going to bed to a Razor" (September 1754).
"Tomorrow is still the fatal time when all is to be rectified; tomorrow comes, it goes, and still I please myself with the shadow, whilst I lost the reality, unmindful that the present time alone is ours, the future is yet unborn, and the rest is dead."	"*To-morrow*, every Fault is to be amended; but that *To-morrow* never comes" (July 1756).
". . . when high blood and generous breeding breake their fast in plenty, and dine in poverty, they often sup in infamy. . . ."	"Pride breakfasted with Plenty, dined with Poverty, and supped with Infamy" (June 1757).
"Half the Truth is often as arrant a Lye, as can be made."	"Half the Truth is often a great Lie" (July 1758).

Immediacy

Franklin often made the old sayings more immediate and dramatic. Thus, "Vanquish thy own Wishes and Desires, and the Chariot of Triumph belongs more truly to thee than to Caesar" became "Caesar did not merit the triumphal Car, more than he that conquers himself" (April 1738).

Original	Franklin's Revision
"Is't not enough Plagues, Wars, and Famines rise / To lash our crimes, but must our wives be wise? / Famine, Plague, War, and an unnumber'd throng / of guilt-avenging ills to man belong."	"Famine, Plague, War, and an unnumber'd throng / Of Guilt-avenging Ills to Man belong; / Is't not enough Plagues, Wars, and Famines rise / To lash our crimes, but must our Wives be wise?" (December 1734).
"Do thou drive thy business; let not that drive thee."	"Drive thy business; let not that drive thee" (November 1738). "Drive thy Business, or it will drive thee" (September 1744).
Franklin combined three sayings: 1) "Calamity is the test of integrity"; 2) "In great Prosperity, as well as in great Calamity, we ought to look into ourselves, and *fear*"; and 3) "Calamity is the touchstone of a brave mind."	"Calamity and Prosperity are the Touchstones of Integrity" (March 1752).
"Most Mens Anger about Religion is as if two Men should quarrel for a lady they neither of them cared for."	"Many have quarrel'd about Religion, that never practis'd it" (June 1753).
"Men should do with their hopes as they do with tame fowl, cut their wings that they may not fly over the wall."	"Cut the Wings of your Hens and Hopes, lest they lead you a weary Dance after them" (February 1754).
"The tongue talks at the head's cost."	"The Tongue offends, and the Ears get the Cuffing" (November 1757).
"Resolving to serve well, and at the same time to please, is generally resolving to do what is not to be done."	"To serve the Publick faithfully, and at the same time please it entirely, is impracticable" (October 1758).

Balance and Antithesis

Franklin emphasized balance and antithesis, often employing natural opposites or continuing a metaphor. "That which is given shines, that which is eaten stinks," a possibly puzzling statement, became an ironic comment on human nature: "What's given shines, What's receiv'd is rusty" (July 1735).

Original	Franklin's Revision
"Do good to all; that thou mayest keep thy Friends, and gain thy Enemies."	"Do good to thy Friend to keep him, to thy enemy to gain him" (July 1734).
"He that payeth beforehand, shall have his Work ill done."	"He that pays for Work before it's done, has but a pennyworth for twopence" (March 1739).
"Who riseth late, trots all day, because he is behind hand with business."	"He that riseth late, must trot all day, and shall scarce overtake his business at night" (August 1742; Preface 1758).
"If you are too fortunate, you will not know yourself. If you are too unfortunate, no Body will know you."	"None know the unfortunate, and the fortunate do not know themselves" (February 1747).

"Despair hath damn'd some, but Presumption Multitudes."

"Despair ruins some, Presumption many" (July 1747).

"The Fox may grow gray but never good."

"Many Foxes grow grey, but few grow good" (March 1749).

"Neglect will kill an Injury sooner than Revenge."

"Neglect kills Injuries, Revenge increases them" (September 1749).

"The greatest punishment that can be inflicted on us would often be the grant of our own wishes."

"If Man could have Half his Wishes, he would double his Troubles" (October 1752).

"Nothing can be humbler than Ambition, when it is so disposed."

"Nothing Humbler than *Ambition*, when it is about to climb" (November 1753).

"Infamy is where it is received. If thou art a mud wall, it will stick; if marble, it will rebound."

"Act uprightly, and despise Calumny; Dirt may stick to a Mud Wall, but not to polish'd Marble" (September 1757).

Alliteration and Rhyme

Franklin made some expressions more memorable with alliteration or rhyme. "A Melon and a woman are hard to be known" became "Men and Melons are hard to know" (September 1733). (The proto-feminist Franklin may have chafed at the singling out women in the old saying.)

Original	Franklin's Revision
"A woman, a guest, and rain are wearisome after three days."	"After 3 days men grow weary, of a wench, a guest, and weather rainy" (June 1733).
"A ship under sail, a man in complete armor, a woman with a great belly are three of the handsomest sights."	"A ship under sail and a big-bellied Woman, / Are the handsomest two things that can be seen common" (June 1735).
"There be more old drunkards than old physicians."	"There's more old Drunkards than old Doctors" (April 1736).
"Dine with little, sup with less, sleep high, and thou wilt live."	"Dine with little, sup with less: / Do better still; sleep supperless" (April 1744).
"A quiet Conscience sleeps in Thunder."	"A quiet Conscience sleeps in Thunder, / But Rest and Guilt live far asunder" (July 1747).
"To a wise Man, Living is Thinking."	"Life with Fools consists in Drinking; With the wise Man Living's Thinking" (April 1748).
"He has a Mouth for every Matter."	"Henry Smatter has a Mouth for every Matter" (September 1748).
"To prove to be like Ears of Corn, viz. The fuller they are, the more they stoop, and humble themselves."	"*Youth* is pert and positive, *Age* modest and doubting: So Ears of Corn when young and light, stand bolt upright, But hang their Heads when weighty, full, and ripe" (May 1751).
"Little boats must keep the shore."	"Great Estates may venture more; / Little Boats must keep near Shore" (October 1751; Preface 1758).
"Men take more pains to hide than to mend themselves."	"Men take more pains to mask than mend" (April 1757).

Sex

Franklin sometimes accentuated or created possible sexual readings. In the first revision below, Franklin featured the sexual interpretation by ending with it. He also made the saying more homely and more American, for apple cider was, after water, the most common colonial drink.

Original	Franklin's Revision
"Nor wife, nor wine, nor horse ought to be praised."	"Never praise your cyder, Horse, or Bed-fellow" (March 1736).
"Who paints her face thinks on her Tail."	"She that paints her Face, thinks of her Tail" (May 1736)
"The good wife is made by the man."	"Good wives and good plantations are made by good husbands" (August 1736).
"Forewarn'd forearm'd."	"Forwarn'd, forearm'd, unless in the case of Cuckolds, who are often forearm'd before warn'd" (September 1736).
"The Woman who hearkens, and the town which treats, the one will yield, the other will do."	"Neither a Fortress nor a Maidenhead will hold out long after they begin to parly" (May 1734).
"Who spins well hath a large frock."	"The good Spinner hath a large Shift" (April 1742). "The diligent Spinner has a large Shift" (June 1756; Preface 1758).

ORIGINAL SAYINGS

The original sayings substantiate major aspects of Franklin's thought. One that reveals his pessimism is "9 Men in 10 are suicides" (October 1749). The Franklin scholar Whitfield J. Bell commented, "On any of several levels we know, to our regret, what he meant."[8] Another original one disclosed his belief that few persons aspired to be thoroughly good, but many attempted to be famous: "Strive to be the *greatest* Man in your Country, and you may be disappointed; Strive to be the *best*, and you may succeed: He may well win the race that runs by himself" (January 1747). A third on human nature was, like the last, somewhat pessimistic. Though the first three parts often occurred separately, the arrangement and conclusion are original: "*Who is wise?* He that learns from every One. *Who is powerful?* He that governs his Passions. *Who is rich?* He that is content. *Who is that?* Nobody" (July 1755).

In an early letter (6 January 1726/7), Franklin told his sister Jane that he had been thinking of sending her a tea table but decided on a spinning wheel. The former represented conspicuous consumption and needless expense, whereas the latter suggested industry and production. Franklin used the opposition in his first almanac to create a new sententia: "Many estates are spent in the getting, / Since women for tea forsook spinning and knitting" (July 1733). When the proto-feminist repeated it years later, he added, "And Men for Punch forsook Hewing and Splitting" (preface, 1758). A seemingly sexist saying also turned out to be feminist: "One good Husband is worth two good Wives: for the scarcer things are the more they're valued" (July 1742). A saying on money was original: "There are three faithful friends, an old wife, an old dog, and ready money" (January 1738).

Franklin's sociability, as well as his appreciation of the difference between appearance and reality, showed in a sententia on hospitality: "If you wou'd have Guests merry with your cheer, / Be so your self, or so at least appear" (December 1734). Another saying showed a cynicism concerning human nature—or what some might consider an insight into psychology. "A quarrelsome Man has no good Neighbours" (February 1746). Another may concern psychology—or simply common sense: "There was never a good Knife made of bad Steel" (June 1755). Attempting to inculcate civility and good manners, *Poor Richard* said, "None but the well bred man knows how to confess a fault, or acknowledge himself in an error" (November 1738). Just as Franklin practiced tolerance in religious beliefs, he recommended forbearance in manners: "He is not well-bred, that cannot bear Ill-Breeding in others" (November 1748).

Franklin wrote new sententiae on industry: "Industry need not wish" (October 1739; preface, 1758); "Industry pays Debts, Despair encreases them" (November 1742; preface, 1758); "Industry, Perseverance, and Frugality, make Fortune yield" (April 1744); and "God gives all Things to Industry" (October 1755; preface, 1758). Two related original proverbs do not use the word: "No man e'er was glorious, who was not laborious" (March 1734), and "Time enough always proves little enough" (November 1747).

Though many of his original proverbs have been mentioned here, others will be found in the following discussion of topics that frequently appear both in Franklin's other writings and in *Poor Richard*.

Subjects of the Proverbs

Franklin appreciated Addison's and Steele's attempts to ameliorate manners through the *Spectator* and *Tatler* essays, and in this purpose, his almanacs imitated them. Franklin was a keen observer of behavior and wanted to make early eighteenth-century society more polite and considerate. The almanacs also reflected Franklin's other values, as well as his interests and opinions. When the sayings echo ideas found in Franklin's writings, they may be read as a guide to his opinions.

Moral philosophy was a frequent topic of eighteenth-century writers and is perhaps the most frequent subject in the proverbs. As seen in Chapter 2, "The Art of Virtue," other than those professionally concerned with religion, Franklin wrote more on human nature, theology, ethics, virtue, and doing good than any other colonial American. Though pessimistic and cynical about human nature, he was also idealistic. Idealism appears in the proverbs on moral philosophy, sometimes in conjunction with cynicism, especially in the proverbs on pleasure and love. The second most important cluster of topics in the proverbs concern democracy and egalitarianism. From his satires in the *New-England Courant* in his teens to his speeches in the Constitutional Convention as an eighty-one-year-old man, Franklin was among the most egalitarian Americans. These subjects are also common in the almanacs' poems and prose.

Some subjects of the almanacs' prose pieces that are among Franklin's major interests are only minor subjects in the proverbs. Fundamental questions of philosophy rarely appear, though Franklin's appreciation of the difference between appearance and reality, his suspicion of absolutes, and his relativism sometimes surface, together with his concern for what constitutes human identity. Science does not occur in the proverbs, though it is often a subject of the longer prose pieces in the almanacs, with brief essays on plants, the Copernican system, and the microscope; but it does not lend itself to treatment in proverbs. Finally, humor and coarseness are mentioned below because they often appear in his writings about pride, human nature, and himself.

The sayings in *Poor Richard* concerning industry and frugality are minor in any single year. They are famous because they were gathered together, and others added, in the preface to the 1758 almanac. That extraordinarily popular preface is what people have generally read, not the original proverbs. The preface, sometimes called "Father Abraham's Speech" or more commonly, "The Way to Wealth," will be discussed in Volume 3.

Behavior

Poor Richard noted in June 1748 that Addison's "writings have contributed more to the improvement of the minds of the British nation, and polishing their manners, than those of any other English pen whatever." Courtesy made life more agreeable. Franklin wrote that "a Person of good Breeding . . . should make it his chief Aim to be well with all" (June 1757). Earlier, he observed, "To be humble to Superiors is Duty, to Equals Courtesy, to Inferiors Nobleness" (October 1735); and "He that can compose himself, is wiser than he that composes books" (April 1737). He advised, "Be not niggardly of what costs thee nothing, as courtesy, counsel, and countenance" (August 1739). Knowing that early American society respected wealthy persons, Franklin, somewhat ironically, defined a *gentleman*: "Money and good Manners make the Gentleman" (March 1742). He was ambivalent about the meaning of *ceremony*, for it had an implication of mere show (and was associated with nobility and courts), though he cited the proverb "A Man without ceremony has need of great merit in its place" (April 1745). Seven years later, he distinguished between ceremony and politeness (i.e., civility): "Ceremony is not Civility; nor Civility Ceremony" (October 1752). And he finally directly condemned ceremony: "*Friendship* cannot live with *Ceremony*, nor without *Civility*" (June 1754).

Franklin said in the *Autobiography* that he paid little attention to what food or drink he was eating, a practice that served him well in foreign countries when his better-instructed companions were unhappy with their food and drink (A 9). He said the same in *Poor Richard*, though he there also suggested his disgust with the supposed gentleman of taste. "How happy is he who can satisfy his hunger with any food, quench his thirst with any drink, please his ear with any musick, delight his eye with any painting, any sculpture, any architecture, and divert his mind with any book or any company! How many mortifications must he suffer, that cannot bear any thing but beauty, order, elegance and perfection! *Your man of* taste, *is nothing but a man of* distaste" (October 1748). That conclusion also exemplifies Franklin's characteristic reversal of ordinary opinions, here captured in its own rhetorical reversal. He stated in October 1751, "Nice Eaters seldom meet with a good Dinner."

Though the former vegetarian included temperance among his list of thirteen virtues in the *Autobiography*, he warned more against eating too much when he was young and slender than he did in middle age: "Eat to live, and not live to eat" (May 1733). In an original saying, he wrote, "To lengthen thy Life, lessen thy Meals" (June 1733). Warnings against overeating occur in most of the early almanacs: "Hot things, sharp things, sweet things, cold things / All rot the teeth, and make them look like old things" (February 1734); "Be temperate in wine, in eating, girls, and sloth; / Or the Gout will seize you and plague you both" (February 1734); "Deny Self for Self's sake" (August 1735); "I saw few die of Hunger, of Eating 100,000" (November 1736); "The excellency of hogs is fatness, of men virtue" (August 1736); "Three good meals a day is bad living" (September 1737); "Eat few Suppers, and you'll need few Medicines" (August 1742).

Franklin warned against drunkenness not only in essays and news articles but also in *Poor Richard*. "Nothing more like a Fool, than a drunken Man" (November 1733). He also wrote an original maxim on drinking in his first almanac, "He that drinks fast, pays slow" (August 1733). "Drink Water, Put the Money in your Pocket, and leave the *Dry-bellyach* in the *Punchbowl*" (September 1734). Denying a commonplace cliché ("Drink drowns care"), he made an original saying, "*Drink* does not drown *Care*, but waters it, and makes it grow faster" (May 1749). "Drunkenness, that worst of Evils, makes some Men Fools, some Beasts, some Devils" (December 1751).

Human Nature

As his newspaper writings testify, Franklin was interested in fundamental questions concerning human nature. After examining the crowd's behavior at the intended execution of Prouse and Mitchel, he concluded that humans were naturally benevolent, wishing well to others. On the other hand, he thought the doctrine that this world was "the true hell" (17:315–16) aptly described the behavior of men to one another. He anticipated Melville's perception in "Hawthorne and his Mosses": "In certain moods, no man can weigh this world, without throwing in something, somehow like Original Sin, to strike the uneven balance."[9] Though Franklin denied the doctrine of original sin (2:114), he was pessimistic about human nature, sarcastically observing that "Providence . . .

has given every Man a natural Inclination to backbite his Neighbour" (7 September 1732). The proverbs in *Poor Richard* confirm his pessimism.

Five cynical proverbs appeared in his first almanac: "He's a Fool that makes his Doctor his Heir" (February 1733). "The poor have little, beggars none, the rich too much, *enough* not one" (May; repeated, April 1740). A third said, "After 3 days men grow weary, of a wench, a guest, and weather rainy" (June); a later variant read, "Fish and visitors stink in 3 days" (January 1736). Fourth, "Distrust and caution are the parents of security" (July). The fifth said, "The old Man has given all to his Son: O fool! to undress thy self before thou art going to bed" (October 1733). Like sons, other family members might not love the deceased: "Onions can make ev'n Heirs and Widows weep" (October 1734).

Franklin said in the *Autobiography* that persons could find or make reasons "for every thing one has a mind to do" (A 35). In creating a reason, one often deceived oneself. "It's common for Men to give 6 pretended Reasons instead of one real one" (February 1745). "Who has deceiv'd thee so oft as thy self?" (January 1738). "It's the easiest Thing in the World for a Man to deceive himself" (April 1746). "Are you angry that others disappoint you? remember you cannot depend upon yourself" (December 1735). Nor could one depend upon others: "None are deceived but they that confide" (February 1740). Repeating a cynical saying (Robert Frost later liked it), Franklin cited: "Love your Neighbour; yet don't pull down your Hedge" (April 1754). In an eighteenth-century version of "No pain; no gain!" he wrote: "The Things which hurt, instruct" (October 1744). He came closer to the modern saying in April 1745: "No Gains without Pains," which became "There are no Gains without Pains" in the 1758 preface.

Pride

Allied to his pessimism concerning human nature was his vision of mankind's vanity. In 1725 Franklin concluded his *Dissertation on Liberty and Necessity* with "Mankind naturally and generally love to be flatter'd: Whatever sooths our Pride, and tends to exalt our Species above the rest of the Creation, we are pleas'd with and easily believe, when ungrateful Truths shall be with the utmost Indignation rejected" (1:71). Vanity characterized human nature. In *Poor Richard* for August 1749, he wrote of pride: "*Pride* is said to be the *last* vice the good man gets clear of. 'Tis a meer *PROTEUS*, and disguises itself under all manner of appearances, putting on sometimes even the mask of *humility*. If some are proud of neatness and propriety of dress; others are equally so of despising it, and acting the perpetual sloven." A number of his proverbs repeated the sentiment: "Sal laughs at every thing you say. Why? Because she has fine Teeth" (November 1735); "*Pride* and the *Gout* are seldom cur'd throughout" (June 1747). Persons constantly blinded themselves to truth or reality by believing whatever they wanted (and especially whatever they needed) to believe.

Concerning pride and the world's end in *Poor Richard* for 1757, he said: "We must not presume too much on our own Importance. There are an infinite

Number of Worlds under the divine Government, and if this was annihilated it would scarce be miss'd in the Universe" (7:91; cf. "Articles of Belief," Volume 1, Chapter 15). Poor Richard remarked in October 1734, "As sore places meet most rubs, proud folks meet most affronts." After Franklin read, "The first degree of folly is to *hold* oneself wise, the second to profess it, the third to despise counsel," he made one change: "The first Degree of Folly, is to *conceit* one's self wise . . ." (January 1754; emphasis is mine). Franklin asserted in March 1745, "*Vanity* backbites more than *Malice.*" He printed the seemingly paradoxical statement, "The Proud hate Pride—in others" (December 1751). That proverb is directly taken from La Rochefoucauld, whose cynical *sententiae* on pride supplied Franklin with more sayings in *Poor Richard* than those of any other single author. As A. Owen Aldridge commented, La Rochefoucauld's worldly maxims are "the *locus classicus* in western literature for the doctrine of self-love."[10] Poor Richard observed, "Men often *mistake* themselves, seldom *forget* themselves" (November 1758). On the other hand, he praised humility: "Humility makes great men twice honourable" (June 1735).

Franklin often expressed cynicism about human nature: "He that speaks ill of the Mare, will buy her" (August 1742). The following year he recommended a constant reserve, "Let all Men know thee, but no man know thee thoroughly: Men freely ford that see the shallows" (July 1743). In June 1739 he printed, "Let thy Discontents be Secrets." And in April 1741 he explained, "Let thy discontents be thy Secrets; if the world knows them, 'twill despise *thee* and increase *them.*" Of secrets, he noted, "Three may keep a Secret, if two of them are dead" (July 1735). He ironically commented in November 1750, "The Golden Age never was the present Age." He came across a saying in 1752 that appealed to him, but he resented its discrimination between farmers and their "betters," so he revised it and added an ironic conclusion. The original saying was "The clown, as well as his betters, practices what he censures, and censures what he practices." Franklin wrote: "Mankind are very odd Creatures: One Half censure what they practise, the other half practise what they censure; the rest always say and do as they ought" (June 1752).[11] He repeated a savage proverb on human nature in February 1751, "Many a Man would have been worse, if his Estate had been better." The same year, he revised the following, "The greatest punishment that can be inflicted on us would often be the grant of our own wishes," shortening it and adding an antithesis and a terminal rhyme: "If a Man could have Half his Wishes, he would double his Troubles" (October 1752).[12] Elsewhere he gave an example of getting one's wish: "All would live long, but none would be old" (September 1749). He observed, "Good Sense is a Thing all need, few have, and none think they want" (June 1746).

Some comments may reflect Franklin's personal history. In 1734, as he was becoming a successful businessman, he wrote, "In success be moderate" (March 1734). In the last *Poor Richard* he prepared, he twice seemed to reflect on his career as an assemblyman and politician: "The first Mistake in publick Business, is the going into it" (July 1758), and "To serve the Publick faithfully, and at the same time please it entirely, is impracticable" (October 1758).

Though most of Franklin's comments on human nature were cynical or pessimistic, many were realistic and shrewd. In April 1734 he wrote, "If you ride a Horse, sit close and tight, / If you ride a Man, sit easy and light." The following proverb might be thought cynical: "Would you persuade, speak of Interest, not of Reason" (June 1734). He gave advice in November 1743 that John Paul Jones read and followed in 1778 and therefore named his ship *Le Bonhomme Richard*, "If you'd have it done, Go: If not, send." Franklin commented on the difficulty of self-knowledge: besides the several proverbs quoted above on deceiving oneself, he wrote, "There are three Things extreamly hard, Steel, a Diamond and to know one's self" (January 1750).

Franklin observed to his son on 16 August 1784, "Our Opinions are not in our own Power; they are form'd and govern'd much by Circumstances, that are often as inexplicable as they are irresistible." In *Poor Richard*, too, he noted that humans had dispositions they could not control: "He that hath no *ill* Fortune, will be troubled with good" (November 1754); and "They who have nothing to be troubled at, will be troubled at nothing" (July 1741 and September 1742). He made the same point in a letter commenting on the characteristics of two old friends, Stephen Potts and William Parsons, saying that happiness depends on internals rather than externals and that "there is such a thing as being of a happy or an unhappy constitution" (8:160). So, too, he wrote in *Poor Richard*, "Some ancient Philosophers have said, that Happiness depends more on the inward Disposition of Mind than on outward Circumstances; and that he who cannot be happy in any State, can be so in no State" (November 1757). He took the thought a step further in a letter of 24 November 1786: "all among us may be happy, who have happy dispositions, such being necessary to happiness even in Paradise" (S 9:548).

Though Franklin wrote that the "greatest of Pleasures to a benevolent Mind, [is] the giving Pleasure to others" (1:249), he wrote as Poor Richard, "Nothing brings more pain than too much pleasure; nothing more bondage than too much liberty, (or libertinism)" (February 1738). He ironically commented, "He that falls in love with himself, will have no Rivals" (May 1739). Most sayings on pleasure and love made good sense: "If you'd be belov'd, make yourself amiable" (November 1744). He revised it in February 1755: "If you would be loved, love and be loveable" (February 1755). And he shortened it in May 1756: "*Love, and be lov'd*." Of pleasure, he wrote, "Fly Pleasures, and they'll follow you" (May 1738; preface, 1758); and "Who Pleasure gives, / Shall joy receive" (May 1734).

Theology and Ethics

As we have seen, though Franklin divorced religion from ethics, he kept the traditional Christian values. Instead of basing them on the Bible or theology, he grounded them on secular utility. As Poor Richard said, "Sin is not hurtful because it is forbidden but it is forbidden because it's hurtful. Nor is a Duty beneficial because it is commanded, but it is commanded, because it's beneficial" (October–November 1739).

The most common criticism of Franklin as a young man was that he was irreligious. He often advised himself to correct the appearance if not the reality of disbelief. He repeatedly advised others and himself not to satirize religion. Finally, on 13 December 1757, he wrote an essay (in the form of a letter) against satirizing religion. Earlier, in *Poor Richard*, he had written, "Eyes and Priests / Bear no Jests" (March 1735; April 1739). In September 1742 he warned, "You will be careful, if you are wise; / How you touch Men's Religion, or Credit, or Eyes." He repeated the moral in September 1751, "Talking against Religion is unchaining a Tyger; The Beast let loose may worry his Deliverer." A prose passage in *Poor Richard* for June 1757 anticipated part of the 13 December letter: "sarcastical Jests on a Man's Person or his Manners, tho' hard to bear, are perhaps more easily borne than those that touch his Religion. Men are generally warm in what regards their religious Tenets, either from Tenderness of Conscience, or a high Sense of their own Judgments. People of plain Parts and honest Dispositions, look on Salvation as too serious a Thing to be jested with; and Men of speculative Religion, who profess from the Conviction rather of their Heads than Hearts, are not a bit less vehement than the real Devotees. He who says a slight or a severe Thing of their Faith, seems to them to have thereby undervalued their Understandings, and will consequently incur their Aversion, which no Man of common Sense would hazard for a lively Expression; much less a Person of good Breeding, who should make it his chief Aim to be well with all" (7:82). In this rationale, the main reason not to satirize religion is simply civility—it offends good manners.

Despite repeatedly warning himself, Franklin willy-nilly succumbed, even in *Poor Richard*. In a clever, original sententia, where the cadence and content both suggest that the last word should be nonsense (rather than things invisible), he wrote, "Men differ daily, about things which are subject to Sense, is it likely then they should agree about things invisible" (January 1743). When he paired two sentences, he insulted both ministers and religion: "When Knaves fall out, honest Men get their goods: When Priests dispute, we come at the Truth" (June 1742). He recalled in his *Autobiography* that he wasted his time reading his father's books of "polemic Divinity" (A 11), and he wrote in November 1743, "Many a long dispute among Divines may be thus abridg'd, It is so: It is not so. It is so; It is not so." He implied in March 1748 that religion was merely self-comfort: "The Heathens when they dy'd, went to Bed without a Candle."

He occasionally directly attacked ministers and sermons. "*Sound*, and sound Doctrine, may pass through a Ram's Horn, and a Preacher, without straitening the one, or amending the other" (June 1750). That anticipated his comment to his daughter on 8 November 1764 that she should pay attention to sermons even though they came from "Preachers you dislike, for the Discourse is often much better than the Man, as sweet and clear Waters come to us thro' very dirty Earth" (11:450). In July 1736 Poor Richard quoted, "None preaches better than the ant, and she says nothing," and in June 1747, "A good Example is the best sermon." Franklin twice contrasted the spiritual world of faith with the practical world in which everyone lives. The first example anticipated the hypocrisies concerning trust that Melville explored in *The Confidence Man*. Franklin wrote, "In the Affairs of this World Men are saved, not by Faith, but by the Want of it" (June 1754; preface, 1758). The second suggested that reason contradicted religion: "The Way to see by *Faith*, is to shut the Eye of *Reason*: The Morning Daylight appears plainer when you put out your Candle" (July 1758). Mark Twain expressed the thought more idiomatically: "Faith is believing in what you know ain't so."[13]

Though Franklin was not a Christian (six weeks before his death, he acknowledged to Ezra Stiles that he had "some Doubts" as to the divinity of Christ), he thought that through the course of time, Christianity had gradually improved (S 9:303). In 1749 he praised the achievements of both Luther and Calvin. That same year he advocated a deistic approach to religion, implying that the fundamentals of religion were generally the same: "Different Sects like different clocks, may be all near the matter, 'tho they don't quite agree" (June). He wrote Benjamin Vaughan on 24 October 1788 concerning Joseph Priestley's reputation as a heretic, "all the heretics I have known have been virtuous men. . . . It is not to my good friend's heresy that I impute his honesty. On the contrary, it is his honesty that has brought upon him the character of heretic" (S 9:677). A similar thought caused him in October 1757 to add an ominous prefatory statement ("Singularity in the right, hath ruined many") to the sententia, "Happy those who are Convinced of the general Opinion."

Nothing was more common than the religious warning that God knew and saw everything one did. Franklin omitted religion and wrote, "Do not do that which you would not have known" (February 1736). Later Franklin came across a classical version of the thought: "Be fearful only of thyself; and stand in awe of none more than thine own Conscience. There is a Cato in every Man; a severe Censor of his Manners; and he that reverences this Judge, will seldom do anything he need repent of."[14] Franklin shortened the thought by replacing God with Cato: "Think Cato sees thee" (February 1741).

Virtue

As we have seen above (Chapter 2), Franklin devised a systematic approach to virtue that emphasized a gradual, bit-by-bit approach toward perfection. He set the approach forth in his list of thirteen virtues and method of attaining them, a discipline he probably began in the spring of 1731 and described in Part 2 of the *Autobiography*. *Poor Richard* condensed Franklin's plan: "Each year one vicious habit rooted out, / In time might make the worst Man good throughout"

(December 1738). Though Franklin borrowed the saying, he revised and improved it (the original read, "If every Year thou wouldst root out one vicious Habit, thou mightest, in some time, become perfect").[15]

In order to attain an end, one should have a "regular plan and design." In the "Plan of Conduct" (1:99) composed while returning from England in 1726, Franklin wrote that a plan was as necessary in life as in writing. Poor Richard echoed Franklin's earlier thoughts in June 1749: "It was wise counsel given to a young man, *Pitch upon that course of life which is most excellent, and CUSTOM will make it the most delightful. But many pitch on no course of life at all, nor form any scheme of living, by which to attain any valuable end; but wander perpetually from one thing to another." Pythagoras said the italicized part, which Franklin read in Addison's *Spectator* No. 447 and reprinted in the *Pennsylvania Gazette* on 24 June 1731.

Just before that "wise counsel" repeated by Poor Richard, he included a poem (I suspect Franklin wrote it) on the importance of habit and custom in preserving virtue (May 1749). Old habits could be changed by perseverance. Franklin believed that persistence was necessary to any success, and wrote an essay on constancy on 4 April 1734 (above, Chapter 2). Poor Richard wrote, "Little Strokes, / Fell great Oaks" (August 1750; preface, 1758), and advised, "In studying Law or Physick, or any other Art or Science, by which you propose to get your Livelihood, though you find it at first hard, difficult and unpleasing, use *Diligence, Patience* and *Perseverance*; the Irksomeness of your Task will thus diminish daily, and your Labour shall finally be crowned with Success" (July 1757; cf. P 14:344).

In his "Man of Sense" essay (Chapter 2), Franklin argued self-interest should make persons be virtuous, because virtue alone would lead them to that most desired ideal in life, happiness. That motif occurred in several other writings, as well as in some of the quotations above. It appeared in brief in the following sayings: "You may be more happy than Princes, if you will be more virtuous" (May 1738); "Virtue and Happiness are Mother and Daughter" (May 1746); and in May 1750, he gave the classical proverb quoted by Cicero: "Beatus esse sine Virtute, nemo potest" ("No one can be happy without virtue").

But what is virtue? At least thrice Franklin gave his fundamental credo: in December 1737 he echoed Cotton Mather when he wrote, "The noblest question in the world is *What Good may I do in it?*"[16] In September 1747 he put the belief in a religious context: "What is Serving God? 'Tis doing Good to Man." In November 1753 he could not resist a jab at praying: "Serving God is Doing Good to Man, but Praying is thought an easier Service, and therefore more generally chosen." On the other hand, perhaps thinking of the indefatigable labors of the sickly George Whitefield, he revised the riddle, "I spend myself to serve others, viz., a candle," and wrote, "The painful Preacher, like a candle bright, / Consumes himself in giving others Light" (February 1742). The civic-minded Franklin knew that persons joined together in associations could usually do more good than a single person. He gave his philosophy concerning associations in April 1757: "Man is but of a very limited Power in his own Person, and consequently can effect no great Matter merely by his own personal Strength, but as he acts in Society and Conjunction with others." The Library Company motto expresses Franklin's belief in the primary purpose of volunteer associations: *Communiter bona profundere deum est* (To pour forth benefits for the common good is divine).

Egalitarianism

Though Franklin frequently expressed egalitarianism, few people cared until he was elected to the Pennsylvania Assembly in 1751. Appreciations of ordinary persons and scorn for the idea of aristocracy appear throughout the almanacs. Two 1734 proverbs affirmed Franklin's democratic beliefs: "There have been as great Souls unknown to fame as any of the most famous" (July). "An innocent *Plowman* is more worthy than a vicious *Prince*" (August). He used the farmer again in 1746: "A Plowman on his Legs is higher than a Gentleman on his Knees" (May). *Clown* had "farmer" as one meaning, but Franklin chafed at that usage and redefined it in January 1736: "He is no clown that drives the plow, but he that doth clownish things." Just as Lord Chesterfield scorned proverbs, he also said that "bad pronunciation" was to be avoided.[17] Franklin, however, said, "Write with the learned, pronounce with the vulgar" (March 1738). He reinforced his satire of affected gentility in May 1746 (repeated in preface, 1758) with an original proverb, "For one poor Man there are an hundred indigent"; in October 1743, "Came you from Court? for in your Mien, / A self-important air is seen." In January 1745 and the 1758 preface, he quoted an egalitarian proverb ("Help, Hands; / For I have no Lands") that Captain John Smith had paraphrased in 1612: "My hands hath been my lands this fifteene yeares in Europ, Asia, Afric, or America."[18]

Complementing Franklin's egalitarianism is his scorn for the idea of aristocracy. In *Poor Richard* for November 1751, he mathematically showed that each "present Nobleman, to exclude all ignoble Blood from his Veins, ought to have had One Million, Forty-eight Thousand, Five Hundred and Seventy-six noble Ancestors" since the time of the Norman Conquest. He concluded that "the Pretension of such Purity of Blood in ancient Families is a mere Joke." In March 1745, he wrote, "All blood is alike ancient." In January 1733 and January 1739, he quoted the proverb "Kings and Bears often worry their keepers." When he came across the saying "The Kings cheese goes half away in parings; *viz*, among so many Officers," he changed it: "The King's cheese is half wasted in parings: But no matter, 'tis made of the peoples milk" (June 1735). In January 1748, "Robbers must exalted be, / Small ones on the Gallow-Tree, / While greater ones ascend to Thrones, / But what is that to thee or me?"

A person who would write such statements during the first half of the eighteenth century had the makings of a good revolutionary.

Appearance and Reality

Among the proverbs and sententiae that seem especially characteristic of Franklin are skeptical ones concerning the nature of reality. As we will see, he wrote on the philosophical nature of truth during the Hemphill trial (1735) and in an essay titled "What is True" (24 February 1742/3). Franklin posed questions concerning truth a number of times, always remaining skeptical: "Historians relate, not so much what is done, as what they would have believed" (March 1739). Moreover, he knew that "Philosophy as well as Foppery often changes Fashions" (January 1753).

Franklin often contrasted appearance and reality. He ironically commented on his failure to learn "humility" in the *Autobiography*: "I cannot boast of much Success in acquiring the *Reality* of this Virtue; but I had a good deal with regard to the *Appearance* of it" (A 90). He repeated two lines from John Gay's *Fables* in September 1740: "We frequently misplace Esteem / By judging Men by what they seem." In March 1744 he wrote his own saying on identity: "What you would seem to be, be really," and he paraphrased the proverb in an essay of August 1758: "Be *really* good, if you would *appear* so" (8:131). He gave excellent advice on entertaining, while adding an original, characteristic awareness of appearance and reality that might make the sentiment seem cynical: "If you wou'd have Guests merry with your cheer, / Be so your self, or so at least appear" (December 1734). At the same time, Franklin was always conscious of the importance and implications of appearance, and he advocated attempting to make infants happy, so that a pleasant expression might become habitual to them (18:253).

Humor and Coarseness

Franklin was famous for his humor, both in conversation and in writing. As a young man, he was esteemed as "a pretty good Riggite, that is a jocular verbal Satirist" (A 47). The English poet Paul Whitehead recognized Franklin's "American jokes" (20:439) even in an anonymous newspaper essay. John Bartram confirmed Franklin's personal and written humor in a letter to him dated 29 July 1757: "Pray my dear friend bestow A few lines upon thy ould friend such like as those sent from Woodbridge. They have A Magical power of dispeling malancholy fumes and chearing up my spirits, they are so like thy facetious discource in thy southern chamber when we used to be together." Franklin's delight in humor is reflected in the numerous punning proverbs cited above and in the revision of a couplet from Rochester, "As Charms are nonsense, Nonsense seems a Charm / Which hearers of all Judgment does disarm." Franklin's version emphasized the play on *charm* as superstition and ended with a neat chiasmus (a reversal of repeated words), "As Charms are nonsence, Nonsence is a Charm" (August 1734). As John Adams conceded, Franklin "was master of that infantine simplicity which the French call *naïveté* which never fails to charm, in

Phaedrus and La Fontaine, from the cradle to the grave."[19] He punned when advocating industry: "Strange, that he who lives by Shifts, can seldom shift himself" (October 1734). He used an ironic humor, homonym, and chiasmus in writing about debts: "'Tis against some Men's Principle to pay Interest, and seems against others Interest to pay the Principal" (January 1753). With a possible sexual application, Franklin quipped, "Old Boys have their Playthings as well as young Ones; the Difference is only in the Price" (August 1752).

An earthy quality often occurs in Franklin's prose and rarely in that of his major contemporaries—except, of course, Jonathan Swift. On 29 January 1722 James Franklin had quoted the Italian proverb "The Man who lives by Hope, will die by Hunger." Franklin's version said, "He that lives upon Hope, dies Farting" (February 1736). Later, he wrote a more genteel version: "He that lives upon Hope will die fasting" (preface, 1758). Franklin thought people too fond of criticizing others, and in 1741 he quoted John Gay, "E'er you remark another's Sin, / Bid your own Conscience look within" (April). But that does not contain the characteristic Franklinian note. Franklin read two other proverbs with the same moral, but neither was as devastating as Franklin's scatological version. One was, "He that commits a fault thinks everyone speaks of it," and the other, "The look of every person will be construed as a reproach, by one who is conscious of having capitally erred."[20] Franklin knew all three and wrote, "He that is conscious of a Stink in his Breeches, is jealous of every Wrinkle in another's Nose" (March 1751). Using anadiplosis (repetition of the last word of a phrase, clause, etc., to begin the next), Franklin wrote a pithy statement on virtue ending with a scatological note: "Relation without friendship, friendship without power, power without will, will without effect, effect without profit, and profit without vertue, are not worth a farto" (April 1733). Franklin used a vulgar pun when remarking on pride in June 1741: "Where yet was ever found the Mother, / Who'd change her booby for another?" He also introduced a scatological note in an anti-aristocracy proverb. The original sententia said, "And when seated upon the most elevated Throne in the World, we are but seated upon our Breech." Franklin changed it to "The greatest monarch on the proudest throne, is oblig'd to sit upon his own arse" (January 1737).

The sententia that I have chosen for the epigraph of this volume seems to me especially revealing of Franklin's taste and qualities. In Thomas Fuller's *Introductio ad Prudentiam* (1727), he read, "If thou wouldst win Immortality of Name, either do Things worth the Writing, or write Things worth the Reading." As he revised it, he thought of a common lugubrious verse on samplers, which in one version said, "When I am dead and all my bones are rotten / If this you see Remember me and never let me be forgotten." He put together and revised the learned saying and the folk rhyme. The combination of a folk and a scholarly saying seems typical of Franklin's egalitarianism, while at the same time the result is a mortifying attack on the high estate of mankind: "If you wou'd not be forgotten / As soon as you are dead and rotten, / Either write things worth reading; / Or do things worth the writing" (May 1738).[21]

A savage note sometimes occurs in Franklin. "The D——l wipes his B——ch with poor Folks Pride" (May 1743). "Force shites upon Reason's Back" (September 1736). He read "No naked man is sought after to be rifled" and wrote, "An hundred Thieves cannot strip one naked Man, especially if his Skin's off" (October 1755). The 1734 almanac contained three maxims concerning sex: "You cannot pluck roses without fear of thorns, / Nor enjoy a fair wife without danger of horns" (January); "Where there's Marriage without Love, there will be Love without Marriage" (May); and "Neither a Fortress nor a Maidenhead will hold out long after they begin to parly" (May). So, too, did the 1736 almanac: "She that paints her Face, thinks of her Tail" (May); "Why does the blind man's wife paint herself" (June); and "Three things are men most liable to be cheated in, a Horse, a Wig, and a Wife" (October). He returned to the face-tail opposition three years later: "Prythee isn't Miss Cloe's a comical Case? / She lends out her Tail, and she borrows her Face" (February 1739). The salacious, bawdy, and coarse elements in Franklin undercut the position of man as a superior, spiritual being and affirm the animality and grotesqueness of the human condition. John Adams wrote Thomas Jefferson about Franklin's scorn for the pretensions of philosophers to a life of pure reason: Franklin said they would happily abandon their high thoughts to "knaw a morsel of a damn'd Hogs Arse."[22]

CONCLUSION

The urban population of colonial America was small; more than 95 percent of the population was rural. Newspapers were delivered to subscribers who lived along postal routes and to those who lived in towns. Almanacs, however, were sold in every country store from November through January, and they were carried by chapmen in their packs throughout the country. They were sold throughout colonial America to an overwhelmingly rural audience. As Franklin noted, most people read little beside elementary schoolbooks, the Bible, and the annual almanac. Franklin had that rural audience primarily in mind in compiling his annual almanac. Nevertheless, he also wrote for himself as well as for the litterateurs among his contemporaries. They would have appreciated the imitations of Swift and Rabelais, whereas the ordinary farmer would have enjoyed the humor without recognizing the allusions. *Poor Richard* was of course more suitable for eighteenth-century farmers than today's readers. Though the proverbs had entertainment as one aim, they were also intended to instruct the reader in manners, values, and philosophy. Naturally the contents of the almanacs sometimes reflected Franklin's personal beliefs, but the contents more often were chosen for the rural audience of colonial America. The almanacs were important agents in the evolution of early American culture.

Franklin's personal style as an almanac writer is apparent in every *Poor Rich-*

ard from 1733 through 1757. Less than one-tenth of the sayings are original, but most of the others have been revised and improved, often not only in style but also in content. Though I have probably cited all the original sayings somewhere in the chapter, numerous additional examples of Franklin's improving the old proverbs could have been listed, as well as other stylistic techniques and further topics. Some materials in the almanacs may be read for intrinsic enjoyment, and some may be read for their insight into Franklin's mind and character. As an almanac maker, he had no peer. Characteristically, he viewed that achievement ironically.

NINE

Franklin and Politics

1730–1736

Franklin's burlesque of Isaac Norris, Sr.: Andrew Hamilton "abuses the Go[ver-no]r, and has endeavoured to displace him, for it is commonly reported, that he should say in a certain Place, that his Honour don't see now so well as when he was but one and twenty; and I my self with these very Eyes of mine, saw him once offer the arm'd Chair to the Pro[prieto]r when the Gov——r was present; Now if this was not a plain Attempt to displace his Honour, judge ye."—"A Half-Hour's Conversation with a Friend," 1:336–37

FRANKLIN'S EDITORIALS, NEWS REPORTING, AND EVEN MANY REPRINTED ITEMS in the *Pennsylvania Gazette* reveal his political positions. Eighteenth-century society was more hierarchical than today's, but Franklin was more egalitarian than most citizens of his society. Further, in his Americanism, he was nearly sui generis. Though some scholars have thought that he was not involved in Pennsylvania politics before being elected to the Pennsylvania Assembly in 1751 and others that he at first identified with the Proprietary (or Prerogative) Party,[1] in fact, he primarily and frequently sided with the Popular or Quaker Party throughout his career as a printer in Philadelphia (1729–47). Philosophically, the Popular Party was more democratic than the Prerogative Party—which, as the name implies, believed that the authorities should have more power than the elected representatives. With a few exceptions, even the members of the Popular Party expected some degree of prerogative in politics as well as in personal relations. Particular issues, however, were rarely a simple matter of prerogative.

The major issues in Pennsylvania politics during the colonial period were military defense, paper currency, taxation of the proprietors' estates, and the proprietors' secret instructions to the governors. During every colonial war, military defense became all-important, though the other matters all bore upon defense. In the colonies, the wars generally began earlier and lasted longer than the corresponding European wars between Great Britain and its enemies. Britain's War of Jenkins' Ear (1739–42) and King George's War (1744–48) were preceded by skirmishes between the English, French, and Spanish in America. The Spanish made warlike preparations in Florida before the outbreak of the War of

Jenkins' Ear, as did the French on the Western frontier before King George's War. During the 1730s, Americans who focused on imperial matters realized that a war with the Spanish and the French was inevitable. At stake was the North American continent. In Pennsylvania, though some Quaker leaders supported defense, the Quaker Party, especially the pacifists, opposed it. Franklin championed military defense. As we will see later in this chapter, on the military issue he was, in effect, a Proprietary Party leader.

Franklin was also the foremost supporter of a Pennsylvania paper currency from the appearance of Busy-Body No. 8 on 27 March 1729. Though paper currency remained controversial, it became less important in internal Pennsylvania politics after the early 1730s because most Pennsylvanians came to agree that it generally benefitted the economy. Nevertheless, the Proprietary Party generally opposed it, as did a number of established merchants (including a few Popular Party members) who were assembly members. Paper currency came to the fore again when British authorities questioned colonial paper currency bills. In 1740 the British government required all colonial currency bills to have royal approval before being approved; in 1751, Parliament forbade the New England colonies to use paper currency except in times of emergency; and in 1764 it prohibited paper money throughout the colonies. Franklin also sided with the Popular Party on three other major issues: 1) taxing the proprietors' estates (an issue that received more publicity later and was the major reason for Franklin's first mission to England in 1757–62), 2) revealing the proprietors' secret instructions to the governors, and 3) charging quitrents in Pennsylvania currency rather than in the more expensive sterling.

With the support of Andrew Hamilton, Speaker of Pennsylvania's House of Representatives, Franklin and Meredith were elected printers of the assembly's *Votes and Proceedings* on 30 January 1729/30 and, on 14 February, of its *Acts* (i.e., its laws). Being printer (the partnership with Meredith ended five months later on 14 July) to the legislature was a political and financial plum. It paid well and, more important, in a society where debts often ran for decades, it paid promptly. The legislature settled its accounts annually. Because the appointment was highly desired, printers to the legislatures were generally political sycophants; Franklin, however, was his own man.

AMERICANISM

Franklin imbibed the Old Charter beliefs of the popular Boston politicians of his boyhood. They replied to English mercantilism by taxing English goods imported into Massachusetts (the impost acts of 1715, 1716, 1717, and 1718). They resisted the British authorities' demand that a fixed salary be settled on the Massachusetts governor. They maintained that the British had illegally deprived them of their charter. They claimed that only the Massachusetts legislature could tax Massachusetts. And they objected to Englishmen being appointed to posts of profit in the Massachusetts government.[2] Franklin echoed these positions. He began the *Pennsylvania Gazette* in 1729 with an editorial on Massachusetts politics, siding with the Old Charter politicians against Governor William Burnet's demand for a fixed salary. The following year, Franklin satirized Burnet's successor, Governor Jonathan Belcher, in a vicious poetic fable ("The Rats and the Cheese") and declaimed against Belcher in a Junto speech in the spring of 1731 (see Volume 1, Chapter 18). He played upon the Americans' objections to "strangers" (i.e., non-Americans) being appointed as officials in American when he featured the news that a new governor had arrived in North Carolina, "accompanied by several Gentlemen, who are to have the chief Places of Profit and Trust in that Government" (27 May 1731). Franklin knew from reading and from talking with his contemporaries that many other Americans, in addition to New Englanders, objected to British claims of supremacy and superiority. In the previous generation, Virginians, especially the historian Robert Beverley, and Marylanders, like Thomas Bordley (d. 1727) and Ebenezer Cook, had manifested strong sentiments of Americanism.

Throughout 1729–36, Franklin waged a campaign to awaken Americans to what he considered the prejudice with which Great Britain treated the colonies. Parliament passed two new Acts of Trade and Navigation in the early 1730s, the Hat Act (1732) and the Molasses Act (1733). Though both especially penalized the New England colonies, they also affected Pennsylvania. The Hat Act tried in various ways to limit the making of hats in the colonies. Since it made its way through parliamentary committees and debates from two to four years before being passed, colonial American alarm against it mainly appeared before 1730. It therefore did not appear in Franklin's *Pennsylvania Gazette*, which began in October 1729. His enmity toward it, however, is clear because he quoted nearly the entire act in his hoax and satire, "An Edict by the King of Prussia" (22 September 1773).[3]

The *Pennsylvania Gazette* followed the progress of the Molasses Act closely. On 17 June 1731, Franklin noted that a bill for prohibiting the importation of rum, sugar, and molasses from the French and Dutch plantations into the New England colonies had passed both houses of Parliament: "What Effect this will have, as to raising or falling the Prices of those Commodities and of our Flour, & c. is left to the Judicious to consider." The act, he suggested, would raise the price of rum, sugar, and molasses purchased by Pennsylvania merchants and consequently depress the price of flour and other foods shipped from Pennsylvania. On 24 June he published "the mortifying News" of the Molasses Act's imminent passage. For at least June 1731 to July 1733, Franklin reprinted a host of articles from other colonial and English papers regarding it and, finally (14 and 21 September 1733), the act itself.[4]

While Parliament debated the Molasses Act, it also contemplated a bill "for Restraining our Northern Colonies from carrying Horses and Lumber to the Foreign Colonies." Franklin reprinted an article against the bill on 1 July 1731 from the (London) *Whitehall Evening Post* of 10 April. More galling to Franklin and to other Americans than the Molasses Act was the Board of Trade's instruction on 10 December 1731 that no duties or other taxes could be laid on slaves or convicts shipped to America.[5] Like the Maryland politician Thomas Bordley, who editorialized against earlier similar prohibitions in the *American Weekly Mercury* (14 February 1720/1),[6] and like Thomas Jefferson (who was not yet born in 1731) in the Declaration of Independence, Franklin chafed at the policy. He reprinted news of the offending instructions twice: once from Virginia (26 June 1732) and the following week in a news report from Massachusetts (3 July). By 1737, when he reported crimes he routinely noted if the criminals were transported felons. Later, as we will see, he viciously ridiculed the British policy in editorials and news reports (8 April 1751) and in his satire "Rattle-Snakes for Felons" (9 May 1751).

No other colonial paper printed so many pieces about the British Acts of Trade and Navigation. The acts irritated Franklin, who wanted Americans to know about them. He evidently believed that if Americans thought about the acts, they would resent them. On 31 July 1731, Franklin reprinted a typical English mercantile attack on goods manufactured in New England from the London *Daily Post Boy*, together with an excellent refutation. The 8 June 1732 *Gazette* noticed several anti-American mercantilist acts: one forbidding the importation of hops into Ireland from America; another forbidding exportation of hats from America; a third limiting the number of hat apprentices in the colonies (these last two were part of the Hat Act); and a fourth about the progress of the Molasses Act. On 28 December 1732, Franklin reprinted a summary of the Board of Trade's actions. He again replied to English mercantilism (31 January and 7 March 1738 *Gazette*) when he supported the Maryland tobacco growers' plan to ship tobacco directly to France rather than through England. Though the southern colonies unanimously supported the idea, the colonies north of Maryland generally ignored the issue. One might attribute Franklin's publicity concerning the plan and backing it simply to Philadelphia's being closer to the tobacco-growing region than more northern newspapers, but Andrew Bradford's *American Weekly Mercury* opposed it.[7]

Franklin followed the news of Parliament's treatment of the colonies and often reprinted it. Years later, he said that the foundation of the American Revolution was laid in Parliament's desire to subject the colonies to being governed by royal instructions.[8] He probably had in mind the memorial presented by the council and representatives of Massachusetts in 1733 to the House of Commons. The appeal set forth the difficulties the Massachusetts government labored under, arising from a royal instruction concerning the issuing and disposing of the public monies. The memorial also represented the problems caused by a royal instruction restraining the emission of bills of credit. The Massachusetts Assembly petitioned the House of Commons to take the case into consideration and become intercessors with the king, imploring him to withdraw the instructions as contrary to their charter. In reply, the House of Commons resolved that the complaint was "frivolous and groundless, an high insult" upon His Majesty's government. Further, Parliament said (10 May 1733) the request attempted "to shake off the dependency of the said colony upon the kingdom, to which, by law and right, they are, and ought to be, subject." The officially expressed fear of the possible future independence of the colonies no doubt made Franklin think that the colonies should indeed become independent—though the time was not ripe.

Franklin's responses to negative English attitudes concerning America can be found throughout his writings and his editorship of the *Pennsylvania Gazette*. We saw above how he satirized John Webbe's essay condescending to Americans (Chapter 6). He indirectly praised America in his obituary and newspaper reporting. Just as Franklin in his first editorial on Massachusetts politics satirized the supposed decline of the "gallant" English cocks and matchless dogs in America (9 October 1729), so he indirectly combated the idea of humans degenerating in America by celebrating the old age and numerous descendants of the first English inhabitants of Pennsylvania (as we saw in Volume 1, Chapter 1, Massachusetts newspapers did the same for early New Englanders). On 5 July 1739, he reported on the 115 descendants of Richard Buffington, aged at least eighty-five, whose "eldest Son, now in the Sixtieth Year of his Age, was the first born of English Descent in this Province."

CURRENCY

Franklin's ongoing interest in paper currency and the economy appeared in his anonymous *Pennsylvania Gazette* essay titled, "Remarks upon a South Carolina Currency Scheme" (31 May 1733). A series of articles in the *South Carolina Gazette* had proposed a new basis for a paper currency. Franklin began by summarizing the writer's proposal. The author had noted that the principal objection to a paper currency was its varying value. Paper money had first been printed in America about the beginning of the eighteenth century. Though intended only as a temporary measure, it had been continued by every government that tried it. Now, the author proposed a South Carolina semi-permanent paper currency to use until the colony's trade would allow the exchange of silver and gold. To prevent the paper's sinking in value, the author proposed that the interest be paid in silver and gold, and the paper bills be taken only in discharge of the principal.

Franklin had three reservations. First, since interest was now 10 percent in Carolina, if £50,000 in paper money (the amount mentioned) was issued out upon loan, £5,000 in silver and gold would be necessary annually to discharge the interest. The yearly demand for so much hard currency must prevent its exportation. Further, the planter must outbid the merchant in order to have silver or gold. If the planter gave 2 or 4 percent in paper currency for the hard currency, Carolina's interest rate would rise from 10 percent to 12 or 14 percent, thereby lessening the value of the Carolina bills, compared with silver and gold.

Second, if the merchant needed hard currency to pay for his merchandise, he would raise the price of his retail goods till he could afford to purchase the wholesale items. If the planter needed the merchandise, he would be forced to give a higher price than the wholesaler. Third, if the interest were all due at one time of the year, the value of silver at that time of the year would be higher and paper would be lower than at other times, thus making the currency continually vary in value. Having devastated the proposal, Franklin diplomatically concluded that his reservations might not be germane.

HAMILTON BESIEGED

In 1726, Hannah (d. 1727) and Springett Penn (d. 1732) had appointed Patrick Gordon the governor of Pennsylvania. After a long lawsuit concerning the proprietorship of Pennsylvania, the legal tangle was resolved in May 1732, with William Penn's three sons, John, Thomas, and Richard, becoming the proprietors. A new commission had to be issued to Gordon, and rumor reported that he was to be replaced. The Pennsylvania Assembly, meeting 6–11 August 1733, cast doubt upon Gordon's authority as governor. When the assembly (11 August 1733) said it would adjourn, Governor Gordon asked that it revive the excise on liquor and pass an act regulating flour. The assembly replied that it had sat a whole week and heard nothing from the governor until then. It called his request unreasonable and added "that entering into a farther Examination of the Reasons why they do not proceed upon Business at this Time, may not be agreeable to the Governor." The assembly then adjourned. The council recorded that the governor "understood that some Objections had been started in the House of Representatives to his Powers as Lieutenant Governor, for want of a new Commission with His Majesty's Royal Approbation from our present Honourable Proprietaries, and that the House for this Reason (tho' they were not willing to assign it publicly,) did not incline to proceed on any Act of Legislature." Governor Gordon found the assembly's reason insulting and held Speaker Andrew Hamilton particularly responsible.

In the small populations of the colonies, personal relations were even more important in politics than they are today. During this same summer of 1733, one of Governor Gordon's daughters charged Hamilton's son James with unbecoming conduct, and the governor and Speaker quarreled. Furthermore, both Isaac Norris, Sr., and Jr., opposed Hamilton. The combined opposition of the governor and a leading Quaker political family spelled trouble for Franklin's friend and patron. Perhaps for the first time since the defeat of Sir William Keith for Speaker in 1726 the Proprietary Party and important elements of the Quaker Party joined together against a politician. A piece in the *American Weekly Mercury* for 9 August attacking traitors probably targeted Hamilton. Franklin therefore wrote a poem, "Against Party-Malice and Levity, Usual at and Near the Time of Electing Assembly-Men," before leaving for a trip to New England, instructing that it be printed in the last issue of the *Gazette* before the election.

Then he set off on 30 August 1733, leaving a journeyman printer (who is not known) in charge of bringing out the paper. While Franklin was in New England, three attacks on Hamilton appeared in the *American Weekly Mercury*. Those on 13 and 20 September satirized (without naming) Hamilton as a traitor, and on 27 September a severe censure appeared under the pseudonym "Cato Jun." (probably Isaac Norris, Jr.), claiming that Hamilton exercised the "artful power" of an "ambitious ringleader."[9]

The next day under the pseudonym "Pennsylvanus," Franklin's poem appeared:

> Happy's the Man, who with just Thoughts, and clear,
> A steady Passage thro' this life can steer;
> Whom from his Course no gainful Bias draws;
> Nor speeds too fast, urg'd on by loud Applause;
> Nor shrinks with Fear, but holds his glorious Way
> Incessant, like the Ruler of the Day;
> Reason his Guide, and Truth his constant Aim,
> The great Protectors of a good Man's Name! (ll. 1–8)

Franklin stated the prevailing class prejudices: the rich versus the poor; the learned versus the unlettered (ll. 35–46). And he reminded the opposing groups that the wheel of fortune constantly revolved (ll. 47–52).

> Still, High for High, and Low for Low, will fight,
> O'erlooking all the mutual Rules of Right:
> By nothing is the Clash of Arms debar'd,
> But Flat'ry here, and there a hop'd Reward! (ll. 53–56)

Franklin urged that all electors vote and that they not be misled by either the candidate's education or his financial condition. The voter should look through appearances to the ability and the virtue of the candidates. Surprisingly, Franklin suggested that though some candidates were "Men of Sense, and Skill / Uprightness, Resolution, and Good-Will" (ll. 191–92), there were not enough to fill the "ticket" (l. 196):

> On his next Choice as hard a Task may lie,
> His part-fill'd Ticket fitly to supply. (ll. 195–96)

(The "ticket" or ballot was usually written by the voter. But sometimes parties gave out a ticket with the names included, which the voter used.) In closing, Franklin reiterated that voters should attempt to see through appearances and choose the virtuous candidates (ll. 205–8).

The poem neither calmed nor influenced the voters.

With Gordon and the Norrises campaigning against him, Hamilton was defeated on 1 October 1733. The opposition rejoiced: Cato Jun. trumpeted in the *Mercury* of 4 October, "When the Wicked Perish there is Shouting." Andrew

Bradford took the opportunity to criticize Franklin, publishing in the same *Mercury*: "Whereas great Complaint is made among the People in *New-Jersey*, for want of the Acts of Assembly which were passed at *Burlington* the last sitting of the Assembly, and many blame *Andrew Bradford*, supposing it his neglect in their not being Printed. These are therefore to acquaint the Publick, That the said Acts are not come to the Hands of the said *Andrew Bradford*, nor to his Father *William Bradford* in *New-York*, and therefore their not being printed cannot be our Neglect." The "Neglect" was Franklin's. Worse, with Franklin still out of town, the *Pennsylvania Gazette* for 4 October failed to appear. The following week, a Hamilton supporter wrote a weak essay for the 11 October *Gazette* satirizing the *Mercury* writers who had attacked Hamilton.

When Franklin returned to Philadelphia on 13 October and found that Andrew Hamilton had failed to be reelected, he must have wondered if he would survive as public printer. The assembly met on Monday, the fifteenth, chose Jeremiah Langhorne, the Bucks County political boss, as Speaker, appointed the standing committees, and elected Joseph Growden clerk for the current year. On 17 October the assembly adjourned for two months. By taking no action, the assembly had temporarily continued Franklin as its printer.

Franklin probably knew the identities of the writers who opposed Hamilton, Cato Jun. and Julius. The printer indirectly apologized on 18 October for the past week's weak satire: "The Printer of this Paper returned but on Saturday last, from a Journey on which he was absent near seven Weeks: If in that Time any Passages have appeared in the Gazette, that may be construed into Personal Reflection, it was without his Knowledge or Approbation, and must be ascribed to the Inadvertence of those who carried on his Business." In that same day's *Mercury*, the Philadelphia doggerel poet John Dommet attacked the weak satirist of 11 October, mistakenly thinking that Franklin was the writer. To discredit him, Dommet raked up Franklin's slur of two years previously on "black gowns." Another item in the 18 October *Mercury*, "A True Letter to a Friend in the Country," charged that Hamilton's control of the assembly, the courts, and the Loan Office had been sinister and dictatorial.

"A Half-Hour's Conversation with a Friend"

On 16 November 1733, Franklin replied to the attacks on Andrew Hamilton with "A Half-Hour's Conversation with a Friend."[10] The interview with a famous person is a standard media feature today, but I don't recall any previous interviews in the English or American newspapers. Some words and writings of contemporaries, like Cotton Mather, had been quoted in New England newspapers, but such writings did not use an interview format. Franklin seems to have written the first press interview. Franklin probably made up the interview. As Hamilton's friend and protégé, the newspaperman must have wanted to defend him. The interview form that Franklin adopted made the piece more dramatic than an essay would have been. Since it was intended as a favor to Hamilton, Franklin no doubt told him about the piece beforehand and showed it to him after writing it. Hamilton may have made suggestions for it.

The piece has a framework or envelope structure, with the reporter opening and closing the article, and with the interview itself taking up the body of the article. Franklin began with a brief note addressed to the editor, "Mr. Franklin," saying that the "Half-Hour's Conversation" replied especially to the *Mercury's* 18 October "A True Letter to a Friend in the Country." The author/Franklin confessed that his purpose was partly to entertain: "As there is nothing can please every body, so who can tell but this may divert somebody." The writer said that he had a conversation with Andrew Hamilton about the "True Letter." He had heard the opinions of numerous people concerning it: "Some say they are persuaded it was not the Author's Love to his Country induced him to publish those Charges in the Manner he has done, and that it would have been much better to have charged that Man with Particulars, and by Name, and likewise to have subscribed his own, by which the People might at the same Time have known the Criminal and the Accuser; but not having done this, they conclude the whole to be no more than the Effects of some private Resentment." But others, who disliked Hamilton, commended the letter, "not, they say, that they can agree it is all true, but approve well of that old Saying, *Throw Dirt enough, and some will stick*" (1:333–34). Franklin thus suggested that there was nothing to the charges against Hamilton.

Adding to the interview's immediacy, the author/Franklin said he met Hamilton "last Night" and repeated to him the various opinions. Hamilton acknowledged that though he was not named in "A True Letter," from the particular description of his various occupations the person attacked must be he. Hamilton added that since "A True Letter" was "commonly agreed to be wrote by nobody, he thought no body should regard it." Franklin, however, pointed out that the author of "A True Letter" objected that Hamilton was charged with "horrid Ingratitude" to both the proprietors and governor, and that if he did not reply, his silence might be interpreted as an acknowledgment of guilt. Franklin portrayed the speaker/interviewer as a diligent inquirer for truth, as well as a friend of Hamilton, and represented the lawyer as a distinguished person reluctant to engage in controversy with an anonymous opponent. Both of Franklin's personae seem reasonable, calm, and trustworthy.

Hamilton answered that he was well aware how power had been used in all ages to destroy innocent men, but Pennsylvanians enjoyed more liberty than other governments and had no reason to fear an arbitrary power because their liberties could only be abridged "by the Judgment of twelve Freemen of Pennsylvania." Consequently, a person falsely charged with crimes "can laugh at the impotent Efforts of the Great and Powerful." Though the speaker/Franklin granted that what Hamilton said was true, it did not answer the charges against him. Hamilton therefore reluctantly began to reply, while at the same time showing his superiority by mocking the abilities of the anonymous slanderer:

Pennſylvania GAZETTE.

Containing the freſheſt Advices Foreign and Domeſtick.

From November 8. to November 16. 1733.

Mr. *Franklin*,

AS Mr. *Bradford* was pleaſed to entertain the Publick with *A true Letter to a Friend in the Country*, as 'tis called, in his Mercury of the 18th of *October* laſt, I deſire you will give this *Half-hour's Converſation with a Friend* a Place in your Gazette, which may at preſent ſerve for an Anſwer to that Letter. As there is nothing can pleaſe every body, ſo who can tell but this may divert ſomebody.

Sir, Your humble Servant.

TO gratify your Curioſity, I ſhall as far as my Memory will ſerve me, let you know, as well the Sentiments of the Publick upon the Subject of the Letter publiſhed in Mr. *Bradford's* Mercury of the 18th of *October* laſt, as what paſs'd between my ſelf and the Perſon who is ſuppoſed to be chiefly pointed out in that Letter. I have had the Opportunity of hearing the Sentiments of a great many People concerning that Performance. Some ſay they are perſuaded it was not the Author's Love to his Country induced him to publiſh thoſe Charges in the Manner he has done, and that it would have been much better to have charged that Man with Particulars, and by Name, and likewiſe to have ſubſcribed his own, by which the People might at the ſame Time have known the Criminal and the Accuſer; but not having done this, they conclude the whole to be no more than the Effects of ſome private Reſentment. Others, who ſeem to be very certain againſt whom all the heavy Charges in that Letter are levelled, and who like the Man no better than the Author does, commend the Letter much, not, they ſay, that they can prove it is all true, but approve well of that old Saying, *Throw Dirt enough, and ſome will ſtick*; and they add, it never having been anſwered, ſuch who know nothing of the Matter are the more enclin'd to believe it. Theſe Reports made me deſirous to ſee the Perſon, who is my particular Friend, againſt whom it ſeems generally agreed the *true Letter*, as 'tis called, was wrote; And meeting with him laſt Night, I acquainted him with the various Sentiments of the People upon the Subject: He frankly own'd, that from the particular Deſcription of his Employments, no body could doubt but he was the Man pointed at; but ſaid, ſeeing it was commonly agreed to be wrote by nobody, he thought no body ſhould regard it. Here I put my Friend in mind, that I had often heard him ſay very hard Things of an ungrateful Man; and foraſmuch as the Letter-writer would have it believed that my Friend was under very great Obligations both to the Proprietor and Governor, and being charged with horrid Ingratitude to both, it might not only draw on him their Reſentment, but the Cenſure of others, who might conſtrue his Silence into a Proof of his Guilt. To which he made me the following Anſwer, as I can remember, and which I think I am bound in point of Friendſhip and Juſtice to his Character, to make as publick as the Letter. ' Sir, I am very ſenſible of the ' Weight of Power in the Hands of a ſupreme Magiſtrate, ' and how it has been made uſe of in all Ages, and moſt ' Countries of any long ſtanding, to deſtroy the moſt inno- ' cent Men. I am likewiſe ſenſible, that *that* ſame Power

' never wants Creatures who are ready to execute Ven- ' geance upon the Heads of thoſe who deſerve it leaſt, not ' always meerly in compliance with the Will of their Su- ' periors, but very frequently becauſe they want his Place ' or hate his Perſon. Howcver, I hope no honeſt Men ' who underſtand or have a true Value for that ineſtima- ' ble Bleſſing of Liberty, which the People here enjoy in ' a greater Degree than moſt of their Neighbours, can with ' juſt Reaſon apprehend any Danger from that Quarter of ' Power. The People of *Pennſylvania* are too wiſe to be ' cheated into an Opinion that a Man is to be deſtroy'd ' becauſe his Superiors and a few of their Creatures appre- ' hend that he ſtands in their Way: No, they know a ' Man can loſe neither Life, Liberty, nor Eſtate, but by ' the Judgment of twelve Freemen of *Pennſylvania*; and ' being ſecure of this, and that it is in no Man's Power to ' prove that he ever deſerted the Intereſt or Cauſe of his ' Country, he can laugh at the impotent Efforts of the ' Great and Powerful." But here I interrupted my Friend, and put him in mind, that tho' all he ſaid was moſt un- queſtionably true, and that I was pleaſed to hear him pre- fer Juſtice to all Powers and Dependencies whatſoever, yet it did not ſeem to anſwer the Charges exhibited againſt him in the Letter before us: And thereupon he proceeded to the Effect following. ' Sir, you know in Law a particular ' Anſwer to a general Charge is never required of any Man, ' and therefore it cannot be expected that I ſhould make ' a particular Anſwer to a Number of general Charges, ſuch ' as, *ſpeaking contemptibly* (I ſuppoſe the polite Author means ' *contemptuouſly*) *of the Proprietor, abuſing and diſplacing the ' Governor, endeavouring to put a Stop to the Proceedings of Go- ' vernment and to the Adminiſtration of Juſtice, Partiality in ' Lending out Money at the Loan-Office, &c.* Now to theſe I ' can only make this general Anſwer, that the Charges ' are moſt unjuſt; and if the worthy Author of that Letter ' will produce any Perſon of Credit (but I deſire it may be ' remembered the Author himſelf is always excepted, for ' who knows but having once told a Lie he will be ſo ' hardy as ſtill to ſtand to it) that can prove I have wit- ' tingly or willingly ſaid or done any Wrong to that honour- ' able Gentleman, or any of his Family, I will in the moſt ' publick Manner make ſuch Acknowledgments as all the ' World ſhall ſay are juſt. Nor have I ever allow'd my ' ſelf the Freedom with the Propr——r which the Author ' has ſeen fit to do, where he (*kind Man*) cautions that ' Gentleman neither to be wheedled, nor frightned by the ' Threats of that dangerous Man; and leſt he ſhould faint, ' for his Encouragement has told him, that all the People ' will ſtand by him, and others (no doubt meaning him- ' ſelf) who don't love Trouble, will be rouſed Now ' whether this be decent Treatment of a Gentleman of the ' Pro——'s Character, in ſuppoſing him to want Reſolu- ' tion to reſent any Injury done him by any Man, but eſ- ' pecially by one out of Favour with his Superiors is moſt ' certain, and, as the Author ſays (and without all doubt ' wiſhes it were true) hated by all the People, the Truth ' of which I leave the World to judge of. As to the diſ- ' placing the Governor, he ſaid, I don't underſtand what is

meant

Figure 11. "A Half-Hour's Conversation with a Friend," the first interview in American journalism, Pennsylvania Gazette, 16 November 1733. Franklin's friend and patron Andrew Hamilton was defeated in the election of 1733 by the combined forces of the leaders of the Proprietary Party and key members of the Quaker Party. Franklin thereafter wrote a supposed interview with Hamilton, who is best known as the defender of John Peter Zenger in a famous 1735 trial involving the freedom of the press. Perhaps partly because of Franklin's defense, when an election for a deceased member of the assembly was held the following month (December, 1733), Hamilton won the seat. The following year he was again elected Speaker of the House. Courtesy, Library Company of Philadelphia, Philadelphia.

"Sir, you know in Law a particular Answer to a general Charge is never required of any Man, and therefore it cannot be expected that I should make a particular Answer to a Number of general Charges, such as, *speaking contemptibly* (I suppose the polite Author means *contemptuously*) *of the Proprietor, abusing and displacing the Governor, endeavouring to put a Stop to the Proceedings of Government and to the Administration of Justice, Partiality in Lending out Money at the Loan-Office, etc.* Now to these I can only make this general Answer, that the Charges are most unjust; and if the worthy Author of that Letter will produce any Person of Credit . . . that can prove I have wittingly or willingly said or done any Wrong to that honourable Gentleman [the governor], or any of his Family, I will in the most publick Manner make such Acknowledgments as all the World shall say are just" (1:335). In arguing that an accusation could not be general but must have specific detail in order to be answered, Franklin echoed the defense of James Franklin and his friends in the *New England Courant* of 6 May 1723, the day before James was tried for contempt of the General Court of Massachusetts.

Hamilton/Franklin pointed out that the author of "A True Letter" placed the proprietor in the position of a fearful, timorous person, who lacked resolution to resent injuries. He suggested that the author had charged Hamilton with an attempt to remove the governor. Franklin indirectly made the point that since only the proprietors could remove the governor, it would be foolishly contradictory for Hamilton to attack the proprietors if he wanted to remove the governor. Further, Hamilton said that the proprietors "will bear me Witness, that I never directly nor indirectly made any Application to them for any such Removal; therefore this part of the Charge is utterly false." Hamilton continued by directly refuting other charges of "A True Letter." He did, however, admit to one: "as to my great Pride and other personal Vices, I shall only say, *Lord I have sinned, have Mercy upon me a miserable Sinner*" (1:336). Herein, Franklin (in his persona as Hamilton) dwelt on the Aristotelian proof of ethos, or establishing the good character of Hamilton, by suggesting his humility and devotion to God.

Then Franklin, still writing as Hamilton, paraphrased the content of "A True Letter," exposing it to savage burlesque, anticipating his parody of the Reverend Joshua Smith's "Meditation on the Vanity and Brevity of Human Life," where he compared Smith's statements to a "Child who laments that he cannot eat his Cake and have his Cake" (8 August 1734). Hamilton wrote, "Was this fine Letter but stript of all the affected simplicities and disguises the Author has been at the pains to dress it up in (for he used to write in the same stile against Sir William [Keith]) and put into plain English, methinks it would read pretty much to the following purpose: '*Loving, Loving, Loving Friends*, hear and believe, and then you will see, there is risen up amongst us a dangerous, proud, wicked, witty Fellow, whose Life is inconsistent with your Lives and Liberties, as by the following Instances will to you my dearest Countrymen be most manifest." The author then ridiculed the charges against Hamilton with a micro-cosmic tall tale: "He speaks contemptibly of the Pr[oprieto]r, for I my self have heard him swear terribly, that Gentleman was not tall enough to touch the Moon, nor strong enough to remove a Mountain."

Franklin also satirized the charges by applying a ridiculously literal meaning to the word *displace*: "He abuses the Go[verno]r, and has endeavoured to dis-place him, for it is commonly reported, that he should say in a certain Place, that his Honour don't see now so well as when he was but one and twenty; and I my self with these very Eyes of mine, saw him once offer the arm'd Chair to the Pro——r when the Gov——r was present; Now if this was not a plain Attempt to displace his Honour, judge ye." Franklin lampooned the charge that Hamilton was proud and then exposed the anonymous author of "A True Let-ter": "He's proud and revengeful to the last Degree, for he will not be thankful to his Betters for abusing him; and upon a certain Time publickly exposed me for insinuating he had taken greater Fees in his Office than by Law he was entitled to" (1:336–37).

The reference to the author of "A True Letter" as a pamphleteering oppo-nent of Sir William Keith shows that Franklin believed him to be Isaac Norris, Sr. The allusion to him as someone who had said that Hamilton took excessive fees in his office and who had subsequently been publicly exposed again pointed to Norris. He had said at a dinner in 1732 that Hamilton took excessive fees as prothonotary. Learning of the charge, the irritated Hamilton brought it up in public when both men were serving as justices in the court of common pleas and excoriated Norris.[11]

Franklin continued his burlesque of the attack in "A True Letter" on Hamil-ton: "He is a great Lawyer, and will not be fool'd out of a good Cause; he is so cunning too, that he will rarely be concerned in a Case but what he believes to be just, he speaks to it with great Zeal, the Court is oblig'd to do right, and often give Judgment for his Client, and thus it is he rules them as he pleases. He has so much Wit as to propose nothing in Assembly but what he thinks reasonable, and so crafty he will always agree with them in what is just, and by these Meth-ods it is that he manages the Whole at Pleasure." Then Franklin again applied tall-tale techniques to ridicule the accuser: "About six Years ago he [this terrible man] eat up your Privileges at a Breakfast; it is but three Years since he made a Dinner of your Liberties; and if you suffer him to live one Year longer, he'll swallow all your Estates for his Supper. In short, he's a Witch; for with his Breath he blows Men blind, and with his Wit and Raillery he strikes them dumb: Is this Man fit to live?"

Having burlesqued the supposed charges, Franklin undercut the anonymous author: "I hope my Word is sufficient Proof for all these Things; and if you presume to doubt the Truth of what I have said, you are no better than the Courts and Assemblies I have been speaking of, that is, a parcel of Idiots, Fools and Miscreants; and what is still worse, I'll take my Oath on't, you are sworn

Enemies to the Prop——r and G——r" (1:337–38).[12] Returning from the mock persona of the author of "A True Letter" to that of the reporter, Franklin ironically concluded the attack on the slanderer: "Tell the People again and again, that nothing but that Humanity and Generosity which is so natural to you, and the *tender* Regard you have for their Liberties and Privileges, but above all the Love you have for their Properties, could have rous'd you from your beloved Retirement" (1:338).

A Bucks County delegate to the legislature, William Paxson, died in mid-December 1733. Hamilton was elected to replace him on 27 December 1733 and took his seat in the House on 31 December. The following October, he was again elected Speaker of the Pennsylvania House. Perhaps Franklin heard in early November that Paxson was ill and wrote a "Half-Hour's Conversation" as political propaganda for Hamilton. At any rate, the essay/interview must have helped him.

Thomas Penn's Agenda

For nine years (12 August 1732 to 20 August 1741), Thomas Penn resided in Pennsylvania and directly managed proprietary affairs. For a year during that period (19 September 1734 to 20 September 1735), his brother John also lived in Philadelphia. The Penns especially wanted to collect money for the land and the quitrents owed them, but the settlers disputed the amount. They believed that quitrents were £10 Pennsylvania currency per hundred acres; Thomas Penn said that it was £10 sterling per hundred—which was approximately one-third more. One consequence of the disagreement was that the Pennsylvania Assembly attacked the chancery court structure. Since the governor was both judge and jury in the chancery court, those who paid their quitrents in Pennsylvania currency feared that Thomas Penn would bring them before the chancery court, where the governor, an appointee of the proprietors, would surely find in their favor. Most Pennsylvanians opposed the chancery court. The *Gazette* favored the popular position and wanted to abolish the chancery court as contrary to the charter, but the *Mercury* took the Proprietary Party position and defended the court. As usual, the *Mercury* attacks descended to personal vituperation against Andrew Hamilton, with occasional glancing blows at Franklin. Newspaper essays on the chancery court appeared from 18 December 1735 through 2 March 1736. The *Mercury* attacks on "Mr. F——" (whom some have assumed was Franklin) were aimed at "Mr. Freeman," the pseudonym of the *Gazette* author who criticized the courts; others have assumed that "Mr. F——" was Andrew Hamilton. Historian Craig Horle, however, suggested that Freeman was the New Jersey attorney and intellectual James Alexander.[13] Though Franklin was not "Mr. F——," he supported the Quaker Party's position on the issue.

The Threat of War

In the 1730s, those who believed that the English colonies would advance into the interior of America knew that another war must ensue with France. France had established a new fort at Crown Point on Lake Champlain in 1731 and a series of forts west to the Great Lakes. The population of Pennsylvania and the other British colonies was continually increasing, with new settlers moving beyond the three established Pennsylvania counties of Philadelphia, Chester, and Bucks. James Logan pointed out to the council on 16 August 1731 that the French claimed land along the western border of Pennsylvania and other colonies. He said that they were attempting to control the Shawnee Indians on the Ohio and argued that the "Attempt of the French" to dominate the Ohio, "if attended with Success," would ultimately destroy the English colonies. Logan realized that William Penn's former Indian policy of dealing with the Delaware chiefs and ignoring the Six Nations Confederacy was no longer viable. Settlements along the Susquehanna and the upper Delaware valleys were outside the traditional Delaware Indian territory. Logan foresaw that the French would attempt to extend their power into western Pennsylvania. The Six Nations traditionally had authority over the Shawnee Indians living along the upper Susquehanna River and the upper Delaware Valley. Logan formed a new Indian policy in 1731, inviting the Six Nations, or Iroquois chiefs, to come to Philadelphia. He hoped that the Six Nations would not only control the Delaware and the Shawnee Indians but influence other Indian tribes in the West to side with the English against the French.

In the late summer of 1731, James Logan wrote a memorial, "Of the State of the British Plantations in America," addressed to Robert Walpole, in effect England's prime minister. It pointed out that the French claimed all the interior of America and were encroaching upon the various British colonies. Franklin found Logan's memorial important and made a personal copy.[14] At Logan's instigation, John Shickellamy, an Oneida chief who was ostensibly in charge of the Pennsylvania-area Indians for the Iroquois League, came to Philadelphia with Conrad Weiser, his interpreter, in December 1731. After Shickellamy reported back to the Six Nations, a delegation of chiefs came to Philadelphia for a treaty on 18 August 1732. Proprietor Thomas Penn, who had arrived in Pennsylvania only six days earlier, opened the treaty on 23 August. It was primarily conducted at the Friends' Meeting House at the southwest corner of Second and Market Streets (then Philadelphia's largest building), with "a very great Audience, that crowded the House and all its Galleries."

Franklin must have observed parts of the treaty proceedings and speculated on their significance. The Pennsylvanians and the Six Nations chiefs both regarded the Delawares and the Shawnees who lived along the Ohio as Iroquois dependents. On 30 August Pennsylvania gave Shickellamy and Weiser special presents for their efforts. The conference ostensibly ended on 2 September, as Franklin reported in the 7 September paper. But that day, at James Logan's home, Sasoonan and a few other Schuylkill Indian chiefs sold land to the Penns. Pennsylvania and the Six Nations intended to meet again the following year, 1733, but they did not do so until 1736. By 1734 Franklin knew that the French

were inciting the Shawnee and other Indians on the Ohio, and he believed that
Pennsylvania should have a militia in case of war to defend itself—from the
French and Indians on the frontier or from the French and Spanish on the
Delaware Bay. The Quaker-controlled assembly opposed a militia, even for de-
fensive warfare, though many good Quakers, like Logan, believed that force was
an essential part of government.

In the 8 January 1734 *Gazette*, Franklin commented that recent New York
papers contained depositions taken from several persons who had lately been in
Canada and at Louisburg. They testified that "there is no want of Provisions in
those Places" and suggested that the sloop *Le Caesar*, which had recently come
to buy "Provisions" in New York, actually came only "to give an Opportunity
to some French Engineers and Pilots to discover the Channel and Way in, and
view the Strength of the Fortifications, that they may be better enabled to execute a Design they have upon that Place in case a War should break out."

Defying the "Stiffrumps"

Considering the war threatening the colonies, Franklin thought the defenseless
situation of Pennsylvania foolish. On 6 March 1734 he published his "Queries
on a Pennsylvania Militia," written in the persona of a Quaker who favored self-
defense. It opened: "B. Franklin, *Thee art desired to insert the following Queries
in the* Gazette, *for the Consideration of People*." The Quaker speaker asked a
series of rhetorical questions in a seemingly unemotional tone. The cumulative
effect, emphasized by the repetition of "whether" at the beginning of almost
every query, was an incontrovertible argument for self-defense. He began with
a geographical fact. Was it not a great disadvantage for the French that from the
"Mouth of *Mississipi* [sic] to St. *Lawrence*, they have no Ports to the Sea . . . but
see them all in the Hands of the English, for 1500 Miles; tho' they possess a fine
Country back of the same Extent?" (W 223). Franklin echoed Logan, who had
made the same point in his 1731 memorial: "But to all this Vast Tract, the French
have no other Inlet from the Sea, than by the Mouths of those two great Rivers
Saint Lawrence and Messisippi [sic] both of which are Tedious and Dangerous."[15] Perhaps Franklin talked with Logan about the "Queries" before publishing them, asking Logan's permission to use his arguments. It would have been
unlike Franklin to borrow someone else's thoughts without citing or asking
them. Logan would not himself have wanted to make such arguments in the
public press without the approval of key Quakers, but he probably welcomed
the publicity given to views he privately endorsed.

In the "Queries," Franklin asked whether the possession of New York, Pennsylvania, and New Jersey would not be very convenient for the French, partially
because of the provisions raised there but especially because of "our Rivers
which run far back towards their present Settlements?" (W 223). This argument
and the following ones were Franklin's. The Quaker persona questioned,
"Whether it is not possible for our Pilots to be compell'd to bring armed Vessels

up this River?" (That was to happen in 1747.) He asked whether vessels did not often turn the point in sight of Philadelphia before Philadelphians knew of their being in the river. If the enemy surprised Philadelphia, was there not "plate, clocks, Watches, and other rich Goods in it" sufficient to make it worth attempting to attack? Both rhetorical questions demanded the answer "Yes."

The Quaker persona also claimed that a small number of well-organized soldiers could ravage the entire city without any considerable risk. He then directly challenged the Society of Friends, arguing against pacifism. Though not all Pennsylvania's Friends were pacifists, many were. "Whether they who are against fortifying their Country against an Enemy, ought not, by the same Principle to be against shutting and locking their Doors a Nights? Whether it be not as just to shoot an Enemy who comes to destroy my Country, and deprive the People of their Substance, Lives and Liberties, as to sit (being either Judge or Juryman) and condemn a Man to Death for breaking open a House, or taking a Purse?" Franklin then cited the Bible, using a quotation that he later repeated in his pamphlet *Plain Truth* (1747), which urged the creation of a volunteer militia association to defend Pennsylvania: "Whether there was not formerly a People, who possessed a large and good Land, where there was plenty of every Thing; and who lived *after the Manner of the Zidonians, careless, quiet, and secure*? Whether this was not an Invitation to an Enemy? And what was the Consequence? See Judges 18" (W 223–24).

Knowing the anti-French prejudice of his audience, Franklin had his Quaker persona ask, "Whether the *French* Soldiers are a good, friendly, harmless Sort of People; or whether they are not composed of the Scum, the most profligate, wicked, and abandoned of the Nation? Whether, if they were in Possession of these Governments, and quarter'd upon the Inhabitants, they would out of Honesty and Scruple of Conscience, forbear to take any Thing which was not their own? And out of Modesty and Bashfulness, forbear to ravish any of our Wives and Daughters?" Franklin reminded the Pennsylvania Quakers that the French soldiers committed such atrocities when they overran Holland in 1675.

The persona questioned how much, if war came, pacifist Quakers could stand: "Whether we are sure that if they should attempt to abuse our Women, our Men could be quiet and peaceable Witnesses of it; and that Attempts to rescue and prevent, would not occasion frequent and daily Murders here, as well as in *Holland* aforesaid?" In war, the English were brutal also. Franklin ironically queried, "Whether" the French "would not take as much Pride in deflouring *Quaker* Girls, as the *English* did in the Nuns of the Town they took in *Spain*?" The persona asked if the Quakers thought heaven would protect them in preference to other persons: "Whether from the Purity of our Lives and the Sanctity of our Manners, we have any more Reason to expect the immediate Protection of Heaven than the rest of our Neighbours?" The speaker reminded the audience of Aesop's fable of the wagoneer and the cart: "Whether the ancient Story of the Man, who sat down and prayed his Gods to lift his Cart out of the Mire, hath not a very good Moral?" (W 224). Thirteen years later, when the French and Spanish privateers were raiding on the Delaware River just south of Philadelphia, Franklin printed a woodcut of this fable at the beginning of *Plain Truth*.

The Quaker speaker added two final arguments: "Whether 500 disciplined Men well armed, are not able to beat an unarm'd, unheaded, undisciplined, and affrighted Mob of 5000?" Franklin repeated the statement in *Plain Truth* (3:193). The Quaker finished by asking, "Whether, if it were known that we fortifyed and exercised ourselves, it would not contribute towards discouraging an Enemy from attacking us?" (W 225). Franklin concluded *Plain Truth* with the same argument (3:203).

Franklin gambled his position as printer for the province when he wrote and published the essay. Though he used a Quaker speaker for it, the assembly members knew he wrote it. He probably gave a talk on the defenseless condition of Pennsylvania at a Junto meeting before publishing it. How many other print-ers for a colony challenged the dominant party position?[16] Fortunately for Franklin, the Quaker Party did not fire him from his position as printer despite his opposition to its pacifism. The Quaker leaders knew that he sided with them on such key issues as a paper currency, secret instructions to the governor, and taxation of the proprietary estates. Though Andrew Hamilton had been re-elected to the House the previous December, he was not now the Speaker. But many moderate Quakers, including James Logan, agreed with Franklin. Had the Quaker Party fired him for this outspoken opposition to the pacifists, it would have irritated and perhaps alienated some Quaker citizens and assemblymen. There was no discernible reaction to Franklin's political disagreement with the pacifist Quakers.

Many Quakers disagreed with the pacifists. The *Autobiography* contains an anecdote concerning William Penn and James Logan. When Logan sailed for America with Penn in the fall of 1699, "It was War Time, and their Ship was chas'd by an armed Vessel suppos'd to be an Enemy. Their Captain prepar'd for Defence, but told William Penn and his Company of Quakers, that he did not expect their Assistance, and they might retire into the Cabin; which they did, except James Logan, who chose to stay upon Deck, and was quarter'd to a Gun." The sail chasing them turned out to be English, so there was no fighting. But when Logan "went down to communicate the Intelligence, William Penn re-buk'd him severely for staying upon Deck and undertaking to assist in defending the Vessel, contrary to the Principles of *Friends*, especially as it had not been required by the Captain. This Reproof being before all the Company, piqu'd" Logan, "who answer'd, *I being thy Servant, why did thee not order me to come down: but thee was willing enough that I should stay and help to fight the Ship when thee thought there was Danger*" (A 113).

Franklin kept the French and Indian threat before the *Gazette* readers. On 28 August 1735 he reported that five French deserters made their way from the

Mississippi to Albany, whence two of them came to Philadelphia and the others to New York. "They reckon they have travell'd 1500 Miles thro' the Woods, subsisting only upon what they could kill by the Way." He reported that few French were yet settled on the Mississippi River, "only here and there a Fort for Security of Trade; and that there are more Soldiers than other Inhabitants." Franklin implied that Americans should advance to the Mississippi and claim that great waterway, which was the key to the heartland of the continent.

CHANGES

On 5 August 1736, after having served the province for eleven years, Governor Patrick Gordon died. James Logan, president of the council, acted as governor for the next two years until Governor George Thomas arrived in Philadelphia on 1 June 1738. During the late summer of 1736, the Indian expert Conrad Weiser learned that a group of Six Nations chiefs, who had been expected two years earlier, were now on their way to Pennsylvania. Weiser guided them to Logan's home at Stenton where the treaty began on 28 September. It continued at the Friends' Meeting House in Philadelphia, where on Saturday, 2 October, "divers Gentlemen, and a very large Audience . . . filled the House and its Galleries."

Franklin reported the treaty in the 7 October *Gazette*, remarking on the Indians' specialized vocabulary and their aids to memory: they met "to *brighten the Chain of Friendship, clear the Road of Communication, &c.* The Speaker among them was prompted by one who sat near him, with a Handful of little Sticks, which served as Memorandums of the Points to be spoken of." Franklin later commented on the wampum belts given by the Indians. The size, he wrote, was "always in Proportion" to the Indians' ideas of "the greater or less Importance of the Matters treated" (8:209). When the chiefs met privately with John Penn, he reminded them that they had previously sold all the land along the Susquehanna and asked why they had lately laid claims to them. On 11 October the Indians confirmed the previous sale. The treaty concluded on 14 October by renewing their 1732 treaty of friendship.

On 14 October the *Gazette* celebrated Pennsylvania's peaceful Indian policy under William Penn, adding that about fifty years prior, New York's governor, Colonel Thomas Dongan, purchased for William Penn all the lands lying upon the Susquehanna River. "We are told that the Chiefs of these Nations, now here, who are about Twenty in Number, have confirmed that Purchase made by Col. *Dongan*, and have absolutely released to Our present Honourable Proprietors all the Lands from about the Mouth of Susquehannah as high up that River as those called by the Indians the *Twhagasachata* or *Endless Mountains*, with all the Lands on both Sides the said River, and its Streams as far Westward as the Setting of the Sun." *A Treaty of Friendship Held with the Chiefs of the Six Nations at Philadelphia* (1737) was the first Indian treaty Franklin printed. He subsequently printed more Indian treaties than any other colonial printer. After the primary treaty, the chiefs went to Conrad Weiser's home, where on 25 October

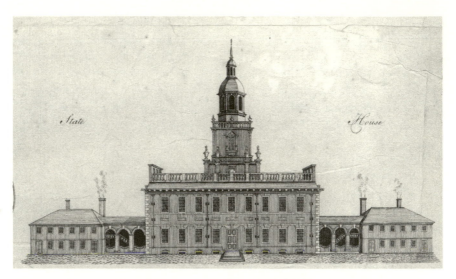

Figure 12. The State House (Independence Hall), Philadelphia. An inset in a map of Philadelphia drawn by John Reed, engraved by James Smithers, and printed by Thomas Man, Philadelphia, 1774. Primarily designed by Franklin's patron Andrew Hamilton, the State House was first used on 23 September 1736 when William Allen, mayor of Philadelphia for the past year, made the annual feast on his retirement. Within a month, the Pennsylvania Assembly began meeting there. Franklin, as Clerk of the House, was present at the State House for every meeting of the Assembly from 1736 to his election as a member in 1751, and for most meetings thereafter until he left for England in 1757. He arranged for the Library Company to use the upper floor of the west wing in 1739; its collections remained there until 1773. Courtesy, American Philosophical Society, Philadelphia.

they sold the land along the Delaware River below the Kittatinny Hills. A group of four chiefs warned the proprietors that the Delaware Indians no longer owned any land and were not to be trusted. Little did the chiefs know that the primary person not to be trusted was Thomas Penn, the son of their faithful friend William Penn.

On 23 September 1736, the almost completed State House (designed by Andrew Hamilton, now called Independence Hall) was first used when William Allen, mayor of Philadelphia for the previous year, made the annual mayor's feast on his retirement. The assembly first met in the statehouse on 14 October 1736. The next day Franklin, no doubt through the influence of Andrew Hamilton, Speaker, was elected clerk of the assembly. Before his election as clerk, Franklin had been an interested observer and writer on Pennsylvania politics. Despite his editorial forays into politics, he had not been an insider. That changed with his election.

TEN

The Hemphill Controversy

It is no matter, whether the particular Judgments Men form, are just and according
to Truth, or not; for Truth consider'd as abstracted from the Discerning of the
Mind, is no Rule of Action to any Man, nor can any Thing be Truth to us but as
we apprehend it to be so, and see the Agreement *between the Ideas* compar'd in
our Minds.—*2:86–87*

FRANKLIN'S WRITINGS IN THE HEMPHILL CONTROVERSY were among his errors
as a young man. He foolishly opposed public opinion. Later, in a letter of 13
December 1757, when giving reasons against satirizing religion, he wrote, "He
that spits against the Wind, spits in his own Face." He may well have had in
mind his writings defending Hemphill. The Hemphill affair was the first heresy
trial in American Presbyterian history.[1] The Reverend Samuel Hemphill came
to Philadelphia in 1734 from Ireland and became an assistant to the Reverend
Jedediah Andrews, minister of Philadelphia's Presbyterian church. Franklin
thought Hemphill gave "excellent Discourses" and attended his sermons frequently. He preached little about the tenets of Presbyterianism but much about
"the Practice of Virtue, or what in the religious Stile are called Good Works."
Andrews and many of the strict orthodox Presbyterians in the congregation
disapproved. After Hemphill was charged with heterodoxy, Franklin "became
his zealous Partisan," defending him with a dialogue in the *Pennsylvania Gazette*
and three pamphlets (A 96). Contemporaries generally assumed that Hemphill
wrote them. Though Franklin had previously revealed his religious doubts (especially in his *Dissertation on Liberty and Necessity* [1725]), these 1735 pieces
announced his theological skepticism more thoroughly and directly than any
previous Philadelphia writings.

BACKGROUND

Having arrived in Philadelphia at summer's end in 1734, the Reverend Samuel
Hemphill was admitted a member of the Presbyterian Synod on Saturday, 21
September. On Monday, 23 September, he joined the other new members in
declaring for and adopting "the Westminister Confession, Catechisms, and Di-
rectory commonly annexed, the former as the confession of their faith, and the
latter as the Guide of their Practice in Matters of Discipline, as far as may be
agreeable to the Rules of Prudence, &c." Fifteen years earlier, the Reverend

George Gillespie had proposed that the Philadelphia Presbyterian Synod adopt subscription to the Westminster Confession as essential to ministerial candidates. The Reverend Jonathan Dickinson, who later became the first president of the College of New Jersey (now Princeton), and others opposed making it essential. From 1721 until 1729, the synod frequently considered the question. Finally, the Adopting Act was passed on 19 September 1729, asserting that all candidates for the ministry had to agree with all the "essential and necessary articles of the confession."[2] On 7 January 1730/1 the synod paid Franklin for printing the act. In 1735, the Hemphill affair tested the American Presbyterian Church's compliance with the Adopting Act.

The Reverend Jedediah Andrews, the sixty-one-year-old minister of the First Presbyterian Church, Philadelphia, had asked for an assistant early in 1734,[3] and in November he invited the newly arrived Hemphill to preach with him. Hemphill proved popular with part of the congregation. Franklin, who had been bored by Andrews, returned to regular attendance. But some church members found Hemphill's theology too liberal. Andrews wrote that "Most of the best of the People, were soon so dissatisfied that they would not come to meeting." According to the old minister, "Freethinkers, Deists and Nothings getting a scent of him flocked to him."[4] Andrews attended Hemphill's sermons throughout the winter and by March had made up his mind. He went "from House to House among his Congregation, declaring Hemphill to be a Preacher of erroneous Doctrine, calling him *Deist, Socinian*, and the like, and was pleased to be very angry with those who could not agree with him in his Notions of Hemphill and his Sermons" (2:40). Then Andrews complained to the Presbyterian authorities.

At its annual fall meeting, the Presbyterian Synod appointed a commission to take care of any problems that might arise during the next twelve months. In answer to Andrews's complaint, the commission that had been appointed in September 1734 met in Philadelphia during April 1735 to investigate Hemphill. The moderator of the 1734 synod had been the Reverend Ebenezer Pemberton. As usual, the former moderator had been appointed to head the commission for the next year. Seven members of the commission attended the Philadelphia meeting. Three were from Pennsylvania: Thomas Creaghead of Salisbury, James Anderson of East Donegal, and John Thomson of Chestnut Level. Two were from New York: Pemberton himself from New York City and Robert Cross of Jamaica, Long Island. Another member was from New Jersey, John Pierson of Woodbridge, and another from what is now Delaware, George Gillespie of White Clay Creek, New Castle County. The most able member appointed to the commission at the 1734 synod, Jonathan Dickinson, is not known to have participated in the trial. But later in the controversy, he played the most important role for the Presbyterians.

For the investigation of Hemphill, thirteen additional synod members were added to the standing committee. Four were from Pennsylvania: William Tennent, Sr., of Warwick, David Evans of Tredyffrin, Richard Treat of Abington, and Adam Boyd of Sadsbury; three were from New Jersey: Nathaniel Hubbel of Westfield, Gilbert Tennent of New Brunswick, and William Tennent, Jr., of Freehold; two were from Maryland: Joseph Houston of Elk River and Alexander Hutchison of Bohemia Manor; and two from what became Delaware: Andrew Archbold of New Castle and Robert Cathcart of Middletown, New Castle County. Elder Robert Jamison and the Reverend Thomas Evans also served on the commission.

Franklin probably knew who had been selected for the commission before he wrote Hemphill's first defense. In the small Middle Atlantic society of the 1730s, Franklin must have been acquainted with every member. Several, like the Reverend David Evans of Tredyffrin, clerk of the commission, turn up frequently in Franklin's financial accounts. He knew the two ministers who lived furthest away, Robert Cross and Ebenezer Pemberton. Cross appears in Franklin's accounts, and Franklin later printed his *Protestation Presented to the Synod of Philadelphia* in 1741. Ebenezer Pemberton (Harvard, 1721) was the son of Franklin's childhood minister, Ebenezer Pemberton (1671/2–1716/7). Pemberton, Jr., was just one year older than Franklin, and they spent their childhood living within a few hundred feet of one another. They knew one another well.

The Charges

On 7 April 1735, Jedediah Andrews brought eight heresy charges against Samuel Hemphill. Franklin listed them in his 17 July 1735 pamphlet, *Some Observations on the Proceedings against the Reverend Mr. Hemphill* (2:41–42). During the course of its investigation, the commission revised several and dropped two. In its *Extract of the Minutes of the Commission of the Synod* (published on 22 May 1735), the commission listed the six charges of which it convicted Hemphill. First, Hemphill taught that Christianity is "an Illustration and Improvement of the Law of Nature, with the Addition of some few positive Things, such as the two Sacraments, and our going to God and making our approaches to him in the Name and Mediation of his Son *Jesus Christ*" (*E* 8).[5] The arraignment reworded and slightly revised Andrews's first accusation. Since Presbyterians believed that the Bible was the Word of God and that the Law of Nature had little to do with Christianity, he was found guilty.

Second, Hemphill denied "the necessity of Conversion to those that are born in the Church, and are not degenerated into vitious Practice" (*E* 9). The indictment reflected Andrews's accusation that Hemphill said "the Sacrament of the Lord's Supper is only a Means to promote a good and pious Life." Andrews was "also not satisfied at his speaking against the need of spiritual Pangs in order to Conversion" (2:41). Presbyterians believed that a new birth was necessary for conversion. Third, the commission agreed with Andrews's claim that Hemphill railed "against the Doctrine of Christ's Merits and Satisfaction, as a Doctrine that represented God as stern and inexorable, and fit only for Tyrants to impose and Slaves to obey." The commission also confirmed Andrews's charge that Hemphill criticized ministers who "made a Charm of the Word *Christ* in their preaching, thereby working up their Hearers to Enthusiasm" (2:41). Hemphill implied that God was loving and kind—a liberal position, not a Presbyterian one.

Fourth, the commission objected to Hemphill's teaching that saving faith was "a firm Perswasion of Mind of the Truths of the Gospel upon good and rational Grounds" (*E* 10). Andrews's charge against Hemphill was essentially the same. Fifth, Hemphill asserted "the sufficiency of the Light of Nature to bring us to Salvation" (*E* 10). Andrews's version was that Hemphill opened "the Door of the Church wide enough to admit all honest Heathens" (2:42). Sixth, the commission claimed that Hemphill perverted "the Doctrine of Justification by Faith" (*E* 10–11). This was the seventh charge brought by Andrews. The commission ignored Andrews's sixth and eighth charges. Both charges rambled, but their substance was: "when an Account was given how our Souls came to be distempered, no Distemper by original Sin, as I heard, was mentioned"; and Hemphill "constantly omits to pray for any Church either Catholick or particular, or any Ministers of it, but only for Mankind in general" (2:42–43).

Though many liberal Anglicans advocated the positions Hemphill preached, the Presbyterian commission believed Hemphill violated the local presbytery's essential doctrines of election and rebirth.[6] Franklin disagreed with those tenets.

THE "DIALOGUE"

Franklin's first publication in the Hemphill affair, "A Dialogue between Two Presbyterians," appeared in the *Pennsylvania Gazette* on 10 April 1735. "S" (who represented Franklin's views) supported Hemphill; "T" opposed him. Franklin thought the dispute mainly concerned the quarrel between faith and works.[7] S declared that Christ and the Apostles mainly preached morality, and instanced the Sermon on the Mount as arguing the superiority of good works to faith. T replied that faith as well as morality was recommended in the New Testament. S argued that faith should produce morality, and morality, salvation but that salvation did not result from faith alone. "I should as soon expect, that my bare Believing Mr. Grew to be an excellent Teacher of the Mathematicks, would make me a Mathematician, as that Believing in Christ would of it self make a Man a Christian" (2:29). (Theophilus Grew was a well-known Philadelphia mathematics teacher.)

T asked S/Franklin if he thought that morality or virtue alone, without faith, could save a man. S replied that "Morality or Virtue is the End, Faith only a Means to obtain that End: And if the End be obtained, it is no matter by what Means." Though heresy to Presbyterian doctrine, that sentiment was one that Franklin evidently believed and frequently cited. Echoing the French intellectual Pierre Bayle,[8] Franklin cited a number of biblical passages to prove that morality or virtue was more important than faith. S claimed that "'tis the Doing or not Doing all the Good that lies in our Power, that will render us the Heirs of

Happiness [heaven] or Misery [hell]." T then asked why Hemphill did not preach up faith as well as morality. S replied that the minister knew that "we all have Faith in Christ already," and that therefore he exhorted the parishioners to good works. T said he did not like "this Sort of Preaching" and was glad the synod would shortly meet to examine it. S replied that he hoped the synod would not "persecute, silence and condemn a good Preacher, for exhorting them to be honest and charitable to one another and the rest of mankind" (2:30–31).

Since Hemphill was a Presbyterian minister, T argued that he should preach "as Presbyterians use to preach." All should "abide by the Westminster Confession of Faith." S countered that just as the "Apostacy of the Church from the primitive Simplicity of the Gospel" came on by slow degrees, so, too, the reformation of the church evolved gradually. "Did not Luther at first preach only against selling of Pardons? . . . He afterwards went further, and Calvin, some think, yet further." He said the Church of England reformed still more but then fixed "her Faith and Doctrine by 39 Articles." The Presbyterians, "being too self-confident to think, that as their Fathers were mistaken in some Things, they also might be in some others; and fancying themselves infallible in *their* Interpretations, they also ty'd themselves down by the Westminister Confession. But has not a Synod that meets in King George the Second's Reign, as much Right to interpret Scripture, as one that met in Oliver's Time? And if any Doctrine then maintain'd is, or shall hereafter be found not altogether orthodox, why must we be for ever confin'd to that, or to any, Confession?" (2:31–32).

Several ideas in the above paragraph recur in Franklin's writings. Concerning religion's progress since the Reformation, Franklin wrote on 13 April 1785, "Our ancestors from Catholic became first Church-of-England men, and then refined into Presbyterians. To change now from Presbyterianism to Popery seems to me refining backwards, from white sugar to brown" (S 9:303).

Franklin often condemned those who subscribed to fixed doctrines as persons who thought themselves infallible, comparing them to the Roman Catholic pope. He expressed that opinion in an anecdote in his final speech to the Constitutional Convention and again in the *Autobiography*. When Michael Welfare, a leader of the Dunkers, complained to Franklin that the Church of the Brethren were "calumniated by the Zealots of other Persuasions, and charg'd with abominable Principles and Practices to which they were utter Strangers," Franklin advised him to publish their articles of belief and rules of discipline. Welfare replied that their principles had been improving and errors diminishing. "We fear that if we should once print our Confession of Faith, we should feel ourselves as if bound and confin'd by it, and perhaps be unwilling to receive farther Improvement; and our Successors still more so, as conceiving what we their Elders and Founders had done, to be something sacred, never to be departed from." Franklin generalized, "This Modesty in a Sect is perhaps a singular Instance in the History of Mankind, every other Sect supposing itself in Possession of all Truth, and that those who differ are so far in the Wrong." Then, using a traditional symbol for ignorance, Franklin wrote a wonderful epic simile: "Like a Man traveling in foggy Weather: Those at some Distance before him on the Road he sees wrapped up in the Fog, as well as those behind him, and also the People in the Fields on each side; but neer him all appears clear.—Tho' in truth he is as much in the Fog as any of them" (A 115–16).

The argument of S in the above paragraph also revealed Franklin's radical skepticism (or Pyrrhonism), and it again testified that Franklin could and did live in a world without certainties. Those qualities were found in the *Dissertation on Liberty and Necessity* as well as in the "Dialogue." Franklin sometimes said that the purpose of most religions was to provide boundaries, spiritual certainties. Poor Richard said, "The heathens when they died went to bed without a candle" (3:250).

Continuing the "Dialogue," T said that if the majority of the synod were against Hemphill, they could justly hinder him from preaching. S/Franklin asked, if the American Presbyterians sent a missionary to Turkey, "would it not be unreasonable in the Turks to prohibit his Preaching?" T agreed that it would be unreasonable. S asked, if the Turks, "should out of the same charitable Disposition, send a Missionary to preach Mahometanism to us, ought we not in the same manner to give him free Liberty of preaching his Doctrine?" T conceded that it "may be so." Franklin concluded, "If it would be thought reasonable to suffer a Turk to preach among us a Doctrine diametrically opposite to Christianity, it cannot be reasonable to silence one of our own Preachers, for preaching a Doctrine exactly agreeable to Christianity, only because he does not perhaps zealously propagate all the Doctrines of an old Confession" (2:32).

S/Franklin next returned to a favorite point: "We have justly deny'd the Infallibility of the Pope and his Councils and Synods in their Interpretations of Scripture, and can we modestly claim *Infallibility* for our selves or our Synods in our way of Interpreting?" (2:33). He then made a characteristic observation, "In the present weak State of humane Nature, surrounded as we are on all sides with Ignorance and Error, it little becomes poor fallible Man to be positive and dogmatical in his Opinions."

The most obvious point of faith, S/Franklin claimed, was that "*Morality* is our Duty, for all" agree in that. "A virtuous Heretick shall be saved before a wicked Christian." Since it was uncertain until we arrive in heaven "what true Orthodoxy in all points is," Franklin hoped that "we shall as heretofore unite again in mutual *Christian Charity*" (2:33).

Surprisingly, the "Dialogue" shows Franklin using the *Pennsylvania Gazette* to argue what he must have known would be an unpopular position. Politically and personally, it was a mistake. The dialogue contradicts not only the view that Franklin did not often take sides in his paper[9] but also his own statements concerning the printer's nonpartisan role in such writings as "An Apology for Printers." Though the "Dialogue" contains some effective arguments and is interesting for Franklin's ideas, it lacks drama and engaging characters. S/Franklin takes up almost all the words; T, merely a strawman, makes no good arguments for his position. The personae are as disembodied as their initials.

THE TRIAL

A week after the "Dialogue" appeared, the Presbyterian commission met on Thursday afternoon, 17 April 1735, to investigate Andrews's charges against Hemphill. Franklin evidently attended all the public proceedings of the trial (Thursday, 17 April, Friday, Saturday, and the following Thursday morning). The hearings were bitter. Andrews exclaimed, "Never was there such a Tryal known in the American world."[10] At the trial's start, Hemphill objected to John Thomson and George Gillespie serving on the commission since both previously condemned him. They denied it, and moderator Ebenezer Pemberton allowed them to serve (2:43). Later, in defending Hemphill, Franklin twice censured the commission for including Thomson and Gillespie (2:43, 97–98).

The commission requested copies of Hemphill's sermons, which he refused to provide, upon which the commission suggested that his refusal proved his guilt. Franklin later commented, "How becoming such a Conduct as this was, in Judges who had not as yet heard any thing more of the Cause than barely the reading of the Charges, let the Reader judge" (2:44). The members of the commission reminded Hemphill that he had told Andrews he would show the elder minister his notes. Hemphill replied that he would have let Andrews examine his notes in private, but Andrews had never called upon him, and the situation was different now that the commission had met. When the Reverend William Tennent, Sr., repeated the charge, Franklin pointed out that the commission "converted an Opinion of Hemphill's of what he might be willing to do . . . into an absolute Promise of what he really wou'd do" (2:100).

The trial proceeded on evidence from those who had heard the sermons. Reports conflicted, even among the accusers. Moderator Pemberton said that the "*plumb* Evidence" was that a member of the congregation testified that Hemphill said "*That to preach up Christ's merits and Satisfaction, his Death and Sufferings, was to preach up a Charm.*" Hemphill and others present on the occasion denied that he had said it. A number of Hemphill's supporters remembered "the very Words of the Sentence in which the Word *Charm* was contain'd," but the moderator ruled that Andrews's charge corroborated what one Hemphill accuser said. A Hemphill supporter who belonged to the Presbyterian congregation asked the accuser if he did not believe his words were false. The accuser replied "*That he was not obliged to answer the Question.*" Later, a member of the commission justified the evasion by calling it "*an innocent Wile,* and said, *there was no harm in admitting a false Evidence in order to force the Accused to confess the Truth.*" Franklin wrote in his *Observations on the Proceedings* that the remark was "sufficient to fill the Mind of every candid Reader with Horror!"

(2:45). In his later *Defense of the Observations*, Franklin attributed the words to the Reverend Nathaniel Hubbell of New Jersey (2:101).

The accusers also charged Hemphill with saying that there were no mysteries in Christianity (thus suggesting that Hemphill believed religion had nothing supernatural in it). But a number of persons present at the time denied that he had said it. Moderator Pemberton, however, would not admit their testimony, calling it negative evidence. The next day the commission agreed to allow Hemphill to present evidence against the accusations. But according to Franklin, "in order to render their Indulgence ineffectual," the commissioners "peremptorily refus'd to let him have a Copy" of the charges. How, asked Franklin, "can any Man invalidate the Testimony of another without knowing what it is?" (2:46).

On Sunday, 20 April, during the investigation, commission members Ebenezer Pemberton and Robert Cross both preached before the commission. Both condemned Hemphill. Pemberton's *Sermon Preached before the Commission* (published in New York by John Peter Zenger) had two doctrines: 1) "That Christ and the Way of Salvation by him, is too often condemned and aspersed" and 2) "That it is the Duty and Character of every Christian, to justify Christ and his ways from the Cavils and Exceptions of prejudic'd Sinners." If Andrews correctly charged that Hemphill declaimed against the doctrine of "Christ's Merits and Satisfaction, as a Doctrine that represented God as stern and inexorable" or that some "made a Charm of the Word *Christ* in their preaching, thereby working up their Hearers to Enthusiasm," then Pemberton's sermon directly attacked him.

In his first charge, Andrews had accused Hemphill of saying that Christianity was nothing but "a Revival or new Edition of the Laws and Precepts of Nature." Pemberton evidently referred to it when he said that "Many begin to be weary of the ancient Doctrines of Religion, and cry up to the Dictates of Nature and the Writings of the Philosophers." Later in the sermon, Pemberton again condemned those who celebrated "the Law of Nature." He also replied to Hemphill's supposed positions on faith (the third charge) and on salvation (the fourth charge). Pemberton preached, "Faith is the great Duty which the Gospel most solemnly and frequently inculcates upon us and declares to be the indispensable Condition of our Justification upon Earth, and acquittance at the Bar of Christ." Finally, Pemberton censured Hemphill's supposed position on communion (the second charge), declaring that the "Ordinances of divine Worship" were held sacred by "the upright Soul."[11]

In his preface addressed "To the Reverend COMMISSION of the Synod," Pemberton may have alluded to Franklin's newspaper essay and first pamphlet when he wrote that his own "Conduct" in giving the sermon exposed him "to the Censure and Reproach of Men of corrupt Principles and abandon'd Morals." Pemberton evidently published the sermon after Franklin referred to it in

Some Observations (17 July) and before 4 September, when Andrew Bradford published *A Vindication of the Reverend Commission of the Synod.*

On the same Sunday that Pemberton preached (20 April), Robert Cross admonished those who followed the "law of nature" rather than the gospel in his sermon, *The Danger of Perverting the Gospel of Christ.* His first proposition was "By the Gospel of Christ, we are to understand the whole Revelation of the Mind and will of the Almighty God, in all Things concerning the Redemption and Salvation of the laps'd perishing World of Mankind, through the Merits and Mediation of our Lord and Saviour Jesus Christ." He claimed, "These are guilty of perverting the Gospel of Christ, who add any Thing to the Terms of Salvation, propos'd and establish'd by Jesus Christ." Likewise, they pervert the gospel "who make the Way to Heaven and Happiness wider and easier than the great *Author and Finisher of our Faith hath made it."* He further said that "there is but one Way of Salvation, and that is in and through Jesus Christ." Those who preach otherwise "are guilty of arraigning infinite Wisdom, at the Bar of blind and corrupt Reason, and of despising the Riches of the free Grace and Mercy of God." Cross concluded, "How cautious all should be who hear the Gospel preached, lest instead of the faithful Stewards of the Mysteries of God, they embrace false teachers."[12]

In *Some Observations*, Franklin declared it unfair of the judges to preach against Hemphill while they were conducting the trial (2:47). Cross replied to the criticism in a note added to the published sermon: "The Occasion of the Meeting of the Commission of the Synod, was to take cognizance of one of their Number, who was accused of Preaching false Doctrine, while the Tryal was depending. This Sermon was Preached before the Commission, and a very numerous audience, the Person accus'd, being likewise present, who found Fault with it as a prejudging the Cause, whether justly or not, is now submitted to the publick."[13] Cross evidently believed that "the person accused" (Hemphill) wrote the anonymous pamphlets.

After hearing Pemberton's and Cross's sermons, Hemphill consented to read his sermons to the commission (2:47). On Monday afternoon, Tuesday morning and afternoon, and Wednesday morning (21–23 April), he read several of his sermons before the commission. The members deliberated that afternoon, then sent Hemphill extracts from his sermons, and asked him to appear the next morning "and offer anything further that he has to say in his own Defence." On 24 April, Thursday, at 9 a.m., Hemphill and "other Gentlemen having said what they thought proper; all Parties were desired to withdraw" so the commission might "proceed to Judgment" (*E* 6). Franklin was probably the chief "other" gentleman speaking for Hemphill. That afternoon, meeting in closed session, the commission found him guilty of the first two charges brought against him. On 25 April, in the morning, the commission found him guilty of the third and fourth articles; that afternoon, he was judged guilty of the fifth and sixth. On 26 April, Saturday, the commission unanimously voted to suspend Hemphill "from all the parts of his Ministerial Office until the next Meeting of our Synod," when the synod would decide what to do (*E* 13).

OBSERVATIONS

Franklin found the commission's policies high-handed and partisan. Of course, the Reverend Ebenezer Pemberton, moderator, was primarily responsible for its procedures. Rumor, no doubt abetted by Franklin, reported that Hemphill had been unjustly tried and condemned. Andrew Bradford published for the commission, *An Extract of the Minutes of the Synod, Relating to the Affair of the Reverend Mr. Samuel Hemphill* (22 May). The prefatory advertisement said, "The late Tryal of the Reverend Mr. Samuel Hemphil, before the Commission of the Synod, being the Subject of much Discourse; we thought it necessary to publish our Minutes upon that Affair, to prevent any Misrepresentations, and unjust Aspersions that might be cast upon us" (*E* 2). Since the *Extract* was compiled from the minutes of the commission, it is in effect the work of the commission's clerk, David Evans, perhaps as revised by a subcommittee appointed to defend the commission.

According to Franklin, the *Extract* misrepresented the case. He announced on 12 June that *Some Observations* was "now in the Press and will speedily be published." But Franklin was sick with pleurisy from early May to October, though he had a partial recovery in July. Despite the 12 June advertisement for *Some Observations*, he had not finished writing it then and was thereafter too sick to complete it for several weeks. Franklin's accounts show that a copy probably sold on 10 July and that frequent sales began on 15 July. The *Pennsylvania Gazette* announced its publication on 17 July. An instant success, the thirty-two-page pamphlet, which sold for six pence, sold out within two weeks, and a second edition was advertised on 31 July. Hemphill, made notorious by the publicity, preached twice on Sunday, 27 July, "to a very numerous Congregation at the House where the [Pennsylvania] Assembly used to meet."

In the anonymous *Some Observations*, Franklin told the story of Hemphill's trial, emphasizing what he judged to be procedural faults. Though the commission promised Hemphill that he would have an opportunity to vindicate any parts of his sermons that the commission objected to, "this was promis'd with a View to end a Dispute between the Moderator and Hemphill" (2:48). But they did not tell him what parts they had in mind. Franklin compared the trial to "that hellish Tribunal the *Inquisition*, who rake up all the vile Evidences, and extort all the Confessions they can from the wretched Object of their Rage, and without allowing him any Means of invalidating the Evidence, or convincing 'em of their own Mistakes, they assemble together in secret, and proceed to Judgment" (2:49). One wonders if Franklin recalled reading the Reverend Samuel Willard's protest against confessions in the Salem witchcraft trials: "there are other ways of undue force and fright, besides, Racks, Strappadoes and such like things as Spanish Inquisitors use."[14] Franklin proceeded to attempt to refute the six charges presented in the *Extract*.

Concerning Hemphill's preaching the law of nature, Franklin argued "that our Saviour's Design in coming into the World, was to restore Mankind to the State of Perfection in which Adam was at first created, and that all those Laws which he has given us are agreeable to that original Law, as having such a natural Tendency to our present Ease and Quiet, that they carry their own Reward, tho' there were nothing to reward our Obedience or punish our Disobedience in another Life" (2:50–51). As we saw in "The Art of Virtue" (Chapter 2), the argument that Christian ethics are good for people, whether founded on supernatural doctrine or not, often occurs in Franklin's writings. He further claimed that all things that God made our duty had "a natural Tendency to our Happiness; and if to our Happiness, then it is agreeable to our Nature, since a Desire of Happiness is a natural Principle which all Mankind are endued with" (2:51). Just a few months before, Franklin said in his "Man of Sense" essay that happiness was "our main End in View" (2:16). As pointed out above, this sentiment echoed numerous writers.

Second, Franklin contended that the commission had changed Hemphill's meaning by adding some words and leaving out others. Hemphill's words, Franklin stated, were "agreeable to the *fundamental* Articles" of the Westminster Confession, "which was all he declared to at his Admittance into the Synod: Surely the commission would not condemn him for differing with them about extra-essentials" (2:52). Since Franklin had printed the 1729 Adopting Act, he must have known the synod's debates concerning its "essentials" and "non-essentials." The members of the commission charged that Hemphill denied the necessity of spiritual rebirth, but Franklin maintained that they did not quote him correctly. Franklin went on, however, to give his own theory of behavior (another recurring motif; see Chapter 2), which contradicted the Puritan requirement for a new birth. "Men don't become very good or very bad in an Instant, both vicious and virtuous Habits being acquired by Length of Time and repeated Acts" (2:53).[15] Franklin next turned from the particular theological issue to the nature of God—and from the nature of God back to the theological issue: "I may add, that whoever preaches up the absolute necessity of spiritual *Pangs* and Convulsions in those whose Education has been in the Ways of Piety and Vertue, and who therefore are not to pass from a State of Sin to a State of Holiness, but to go on and improve in the State wherein they already are, represent Christianity to be unworthy of its divine Author" (2:54). Few good Puritans, Protestants, or even Christians would raise questions that presumed to judge God "unworthy."

The commission's third article against Hemphill was that he took no notice of Christ's making satisfaction to the Justice of God (i.e., to Christ as a Redeemer). Franklin observed that Christ as a Redeemer was "by all Christians . . . esteem'd a fundamental Article of Belief" and that Hemphill in fact repeatedly expressed this opinion. Franklin quoted several passages from Hemphill's sermons and prayers proving his point. He expressed amazement that the vote against Hemphill was unanimous. He claimed that "one of the chief Managers in the whole Tryal, being shewn the very Paragraph upon which they pretend to ground their Censure concerning the Satisfaction of Christ . . . declared his Sentiments in this Manner, *For my part, I do not know what other People may think of it, I can't see any Heresy in it, it is all very right.*" Franklin protested that the judge "wanted either Courage or Honesty afterwards, when he did not dissent from the rest" (2:58).

Franklin noted that the commission also condemned Hemphill for saying "God hath no Regard to any thing but Mens inward Merit and Desert." He then revealed another characteristic turn of mind when he asked, "Does God regard Man at all?" In his "Articles of Belief" (20 November 1728), Franklin had written, "I imagine it great Vanity in me to suppose, that the *Supremely Perfect*, does in the least regard such an inconsiderable Nothing as Man" (1:102). In a letter to George Whitefield (prior to 2 September 1769), he voiced a similar thought. Here in 1735, he replied, "The Answer I suppose will be, That he does, but that it is upon the Account of Christ's Merits; which I shall grant them, and allow it to be the Merits and Satisfaction of Christ that purchased such easy and plain Conditions of Happiness; but still it is our Compliance with these Conditions that I call inward Merit and Desert which God regards in us. For to say that God regards Men for any thing else besides Goodness and Virtue, is such a Notion as makes all Men both virtuous and vicious capable of being equally regarded by him, and consequently there is no Difference between Virtue and Vice" (2:59). Having made the question a reductio ad absurdum (a conclusion similar to making pleasure and pain equivalent in *A Dissertation on Liberty and Necessity*), Franklin thought its supposed imbecility self-evident.

Fourth, the commission claimed that Hemphill's description of "Saving Faith" was too general. Franklin ridiculed their condemnation as being more general than Hemphill's description. Fifth, the commission charged that Hemphill denied the necessity of a divine revelation. Franklin argued that the commission's extract from Hemphill's sermon changed its meaning and that the commissioners then asserted a falsehood. Franklin closed this refutation with another indictment of the ministers: "And this is sufficient to show the base Conduct of these Men, who to accomplish their wicked Ends, will not only venture to change the Meaning but the very Words themselves" (2:61).

The sixth accusation said Hemphill perverted the doctrine of justification by faith. Franklin impatiently asked, "What is it that they would not find supported from his Sermons, if Andrews had charged him with it?" Franklin then summarized the unexceptional doctrines of Hemphill's sermon on Ephesians 3:8. The ministers denounced Hemphill for asserting "that all Hopes of Happiness but what are built on Purity of Heart and a virtuous Life, are, according to the Christian Scheme vain and delusory, and will certainly end in Disappointment and Confusion." Though they "absolutely condemn" these words in Hemphill, they "zealously maintain the very same thing; or, in their own orthodox Words, the indispensable necessity of universal Holiness in order to Salvation" (2:62–63). The commission finished by condemning Hemphill's doctrines as "Unsound and dangerous, contrary to the sacred Scriptures and our excellent Confession and Catechisms," and by implying that Hemphill was a hypocrite for assenting to the Westminster Confession the previous September (*E* 12). Franklin again said that Hemphill only assented to its *"fundamental Articles."* In "late Years" Franklin added, the ministers "agreed, that there were some Articles in it of no great Moment whether Men believed 'em or not, nay some publickly declared they did not understand many of 'em, (which I sincerely believe was very true) yet they would now make 'em all Fundamentals, in order to serve a Turn." In his conclusion, Franklin quoted the English Whig Thomas Gordon, an author of *Cato's Letters*, that "all Persecution is Popery, and every Degree of it, even the smallest Degree, is an Advance towards the Inquisition" (2:65).

Vindicated

Franklin's defense of Hemphill caused a flurry of publications. Since he had blamed both Ebenezer Pemberton and Robert Cross for preaching against Hemphill while the trial was taking place, the two published their sermons in self-defense. And the Reverend George Gillespie, another commissioner, brought out *A Treatise against the Deists or Free-Thinkers; Proving the Necessity of Revealed Religion.* (Bradford advertised it on 7 August.) According to a mid-nineteenth-century historian of American Presbyterianism, "Gillespie was zealous for strict discipline, and three times entered his dissent when offenders were dealt with too leniently for their immoralities."[16] Gillespie's "Appendix, Proving that the Preaching of *Meer Morality*, is not the best way of Preaching: against Free Thinkers or Deists" (pp. 58–62) replied to Hemphill and to his unknown apologist, Franklin.

On 14 August, Bradford's *American Weekly Mercury* advertised as "in the Press" *A Vindication of the Reverend Commission of the Synod: In Answer to Some Observations on Their Proceedings against the Reverend Mr. Hemphill.* The *Vindication*, which appeared on 4 September, was authored by Ebenezer Pemberton (pp. 1–14) and Jonathan Dickinson (14–48), with Robert Cross writing two pages (37–38) in his own defense.[17] By then the *Mercury* had published two articles (14 and 21 August), indirectly condemning Franklin's positions. From a Presbyterian viewpoint, the *Vindication* thoroughly refuted Franklin. Pemberton evidently still believed that Hemphill, not Franklin, had written *Some Observations* (*Vindication* 3). In its *Vindication*, the commission charged that Hemphill "borrowed much of what he deliver'd" (6), and identified one extract from "*Forster's* Sermons" (37).

Dickinson's method (14–48) was to consider each of the six charges in detail, then to refute Franklin's defense. Thus, concerning the first charge (that Christianity is the same as the law of nature), Dickinson said, "Among all which peculiars of Christianity, wherein (if in any thing) it is distinguished from the Law of Nature, we hear not one Word of Faith in Jesus Christ, of the Necessity of our Interest in the Benefits of his Redemption, of Justification by his Righteousness, or of our Sanctification by his Holy Spirit; nor one Word of any thing but what we find urged by the heathen Moralists, from the same sort of Arguments" (16).

Perhaps Franklin's most appealing argument concerned the third charge. Franklin said that when a member of the commission was shown the extract, he said there was nothing wrong with the doctrine. (Robert Cross's rebuttal, pp. 37–38, disclosed that he was the person Franklin had in mind.) Franklin said he therefore lacked either honesty or courage in voting with the commission. Cross countered, "When the Gentleman in *Philadelphia* shew'd that Paragraph, it was intirely new to the Person to whom he shew'd it . . . and as the Propositions were chiefly Negative, he did not then see the Heresy that was couched in them. . . . [But when] the Members of the *Commission* had reason'd upon it, and the Person accused [Cross] had in his own mind resolved the Negative Propositions into Positive, he saw Cause enough to be of another Opinion . . . and to join with the rest of the *Commission* in judging, that the most plain and obvious Scope of it is Subversive of the true and proper Satisfaction of Christ" (37–38).

At the end of his rebuttal of every Franklin argument, Dickinson printed as an appendix "every thing that was taken out of his Sermons by the Commission's Order" (49–63). Pemberton, Cross, and Dickinson not only had the better arguments from a Presbyterian viewpoint, they also presented a far more reasonable, judicious, and careful tone and persona than did Franklin. Only freethinkers would have agreed with Franklin—his criticisms were heavy-handed, his tone was rude, and his persona intemperate. Like Pemberton, Dickinson made surprisingly little of Hemphill's plagiarism. Franklin evidently misremembered, exaggerating the role of the plagiarisms when he wrote in his *Autobiography*: "During the Contest an unlucky Occurrence hurt his Cause exceedingly. One of our Adversaries having heard him preach a Sermon that was much admired, thought he had somewhere read that Sermon before, or at least a part of it. On Search he found that Part quoted at length in one of the British Reviews, from a Discourse of Dr. Forster's." The quotation from Forster came from a sermon Hemphill read before the commission, from which the commission copied extracts. Dickinson had recognized it. Franklin continued, "This Detection gave many of our Party Disgust, who accordingly abandoned his Cause, and occasion'd our more speedy Discomfiture in the Synod. I stuck by him, however, as I rather approv'd his giving us good Sermons compos'd by others, than bad ones of his own Manufacture; tho' the latter was the Practice of our common Teachers. He afterwards acknowledg'd to me that none of those he preach'd were his own; adding that his Memory was such as enabled him to retain and repeat any Sermon after one Reading only.—On our Defeat he left us, in search elsewhere of better Fortune, and I quitted the Congregation, never joining it after, tho' I continu'd many Years my Subscription for the Support of its Ministers" (A 96–97).

A Letter to a Friend

Franklin acknowledged defeat in the *Autobiography*, but he did not do so in 1735. Before Pemberton and Dickinson's *Vindication* appeared on 4 September, Franklin had written another tract, *A Letter to a Friend in the Country, Containing the Substance of a Sermon Preach'd at Philadelphia, in the Congregation of the Reverend Mr. Hemphill, Concerning the Terms of Christian and Ministerial Communion.* Though dated 30 August, it was not published (probably because Franklin was sick) until 22 September, by which time the regular synod meeting was in session. The editors of *The Papers of Benjamin Franklin* cautiously attributed the preface to Franklin, saying it was "probably" his, "though it is by no means certain that he wrote the body of the pamphlet. He may, however, have revised it" (2:65). Melvin Buxbaum subsequently ascribed the whole to Franklin, saying that the tone and style were the same as Franklin's other writings in the Hemphill affair.[18] I agree. The preface to the pamphlet, titled "The Publisher ["B. Franklin"] to his Lay-Readers," which is signed "A Layman" (2:66–67), is obviously by Franklin. The same voice recurs in the "sermon," and the unusual opinions expressed in the preface are repeated there. The postscript continues the same voice and opinions. Details of content and style given below confirm Franklin's authorship, though during 1735 *A Letter* was also ostensibly ascribed to Hemphill. It supposedly contained extracts from a sermon preached "in the congregation of the Reverend Mr. Hemphill," together with the writer's comments on the sermon. A logical assumption would be that Hemphill preached the sermon, that someone in the country heard reports of it and wrote Hemphill asking for a copy, and in reply, the author (supposedly Hemphill) of *A Letter* quoted from his sermon and commented on it.

The layman/Franklin began by observing "how difficult it is to alter Opinions long and universally receiv'd. The Prejudices of Education, Custom and Example, are generally very strong." Franklin argued this common idea in his early *New-England Courant* "Timothy Wagstaff" essay (15 April 1723), and repeated it in his letter to his parents of 13 April 1738, on "the unavoidable Influence of Education, Custom, Books, and Company upon our Ways of thinking." In a slightly earlier essay, "On a Pertinacious Obstinancy in Opinion" (27 March 1735), Franklin said it was a glorious "Conquest" when people did abandon all prejudice and brought themselves "to think *freely, fairly,* and *honestly*" (2:66).

The layman complained to his "Brethren of the Laity" that most clergymen were too fond of power (the criticism echoed the *New-England Courant*'s position of 1721–23). He suggested that the laity unite against the clergy's "temporal Interests." In effect, Franklin suggested that laymen should not pay the clergy.

Franklin's anticlericism and his suggestion echoed the deist writers and anticipated criticisms of organized religion during the Great Awakening (1740–48).[19]
He said, "Their pretending to be the Directors of Men's Consciences, and Em-
bassadors of the meek and lowly Jesus, ('twere greatly to be wish'd they study'd
more to imitate so perfect a Model of Meekness and Humility, and pretended
less to a Power that belongs not to 'em) and their assuming such like fine Titles,
ought not to frighten us out of a good Cause, *The glorious Cause of Christian
Liberty.*" He expected, however, that the clergy would "make very free with the
Characters of those that oppose their Schemes, and like sound, orthodox Divines, call them Hereticks, unsound in the Faith, and so on; but there is no
Argument in such kind of Language, nor will it ever persuade" (2:66–67).

     The laity should oppose the clergy for two reasons. First, whenever men
"submitted themselves to the Impositions of Priests, whether Popish, Presbyterian or Episcopal, &c., [then] Ignorance and Error, Bigotry, Enthusiasm and
Superstition, more or less, and in Proportion to such Submission, most certainly
ensu'd." Second, "all the Persecutions, Cruelties, Mischiefs and Disturbances,
that ever yet happen'd in the Church, took their rise from the usurp'd Power
and Authority of her lawless Sons." The only thing that could make America,
"our infant and growing Nation," miserable would be to allow "the Clergy to
get upon our Backs, and ride us, as they do their Horses, where they please"
(2:67). Before the Great Awakening, such anticlerical sentiments rarely surfaced
in America,[20] though they were typical of deistic thought and of the young
Franklin. There may also have been some class resentment in the charge, for
most artisans in America could not afford to own a horse. In the main part of
the letter, the author refers to the "Priest-ridden Laity" (2:68), thereby continuing the anticlerical expressions in Franklin's preface (note, too, how unusual an
opinion this would be for Hemphill or any minister to hold).

     In reviewing the supposed sermon, the author of the letter to the layman
said it had an introduction and a textual explication (part of the normal sermon
structure), but instead of a "doctrine" (i.e., a truth deduced from the text) he
called the thesis "the Question propos'd to be consider'd" (2:69). These words
challenge the whole tenor and manner of the usual "sermon": instead of dem-
onstrating an undoubted truth, the author questions a philosophical possibility.
That was not what eighteenth-century Presbyterian ministers did. The "Question" was "*Whether it be lawful to impose any other Term of Communion, Christian or Ministerial, than the Belief of the Holy Scriptures? Or, Whether a Man that
professes to believe the Holy Scriptures, and the Christian Scheme of Religion as
contain'd in them, ought not to be admitted to Christian and Ministerial Communion, if no Reason can be alledg'd against him in other respects, why he should
not?*" Franklin's method was to advance a series of arguments against the
"Question" and to discredit them.

     The first argument was that certain conditions and creeds had been deemed
necessary by all Christian churches since early times. Franklin replied that such

conditions were not found in the Bible. "Nothing more was required of . . . new Converts, but that they should acknowledge Jesus Christ to be the Messiah . . . and that they should to the best of their Power, act agreeable to his Precepts, and obey his Laws. And really there was hardly a Possibility, that one Discourse should inform them of all the metaphysical Notions, nice Distinctions, which are now brought into our Confessions of Faith as necessary Articles." That sentence recapitulates Franklin's skepticism concerning "metaphysical useless Points," which he verbalized elsewhere (3:88–89, 31:59)—and below. The speaker argued that there was no such requirement in the first two centuries. The Apostles Creed was the earliest. Composed in the beginning of the third century, it "is couch'd in so loose a Manner, with respect to the Points chiefly controverted among Christians, that it is highly probable it was fram'd on purpose with that remarkable Latitude, in order to let into the Church all such as in general sincerely believe the Holy Scriptures, tho' with respect to many metaphysical Speculations, they should widely differ from other Christians" (2:70–71).

The second argument of those who believed in creeds (belittling such persons, Franklin called them "Creed-Imposers") was that every society "*has a Right to make such Laws as seem necessary for its Support and Welfare: The very Nature of a Society requires, nay supposes this; else it would lie open to all kinds of enemies; there would be no Provision, no Remedy against the Intrusion of Adversaries, that might destroy its very Vitals.*" Dickinson argued for this position in his *Vindication*, but Franklin contended that a difference existed between a civil and a Christian society. The former could make what laws it thought best for its defense and preservation, but the latter was responsible only to Jesus. "Every Subject is equal to any other Subject; their Concerns have nothing to do with this World; every one is accountable for his Belief to Christ alone. . . . One Man's Salvation does not interfere with the Salvation of another Man, and therefore every Man is to be left at Liberty to work it out by what Method he thinks best" (2:72–73). Franklin's statement denied any theological reason for organized religions to exist, though they could still have communal and social functions.

Though the speaker was dealing with abstract theological matters, he showed Franklin's ability to write *sententiae*: "In abundance of Things in Life, but most peculiarly in Religion, a rational Creature may easily be led, but will not be driven" (2:74). The author went from the generalization to the particular: "And tho' a Thing be in itself of little Consequence, yet the Making or Declaring it essential, renders it highly prejudicial to Religion; and therefore out of a discreet Zeal, not any Obstinacy, a good Man may reject and oppose it, because enforc'd as material: Whereas if look'd upon and left as what it really is, he would scarcely mind it, much less would he scruple to comply." He believed that if truth had "full Room to play," it "would soon diffuse it self, and settle in almost every Man's Breast, at least with respect to Matters of Importance in Religion" (2:74–

75). The speaker echoed Franklin's opinion in his "Apology for Printers" (10 June 1731) where he said that "when Truth and Error have fair Play, the former is always an overmatch for the latter" (1:195). The locus classicus for that position, as noted above, was Milton's *Areopagitica*.

The letter writer next said that liberty "would probably soon lead People to lay aside all impertinent Practices, and cause them perfectly to forget, or at least hardly to think it worth while Disputing about a Number of metaphysical useless Points, which the Spirit of Pride and a Love of Power and Authority on one side, and Impatience of spiritual Servitude on the other, turn into so many Engines of Contention and War" (2:75).

What should be done with a person who disagreed with you? "Why truly, just nothing," for "he *may* be in the right" (2:75–76). The speaker's relativism, his ability to exist comfortably with a variety of possible realities, was unusual. The author exhibits the radical relativism of Franklin—an extraordinary attitude in colonial America, embraced only by Franklin, so far as I know. His reading of the classics, especially Lucretius, and of such moderns as Montaigne, Pascal, Locke, Pierre Bayle, and Mandeville all provided key elements of his philosophy and theology.[21] The author of the letter said that "to invest any Set of Men with a Power of thus Judging, and Censuring and Excommunicating according to their Determination" is to make "such Judges just so many *Popes*" (2:76). He had used the comparison above in "A Dialogue" (2:33).

Third, according to the speaker, "Creed-Imposers" claimed they should have "the Liberty of chusing their Teachers. If a Man that offers to be a Minister or Teacher, refuse to subscribe the Confession of Faith receiv'd in that Society into which he would be introduc'd as a Teacher, that Society has reason to think that that man entertains and might broach Heretical Doctrines; and if they have a Right to reject him, 'twould be very imprudent to admit him" (2:77). Franklin first boldly replied: "Perhaps it will be said, that a Man may dispute even the Truth of Christianity itself, reject Christ, look upon him as an Impostor, &c. Well, what then? Why, say they, must even that Man be admitted into Christian Communion with us? The Answer is obvious: That Man does not at all pretend to Communion, for he declares himself no Christian; he denies the Truth of Christianity in general. We don't exclude him, he excludes himself" (2:77).

In actuality, Franklin here examined his own case: if he were outspoken about his religious beliefs with the normal persons around him, he would exclude himself from their society. He had done so in Boston (and to some degree in the much larger society of London), though he knew one had to live with one's contemporaries. Franklin liked and respected most people. The seventeen-year-old iconoclast who ran away from Boston and was befriended by an "old woman" in Burlington (A 23) would never have questioned her religion or insinuated to her his religious doubts. She did not deserve anything other than respect and fine treatment because of her humanity and generous spirit. But pastors who thought respect automatically due them because they were ministers drew forth Franklin's sarcasm.

The letter writer went on to say that Hemphill was a Christian. But if one defines a Christian as a person who believes in the divinity of Christ (as Franklin defined it above), then Franklin was himself not a Christian (see his letter to Ezra Stiles, 9 March 1790, written just a few weeks before his death). The reason for not proclaiming his iconoclasm was that it would exclude him from the society and friendship of his fellows. As he had observed in his sea journal of 1726, "it is for aught I know one of the worst of punishments to be excluded from society" (1:85).

The main argument against the "Creed-Imposers" was that they had no authority to set up any religious tests other than a belief in the Scriptures. "Why should I pretend to impose my Sense of the Scriptures, or of any part of them, upon you, any more than you yours upon me? and since a Pretence to Infallibility is absurd, these Interpretations may in many Instances be wrong, and when this is the Case (as it is much to be fear'd, it but too often happens) Error and Falshood is impos'd instead of Truth" (2:78). Franklin may have recalled the arguments over Stoddardism in his youth. Increase and Cotton Mather and the other conservative ministers believed in the necessity of a spiritual relation before a person could become a full church member. Solomon Stoddard, Benjamin Colman, and others thought such public confessions were not essential. Some personalities were daunted by the public confession; some were not. It seemed to Samuel Willard, who baptized Franklin, that the public confession had little to do with whether or not one lived like a "visible saint." Willard stoutly declared that to censure anyone who conformed to the outward forms of religion was "to usurp Gods Prerogative in judging the heart."[22] Though a pillar of the New England Congregational Church, Willard's position on the issue was closer to that of St. Augustine and Roger Williams than to the theocratic tendencies of Massachusetts puritan ministers. Of course Franklin's position was more radical than Willard's.

Instead of censuring a person for his error, the speaker recommended that "the only Way to convince a Man of his Errors, is to address his Understanding. One solid Argument will do more than all the human Creeds and Confessions in the Universe; and if a Man once clearly sees the Truth of any Proposition or Article, his assent necessarily follows, and in all Cases of this Nature his Asssent will be in Proportion to Evidence perceiv'd" (2:79). Here Franklin echoes the Port Royal *Logic* and Locke's *Essay Concerning Human Understanding*, particularly the chapters "Of True and False Ideas" and "Of the Degrees of Assent."[23]

The author of the letter maintained that one should "never do any Thing that may hinder the Discovery of any useful and important Truth. You say, you may be led into Error, but if you be sincerely persuaded an erroneous Opinion is a true one, do you imagine our good and just God will punish you for it? No, surely; or else what would become of all Mankind. Sincerity is the Touchstone.

'Tis that will decide our future Condition" (2:79). Sincerity was one of Franklin's thirteen virtues in the *Autobiography*. Further, the writer, like Franklin in his private 1726 sea journal, linked truth and sincerity: "Truth and sincerity have a certain distinguishing native lustre about them which cannot be perfectly counterfeited, they are like fire and flame that cannot be painted" (1:78–79). "The Justness of our Reasonings, in all Instances, we cannot absolutely answer for; but we can know whether we be sincere in our Enquiries and Searches after, or Love for any Truth, whereby we suppose God's Glory, and the Good of our Fellow-Creatures may be promoted" (2:79). The author, like Franklin, lived in a state of metaphysical uncertainty.

The writer declared that to reject a minister "because he does not in the Whole believe as we do, is to declare we will not upon any Account, or for any Reason, alter our Opinions whatever they be. It is to declare that we are infallibly in the right" (2:80). He further contended that "To confine our selves to listen only to such Teachers as are sworn to tell us nothing but what we do sufficiently know and believe, is actually to forsake our Liberty, to fetter our Understandings, and limit ourselves to a poor, slavish, narrow Circle of Thought" (2:81).

The speaker then left the topic of freedom of thought to take up a surprising financial argument. The opinion anticipates Franklin's proposal during the Constitutional Convention that elected officials (representatives, senators, etc.) should not receive salaries (2 June 1787). The letter writer said "it were greatly to be wish'd that we had Teachers among us, who could live independently of the Gratuities and Voluntary Contributions of the People." No ministers wanted to hear that! The declaration fulfilled Franklin's threat in the preface that laymen "could make use of more prevailing Arguments than any that have been yet advanc'd, I mean such as oppose their temporal Interests" (2:66). The author continued, "Any Man in easy Circumstances, that had a competent Share of Learning, and a fair Character in the World, should at first Request be with Gratitude admitted into the Number of our Teachers" (2:81). Franklin's implied threat to the clergy was that none but voluntary teachers who had "easy Circumstances" would be admitted.

A minister who was denied "Communion with a Society of Christians" suffered first in reputation and second in his "Worldly Circumstances." The author revealed Franklin's occasional coarseness when he wrote that the case is worst with a person who has been a minister for some time who "is immediately depriv'd of Office and Benefice," for "he and his Family" may have to "go and starve on a Dunghill." The persona carried his logic to an extreme conclusion: "And tho' these Men tell us, they would not be for making use of Racks, Tortures, Gibbets, Death, &c. yet it is plain that if they have a Right to make Use of the lowest Degrees of Persecution, or to lay a Man under any Restraints for religious Speculations; they have a Right to proceed to higher degrees, if the lowest don't answer the End, and so to go on to the highest that even a Spanish

Inquisition cou'd invent, if nothing less will do" (2:81–82). The speaker again undermined his argument by being too strident.

The speaker then expressed a characteristic Franklin opinion concerning the effects of heredity, environment, education, and personality: "For as long as Men are made by God himself, of different Constitutions, Capacities, Genius's, &c. and since in his all-wise Providence he affords them very different, very various Opportunities of Education, Instruction and Example, a Difference in Opinion is inevitable. Besides a Man's Sentiments *are not in his own Power*; Conviction is the necessary Result or Effect of Proof and Evidence; and where the Proof does not appear sufficient, a Man cannot believe or assent to the suppos'd Truth of any Proposition if he would" (2:83, emphasis mine). Franklin wrote his son the same sentiments, using some of the same words on 16 August 1784: "I ought not to blame you for differing in Sentiment with me in Public Affairs. We are Men, all subject to Errors. Our Opinions *are not in our own Power*; they are form'd and govern'd much by Circumstances, that are often as inexplicable as they are irresistible" (emphasis mine).

The last argument of the "Creed-Imposers" was that "The strange Mixture of various and jarring Opinions, the Confusion which it is imagined would inevitably, upon the Principles here asserted, rush into the Church of Christ, is the grand Difficulty" (2:83). The speaker countered that these differences exist anyway: "Even in this City we have half a Dozen, for aught I know half a Score, different Sects; and were the Hearts of Men to be at once opened to our View, we should perhaps see a thousand Diversities more." Consciousness of the possible difference between appearance and reality is another Franklin trademark. In the following sentence, Franklin specifically referred to the supposed practice of the Catholic Church, which had recently erected a church in Philadelphia.[24] The author argued that "the greatest Absurdities and Falshoods are supported by this goodly Method of imposing Creeds and Confessions: Such as Cringings, Bowings, Mortifications, Penances, Transubstantiations, praying to Saints and Angels, Indulgences, Persecution or playing the Devil for God's Sake, &c. and if the Church has a Power of imposing at all, she has a Power of imposing every thing she looks upon to be Truth, and consequently the aforesaid Impertinences, if she in her great Wisdom thinks proper to do so" (2:84–85).

The speaker claimed that good would follow from abandoning fixed creeds. First, "there would be among Christians a full Liberty of declaring their Minds or Opinions to one another both in publick and private. And secondly Heresy, that huge Bugbear would no more frighten People, would no more kindle among us the hellish Fires of furious Zeal and Party Bigotry. We might peaceably, and without the least Breach upon Brotherly Love, differ in our religious Speculations as we do in Astronomy or any other Part of natural Philosophy" (2:85). Like Franklin, the persona used proverbs, and Franklin quoted the same one in his "Apology for Printers": "As many men, as many Minds" (2:85, 1:194).

The author again reveals Franklin's relative serenity in facing the voids of philosophical and theological speculation.

In a postscript the speaker said, "That even where the religious Rights of others are affected by our private Judgments, we must judge for our selves, and are in so doing only maintaining our own just Rights." Franklin echoed an eighteenth-century opinion that had been popularly expressed in "The Right of Private Judgment," which appeared in the London *Old Whig* on 10 April 1735 and had been reprinted in the April *London Magazine*. Franklin took its thesis to a more sophisticated philosophical level when he argued, "It is no matter, whether the particular Judgments Men form, are just and according to Truth, or not; for Truth consider'd as abstracted from the Discerning of the Mind, is no Rule of Action to any Man, nor can any Thing be Truth to us but as we apprehend it to be so, and *see* the Agreement *between the Ideas* compar'd in our Minds. So that in *receiving* the Truth ourselves, or *imposing* it upon others it must be the *Apprehension* or *Perception* of our Minds that must be our Rule. And this Rule must equally direct Men, whether they are really in the Right, or only *think* themselves so, seeing Truth not known or perceiv'd by the Mind, can be no Rule at all" (2:86–87). In short, truth, or what was usually meant by truth, was subjective. The author's logic and his awareness of truth as the perhaps wrong perception of an individual are Franklinian. One of the queries he had posed for discussion in the Junto about 1732 was, "If the Sovereign Power attempts to deprive a Subject of his Right (or *which is the same Thing, of what he thinks his Right* [emphasis mine]), is it justifiable in him to resist if he is able?" (1:263). We will return to Franklin's ideas of truth in discussing the draft of a letter to his father on 13 April 1738 (Chapter 12).

DECISION

At its annual fall meeting, the Presbyterian Synod ordered on 20 September "that Mr. Hemphill be notified to appear . . . if he sees cause, or has any thing to offer unto them." On 22 September, *A Letter to a Friend* came out, and that same day, Hemphill replied to the synod, saying that "what I have at present to offer to the Synod, is contained in an Answer to the Vindication of the Reverend Commission now in the press." Perhaps emboldened by Franklin's *Letter*, he added that he despised the synod's claim to authority and said, "I shall think you'll do me a deal of Honour, if you entirely excommunicate me." The synod ignored his challenge (which implied that it assumed the infallibility of the Catholic Church), but on that day, Monday, 22 September, declared him "unqualified for any future Exercise of his Ministry within our Bounds."

The synod also requested that "the brethren appointed to justify the Commission against any Complaints from Mr. Hemphill, if he should publish any such, having complied with the Commission's Order in that Matter, are desired by the Synod to continue to answer any further Publications of Mr. Hemphill's *or his Friends* [emphasis mine] in that Cause, if they shall think it necessary."

Publication costs were to be paid by the synod.[25] The reference to "or his Friends" suggests that some synod members now suspected or knew that Hemphill might not be responsible for the tracts defending him. Franklin, however, was not named.

A DEFENSE

In October, Franklin answered the commission's *Vindication*. His *Defense of Mr. Hemphill's Observations; or, an Answer to the Vindication of the Reverend Commission* was advertised as "Just Published" on 30 October. Franklin used the first person in the *Defense*, and his contemporaries again generally assumed that the author was Hemphill. Franklin began by attacking the ministers of the commission, quoting Shaftesbury's "Miscellaneous Reflections" in the *Characteristics* concerning the "high Characters, Appellations, and Titles" that ministers should support.[26] He again criticized Robert Cross and Ebenezer Pemberton for preaching against Hemphill during the trial (2:93). Franklin declared that the ministers had no right to censure Hemphill and expel him from their society, repeating his comparison to the Spanish Inquisition. As in *A Letter to a Friend*, he argued that if Hemphill's opinions were wrong, they should be heard and truth would win out (2:95).

Replying to the charge that some of Hemphill's sermons were borrowed, Franklin argued that all ministers borrowed. We are told "that Ministers ought to have a good Salary, because they are at great Expence in Learning, and in purchasing Books. If they preach from their own natural Fund or by immediate Inspiration, what need have they either of Learning or Books?" The only difference between Hemphill and other ministers was that the others "chuse the dullest Authors to read and study, and retail the dullest Parts of those Authors to the Publick. It seems as if they search'd only for Stupidity and Nonsense." In contrast, Hemphill "gave us the best Parts of the best Writers of the Age." Franklin adopted and revised the apologue of the spider and the bee, which he knew from several sources, including Jonathan Swift's *Battle of the Books* and Bernard Mandeville's *Fable of the Bees*: "Thus the Difference between him and most of his Brethren, in this part of the World, is the same with that between the Bee and the Fly in a Garden. The one wanders from Flower to Flower, and for the use of others collects from the whole the most delightful Honey; while the other (of a quite different Taste) places her Happiness entirely in Filth, Corruption, and Ordure" (2:96–97).[27] The assertions were impassioned and the tone insulting.

Franklin returned for the third time to the supposed impropriety of admitting Thomson and Gillespie among the judges when they were already prejudiced against Hemphill. He said that "three Gentlemen of undoubted Credit" declared that they had seen Thomson's letters condemning Hemphill. Franklin asked, "Did they not repeat one Sentence that made it [their prejudice] obvious to the whole Congregation?" (2:97). He referred to the first day's hearing, 17

April, when Hemphill challenged two judges. Franklin said that according to their procedure, "no Fact, how atrocious soever, and witness'd by ever so many credible Persons, shou'd be punish'd unless done in open Court, that the Judges themselves might see it." He declared that the commission outdid "the Jesuits themselves, in *Subterfuge, Distinction and Evasion*," and quoted two passages from *Hudibras* that insulted Presbyterians (2:97–98).

The witnesses for Hemphill were stifled, according to Franklin, by moderator Ebenezer Pemberton, who cried out that "He wou'd have no clashing of Evidences." Franklin said that "the Evidence in Hemphill's Favour was beyond Comparison," but the very fact that witnesses appeared for Hemphill was "Cause sufficient to make the impartial Commission disregard or suppress their Testimony" (2:99–100). Franklin also disclosed the name of the minister (Nathaniel Hubbell) who had seemingly justified lying in order to entrap the accused (2:101).

Franklin outrageously claimed that the six arguments in the *Vindication* actually propagated "Enthusiasm, Demonism, and Immorality in the World." His premise was that "the main End and Design of . . . Religion" was "to promote the Practice of Piety, Goodness, Virtue, and Universal Righteousness among Mankind, or the Practice of the moral Duties both with Respect to God and Man, and by these Means to make us happy here and hereafter" (2:102–5). In other words, Franklin made religion merely ethics. The first article in the *Vindication* concerned Christianity as a second revelation of God's will, the first being the Light of Nature. The most surprising feature of Franklin's rebuttal of this argument is his familiarity with the theological polemics of the Reverend Joseph Boyse (1660–1728). The mature Franklin either remembered his father's books of divinity or had read Presbyterian theology since then (2:107–10).

Franklin's persona had increasingly lost its decorum and sense of audience as the quarrel went on. In replying to the charge that Hemphill denied the necessity of a new birth to those born in the church, Franklin seemed only to be appealing to deists and freethinkers. He retorted that Hemphill merely discriminated between heathens and wicked Christians on the one hand and those who were always good Christians on the other. Franklin claimed that Christians who make daily progress in virtue do not necessarily become "new Creatures." Belief in a new birth, however, was a fundamental tenet of Presbyterians—and of Puritans in general. Franklin travestied their old syllogistic reasoning while viciously assaulting them: "Asses are grave and dull Animals, / our Authors are grave and dull Animals; therefore / Our Authors are grave, dull, or if you will, Reverend Asses" (2:113). Hemphill may have agreed with him but would never have been so insulting. Franklin, however, went even further and denounced the doctrine of original sin.

The doctrine of *"our lost and undone State by Nature,"* proceeding from "old Father Adam's first Guilt," is a "Bugbear set up by Priests (whether *Popish* or *Presbyterian* I know not) to fright and scare an unthinking Populace out of their Senses." Franklin undercut the Presbyterians by suggesting that the doctrine was Roman Catholic. He declared that the teaching was "absurd in it self" and could not "be father'd upon the Christian Religion as deliver'd in the Gospel." Moral guilt, he said, "is so personal a Thing, that it cannot possibly in the Nature of Things be transferr'd from one Man to Myriads of others, that were no way accessary to it" (2:114). If original sin existed, it was unjust and cruel. In several satires, Franklin had implicitly condemned the nature of a God who could create such a system. Here, however, he went further and directly expressed what he thought the Calvinistic position said about the nature of God— God was unjust and cruel. He sarcastically echoed this opinion on original sin in a letter of 9 November 1765 to his wife. Upon hearing from her that Provost William Smith had accused Franklin of planning the Stamp Act, he wrote, "I thank him he does not charge me (as they do their God) with having plann'd Adam's Fall, and the Damnation of Mankind" (12:360).

Though Franklin had drawn support from biblical texts several times in the controversy, he now rejected its authority. If passages supporting the doctrine of original sin exist in the Bible, they "could not be genuine, being so evidently contrary to Reason and the Nature of Things." Thus, reason is supposedly superior to the Bible. He compounded his unorthodoxy by stating that the doctrine of original sin "has no other Tendency than to represent the great Father of Mercy, the beneficent Creator and Preserver of universal Nature, as arbitrary, unjust and cruel." Franklin actually claimed that teaching the doctrine of original sin was "teaching . . . Demonism" (2:114–15). He could not have opened himself more directly to the charge of heresy. Hemphill may earlier have been grateful for Franklin's defense, but if he had ever hoped to preach again, this tract (ostensibly by Hemphill) would certainly have ended his ministry.[28]

In questioning the nature of God, Franklin revealed his skepticism. The same ideas appeared earlier in *A Dissertation on Liberty and Necessity* (1725), and recently in several short tracts, like "The Death of Infants" (20 June 1734), though in these writings Franklin did not so directly and openly express his opinions. He wrote to his sister Jane on 30 December 1770 that in order to think God was all-powerful and all-good, one must suppose that this world was the true hell. Franklin's opinions are neither Presbyterian nor Christian. They show him to be a skeptic who sometimes seems agnostic and sometimes atheistic. He not infrequently, however, suggested that some other possibility concerning God might be correct. As we will see, he thought his own beliefs were probably wrong. An element of his theological thought was fideism. Since ultimate realities were unknowable through our reason and sensory perceptions, there might be a God.

Franklin took up Hemphill's supposed declamation "against the Doctrine of Christ's Merit and Satisfaction." The commission's excluding non-Christians from salvation roused Franklin's ire. "Pray, how came these Reverend Gentlemen to know that the Heathen, living up to the Light of Nature, may not have an Interest in the Merits and Satisfaction of Christ, or that they may not be accepted of God upon account thereof." Again, Franklin judged the nature of God: "And can any imagine that our good God, as is here suppos'd, will eternally damn the Heathen World for not obeying a Law they never heard of; that is, damn them for not doing an Impossibility." Franklin returned to this line of thought, as well as to other ideas in the Hemphill tracts, a few years later in *A Speech Delivered by an Indian Chief, in Reply to a . . . Swedish Missionary*. Franklin continued, "Surely none can imagine such a thing; except such as form their Ideas of the great Governor of the Universe, by reflecting upon their own cruel, unjust and barbarous Tempers, as our Authors seem to do." The skeptic found it impossible to think that "a good and just God" could condemn the heathens who followed the "Light of Nature" (2:118–19). He repeated that he would reject any passages of the Bible that contradicted the clear "Decisions of Reason." Instead of a God of "infinite Justice, Goodness and Mercy," the ministers created a "stern, arbitrary, inexorable" God (2:120).

The remarks on original sin and the nature of God did not belong in a pamphlet ostensibly defending Hemphill from a group of Presbyterian ministers. Franklin's statements were more damning than anything the commission had excerpted from Hemphill's sermons.

After briefly opposing the fourth and fifth accusations, Franklin answered the sixth at length. The ministers found that "Hemphill has subverted the Doctrine of Justification by Faith" (2:122). Hemphill had claimed that good works as well as faith were necessary to salvation. Following Franklin's defense of Hemphill in *Some Observations*, Pemberton and Dickinson had further condemned him in *A Vindication*. Writing the liveliest prose in the Hemphill pamphlets, Franklin countered:

> *It is scarce possible for a Man to bind together a great[er] Bundle of Error, Ignorance and Impertinence in so few Words, than this Gentleman has done.* Hah! a home Thrust! a bold Stroke! next Turn's mine. Here they suppose this Position of Hemphill's to be erroneous, &c. And yet in the next Paragraph tell us, with a sanctify'd Leer, that *the whole Protestant World, the Antinomians only excepted, have constantly taught, that those Men who have been educated in the Christian Religion, are justifyed by a Faith, that from the very Nature of it is necessarily accompanied with Good Works, by a Faith that can no more exist without good Works, than the Body can live without the Spirit,* &c. So then we are now justify'd by a Faith, the very Life and Soul of which consists in good Works, as certainly as the Life of the Body consists in the Spirit. Such Inconsistency! Such Self-contradiction! Surely these Men's Spirits must be strangely muffled up with Phlegm, and their Brains, if they have any, *encompass'd with a Fence of a most impenetrable Thickness.* (2:124–25)

From the lively, informal exclamations to the concluding "s" alliterations, the paragraph uses a highly literary and declamatory style.

Franklin concluded the pamphlet with repetitions of the words *sense* and *honesty*, dividing the commission into three classes: "first, the Men of Honesty who wanted Sense; secondly the Men of Sense, who wanted Honesty; and lastly those who had neither Sense, nor Honesty." *The Papers of Benjamin Franklin* omitted a postscript supposedly added by Samuel Hemphill: "Since the Writing of this, Mr. *Hemphill* has been inform'd that the Reverend Synod has with great Formality, Gravity and Solemnity, excommunicated him entirely out of their Society. As Gratitude is a Debt always due for a Favour bestow'd, and as expelling the said *Hemphill* out of so bad Company, was the greatest Favour and Honour these Reverend Gentlemen were capable of doing him, he takes this publick Opportunity of thanking them very heartily for it."[29]

REPLIES

The same day that Franklin's *Defence* appeared (30 October), the *American Weekly Mercury* advertised that *Remarks upon a Pamphlet, Entitled A Letter to a Friend in the Country* was "now in the press." Even though Franklin was ill during 1735, he wrote pamphlets in the Hemphill controversy faster than the commission. The commission's writings, however, had to be approved by at least its key members, and we know that their *Vindication* had been written by three persons. In effect, the commission's previous writings were produced by a committee. The next document, however, was evidently by Jonathan Dickinson. His reply did not appear until December. In a reasonable and conciliatory tone (completely unlike Franklin's last pamphlet), Dickinson lamented past persecutions in the name of faith (thus granting one of Franklin's points in the *Letter*) but added that under the present liberty, the opposite extreme was now a danger and accused Franklin's *Letter*, "notwithstanding the many valuable Truths, so fairly stated, and rationally established by it," of opening the "Door to *Infidelity*" (2).

In his *Remarks*, Dickinson objected to the invectives in the preface and excerpted examples. Mainly, however, he quarreled with the substance of the supposed sermon. He asked, "Whether any Man may be esteemed an *Heretick*, who professeth a Belief of the holy Scriptures?" (9). He argued that such heretics were numerous. He also took up Franklin's argument against imposing one's opinions on others: "For tho' it be true, that I have no juster Pretence than any other Person, to determine what is a fundamental Article of Religion; and on that Account to impose my Opinion upon others: Yet I have an undoubted Right, to judge for my self, and to reject those Opinions which I think fundamentally erroneous; and consequently to enjoy the Liberty of my *Conscience*, by refusing Communion with those, that I think unqualified for it. . . . As I may not impose my *Credenda* on other Men, neither may they impose theirs on me. If I think in my Conscience, *Arianism* (for Instance) unqualifies a Man for my Communion, must I be forced against my *Conscience*, to have either Christian or Ministerial Communion with such a Person? What then becomes of the *Free-*

dom and *Liberty* that this Author so strenuously argues for?" (15–16). Dickinson concluded by quoting John Locke's *Letter Concerning Toleration*: "This is the fundamental and immutable Right of a spontaneous Society, that it has Power to remove any of its Members, who transgress the Rules of its Institution. But it cannot by the Accession of any new Members, acquire any Jurisdiction over those, that are not joined with it. And therefore Peace, Equity, and Friendship, are always mutually to be observed, by particular Churches, in the same Manner, as by private Persons, without any Pretence of Superiority or Jurisdiction over one another."

Dickinson argued that he and the Presbyterian Synod had every right to reject Hemphill, for he disagreed with them in the fundamental beliefs of Presbyterianism.

Before Dickinson's *Remarks upon* appeared on 4 December, Franklin's *Defence* had been published. A rebuttal to it, according to the synod's September agreement, was called for. "Obadiah Jenkins" was the pseudonymous author of *Remarks upon a Defense of the Reverend Mr. Hemphill's Observations*. A contemporary annotation on the Princeton copy says, "Chiefly by Mr. [Jonathan] D[ickinson] to p. 15," and "Partly by Mr. [Ebenezer] P[emberton] from p. 16."[30] *Remarks upon the Defence* was dated New York, 24 November. The *American Weekly Mercury* advertised it as "now in the Press" on 18 December and finally as "Just Published" on 6 January 1735/6. The full title, *Remarks upon the Defence of the Reverend Mr. Hemphill's Observations: In a Letter to a Friend. Wherein the Orthodoxy of His Principles, the Excellency and Meekness of His Temper, and the Justice of His Complaints against the Reverend Commission, Are Briefly Considered; and Humbly Proposed to the View of His Admirers*, did not quite say it all: Dickinson proved, however, that Franklin's statements were unorthodox, that he poured contempt and irate expressions upon the ministers, and that he denied the truth of the Bible. Dickinson also listed in parallel columns Franklin's statements on original sin, on conversion and sanctification, on the satisfaction of Christ, on the end and design of Christ's incarnation and obedience, on justification, and on faith in Jesus Christ—all compared with the standard Presbyterian positions. Franklin's were "new fangled Notions" (15). Then Pemberton took over, thoroughly documenting Hemphill's plagiarisms: "His Sermon on *Mark* xvi.16. was borrowed (or rather stolen) from Dr. *Clarke*, an open *Arian*. His Sermons on *Gal.* vi.15. on *Rom* viii.18. and on *Psal* xli.4. from *Clarke's* assistant Dr. Ibbors. And his Sermon on *Acts* xxiv.25 from Mr. *Foster*. And how ingenious soever these Authors may be, they are the most noted Underminers of those Doctrines which have ever been esteemed the peculiar Glory of the Protestant Churches" (18). Hemphill's sources, Pemberton suggested, were even more objectionable than his plagiarism.

In the *Autobiography*, Franklin said that the plagiarism charge discredited Hemphill. He completely dropped out of sight after his contemptuous reply, which the Presbyterian synod received on 22 September (reprinted in the postscript to Franklin's *Defense*). But Franklin's *Defense* would have buried him more effectually than any number of plagiarisms from liberal theologians. By 1736, Hemphill was long gone, the public was tired of the quarrel, and even the tenacious Franklin seemingly gave up—at least on Hemphill. After Hemphill left, Franklin again stopped attending Philadelphia's Presbyterian church, though he continued to support its ministers. At the same time, he had been paying for his wife's seat in the Anglican Christ Church, and by 1736 he must also have been paying for William's seat there.

Why?

Why did Franklin do it? He wrote four pieces supporting Hemphill, none of which could gain him anything but infamy in 1735 Philadelphia. He repeated the pattern he had established as an adolescent in Boston in 1722–23, where his writing and discourse made him "pointed at with Horror by good People, as an Infidel or Atheist" (A 20). Though the *Autobiography* does not list the Hemphill tracts among the "errata" he committed, they were.

Two reasons for Franklin's replies are straightforward. First, he became caught up in the controversy, one tract leading to the next. He wrote the "Dialogue" (published 10 April) to defend Hemphill and make some commonsensical observations on his behalf. The tone of the "Dialogue" is reasonable, and though Franklin betrays a radical skepticism, one has to read between the lines to detect it. The "Dialogue," however, had little effect other than to stir up some possible questions among the public about the trial's procedures. When the commission's *Extracts* appeared, attempting to justify its decision, Franklin became angry about what the authors did not say. Since his "Dialogue" had occasioned the *Extracts*, he felt he should reply to it. He believed that Hemphill was maligned and that pertinent evidence was being suppressed or overlooked. He therefore wrote *Some Observations*. The commission's subcommittee replied to it with their *Vindication*. Before it appeared, Franklin wrote *A Letter*, setting forth his own religious beliefs, though ostensibly in the persona of Hemphill.

He wrote *A Defense* in reply to the commission's *Vindication*. It contained a much more strident tone, castigated particular members of the commission, and divulged his own heretical beliefs. Perhaps young Franklin (then twenty-nine) had persevered in the Hemphill quarrel partially through pride. Two more replies by the commission's subcommittee followed: *Remarks upon . . . A Letter*; and *Remarks upon a Defense*. Franklin wisely gave up the contest and left these tracts unanswered.

A second reason Franklin defended Hemphill is equally obvious—he thought Hemphill's sermons were good, and he enjoyed them. He believed Hemphill was right in preaching morality and works rather than faith and right in praying for all humankind rather than for just Presbyterians.

At least four additional reasons may be partially responsible, and a fifth should probably be considered. First, Franklin's authorship was not recognized.

Though he appeared as the publisher in the preface to *A Letter to a Friend*, no replies were addressed to Franklin. Dickinson and the other members of the subcommittee who replied to Franklin all believed (or pretended to believe) that they were answering Hemphill. That allowed Franklin to try out his subversive religious opinions in public and to see what the reaction to them would be without venturing his reputation (and his young printing business) in the battle. Further, as I have pointed out, Franklin repeatedly revealed that he took special pleasure in witnessing the reactions to his writings when he was not known to be the author. There are, however, three hints that some people suspected he was writing the Hemphill defenses. As noted above, Ebenezer Pemberton may have alluded to Franklin in the preface to his sermon. Second, the synod referred to "further publications of Mr. Hemphill *or his Friends*" (emphasis mine). And third, a mock advertisement in Bradford's 28 August 1735 *Mercury* dated "Boston, August 18" seemed to point at Franklin: it announced, "shortly will be Publish'd, a Notable Piece, Intitled, *The Venal Advocate, Or, The Character of Janus and Proteus display'd, in a Dialogue between Philadelphia and New York*." Since Hemphill/Franklin wrote from Philadelphia and Dickinson and Pemberton wrote partly from New York, the advertisement probably referred to the Hemphill tracts. Franklin was already well-known for his multiple personae and his literary shape-shifting. Someone may have been calling Franklin "The Venal Advocate," for "Janus," the two-faced god, was a symbol for a printer, and "Proteus," the shape-shifter, was an apt name for a writer who assumed numerous personae.

Second, the defense of Hemphill may relate to Franklin's grave illness during 1735. He must have thought that he might die. When he was sick for a shorter period in 1727, he wrote that he "suffered a good deal, gave up the Point in my own mind, and was rather disappointed when I found my self recovering" (A 52). Though "A Dialogue" was written before he became seriously ill, the three pamphlets were written during his illness. Perhaps he wanted to spread his doctrine of universal toleration for all speculative opinions as a contribution to society. Perhaps, too, his illness affected his judgment and made him impatient and irritable with the others' opinions. Certainly, the intemperate tone and castigations in Franklin's Hemphill pamphlets are unusual in his writings.

Third, James Franklin died on 4 February 1734/5, only a few weeks before Franklin published the "Dialogue," his first defense of Hemphill. Though the brothers had a stormy relationship, they were close, and Franklin must have grieved for his brother. Franklin surely remembered his brother's ambitions and his triumphs and disasters in Boston. He probably thought that his older brother had failed to realize his potential. The younger sibling may have partly blamed himself for leaving James Franklin alone to carry on the fight against the Boston theocracy. Franklin had to know that his older brother never did as well, either financially or literarily, after Franklin left Boston in 1723. Perhaps he felt that in challenging the Presbyterian commission and synod, he was once again joining in spirit with his redoubtable brother, fighting against authority.

Fourth, the Reverend Ebenezer Pemberton, moderator of the commission and the son of Franklin's childhood minister, had been a schoolmate at the Boston Grammar School. He was probably one of the slightly older boys whom Franklin surpassed. Though the older Pemberton had died in 1717, the community supported young Ebenezer, who went to Harvard on scholarships.[31] Thinking of Ebenezer Pemberton as Hemphill's judge may have brought back all the old resentments that Franklin felt when his father took him out of the grammar school and seemed to condemn him to the comparatively unimportant life of an artisan. For Franklin, Pemberton probably represented the Boston theocracy that James and he had opposed in the *New England Courant*. Franklin held Pemberton, as moderator of the commission, primarily responsible for its unfair procedures. In defending Hemphill against Pemberton, Franklin probably relived his early struggles against Boston's religious hegemony.

A final possibility (which might occur to some persons but which I do not believe) concerns finances and the business rivalry with Andrew Bradford. Franklin's "Dialogue" in the *Pennsylvania Gazette* was notorious and sold extra copies of that issue. *Some Observations* likewise became the talk of the town and had two editions. It seems unlikely, however, that Franklin's motivation in taking up Hemphill's cause was economic. The fact that a pamphlet had two editions, though it proves its popularity, also proves that the printer misjudged its probable sale and printed too few copies. There is also no evidence that either his *Letter to a Friend* or his *Defense* sold well. It is likely that the public had tired of the controversy by the time they appeared. And though all four of the commission's pamphets were published by Andrew Bradford, that only seems logical. The controversy was centered in Philadelphia, and the only other Philadelphia printer, Benjamin Franklin, supported Hemphill and was publishing the pamphlets in his favor.

Whatever the explanation, Franklin's involvement in the Hemphill affair was a failure and a mistake. Though the writings were generally attributed to Hemphill at the time, the irreligious opinions in them shocked Philadelphia's ordinary citizens. Franklin lost the battle to defend Hemphill, but he returned to some of the basic questions in refashioning within the next several years *A Speech Delivered by an Indian Chief, in Reply to a . . . Swedish Missionary*. In the *Autobiography*, he had the last word on Hemphill and on the preaching of Jedediah Andrews, which he said was "dry, uninteresting and unedifying, since not a single moral Principle was inculcated or enforc'd, their Aim seeming to be rather to make us Presbyterians than good Citizens" (A 77).

Francis Bacon's Idols and Franklin's Hemphill Tracts

In the *Novum Organum*, Francis Bacon defined four species of idols that beset human beings: idols of the tribe, idols of the den, idols of the market, and idols of the theater. In Franklin's Hemphill tracts, written for an obscure occasion that affected at most a few hundred people in 1735 and was soon forgotten, the printer touched on most of Bacon's idols. Franklin had surely read the *Novum Organum* and may have had it in mind.

The idols of the tribe are those mistakes inherent in human nature, especially the tendency for humans to judge everything by their own standards. Franklin's frequent castigations of the commission's judgments in assuming authority over the beliefs and opinions of others (which he compared to the Roman Catholic pope's claims of infallibility) could be considered idols of the tribe. The idols of the den are the mistakes of individuals caused by heredity, education, and custom. These are different for every individual, but all persons are subject to these immediate influences—which, in turn, are simply due to chance. Thus there are a bewildering variety of beliefs in the world and different beliefs even within one small village. In *A Letter*, Franklin twice dwells on the idols of the den. The idols of the market are those factors brought about by the exchanges between persons, exchanges primarily dependent on words, which, in turn, depend on the common usage of a particular society. The words themselves often necessarily convey mistakes, thus bolstering Franklin's recurring epistemological skepticism. Finally, there are the idols of the theater, which include dogmatic structures of philosophy, theology, or logic. The Philadelphia Synod's subscription to the Westminster Confession was, of course, the basic reason for Hemphill's heresy trial. As we saw, Franklin objected to making it an article of necessary faith, as well as to the particular doctrine of original sin and the belief that faith was more important than good works.

All in all, Franklin dwelt on various versions of Bacon's four idols in defending Samuel Hemphill; but his impassioned and overzealous argument revealed that he, too, was guilty of the idols of the tribe.

ELEVEN

Assessing Franklin as a Young Man, Age 24 to 30

For as long as Men are made by God himself, of different Constitutions, Capacities, Genius's, &c. and since in his all-wise Providence he affords them very different, very various Opportunities of Education, Instruction and Example, a Difference in Opinion is inevitable.—Franklin, defending Hemphill (2:83)

THOUGH HIS MAJOR WRITINGS and scientific achievements were yet to come, the essential Franklin emerged in these years of early adulthood—a person of great self-discipline, a shrewd businessman, an extraordinarily hard worker, a brilliant man of letters, a doer of good, and a civic-minded citizen. He was also proud and sometimes rash; moreover, he could be a subtle and fierce enemy.

In a common-law marriage, Franklin took Deborah Read Rogers to wife on 1 June 1730. Since her former husband was rumored to have a wife in England, and since he had absconded in December 1727 owing money, the form of marriage was sensible. She immediately became a partner in the business, caring for the shop and assisting in some printing chores like sewing the pamphlets. Franklin was evidently caring for his young son, William (born about 1728), when he married. Franklin's decision to raise his son himself continually reminded some Philadelphians that he had not been chaste before marriage. William's mother remains unknown. As Poor Richard said, "Three may keep a Secret, if two of them are dead" (July 1735). Franklin's reputation as a sexual roué owes something to having fathered an illegitimate child.

Though he reported being "much hurryed in Business" in June 1730, Franklin continually added organizations and responsibilities to his business activities. He had met Pennsylvania's eminent lawyer and politician, Andrew Hamilton, in London during 1725. Hamilton became his major patron, responsible for appointing Franklin and Meredith printers to the Pennsylvania Assembly in 1730 and Franklin as clerk to the assembly in 1736. Franklin, in turn, defended Hamilton in the *Pennsylvania Gazette*, especially in the interview, "A Half-Hour's Conversation with a Friend" (16 November 1733). Franklin joined the Philadelphia Freemasons early in 1731 and was elected its grand master in 1734. In the spring of 1731, he organized the Library Company of Philadelphia, which soon thereafter became a flourishing institution. In this and later endeavors he began by enlisting the opinions and support of the cadre of friends that constituted the Junto. Through the Library Company and his love for books, he became allied with the older Philadelphia intellectual James Logan. At the end of 1732, he started *Poor Richard*, which immediately became the best-selling almanac of the Middle Colonies.

Franklin's private course of study more than compensated for his lack of formal education. He developed a reputation as an intellectual during these years. He read and translated German by 1731 and French by 1732. From French, he went on to study Spanish, Italian, and Latin (though he may have studied Latin as an adolescent). He continued reading widely in history, philosophy, and literature and wrote numerous essays, skits, and philosophical discussions for private circulation and for his newspaper. He also pursued interests in natural philosophy while forming friendships with such men as John Bartram and Peter Collinson in the international natural history circle.

By his thirtieth birthday, 6 January 1735/6, he was better-off financially and socially than his parents or any of his siblings—and almost all of Philadelphia's artisans. In the *Autobiography*, he contrasted his 1727 entry into Philadelphia "with the Figure I have since made there" (A 24). The first time he made a "figure" in Philadelphia was on Monday, 24 June 1734: as grand master of the Masons, he provided "a very elegant Entertainment" when "the Proprietor, the Governor, and several other Persons of Distinction honour'd the Society with their Presence."

As his status changed, he assumed responsibilities for an extended family. When his brother James died early in 1735, Franklin began helping his widow, Anne (Smith) Franklin, by sending her gratis every year hundreds of copies of *Poor Richard*. He probably gave her copies of his other imprints for free as well. Within a few years, he gave his brother's widow his old types, took in her son James ("Jemmy"), paid for his education, and, in 1740, made him an apprentice.

Had Franklin changed his metaphysical or his religious beliefs since writing *A Dissertation on Liberty and Necessity*? Perhaps not. Even his series of responses to such a simple matter as the case of the missing horse (25 January 1731/2) displays numerous bewildering and contrasting opinions, suggesting that he believed reality had numerous possible complexities with little or no metaphysical certainty. In Philadelphia during 1730–36, as earlier in Boston and London, Franklin wrote literary satires rashly attacking religion and ministers, thereby continuing his reputation as an infidel. After being accused of "abundant Malice against Religion and the Clergy," Franklin apologized for printing "No Sea Hens nor Black Gowns will be admitted on any Terms" in an advertisement for a voyage. His "Apology for Printers" (10 June 1731) made light of the criticism, even while continuing it by saying that writing against the clergy was "a fruitful Topic, and the easiest to be witty upon of all others." Further, he continued to mock religious opinions in his "Meditation on a Quart Mugg" (19 July 1733) and in his parody and reply to a religious meditation (8 August 1734). His essay

"The Death of Infants" (29 June 1734) satirized physico-theology and the Argument from Design. It continued his bleak pessimism concerning the nature of God.

He remained obsessed with theology, morality, and philosophy, writing more on them in 1735 than in any other year. During the Hemphill affair he denounced some individual doctrines that most Christian religions accepted and revealed that his skepticism extended to his own beliefs. He valued Christian ethics because they were good for people and tended to make them happy: "they carry their own Reward, tho' there were nothing to reward our Obedience or punish our Disobedience in another Life" (2:50–51). Truth may be unknowable; other opinions concerning religion may be right; all one can ask is sincerity in the pursuit of truth. Opinions about ultimate realities necessarily differ. Franklin's skepticism concerning reason led him, at times, toward fideism.

Franklin wrote in the *Autobiography* that his father advised him to "avoid lampooning and libeling to which he thought I had too much Inclination." He had not yet, however, learned to do so. The *Gazette* for 29 February 1731/2 contained an essay by "A. Z." satirizing quacks, punning on worms and wormers. The piece boldly reflected on the Philadelphia Common Council. "For my Part, having considered the whole Affair, I must needs say, I think it deserves a more effectual Animadversion than mine; and that (with the utmost Humility I offer it) should our worthy—[Mayor] and C—M-n [Council Men] take it under theirs, it would become the sagacity and Vigilance so often shown for the Interest and Honour of our wise and religious City." Even if Franklin did not write the ironic attack (he may have), its publication must have aggrieved the corporation. The Philadelphia Corporation had faults, but Franklin could hardly have thought that satirizing the mayor and councilmen and ironically repeating the cant about the "wise and religious" city would serve any useful purpose.

Franklin continued to reveal faults. By threatening adverse publicity, he manipulated his election into the Philadelphia Freemasons. His satire on the parents of the girl he had been courting was, to the Godfreys and others in the know, vicious. There seems to have been no reason for his mocking the almanac maker John Jerman. The maxim that he wrote for himself under the virtue "Moderation" was "Forbear resenting Injuries so much as you think they deserve" (A 79). Perhaps he never quite learned to do so.

In some ways Franklin's faults complemented his virtues: he exuded intellectual and physical energy (though he had a second prolonged sickness in 1735), writing much, engaging in controversies, rushing in to aid anyone he thought poorly treated, and creating or joining civic and social organizations. Early eighteenth-century America, though more democratic than England or Europe, was nevertheless deferential and hierarchical. The egalitarian Franklin, who identified with what was commonly called the "lower sort," could not help but jeer at some aspects of his society and at the pretensions of his "superiors." As he wrote in the "Outline" for the *Autobiography*, "Costs me nothing to be civil to inferiors, a good deal to be submissive to superiors" (A 205). Note, however, that he automatically accepts the existence of "inferiors" and "superiors" in eighteenth-century society.

Ethically, Franklin tried to hold himself to high standards. In the spring of 1731, he drew up his scheme of self-discipline (the list of thirteen virtues and the chart of how to spend the hours of a day) to impose control over his private life. He did not think the list was especially suitable for others; it was drawn up to correct his own faults, but he thought the systematic method might be generally useful. He wanted to make himself better morally, though he still committed the personal and intellectual blunders of a young iconoclast. Yet, how many young artisans in his circumstances in his day assumed responsibility for a bastard child?

Franklin's political positions were becoming clear during this period. As champion of a paper currency, he was identified with Pennsylvania's Popular or Quaker Party. On the other hand, he advocated a strong militia (6 March 1733/4) and became known as Pennsylvania's foremost proponent of military preparedness, which was a Proprietary Party position. Generally, however, his egalitarianism placed him in opposition to the Proprietary Party, which, as the name implied, favored proprietary privileges. He met Thomas and John Penn during this period, and he was disgusted by their repeated avariciousness and selfishness (especially when they demanded that their quitrents be paid in sterling, thus undercutting Pennsylvania's paper currency). His identification with the Popular Party was clear in his first editorial in the *Pennsylvania Gazette*, when he sided with the Old Charter Party in Massachusetts against the governor's demand for a fixed salary. That same editorial also expressed his Americanism, which was restated in this period not only in his satire of English condescension but in his attacks on the Acts of Trade and Navigation. He publicized and implicitly criticized the Board of Trade's rejecting acts passed by various colonies that would have taxed and therefore impeded the importation of slaves and transported felons.

He mocked his own pride and satirized himself as well as others. In the *Pennsylvania Gazette* on 23 September 1731 he wrote, "Thursday last, a certain P—r ['tis not customary to give Names at length on these Occasions] walking carefully in clean Cloaths over some Barrels of Tar on Carpenter's Wharff, the head of one of them unluckily gave way, and let a Leg of him in above his Knee. Whether he was upon the Catch at that time, we cannot say, but 'tis certain he caught a Tartar. 'Twas observ'd he sprung out again right briskly, verifying the common Saying, As nimble as a Bee in a Tarbarrel. You must know there are several sorts of Bees: 'tis true he was no Honey Bee, nor yet a Humble Bee, but a Boo bee he may be allow'd to be, namely B.F."

PART II

Expanding Personal Interests, Age 30 through 41 (1736–1747)

TWELVE

Personal Life

God only knows whether all the Doctrines I hold for true, be so or not. For my own part, I must confess, I believe they are not.—Franklin to his parents, 13 April 1738 (2:202n.)

DEBORAH FRANKLIN

Franklin loved and identified with Deborah. Their great tragedy was the death of their son Francis at age four in 1736. Deborah, like Franklin, was approximately thirty years old at the time. Since they had only one child in their first six years of marriage, it seemed unlikely that the couple would have another. The thought must have been an unhappy one: they were both from large families, and they had probably expected to have several children. But as the years passed and Deborah progressed through her early and middle thirties without a second child, they probably resigned themselves to being childless. It was no doubt harder for Deborah than for Franklin; he had a son. Indeed, the presence of the illegitimate William probably only added to Deborah's dejection. The couple were no doubt overjoyed to realize in the spring of 1743 that Deborah was pregnant, due early that fall.

Franklin celebrated Deborah as a faithful wife and partner in the *Autobiography*. Throughout these years, she helped in Franklin's various businesses. She continued working in the printing office and in the shop. After Franklin was appointed postmaster in 1737, Deborah, with a clerk, supervised the post office. She was a good cook, housekeeper, and hostess. She was loyal, courageous, and loved Franklin.

Deborah was impatient with pretentious persons but rarely showed it. Instead, she had a saying that Franklin, when considering the ostentatious displays of the Society of the Cincinnati, recalled long after her death. He wrote their daughter, Sarah, that the patrician trappings of the society reminded him of a favorite expression of Deborah's concerning "punctilious Persons, who are always exacting little Observances of Respect . . . *if People can be pleased with small Matters, it is a pity but they should have them*" (26 January 1784).

A testimony to Franklin's feelings for her is their wedding anniversary song. According to the Philadelphia physician John Bard, he and Franklin were at a club where someone objected to married men singing songs in praise of mistresses. Franklin had often ridiculed the common satires against marriage and

women. The morning after the club meeting, Franklin gave Bard a song celebrating Deborah and asked that he sing it at their next gathering.[1]

A different origin for the song was recorded in the early 1780s by Franklin's
young friend Pierre Cabanis, who lived at the home of Mme. Helvétius. Cabanis
wrote that Franklin composed it to sing to Deborah on their marriage anniversary. Cabanis is right (though Bard's account could be reconciled with it), for
the first stanza mentions the Franklins' wedding day, with one version identifying it as twelve years ago and another as "Twice twelve" years ago. Written to
the tune of the popular song, "The Hounds Are All Out," Franklin's wedding
anniversary song appeared anonymously in at least two early nineteenth-century
songbooks.[2] To judge by line 3 of the earlier version, "Now twelve Years my
Wife," one text dates from 1 September 1742, their twelfth anniversary.[3] It was
printed by Franklin's nephew Benjamin Mecom in a 1758 chapbook featuring
the first separate printing of "The Way to Wealth."[4] Though Bard and Cabanis
are the only persons who left manuscript copies of the song, other friends knew
it. Franklin sang it to friends in England when Deborah was not present. In a
letter of 13 December 1757 to Deborah attempting to persuade her to come to
England, William Strahan called her "Joan," obviously referring to the song.

As Ellen Cohn has noted, the reference to "Chloes and Phillisses" in the first
line parodied the "pervasive practice of addressing poems to classically named,
idealized women." Two popular songs of the time had already mocked the practice and singled out "Philis and Chloe" as the names so often used by lovesick,
hackneyed songwriters.[5] Franklin's audience therefore would have immediately
appreciated in the opening line of the song that Franklin's was satirizing the
usual cant.

The Wedding Anniversary Song [my title]

1) Of their Chloes and Phillisses Poets may prate
I sing my plain Country Joan
Now twelve Years my Wife, still the Joy of my Life
Blest Day that I made her my own.
          My dear Friends,
Blest Day that I made her my own.

2) Not a Word of her Face, her Shape, or her Eyes,
Of Flames or of Darts shall you hear;
Tho' I Beauty admire, 'tis Virtue I prize,
That fades not in seventy Years,
          My dear Friends, etc.

3) In Health a Companion delightfull and dear,
Still easy, engaging, and Free,
In Sickness no less than the faithfullest Nurse
As tender as tender can be,
          My dear Friends, etc.

4) In Peace and good Order, my Houshold she keeps
Right Careful to save what I gain
Yet chearfully spends, and smiles on the Friends
I've the Pleasure to entertain
    My dear Friends, etc.

5) She defends my good Name even when I'm to blame,
Friend firmer was ne'er to Man giv'n,
Her Compassionate Breast, feels for all the Distrest,
Which draws down the Blessing from Heav'n,
    My dear Friends, etc.

6) Am I laden with Care, she takes off a large Share,
That the Burthen ne'er makes [me] to reel,
Does good Fortune arrive, the Joy of my Wife,
Quite Doubles the Pleasures I feel,
    My dear Friends, etc.

7) In Raptures the giddy Rake talks of his Fair,
Enjoyment shall make him Despise,
I speak my cool sence, that long Experience,
And Enjoyment have chang'd in no wise,
    My dear Friends, etc.

8) Some Faults we have all, and so may my Joan,
But then they're exceedingly small;
And now I'm us'd to, 'em, they're just like my own,
I scarcely can see, 'em at all,
    My dear Friends, etc.

9) Were the fairest young Princess, with Million in Purse
To be had in Exchange for my Joan,
She could not be a better Wife, mought be a Worse,
So I'd stick to my Joggy alone
    My dear Friends
I'd cling to my lovely ould Joan.

Franklin's anniversary song is too realistic to be entirely complimentary. Besides celebrating Deborah as a wife, the song (as Bard's anecdote reinforces) mocks and replies to the usual extravagance found in songs to a mistress. Realism was called for, and Deborah no doubt appreciated the tribute. Franklin's compliments are confirmed by evidence. For example, her loans of small sums to "my madman" (27 August and 27 November 1731) substantiate that she had a "Compassionate Breast," which felt "for all the Distrest."

It may be reading too much into the song to note that it says nothing about Deborah as a mother. Abstractly considered, a song in praise of a wife might well be expected to celebrate her as mother. But in 1742 Deborah had no children of

Poor RICHARD's Description of his
Country WIFE JOAN.

A SONG --- TUNE, *The Hounds are all out.*

1. OF their *Chloes* and *Phyllises* Poets may prate,
   I will sing my plain COUNTRY JOAN;
Twice twelve Years my Wife, still the Joy of my Life;
Bless'd Day that I made her my own,
                        My dear Friends.
Bless'd Day that I made her my own.

2. Not a Word of her Shape, or her Face, or her Eyes,
   Of Flames or of Darts shall you hear:
Though I BEAUTY admire, 'tis VIRTUE I prize,
   Which fades not in seventy Years.

3. In Health a Companion delightful and gay,
   Still easy, engaging, and free;
In Sickness no less than the faithfullest Nurse,
   As tender as tender can be.

4. In Peace and good Order my Houshold she guides,
   Right careful to save what I gain;
Yet chearfully spends, and smiles on the Friends
   I've the Pleasure to entertain.

5. Am I laden with Care, she takes off a large Share,
   That the Burden ne'er makes me to reel;
Does good Fortune arrive, the Joy of my Wife
   Quite doubles the Pleasure I feel.

6. She defends my good Name, even when I'm to blame,
   Friend firmer to Man ne'er was given:
Her compassionate Breast feels for all the distress'd,
   Which draws down the Blessings of Heaven.

7. In Raptures the giddy Rake talks of his Fair,
   Enjoyment will make him despise.
I speak my cool Sense, which long Exper'ence
   And Acquaintance has chang'd in no Wise.

8. The Best have some Faults, and so has My JOAN,
   But then they're exceedingly small,
And, now I'm us'd to 'em, they're so like my own,
   I scarcely can feel them at all.

9. Was the fairest young Princess, with Millions in Purse,
   To be had in Exchange for My JOAN,
She could not be a better Wife, might be a worse,
   So I'll stick to My JUGGY alone.

Figure 13a. A wedding anniversary song: "Poor Richard's Description of his Country Wife JOAN" from Father Abraham's Speech (Boston: B. Mecom, [1758]). Franklin's nephew, Benjamin Mecom, printed the song in the first separately published edition of what came to be called The Way to Wealth. All manuscript and printed versions of the song display some differences. Here, the third line in the first stanza reads "Twice twelve Years my Wife," which would date this text 1 September 1754; another has "Now twelve Years my Wife," which would date it 1 September 1742 (2:352–54). Courtesy, John Carter Brown Library, Brown University.

I SING MY PLAIN COUNTRY JOAN

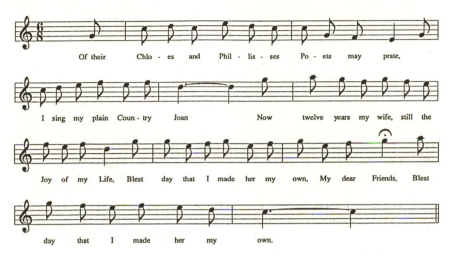

Figure 13b. *Music to the wedding anniversary song. Ellen R. Cohn printed the song set to music in "Benjamin Franklin and Traditional Music," in* Reappraising Benjamin Franklin *(1993), pp. 301–2.*

her own and behaved something like the stereotypical stepmother toward William.[6] Without being ironic, Franklin could not have celebrated the thirty-six-year-old Deborah as a mother. Even in 1754, the probable date of a later version of the song, Franklin added nothing about her role as a mother, though, as we will see, she was a loving parent to Sarah.

Deborah was a good partner, but, like everyone, she had foibles. She occasionally failed to keep exact business records and was sometimes extravagant. Although Franklin always celebrated her to others, he revealed on several occasions some irritation concerning her financial negligence. Perhaps the most significant time was recorded by Deborah herself. Keeping track of sales on credit in the shop on 16 August 1737, she forgot to specify the quality of a quire of paper bought by the poet and schoolmaster William Satterthwaite. When Franklin compiled the accounts (he did so every few days) from the running record in the shop book, she did not remember the quality of the paper. The irritated Franklin told her that she was careless and now he would have to trust Satterthwaite's word concerning what he owed. In distress, Deborah recorded in the accounts what Franklin said to her.

Deborah could be difficult and had occasional bouts of anger. She squabbled with a neighbor, Sarah Broughton, about money.[7] In 1745 she quarreled with James Read, her cousin by marriage who lived next door. Lawyer Read wrote Franklin his side of the affair (his letter is not extant). Franklin was amused that

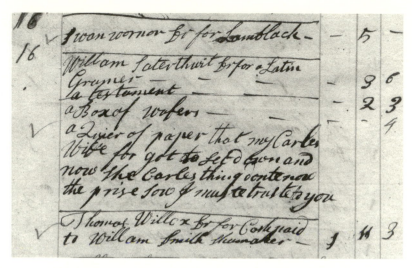

Figure 14. Criticized by Franklin, Deborah writes an anguished shop book entry, 16 August 1737. The shop book, 14 November 1735 to 7 December 1739, recorded items sold on credit in the shop, which Deborah Franklin generally minded while Franklin worked at printing on the second floor. Most shop book entries are in Deborah's hand. Her agonized comment in the midst of the shop book entries documents one time that Franklin became upset with her for careless bookkeeping. The statement evidently paraphrased what an irritated Franklin told her he would have to say to the customer, schoolteacher and poet William Satterthwaite.

A transcription follows:

Swan Wornor Dr. For Lamblack   5.0.

————. Willam Saterthwit, Dr. for a Latin
Gramer,   3.6.
a testament,   2.3.
a Box of Wafers,   0.4.
a Quier of paper that my Carles Wife for got to set down and now the carles thing donte now the prise sow I muste truste to you.

————. Thomas Wilcox, Papermaker, Dr. For Cash paid
to William Smith Shumaker,   1.11.3.

Courtesy, American Philosophical Society, Philadelphia.

Read thought he might side with him against Deborah and did not answer. The lawyer, however, pressed him for a written reply. So Franklin, in a letter of 17 August, joked about the affair. Read especially admired the writings of Thomas á Kempis and had quoted Kempis in his letter. Franklin wrote that Read's copy must be corrupt if it contained the passage as Read quoted it: "*In omnibus requiem quaesivi, sed non inveni, nisi in angulo cum libello*" (Everywhere have I sought rest and found it not, except sitting apart in a nook with a little book). Franklin said that "the good father understood pleasure (*requiem*) better, and wrote, *in angulo cum puella* [in a corner with a girl]." Franklin joked: first, about the meaning of *requiem*, which in the original quotation is better translated as *rest* than *pleasure*, though the latter is also possible; second, he introduced a sexual suggestion which the ascetic saint certainly would not have meant. Franklin carried the sexual suggestion further: "I know there is another reading, *in angulo puellae* [in a girl's corner or angle]; but this reject, tho' more *to the point*, as an expression too indelicate."

Having made the erotic jokes, Franklin turned to Read's profession: "Are you an attorney . . . and do you know no better, how to chuse a proper court in which to bring your action? Would you submit to the decision of a husband, a cause between you and his wife? Don't you know, that all wives are in the right?" Thus Franklin gave his opinion while at the same time trying to maneuver him into good humor. "It may be you don't, for you are yet but a young husband." Franklin and Deborah had no doubt attended Read's marriage to Susanna Leacock on 20 April 1745. Susanna ("Suky") was Deborah's second cousin on her mother's side. Franklin continued, "But see, on this head, the learned Coke, that oracle of the law, in his chapter *De Jus Marit. Angl.*" Of course, there is no such chapter. Franklin then created a sententia and, to give it more force, attributed it to Socrates: "*that in differences among friends, they that make the first concessions are the WISEST.*" He concluded with his "sincerest love to our dearest Suky, Your very affectionate friend and cousin, B. Franklin." Even if the letter reconciled Deborah and James Read, cousin "Jemmy" was shortly to earn Franklin's animosity by opposing him for clerk of the assembly, by neglecting to pay for the books that he bought from the London printer William Strahan, and by prosecuting Franklin's good friend Robert Grace. No one knows what the quarrel between Read and Deborah was about, but to judge by Read's later behavior, I like to think that Deborah was in the right.

THE FRANKLIN HOUSEHOLD

Ever since Franklin and Hugh Meredith had rented a house from Simon Edgell in 1728, Franklin and his growing family lived at the site of the present 139 Market Street, often with a boarder in the garret and with a tenant renting one of the two front rooms on the first floor. On 14 August 1737, Edward Lewis, who worked for Franklin, began boarding with the Franklins. After Franklin was appointed postmaster of Philadelphia in October 1737, he probably stopped renting out half of the first floor front, using it instead as the post office. During the decade after 1736, the Franklin household included his nephew James Franklin, Jr. (about six or seven years old in 1736, when he came to live with them), and his son, William (seven or eight years old in 1736). The boys studied with Theophilus Grew, and on 12 December 1738, just before the Franklins moved to 131 Market Street, they became students of Alexander Annand.

The Franklins' improving finances allowed them to employ servants. Franklin said in the *Autobiography* that he and Deborah "kept no idle Servants" (76), but Deborah had a series of maids beginning in 1736 or earlier. The first reference is for 24 April 1736 when shoemaker Warner charged Franklin five shillings for making a pair of shoes for "the maid." Francis Folger Franklin was then still alive and four years old. Perhaps Deborah had help after his birth in 1732. The Franklins continued to employ maids after the boy died in 1736. Warner made shoes for a maid named Scull on 5 March 1737 and for an unnamed maid on 30 June 1737. Deborah referred to a maid named Catren several times between 6 September and 21 December 1737, and then Hannah turned up in the accounts on 13 February 1738 and reappeared frequently for the next six weeks. The following year found the maid Scull again in the records (3 July 1739). Perhaps she had worked continuously for the Franklins since early 1737; perhaps Catren and Hannah were temporary. The maid Scull may have been related to Franklin's Junto friend, the surveyor Nicholas Scull. By 16 October 1747, the Franklins had a mistress for their four-year-old daughter, Sarah.

Scholars have written about Franklin's slaves.[8] Owning slaves was not uncommon in the mid-eighteenth century. Until recently, the earliest known record of Franklin's owning a slave was 12 April 1750, when he owned two slaves, presumably a married couple. The financial accounts, however, reveal the possibility of slave ownership fifteen years before. On 16 December 1735, Franklin bought a pair of shoes from Warner for a "negro boy." Perhaps the boy was named Joseph, for on 24 March of that year, Franklin bought a "Pair of Breeches for Jos." for one pound from the merchant Isaac Cosin. Joseph may, however, have been Joseph Rose, an apprentice working for Franklin. He and Deborah often used just the first name of persons in the accounts for servants and children. "Joseph" occurred again in the 1742 accounts (prior to 2 August), where Charles Moore recorded a debt of £1.10 for "a beaver hat by your order for your man Joseph." The words "your man Joseph" seem more likely to refer to a slave than to an apprentice.[9] Further, by 1741, Joseph Rose may have been the foreman of Franklin's shop. Nevertheless, the "Joseph" references may be to Joseph Rose.

Another early account may also suggest that Franklin owned a slave. On 13 July 1738, Franklin recorded in the shop book loaning a person simply called "Cesar" 4 shillings (the entry is in Franklin's hand). Classical names were often given to slaves, so Cesar may have been a slave and may have been working for Franklin. Since the name appears only once in the accounts, he must remain enigmatic.

Franklin definitely owned a slave by 1745. On 14 August the hatter Charles Moore charged Franklin 15 shillings "To a Racoon hat for your Negro," and on 21 December 1745 Moore charged him for "dressing a hat for your Negro." No further references to Franklin's slave occur until five years later. The man mentioned in Moore's accounts may have been sold or died shortly thereafter, but he may be the same slave Franklin owned in 1750. The previous references

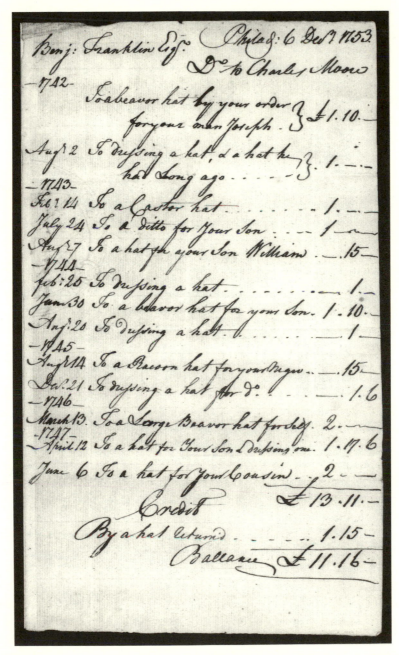

Figure 15. *A hat for Franklin's slave, 1745. A bill from Charles Moore, hatter, provides evidence that Franklin owned one slave, and perhaps two, before 1750. In 1742, the entry "your man Joseph" may have referred to a slave, though it probably referred to Joseph Rose, the son of Aquila Rose (d. 1723), who had begun working as an apprentice for Franklin in 1730. (By 1742, Joseph Rose was a young man.) Franklin did have an unnamed slave by 14 August 1745. "To a Racoon hat for your Negro, 15.0"; and "Dec 21 [1745], To dressing a hat for d[itt]o, 1.6." Courtesy, American Philosophical Society, Philadelphia.*

to an unnamed slave or servant might all be to a slave named Peter, who accompanied Franklin to London in 1757. He may be the same person who was a "negro boy" in 1735.

Like other printers, Franklin advertised slaves for sale in his newspaper, the *Pennsylvania Gazette*. Advertisements often said to "enquire at the printing shop." Though some persons have interpreted such words as proof that Franklin was selling slaves, the phrase meant that more information was available at the printing shop. That general form was commonly used for homes, ships, plantations, and slaves in the colonial newspapers. Though he did not personally trade in the buying and selling of slaves, no evidence exists that Franklin had any reservation about the institution of slavery itself until later, but Franklin did print George Whitefield's essay against slavery (discussed in Chapter 17).

Social Life

As a young man, Franklin was a merry companion, famous for punning, humor, and laughter. That characteristic does not strongly appear in the *Autobiography*, though he refers to his reputation as "a pretty good Riggite, that is a jocular verbal Satirist" while working as a printer in London (A 47). His humor, however, was celebrated by numerous contemporaries and appears frequently in his letters, as well as in his hoaxes and satires. As we have seen, he was a vegetarian as a teenager in Boston, and during his early life as a printer in Philadelphia he was evidently abstemious. By the 1740s, Franklin was well-off and evidently enjoyed social drinking with his friends at taverns and at home. Since there are no records of Franklin being drunk and since he satirized excessive drinking throughout his life, we can be fairly certain that he was a temperate drinker.

Franklin made his first documented purchase of an alcoholic beverage on New Year's Eve 1739—1s, 6d, worth of beer; he was then thirty-three. But the large amount that he paid for beer eight years later proves that well before then Franklin frequently entertained friends with beer: on 6 October 1747 he paid Timothy Matlock "his Acct. for Sm[all] Beer in full, 10.13.19." Ten pounds, thirteen shillings, and nineteen pence bought a lot of beer.

Playing musical instruments and singing were favorite eighteenth-century recreations. Franklin's father "was skill'd a little in Music and had a clear pleasing Voice, so that when he play'd Psalm Tunes on his Violin and sung withal as he some times did in an Evening . . . it was extreamly agreable to hear" (A 8). Franklin's early biographer James Parton wrote in 1864 (1:246) that Franklin played several instruments, including the harp, the guitar, the violin, and the violincello, but Parton cited no evidence. Carl Van Doren repeated Parton's statement, minus the violincello.[10] Franklin's inventory, taken 26 April 1790, lists a harmonia appraised at £15; a spinnet appraised at £5; a harpsichord, £25; a glassichord, £8.15.0; and a viola de gamba and bells at £8.15.0.[11] Franklin probably could play them all. Apparently they were all in good condition and had a total appraised value of £69. The early account books show that in 1731 he purchased a hautboy from James Wilmot for eight shillings,[12] so either he or Deborah probably played the oboe.

Since the violin was such a common instrument in the eighteenth century, and since Franklin's father played it well, Franklin may have learned to play it. If so, he must not have played it well, as there are no references to it. The English man of letters Leigh Hunt (whose parents knew Franklin in Philadelphia) wrote that Franklin offered to teach Hunt's mother to play the guitar, but it seems unlikely that he had either the time or the skill to do so.[13] Franklin is well-known for inventing the harmonica/glassichord, which he described in a letter of 13 July 1762. The "harmonia" of the inventory was probably a harmonica.

During the 1740s Franklin wrote several songs: two were drinking songs and one was the wedding song for Deborah. He did not compose music for them, but, as he advised his brother Peter (11:539), he followed the common method of setting them to well-known tunes. No testimony exists of Franklin's playing an instrument while singing the songs—though he probably did. Neither song has an exact date, but he said in a 1781 letter that he composed "Fair Venus Calls" forty years previously.

"Fair Venus Calls"

About 1741, Franklin wrote "Fair Venus Calls" and sang it at Masonic meetings. In addition to a copy in his 29 March 1781 letter to Abbé de la Roche (34:495–97), an anonymous version turned up in a collection titled *The Masonic Minstrel* (1816).[14] The song is a dialogue, with stanzas successively praising various pleasures and/or follies, and the chorus answering, "O no! / Not so! / For honest Souls know, / Friends and a Bottle still bear the Bell." (Franklin explained to French friends in 1781 that to "bear the Bell" was to win the prize.) Part of the song's verbal success is the way Franklin used different voices and levels of diction to celebrate love, riches, and power. The first voice, celebrating love, is elevated and formal:

> Fair Venus calls, her Voice obey;
> In Beauty's Arms spend Night and Day.
> The Joys of Love all Joys excell,
> Loving is certainly Living well.

The chorus disagrees:

> Oh no!
> Not So!
> For honest Souls know,
> Friends and a Bottle still bear the Bell.

From a lover, the persona changes to a wealthy miser, and the lines convey his pleasure in money with a wonderful, colloquial last line:

FAIR VENUS CALLS.

SONG.

Fair Venus calls, we must obey, In love and sports spend night and day; The joys of love, all joys ex-cel, For loving is certainly living well,

CHORUS.

Oh, no, not so, all honest souls no, A friend and a bottle still bear the bell.

If that will not fit ye, we'll govern the city,
  There's pleasure in pride no tongue can tell;
Though by numbers we're teas'd, yet our pride is well pleas'd,
  And that would make Lucifer happy in hell.
      Oh, no, not so, &c. &c.

Then let us get money, as bees lay up honey,
  We'll build large hives, and store each cell;
The sight of our treasure, will yield us much pleasure,
  We'll jingle, and jingle it wond'rous well.
      Oh, no, not so, &c. &c.

Figure 16. Words and music to Franklin's song "Fair Venus Calls" from David Vinton, The Masonic Minstrel (Dedham, Mass.: H. Mann, 1816). The differences between Franklin's holograph manuscript at Yale University (34:496–97) and the anonymous song printed by David Vinton in 1816 may suggest that "Fair Venus Calls" had passed into the oral tradition. One key difference between the two texts is in line 2: where Franklin has "Beauty's Arms," Vinton has "love and sports." The musicologist Carleton Sprague Smith suggested that Franklin's son-in-law Richard Bache, who was a founder of the Gloucester Fox Hunting Club of Philadelphia in 1766 and who was known for his bass voice, may have been responsible for introducing the reference to "sports"—and thus to fox hunting.

In stanza 2, line 2, I slightly prefer the Vinton text's "each cell" to "them well"; but in line 4, I prefer Franklin's "count it, & chink it, & jingle it" to Vinton's "jingle, and jingle it wond'rous." I also slightly prefer Vinton's concluding line "A friend and a bottle still bear" to "Friends and a Bottle still bore." The Vinton 1816 text may reflect a different Franklin text (perhaps even an earlier one) of the song than the one he recalled in France some forty years after writing it in Philadelphia. Courtesy, American Antiquarian Society, Worcester, Massachusetts.

> Then let us get Money, like Bees lay up Honey,
> We'll build us new Hives, and store them well;
> The Sight of our Treasure shall yield us great Pleasure,
> We'll count it, and chink it, and jingle it well.

Then the chorus counters with "Oh no!" etc.

The third speaker is a politician who celebrates power, which is identified with fame and pride. The last line undercuts him (and may echo *Paradise Lost*):

> If this does not fit ye, lets govern the City;
> In Power is Pleasure, no Tongue can tell.
> By Crouds tho' you're teased, your Pride shall be pleased,
> And this can make Lucifer happy in Hell.

The fourth stanza at first seems to summarize the first three and to tell us, in the voice of Solomon, that life is vanity.

> Then toss off your Glasses, and scorn the dull Asses,
> Who missing the Kernel, still gnaw the Shell.
> What's Love, Rule or Riches? Wise Solomon teaches
> They're Vanity, Vanity, Vanity still.

The typical and expected conclusion would be to turn our eyes from earthly things and to regard the spiritual, but Franklin suddenly reverses the moral. The chorus is all the more striking because the last line changes from the expected conclusion that all is vanity to the carpe diem theme—celebrating life, drinking, and good fellowship.

> Chorus: That's true,
>   He knew;
> He 'ad try'd them all through,
> Friends and a Bottle still bore the Bell.

The celebration of drinking, social life, and friends provides a fresh note in Franklin's belletristic writings, though it confirms other ample evidence of his sociability and humor.

"The Antediluvians Were All Very Sober"

Franklin composed another drinking song about 1745, taking as his mock inspiration the biblical story of Noah and the flood. The hint of sacrilege made the song slightly daring and more fun. "Derry Down" indicated the popular refrain "Derry down, down, down derry down," a tune with many variations.

> The Antediluvians were all very sober
> For they had no Wine, and they brew'd no October;
> All wicked, bad Livers, on Mischief still thinking,

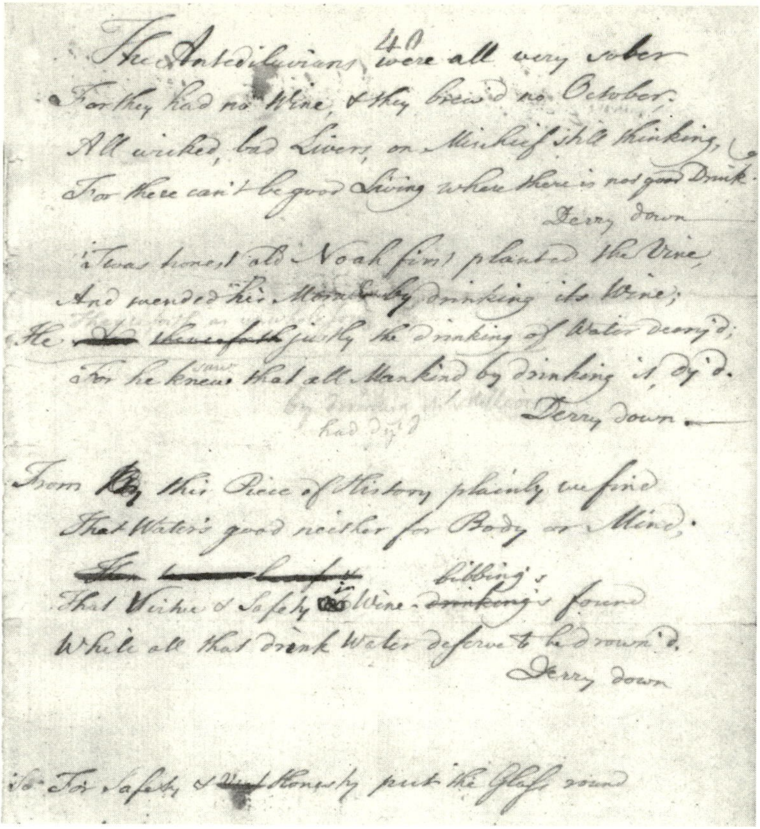
40
The Antediluvians were all very sober
For they had no Wine, & they brew'd no October;
All wicked, bad Livers, on Mischief still thinking,
For there can't be good Living where there is not good Drink.
Derry down

'Twas honest old Noah first planted the Vine,
And mended his Morals by drinking its Wine;
He And thenceforth justly the drinking of Water decry'd;
For he knew saw that all Mankind by drinking it, dy'd.
Derry down

From By this Piece of History plainly we find
That Water's good neither for Body or Mind;
That Virtue & Safety in Wine-drinking's bibbing's found
While all that drink Water deserve to be drown'd.
Derry down

So For Safety & Virt Honesty put the Glass round

Figure 17. The manuscript of Franklin's drinking song ("The Antediluvians Were All Very Sober"). The holograph at the American Philosophical Society has revisions in the second and third stanzas (insertions are shown by ↑. . .↓; cancellations by <. . .>; italics within brackets are editorial comments). Beginning in line 3, stanza 2:

↑tHe↓ <And thenceforth> justly the drinking of Water decry'd;
For he knew ↑<saw>↓ that all Mankind by drinking it, dy'd.
Derry down

[later penciled alternative to the last two lines; words in brackets retained from first version:]

Thenceforth as unwholesome he [Water decry'd']
[For he] saw [that] by drinking it Millions had dy'd.

↑From↓ <By> this Piece of History plainly we find
That Water's good neither for Body or Mind;
<Then [?? be? safe? [undeciphered]] &>
That Virtue & Safety <&> õin' Wine-<drinking's> ↑bibbing's↓ found
While all that drink Water deserve to be drown'd.
Derry down

↑So↓ For Safety & <Virt> Honesty put the Glass round.

Courtesy, American Philosophical Society, Philadelphia.

For there can't be good Living where there is not good Drinking.
Derry down
'Twas honest old Noah first planted the Vine,
And mended his Morals by drinking its Wine;
He justly the drinking of Water decry'd;
For he knew that all Mankind, by drinking it, dy'd.
Derry down.

From this Piece of History plainly we find
That Water's good neither for Body or Mind;
That Virtue and Safety in Wine-bibbing's found
While all that drink Water deserve to be drown'd.
Derry down
So For Safety and Honesty put the Glass round.

Franklin's free use of the Bible and religion in the song anticipated his biblical parables of 1755, and the combination of religion and wine foreshadowed his 1779 bagatelle "On Wine."

Franklin's Friends

During the years 1736–47, most of Franklin's close friends continued to be Junto members: Joseph Breintnall, Thomas Hopkinson, Robert Grace, Hugh Roberts, William Coleman, and Philip Syng. The latter two were both named as advisors in his 1750 and 1757 wills, and all these friends entered into Franklin's various civic associations. Breintnall and he performed early scientific experiments together; later Hopkinson and Syng were two of his three collaborators in electrical experiments (the other was his neighbor Ebenezer Kinnersley). Dr. John Bard was another longstanding friend, presumably Franklin's early physician and a Junto member. Naturalist John Bartram and Dr. Thomas Bond both became Franklin's good friends and were involved in the 1743 attempt to create the American Philosophical Society.

Franklin had two older patrons: Andrew Hamilton and James Logan, both of whom have been mentioned but deserve notice here. Hamilton became interested in Franklin in London, and as Speaker of the Pennsylvania Assembly (beginning in 1729) he was in a position to help his young friend. Franklin, in turn, used his literary ability to help Hamilton. The brilliant lawyer evidently found the young printer likable, efficient, and intellectually sympathetic. Both had a reputation for irreligion, and both were ostensibly deists. Hamilton had begun in America as a schoolteacher and probably saw Franklin as a younger version of himself—someone who was achieving a place in society by sustained application and superior ability. Hamilton had Franklin appointed printer to the legislature in 1730 and clerk of the assembly in 1736. Franklin, in turn, wrote a shrewd defense of his older friend on 16 November 1733 after Hamilton had been defeated in a bid for reelection. Franklin's "Half-Hour's Conversation with a

Friend" probably aided in his friend's election a month later. Without Hamilton's patronage, Franklin's career would have been much different—and less financially successful.

James Logan took an interest in the Library Company and conferred with Franklin in 1731 on the books to be purchased. That same year, Logan wrote a memorial, "Of the State of the British Plantations in America," which Franklin copied and which influenced his thinking on the relations between America and the rest of the British Empire. Logan was partially responsible for giving young Franklin the commission to print Alexander Arscot's *Some Considerations Relating to the Present State of the Christian Religion* (part 1, 1731; part 2, 1732). He chose Franklin to print his *Latter Part of the Charge to the Grand Inquest, September 24, 1733.* In 1735, Franklin asked Logan if he could print Logan's version of *Cato's Moral Distichs*, which the classical scholar had translated for his daughters. Logan consented, though he modestly would not allow Franklin to put his name as translator in the volume. When Logan retired as a judge, Franklin printed his "Farewell" to the law, *The Charge Delivered . . . to the Grand Inquest . . . April 13, 1736.* It contained a brief version of Logan's philosophical treatise, "The Duties of Man Deduced from Nature."

About 1740, Franklin requested permission to print Logan's translation of Cicero's *de Senectute*. Logan consented, and Franklin sent him the first sheet in the winter of 1741–42. Swamped with printing George Whitefield's and others' religious works, Franklin continually postponed printing Logan's *Cicero's Cato Major or His Discourse of Old-Age* until 1744. Logan and Franklin both knew that it was unlikely the book would be successful—but both hoped well for it. Franklin sent three hundred copies to the London printer William Strahan, who simply turned them over to a bookseller and forgot about them. Franklin concluded his preface to Logan's translation with an expression of the *translatio* motif: "I shall add to these few Lines my hearty Wish, that this first Translation of a *Classic* in this *Western World*, may be followed with many others, performed with equal Judgment and Success; and be a happy Omen, that Philadelphia shall became the Seat of the American Muses." Like Cotton Mather, Richard Lewis, and George Webb earlier and like Philip Freneau and Hugh Henry Brackenridge later, Franklin used the westward movement of civilization to suggest his love for America and to proclaim its future greatness.[15]

In 1736 or 1737, Logan asked Franklin to read and criticize a chapter from his philosophical treatise "On Moral Good or Virtue." Franklin did so. He suggested, in view of Logan's "dilate Manner of Writing," that Logan supply a short summary of each chapter at the beginning and a brief topical note on each paragraph in the margin. Revealing his own pessimistic view of life, Franklin wrote: "It seems to me that the Author is a little too severe upon Hobbes, whose Notion, I imagine, is somewhat nearer the Truth than that which makes the State of Nature a State of Love." And then, with a characteristic compromise, Franklin added, "But the Truth perhaps lies between both Extreams" (2:184–85).

He commented on Logan's consideration of music: "I think what is said upon Musick, might be enlarg'd to Advantage by showing that what principally makes a Tune agreeable, is the Conformity between its Air or Genius, and some Motion, Passion or Affection of the Mind, which the Tune imitates." Franklin may echo Francis Hutcheson (who said that music could raise "agreeable Passions").[16] The sentiment also anticipates Franklin's later opinions on music, for example, the list he drew up for the Abbé Morellet in 1772 of forty-five human emotions that music could express. Franklin further suggested that Logan should number and define each virtue, "which I have not yet seen, scarce two Authors agreeing therein, some annexing more, others fewer and different Ideas to the Same Name." Franklin had followed his own recommendation in defining thirteen virtues when he drew up his scheme for self-improvement in 1731.

Routines

Franklin's chart of a working day in the *Autobiography* ignores his numerous duties and meetings other than those related to his printing business. He did specify that the hours between 6 and 10 p.m. were devoted to putting "Things in their Places," followed by "Supper, Musick, or Diversion, or Conversation" and then came "Examination of the Day" (A 83). Perhaps he managed to follow the schedule on many working days when he was a young printer, but the number of Franklin's obligations was growing. As Pennsylvania's government printer, he was expected to be in Philadelphia when the assembly was in session in order to do the required printing. After he was elected its clerk on 15 October 1736, he had to attend every meeting. Some legislators from the counties, like Samuel Blunston (1689–1745) and John Wright (1667–1749), both from Lancaster County, became good friends. Franklin must have spent time with such persons after the assembly sessions. The assembly convened at what is now called Independence Hall for the first time on 14 October 1736, the day before Franklin's election as clerk. He attended meetings there until 1757, then off and on for the rest of his life, concluding with the meetings of the Constitutional Convention in 1787 and with those of the Supreme Executive Council of Pennsylvania in 1788.

In addition to the sessions of the legislature, Franklin had a number of fixed routines. Since organizing the Junto in the fall of 1727, he was present at its meetings on Friday evenings. I suspect, however, that once he was elected clerk of the assembly in 1736, the Junto meetings were cancelled on the Fridays when the legislature was in session. This would not have been just for Franklin's sake, for all the members of the Junto had more responsibilities as they aged, and during the assembly's meetings all the Junto members would have been busier than normal. Beginning in February 1730/1, Franklin appeared at the Freemasons' monthly meetings on the first Monday night of the month, as well as the annual meeting on St. John the Baptist's Day, 24 June. After organizing the Library Company of Philadelphia in 1731, he attended the normal meeting of the Library Company directors on the second Monday night of every month, in addition to numerous special meetings and the annual election on the first Monday in May. Beginning on 7 December 1736, he went to the Union Fire Company meetings on the last Monday night of every month. In 1744 the fledgling American Philosophical Society evidently met on the first Thursday night of the month. In addition to the fixed routines, Franklin made time for civic duties, clubs, chess, and coffeehouses while all the time working as printer, postmaster, and clerk of the assembly.[17] He was extraordinarily energetic, hardworking, and efficient—and withal, always thinking of what additional institutions would be useful to his society and how he could be more serviceable.

SCANDAL: THE DEATH OF DANIEL REES

While fulfilling a civic duty Franklin became involved in the most serious slander he suffered as a young man.[18] The Court of Common Pleas appointed Franklin, John Danby, and Harmanus Alrichs as auditors to settle a dispute between Dr. Evan Jones, pharmacist, and Armstrong Smith. The parties met at a Market Street tavern on Saturday, 11 June 1737. Smith was late. While the others waited, Jones and his lawyer, John Remington, told the auditors about hoodwinking Daniel Rees, Jones's apprentice. Franklin laughed heartily ("as my Manner is") at the beginning of the account.

Young Rees wanted to become a Freemason. Jones, Remington, and some friends had pretended that they were Masons and had initiated Rees in a scurrilous mock ceremony. Remington read the initiation oath that he had written for Rees, and Franklin asked for and received a copy. As Jones and Remington continued the story, Franklin, Danby, and Alrichs all became uncomfortable and then expressed their disapproval. Jones, Remington, John Tackerbury, and a group of cronies had led the blindfolded Rees into Jones's garden and made him kneel and repeat after Remington the "diabolical Oath." The oath affirmed that Satan "was acknowledged and adored as a supream and mighty Power." They then had given Rees a cup containing "a violent Purge" under the guise of a communion; and had led him to kiss Tackerbury's ass under the supposition that it was the Bible. Danby said that in England they would have been prosecuted. Alrichs objected to the mock initiation. Franklin said "That when the Young Man came to know how he had been impos'd on, he would never forgive them."

Dr. Jones and Remington nevertheless said that they intended to have further fun with Rees. Remington intended "to introduce him blindfold and stripp'd into a Room where the Company being each provided with a Rod or Switch should chastize him smartly." But Dr. Jones "had a better Invention; they would have a Game at *Snap-Dragon* in a Dark Cellar, where some Figures should be dress'd up, that by the pale Light of Burning Brandy would appear horrible and frighten him Damnably." About then, the gullible Rees himself came to the tavern to speak with Jones, who pointed at Franklin and said, "*Dan-*

iel, that Gentleman is a Free-Mason; make a Sign to him." The embarrassed Franklin turned away and looked out of the window into the garden.

The following Monday night, 13 June 1737, Dr. Jones, Remington, Tackerbury, "Sulevan," "E. W." (a tailor), and some others met at Jones's house with the credulous Rees. After supper, the company retired to the cellar, and the blindfolded Rees was led down to them. Dr. Jones twice attempted to set fire to the fluid in an earthen pan, without effect. He went upstairs and returned with a large bottle, poured additional spirits into the pan, and then ignited the spirits. The pan had raisins at the bottom, and Dr. Jones and others dipped in their hands for the raisins and flicked the flames about. "Some of the Company then diverted themselves at a Play called Snap-Dragon, holding their Heads over the Pan, that their Countenances, from the blue Reflection of the Flames, might appear ghastly and hideous; hoping from thence, that the Youth, upon taking the Bandage from his Eyes would imagine he saw the real Servants of the Devil, who was personated by a Fellow ["Sulevan"] dressed in a Cow's Hide with Horns." But young Rees did not seem scared. "His Master asked him if he was not afraid." He answered that he was not. Then Jones either deliberately threw or accidentally spilled the burning spirits on Rees. He cryed out, "*Master, I'm kill'd, I'm kill'd.*" Severely burned, Rees lived in agony for several days and died on Thursday morning, 16 June.

Both the *Gazette* and the *Mercury* for 16 June briefly reported the incident and Rees's subsequent death and noted that "The Coroners inquest are now met about it." In the same papers, the Philadelphia Masons Thomas Hopkinson (grand master), William Plumsted (deputy Master), and Joseph Shippen and Henry Prat (grand wardens) all signed an advertisement on behalf of the members of St. John's Lodge "declaring the Abhorrence of all true Brethren to such Practices in general, and their Innocence of this Fact in particular; and that the Persons concerned in this wicked Action, are not of our Society, nor of any Society of *Free and Accepted Masons* to our Knowledge or Belief."

The next week, both newspapers reported that the coroner's inquest found that Rees was killed "by the burning Spirits thrown upon him," but the evidence showed that the "throwing those Spirits on him was accidental." The reports concluded, however, "since the inquest, farther Evidence has been given to the Magistrates, that it was a voluntary Action." The papers repeated the Freemasons' advertisement declaring their detestation of such wicked actions. Despite the current bad publicity for the Freemasons, Franklin nevertheless published on 30 June the results of an election at the Indian King on Friday, 24 June, when William Plumsted "was unanimously chosen Grand-Master of this Province, for the Year ensuing, who appointed Joseph Shippen, jun. to be his Deputy, and Messrs. Henry Pratt, and Philip Syng, were nominated and chosen Grand-Wardens." Bradford, however, used the current scandal to attack the Freemasons, reprinting an anti-Masonic article in his next *Mercury* (4 August).

When the grand jury met, Franklin and other persons gave what evidence they knew. The grand jury indicted Dr. Evan Jones, John Remington, and "E—— W——, Taylor." At the next session of the court of oyer and terminer, Dr. Jones was tried (Wednesday, 1 February 1737/8). The jury, which began hearing the case at 9 a.m., debated it until nearly 2 a.m., when the members turned in their verdict—manslaughter. The next day, Remington and "E. W." were tried; Remington was also convicted of manslaughter, but "E. W." was acquitted. Remington immediately appealed to James Logan, president of the Provincial Council, for a pardon. Remington said that "no Evidence did or could appear to prove that the Petitioner had any hand in the throwing or spilling the said Liquor on the Body of the said Daniel, or was privy to any Design or Intention of doing harm to the said Daniel, or to any other Person." The board pardoned Remington on 3 February but stipulated that he could be tried in the future for the "wicked & irreligious" mock oath.

"A. B.," a writer in Franklin's *Gazette*, reported the trial on 7 February 1737/8, including the opinion of "One of the King's Council" that Dr. Jones was guilty of murder: "no Government could subsist, nor could any thinking Man believe he had any reasonable security for his Life, where such cool Villany should be perpetrated with Impunity; or where a Man flinging Fire, Flames, and Death around him, shall be allow'd to excuse it, by saying he was only in Jest." The news account also noted that Joseph Growden, the king's attorney general, testified that he had read all the precedents "with the strictest Attention, and finding none in Point with this, his Conscience obliged him to declare, he did not think the Prisoner guilty of Murder." The briefer account in the *Mercury* (7 February), was superior, giving the actual date of the trial, the time it began and ended, and the result: Dr. Jones "was accordingly, at the breaking up of the Sessions, burnt in the Hand, and order'd to find sufficient Security for his good Behaviour." Bradford also recorded that "There was the greatest Throng of People to hear the Trial, which perhaps ever appear'd at any Trial in this Province." Only the *Mercury* mentioned that the trial of John Remington and "E. W., Taylor" occurred the next day.

Insulting the Freemasons, William Bradford claimed in this *Mercury* that a band of negro thieves was really a "Lodge of Free Masons." Since it was well-known that Franklin was a Freemason, Bradford was probably pleased to have a chance to implicate his competitor, though so far the attack was only implied. That changed, however, with a scandalous article in the *American Weekly Mercury* for Tuesday, 14 February, which supposed Franklin to be A. B. But as I will show below, I do not believe Franklin wrote it. The *Mercury* author, "C. D.," accused A. B. of cowardice and cruelty in attacking Dr. Jones when he was in distress and of envy and malice in asking a greater penalty for him than the law had found. Actually, A. B. had reported not his own opinion but what one of the council said, though A. B. seemed to support the charge. C. D. further claimed that John "*Tackerbury*, the principal Evidence against Dr. *Jones*, hath long assumed the Character of one of the *Fraternity of Free-Masons*, but was expelled the *Common Lodge* (as is reported) for some scandals in his Behavior (which are too notorious in general)." But John Tackerbury's name does not occur in Ledger B of St. John's Lodge, the only lodge in Philadelphia before 1737. He could have previously been a member of some other lodge, but at this date, there were comparatively few lodges in Great Britain or the colonies. Tackerbury was probably not a Mason.

C. D. sneered that A. B.'s "Character when discovered and displayed, will perhaps afford more Instances of *Blasphemy* and *Profaneness*, than is contained in that Writing [referring to Remington's mock oath] or any other Writing or Words (except his *own*) known or uttered in *Pennsylvania*." Here is the standard charge that Franklin was irreligious, but this author takes it further in accusing Franklin of blasphemy and profanity. C. D. continued, "Nor can I see the justice or reasonableness of his pecuniary [*sic*], that some of the ridiculous Ceremonies used in the Garden, was in allusion to any sacred Rites, unless to shew how Agreeable such is, to his *wonted Air* and *accustomed Eloquence*, in ridiculing those and other religious and sacred Points of Divine Worship."

The libeler then said that Franklin, about four days prior to the fatal mock initiation, expressed his approbation of the mock oath "by a most hearty Laughter," that "in several Companies he diverted himself" by reading the scandal aloud, that "he candidly saluted" Daniel Rees "by the Name of *Brother* . . . and congratulated him on being admitted into the *Brotherhood*," and that he "desired to have Notice to be present at the Diversion of *Snap-Dragon*." The *Mercury* author further claimed that Franklin, "to the surprise of his Friends, who at his request had entrusted him with the Writing [the mock oath] for his Diversion, went and informed a *Magistrate* thereof, and appeared as an *Evidence* upon the same at the Trial, which doubtless conduc'd to the finding a *Verdict* against one of the Prisoners." C. D. evidently referred to the verdict against John Remington. C. D. then cast doubt upon the guilt of Dr. Jones by claiming that Tackerbury jogged Jones's elbow and also claimed that Sulevan said that the cellar was so dark "he could not tell *how* or *by whom* the Spirit was thrown."

Franklin must have heard that he would be maligned in the *Mercury*, for he put off printing Tuesday's *Gazette* until Wednesday, 15 February 1737/8. He defended himself with dignity; told the story of meeting with Jones and Remington in the tavern in the company of Danby and Alrichs; said that he laughed "at the *Beginning*" of the story; professed that before the end of the story, he, Danby, and Alrichs all expressed their disapproval; and declared that he deliberately did not look at Rees when Jones asked him to give a Masonic sign. He wrote that C. D.'s charges "And all those Circumstances, with that of my *desiring to have Notice that I might be present at the Snap-Dragon*, are absolutely false and groundless." As for Remington's mock oath, Franklin said, "I communicated it to one, who mention'd it to others, and so many People flock'd to my House for a Sight of it, that it grew troublesome, and therefore when the Mayor sent for it, I was glad of the Opportunity to be discharg'd from it." He was subpoe-

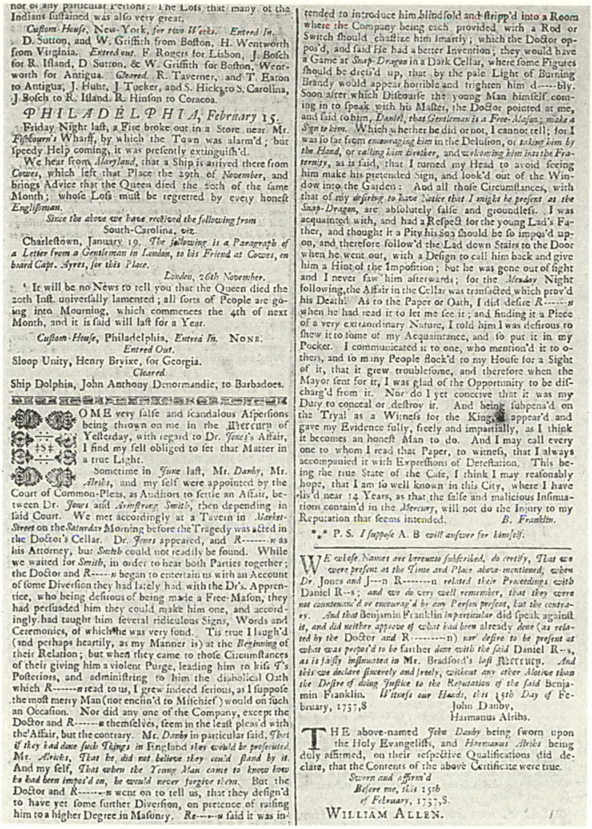

Figure 18. *Charged with complicity in the hazing and death of Daniel Rees, Franklin defended himself in the* Pennsylvania Gazette, *15 February 1737/8, p. 3. Along with merchants John Danby and Harmanus Alrichs, Franklin met the pharmacist Dr. Evan Jones and the lawyer John Remington in a Market Street tavern, where Jones and Remington told of a mock Masonic initiation of Jones's apprentice, Daniel Rees. Franklin laughed heartily, "as my Manner is," at the beginning of the relation. Remington read the sacrilegious oath he had written for the occasion, and Franklin asked for a copy of it. But as the details of the initiation emerged, Franklin, Danby, and Alrichs all expressed their disapproval. Nevertheless, Jones and Remington said they intended to have further fun with the gullible Rees.*

At the second mock initiation, Jones accidentally spilled boiling oil on Rees, who died of the burns. Jones, Remington, and others involved in the hazing of Rees were tried. Franklin turned the oath over to the authorities and gave evidence at the trial concerning the conversation with Jones and Remington. Jones and Remington were found guilty of manslaughter. Though no one involved was a Mason, Franklin's competitor William Bradford took the opportunity to besmirch the Masons, and someone, probably Remington, published an article in Bradford's American Weekly Mercury *slandering Franklin. Though the attack on Franklin was clearly fallacious, rumors that he was involved circulated widely and caused his parents concern. Franklin therefore wrote an account of the meeting with Jones and Remington. Franklin also secured depositions from Danby and Alrichs, the other persons present when Jones and Remington told the three of them about the first hazing. Courtesy, Library Company of Philadelphia.*

naed as a witness at the trial, "appear'd and gave my Evidence fully, freely and impartially, as I think it becomes an honest Man to do." He added, "And I may call every one to whom I read that Paper, to witness, that I always accompanied it with Expressions of Detestation. This being the true State of the Case, I think I may reasonably hope, that I am so well-known in this City, where I have liv'd near 14 Years, as that the false and malicious Insinuations contain'd in the *Mercury*, will not do the Injury to my Reputation that seems intended."

Franklin added to his vindication the sworn depositions of John Danby and Harmanus Alrichs. They testified that Franklin's statement was the truth, that none of the three countenanced or encouraged Jones or Remington, "And that Benjamin Franklin in particular" spoke against the mock initiation "and did neither approve of what had been *already* done (as related by the Doctor and R[emingto]n) nor desire to be present at what was propos'd to be *farther* done with the said Daniel R[ee]s, as is falsely insinuated in Mr. Bradford's last *Mercury*." The sworn testimony of Danby and Alrichs, recorded before magistrate William Allen, was dated 15 February 1737/8, the same day Franklin's rebuttal appeared. Their depositions concluded Franklin's defense.

One would have thought the testimony of the three would have ended the affair, but C. D. replied in the following *Mercury* (21 February). He said that the meeting of the auditors with Dr. Jones and Remington occurred on Friday, not Saturday; that Tackerbury's name was often mentioned in the discourse; and that Dr. Jones and not Remington took out and read the mock oath. After these assertions, he again affirmed that Franklin "did Salute the young Man by the Name, give a Sign, and congratulate him upon the Occasion; and signified his desire and design to be present at the then proposed Diversion . . . tho' some present either forgot or did not hear all that passed." The *Mercury* defamer asked why Franklin "did not (since he had several Days opportunity for it) sooner inform the Magistrate, or advise the Young Man, so as to prevent that Imposition, and the unhappy Consequences that happened in the Cellar?" The *Mercury* writer also said that Franklin's "appealing to several who heard him read this profane Writing, to witness that his Reading was accompanied with Expressions of Detestation, may possibly imply more of Hypocrisy than Sincerity. And I think it more consistent with the part or duty of a good Man, to conceal or destroy so profane a Writing, than to repeat or publish it to his Neighbours, which in my Opinion shews more of his *pleasure* in it than *detestation* of it, since his so doing could not tend to the publick nor private good." In the same 14 February *Mercury*, William Bradford noted, "The Letter signed *BOAZ* giving an account of Tackerbury's being a Freemason, must be omitted this week." The letter never appeared.

Franklin made no reply, and the affair died.

WAS FRANKLIN COMPLICIT?

One wonders about several things. First, should Franklin have informed a magistrate about the hoodwinking of Rees? The affair was hardly serious before the accident on Monday night, 13 June. If Franklin had informed a magistrate about the first mock initiation, he would have seemed to be acting like an officious busybody. Only Rees's tragic death made the earlier proceedings important. If Franklin should have informed a magistrate, shouldn't Danby and/or Alrichs have done so? None of the three judged it necessary.

Second, was Franklin A. B.? The editors of the *Papers* thought not and did not print A. B. One scholar has suggested that Franklin was A. B. He said that A. B.'s piece "was written by someone with his naturalist's interest in unusual phenomena, for the writer stopped briefly to describe the appearance of Rees's fatal burns."[19] A. B.'s report is not well organized, does not give essential information (e.g., when the trial occurred), and fails to describe the trial clearly. Indeed, using only the *Gazette* report, several persons have written that Tackerbury was the third person arraigned with Jones and Remington,[20] but the *Mercury* report (7 February), reveals that the third person tried and acquitted was "E. W., Taylor." The summary of the trial in the *Mercury* for 7 February is superior; Franklin would not have written A. B.'s vague and inferior report.

The third and fourth considerations are related. Who was C. D.? He was present at the meeting of the auditors (Franklin, Danby, and Alrichs) with Jones and Remington. C. D. protested that Franklin's turning over the oath to the authorities betrayed a trust, and he objected to Franklin's testimony at the trial. Remington, the attorney who wrote the scandalous oath, and Jones are the likely candidates. C. D., however, seems especially concerned with the oath. Remington had reason to be; Jones did not. Further, Jones had been punished, and for him, the affair was over; Remington could be tried for writing the oath in the future. The author seems more likely to be Remington than Jones. Fourth, did Franklin violate any trust in making the oath public? Of course not. It was germane evidence in a murder trial. The only person who might possibly think that Franklin violated a trust would have to be a prejudiced participant. Remington was probably C. D.

One final consideration concerns Franklin's initially laughing at the oath, asking for and receiving a copy, and showing it to someone else. The oath and Franklin's initial reaction to it hardly seemed important until after Rees was burned and died. That outcome made not telling the authorities, Rees, or his parents about the initial hazing a mistake; and the outcome made Franklin's reaction to the oath a mistake. But Franklin, Danby, and Alrichs could not know the future.

Though the Freemasons, through no fault of their own, had been temporarily given a bad name, Franklin continued publicly supporting them. Just as in the previous year, when the news of the Rees affair was breaking, he printed news of the local Masonic election; a few months after the trial, Franklin did again: "On Saturday the 24th past, was held at the Indian King in this City, a Grand Lodge of Free and Accepted *MASONS*; when Mr. *JOSEPH SHIPPEN* was unanimously chosen Grand-Master of this Province, for the Year ensuing; who appointed Mr. Philip Syng, to be his Deputy; and Dr. Thomas Cadwalader, and Mr. Thomas Boude, were nominated and chosen Grand-Wardens" (6 July 1738). Franklin did not abandon his associates and friends merely because they had temporarily received adverse publicity. His reporting not only showed his loyalty to them but also implicitly repeated the statement that the Freemasons had nothing to do with Rees's death.

In addition to the persons who took part in the mock initiation, one must lament the role of Andrew Bradford, who was generally a decent person. In printing the anti-Masonic notes and the libel on Franklin, he revealed that he had, evidently in his eagerness to damage a competitor, lost responsible judgment in editing the *Mercury*.

THE COMFORTABLE PYRRHONIST

The *Boston Evening Post* (6 March), the *New England Weekly Journal* (7 March), and the *Boston-News-Letter* (9 March) all reprinted the 7 February *Mercury* report of the crime and trial. Though no Boston paper mentioned Franklin's supposed connection to the sacrilegious mock initiation and the death of Rees, Franklin's parents heard of it and were upset. Each wrote him on 21 March 1737/8, expressing concern about his religious beliefs. Their letters have been lost, but from the drafts of Franklin's reply (13 April 1738), we can surmise the contents. In his first draft, Franklin wrote, "You both seem concern'd for my Orthodoxy. God only knows whether all the Doctrines I hold for true, be so or not." He then reversed the expected conclusion: "For my part, I must confess, I believe they are not, but I am not able to distinguish the good from the bad." Instead of being sure that he was right, or thinking he probably was right, or even supposing that he might be right, Franklin was sure that his beliefs were wrong.

"I believe they are not." Those words are among the most surprising and the most revealing that Franklin ever wrote. What a paradox! How could anyone say that he believed that the doctrines he held to be true were not true? One might almost think that he was trying to write an oxymoron concerning God and truth. He probably knew that he was reversing paradoxes of devotional poetry, which attempted, as in Milton, to express the Christian mysteries that transcend reason. Franklin said that since no one could know such absolutes as God or the Truth, our thoughts about the ultimate absolutes were probably wrong. He explained the reasons for his radical skepticism: "And Knowing my self, as I do, to be a weak ignorant Creature, full of natural Imperfections, subject to be frequently misled by my own Reasonings, or the wrong Arguments of others, to the Influence of Education, of Custom, of Company, and the Books I read, It would be great Vanity in me to imagine that I have been so happy, as out of an infinite Number of Opinions of which a few only can be true, to select those only for my own Use." Not only are the "Prejudices of Education, Custom and Example" (2:66) extremely strong, but every individual has his own

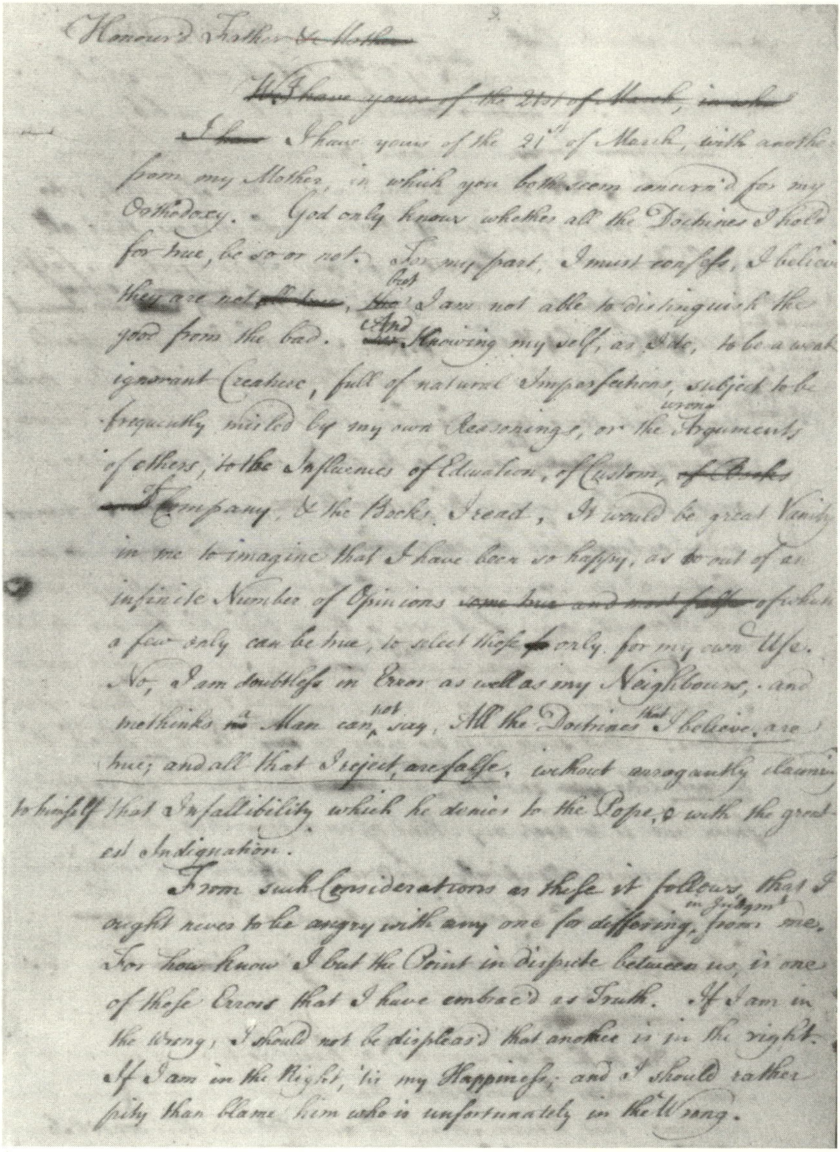

Figure 19. Franklin's religion, described in a letter to his parents, 13 April 1738. In March 1738, after three Boston newspapers reprinted a report of the trial of Evan Jones and John Remington for the possible murder of Daniel Rees, Franklin's parents wrote him, 21 March, expressing concern for his religious beliefs. Franklin drafted a reply on 13 April. His reply is not extant, but in the draft, Franklin wrote, "You both seem concern'd for my Orthodoxy. God only knows whether all the Doctrines I hold for true, be so or not." One would expect him to then say that he believed they were true. Instead, he wrote, "For my part, I must confess, I believe they are not, but I am not able to distinguish the good from the bad."

Who ever heard of anyone saying that what he thought was true he did not believe was true? In effect, Franklin was saying that if truth existed, persons could not be certain that they knew it. Courtesy, Historical Society of Pennsylvania, Philadelphia.

makeup, which often determines his opinions. If absolute truth exists, we cannot know it.

Franklin's brief draft gathers together most of the intellectual threads we have seen in the Hemphill tracts, and his statement "I believe they are not" pithily expresses the paradox of trying to find absolute certainties when one believes that there is none.

Perhaps the recent predecessor closest to Franklin's position is Pascal. Like Franklin, he repeatedly emphasized that reason was weak ("the farthest Reason can go, is to confess that there are infinite numbers of things that are above it"), that custom created the beliefs of most people ("Custom . . . forms and inclines Nature"), and that there was little possibility of any certainty in metaphysics or in life. Pascal's most famous passage, the wager, granted that there was no proof of God's existence but said that "in betting to believe God is, if you win you win all; if you lose you lose nothing."[21] Pascal and Franklin both characteristically saw paradoxes concerning belief, though Pascal suffered more metaphysical despair in affirming religion than did Franklin—who sometimes affirmed belief, sometimes doubt, and sometimes nonbelief.

Franklin thought that if truth existed, persons could not know it because it was too complex. He expressed its moral complexity when he was nineteen in the *Dissertation on Liberty and Necessity*: "Now there is every Moment something *best* to be done, which is alone then *good*, and with respect to which, every Thing else is at that Time *evil*. In order to know which is best to be done, and which not, it is requisite that we should have at one View all the intricate Consequences of every Action with respect to the general Order and Scheme of the Universe, both present and future; but they are innumerable and incomprehensible by any Thing but Omniscience" (1:62). He showed in his "Casuist" essays of 1732 on the case of the missing horse that the potential explanations and opinions on even a simple legal matter are subject to numerous possibilities. With questions of metaphysical absolutes, like God or Truth, we are all probably wrong. Franklin agreed with the Greek philosopher Carneades, who did not deny that there were absolutes "but maintained we could not certainly discern them."[22]

Franklin's view of the metaphysical complexity of reality led him, on the one hand, to a radical skepticism concerning ultimate realities and, on the other, to a belief that the existing condition of his life, and of most people in his society, was about as good as it was possible to be. That did not mean that he did not want to change conditions for those who were subjected to prejudice. He sought social amelioration. Even as an old man, he was the most radical member of the Constitutional Convention. He wanted life to be better for all people. But he was leery of panaceas and of changes that did not take into consideration the psychology of human nature. As we will see elsewhere, he applied his view of reality's complexity to society, history, and ecology.

Franklin's letter to his parents said that no one could be certain of an absolute truth. "No, I am doubtless in Error as well as my Neighbours, and methinks a Man can not say, *All the Doctrines that I believe, are true; and all that I reject, are false,* without arrogantly claiming to himself that Infallibility which he denies to the Pope." Knowing that his radical skepticism would upset his parents, who believed in the traditional New England Congregationalism, he revised the letter. In his second draft, he wrote, "Doubtless I have my Share [of erroneous opinions], and when the natural Weakness and Imperfection of Human Understanding is considered, with the unavoidable Influences of Education, Custom, Books and Company, upon our Ways of thinking, I imagine a Man must have a good deal of Vanity who believes, and a good deal of Boldness who affirms, that all the Doctrines he holds, are true; and all he rejects, are false."

The skepticism in the second version is not nearly so obvious. Franklin could live comfortably in a world without absolutes, but he knew that many people could not. In his wills of 1750 and 1757, Franklin thanked God (though his definition of God is uncertain) for giving him "such a Mind, with moderate Passions, or so much of his gracious Assistance in governing them" that he was relatively content with life. Though he wrote repeatedly on theology and other metaphysical questions, he was personally comparatively untroubled by metaphysical uncertainties. He wrote Jane Mecom on 17 July 1771, "I am much disposed to like the World as I find it, and to doubt my own Judgment as to what would mend it. I see so much Wisdom in what I understand of its Creation and government, that I suspect equal Wisdom may be in what I do not understand. And thence have perhaps as much Trust in God as the most pious Christian."

Replying to his parents, he defended speculative opinions so long as they did not result in evil actions: "I think Opinions should be judg'd of by their Influences and Effects; and if a Man holds none that tend to make him less Virtuous or more vicious, it may be concluded he holds none that are dangerous; which I hope is the Case with me." Franklin assured his mother that Freemasons "are in general a very harmless sort of People; and have no principles or Practices that are inconsistent with Religion or good Manners." He did, however, reveal his usual proto-feminist feelings when he added that his mother had "some reason to be displeas'd" with Freemasons, "since it is not allow'd that Women should be admitted into that secret Society." Was he attributing his own proto-feminist attitudes to his mother, or might his statement suggest that his mother was the source of this perspective? "My Mother grieves that one of her Sons is an Arian, another an Arminian. What an Arminian or an Arian is, I cannot say that I very well know." But, of course, Franklin knew. He then wrote, "My good Mother is I believe the first that gave me either of those Names." He recognized that the last sentence was unfilial and would have hurt her feelings, so he cancelled it. Instead, he wrote, "The Truth is, I make such Distinctions very little my Study; I think vital Religion has always suffer'd, when Orthodoxy is more regarded than Virtue."

He concluded with his fundamental belief, one that had nothing to do with absolutes. He believed in attempting to do good for his fellow human beings. In consideration of his parents' religious beliefs, he gave it a biblical certification by paraphrasing Matthew 25:34–46: "And the Scripture assures me, that at the last Day, we shall not be examin'd what we *thought*, but what we *did*; and our Recommendation will not be that we said *Lord, Lord*, but that we did *GOOD* to our Fellow Creatures" (2:203–4). Thus, he repeated the position reflected by his early pseudonym, Silence Dogood, which he echoed throughout his life. Since only a draft of the letter exists, we cannot be certain what he actually sent, though it was probably more deferential than the drafts.

131 MARKET STREET

By the end of 1738, Franklin decided that the family and business needed more room, and he leased Robert Grace's property (11 January 1739). Grace owned a lot and the four structures on it, now the site of 131 Market Street and 120 and 122 Church Alley. The house on Market Street was just four buildings down the street toward the river from the Franklins' previous home. The Grace house was larger, 17 feet wide by 45 feet deep with a two-story kitchen, 20 by 11 feet, behind it. Two smaller structures on Church Alley served as the printing shop and the post office.[23] The Franklins lived at the Grace house on Market Street for nine years, until approximately 1 January 1748, shortly before Franklin retired from printing. Then the Franklins rented a home from John Wister at the present site of 325 Market Street. The printing office and post office remained in Church Alley. On 14 January 1752, Franklin moved the post office to his home. The printing office of Franklin and Hall continued at the Grace property throughout their partnership, which ended in 1766, when the imprints still read "at the New-Printing-Office, near the Market."

Shortly after moving, the Franklins were burglarized. On 15 February 1739, a tall, thin Irishman named William Lloyd stole "an half-worn Sagathee Coat lin'd with Silk, four fine homespun Shirts, a fine Holland Shirt ruffled at the Hands and Bosom, a pair of black broadcloth Breeches new seated and lined with Leather, two pair of good worsted Stockings, one of a dark colour, and the other a lightish blue, a coarse Cambrick Handkerchief, mark'd with an F in red Silk, a new pair of Calfskin Shoes, a Boy's new Castor Hat, and sundry other Things." Evidently the Franklins at this time still had little that was valuable and easily portable. The thief took no silver or jewelry, no expensive watches or small clocks. Used clothing was worth more in the eighteenth century than today, but the burglar hardly had a good haul. The press and types were valuable, but they were too big, too heavy, and too specialized to steal.

THE *GENERAL MAGAZINE*

The story of the *General Magazine* provides more revealing information about Franklin's character than almost any other event in the period 1736–47, and therefore it will be related here rather than in Chapter 15, which deals with his business ventures.[24] By 1740, Franklin planned to start an American magazine. Like the *Gentleman's Magazine* (founded 1731) and other English journals, it would appear monthly and mainly reprint materials from the newspapers. But the American magazine would specialize in reprinting American materials— primarily from the colonial newspapers. By 1741, America had eleven: five in Boston, two in New York, two in Philadelphia, one in Virginia, and one in South Carolina. A decade earlier, when the seven existing American newspapers had smaller formats and less American content, it would have been impossible to have put together a monthly magazine consisting primarily of American materials. It was possible in 1741.

Franklin thought the attorney John Webbe might make a good editor. He had written a number of essays attacking Franklin and Hamilton in the *American Weekly Mercury* during 1732, as well as a series of essays on government in the *Pennsylvania Gazette* during 1736. Franklin told Webbe about the projected magazine. An issue would consist of three sheets, making (at 19 pages per sheet) 57 pages. He would print 1,000 copies at first. The price would be 15 shillings a year or 15 pence per issue. Merchants who retailed the magazine could purchase it at 12 shillings a dozen. Franklin would shoulder the expense for the paper, printing, correspondence, selling, and keeping accounts. Webbe would select the materials, make abstracts, and write promotions for the magazine. Franklin proposed that for bearing all expenses, he would be paid one-half of the income, and the other half would be equally divided between Webbe and himself. The royalties would remain the same (three-fourths to Franklin, one-fourth to Webbe) for all magazines sold under 2,000; for all above 2,000, the receipts would be equally divided. The printer supposed that editing the magazine would require three or four days a month. He said he had the only small type in America suitable for printing it (he had purchased a Caslon brevier type a few months earlier and first used it in the 17 July 1740 *Gazette*).[25] He pointed out that his position as Philadelphia's postmaster would facilitate the delivery of the magazine throughout the colonies.

Webbe liked the idea and agreed. But after considering it, he thought that "every Moment of my Time would be necessarily ingrossed in the Execution of the Undertaking" (2:268). History repeated itself. When Franklin had told the printer George Webb (no relation to John Webbe) about his plan to start a newspaper, Webb told Samuel Keimer about it, who promptly started one. John Webbe told Andrew Bradford about Franklin's plan for a magazine, proposed editing one for him, and asked for a larger share of the profits. Bradford agreed. Franklin heard of Webbe's perfidy before 6 November, and it may be, as James A. Sappenfield speculated, that some Poor Richard sayings for 1741 were influenced by the controversy with Webbe and Bradford: "If you would keep your Secret from an enemy, tell it not to a friend" (2:296).[26]

Webbe thereupon wrote an advertisement for the projected *American Magazine* (was that Franklin's prospective title?), which Bradford printed in the

American Weekly Mercury on 6 November 1740. Each issue would contain four sheets, or the equivalent, of the size of the *Mercury*; the price would be twelve shillings a year, Pennsylvania currency; and the first number would appear in March. Though with a larger type, it would be both one sheet larger and three shillings per year cheaper than Franklin's proposed magazine. The Bradford-Webbe *American Magazine* would publish the speeches of the colonial governors, the addresses and answers of the assemblies, and "their Votes, Resolutions and Debates." Webbe planned an ambitious political magazine. Further, "at the End of every Session, we shall give an Extract of the Laws therein passed, with the Reasons on which they were founded, the Grievances intended to be remedied by them, and the Benefits expected from them."

Though the political commentary alone was far too ambitious, Webbe also promised to explain the key socioeconomic factors affecting each colony: "That the Reader may be the Better enabled to form a Judgment of the various Transactions intended to be set in View; Succinct Accounts will be given, in the Course of the Work, of the Situation, Climate, Soil, Productions, Trade and Manufactures of all the British Plantations; the Constitutions of those several Colonies, with their respective Views and Interests, will be opened and explained; and the Nature and Extent of the various Jurisdictions exercised in each Government particularly described."

The *American Magazine* would also contain accounts of remarkable civil and criminal trials, the rates of exchange between each colony and England, and the prices of goods in the principal colonial trading centers. Near the end of the long rambling advertisement, Webbe said the magazine would include a digest of "the General Affairs of Europe, Asia and Africa" that "will yield greater Pleasure and Profit, than the scattered, unconnected Articles of News in the common Prints." Webbe's editorial plan would take a great deal of time. Every student of American history must wish that he had succeeded.

Angry that Webbe had stolen his idea and sold it to Bradford, Franklin nevertheless determined to proceed. He advertised in the *Pennsylvania Gazette* on 13 November 1740 the following: "in January next will be published, (To be continued Monthly), *The General Magazine, and Historical Chronicle, For all the British Plantations in America.*" Each issue would feature eight subject headings:

1) "Extracts from the Votes, and Debates of the Parliament of Great Britain." That was a standard feature of the *Gentleman's Magazine*.

2) "The Proclamations and Speeches of Governors; Addresses, Votes, Resolutions, &c. of Assemblies, in each Colony." Each American newspaper printed the proclamations and speeches of the local governors and the responses of the assemblies, and some newspapers reprinted these from the other colonies, often simply as filler; none currently printed them all. Franklin may have taken this idea from Webbe, or perhaps he had proposed it as a feature to Webbe.

3) "Accounts of, and Extracts from, all new Books, Pamphlets, &c. published in the Plantations." The *Gentleman's Magazine* contained lists of London books, sometimes with short notes about the contents; no publication currently did this for America. American pamphlets and books, however, were often advertised in the local American newspapers, and Franklin advertised his imprints in the *Pennsylvania Gazette*.

4) "Essays, controversial, humorous, philosophical, religious, moral or political." A standard feature of the *Gentleman's Magazine*, the essays were generally reprinted from newspapers.

5) "Select Pieces of Poetry." Again, a standard feature of the *Gentleman's Magazine*, mainly from the newspapers.

6) "A concise chronicle of the most remarkable Transactions, as well in Europe as America." Another *Gentleman's Magazine* characteristic, though it largely ignored American affairs.

7) "Births, Marriages, Deaths, and Promotions, of eminent Persons in the several Colonies." The *Gentleman's Magazine* carried similar contents, featuring English nobility and personages and, with a few exceptions, ignoring Americans.

8) "*Course* of Exchange between the several Colonies, and London; Prices of Goods, &c." Franklin may have borrowed this, too, from Webbe, though Franklin occasionally featured such information in the *Pennsylvania Gazette*.

Franklin continued, "This Magazine, in Imitation of those in England, was long since projected." One suspects that he did indeed intend to start a magazine when he ordered that small brevier type about a year earlier. Then Franklin attacked Webbe: "It would not, indeed, have been published quite so soon, were it not that a Person, [Franklin footnoted "John Webbe"] to whom the Scheme was communicated *in Confidence*, has thought fit to advertise it in the last *Mercury*, without our Participation; and, probably, with a View, by Starting before us, to discourage us from prosecuting our first Design, and reap the Advantage of it wholly to himself." He at first intended (as Bradford did later) to sell the magazine through subscriptions (thus the annual fee), but now he decided to beat out Bradford: "we desire no Subscriptions. We shall publish the Books at our own Expence, and risque the Sale of them." So every issue was a gamble. If Franklin had collected subscriptions (as he had for the journals and sermons of Whitefield, and as the English and later American magazines did), the venture might have succeeded. To meet the competition, Franklin also increased the size of an issue: "Each Magazine shall contain four Sheets, of common sized Paper, in a small Character," and undercut Bradford's announced price of twelve shillings a year: "Price *Six Pence* Sterling, or *Nine Pence* Pennsylvania Money; with considerable Allowance to Chapmen who take Quantities." He had intended to sell the magazine for fifteen pence but now charged only nine. By not arranging for subscriptions and by reducing the price of the magazine, Franklin doomed the venture.

"The Detection"

Webbe felt maligned. He replied to Franklin with articles, titled "The Detection," in the next three issues of the *American Weekly Mercury*. In the first (20 November) he began by accusing Franklin of "insinuated" falsehoods. Such lies were "the most mischievous Kind of Lying; for the Strokes being oblique and indirect, a Man cannot so easily defend himself against them, as he might do, if they were straight and peremptory." Franklin's method was "more mean and dastardly." It had "the Slyness of a Pickpocket." Franklin's "first Falsehood" (Webbe never specified a second) was suggesting that he communicated the project to Webbe in private and that Webbe agreed to edit the magazine. Webbe conceded that Franklin had communicated the proposal, but then equivocated: "surely his making the Proposal neither obliged me to the writing of one for him to print, nor restrained me from the printing of it at any other Press without his Leave or Participation." Webbe claimed that it was comparable to Franklin's offering to print everything to anyone "that he thinks has a Talent for Writing, and they shall from thenceforth be restrained from publishing any Thing without his Consent" (2:266). The comparison was ludicrous—among other considerations that might be mentioned is the fact that no magazine had ever been published in America though thousands of books and pamphlets had been.

Webbe claimed sole credit for the plan for the proposed magazine. Though it had similarities to the contents of the usual English magazine, the plan emphasized Webbe's original contributions. That was, to be sure, different from Franklin's plan. Franklin projected mainly reprinting items from the colonial American newspapers. Webbe projected a painstaking history and analysis of contemporary American politics, along with some reprints, but he was only partially successful in carrying out his proposal. Webbe thought that Franklin's proposal to take three-quarters of the money arising from the sale was too much. Though Franklin had told him it would only take three or four days a month to edit the magazine, Webbe believed that the kind of magazine he would edit would require all his time. Of course Webbe did not mention that he had taken Franklin's details of size and price to Bradford.

Franklin did not reply. He merely reprinted his advertisement of 13 November, which specified that a certain person "to whom the Scheme was communicated *in Confidence*, has thought fit to advertise it in the last *Mercury*." In the *Mercury* of 27 November, Webbe continued with a rambling second "Detection." He said that he gave the plan of the magazine at large to give a sample of his writing and then wrote a discourse on good prose. Evidently Franklin had privately ridiculed Webbe's first long proposal. Though Franklin's criticism is not extant, Webbe (tongue in cheek) granted its validity but concluded that though he might be a bad writer, he was not, unlike Franklin, "a *bad Man*" (2:273). Webbe probably had in mind Franklin's reputation for irreligion. Again, Franklin made no reply; he again reprinted the *Gentleman's Magazine*'s advertisement that had originally appeared on 13 November.

In a third "Detection" (4 December), Webbe went too far. He said that Franklin's silence was "the *highest* Justification I can desire. *While* he continues in that Humour I shall suppress the Remainder of the Detection. This is a Kindness he could not reasonably expect at my Hands; Considering that he has since my first Letter, in Quality of Post-Master, taken upon him to deprive the *Mercury* of the Benefit of the Post, and will not permit it to travel with his *Gazette*. . . . His Resentment against his Brother Printer is altogether unreasonable" (2:274).

Franklin replied on 11 December 1740 that it was "now upwards of a Twelve-month since I refus'd to forward Mr. Bradford's Papers free by the Post, in Obedience to a positive Order from the Hon. Col. Spotswood, then Post-Master General." Franklin explained that he had been ordered not to allow Bradford's papers to be carried free by Alexander Spotswood because Bradford had not paid his accounts to Spotswood. Franklin printed Spotswood's letter of 12 October 1739. Franklin next turned the tables on Webbe. He began with an ostensible defense of Bradford: "I must however do Mr. Bradford the Justice, to vindicate him from an injurious Suspicion which I apprehend may arise on this Occasion, to wit, That he has impos'd that Story on his unhappy Writer, and misled him by a wrong Account of Facts he might be ignorant of. For this, in my Opinion, cannot possibly be: Inasmuch as that Person is thoroughly acquainted with the Affair, was employ'd as Attorney in the Action against Bradford, and had, at the very Time he was writing the Paragraph in Question, the Original Letter from Col. Spotswood, in his own Possession" (2:276).

In a two-page supplement to the 18 December *Mercury*, Webbe responded that after the order from Spotswood, Bradford "never sent him [Franklin] any of his Papers to be forwarded in the Mail," but "he sent them to the Riders who used to distribute them on their several Routs." Webbe said that Franklin "had declared, some Time before he laid me under the Necessity of writing against him in my own Defence, that as he favoured Mr. Bradford by permitting the Postman to distribute his Papers, he had him therefore *under his Thumb*; and was confident, in Regard he could at any Time deprive him of that Privilege, that he would not, if he understood his own Interest, be prevaild upon to publish any Thing against him." After Webbe's first "Detection" appeared, the post rider who generally carried Bradford's paper told him that "he was apprehensive it wou'd be displeasing to Mr. Franklin, were he to know he distributed them" (279). The post rider refused to carry any more of Bradford's papers. As usual, Webbe could not end. He rambled on, lamely attempting to criticize Franklin's 11 December reply. The following week, 25 December, Franklin again repeated the 13 November advertisement for the *General Magazine*.

If Franklin said he had Bradford "under my Thumb," and if he did order the post riders not to carry Bradford's paper privately, then he deserves censure. But there is no proof that he did so. If we take what Webbe said literally, the post riders, seeing the *Mercury* attack Franklin, decided on their own not to carry it. That may have happened. It seems out of character for Franklin to boast that he could squelch Bradford or refuse him the possibility of bribing the post riders. Indeed, Franklin twice mentioned in the *Autobiography* that Bradford forbade him the use of the post, "and I thought so meanly of him for it, that when I afterwards came into his Situation, I took care never to imitate it" (A 69, 101).

But the race was on. Franklin had advertised that he would publish the *General Magazine* for January. That meant he would publish in February, for eighteenth-century magazines appeared in the month following their dates. The *Gentleman's Magazine* for January appeared about mid-February and reprinted materials that had been published in the English newspapers and elsewhere during January. Bradford resolved to publish first. On 5 February, both the *Pennsylvania Gazette* and the *American Weekly Mercury* advertised that their magazines would appear in the following week. Neither did. On 12 February, the *Mercury* advertised that the *American Magazine* would appear "tomorrow." The *Gazette* on 12 February advertised that the *General Magazine* would appear on "Monday next," 16 February. Presumably, that happened. Bradford and Webbe's *American Magazine* appeared three days before Franklin's *General Magazine*.

Contents: Webbe's American Magazine

Both magazines were ambitious. Webbe's first *American Magazine* printed abstracts of the assembly proceedings of New Jersey, Pennsylvania, and Maryland, often citing John Locke's essays on government, as Webbe had done in 1736. He wrote an account of Pennsylvania, refuting Jonathan Swift's remarks in the *Drapier's Letters* that the Irish had been lured to Pennsylvania to provide a screen and defense for the inhabitants against the Indians. His "Remarks on the *Maryland* Government" included several shrewd observations. In the February issue, Webbe continued his remarks on the Maryland government, printed its assembly's proceedings and those of Pennsylvania and New York, and gave extracts of the speeches between the governor and assembly in New Jersey.

Webbe printed one extraordinary item in the third and last issue, for March: "The Religion of the *Indian* Natives of *America*, explained, in an Argument held by one of them at *Connestogoe* in *Pennsylvania*, with a *Swedish* Minister, in the Year 1690. *Translated from the Latin*." Franklin, I believe, wrote it. He often circulated copies of his writings in manuscript and often others printed them. Webbe evidently received a copy and decided to scoop Franklin with Franklin's own writing. (As we have seen, Bradford did that on 15 February 1731/2 with "The Palatines' Appeal.") I suspect that only Franklin's authorship explains why Bradford dared publish it. When Franklin's partner James Parker printed a version of it several years later, he was prosecuted for heresy in New York. Franklin interceded for him with Cadwallader Colden, and the prosecution was dropped. Bradford knew that if he was prosecuted, he could say that Webbe, not he, edited the magazine, and Webbe could reveal the author, who would be the primary person blamed. Franklin's authorship was probably known, however, and no one would want to try to prosecute him, for everyone knew that Andrew Hamilton, the former attorney general and former Speaker of the House, was not only Franklin's friend and a deist but also the best lawyer in Pennsylvania. It would have been time-consuming and finally unprofitable to prosecute Franklin. The *Indian Speech* became the most reprinted Indian speech before Jefferson popularized "Logan's Speech" in *Notes on the State of Virginia* (1785). Franklin echoed the *Indian Speech* in writing similar deistic Indian satires. (It will be discussed in Chapter 19.)

Webbe also printed a surprising and interesting item in the March issue: "Some Reflections on the *exorbitant* Grants made to private Persons of unculti- vated Land in America." The radical economic article argued that the land should belong to the person who cultivated it—an argument advanced by Cap- tain John Smith over a century before.

Contents: *Franklin's* General Magazine

Franklin's *General Magazine* began with "Brief Historical and Chronological Notes of several Princes, States, Governments, &c.," on pages 1–6, including the British plantations. The information was more complete than similar surveys that he had printed in *Poor Richard*. He reported the "Proceedings in Parliament of Great Britain on the Affair of Paper Money in the American Colonies" (6–9), with the "Instructions thereupon sent to the Governors of the Plantations" (9–11); "New England Scheme for emitting Notes to pass in Lieu of Money" (11–16); "Proclamation issued in New York, relating to the Coin" (16–18); "Proceedings in the Assembly of Pennsylvania" (18–21); "Report of the Lords Commissioners for Trade and Plantations, on Six Pennsylvania Laws" (21–22); "Report of the King's Attorney and Solicitor General, on one of the said Laws" (22); "Act of Parliament for Naturalizing Foreigners in the British Colonies" (22–26); "Pro- ceedings of Assembly in New-England" (26–34); extracts from new books pub- lished in the colonies (34–57); essays from the colonial newspapers (57–61); poetry (62–70); a historical chronicle of the most important events (especially in the colonies) for the past month (71–74); the price of bills of exchange in the different colonies (74); price current in Philadelphia (74); and "An Account of the Export of Provisions from the Port of Philadelphia, in Pennsylvania, betwixt the 25th of December 1739, and the 25th of December 1740" (75). On the last page, Franklin advertised four books from his own press.

Except for the introductory historical and chronological notes and the his- torical chronicle of the most important events of the past month, Franklin's only writing in the first issue of the magazine accompanied the account of Phila- delphia's exports. Like many newspaper articles discussed in the chapter on Franklin as a newspaperman (Volume 1, Chapter18), the report shows Franklin's characteristic statistical approach, as well as his proto-Americanism: "The above Account is a Proof of the Fertility of this Province, and of the great Plenty wherewith *GOD* has bless'd the Industry of the Inhabitants; who in a few Years have made a Garden of a Wilderness, and, besides living well themselves, have so much Food to spare to other Countries. By means of this and the neighbouring *Provision Colonies*, the British Fleet and Forces in the West-Indies are at this Time supplied with Provisions at a moderate Price, while the Enemy is starving in Want; which shows that these Colonies give Great Britain a considerable Advantage over its Enemies in an American War, and will no doubt be an additional Inducement to our Mother Country to continue us its Protection."

Franklin Insults Webbe

An advertisement for the *American Magazine* appeared in the 19 February 1741 *Mercury*. Bradford signed it, but evidently Webbe wrote it. Smarting from having lost the race to print first, Franklin found the advertisement irritating. He travestied it under the title "Teague's Advertisement" in the 26 February *Gazette*. The title alluded to Webbe's Irish background, and Franklin mainly used a mock Irish brogue. His model was "Teague's Orashion," a poem that appeared five years before in the *Gentleman's Magazine* for January 1735, beginning "Arah, dear joy." Webbe had advertised that each issue of the *American Magazine* would contain "something more than four Sheets . . . so that there will be not less than fifty two Sheets published in one Year, which will comprehend double the Quantity of Matter . . . contained in a common News Paper during a like Course of Time." Franklin wrote: "Arra Joy! My monthly *Macasheen* shall contain Sheets four, / Or an Equivalent, which is someting more; / So dat twelve Times four shall make fifty two, / Which is twice as much as fifty two Newsh-Papers do" (2:305).

Webbe had continued: "Price single, one Shilling; to Subscribers twelve Shillings per *ann*. Pennsylvania Currency. It seems unnecessary to add that every Body will be at Liberty as being a Thing of Course, to withdraw his Subscription when he pleases." Franklin burlesqued: "Prishe shingle *One Shilling*: But shubscribe for a Year, / You shall have it sheaper, at de shame Prishe, Honey dear: / And if you will but shubscribe to take it de Year out, / You may leave off when you pleashe, before, no doubt." Franklin noted, "The Word *cheaper*, I own, is not express'd in the Original; but it must have been intended to be understood; otherwise, what Encouragement is there to take by the Year, or where is the Inducement to subscribe?"

Puffing its future contents, Webbe wrote, "As the principal Part of this Magazine is not a Transcript from printed Copy, but is a Work that requires a continual Study and Application, it cannot be afforded for less Money than is mentioned." Franklin wrote, "'Tis true, my Book is dear; but de Reashon is plain, / The best Parts of it ish de Work of my own Brain: / How can odher Men's Writings be wort so much! / Arra! if you tink so, you're no vhery good Shudge." Webbe said, "The News will be inserted in the next, which was omitted this Time, as not being thought proper to repeat, what had been so often told over in other publick Papers." Franklin ridiculed, "De Newsh which I left out, becaush it was old, / And had been in odher Papers so often told, / I shall put into my nexsht (do 'tis shince told onesh more) / Becaush 'twill be newer dan it wash before" (2:305).

In a foolish conclusion Webbe said, "Care is also promised for the Buyer's Sake, as well as from a Regard to the Reputation of the Country, to avoid re-printing any of the Rubbish or Sweepings of Printing-Houses." Franklin ridi-culed him: "For de dear Buyer's Shake, and de Land's Reputaish' / No Shweepings, but dose of my own Shcull shall have plaish; / And dose, you must tink, will be vhery fine: / For do dis Advertisement my Printer does Shign, / To tell you de Trute, de Shense is all mine. / Signed A. Bradford."

Litterateurs of the neighboring colonies relished and remembered Franklin's satire. Dr. Adam Thomson imitated it in his poem "Teague Turn'd Planter" in the *Maryland Gazette* on 28 July 1747, and Dr. Alexander Hamilton of Annapolis, in his literary history of the *Maryland Gazette* (29 June 1748), burlesqued Webbe (or Webb) as Teague, "the Author of the *Advertisement.*"[27]

In the *American Weekly Mercury* of 5 March 1741, Andrew Bradford took the high road. He claimed that the advertisement was his own (Webbe must have been responsible at least for the brag about the original materials in the *Ameri-can Magazine*) and censured Franklin for using invidious nationalistic prejudice. Bradford noted that Franklin's mimicry echoed the standard Teague humor and added that it was partially written in "broken Dutch" (*Dutch* was a common Pennsylvania term for *German*), thus trying to win German subscribers for him-self and to turn them against Franklin. In satirizing national stereotypes, Frank-lin was, by today's standards, insensitive, but such insults were standard eighteenth-century English humor. Witness Franklin's source in the *Gentle-man's Magazine* or Dr. Johnson's definition of *Oats* in his *Dictionary*: "A grain, which in England is generally given to horses, but in Scotland supports the people."

The succeeding five issues of Franklin's *General Magazine* were similar to the January number. Franklin did, however, publish two of his own compositions in the magazine, "Essay on Paper-Currency" in February and "Theophilus" on "The Divine Prescience" in March. The "Essay on Paper-Currency" proposed to fix the value of colonial paper currency by having a loan office for the colonies that would lend money just as the Pennsylvania Loan Office did within Pennsyl-vania. The interest would establish a bank for the colonies in England that could adjust the rate of exchange and thus invalidate the English complaint against the uncertainty of the value of colonial paper money. In some ways, the idea resembled today's Federal Reserve Board.

" "Theophilus" on "The Divine Prescience" claimed that everything was pre-destined. If everything had not been decreed from eternity, "there is no Possibil-ity . . . of defending the Doctrine of the *Divine Prescience*." He concluded that "whoever denies God's immediate Concourse with every Action we produce, must of Consequence deny God's Foreknowledge." The argument was basically the same that Franklin had presented in the *Dissertation on Liberty and Necessity* and implied that God was responsible for all evil in the world. (Both *General Magazine* contributions will be briefly discussed in Chapter 19.)

The first two American magazines, Webbe and Bradford's short-lived *American Magazine* (a total of 120 pages) and Franklin's *General Magazine* (a total of 426 pages, with at least one-third more type per page than the *American Magazine*) are tributes to Franklin's entrepreneurial genius. Though both failed, both have notable contents. Franklin's account of new books and pamphlets published in the plantations was a valuable compilation, not to be duplicated in the colonial period, and his reprinting excerpts of Robert Beverley's *History of Virginia* demonstrated his high regard for the literary artistry and proto-American ideals of the Virginian.

Franklin's entrepreneurial attempts and aptitude, however, appear throughout his business career. More succeeded than failed. What rarely appears is a passionate, angry, and impractical Franklin. In his anger, he ruined both magazines. He changed the projected price of his magazine, its format, and the plan for subscriptions. He undercut Webbe and Bradford's *American Magazine*, but he also destined his own *General Magazine* to financial failure. What should he have done? Though Webbe promised much, the actual *American Magazine* delivered little. Its small and specialized contents would probably not have won a large audience. It would have failed even if Franklin's *General Magazine* had not appeared. If Franklin had simply waited a year and then proceeded with his original plan, his magazine might well have succeeded.

Personal Affairs, 1740–1742

Deborah suffered a major loss when her younger sister Frances, who had married John Croker, died. The Franklins no doubt attended her funeral at Christ Church on 8 April 1740. Since Franklin had loaned John Croker money throughout his wife's sickness and after her death, we have a detailed record in Franklin's accounts of expenses for a nurse, winding sheet, pall, coffin, burial fees, mourning gloves, wine, spice, and sugar. Deborah's only remaining sibling was her brother, John, who had been baptized at Christ Church on 11 August 1712. He was a carpenter and occasionally turns up in Franklin's accounts doing odd jobs. In barter, Franklin took a walnut table from him on 9 April 1743.

Having educated his nephew James Franklin, Jr., for about five years, Franklin made him an apprentice on 5 November 1740, while William Franklin continued studying with Alexander Annand until at least December 1743 (2:388). Jemmy, who was about eleven in 1740, lived with the Franklins and worked as an apprentice until 5 November 1747.

Franklin purchased two parcels of real estate in the summer of 1741. On 31 July he bought a pasture of about three acres in the Northern Liberties from the brick maker William Coats. He probably purchased it for William Franklin's pony. The next summer, William advertised: "*STRAY'D*, about two Months ago, from the Northern Liberties of this City, a small bay Mare, branded IW on the near Shoulder and Buttock. She being but little and barefooted, cannot be supposed to be gone far; therefore if any of the Town-Boys find her and bring her to the Subscriber, they shall, for their Trouble, have the Liberty to ride her when they please, from William Franklin. Philad. June 17. 1742." Five years later (6 August 1747), Franklin advertised that the horse had been stolen. On 1 August 1741, Franklin purchased a house and lot from Christopher Thompson, a bricklayer, on the north side of Mulberry or Arch Street, between Fourth and Fifth Streets. Franklin paid the annual ground rent on the property to Thompson until he purchased the land on 13 December 1771. Presumably, Franklin bought the house as an investment and rented it out.

Franklin's friend and patron Andrew Hamilton died on 4 August 1741. Franklin and Deborah probably attended his funeral at Bush Hill the next day, and on 6 August the *Pennsylvania Gazette* carried Franklin's long, appreciative obituary of him. After Hamilton's death, the older man closest to Franklin was James Logan. Though he did fewer favors for Franklin than Hamilton, Logan was evidently Franklin's favorite intellectual conversationalist in the Philadelphia area.

Franklin set up a third printing partner, James Parker, on 20 February 1741/2, with terms almost identical to those of his earlier agreements with Thomas Whitmarsh and Lewis Timothy. Franklin had learned, however, that an annual accounting was difficult for some people, and so he now made it quarterly. Parker had served his apprenticeship with William Bradford of New York but ran away in 1733 and worked briefly for Franklin. He supposedly ran away because he believed he was already a better printer than Bradford and had nothing more to learn from him.[28] At Franklin's urging, Parker had returned to New York and completed his apprenticeship in 1735, and may then have returned to work for Franklin. On 29 November 1739, Parker was living and boarding with the Franklins. The financial accounts suggest that he remained with Franklin until late 1741. With William and Jemmy Franklin and James Parker all living with the Franklins, the house at 131 Market Street must have been bustling with activity. Early in 1742, Franklin sponsored Parker as his printing partner in New York, hoping that Parker would become the printer for the New York legislature, replacing William Bradford (1663–1752), who was seventy-eight years old. That happened: Bradford retired in 1742, and Parker became the printer for New York in 1743. He started a newspaper, the *New York Weekly Post Boy*, on 3 January 1742/3. Though Franklin and Parker's partnership officially ended on 20 February 1747/8, Parker continued to work with and for Franklin in various positions. Franklin set him up as a printer in New Haven, Connecticut, and appointed him postmaster there in 1753. When Franklin prepared to go to England as Pennsylvania's agent in 1756, he appointed Parker comptroller of the post office, a position Parker held until his death at age fifty-six on 2 July 1770.

NEW ENGLAND TOUR, 1743

In the late spring and early summer of 1743, Franklin made his third visit to Boston and New England, vacationing and making contacts with other printers and postmasters. He had last visited Boston ten years before, in 1733. Because of the war with Spain, travel by ship was dangerous, so Franklin went overland, no doubt renting a horse for the journey. Before leaving, he drafted *A Proposal for Promoting Useful Knowledge among the British Plantations in America* and printed it on 14 May 1743. He was thinking of discussing the proposal with other colonial intellectuals. He probably left for New York the next day, 15 May. Franklin certainly visited his partner James Parker in New York. Although Parker had started the *New York Weekly Post Boy* at the beginning of 1743, he made no references to Franklin in the newspaper, and no records of Franklin's stay in New York have turned up. In addition to Parker, Franklin probably visited the New York postmaster, Richard Nicholls (we know he talked with Nicholls the next year on a brief New York visit in early April), and perhaps the merchant James Burling, who, along with James Parker, sold Franklin's new stoves in New York in 1744.

In Boston, Franklin probably stayed with his parents, Josiah and Abiah, and visited his brother John and his sisters Elizabeth Douse and Jane Mecom (Jane now had seven living children). Franklin must have told them with pleasure that Deborah was pregnant. Franklin's brother John was, like their father, a tallow-chandler, but he had various business interests and was well-off. John took in subscriptions for Whitefield's works for Franklin in 1739–40 and sold Franklin's stoves, or Pennsylvania fireplaces, in 1744. Franklin probably spent more time with him than with anyone else in Boston.

Boston's First Lodge of Freemasons recorded Franklin's presence (Wednesday, 25 May) when he attended with Henry Price, provincial grand master of the North American Freemasons. The itinerant lecturer Dr. Archibald Spencer had been admitted a member at the previous meeting, 11 May, and no doubt was present on 25 May. Spencer was already a Freemason and brought testimonials with him. In the *Autobiography*, Franklin attributed his introduction to electricity to Spencer, who advertised in the *Boston Evening Post* and the *Boston Post Boy* for 30 May and the *Boston Gazette* for 31 May 1743 a course of lectures on natural philosophy. Franklin attended them, paying the expensive price of six pounds. He recalled in 1788 that Spencer's experiments "were imperfectly perform'd, as he was not very expert; but being on a Subject quite new to me, they equally surpris'd and pleas'd me" (A 152).[29] The Boston engraver Lewis Turner had been "made" a Mason at the previous meeting and probably attended the 25 May meeting. Franklin also attended the Freemasons' meeting two weeks later, 8 June, when Turner was admitted a member. Franklin employed him the following year to engrave the plates illustrating the construction of Franklin's new stove, *The New-Invented Pennsylvania Fireplace* (1744).

On 6 June, Franklin watched the pageantry of Boston's Artillery Company. John Franklin belonged to it, having joined in 1739. In the morning, the company's colors were displayed at Major Henchman's corner (the south corner of State and Washington Streets) as a signal that a training session would be held that day. After the procession formed at the recently completed Faneuil Hall armory, the lieutenant with the color guard proceeded to bring the standard to its place. The sergeants bore halberds, which had just been ordered the preceding May. The Reverend William Hooper, minister of the West Church, gave the artillery election sermon. After the election, the company went to Castle Island and practiced firing the great cannon defending the Boston seaport. Four years later (7 December 1747) Franklin told James Logan that Philadelphia's voluntary militia association proposed "to breed Gunners, by forming an Artillery Club, to go down weekly to the [Philadelphia] Battery & exercise the great Guns. The best Engineers against Cape Breton, were of such a Club, Tradesmen & Shopkeepers of Boston; I was with them at the Castle at their Exercise, 1743."

Franklin visited a series of Boston booksellers, printers, and publishers. Franklin's accounts reveal that he was selling books and almanacs to his brother James's old friend Thomas Fleet, to the Boston bookseller Joshua Blanchard, and especially to the Boston bookbinder Charles Harrison. Franklin had previously done business with Benjamin Eliot (d. 1741) and with the printing partners Samuel Kneeland and Timothy Green. When Gamaliel Rogers and Daniel Fowle started the *American Magazine and Historical Chronicle* in September 1743, they asked Franklin to sell the magazine in Philadelphia. They must have planned to start the magazine before Franklin came to Boston and no doubt enlisted his aid on this visit. Franklin called on most, if not all, of the Boston printers. He also would have visited William Brock, the deputy postmaster for Boston and, if he were in town, Ellis Huske, the postmaster of New England (who lived in Portsmouth, New Hampshire, but maintained a Boston office). Franklin probably also saw Richard Clark, who, along with Franklin's brother John, would sell Franklin's new stoves in 1744. During this Boston visit he met William Vassall, a Harvard graduate of 1733 to whom he wrote concerning inoculation on 29 May 1746.

Though Franklin may not have attended church in Boston, he talked with his sister Jane about religion. Despite fearing that her admonition might give him offense, she wrote him a concerned letter about religion shortly after he returned to Philadelphia. He replied on 28 July 1743 that he "was far from being offended at you for it." He explained, "If I say any thing about it to you, 'tis only to rectify some wrong Opinions you seem to have entertain'd of me, and that I do only because they give you some Uneasiness, which I am unwilling to be the Occasion of. You express yourself as if you thought I was against Worshipping of God, and believed Good Works would merit Heaven; which are both Fancies of your own." He wrote Jane that he had composed an entire book of devotion and prayer for his own use. (He did not mention that his 20 November 1728 "Articles of Belief and Acts of Religion" postulated a polytheistic system, with only the possibility of a subordinate God being concerned with "such an inconsiderable Nothing as Man.") He wrote Jane that "there are few, if any, in the World, so weak as to imagine, that the little Good we can do here, can *merit* so vast a Reward hereafter."

Franklin then said he had some reservations about New England Puritanism: "There are some Things in your New England Doctrines and Worship, which I do not agree with, but I do not therefore condemn them [of course he did so in various writings, especially the Hemphill tracts], or desire to shake your Belief or Practice of them. We may dislike things that are nevertheless right in themselves. I would only have you make me the same Allowances, and have a better Opinion both of Morality and your Brother." He then revealed that he had read Jonathan Edwards's *Some Thoughts Concerning the Present Revival of Religion in New England* and recommended that she read pages 367 to 375. Continuing, he cited Matthew 7:16: "and when you judge of others, if you can perceive the Fruit to be good, don't terrify your self that the Tree may be evil, but be assur'd it is not so; for you know who has said, *Men do not gather Grapes of Thorns or Figs of Thistles.*" He closed saying that "I shall always be Your affectionate Brother" and then added a postscript to Jane, who frequently revealed that she could be too sensitive to supposed criticisms: "It was not kind in you to imagine when your Sister commended Good Works, she intended it a Reproach to you. 'Twas very far from her Thoughts." Evidently the religious discussion between Jane and Franklin had taken place before at least one other person, a "sister" of Jane and Franklin, probably the wife of John Franklin or perhaps their much older sister Elizabeth Douse.

Returning from Boston in mid or late June 1743, Franklin went by way of Newport, Rhode Island, to call upon his sister-in-law Anne (Smith) Franklin, bringing news of her son James (now about thirteen) who was serving an apprenticeship with Franklin. If his seafaring brother Peter Franklin, a ship captain who lived in Newport, had the space, Franklin probably stayed with him. Dr. Thomas Moffatt, who was to become the first librarian of the Redwood Library (1747), and the artist Robert Feke, who first painted a portrait of Franklin, are among the Newport inhabitants he probably knew. If Franklin chanced to be in Newport on a Monday night, an acquaintance would have invited him to the Philosophical Club.[30] Traveling on to Connecticut, Franklin met Cadwallader Colden, and for the next twenty years the New York physician, intellectual, and politician was among his faithful correspondents. Franklin stopped by New London, Connecticut, to see Timothy Green (1679–1757), printer and bookseller, who had taken in subscriptions for Franklin's printing of Whitefield's journals in 1739 and who had recently purchased 100 copies of Franklin's 1743 *Pocket Almanac.* In New Haven, Franklin called on Yale's president, the Reverend Thomas Clap, who commissioned him to reprint Increase Mather's *Soul-Saving Gospel Truths.*

WILLIAM AND SARAH FRANKLIN

Two and a half months after Franklin's return from Boston to Philadelphia, Sarah Franklin was born (11 September 1743). Less than two months after birth, she was baptized in Deborah's Christ Church (27 October 1743). Recalling the death of their son Franky from smallpox, Franklin and Deborah had Sarah inoculated when she was two and a half years old on 18 April 1746. By 16 October 1747, Franklin proudly reported to Abiah Franklin that her four-year-old granddaughter was "the greatest lover of her book and school, of any child I ever knew." Sarah was also "very dutiful to her mistress as well as to us."

According to Sarah's granddaughter, when Sarah as a child was learning to sew, she tried to make a good buttonhole. She tried and tried, and finally gave up. "Not one word or look of reproach came from her father . . . but the next day he said, 'Sally, I have made an arrangement with my tailor to have you go to him every day. . . . He will teach you to make button-holes.'"[31] Evidently she learned how. When she was five, she made a beautiful cross-stitch pocketbook for her grandmother Abiah Franklin. After Abiah's death on 8 May 1752, Jane Mecom gave it to a Nantucket cousin, Kesia Coffin, who had admired it and thereafter "always used it when she went abroad." As late as 29 May 1786, Jane wrote of the pocketbook with admiration.

Sarah attended Christ Church with her mother and her brother William. After hearing of the successes of Philadelphia privateersmen like John Sibbald and William Dowell, around 1742 young William ran away from home and "got on board a privateer, from whence I fetched him" (3:303). Several years later, William still craved excitement. When Pennsylvania forces were being raised for the invasion of Canada in 1746, William begged his father to give him permission to join. By then about eighteen, William could not easily be refused. He received permission, joined Captain John Diemer's company as an ensign (9 June), marched off with the troops (4 September), and arrived at Albany (30 October). There the campaign fizzled while awaiting orders from the British authorities. The inactive troops, poorly provisioned, ill clad, and unpaid, began sneaking away.

Franklin was disgusted with the British handling of military affairs in America. Though he almost always took the feelings of his correspondent into account, he allowed a note of pique with the British to enter into his correspondence with the London printer William Strahan on 4 January 1746/7. A powerful French fleet and an army had been sent out to retake Louisbourg and Cape Breton in 1746 but met with disastrous storms and returned to France. Franklin wrote Strahan that "Your Government sent no Fleet to protect us from the French under D'Anville. But they have been defeated by the Hand of God." By 7 May 1747 William had returned to Philadelphia from Albany and advertised three pounds reward each for the deserters from Captain Diemer's company. That fall, the campaign was dissolved. Thirteen years later, Franklin recalled his scorn for the British conduct of the campaign in a letter to David Hume (27 September 1760).

THE DEATH OF JOSIAH

Sometime in the summer of 1744, Franklin's father questioned him about medicines for kidney stones. In his reply, 6 September, Franklin said, "I apprehend I am too busy in prescribing, and meddling in the Dr's Sphere, when any of you complain of Ails in your Letters: But as I always employ a Physician my self when any Disorder arises in my Family and submit implicitly to his Orders in every Thing, so I hope you consider my Advice, when I give any, only as a Mark of my good Will, and put no more of it in Practice than happens to agree with what your Dr. directs." When Franklin wrote the Mecoms about the end of 1744, he thanked Jane: "Dear Sister, I love you tenderly for your care of our father in his sickness." Josiah Franklin died on 16 January 1744/5 at the age of eighty-seven. His obituary appeared in the *Boston News-Letter* on 17 January. "Last night [16 January] died Mr. Josiah Franklin, Tallow-Chandler and Soap-maker. By the Force of a *steady Temperance* he had made a Constitution, naturally none of the strongest, last with comfort to the Age of Eighty-seven Years; and by an entire Dependence of his *Redeemer* and a constant Course of the strictest *Piety* and *Virtue*, he was enabled to die, as he liv'd, with Chearfulness and Peace, leaving a numerous Posterity the Honour of being descended from a Person, who thro' a long Life supported the Character of an *Honest Man*." Franklin did not reprint it in the *Gazette*, though he did reprint Boston news from immediately before and immediately after it. Andrew Bradford, however, reprinted it in the *American Weekly Mercury* on 12 February.[32]

Since the obituaries of tallow-chandlers rarely appeared in the newspapers, perhaps the *Boston News-Letter* printed the notice of Josiah because he was the father of Benjamin Franklin, who by this time (as printer and editor of the best colonial newspaper and almanac, founder of the Library Company of Philadelphia, postmaster of Philadelphia, clerk of the assembly, and former grand master of the Philadelphia Masons) was a well-known colonial American. Saddened by the death, Franklin no doubt regretted that his father had not had an easier and more successful life. He was probably unhappy that Josiah's fellow members of the Old South Church had not selected him a praecentor in 1718 and a deacon in 1719. Those would have been crowning achievements for the devout Josiah. Franklin praised him in the *Autobiography* for his mechanical ability, ingenuity, conversation, drawing, and music. Though the obituary reported that Josiah's constitution was "naturally none of the strongest," it reflected Josiah in his old age. Franklin, remembering him in his middle age, said that he was well set and strong. All in all, Franklin's portrait of Josiah is flattering. On a later trip to Boston (probably the 1763 visit), Franklin had an obelisk erected over the graves of Abiah and Josiah Franklin.

NEW YORK TRIPS, 1744–1745, FRIENDS, AND THE NEW ENGLAND TOUR, 1746

In early April 1744, Franklin made a brief trip to New York, probably to confer with his New York printing partner James Parker. While there, he talked with the New York postmaster Richard Nicholls. He was back in Philadelphia by 9 April. Writing to Cadwallader Colden on 29 April, the botanist John Bartram used Franklin as a touchstone for a busy person: "I am full as much hurried in business as our friend Benjamin for I can hardly get any time to write but by Candle light after A very hard days labour."

In the beginning of November 1745, Franklin again briefly visited New York, no doubt seeing Parker. Since French privateers had joined the Spanish ones preying on English and American ships, he again journeyed overland. He was gone for about ten days and brought back news of opportunities for physicians in New York, thus encouraging Dr. John Bard to move there. On 16 March 1745/ 6, Joseph Breintnall, Franklin's close friend, drowned himself in the Delaware River. In the *Autobiography*, Franklin recorded that after becoming a deist, he "perverted some others, particularly" his early friends John Collins and James Ralph, "but each of them having afterwards wrong'd me greatly without the least Compunction, and recollecting [Governor] Keith's Conduct towards me, (who was another Freethinker) and my own towards Vernon and Miss Read which at Times gave me great Trouble, I began to suspect that this Doctrine tho' it might be true, was not very useful" (A 58). Franklin did not mention Breintnall, a Quaker who also became a deist. When Franklin learned of his friend's suicide, he may have wondered whether religion would have helped preserve his life.

Franklin's letters often contain striking passages. When Franklin complimented Cadwallader Colden (16 October 1746) on learning that Linnaeus had named an herb for him, Franklin wrote, "I congratulate you on the Immortality conferr'd on you by the learned Naturalists of Europe. No Species or Genus of Plants was ever lost, or ever will be while the World continues; and therefore your Name, now annext to one of them, will last forever." Franklin meant the sentiment to be a great compliment, though he may have known that some species of plants were extinct.

After the death of Postmaster General Alexander Spotswood (1740), Elliott Benger, who had been in charge of the General Post Office on Spotswood's land at New Post, Virginia, was made postmaster general of the colonies on 18 August 1743. Within a few years, he made Franklin his comptroller. When Franklin made the fourth of his eight return trips to New England[33] in November 1746, he was probably inspecting the post offices and the postal routes. Franklin planned the trip so he would return before the Pennsylvania Assembly reconvened on 5 January 1747. He was back in Philadelphia by 29 December, when he attended a Union Fire Company meeting. Once again, he must have traveled overland. In New York he would have visited Parker, Richard Nicholls, and his friend Dr. John Bard; then on to New Haven, and to Newport, Rhode Island, where he saw his sister-in-law, Anne Franklin, no doubt bringing news and a letter from her son James, who was still an apprentice (now about seventeen) with Franklin. Inspired by the article on electricity in the *Gentleman's Magazine* for April 1745 (reprinted in the Boston *American Magazine* for December 1745), the Newport clockmaker William Claggett began astonishing his neighbors in February 1745/6 with repetitions of the experiments described in the *Gentleman's Magazine*. When Franklin was in Newport in November, he may have seen Claggett's experiments, but by then Franklin was performing his own.

In Boston Franklin visited his mother, his sisters Elizabeth and Jane, and his brother John. He again sought out the Boston printers, booksellers, and bookbinders, and he had business with William Brock, deputy postmaster, and (if he was in town) Ellis Huske, postmaster. Though no records of any Boston Masonic meetings for the period exist, Franklin probably attended one or more meetings. His route back to Philadelphia included stops at New Haven and New York. In New Haven, he visited the Reverend Joseph Noyes and probably, once again, the Reverend Thomas Clap, president of Yale, and he talked about glass manufacturing with Thomas Darling. Subsequently, he and Darling exchanged letters on the subject, with Darling asking questions and Franklin describing Caspar Wistar's glass production in Wistarburg, New Jersey. As usual, Franklin had some shrewd thoughts on the subject, recommending an ecological scheme of sustainable economics. Since the cost of wood for fuel was a major expense in manufacturing glass, Franklin advised Darling (10 February 1746/7) "to procure a Tract of Land well wooded, 1500 or 1000 acres may do, seated on or near some navigable Water. By dividing your land, and cutting suppose a Thirtieth Part of your Wood yearly, suffering it to grow again, you may always be supply'd. And by Means of the navigable Water, carry your Glass to Market cheaper and with less Risque of Breakage." Sometime during this New England trip Franklin met the Reverend Jared Eliot of Killingworth, Connecticut, an intellectual and natural philosopher. Franklin's first letter to Eliot (16 July 1747) bespeaks a warm personal acquaintance. Cadwallader Colden wrote John Bartram on 27 January 1747 that he had hoped to see Franklin in New York on his return from Boston. Franklin stayed in Boston so long, however, that Colden had to leave New York before Franklin arrived.

THE NATURE OF BOYS

When Franklin's sister Jane suggested that she would like to have her son Benjamin trained as a printer, Franklin's own home was too full to accommodate the boy, so he suggested that Mecom be apprenticed to his New York partner, James Parker. Franklin wrote Edward and Jane Mecom about the end of 1744 that their son would be well treated by Parker, and that "I shall hear from him every week." Franklin also sent along some good advice: "You will advise him to be very cheerful, and ready to do every thing he is bid, and endeavour to oblige every body, for that is the true way to get friends." But Benjamin Mecom was giddy and always whining, and he wanted a shortcut to success. He complained frequently to his mother, and she finally wrote Franklin, about June 1748, enclosing two of his letters and listing his grievances. Neither his letters nor Jane's are extant, but some of their contents can be deduced from Franklin's reply.

With a remarkable appreciation of human nature, Franklin took into account Jane's worry as mother, Parker's role as master, and Benjamin's as apprentice. To the charge that when Mecom was sick, Mrs. Parker did not serve him quickly and sometimes not at all, Franklin pointed out that both Mrs. Parker and her child were also sick during the 1747 New York epidemic. Mecom "had the distemper favorably, and yet I suppose was bad enough to be, like other sick people, a little impatient, and perhaps might think a short time long, and sometimes call for things not proper for one in his condition" (3:302). Mecom also complained that he did not have suitable clothes. Franklin replied that he was frequently in New York, "and I never saw him unprovided with what was good, decent, and sufficient. I was there no longer ago than March last, and he was then well clothed, and made no complaint to me of any kind." Franklin continued that on Sunday morning, he heard both Parker and his wife repeatedly call to Mecom to prepare for church, but he put it off until it was too late, "and he made not the least objection about clothes." Franklin then shrewdly commented, "I did not think it any thing extraordinary, that he should be sometimes willing to evade going to meeting, for I believe it is the case with all boys, or almost all. I have brought up four or five myself, and have frequently observed, that if their shoes were bad, they would say nothing of a new pair till Sunday morning, just as the bell rung, when, if you asked them why they did not get ready, the answer was prepared, 'I have no shoes' . . . or if they knew of any thing that wanted mending, it was a secret till Sunday morning, and sometimes I believe they would rather tear a little, than be without the excuse" (3:302).

Young Mecom further protested to his mother that Parker sent him on petty errands. Franklin replied that "no boys love it, but all must do it. As soon as they become fit for better business, they naturally get rid of that, for the master's interest comes in to their relief." And Mecom, like so many other boys, tried to run away and join a privateer. Franklin observed, "I do not think his going on board the privateer arose from any difference between him and his master, or any ill usage he had received. When boys see prizes brought in, and quantities of money shared among the men, and their gay living, it fills their heads with notions, that half distract them, and put them quite out of conceit with trades, and the dull ways of getting money by working." And Franklin told of William's attempt to join a privateer, adding that it was not "hard usage at home, that made him do this. Every one, that knows me, thinks I am too indulgent a parent, as well as master" (3:302–3). Franklin did not need to remind her that he himself wanted to run off to be a sailor when a boy or that their older brother Josiah had done so (A 10).

James Parker had just, "by a letter this post, desired me to write to him about his staying out of nights, sometimes all night, and refusing to give an account where he spends his time, or in what company. . . . I do not wonder at his correcting him for that. If he was my own son, I should think his master did not do his duty by him, if he omitted it, for to be sure it is the high road to destruction." Franklin concluded, "I have a very good opinion of Benny in the main, and have great hopes of his becoming a worthy man, his faults being only such as are commonly incident to boys of his years, and he has many good qualities, for which I love him. I never knew an apprentice contented with the clothes allowed him by his master, let them be what they would. Jemmy Franklin, when with me, was always dissatisfied and grumbling. When I was last in Boston, his aunt bid him go to a shop and please himself, which the *gentleman* [emphasis is mine] did, and bought a suit of clothes on my account dearer by one-half, than any I ever afforded myself, one suit excepted; which I don't mention by way of complaint of Jemmy, for he and I are good friends, but only to show you the nature of boys."

Franklin may have been too generous in his judgment of Benjamin Mecom. For the sake of his sister Jane, Franklin looked out for her son time and again, though the young man was increasingly flighty. The apprentice no doubt knew that Franklin himself had run away as an apprentice and had succeeded in the business. Young Mecom evidently thought that success would be easy, but he revealed throughout his comparatively short life that he was impatient with work, never appreciating that drudgery and continued application are necessary for all who have to make their own way.

BECOMING WELL-OFF

When he wrote his mother on 16 October 1747, Franklin began by apologizing for Deborah: "This has been a busy day with your daughter and she is gone to bed much fatigued and cannot write." He was gradually taking on the role of the pater familias for his extended family and sent his mother some money "towards chaise hire, that you may ride warm to meetings this winter." He wrote news of her granddaughter Sarah, "the greatest lover of her book and school, of any child I ever knew." If she were really a lover of books, she must have reminded Franklin of the stories about himself as a child—which he knew Abiah would recall. Evidently the Franklins had hired a tutor-maid for four-year-old Sarah: she was "very dutiful to her mistress as well as to us."

On 4 November 1747, nephew Jemmy Franklin finished his apprenticeship with Franklin and returned to Newport to join his mother and sisters in printing there. Franklin gave his sister-in-law Anne hundreds of *Poor Richard* almanacs every year and copies of other imprints gratis, and he also gave Jemmy some secondhand but valuable type when he finished his apprenticeship. In 1753

Franklin offered to set him up in New Haven (27 October 1753) and purchased real estate near Yale College for a printing shop (8 November 1753), but Jemmy preferred to remain in Newport (25 November 1754) with his mother and sisters.

Minor details in the accounts reveal that the Franklins were enjoying an increasingly high standard of living. Franklin repeatedly purchased linen, probably for clothes, sheets, or tablecloths. From 1734 through 1739, Franklin bought £29.10 worth of linen from various merchants. Deborah mentioned sheets, tablecloths, and napkins in an account of material to be bleached (14 March 1738): "Sent to be whitened att Jarmanton [Germantown], seven sheets att a shilin a sheet, 7.0.; fore tabl Clathes ten pens a peas, 3.4.; Six napkins att a peney a peas, 0.6.; and a litel peas of lining, 0.8.; in all that I am to pay, Total 11.6."

The Franklins gradually accumulated furniture, plate, and silver during these years, but few records of these objects exist. They bought a five-shilling "Nurse Chair" from Solomon Fussell on 19 December 1739. A nurse chair was an upholstered low chair without arms. While sitting in the chair, one could hold an infant on either the left or right side, but the chair was also a fashionable piece of furniture. The Franklins had no infant in 1739. William was then ten or eleven, Francis had died in 1736, and Sarah was not born until 1743. On 26 May 1740, Franklin indulged himself and bought a desk from John Gillingham, joiner, for £7.

On 1 May 1744, Franklin bought a light wig for £5.5. Tradesmen had few occasions to wear wigs. It may have been the same wig Franklin wore in his first portrait, painted by Robert Feke, probably in 1746. One excellent historian has written that Franklin "commissioned Robert Feke to paint a mannered and foppish portrait to honor the occasion" of his retirement and remarked that a portrait revealed aristocratic pretensions. But Franklin's brother John, not Franklin, commissioned the portrait and hung it next to his own in his Boston home. The portrait may show John Franklin's aristocratic pretensions, but not Franklin's.[34] Franklin no doubt decided how to present himself. The authority on Franklin's portraits, Charles Coleman Sellers, said that Franklin dressed "in the style of a successful tradesman, neither wearing his own hair as many contemporaries did, nor assuming the wig style of professional men and gentlemen of leisure." Beside the simple and short style of the wig, its color bespoke Franklin's status. White or gray was the standard color of a professional man's wig. Franklin's was brown. The art historian Wayne Craven pointed out that Franklin was portrayed in an "almost painfully plain and unpretentious manner." He was represented as a successful member of colonial mercantile society but not as one especially wealthy. Nevertheless the portrait marked a major step in Franklin's progress to gentility.[35] It attested not only to John Franklin's love for his younger brother but also to Franklin's increasing reputation.

As noted above, Franklin purchased a horse for his son William in 1736. Eleven years later, the printer bought a horse named Jack for himself. On 30 April 1747, he paid William Maugridge 24 shillings 5½ pence for keeping and shoeing him. Both horses were stolen from Franklin's pasture on 5 August 1747, and Franklin described Jack as "a likely young sorrel Horse, about 14 hands high, with silver Mane and Tail, four white feet, a glaze in his face, no brand, a large belly, and is in good case, paces well, but trots sometimes, very small ears, and is shod all round." William's horse was "a small bay horse, without shoes, low in flesh, long dark tail and mane." Five days later, 10 August 1747, the carpenter Joseph Thornhill charged him £5.14.6 "in full for Stuff and Work of a Shaise [Chaise] House." A carriage was a mark of status. During the next decade, there are many references to Deborah's using and lending the carriage, though I have found none to Franklin's doing so. He must have on occasion, but perhaps he purchased it primarily for Deborah.

By 1747 Franklin was a leading Philadelphia citizen. His role as a public leader had been foreshadowed by his election as grand master of the Freemasons in 1734. As the founder of the Library Company of Philadelphia (1731) and the Union Fire Company (1736), he had used his time and energy to benefit his fellow citizens. The Pennsylvania fireplace (1744) was an important contribution to well-being and earned him an international reputation as an ingenious man. Though his area of influence through this period of his life was generally restricted to Philadelphia, he was on his way to realizing his great ambition, fulfilling the role of the *amicus humani generis*, the friend of humankind.

In 1746, Franklin had begun devoting dozens of hours every week to electrical experiments, and he believed he was making more interesting advances than those he read about from England and Europe. He wanted to devote full time to those experiments and so began to think of retiring. Besides printing and book selling, he had two other profitable pursuits, postmaster of Philadelphia and wholesale paper merchant. On 1 January 1747/8, age 41, he took the decisive step and signed a partnership agreement with his foreman, David Hall. The partnership was to begin on 21 January 1747/8, four days after Franklin became 42. On that date, he retired as a printer and book-seller, but he continued to work as postmaster and as wholesale paper merchant.

Economically, Franklin had become a comparatively well-off (though well below the top one hundred wealthy persons in Philadelphia),[36] but his economic rise did not affect his egalitarianism. I have shown often in Volume 1 and in this volume that Franklin scorned the idea of aristocracy and of a superior class.[37] In this regard, Franklin did not change. He retired as a printer and bookseller, not to become a gentleman (he continued to collect rags for the papermakers), but because he was more interested in science, the safety of the citizens, and doing good than in making money. He wrote Cadwallader Colden on 29 September 1748 that since he was now free from the "little Cares and Fatigues of Business," he hoped to "produce something for the common Benefit of Mankind" (3:318). Later, on 12 April 1750, he wrote his mother that at his death, he "would rather have it said, *He lived usefully*, than, *He died rich*" (3:475).

THIRTEEN

The Assembly Clerk and Pennsylvania Politics

It was thought by some of my Friends that by my Activity in the defense of Pennsylvania, "I should offend" the Quakers, and "thereby lose my Interest in the Assembly where they were a great Majority."—A 111

FRANKLIN ENTERED PENNSYLVANIA POLITICS when he advocated a paper currency in the suppressed Busy-Body No. 8 and again when he published a pamphlet titled *The Nature and Necessity of a Paper Currency* in 1729 (Volume 1, Chapters 16 and 17). Despite being appointed printer to the assembly in 1730, Franklin continued to take political positions that were sometimes unpopular with each party. He defended Andrew Hamilton in 1733 with "A Half-Hour's Conversation with a Friend" (1:333–38), thereby irritating both the Proprietary Party and elements of the Quaker Party. He urged on 6 March 1733/4 that a Pennsylvania militia be established, thereby vexing many Quaker assemblymen. He often inserted political comments in the *Pennsylvania Gazette*. Even after gaining another political plum at the disposal of the assembly, the position of clerk, Franklin continued to be his own man, sometimes supporting particular assembly members and sometimes opposing them and the dominant Quaker Party. Personal friendships with Andrew Hamilton and James Logan had a role in Franklin's political activities, but he seemed mainly concerned with issues rather than people. He thought paper currency was generally good for Pennsylvania's economy, and he thought military defense was a necessity. Though he had written and published a poem as part of an election campaign in 1733, it was comparatively innocuous. During the period from 1736 through 1747, however, he twice directly tried to influence Pennsylvania's elections, once in 1737 and again in 1741.[1]

Andrew Hamilton was reelected to the Pennsylvania Assembly from Bucks County on 1 October 1736. When the assembly met on 14 October, he was elected Speaker for the eighth time. In the assembly on 15 October 1736, "It was moved, that *Joseph Growdon* be appointed clerk to this House for the ensuing Year; and the Question being put, it *passed in the Negative*." Growdon, the son and the brother-in-law of former Speakers (Joseph Growdon, Sr. [1652–1730] and David Lloyd [1656–1731]), had been clerk of the assembly from 1730 through 1735. He was also attorney general from 1726 to 1737. But he was unsatisfactory to Hamilton and to the assembly, and he was feuding with Assemblyman Lawrence Growdon, his older half-brother.[2] Further, he was in debt and failing in health. When he died "greatly indebted" the following year, his son called a meeting of his creditors and sold off his land (28 July 1737). After the vote for Growdon failed, Franklin petitioned the assembly, "setting forth, That he hath been informed this House have a Disposition to change their clerk, and if so, he humbly offers his Service to them in that Station; *Resolved*, That *Benjamin Franklin* be appointed clerk to the House of Representatives for the current Year. And he was called in and qualified accordingly." Since the Speaker of the House generally had the office of the clerk at his disposal, Franklin presumably owed his election to Hamilton.

THE OATHS OF ALLEGIANCE, SUPREMACY, AND ABJURATION

To be "qualified accordingly" meant that one took the oaths of allegiance, supremacy, and abjuration. The Quaker members were allowed simply to affirm, but others took the oaths. Franklin took them annually (later, several times a year for his different offices) until he went to England in 1757—and frequently thereafter until the American Revolution. The oath of allegiance was simple: "I, Benjamin Franklin, do sincerely promise and swear, that I will be Faithful and bear true Allegiance to his Majesty King George II. So help me God."

The oath of supremacy was primarily directed against the Roman Catholic Church: "And I, Benjamin Franklin, do solemnly promise and declare that I from my heart abhor, detest, and renounce as impious and heretical that damnable doctrine and position that Princes excommunicated or deprived by the Pope or any other authority of the See of Rome may be deposed or murdered by their subjects, or any other person whatsoever. . . . in the Sacrament of the Lord's Supper there is no transubstantiation of the elements of bread and wine into the body and blood of Christ." The oath of supremacy concluded by acknowledging "the Holy Scriptures to be given by Divine inspiration."

The oath of abjuration was directed against the Jacobites, those who supported the claim of James II's descendants to the English throne. "I, Benjamin Franklin, do truly and sincerely acknowledge, profess, testify and declare, in my Conscience, before God and the World, that our Sovereign Lord King George II is lawful and rightful King of this Realm. . . . And I do solemnly and sincerely declare, that I do believe in my Conscience that the Person pretended to be the Prince of Wales, during the Life of the Late King James II and since his Decease pretending to be, and taking upon himself the Stile and Title of King of England, by the Name of James III or of Scotland by the Name of James VIII or the Stile and Title of King of Great Britain, hath not any Right or Title whatsoever to the Crown of this Realm."[3]

THE CLERK'S DUTIES

Immediately after electing Franklin clerk, the assembly ordered members Job Goodson and Thomas Leech to "call for and receive of *Joseph Growdon*, late clerk of the Assembly, all such Papers or other Things as belong to the Publick, and are remaining in his Hands as late clerk to the House of Representatives of this Province, and deliver the same to the present Clerk, to be kept and preserv'd among the Journals, &c. of this House." The clerk of the assembly took the minutes, kept the records, served as the assembly's historian, and kept track of the assembly's business. At the opening of a session, "he had to call over the election returns, read the forms by which the members were qualified for their seats, and enter the qualifications in books prepared for that purpose."[4] He reported the unfinished business from the last assembly and conducted the election of the Speaker.[5] The clerk was, after the Speaker, the most important functionary of the assembly—though not a voting member. "By order of the House," the clerk "had frequently to amend bills, transcribe copies of particular acts, make a copy of the sessional laws for the printer, search the journals for precedents, prepare an account of unfinished business, and, in the Speaker's absence, adjourn the House." For such tasks he was paid sums in addition to the six shillings a day he received while the assembly was in session.

The modern authority on the clerk's duties and the organization of the assembly, Sister Joan de Lourdes Leonard, found it surprising that Franklin had time to create arithmetical magic squares and circles while clerk and pointed out that by 1772, the clerk's business was deemed too much for one person, and an assistant clerk was appointed.[6] The procedure in the Pennsylvania Assembly, however, differed dramatically from the British Parliament and from that of most colonial American assemblies—where shouting, vituperative speeches, and even fights sometimes occurred. Pennsylvania's colonial assembly had frequent periods of silence, no doubt reflecting the Quaker religious services. In brief notes on a hotly debated issue in the assembly, Franklin noted "after some Minutes Silence" at one point and "Some Pause intervening" at another (3:15–16). In June 1748, when a Quaker minister spoke to the assembly, he first waited in silence "perhaps ten or twelve minutes." The deliberate silences continued when committees of the assemblymen met with the Pennsylvania Council (P 6:505). As late as 21 July 1774, an observer described the assemblymen as "a parcel of Countrymen sitting with their hats on, great Coarse Cloth Coats, Leather Breeches, and woollen Stockings, in the month of July; there was not a Speech made the whole time."[7] Franklin probably busied himself during times of silence, as well as during the more boring speeches.

Franklin was doubly responsible for the assembly records. As clerk, he took the minutes and submitted them to the committee appointed annually to revise and correct the clerk's minutes; and then, as the printer of the House, he published the *Votes and Proceedings of the House of Representatives*. On 16 October 1736, the House "Ordered, That the Minutes of this House be printed; and that John Kinsey, John Kearsley, Job Goodson, and Thomas Leech, be a Committee to revise them before they are put to the Press."

THE INDEPENDENT CLERK

Franklin recorded, "My first Promotion was my being chosen in 1736 clerk of the General Assembly. The Choice was made that Year without Opposition; but the Year following when I was again propos'd (the Choice, like that of the Members being annual) a new Member made a long Speech against me in order to favour some other Candidate. I was however chosen; which was the more agreable to me, as besides the Pay for immediate Service as clerk, the Place gave me a better Opportunity of keeping up an Interest among the Members, which secur'd to me the Business of Printing the Votes, Laws, Paper Money, and other occasional Jobs for the Public, that on the whole were very profitable. I therefore did not like the Opposition of this new Member, who was a Gentleman of Fortune, and Education, with Talents that were likely to give him in time great Influence in the House, which indeed afterwards happened" (A 100).

The member who opposed Franklin in October 1737 was probably Isaac Norris, Jr. He had reason to dislike Franklin. Isaac Norris, Sr., was among the rich men who resented Franklin's 1729 writings on paper money. The Norrises and Governor Patrick Gordon had opposed Andrew Hamilton in 1733, causing him to lose his assembly seat in the election. After Isaac Norris, Sr., wrote "A True Letter to a Friend in the Country" attacking Hamilton, Franklin lampooned the elder Norris in "A Half-Hour's Conversation with a Friend" on 16 November 1733. But the major reason for the younger Norris's opposition was a short, anonymous article of election propaganda that appeared in the 29 September 1737 *Gazette*—only two days before the 1 October election. It was probably written by Franklin. It began with an amazing statement, one certain to gain attention: "Friends and Countrymen, I am of Opinion that the Majority of the Members of the last Assembly, are entirely unworthy your Notice in the next Election." The author gave three numbered reasons and followed them with two concluding brief paragraphs.

First, the current assemblymen should all be rejected for refusing "to allow the Treasurer's Accounts of near 250£ expended for *Indian* treaties. Altho' he had an Order of Council for advancing that Money." Every knowledgeable Pennsylvanian was aware that only the representatives had the authority to spend funds. The Pennsylvania Council, which was composed of appointed proprietary partisans, could not do so. The article could only be serious if it were written by a proprietary partisan. Even so, the idea of rejecting most of the current assemblymen (they were primarily Quaker Party members) was unrealistic—and in itself mocked the authoritarian attitude of the Proprietary Party. Therefore, every sophisticated reader immediately suspected that the piece really favored the present assemblymen and burlesqued arguments advanced against them.

Second, the author declaimed against the legislators for denying "that the Council had any Right to draw Orders on the Treasurer; and have caused it to be inserted in their Minutes, and even prevail'd with the Council itself to acknowledge, *That the People alone by their Representatives have a Right to dispose of their own Money*: Which Position is contrary to all Reason, and the Fundamentals of our Constitution." The anonymous author thus spelled out the criticism that had been merely implied in the first charge. "No taxation without representation" was a sacred principle of democracy. The article satirized the Proprietary Party's position—and perhaps a specific person who espoused its party line. (As we will see in Volume 3, Franklin fiercely maintained this position after being elected an assemblyman in 1751.)

Then came a surprising turn: in the third point, the author protested against giving money to support the Pennsylvanians "who had been imprison'd, fin'd, &c. By the Government of Maryland. Now what Business had we with those Inhabitants? None surely; unless we consider them as they are Fellow-Countrymen and Members of the same Common-Wealth, united together with us as Parts of the same Body; which Way of Thinking is absolutely wrong, for we ought to look on one another ONLY as TENANTS to the Proprietor and leave it to him to take Care of us or neglect us—*as he pleases*." In the first part of the third reason, the actual author breaks down the mask of the persona—a conservative defender of proprietary privilege. Instead of caricaturing the Proprietary Party's position (which the last part of the last quoted sentence returns to), the author stresses that the government should help those people who suffered in the border war. The underlying author appears again in the next sentence: "And if the President advanc'd any Money in the Behalf of those People, or in the Treaties and Messages aforesaid, it ought to have been out of his own Pocket." The author thus defended James Logan, president of the council and acting governor, for supporting financial aid to the neighboring Indian tribes and for attempting to reimburse the Pennsylvanians who had suffered in the Maryland-Pennsylvania border wars. The author/persona, like Franklin, did not follow party lines.

The author of the 29 September political attack resumed his satirical mask in the conclusion: "Gentlemen, You should consider you have too much Liberty, which is a great Misfortune. There are several wholesome Restraints to be made upon that Liberty, in which I would willingly assist for your Good. I am, as my father was before me, your sincere Friend and Well-Wisher in those Respects, and therefore hope you will chuse me one of your Representatives in the next Assembly." The piece was thus revealed primarily as a satire on a particular candidate, who hoped to be, like his father, an assemblyman, and one who identified with a conservative point of view.

As electioneering propaganda, the article is too complex. It ostensibly criticized the council and James Logan, and indirectly said the assembly was correct. Then it defended Logan for doing what was best for the colony. The propaganda also criticized the assembly—saying that although it was correct in affirming its principles, it should also have repaid Logan's expenditures. Finally, despite its complexity, the piece clearly burlesqued the opinions of a particular conservative would-be assemblyman who thought himself superior. The underlying opinions are similar to Franklin's, but it is surprising that the persona is not a more coherent figure and that the sense of audience is not clearer. As literature, it is comparatively poor. Whether or not Franklin wrote it, he published it in the *Pennsylvania Gazette*, thereby endorsing its political commentary. Though he claimed to be an impartial publisher and though he often was neutral, he also frequently took political positions, as we have seen in his relations with Andrew Bradford and with Andrew Hamilton.

A reply to the *Gazette* attack appeared in the *American Weekly Mercury* on 20 October 1737. It celebrated a deceased legislator (obviously the person criticized in the *Gazette*) with "filial" affection and defended him from "Insatiate Envy" here on earth. A copy of the tribute in Joseph Norris's commonplace book shows that the Norris family was involved. Evidently the *Gazette* satire pointed at Isaac Norris, Jr., who ran for and won a seat in the assembly of 1737–38. No wonder Norris opposed Franklin as clerk. Norris must have held Franklin responsible for the attack. On the other hand, Isaac Norris, Jr., might not seem to fit Franklin's description of a "new" member who opposed his appointment as clerk, for Norris was first elected in 1735. He was not, however, returned in 1736 or 1738, and Franklin, writing in 1771, might well have thought of Norris as new member in 1737.

Franklin reported in the *Autobiography* that he did not attempt to win the new member's

> Favour by paying any servile Respect to him, but after some time took this other Method. Having heard that he had in his Library a certain very scarce and curious Book, I wrote a Note to him expressing my Desire of perusing that Book, and requesting he would do me the Favour of lending it to me for a few Days. He sent it immediately; and I return'd it in about a Week, with another Note expressing strongly my Sense of the Favour. When we next met in the House he spoke to me, (which he had never done before) and with great Civility. And he ever afterwards manifested a Readiness to serve me on all Occasions, so that we became great Friends, and our Friendship continu'd to his Death. This is another Instance of the Truth of an old Maxim I had learned, which says, *He that has once done you a Kindness will be more ready to do you another, than he whom you yourself have obliged.* And it shows how much more profitable it is prudently to remove, than to resent, return and continue inimical Proceedings. (A 100–101)

In addition to the contents of the satire and the reply to it, two bits of information support the hypothesis that Norris was the person who opposed Franklin's appointment as clerk of the assembly. Norris was, after Logan and Franklin himself, Philadelphia's major book collector. He was a logical person to own a "scarce and curious" book. Second, Norris did indeed later come to have "great Influence on the House"—he became its Speaker in 1750 and became Franklin's friend. (Beginning in 1758, Norris addressed him in correspondence as "My Dear Friend.") Incidently, Franklin's "old Maxim" seems to be original. He probably called it a known saying in order to suggest its truth—which otherwise might well seem unlikely. One wonders if the proud young Franklin did not have difficulty in bringing himself to make the overture to Norris and perhaps thought the advice (which he may have made up at the time and addressed to himself) worth emphasizing.

THE 1740 CENSURE

Though the main reproach against Franklin continued to be impiety, political criticisms became common as his egalitarian beliefs became widely known. A knowledgeable proprietary supporter who identified himself as a member of the Philadelphia Corporation attacked Franklin in the *American Weekly Mercury* on 12 February 1739/40. Bradford so relished the piece that he published it in a special postscript.[8] The *Mercury* author accused Franklin of suppressing information favorable to Governor George Thomas: "A Few Members of the Corporation of the City of *Philadelphia* being met to spend a Part of an evening, your printed Copy of the Votes of our Assembly was brought us, as the News of the Day." They focused on the bill "for the better raising money on the Inhabitants of *Philadelphia*." Though they were pleased that the governor had rejected it, they were irritated that Franklin had omitted "the Reasons asigned by the Governor for refusing his Assent to that Bill." (The governor's main reason was that, according to its charter, the Philadelphia Corporation, not the assembly, was charged to make such laws.) The critic must have known that the legislators had instructed Franklin not to print the governor's reasons. The writer nevertheless took Franklin to task: "Now Mr. Franklin, it is very certain you are Master of your own Press, and 'tis as certain you are Clerk to our Representatives, but neither your being Clerk or Printer can in our Opinion, justify your publishing to the World a Message to the Governor, from that honourable House expressing their Dissatisfaction with his Reasons for, and his manner of refusing his Assent to that Bill, and not publish the Refusal itself; for whether the Reasons Assigned by the Governor be good or bad, or whether the Manner of sending them to the House be right or wrong, yet all this can neither justify nor excuse you for suppressing them."

The author disliked Franklin and accused him of insulting the mayor and members of the Philadelphia Corporation. He said that Franklin not infrequently escaped censure after committing an indiscretion through his wit and that the assembly should fire him: "We considered your present Situation, the Caution with which you usually act in Matters where your Interest is concerned, and tho' we know you can, upon some Occasions, strike a bold Stroke, and then depend upon your Wit to bring you off, yet sure you will never have the Face to pretend any Directions from our Honourable Assembly to warrant, such a Piece of low Craft. On the contrary it ought not to be questioned but you'll receive your Reward from that Honourable Body, whose Wisdom and Justice and Truth &c. must detest such Tricking." The charge that Franklin (rather than the assembly) suppressed the governor's reasons must have made Speaker Andrew Hamilton and other Franklin friends sympathize with him. Consequently, they gave him permission to publish the governor's reasons. The writer further attacked Franklin for using various personae in his newspaper writings: "It was observed of you too, that you're never at a Loss for something to say, nor for some Body to say it for you, when you don't care to appear yourself." In concluding, the anti-Franklin writer charged him with being a monetary opportunist, having "a Place worth 60 or 70 l. a year." Though he objected to Franklin's using personae, he signed the piece "A. B. C. D. E. F. &c. &c. &c."

Franklin defended himself by printing the bill, together with the governor's reasons.[9] He wrote a surprisingly convoluted prefatory sentence justifying printing the bill and the governor's rejection: "As the Bill, whereof that which follows is a true Copy, and the Reasons against its being past into an Act, have been the Subject of some Conversation in this City, That any who are willing to give themselves the Trouble of Reading them, may be able to form the better Judgment, it is thought necessary to print them."

The person who attacked Franklin wrote the most acute criticism of Franklin to that time. Andrew Bradford's opposition in the early 1730s reflected business rivalry. Isaac Norris, Jr., in 1736, mainly attacked Andrew Hamilton, though he also cast aspersions upon Franklin for his egalitarian politics and his impiety. New York's William Bradford in 1736 accused him of political favoritism with the New Jersey legislature (not knowing that Franklin had invented a new process for printing paper money). John Remington (if he were, as suggested in the previous chapter, the defamer in the Rees affair in 1738) reflected the common charge of irreverence and the misplaced feeling of being betrayed. John Webbe, editor of Andrew Bradford's *American Magazine*, rambled on and on in denouncing Franklin later in 1740. As shown in Chapter 12, Webbe was proven to be a hypocrite when Franklin disclosed that Webbe not only knew that Postmaster General Spotswood had forbidden Franklin to allow post riders to carry Bradford's *Mercury* but also that Franklin actually employed him as a lawyer in the case.

The current anti-Franklin writer, however, combined the old charges and added to them. The calumniator's accuracy in estimating that Franklin's positions as clerk and printer to the Assembly paid £60–70 a year proved that he was knowledgeable about the assembly's finances. He was also the first person to object to Franklin's using various personae in his writings, as well as the first to find Franklin reprehensible in holding government offices (printer to the assembly, clerk of the assembly, and postmaster of Philadelphia) even though he did not support the government's executive branch. That condemnation anticipated a common criticism by conservative Americans and by the British authorities against Franklin during the pre-Revolutionary period when he was the deputy postmaster general for North America—and yet was the foremost American spokesman against the British authorities. I have no idea who this shrewd opponent was.

SALARY

Assemblymen received five shillings a day for attending sessions, but the clerk was paid six, plus "certain fees."[10] It is difficult to tell how much Franklin earned as clerk, for the assembly's annual accounts (typically paid on the last day of the session) lump together Franklin's pay as clerk and as public printer. His predecessor Joseph Growdon was paid £34 for each of the previous two years—almost three times more than his attendance as clerk warranted. The assembly for 1734–35 met for 43 days: at six shillings a day, Growdon's salary would have been £12.18s. The assembly for 1735–36 met for 42 days: at six shillings per day, Growdon's salary would have been £12.12s. The same assembly of 1735–36 paid Franklin as official printer £31 for printing its votes and acts (14 August 1736). In the first year that Franklin served as clerk, 1736–37, the assembly met only 18 days: at six shillings per day, the salary would have been £5.8s. At the end of that legislative year, however, Franklin was paid £24.9.6 as clerk of the House and for printing (13 August 1737; in addition, the Loan Office trustees paid him £1.10 for advertisements on 10 August 1737).

Franklin's successor, his son William Franklin, was paid six shillings a day while the House was in session: for the assembly year 1752–53, William Franklin was paid £12 for 40 days—the exact amount for the days served. At the same time, however, he was paid "on his Account, 35.1.0."[11] Like other clerks, William performed extra services for the assembly, and by then the legislature's report of expenses was normally more detailed than in the earlier years. After Franklin became Philadelphia's postmaster on 5 October 1737, the assembly occasionally recorded payments to him for the mail.

For the eleven legislative years (which ran from October to October) from 1736–37 to 1746–47, Franklin received an average of £71.10 per year for serving as clerk and for doing the normal printing of the votes and acts. For the special printing jobs he averaged a little over £111. Altogether, the legislature paid him nearly £183 a year (see appendix 3). Franklin was paid more than £11 per annual assembly as clerk, and he made additional money for the clerk's extra duties. He was paid, however, more as printer for the Pennsylvania legislature than as clerk (see table A.2). Franklin remained clerk of the House for fifteen years, until winning a seat in the assembly in a special election on 9 May 1751. He actually continued as clerk slightly longer—until his son William was elected in his stead on 13 August 1751. With a few exceptions, he printed all the official Pennsylvania documents until he retired in January 1748, and after that he and his partner David Hall remained printers to the assembly until 25 September 1767.[12]

PENNSYLVANIA POLITICS

Virginia's Governor William Gooch wrote James Logan on 20 December 1736, proposing that Pennsylvania invite the Iroquois League to a conference at Williamsburg to negotiate peace between the Six Nations (or Iroquois) and the Southern Indians (the Cherokee and Catawba). Logan consulted the Indian expert Conrad Weiser, who went to Onondaga at the end of the winter with the message. Not wanting to travel to Williamsburg, the Iroquois invited Virginia's and Pennsylvania's governors to Albany. A cessation of arms for one summer and one winter was agreed upon (11 April 1737). Meanwhile, Iroquois raiders who knew nothing of the truce killed eight Catawbas. The Catawbas consequently refused Gooch's overture and vowed revenge (27 September). Warfare between the tribes continued.

Pennsylvania's relations with its Indian neighbors deteriorated. William Penn had purchased lands in Bucks County from the Delawares in 1686, which extended into the woods as far as a man could walk in a day and a half. The Indians probably meant to sell an area about thirty miles long and a few miles deep. To settle the boundary, Thomas Penn met with the Delawares in Philadelphia on 25 August 1737. The walk was performed on 19–20 September. Thomas Penn had ordered a path cleared for the walk, had hired excellent athletes, and had arranged for the walkers to be supplied with provisions sent by horse. Penn orchestrated the Walking Purchase to grasp as much land as possible. He disgusted the Delaware Indians and alienated many Pennsylvanians, including Franklin.[13]

William Penn had paid many of the expenses for Indian treaties, but his descendants would not. By the 1730s, though only the proprietors could purchase land from the Indians, and though most treaties partially or wholly concerned such purchases, the proprietors refused to share in the expenses of Indian affairs. The issue of expenses for Indian affairs first became a recurring bone of contention between the Proprietary and Popular Parties during the administration of the new lieutenant governor, George Thomas, who arrived in Pennsylvania on 1 June 1738. He assumed gubernatorial duties from James Logan, president of the council, who had been acting governor since the death of Patrick Gordon on 5 August 1736. Governor Thomas served for nine years, until ill health caused his resignation, and he left for London on 1 June 1747. As usual, relations between the new governor and the assembly began amicably, with the assembly granting Governor Thomas £600 on 10 August 1738, just over two months after he arrived. But the good relations were brief.

Thomas's chief controversy with the assembly in his first two years as governor concerned paper currency. The proprietors (through Thomas Penn, who acted for his two brothers) had instructed him not to assent to any currency bill that did not state that proprietary quitrents (an old feudal obligation consisting of an annual rent in lieu of service that might be required of the freeholder) were to be paid in sterling rather than in the Pennsylvania paper currency. Since the former Re-emitting Act for Pennsylvania's paper currency expired in October 1737 and since the currency was gradually disappearing from circulation, the assembly passed a new currency bill. Governor Thomas did not reveal his instructions but claimed on 1 September 1738 that he had not had sufficient time to consider the bill and postponed it until the next session (scheduled for January 1738/9). Then he argued that the quitrents should be paid in sterling or its equivalent. Speaker Hamilton replied on 19 January 1738/9 that sterling payments would cause the exchange rates to fall and thereby work against the good of all Pennsylvanians, including the proprietors.

At the following legislative session, Hamilton arranged a compromise. The assembly would make the proprietors "an Allowance . . . in Consideration of their accepting our Bills of Credit instead of Silver Money" (9 May 1739). The assembly considered the vote so important that the division (i.e., the names of the persons voting for and against) was recorded by Clerk Franklin and printed in the minutes. As official printer and clerk, Franklin knew that it was the first time the positions of Pennsylvania's assemblymen on an issue were recorded and published. That act marked a significant step in the progress toward modern democracy. The only previously recorded division in the English-speaking world was the Massachusetts legislature's vote to accept the Explanatory Charter, which James Franklin had published on 22 January 1725/6.[14] Speaker Hamilton worked out the details the next day, and the act passed on 19 May 1739. The same day, the assembly voted to pay Governor Thomas £1,000 (the usual annual amount) for his support for the current legislative year (1 October 1738 to 1 October 1739).

Franklin printed the result in the 7 June *Gazette*. He explained the bill and editorialized in its favor: "The Bill passed; by which all the present Money is to be reprinted and re-emitted for 16 Years, with the additional Sum of £11,110. 5s. half the Interest of which additional Sum will be sufficient to discharge the Allowance to the Proprietors: And the remaining Interest on the whole Sum to be current, being fully sufficient to support the Government without a Tax, no Man can possibly feel the least Inconvenience by that Allowance. Add to this, that all Persons renewing their Mortgages in the Loan-Office, or borrowing Money on this Act, may do it without the usual Fees for drawing the Mortgage, Recording, &c. which are to be paid out of the Interest Money, much to the Ease of Poor People. And the Proprietors agreeing to take our Paper-Money instead of Silver for their Arrearages, &c. at 16d for 1s Sterl. the Credit of the Money is by this Expedient supported and preserved, which is a Matter of the utmost Importance to the whole Province." Franklin's remarks constituted not only a beautifully clear explanation of the act and the reasons for it but also, for the times, an unusual political editorial.

Three weeks later, Franklin must have felt betrayed. On 28 June 1739, the new Land Office secretary, Richard Peters, advertised that all persons in arrears on their quitrents must pay their debts before December or lose the land. Penn had revealed himself as an avaricious landlord. Franklin must have regretted writing the editorial. His feelings of contempt for Thomas Penn escalated.

Andrew Hamilton, who had been ill off and on during the previous two years, retired as Speaker of the House, making his farewell speech on 11 August 1739. At the opening of the next legislature in October, John Kinsey, clerk of the Pennsylvania and New Jersey meetings of the Society of Friends (and, as such, the Quaker religious leader), was elected Speaker. Though a Quaker, Kinsey was a moderate and a politician, willing to compromise when he deemed it necessary.

By the fall of 1739, it was rumored that Great Britain would soon declare war against Spain. For the remainder of Governor Thomas's time in Pennsylvania, the key political issue became support of the militia. The governor and the Proprietary Party wanted to finance a militia, but the Quakers refused. On this issue, Franklin supported the Proprietary Party. On 16 October, Governor Thomas asked the assembly to raise a militia, but the assembly promptly postponed considering the request until the next session. Partially because of Spanish mistreatment of English merchant seamen, Great Britain declared war on Spain (the War of Jenkins' Ear) on 19 October 1739. Beginning in 1740, Spanish privateers threatened the shipping and the colonial seaports, and Spanish troops from Florida endangered Georgia. A number of Pennsylvanians (probably including Franklin) petitioned the Pennsylvania Assembly for a military force on 1 January 1739/40, but the assembly refused to act (5 January).

Governor Thomas received instructions that Pennsylvania should raise and equip militia companies to support Admiral Edward Vernon's assault on Cartagena. (George Washington's estate is named for Admiral Vernon.) At the courthouse on 14 April 1741, "where a vast Concourse of People were assembled," Governor Thomas issued a proclamation declaring war. Franklin reported in the 17 April *Pennsylvania Gazette*: "The People express'd their Joy in loud Huzzas; And the Cannon from the Hill, and the Ships in the Harbour, were discharged, while the following Healths were drank, viz. The KING. . . . Success to the new Levies, and intended Expedition, &c. Plenty of Liquor was given to the Populace; and in the Evening they had a Bonfire on the Hill." Franklin added an editorial comment: "As a Design against some of the rich Spanish Settlements appears exceedingly agreeable to the People in general, and there is truly a great Prospect of Success, it is not doubted but a considerable Body of Men will be raised on this Occasion, even in Pennsylvania." Franklin's prediction proved false. Despite the king's request and the governor's urging, Speaker Kinsey and the Quaker Party refused to finance the war effort.

Since the legislature declined paying for volunteers, an insufficient number of freemen volunteered to raise a substantial army. Consequently Governor Thomas allowed indentured servants to enlist (16 April). Thereby he raised seven companies from Pennsylvania and one from the Three Lower Counties.

The Pennsylvania Assembly complained that by enlisting indentured servants, the governor deprived citizens of their property. On 7 August 1740, the retired Andrew Hamilton and a large number of Philadelphians again petitioned the assembly, requesting funds to prosecute the war, telling the assembly that "We most sincerely wish that the inlisting of Servants had been timely prevented, which was very much in your Power to have done by . . . giving a Bounty to encourage Freemen." The assembly ignored the petition. The House voted £3,000 for the king's use provided the money be paid only after all the Pennsylvania servants enlisted in the king's service were returned to their owners. As the legislators knew, this was impractical. If the servants were returned, there would not be enough time to raise more, and without a bounty for enlisting, few new ones would join. On 2 September the assembly complained to England (19 August 1740) concerning the enlisting of servants and voted to hire a new Pennsylvania agent, Richard Partridge.

A colony's agent looked after its interest in London and represented its views to the British authorities. As the positions of the political parties within the colony diverged, each party wanted its own agent, who would present its point of view. The former agent, Ferdinando John Paris, identified with the proprietors. The new agent, Partridge, was hired by the assembly, not the proprietor, and would represent its position to the British authorities. Though both parties sometimes agreed on what was best for Pennsylvania, they often differed. Partridge thought that the assembly's remonstrance against Governor Thomas, who was trying to fulfill the king's orders, would be at best futile and would at worst cause the Pennsylvania legislature to be regarded as traitors, so he wisely put off presenting the complaint.[15] Though the assembly voted to pay Governor Thomas £500 on 14 May, it refused any further support on 3 September 1740, thus depriving him of half the usual annual support.

At the election on 1 October 1740, the voters returned the past assembly members, vindicating the assembly's intransigent stand against the war. The Quaker-controlled assembly continued to refuse to contribute to the war except by agreeing to pay for the time of the indentured servants. The disgusted Governor Thomas wrote to the Board of Trade on 20 October 1740, complaining about the Quaker legislators and about the privileges of the Pennsylvania Assembly. (As we will see, Franklin published the letter, which became a key document favoring the Quaker Party in the 1741 election.)

The early English victories at Cartagena (7 and 14 May 1741) were followed by enormous numbers of deaths from disease. The *Pennsylvania Gazette* reported on 2 July 1741 the campaign's collapse. Governor Thomas was instructed to raise more troops in August 1741. By that time, colonials had heard that the British resented and scorned the military raised in the colonies. The colonists were called (and called themselves) "Americans," while the other British troops were called "Europeans." (Franklin echoed this usage when he praised the Americans who entered the military because they did not do so for the pay or from any hope of preferment, "for the Provincials are shut out from such expectations, their own forces being always disbanded on a peace, and the vacancies among the Regulars filled with *Europeans* [emphasis mine], but merely from *public spirit* and a sense of duty" [8:347].) Adding to their discontent, American troops serving in the West Indies were often impressed into the navy, where they had to perform the most "slavish" tasks. Less than half of the 3,500 Americans who went to the Caribbean returned, and they had bitter memories of the expedition. Even Virginia's Governor William Gooch, colonel of the American Regiment, said that the troops who had served in the expedition were disgusted and would not again serve with the British, "not having digested the hard Usage of being Broke in Jamaica, and sent Home without a farthing in their Pockets."[16]

Franklin printed in the 4 January 1742/3 *Gazette* news of the collapse of the campaign and the discharge of the American troops in four ships, one being sent to New York, two to Virginia, and one to North Carolina. A report reprinted in the *Pennsylvania Gazette* from a Boston newspaper lamented that from nearly a thousand troops raised in New England, not enough men were left alive for the British authorities "to employ one Vessel to bring them home." Franklin's unstated addition was that from more than five hundred men raised in Pennsylvania and Delaware, the same was true. The campaign had been a fiasco. The Americans were also angry with the British Navy for impressing Americans in the colonies, including many men who were not seamen. Admiral Vernon's officers had impressed Americans at various colonial ports, including Philadelphia. On 26 September and 1 October 1743, the British authorities wrote Governor Thomas that the act of the "sixth of Anne" (i.e., the law 6 Anne, c.37) had expired at the Peace of Utrecht in 1713. Contrary to what Americans commonly claimed, it did not prohibit the impressment of Americans for the British Navy or for militia.[17] Franklin, who lived in Boston and Philadelphia while an adolescent and a young man, was well aware of the danger of arbitrary impressment and must on some occasions have feared that he himself might be seized by a press gang.

The assembly, still furious with Governor Thomas over the enlistment of servants, paid him nothing for the 1740–41 year. James Logan tried to have the Quakers reconsider their antimilitary position in the annual Quaker yearly meeting but failed. Franklin printed a few copies of James Logan's letter to the yearly meeting (22 September 1741), in which Logan argued that civil government is founded on force and that Friends "who for conscience-sake cannot join in any law for self-defense [should] decline standing candidates at the ensuing election." Logan's position anticipated the stand taken by the English Quakers (and reluctantly accepted by most Pennsylvania Quakers) in 1755. But in 1741, the Pennsylvania Quakers ignored Logan. In reply to the Spanish privateers, a group of Philadelphia merchants built and manned their own ship. Captain John Sibbald, on the privateer sloop *Victory*, began his amazingly successful career in 1741, which climaxed late the following year when he took Spanish prizes worth more than £90,000 (21 December 1742). Adolescents like William Franklin (ca. fourteen in 1742) must have yearned for the honor, glory, and wealth that the privateersmen shared with Sibbald.

THE 1741 ELECTION

Franklin lobbied against Governor George Thomas and the Proprietary Party when he published Thomas's letter of 20 October 1740 to the Board of Trade. Pennsylvania's agent Richard Partridge had surreptitiously obtained a copy and sent it to the Pennsylvania Assembly.[18] Franklin brought it out as an eight-page pamphlet in late July 1741, in time for it to affect the 1 October election. Though the pamphlet has no title, printer, or publisher and was not advertised, contemporaries knew that Franklin printed and sold it: the merchant John Read of Christeen bought two dozen copies on 31 July; the Philadelphia brush maker John Wilkinson bought a copy on 19 August; and Samuel Norris bought 30 copies on 12 September. (As usual, Franklin gave a discount for large orders: Wilkinson paid 4 pence for his copy; Norris paid 3 pence apiece for 30.) It was no secret that Franklin printed it. (As said before, the surviving accounts record little except items purchased on credit.) Governor Thomas probably wanted to prosecute him for the publication, but that would only have made Franklin a hero to the Quaker Party.

Since Franklin sold the pamphlet, he presumably printed it on his own venture. Though he supported Governor Thomas's attempts to raise a militia, he resented several arguments that the governor made. Thomas told the Board of Trade that he had done his utmost to persuade the Pennsylvania Assembly "to a Sense of their Duty to his Majesty, and of their own Danger; and am now left without hope of their doing any thing for their Security." He appealed to the Lords of Trade "to make such a Representation" of the assembly "to his Majesty as you in your superior Judgment shall think necessary."[19] Though Thomas did not say what the board should recommend, he clearly wanted the pacifist Quakers—or perhaps all Quakers—barred from serving as assemblymen. He claimed that because of the war with Spain and France, the Quakers had redoubled their efforts to have only Quakers elected to the assembly and had been successful. When, during the year 1739–40, he had repeatedly asked them to support Great Britain and to protect themselves, the assembly replied "that I was to look upon them as an Assembly of *Quakers*; and that any Proposition relating to Arms was an Invasion of their Rights, and of the Liberty of Conscience granted to them by the first Proprietor" (*Letter* 2). Thomas complained that before the last election (1 October 1740), the yearly Quaker Meeting, "which was at first designed for the Regulation of the Religious Concerns of that Society (but in this Instance have taken upon them to direct the civil Affairs of the Government)," decided on the candidates, so that only three assemblymen out of thirty were not Quakers.

Octob. 20. 1740.

My LORDS,

AS his Majefty's Honour and Intereft, in regard to this Part of his Dominions, may be affected by the Proceedings of the Affembly of this Province; and as I have ufed my utmoft Endeavours to perfuade them to a Senfe of their Duty to his Majefty, and of their own Danger; and am now left without hope of their doing any thing for their Security; I cannot, confiftent with the Truft committed to me, any longer defer laying thofe Proceedings before your Lordfhips, that you may be enabled to make fuch a Reprefentation of them to his Majefty as you in your fuperior Judgment fhall think neceffary.

BUT that I may not appear too fparing of my own Trouble, by barely referring to the Votes of the Affembly, which are tranfmitted by this Opportunity; I fhall take the Liberty of informing your Lordfhips, that immediately after receiving his Majefty's Commands fignify'd to me by his Grace the Duke of *New-Caftle*, for granting Commiffions of Marque and Reprifal againft the Subjects of the King of *Spain*, my Endeavours were ufed to make the principal Inhabitants fenfible of the defencelefs State of this Province, and of the Neceffity I fhould be under of recommending to the Affembly at their next Meeting, to make fuch a timely Provifion as might not only fecure it againft any Attempts from the *Spaniards*, but the *French* likewife, in cafe they fhould take Part in the War. This, I hoped, would induce the People called *Quakers* to agree to fending fuch Members to the fucceeding Affembly, which is chofen annually here, as were not, like themfelves, tied up by Religious Confiderations, from doing what is fo abfolutely neceffary for the King's Honour, and the Prefervation of their Liberties and Eftates: But it had a very different Effect; for they immediately enter'd into Confultations, and came to a Refolution to exert their whole Power and Influence to procure a confiderable Majority of their own Perfuafion to be chofen, to oppofe all Expence on warlike Preparations, as they call it. And this was not done with their ufual Caution and Secrecy, but was publickly avow'd; and fuch as advifed them to more Moderation

A   were

Figure 20. Franklin influences the election of 1741: the first page of Governor George Thomas's letter to the Lords of Trade (Philadelphia: B. Franklin, 1741). Richard Partridge, the Pennsylvania Assembly's agent, surreptitiously obtained a copy of Pennsylvania governor George Thomas's letter to the Lords of Trade and sent it to Pennsylvania, probably to Speaker Issac Norris. Franklin obtained a copy and printed it at his own risk. Franklin's publication and sale of this letter marks at least the fourth time that he tried to influence Pennsylvania politics.

In his letter to the Lords of Trade, Governor Thomas suggested that at least the pacifist Quakers should be disqualified for political office. He also objected to the importation of indentured servants and said that they often brought over the knowledge to manufacture goods. He claimed that the production of such goods in the colonies was detrimental to the trade of the "Mother Country." Franklin chafed at Thomas's typically English mercantilistic attitudes, at his request for a fixed salary, and at his suggestion that Quaker Pennsylvanians were traitors. Franklin's publication and sale of the letter, which began in late July 1741, influenced the 1741 election in favor of the Quaker Party. Courtesy, Annenberg Rare Book and Manuscript Library, University of Pennsylvania.

Moreover, Governor Thomas contended that the Quakers had secured victory by deceiving the Germans "(who are very numerous here) . . . into a Belief, that a Militia will bring them under as severe a Bondage to Governors as they were formerly under to their Princes in *Germany*; that the Expence would impoverish them; and that if any other than *Quakers* should be chosen upon the Assembly, they would be dragg'd down from their Farms, and obliged to build Forts, as a Tribute for their being admitted to settle in the Province." (Franklin learned from the Quakers and used a similar implied threat in 1755 to secure wagons for General Braddock.) Governor Thomas also reported to the Board of Trade that the Pennsylvania Assembly was wealthy but would not use its money for defense: "it has now near *Ten Thousand* Pounds in Bank, from the Interest of Paper-Money, allowed to be struck here by the Grace and Favour of his Majesty, besides an annual Interest of *Four Thousand* Pounds *per Annum*, and *Three Thousand Five Hundred* Pounds *per Annum* arising out of the Excise upon Liquors: But so long as the House of Assembly shall be composed of" Quakers, no money will be spent for defense (*Letter* 3). Since the British authorities objected to the colonies' issuing their own paper money, Franklin and other supporters of a paper currency could think that the governor was indirectly arguing against colonial paper currency. The governor claimed that the Quakers were "so fond of Power, that no Pains is spared to exclude all others from the Exercise of it, even to the Prejudice of the King's Service" (*Letter* 4).

Not only was Thomas's letter anti-Quaker, but it also seemed anti-American when he objected to the importation of indentured tradesmen and to American manufactures. Governor Thomas expressed the usual mercantilist point of view, in which the colonies existed for the benefit of England. The "Merchants and masters of Vessels, by deluding Promises of mighty Advantages, persuade a great Number of Tradesmen to enter into Indentures with them; and, when brought here, sell them for their own Benefit, the Tradesmen not receiving *One Shilling* in Wages during the whole time of a very hard Servitude; and by this Means the Inhabitants here are enabled to carry on, at a very cheap Rate, Manufactures of several Sorts, directly interfering with those of *Great Britain*" (*Letter* 5). Governor Thomas thus seemed to be calling for further Acts of Trade and Navigation—acts that Franklin, like many Americans, resented.

Governor Thomas protested that since the governor of Pennsylvania depended for his salary on the Pennsylvania Assembly, the governor was "not at Liberty to exercise his own Judgment upon any Bills the Assembly shall think fit to present to him, or even to assert his Majesty's just Prerogatives in any Case whatsoever: *Starve him into Compliance, or into Silence*, is the common Language both of the Assembly and People here, when a Governor refuses his Assent to a Bill, or presses what they dislike, let the Honour of his Majesty, or the Security of this Part of his Dominions be ever so much concerned." Consequently he requested that the Board of Trade interpose and demand that the Pennsylvania Assembly be required for the future to settle a fixed salary on the governor, "as is done in other his Majesty's Governments" (*Letter* 6). New Hampshire and Virginia both had fixed salaries for their governors, but most colonies did not. Franklin had begun the *Pennsylvania Gazette* in 1729 with an editorial on Massachusetts governor Burnet's demands for a fixed salary, wherein Franklin argued that "there should be a mutual Dependence between the *Governour* and the *Governed*, and that to make any Governour independent on his People, would be dangerous, and destructive of their Liberties, and the ready Way to establish Tyranny" (1:160). Naturally the printer objected to Governor Thomas's request.

Worse still, Governor Thomas even suggested that the Pennsylvania legislators might be traitors. He protested against the Pennsylvania Assembly's power to spend its money "since they pretend not to be accountable either to his Majesty, or his Governors," and he feared that "they may . . . apply the publick Money to Purposes injurious to the Crown, and to their Mother-Country." He also remonstrated against their power to adjourn themselves, by which means they supposedly avoided doing their duty. "The Governor, it is true, has a Power of Calling them together by Writ; but to what Purpose will that be, since they can immediately adjourn themselves again" (*Letter* 7). He concluded that he was "too well acquainted with the narrow bigoted Views of the governing Sect here, not to be convinced that it is impossible for me to serve his Majesty faithfully," and therefore "with his Majesty's Permission, I should gladly resign the Government." His final sentence stated that "at present his Majesty's Measures, and the Sentiments of these People, are diametrically opposite."

Publication and sale of the letter embarrassed Governor Thomas. He complained on 27 August 1741 that his confidential letter to the board was in print and "dispersed all over the Province."[20] His appeal of 20 October 1740 to the Board of Trade had backfired. Governor Thomas's implied recommendation that Quakers not be allowed to be legislators caused a wave of sympathy for them. Besides, other sects generally feared the establishment of an Anglican church (25 July 1741) and partially for that reason voted for the Quakers. Further, the Quaker position was popular because by refusing to pay for war, Pennsylvania's taxes were the lowest in the colonies. When war came and the unprotected frontier was in danger opinions changed, but as the war had not yet intensified on the frontier, the governor's letter was used against him and against the Proprietary Party. In its speech to the governor on 27 May 1742 the assembly said, "Among other Privileges we at present enjoy, the Assembly have the Right to sit on their own Adjournments; to dispose of the Publick Money; and the People called *Quakers* have Right, when duly elected, to sit in the Assembly.—All these Privileges, it is plain, from the Tenor of the Governor's Letter to the Lords for Trade and Plantations, he represented as inconsistent with his Majesty's Service; and left no Room to doubt, but that it was thus done to the Intent those Privileges should be taken from us." Franklin printed the assembly's speech separately and distributed it with the *Gazette* for 3 June.[21]

As usual, tension and occasional rowdiness characterized the annual election. On 1 October 1741, Richard Peters, a proprietary supporter, was accused of casting two ballots, and someone hit him. He started fighting back, but, seeing the exchange, Quaker Party member Israel Pemberton separated the would-be combatants. James Hamilton, the future governor and a Proprietary Party leader, threatened to beat Pemberton, but the pacifist replied that he did not fear Hamilton. The turmoil continued as the chief proprietor, Thomas Penn, was hanged in effigy. The small landowners were outraged with him because of his forcing them to pay the old quitrents—and his forcing some off the land they had worked for years. With money rolling into the proprietors' coffers, Penn had sailed for England just over five weeks earlier on 20 August 1741, leaving behind a legacy of resentment—which Franklin no doubt shared.

The Quaker Party won the 1741 election—partly because Franklin had published Governor Thomas's letter. When the legislature met, the Quakers knew that Governor Thomas had complained to the English authorities about them, and they feared that the English authorities might prohibit them from serving as legislators. They voted on 21 October 1741 £3,000 for the king's use. They claimed that they passed the bill in view of the large taxes being paid by the people of Great Britain to support the war. Despite the grant, Pennsylvania remained unprotected.

The quarrel over military spending also took place in the Three Lower Counties and involved Franklin. Governor Thomas had better luck with its assembly. It passed a militia law and made provision for arms and ammunition, among other things. The Delaware Quakers, however, objected, claiming that the law was contrary to their charter of privileges. Samuel Chew, chief justice of the Three Lower Counties, defended the assembly's action to the grand jury of New Castle County on 21 November 1741. The Quaker Chew, like James Logan, saw nothing wrong with defensive war. At the request of the grand jury, Chew sent the speech to Franklin, who published it. After "a certain scurrilous abusive Paper entitled Some Remarks upon a late Speech Said to be made by Samuel Chew" appeared,[22] Chew paid Franklin fifteen shillings for a long advertisement in the 3 March *Pennsylvania Gazette*, claiming that the anonymous author was no Quaker, for the charges he brought were antithetical to the Quaker principles of meekness, humility, and charity. The Quaker Duck Creek Monthly Meeting, however, ordered Chew on 21 June 1742 to make a public retraction of his speech or be dismissed. He refused to do so and stated, in his *Speech Delivered to the Grand-Jury* (20 August 1742), that a religious society should not interfere in matters of state. The grand jury, with Jehu Curtis as its foreman (he had served on the assembly committee to establish the militia and was Speaker of the Three Lower Counties), asked that Chew publish that speech as well. Chew sent it off to Franklin, who did so. The Duck Creek Monthly Meeting expelled Chew on 18 October 1742. Since Franklin sold copies of Chew's pamphlets, he may have published them at his own risk.

Chew then wrote a piece accusing the Quakers of "Church Insolence and

Religious Tyranny" and sent it to Franklin for publication. Several weeks passed and it did not appear. Chew wrote the printer, saying that he had heard that Franklin would not print it. Franklin replied that he "had not declin'd printing it, but only postpon'd it for prudential Considerations." Franklin agreed with Chew's position but realized that if Chew replied, the Quakers would only condemn him further. Had Franklin been younger, he probably would have immediately published Chew's reply. Perhaps his circumspect behavior in the controversy marks his realization that he could not change others' religious principles; perhaps he thought Chew's reply was too personal; or, perhaps he thought it was not newsworthy.

Irritated, Chew turned to Bradford, asking him to print it. Bradford refused. So Chew sent it to James Parker in New York, perhaps not knowing that he was Franklin's partner. Parker may have consulted Franklin, and he printed the reply as a postscript to the *New York Weekly Post Boy* on 21 May 1744. In a prefatory note, Chew declared that the "extream Caution" of the Philadelphia printers was unusual and that he believed "the Religious Party, who are principally concern'd in the Consequences, have interested themselves in the Suppression of it." Using a comparison that echoed Franklin in the Hemphill case (2:33), Chew claimed that the Quakers had become as bad as the pope, assuming to themselves infallibility and dismissing members of the Society of Friends "for Differences even concerning speculative Matters."

On 4 June 1741, Andrew Hamilton and others (probably including Franklin) again petitioned the assembly, requesting the House to make "some Provision to guard us against" the Spanish privateers. After the Quaker-controlled assembly refused to act (6 June 1741), a group of 265 Pennsylvanians petitioned the crown that the assembly was not protecting the province. On 19 February, the Privy Council referred the petition to the Board of Trade, which discussed it on 9 and 30 March and 1 April 1742. London Friends who handled political matters in England for the Pennsylvania Quakers asked the board on 7 April for time to reply. On 24 June, the board heard both sides. Arguing on behalf of the assembly, Hugh Campbell maintained that, according to the Charter of Pennsylvania, the proprietor was responsible for the colony's defense.

The Privy Council, acting on the advice of the Board of Trade, gave its ruling (11 May 1743): the Lords Justices agreed that there was no right of exemption from a duty of self-defense, "The Law concerning liberty of Conscience relating merely to matters of Religion, and not to affairs of Government, and that, to what was insisted on by the Counsel for the Assembly, that their Proprietor was alone, obliged, in case of Emergency, to be at the expence of providing for their Security, founded upon a clause in the Charter which gives him all the powers usually granted to any other Captain General; The said Lords Commissioners are of opinion, that their Proprietor is no more obliged to be at that expense, than the Governor of any other Colony, who has the like power in his Commission."[23]

Franklin reported the upshot in the *Pennsylvania Gazette*, 8 September 1743, noting that "the Counsel's Pleadings lasted Three Hours," and that the only result was "to advise the King to order Governor Thomas to give his Opinion of what he shall judge necessary for putting the Province into a State of Defence." Franklin commented: "This we take to be a soft way of closing the Affair, and that it will die; and we earnestly desire the Disputes between the Governor and Assembly may cease, and all former Animosities to be bury'd in Oblivion." That last sentence expressed Franklin's hope that the assembly and the proprietors would work together for Pennsylvania's defense, though there is some reason to think that he at least partially sympathized with the assembly's position that the proprietors were responsible for the defense of Pennsylvania, but he also believed that Pennsylvanians should defend themselves.[24]

THE 1742 ELECTION

The "knock-down election" of 1 October 1742 was probably the most hard-fought (literally and figuratively) Pennsylvania political contest to that date. Franklin again was involved. The Proprietary Party suggested in mid-September that he was deliberately slow in printing the *Votes and Proceedings of the House of Representatives* for the last session (16–28 August). Since the financial accounts of the Loan Office appeared in the last session, the Proprietary Party was suggesting that the accounts would reveal financial mismanagement by the Quaker Party and that Franklin was covering it up. He replied in the *Pennsylvania Gazette* on 23 September 1742 that the assembly had not instructed him to delay printing the *Votes*, and that he had not "the least Intimation from any Member that such delay would be agreeable." The only reason for any delay was that he was busy working on the complete collection of all the Pennsylvania laws, "the minutes being very little enquired after."

During the previous year, Speaker John Kinsey and the Pennsylvania Assembly had continued to suspend Governor Thomas's financial support, arguing that the funds he received from fines and licenses were sufficient pay. By the end of the 1741–42 assembly, he had been paid nothing for two and a half years. Consequently, the governor withheld approval of the assembly's bills. The Proprietary Party was determined to try to win seats at the election. The Germans generally voted with the Quaker Party. William Allen, the Proprietary Party leader, was recorder of the city of Philadelphia, and as recorder was responsible for the magistrates and the watch or police of the city. Allen ran for inspector against Isaac Norris. When Norris won, a group of seventy or eighty sailors, wielding cudgels, attempted to seize control of the stairs. (The Philadelphia elections were held at the courthouse at Second and Market Streets. The courthouse had an exterior stairway that went up to an entrance on the second floor. The electors walked up the stairs to drop their ballots in the box on the second floor, passing by the inspectors at the landing on the stairway.)

Figure 21. The site of the annual "fight for the stairs" at Philadelphia's elections. Detail from The Paxton Expedition, *cartoon by Henry Dawkins (1764), of the courthouse and the stairs. The annual elections for Philadelphia County on 1 October and for the city of Philadelphia on 2 October were held at the entrance to the courthouse at the top of the stairs. During hotly contested elections, fights broke out before the courthouse and sometimes a "fight for the stairs" ensued. The party that controlled the stairs could control the election. The "knock-down election" of 1742, with sailors wielding cudgels fighting the citizens with sticks of firewood, was the most fiercely fought election to that date. Courtesy, Library Company of Philadelphia.*

The sailors, who worked for the wealthy merchants and ship owners like William Allen, tried to keep the Quakers and Germans from voting. One captain called out to the sailors, "Damn you, go and knock those Dutch Sons of Bitches off the Steps." A sailor yelled, "There goes a Parcel of Quaker Sons of Bitches; they are the Men we want, Men with broad Hats and no Pockets." When the Quakers appealed to William Allen, he answered that the sailors "have as much right here as the unnaturalized Germans."

The tide of battle turned when the sailors attacked the assemblyman Thomas Leech on the steps. Leech, who received the highest number of votes in the election, called for those inside the courthouse to give out firewood and cudgels to the Quakers and Germans. He instructed them to arm themselves "with Billets of Wood or anyThing that comes to Hand, and drive these Sailors off the Ground." Since the Quakers and Germans greatly outnumbered the sailors, they did just that. The riots thoroughly disgraced the Proprietary Party.[25]

Franklin described the election in a news article on 7 October 1742: "In this City, when the People of City and County were assembled in the Market Place, and had just begun the Choice of Inspectors, a Body of Sailors, suppos'd to be about 70 or 80, collected from several Ships in the Harbour, appear'd at the Foot of Market-Street, arm'd with Clubs, and huzzaing march'd up in a tumultuous Manner towards the People." Franklin's report condemned the sailors and, indirectly, William Allen and the Proprietary Party:

> As they [the sailors] were mostly Strangers, and had no kind of Right to intermeddle with the Election, and some ill Consequence was apprehended if they should be suffer'd to mix, with their Clubs, among the Inhabitants, some of the Magistrates, and other persons of Note, met them, and endeavour'd to prevail with them to return peaceably to their Ships, but without Effect. For they fell on with their Clubs, and knocking down Magistrates, Constables, and all others who oppos'd 'em, fought their Way up to the Court-House, and clear'd the Place of Election, the People retiring into the Market-House and Second-Street in a kind of Amaze at such unexpected and unusual Treatment. After the Sailors had triumph'd awhile before the Court-house, they march'd off, and the People, without pursuing them, continued and finished their Election of Inspectors; which was no sooner done but the Sailors returning more numerous and furious than at first, fell upon the People a second time, and knock'd down all they came a-near, several were carried off for dead, and the Confusion and Terror was inexpressible. But the Inhabitants, losing at length all Patience, furnished themselves with Sticks from the neighbouring Woodpiles, and turn'd upon the Sailors, who immediately fled to their Ships and hid themselves, from whence they were drag'd out one by one, and before Night near 50 of them were committed to Prison. A good Watch was kept that Night to prevent any new Tumult, and the City has ever since been quiet.

Franklin's friend and fellow punster Hugh Roberts recalled the "knockdown election" of 1742 when reporting the latest political news to Franklin on 1 June 1758. He said that Allen, the dictator of the Proprietary Party, "who still remains their primum MO BILLY vel primum MOB ILLE," still controlled the party. Then, alluding to the former sheriff of Philadelphia, Septimus Robinson, who cowardly failed to try to maintain order, Roberts reported that the other members of the Proprietary Party were so entirely controlled by Allen that "they appear allmost degenerated into a state of SEPTYCISM tho I would not ROBHISON nor the son of any man living to explain my thoughts" (8:83).

Though the Quaker Party won the election, its position on the military was condemned by both the English Friends and the British government.[26] At the same time, the proprietors were unhappy that the quitrent payments had dramatically shrunk because of rumors of an appeal to England for a royal government to replace the proprietary government. Indeed, the threat of an appeal for royal government had been common during the previous past two years, fueled in part by Penn's forcing landowners to pay the quitrents.[27] Both sides had reason for compromise. The assembly promised on 2 February 1742/3 to pay the governor £500 upon his signing the bills currently before him and another £1,000 when the bills were passed. On 3 February 1742/3, Governor Thomas approved the bills. Two months later (5 April), he appointed Speaker John Kinsey as chief justice. And finally, as we have seen, the 1741 petition to the crown, which the Privy Council originally took up on 18 January 1741/2, was resolved on 11 May 1743. Franklin's editorial comment of 8 September 1743 stressed reconciling party differences.

THE CEREMONY

While internal politics improved, foreign relations worsened. On 25 October 1743, France and Spain signed the Second Family Compact, auguring that France would soon join Spain in the war. On 15 March 1743/4, France declared war against Great Britain, which replied with its own declaration on 29 March. With war impending and relations between the governor and assembly improving, the House voted on 17 May to pay the governor for the current legislative year, and on 26 May 1744 it paid him £1,000 for the current year and an additional £1,000 toward his past support. So he was now owed (or believed he was owed) £1,000 for past support. After news of Great Britain's declaration reached Pennsylvania, the authorities announced that Governor Thomas would proclaim war on 11 June 1744.

The ceremony was typical. Visiting dignitaries (on this occasion, the Virginia commissioners to the Indian treaty at Lancaster) were invited to wait on the governor. At the appointed time (4 p.m.), the important visitors, the governor's council, the mayor, and the Philadelphia City Corporation arrived at the governor's home. Though not mentioned in the extant descriptions, church bells probably pealed at 4:00. The procession from the governor's to the courthouse began a few minutes later, led by about thirty flags and ensigns taken from privateer vessels in the harbor, which were carried by a parcel of roaring sailors. They were followed by eight or ten drums that made a martial noise, then by an African American fiddler whose music could not be heard over the noise and clamor of the people and the rattle of the drums. Then came the constables with their staffs, the sheriffs and the coroner with their white wands, Governor Thomas, with Mayor Benjamin Shoemaker on his right and Recorder William Allen on his left, followed by the Virginia colonels Thomas Lee and William Beverley, then the other Virginia commissioners, next the governor's councillors, after them the City Corporation, and last in the procession came the town gentlemen, including Franklin.

The procession marched with solemn pace two-by-two to the courthouse stairs, where 4,000 people had gathered in the street and more watched from the windows and balconies of the nearby houses. Secretary Richard Peters read three proclamations: first, the king of England's proclamation of war against the French; second, a proclamation to encourage those who fitted out privateers against the enemy; and third, the governor's proclamation of war with France. Then Governor Thomas "with a very audible voice, desired all such persons as were fit to carry arms to provide themselves—every man with a good musket, cartouche box, powder and shot, and such implements as were requisite either to repel or annoy the enimy, if there should be any necessity or occasion." Thomas said he would "call upon each of them to see that they were provided." He vowed, "Depend upon it . . . this Province shall not be lost by any neglect or oversight of mine."

A stentorian voice in the crowd bawled out, "Please your Honour, what you say is right, but I and many others here, poor men, have neither money nor credit to procure a musket or the third part of a musket, so that unless the publick takes care to provide us, the bulk of the people must go unfurnished, and the country be destitute of defence." The governor made no reply, but smiled in silent acknowledgment. The ceremony concluded with a discharge of the privateers' cannons that had been hauled out for the purpose, then two drums beat the point of war, and finally Peters proclaimed, "God save the king!" The crowd replied, "Huzzah! Huzzah! Huzzah!" Then Governor Thomas entered his chariot with Colonel Thomas Lee of Virginia and Secretary Peters, drove home, and the crowd dispersed.[28]

The celebration on the occasion of the taking of Cape Breton (described below) presents some of the similarities and differences between colonial rituals. Had the occasion been a celebration the ritual would have concluded with a bonfire and a few barrels of rum supplied by the government. The citizens would have put lights in their windows signaling their happiness. And later, if the mob had suspected any deviance, rowdies would have roamed the streets and broken the unlit windows.

Governor Thomas requested funds from the assembly on 31 July 1744 for a militia to protect the colony, but the assembly replied on 11 August that a militia was understood as a part of the colony's charter and a militia bill need not therefore be passed by the assembly. The assembly implied that the proprietor should pay the militia. The assembly had previously argued that the British Navy protected Pennsylvania from attacks by sea and that friendly Indians protected Pennsylvania from attacks by land. A split between the conservative pacifist wing of the Quaker Party and the moderates, who were willing to give some support to the authorities for military purposes, became more visible than ever, with Israel Pemberton leading the pacifists and John Kinsey the moderates. At the 1 October 1744 election, the moderates prevailed.

THE LANCASTER INDIAN TREATY, 1744

In late 1742, a series of skirmishes between Iroquois League Indians and Virginians occurred on the Virginia frontier. Pennsylvania proposed that the two parties settle their differences at a treaty. The Iroquois agreed to meet with delegates from Virginia, Maryland, and Pennsylvania at Lancaster in the summer of 1744. Governor Thomas saw no reason to attend, but Indian expert Conrad Weiser feared that the Marylanders and especially the Virginians would behave rudely to the Indians. Weiser convinced Speaker John Kinsey that it was essential for Governor Thomas to be present. Because of William Penn's policies, most Indian tribes knew and trusted the early Pennsylvania governors, who successively inherited the name that the Iroquois had first given William Penn, "Onas" (the Indian name for a pen/quill/feather). Of course the Delaware Indians had learned from the Walking Purchase that the present proprietors were nothing like William Penn, but the Six Nations of the Iroquois did not yet fully appreciate the difference. Kinsey convinced Governor Thomas he should attend. Meanwhile, the commissioners from Virginia arrived in Philadelphia early in June and were, as we have seen, present on 11 June 1744 when Governor Thomas proclaimed war against France.

The war with France made the Lancaster Indian treaty (22 June to 4 July) crucial. If the Six Nations sided with France, the Americans would have had a war on the frontier and could have lost the interior of the continent to the French. Fortunately, through the agency of the Indian expert Conrad Weiser and Governor Thomas, the treaty not only renewed Pennsylvania's alliance with the Six Nations but also extended the alliance to include Maryland and Virginia. The historian Paul A. W. Wallace noted that since the Six Nations "held suzerainty over many of the Indians in the West, nominally under French influence," the treaty "made an actual break in the chain of settlements and protectorates by which the French designed to lock the English colonies in between the mountains and the sea."[29] In the future the Six Nations would protect the frontiers of the English settlements from New England to Virginia. It was a great diplomatic defeat for the French. One could also view it as the beginning of cooperation among the colonial American colonies.

Virginia not only allied itself with the Six Nations but also bought land westward "to the setting of the sun" that the Iroquois had seized from other tribes. In return, the Iroquois gained the right to use the "Virginia road," thus providing convenient access for them to raid enemy tribes in the South. The treaty was a diplomatic victory for the English.

Though not present at Lancaster, Franklin printed the treaty and admired the sentiments of the Onondaga chief Canasatego and of the Cayuga chief Gachradodow. Later Franklin echoed their speeches in letters of 20 March 1751 and 9 May 1753, in his mock "Captivity of William Henry" (1768), and in *Remarks*

Concerning the Savages of North America (1783). At Lancaster, in the morning session of 30 June 1744, the Cayuga chief Gachradodow stressed that the whites and the Indians had different cultures: "You have your Laws and Customs and so have we." He said that when the whites first came to America, they were poor, but now "they have got our Lands, and are by them become Rich, and we are Now poor. What little we had for the Land does soon away, but the Land lasts forever."[30]

The Virginians proposed to the Iroquois that, in order to continue to have expert interpreters, some of the Indians' sons should be sent to the lower schools at William and Mary, where "they shall have the same Care taken of them, and be instructed in the same Manner as our own Children, and be returned to you again when you please." Canasatego politely refused and, like Gachradodow, showed an appreciation of cultural relativism: "We must let you know we love our Children too well to send them so great a Way, and the *Indians* are not inclined to give their Children Learning. We allow it to be good, and we thank you for your Invitation; but our Customs differing from yours, you will be so good as to excuse us."[31]

In a memorable speech at the treaty's conclusion on 4 July 1744, the Onondaga chief Canasatego advised the governors of Virginia, Maryland, and Pennsylvania, as well as the English colonists in general, to join together, citing the example of the Iroquois: "Our wise Forefathers established Union and Amity between the *Five Nations*; this has made us formidable; this has given us great Weight and Authority with our neighbouring Nations. We are a powerful Confederacy; and, by your observing the same Methods our wise Forefathers have taken, you will acquire fresh Strength and Power; therefore whatever befals you, never fall out with one another."[32]

In Franklin's letter to James Parker giving his first tentative plan for a union of the colonies, (20 March 1750/1), he mentioned Canasatego's speech, as well as the example of the League of Six Nations itself (4:118–19). In a letter to Peter Collinson of 9 May 1751, Franklin echoed Canasatego's speech about the education of Indian children in a comment on the "little value" that Indians set on the "Learning" that whites value so highly. Franklin, however, added to the Indian speech, a further note of cultural relativism: "The Indians after consulting on the proposal replied that it was remembered some of their Youths had formerly been educated in that College, but it had been observed that for a long time after they returned to their Friends, they were absolutely good for nothing being neither acquainted with the true methods of killing deer, catching Beaver or surprizing an enemy." Nevertheless, they appreciated that the Virginians meant the proposition as a mark of kindness and goodwill. They therefore replied that if the Virginians "would send a dozen or two of their Children to Onondago, the great Council would take care of their Education, bring them up in really what was the best manner and make men of them" (4:483).

The cultural relativism of Gachradodow and Canasatego also appeared in

Franklin's June 1768 mock "Captivity of William Henry," featuring Canasatego and Alaguippi. When Henry cast doubt upon the Indian myths of origin, Canasatego upbraided him for his poor manners: "you are yet almost as rude as when you first came among us. When young, it seems you were not well taught, you did not learn the civil behaviour of men. We excused you: it was the fault of your instructors. But why have you not more improved, since you have long had the opportunity from our example? You see I always believed your stories, why do you not believe mine?" Henry then observed that Alaguippi "kindly made some apology for me." Henry would be wiser in time. The two Indians agreed on an "observation which they thought very polite and respectful towards me, that my stories indeed might be best for white people, but Indian stories were undoubtedly best for Indians" (15:157).

"Remarks Concerning the Savages of North America" is of course filled with cultural relativism, but its opening especially seems like an echo of Gachradodow's speech on the difference of the cultures of the Indians and whites. He concluded, "You have your Laws and Customs and so have we." Franklin began, "Savages we call them, because their manners differ from ours, which we think the Perfection of Civility; they think the same of theirs" (W 969).

AMERICANISM AND POLITICAL CHANGE, 1744

In a news note of 30 August 1744, Franklin celebrated the number and prowess of the American privateers: "'Tis computed that there are and will be before Winter 113 Sail of Privateers at Sea, from the *British American* Colonies; most of them stout Vessels and abundantly well mann'd. A Naval Force, equal (some say) to that of the Crown of *Great Britain* in the Time of Queen *Elizabeth*." Despite the "some say," the observation was Franklin's, and he repeated the remark in his "Observations Concerning the Increase of Mankind" (4:233).

We remarked above on the significance of Franklin's publishing the "division" or how members voted (9 May 1739). A second small but telling change in Pennsylvania politics during this period concerned the candidates' advertising. Colonial politicians pretended that they were not interested in being elected to office and that they only served because they were, in effect, drafted by the electorate. But on 16 August 1744, Mordecai Lloyd advertised in English and German in both the *Pennsylvania Gazette* and the *Pennsylvania Journal*, asking the freeholders of Philadelphia City and County to elect him sheriff. He repeated the advertisement on 23 August, and 6 and 27 September. His rival for sheriff, Nicholas Scull, Franklin's friend and fellow Junto member, replied on 23 August in both the *Gazette* and *Journal* in English and German, asking that the freeholders of Philadelphia city and county elect him. "Tho' it had not till this Time been customary to request your Votes in Print; yet that Method being now introduced, I think my self obliged in this publick Manner to return you my hearty Thanks for the Favour I have already receiv'd." His advertisement was repeated 30 August, 6 and 27 September. At the 1 October election, Scull was reelected. Similar advertisements for sheriff appeared in the following years. These seem to be among the earliest American political advertisements directly avowed by the candidates.

Cape Breton

In January 1745, Massachusetts Governor William Shirley suggested that the colonies from New England south through Pennsylvania join together to attack the French stronghold, Fort Louisbourg on Cape Breton, Nova Scotia. French vessels from Louisbourg repeatedly assaulted the New England fishing fleets and the British merchant vessels. Shirley organized the expedition, appointed the Massachusetts militia general William Pepperell its head, asked for and secured help from Commodore Peter Warren of the British Navy, and appointed fast days on 28 February and 4 April 1745 to pray for the expedition's success. Governor Thomas, presenting Shirley's request for aid to the Pennsylvania Assembly, declared, "Dispatch . . . is the Life of the Undertaking" (25 February). Though his love for Pennsylvania was stronger, throughout his life Franklin also identified with Massachusetts. He made private notes on the assembly debates and gave as his summary opinion that "the Governor and Assembly have been only acting a Farce and playing Tricks to amuse the World" (26–28 February). He did not specify what farce and tricks he had in mind, but perhaps he thought the governor was insincere in his request, knowing that the assembly would decline.

On 28 February 1745 the Pennsylvania Assembly refused to support the expedition, saying that the plans had been made without consulting Pennsylvania and that any credit for the victory would certainly go to New England. Franklin disgustedly noted, "Several of the Members told me to day that they heartily wished the N E People Success. I told them those People were as much oblig'd to them for their Good Wishes as the Poor in the Scripture to those that say Be ye warmed be ye filled &c. I ask'd them what should hinder the House from sending a little Provision to their fellow Subjects who were going [to be at?] so useful an Undertaking." But the Quaker members answered, "That would be encouraging War" (3:17).

Franklin reprinted accounts of the preparations for the invasion of Louisbourg on 12 April and 2 May. On 23 May the *Gazette* carried a description of Cape Breton, emphasizing its military and economic importance. The report concluded with a note, implicitly condemning the Quaker Party and the Pennsylvania Assembly: "The only Reflection I shall make on these Facts is, that every Man who loves his Country, ought to pray for the Success of the present Expedition." In private, Franklin revealed his humor and skepticism about the outcome—and used, for the first recorded time, a version of the later common expression "a hard nut to crack." He wrote to his brother John: "Our people are extremely impatient to hear of your success at Cape Breton. My shop is filled with thirty inquires at the coming in of every post. Some wonder the place is not yet taken. I tell them I shall be glad to hear that news three months hence. Fortified towns are hard nuts to crack; and your teeth have not been accustomed to it. Taking strong places is a particular trade, which you have taken up without serving an apprenticeship to it. Armies and veterans need skilful engineers to direct them in their attack. Have you any? But some seem to think forts are as easy taken as snuff."

After expressing his doubts, Franklin ironically mentioned the hyperbolic injunction of the Reverend Samuel Moody, who combined a spiritual other-worldliness with fierce frontier fighting. When the sixty-nine-year-old minister was embarking with the troops for Louisbourg, he seized a hatchet and cried out, "The sword of the Lord and of Gideon!"[33] Franklin then referred to the Massachusetts fast days appointed by Governor Shirley: "in which I compute five hundred thousand petitions were offered up [to God] . . . in New England, which added to the petitions of every family morning and evening, multiplied by the number of days since January 25th, make forty-five millions of prayers; which, set against the prayers of a few priests in the garrison, to the Virgin Mary, give a vast balance in your favor." He added, "If you do not succeed, I fear I shall have but an indifferent opinion of Presbyterian prayers in such cases, as long as I live."

Franklin continued his ironic treatment of prayers and religion: "Indeed, in attacking strong towns I should have more dependence on *works*, than on *faith*; for, like the kingdom of heaven, they are to be taken by force and violence; and in a French garrison I suppose there are devils of that kind, that they are not to be cast out by prayers and fasting, unless it be by their own fasting for want of provisions." He concluded on a note mildly satirizing himself: "I believe there is Scripture in what I have wrote, but I cannot adorn the margin with quotations, having a bad memory, and no Concordance at hand; besides no more time than to subscribe myself, etc." (3:26–27).

On 4 June, Governor Thomas again notified the assembly of the requests he had received from Commodore Warren and Governor Shirley for help in the attack on Cape Breton. Two days later, the House answered that New England undertook the enterprise without consulting the neighboring colonies. If it succeeded, New England would receive the principal benefit, and therefore had "no Right to involve us in the Expence." The House said it would wait until the English authorities contacted the governor. With that, the assembly adjourned. The same day, 6 June 1745, Franklin published a woodcut of the "Plan of the Town and Harbour of Louisbourg," the first illustrated news event in American journalism. Since he apologized for its quality, ("rough as it is, for want of good Engravers here"), he probably made the cut himself. Franklin editorialized, "It is therefore in their own Necessary Defence, as well as that of all the other *British* Colonies, that the People of *New-England* have undertaken the present Expedition against that Place, to which may the *GOD OF HOSTS* grant Success. *Amen*." Franklin's religious rhetoric in his public support of the project con-

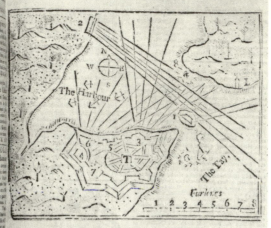

PHILADELPHIA, June 6. 1745.

As the CAPE-BRETON Expedition is at present the Subject of most Conversations, we hope the following Draught (rough as it is, for want of good Engravers here) will be acceptable to our Readers; as it may serve to give them an Idea of the Strength and Situation of the Town now besieged by our Forces, and render the News we receive from thence more intelligible.

PLAN of the Town and Harbour of LOUISBURGH.

EXPLANATION.

1. The Island Battery, at the Mouth of the Harbour, mounting 34 Guns,-----Pounders. This Battery can rake Ships fore and aft before they come to the Harbour's Mouth, and take them in the Side as they are passing in.
2. The Grand Battery, of 36 Forty-two Pounders, planted right against the Mouth of the Harbour, and can rake Ships fore and aft as they enter.
3. The Town N. East Battery, which mounts 18 Twenty-four Pounders on two Faces, which can play on the Ships as soon as they have entered the Harbour.
4. The Circular Battery, which mounts 16 Twenty-four Pounders, stands on high Ground, and overlooks all the Works. This Battery can also gaul Ships, as soon as they enter the Harbour.
5. Three Flanks, mounting 2 Eighteen Pounders each.
6. A small Battery, which mounts 8 Nine Pounders. All these Guns command any Ship in the Harbour.
7. The Fort or Citadel, fortified distinctly from the Town, in which the Governor lives.
8. A Rock, called the Barrel.
T The Center of the Town. L. The Light-House.
Every Bastion of the Town Wall has Embrasures or Ports for a Number of Guns to defend the Land Side.
The black Strokes drawn from the several Batteries, shew the Lines in which the Shot may be directed.

CAPE-BRETON Island, on which Louisburgh is built, lies on the South of the Gulph of St. Lawrence, and commands the Entrance into that River, and the Country of Canada. It is reckon'd 140 Leagues in Circuit, full of fine Bays and Harbours, extreamly convenient for Fishing Stages. It was always reckon'd a Part of Nova-Scotia. For the Importance of this Place see our Gazette, No. 858. As soon as the French King had begun the present unjust War against the English, the People of Louisburgh attack'd the New-England Town of Canso, consisting of about 150 Houses and a Fort, took it, burnt it to the Ground, and carried away the People, Men, Women and Children, Prisoners. They then laid Siege to Annapolis Royal, and would have taken it, if seasonable Assistance had not been sent from Boston. Mr. Duvivier went home to France last Fall for more Soldiers, &c. to renew that Attempt, and for Stores for Privateers, of which they proposed to fit out a great Number this Summer, being the last Year unprovided: Yet one of their Cruisers only, took 4 Sail in a few Days, off our Capes, to a very considerable Value. What might we have expected from a dozen Sail, making each 3 or 4 Cruises a Year? They boasted that during the War they should have no Occasion to cut Fire-Wood, for that the Jackstaves of English Vessels would be a Supply sufficient. It is therefore in their own NECESSARY DEFENCE, as well as that of all the other British Colonies, that the People of New-England have undertaken the present Expedition against that Place, to which may the GOD OF HOSTS grant Success. Amen.

Figure 22. A map of Louisbourg, Cape Breton, which the New England militia was attacking; the first map and illustrated news event in American journalism, Pennsylvania Gazette, 6 June 1745. It portrayed the defenses of Louisbourg, the supposedly impregnable French fortress on Cape Breton. Since Franklin apologized for the woodcut, "rough as it is, for want of good Engravers here," he probably made it himself. After using it, Franklin sent the cut on to his partner James Parker, who employed it in the New York Weekly Post Boy, 10 June. For the next thirty years, Franklin referred to the militia's victory at Louisbourg on 16–17 June 1745 as a touchstone of American military ability and courage. Courtesy, Library Company of Philadelphia.

trasted markedly with his ironic references in the private letter to his brother John.

On 18 July, Franklin reported Louisbourg's surrender. "Wednesday last [10 July], a great Number of Guns were distinctly heard in several Places round this City, the Occasion of which, as well as the Place where they were fired, was unknown till the Evening of the Day following, when an Express arriv'd with Advice of the Surrender of Louisbourg, which had caus'd great Rejoycings at New-York. 'Twas near 9 o'Clock when the Express came in, yet the News flying instantly round the Town, upwards of 20 Bonfires were immediately lighted in the Streets. The next Day was spent in Feasting, and drinking the Healths of Gov. Shirley, Gen. Pepperel, Com. Warren, &c. &c. under the Discharge of Cannon from the Wharffs and Vessels in the River; and the Evening concluded with Bonfires, Illuminations, and other Demonstrations of Joy. A Mob gathered, and began to break the Windows of those Houses that were not illuminated, but it was soon dispersed, and suppress'd." The other two Philadelphia newspapers lacked the anticipatory news of mysterious guns being fired the night before, and thus both lack the drama of Franklin's account. The unlit windows were those of Quaker pacifists, who objected to war. Quaker John Smith recorded that on both Thursday and Friday, 11 and 12 July, "the mob were very rude in this City, breaking many Windows that were not Illuminated, but by the Vigilance of the Inhabitants and the prudent Conduct of the then Mayor Edward Shippen they were suppressed before they had done much mischief."

The New Englanders' victory on 17 June 1745 at Fort Louisbourg amazed the world. Poems in the English and American periodicals celebrated the triumph. In New England, the victory inspired the early military verses of the American folk song "Yankee Doodle."

> Brother Ephraim sold his Cow
> and bought him a Commission
> and then he went to Canada
> to fight for the Nation.
>
> But when Ephraim he came home
> he prov'd an arrant Coward
> He wou'dn't fight the Frenchmen there
> For fear of being devour'd.[34]

Like several colonial American humorous writings, the song was a put-on. English soldiers often expressed a supercilious contempt for Americans and for the American militia. The song exaggerated and burlesqued that attitude. It portrayed the New Englanders as ignorant, backward provincials who were afraid of guns, fighting, and warfare and who feared Frenchmen as cannibals. But everyone knew that the American rabble had achieved the supposedly impossible—they had defeated a large French force defending a reputedly impregnable fortress.

AFTER VICTORY

On 23 July Governor Thomas reported to the assembly the victory at Cape Breton and asked for soldiers, ammunition, and supplies for securing the conquest. Keeping in mind the House's 6 June excuse that it had not received a request from the English authorities, Governor Thomas told the assembly of "his Majesty's Order signified by the Duke of Newcastle" that "if Mr. Warren shall apply to you for Assistance, either of Men, Provisions, or Shipping . . . you should in all such Cases be aiding and assisting to him." The following day, the House finally voted £4,000 for "the King's Use; to be paid into the Hands of *John Pole* and *John Mifflin*, of the City of Philadelphia, Merchants . . . to be laid out by them . . . in the purchase of Bread, Beef, Pork, Flour, Wheat or other Grain . . . within this province; and to be shipped from hence for the King's Service, as the Governor shall think most fit." In its message to the governor, the assembly said, "Although the peaceable Principles professed by divers Members of the present Assembly, do not permit them to join in raising of Men or providing Arms and Ammunition, yet we have ever held it our Duty to render Tribute to Caesar, and have therefore, on the present Occasion, come to the Resolution herewith sent, which we hope will give Public and substantial Proof of our Zeal for the King's Service and the common Good of our Fellow Subjects."[35]

The vote was a breakthrough, and Franklin featured it in a supplement to the *Pennsylvania Gazette* of 25 July 1745. Most supplements were mere additions to the regular newspaper, usually called for by a large number of advertisements. They contained the same typographical layout of the normal issue. This *Extra!* contained no other matter, and Franklin used only one side of a sheet with large blank spaces to feature the vote that he, as clerk, had taken at the assembly. He remarked in his *Autobiography* that some councillors were irritated with the Quaker assembly and advised the governor not to accept the vote, since it did not specify the military supplies needed. Governor Thomas responded, "I shall take the Money, for I understand very well their Meaning; *Other Grain*, is Gunpowder" (A 114). When Franklin reprinted the *Boston Evening Post*'s detailed report of the capture of Louisbourg, on 1 August, he editorialized, "The late Reduction of the City and Harbour of Louisbourg, not only appears wonderful to us in America, but must surprize all the People of England, and make a considerable Noise thro' all Europe. Take it in all its Circumstances, it can scarce be parallel'd in History." In defending Americans and the courage of colonial troops during the pre-Revolutionary period, Franklin used the amazing victory at Cape Breton as a touchstone of American fighting ability.

Contrary to the Cartagena expedition of 1740–42, the Louisbourg expedition of 1745 was a resounding victory, but it, too, turned sour. The American troops expected to receive money and land in Canada, but they found that the British Navy took rich prizes while the American troops did not receive even sufficient food, clothing, or, as the bitter winter approached at Louisbourg, fuel. Thomas Fleet's *Boston Evening Post* reported on 23 September 1745 that the British naval forces at Louisbourg had taken £500,000 sterling, but the American troops, "the poor Men in the Garrison," had so far received nothing, despite their belief that all the treasure seemed "intended for *them*, as a Reward for their signal Service." During the miserable winter following their triumphant victory, about one-third of the Americans died of disease and exposure. Fights broke out between the English navy forces and the American troops, and a joint declaration by the American general and the British admiral forbade their forces to "cast any national reflections on any of his Majesty's subjects."[36] Franklin wrote later that though the American troops "undertook the service on a promise of being discharged as soon as it was over," they had to stay for the following winter when they "suffered ten times more loss by mortal sickness, thro' want of necessaries, than they suffered from the arms of the enemy" (8:349).

The Pennsylvania Assembly paid Governor Thomas £500 on 10 January 1744/5 and £500 on 23 August, "in full of his Support for the current Year," for the usual total for the year of £1,000, but he was still owed £1,000 in past salary. On 14 October 1745, with Speaker John Kinsey attending the Six Nations treaty at Albany, the pacifist Israel Pemberton was chosen Speaker, but he declined; and so John Wright was elected Speaker. Wright, however, fell sick, and on 6 January 1745/6, the moderate John Kinsey (who had been Speaker since 15 October 1739 until the election on 14 October) was again elected. He continued in this office until his death in 1750. With Kinsey as Speaker, the assembly voted "That in order to render the Governor's Support equal to what has been usually given to his Predecessors, an Order be drawn on the Treasurer for the Sum of *One Thousand Pounds*, payable to him," and at the same time the legislators voted him £500 for his current year's support. Early in June 1746, Governor Thomas received instructions to raise volunteers to fight in Canada. He therefore called a special Assembly to meet on 9 June 1746. On that date he issued a proclamation asking for troops for the immediate reduction of Canada. The House finally passed a bill on 24 June, giving £5,000 for "the King's Use" and tying it to an emission of £5,000 in paper currency. Pennsylvania raised three companies. At the end of the legislative year, the assembly voted to pay Thomas £500 "as the Remainder of his Support for the current Year." That brought his salary back to what it would have been had he been paid the customary £1,000 per year.

Though the assembly had voted £5,000 to raise and equip four Pennsylvania companies to participate in the Canadian campaign, it refused all further requests for aid. By 14 October 1746, the Pennsylvania soldiers' wages were in arrears, and they threatened to mutiny if they were not supplied with blankets. New York's governor Clinton purchased blankets for them and charged them to Pennsylvania. When the Pennsylvania Assembly refused to reimburse New York (13 January 1747), Governor Thomas personally paid part of the Pennsylvania soldiers' bills. The Canada campaign gradually fizzled out, with desertions increasingly common. As we have seen, William Franklin served in this failed campaign.

When a number of sailors ran off from the British naval ships in Boston on 16 November 1747, Commodore Charles Knowles ordered an impressment, but the Bostonians had had enough. As mentioned above, Americans liked to believe that "the sixth of Anne" against impressing Americans, that had been passed in 1708, was still in force. Further, they were angry that a law just passed in 1746 (19 George II, c.30) expressly forbade the impressment on the Sugar Islands—but said nothing about the mainland colonies. On 17 November 1747, a Boston mob gathered to resist the press gang. More and more citizens joined the mob. By the late afternoon, it numbered several thousand people. They captured the British naval officers in town and demanded that Knowles release the impressed persons in exchange for the British officers. Governor Shirley called out the militia—but nothing happened. No doubt some Massachusetts militiamen were part of the mob, and others sympathized. For the next two days, anarchy threatened. The Massachusetts General Court (i.e., the governor, council, and assembly) condemned the lawless activity on the twentieth, and the riot subsided. Franklin, who later wrote the strongest American satire against impressment, no doubt followed the course of the incipient revolution and agreed with the mob.[37]

Meanwhile, because of ill health, Governor Thomas sailed for London on 1 June 1747. He had been lieutenant governor since 1 June 1738. Some governors were dishonest and many merely wanted all the money they could get. Thomas was an exception. Though the Philadelphia Corporation was mainly composed of proprietary supporters and therefore would be expected to support the governor, the mayor and Common Council on this occasion spoke for the general sentiment in appraising Thomas: "We may, with the greatest Truth, say You have had clean Hands, and have acquired No Money amongst us, unjustly." Despite his series of political quarrels with the Pennsylvania Assembly, he had gradually won the respect of most Pennsylvanians. After Thomas's departure, the president of the council, Anthony Palmer, assumed the executive duties on 8 June 1747.

Writing Peter Collinson on 20 July 1747, the Philadelphia naturalist John Bartram voiced a new complaint about Thomas Penn. Since Bartram was Franklin's close friend and since Bartram rarely expressed a political opinion (while Franklin often did), Bartram may have echoed Franklin's personal opinion: "Our proprietor is allmost as crafty as covetous. He wont sell land because the people being necessitated for land to live upon raiseth its price prodigiously so that in a few years he may get 5 times as much as he could now or may set it at an extortionate ground rent" (20 July 1747). In the summer and fall of 1747, Spanish and French privateers raided up the Delaware Bay close to Philadelphia.

As the crisis mounted, Franklin took action—but that will be a major subject in Volume 3.

Conclusion

Previous biographers have generally said that Franklin took little interest in politics until elected to the Pennsylvania Assembly in 1751. In fact, he was active in politics throughout his time in Philadelphia, but until 1748 he had to spend most of his time earning a living. Nevertheless he made time for politics as well as engaging in mechanical engineering (e.g., the Pennsylvania stove), natural philosophy, and civic projects. Sometimes printing and publishing allowed him to unite politics with his business; more often his active roles in politics took precious time from his various business activities and from his numerous vocations.

FOURTEEN

Firefighter

As this Association is intended for a general Benefit, we do further agree, that when a Fire breaks out in any part of this City, though none of our Houses Goods or Effects may be in any apparent Danger, we will nevertheless repair thither with our Buckets, Bags and Fire Hooks, and give our utmost Assistance to such of our Fellow Citizens as may stand in need of it, in the same Manner as if they belonged to this Company.—2:375

MOST URBAN COLONIAL HOUSES were made of wood and were heated during the winter by brick fireplaces. Every colonial city had occasional fires, all of which were potentially disastrous. At the cry of "Fire! Fire!" citizens rushed from bed to help fight the inferno. Thieves and crooks as well as honest citizens turned out; criminals often looted burning buildings. But most people tried to help, bringing their own buckets to the fires, manning pumps, trying to save the goods of threatened or burning households, and sometimes performing heroic feats. Franklin, like almost all able-bodied city dwellers, fought fires. He knew Boston's fire-fighting system and something of the laws supporting it. No doubt he had also, in 1725 and 1726, observed London's firemen. After making Philadelphia's citizens aware of the need for concerted fire-fighting efforts, he cited the Boston system as a possible model, though he probably realized that until Philadelphia had a disastrous fire, the citizens would not want to pay for an efficient citywide system. Private fire companies might, however, accomplish many of the same ends as the public ones.

Fire broke out about 11 p.m. Friday, 24 April 1730, in a store near William Fishbourne's wharf. Franklin reported in the *Gazette* on 30 April that "before it could be master'd," the fire "consumed all the Stores, &c. on the Wharff, damaged several Houses on that Side the Street, and crossing the Way, seized the fine House of Mr. *J. Dickinson*, with two other Houses adjoining towards *Walnut Street*, which are all ruined. The Loss in the Whole is supposed to be four or five Thousand Pounds." He editorialized, "It is thought that if the People had been provided with good Engines and other suitable Instruments, the Fire might easily have been prevented spreading, as there was but little Wind. There is now a Subscription on Foot for supplying the Town with every Thing necessary of that Nature, which meets with great Encouragement. There was much Thieving at the Fire, and several ill Persons are now in Prison on that Account." Franklin knew that after the fire, the Philadelphia Common Council had resolved on 29 April to purchase three fire engines, 400 buckets, 20 ladders, and 20 fire hooks. Eighteenth-century fire engines, like modern ones, would pump and shoot (though not far) water. The hoses and buckets were made of strips of leather. "Fire hooks" were used to tear off burning wood, especially shingles. At the next major Philadelphia fire, Franklin was able to report (28 December 1732) that "the Engines did abundance of Service."

Brave Men at Fires

Writing under the pseudonym "Pennsilvanus" in the 20 December 1733 *Gazette*, Franklin celebrated brave men at fires. He used the occasion to imply that the heroism displayed by men at fires proved the existence of abstract virtue in most men—though not in all. "Accidental Fires in Houses are most frequent in the Winter and in the Night Time: But neither Cold nor Darkness will deter good People, who are able, from hastening to the dreadful Place, and giving their best Assistance to quench the Flames; nor wicked People from making as much Haste to pilfer; nor others to be idle Spectators. The two latter Sort are not to be easily instructed and made good; and as it is not in my Power to punish them otherwise than by despising them, as all good People do, I shall here neglect to characterize them further." What good would it do to dwell on the wicked or on the lazy? When Franklin reported trials like that of James Prouse and James Mitchel, he did not focus on the crime. Later newspapermen knew that crime stories sold newspapers; if Franklin knew it, he did not use the knowledge. Franklin praised brave men at fires because he thought they deserved praise and because such celebration might inspire future brave actions:

> How pleasing must it be to a thinking Man to observe, that not a Fire happens in this Town, but soon after it is seen and cry'd out, the Place is crowded by active Men of different Ages, Professions and Titles; who, as of one Mind and Rank, apply themselves with all Vigilance and Resolution, according to their Abilities, to the hard Work of conquering the increasing Fire. Some of the chiefest in Authority, and numbers of Good Housekeepers, are ever ready, not only to direct but to labour, and are not seen to shun Parts or Places the most hazardous; and Others who having scarce a Coat in the World besides that on their Backs, will venture that, and their Limbs, in saving of Goods surrounded with Fire, and in rending off flaming Shingles. They do it not for Sake of Reward of Money or Fame: There is no Provision of either made for them. But they have a Reward in themselves, and they love one another.

The appreciative and egalitarian sentiments are a Franklin hallmark. President Bill Clinton quoted parts of the above in his memorial remarks on 9 December 1999 on the six firemen who died fighting a fire in Worcester, Massachusetts.[1] The deaths of hundreds of brave New York firemen on 11 September 2001 reaffirms Franklin's sentiments.

Franklin encouraged his readers in the belief that "every good Man who sees your Performances" will recognize that "here are brave Men, Men of Spirit and Humanity, good Citizens, or Neighbours, capable and worthy of civil Society, and the Enjoyment of a happy Government. We see where these Men are, and what they are busy about; they are not snoring in their Beds after a Debauch; they are not employ'd in any Crimes for Concealment whereof the Vicious chuse the Night Season, nor do they prefer their own Ease at Home to the Safety of other Peoples Fortunes or Lives." He then used a declamatory style[2] to imagine a series of scenes: "See there a gallant Man who has rescu'd Children from the Flames!—Another receives in his Arms a poor scorch'd Creature escaping out at a Window!—Another is loaded with Papers and the best Furniture, and secures them for the Owner.—What daring Souls are cutting away the flaming Roof to stop the Fires Progress to others!—How vigorously do these brave Fellows hand along the Water and work the Engines, and assist the Ladders; and with what Presence of Mind, Readiness and Clearness, do these fine Men observe, advise and direct. Here are Heroes and effective Men fit to compose the Prime of an Army, and to either lay or defend a Siege or Storm." Franklin implicitly compared brave men at fires to Homeric demigods. With exceptions (e.g., the picaresque novel), the heroes of eighteenth-century fiction were usually aristocrats or persons of supposedly high station (thus Henry Fielding's Tom Jones turns out to be the son of Mr. Allworthy's sister), but Franklin's colonial firefighters anticipate the ordinary persons who are the heroes of later American fiction. He asks and answers the question, is it the times or the particular individual qualities that make persons great? It is the occasion; when needed, normal people often become heroes.

Pennsilvanus, as the pseudonym implies, identified with the area: "This little City, but esteem'd great of its Age, owes not more at this Day for its long Streets and fair Stories, to Architects of any kind, than to those worthy Inhabitants, who have always started at the first Warning, to oppose and vanquish the Rage of Fire." Franklin's speaker also reveals a class consciousness in expressing contempt for wealthy persons concerned about their dress (some persons, besides those wearing "costly Clothes," might be concerned about ruining their clothing): "Besides the Pains freely taken by a great many good People in putting out Fires, some are at the Expence of Buckets and Ladders; without which the Business could not be done. And if it be a Duty incumbent on all that can afford it, to provide such useful Implements, I am of Opinion that it is most so on those, who being decrepit or infirm, cannot assist in Person; or who wearing costly Clothes, would not risque their being spoil'd."

The purpose of Franklin's 1733 piece "Brave Men at Fires" was primarily to praise the heroic actions of those who voluntarily helped in emergencies, partly to assess the basic nature of human beings, and partly to encourage future bravery in emergencies. The conclusion, typical of Franklin's practical turn of mind, made recommendations to improve fire fighting. Franklin deliberately pub-

Pennſylvania GAZETTE.

Containing the freſheſt Advices Foreign and Domeſtick.

From December 13. to December 20. 1733.

To the Publiſher of the GAZETTE.

AN experienc'd Writer has ſaid, there was never a great Man that was not an induſtrious Man, and I believe that there never was a good Man that was a lazy Man. This may ſerve to introduce a few Thoughts I have had while meditating on the Circumſtances of Buildings on Fire, and the Perſons there gather'd. Accidental Fires in Houſes are moſt frequent in the Winter and in the Night Time: But neither Cold nor Darkneſs will deter good People, who are able, from haſtening to the dreadful Place, and giving their beſt Aſſiſtance to quench the Flames; nor wicked People from making as much Haſte to pilfer; nor others to be idle Spectators. The two latter Sort are not to be eaſily inſtructed and made good; and as it is not in my Power to puniſh them otherwiſe than by deſpiſing them, as all good People do, I ſhall here neglect to characterize them further.

The brave Men who at Fires are active and ſpeedy with their beſt Advice and Example, or the Labour of their Hands, are uppermoſt in my Thoughts. This kind of Induſtry ſeems to me a great Virtue. He that is afraid to leave a warm Bed, and to dawb or tear his Clothes or his Skin; He that makes no Difference between Virtue and Vice, and takes no Pleaſure in Hoſpitality; and He that cares not who ſuffers, if he himſelf gains by it, or ſuffers not; will not any one of them, be induſtriouſly concern'd (if their own Dwellings are out of Danger) in preſerving from devouring Flames either private or publick Buildings.

But how pleaſing muſt it be to a thinking Man to obſerve, that not a Fire happens in this Town, but ſoon after it is ſeen and cry'd out, the Place is crowded by active Men of different Ages, Profeſſions and Titles; who, as of one Mind and Rank, apply themſelves with all Vigilance and Reſolution, according to their Abilities, to the hard Work of conquering the increaſing Fire. Some of the chiefeſt in Authority, and numbers of good Houſekeepers, are ever ready, not only to direct but to labour, and are not ſeen to ſhun Parts or Places the moſt hazardous; and Others who having ſcarce a Coat in the World beſides that on their Backs, will venture that, and their Limbs, in ſaving of Goods ſurrounded with Fire, and in rending off flaming Shingles. They do it not for Sake of Reward of Money or Fame: There is no Proviſion of either made for them. But they have a Reward in themſelves, and they love one another. If it were prudent to mention Names, and could Virtue be prais'd without Danger of Envy and Calumny riſing againſt her, I ſhould rejoyce to know a ſkilful Pen employ'd, to diſtinguiſh, in lively Expreſſions and ſignificant Language, Men ſo deſerving.

This poor Paper ſhall praiſe them altogether; and while neither its Author nor they are nam'd, Virtue will be its

own Reward, and Envy and Calumny have no Body to point at. Ye Men of Courage, Induſtry, and Goodneſs, continue thus in well doing; and if you grow not oſtentatious, it will be thought by every good Man who ſees your Performances; here are brave Men, Men of Spirit and Humanity, good Citizens, or Neighbours, capable and worthy of civil Society, and the Enjoyment of a happy Government. We ſee where theſe Men are, and what they are buſy about; they are not ſnoring in their Beds after a Debauch; they are not employ'd in any Crimes for Concealment whereof the Vicious chuſe the Night Seaſon, nor do they prefer their own Eaſe at Home to the Safety of other Peoples Fortunes or Lives. See there a gallant Man who has reſcu'd Children from the Flames!— Another receives in his Arms a poor ſcorch'd Creature eſcaping out at a Window!—Another is loaded with Papers and the beſt Furniture, and ſecures them for the Owner.— What daring Souls are cutting away the flaming Roof to ſtop the Fires Progreſs to others!—How vigorouſly do theſe brave Fellows hand along the Water and work the Engines, and aſſiſt the Ladders; and with what Preſence of Mind, Readineſs and Clearneſs, do theſe fine Men obſerve, adviſe and direct. Here are Heroes and effective Men fit to compoſe the Prime of an Army, and to either lay or defend a Siege or Storm.

This little City, but eſteem'd great of its Age, owes not more more at this Day for its long Streets and fair Stories, to Architects of any kind, than to thoſe worthy Inhabitants, who have always ſtarted at the firſt Warning, to oppoſe and vanquiſh the Rage of Fire.

Beſides the Pains freely taken by a great many good People in putting out Fires, ſome are at the Expence of Buckets and Ladders; without which the Buſineſs could not be done. And if it be a Duty incumbent on all that can afford it, to provide ſuch uſeful Implements, I am of Opinion that it is moſt ſo on thoſe, who being decrepid or infirm, cannot aſſiſt in Perſon; or who wearing coſtly Clothes, would not riſque their being ſpoil'd. But ſuch as can neither adviſe nor labour, ſhould not ſtand in the Way of others who can, and are willing.

It is true indeed, as well among Men as Bees, that ſome Drones are in every Hive or Swarm; but I hope there are few ſo void of Conſideration, and Regard to private and publick Safety, as a vagibond Fellow at the late Fire, who, being ſmartly aſk'd by an induſtrious young Man, why he did not lend a Hand to the Buckets, anſwer'd, He car'd not if all the Houſes in Town were o'Fire: For which he receiv'd a Bucket of Water on his impudent Face. This was a fit Reward, as it was near at Hand and took up a little Time to give it, but I doubt not a large Majority of People think with me, that he deſerves a Puniſhment much greater and more exemplary.

December 1. 1733. *Pennſilvanus.*

Figure 23. Franklin celebrates "Brave Men at Fires," Pennsylvania Gazette, 20 December 1733. Franklin probably wrote this essay on firefighters initially for presentation in the Junto as a first step in his effort to start a volunteer fire company. Three years later, after he had published another piece on fires, he succeeded in starting the Union Fire Company. President Bill Clinton quoted parts of Franklin's essay in his memorial remarks, 9 December 1999, on the six firemen who had just died fighting a fire in Worcester, Massachusetts. The deaths of numerous New York firemen on 11 September 2001 reaffirmed for many persons Franklin's appreciation of brave men at fires. Courtesy of the Library Company of Philadelphia.

lished the essay while the Pennsylvania Assembly was meeting in Philadelphia. The assembly, however, did nothing.

Perhaps Andrew Bradford chafed at the good reception of Franklin's civic-minded article on fire fighting. The *American Weekly Mercury* ostensibly scooped Franklin on 22 January 1733/4 by reporting that "On Wednesday last was play'd at the Court-House, a new *Fire-Engine*, made in this City, which threw the Water much higher than the largest this City had from London. 'Tis said that several others are to be made by the same Man, which 'tis thought will be much better than this, it being the first he ever made." Anthony Nicholas made the fire engine. He attempted to sell it to the Philadelphia Common Council on 21 July 1735, asking £89.11.8 for it. But the committee that examined the engine, Alderman Samuel Hassell and councilmen Israel Pemberton, Peter Stretch, and James Steel, reported to the Philadelphia Common Council on 28 July 1735, that "the sd Engine made by Anthony, is very heavy, Unwieldy, & requires much Labour to Work the Same, that some parts are made of wood which ought to have been Brass, & that they conceive that the sd Engine will not last Long." Nothing further was heard of Nichols's fire engine. Though Nichols's machine was inferior, fire engines were useful. On 18 April 1734, reporting the news of Philadelphia's latest fire, Franklin wrote, "It is thought by some that the Engines sav'd the Town several Thousand Pounds that Day." Just over a year later, he attempted to make some useful suggestions concerning fire fighting.

HINTS ON THE SUBJECT OF FIRES

After the 1730 fire Franklin wrote a paper, which he first read in the Junto, "on the different Accidents and Carelessnesses by which Houses were set on fire, with Cautions against them, and Means proposed of avoiding them" (A 102). Revising it for publication on 4 February 1735, Franklin echoed a thought from his earlier piece "Brave Men at Fires" and adopted the persona of a "decrepit or infirm" person who wanted to help fight fires but could no longer physically do so. Since the benevolent old man could no longer physically help, he tried to serve in another way. He (i.e., Franklin) wrote, "Being old and lame of my Hands, and thereby uncapable of assisting my Fellow Citizens, when their Houses are on Fire; I must beg them to take in good Part the following Hints on the Subject of Fires." He began with fire prevention. "Take Care how they suffer living Brands-ends, or Coals in a full Shovel, to be carried out of one Room into another, or up or down Stairs, unless in a Warmingpan shut; for Scraps of Fire may fall into Chinks, and make no Appearance till Midnight; when your Stairs being in Flames, you may be forced, (as I once was) to leap out of your Windows, and hazard your Necks to avoid being over-roasted" (2:12). Franklin's diction undercut what could be a serious predicament and turned it into a slightly ludicrous picture of the man leaping out a window "to avoid being over-roasted."

The old man urged that the "Act for preventing Fires" be revised to prohibit "too shallow Hearths" and "the detestable Practice of putting wooden Mould-ings on each side the Fire Place, which being commonly of Heart-of-Pine and full of Turpentine, stand ready to flame as soon as a Coal or a small Brand shall roul [roll] against them." Chimneys should be frequently and carefully cleaned, and chimney sweeps "ought to be licensed by the Mayor; and if any Chimney fires and flames out 15 Days after Sweeping, the Fine should be paid by the Sweeper; for it is his Fault." Though the town had enough fire engines, he questioned whether "water enough can be had to keep them going for half an Hour together" (2:12–13). Public pumps were wanting.

Philadelphia lacked neither hands nor goodwill at a fire, "yet we seem to want Order and Method." The infirm persona cited the example of Boston, where "a Club or Society of active Men" belonged "to each Fire Engine; whose Business is to attend all Fires with it whenever they happen; and to work it once a Quarter, and see it kept in order: Some of these are to handle the Firehooks, and others the Axes, which are always kept with the Engine." When fires broke out, the "Officers appointed by Law, called *Firewards*" took charge. They were instantly recognized as fire authorities by "a red Staff of five Feet long, headed with a Brass Flame of 6 Inches." They directed the fire efforts. On their orders, the axe men opened and stripped roofs, the hook men pulled down burning timbers, and the men on the fire engines directed water at their commands. Disobeying the fire marshals in an emergency was punishable by a fine of 40 shillings or ten days' imprisonment (2:13–14).

As Franklin knew, the Boston system required a public law. Perhaps he hoped the Philadelphia Common Council would make one, though he must have known that the system would cost more than the council would want to spend. In Boston the "Officers, with the Men belonging to the Engine, at their Quarterly Meetings, discourse of Fires, of the Faults committed at some, the good Management in some Cases at others, and thus communicating their Thoughts and Experience they grow wise in the Thing, and know how to com-mand and to execute in the best manner upon every Emergency" (2:14).

The old man/Franklin noted that after Boston established its fire-fighting system, the town had limited the spread of fires. Previously, it had suffered several major conflagrations—and Philadelphia would in the future unless it adopted similar strategies. "For Englishmen feel but cannot see; as the Italian says of us." Franklin later began *Plain Truth* (1747) with this same proverb, meaning that Englishmen felt the present circumstances but did not foresee future probabilities. "And it has pleased God, that in the Fires we have hitherto had, all the bad Circumstances have never happened together, such as dry Sea-son, high Wind, narrow Street, and little or low Water: which perhaps tends to makes [sic] us secure in our own Minds; but if a Fire with those Circumstances, which God forbid, should happen, we should afterwards be careful enough." He argued that roofs should be made of tile or that builders should make "their

Roofs more safe to walk upon, by carrying the Wall above the Eves, in the Manner of the new Buildings in London, and as Mr. [Robert] Turner's House in Front-Street, or Mr. [Edward] Nicholls's in Chestnut-Street." In closing, he asked that "others communicate their Thoughts as freely as I have done mine, and perhaps something useful may be drawn from the Whole" (2:14–15).

Franklin noted in his *Autobiography* that the essay "was much spoken of as a useful Piece, and gave rise to a Project, which soon followed it, of forming a Company for the more ready Extinguishing of Fires, and mutual Assistance in Removing and Securing of Goods when in Danger" (A 102). When a fire occurred in the spring of 1736, Franklin praised the "Diligence, Courage, and Resolution of some active Men" who saved several buildings (20 May).

THE UNION FIRE COMPANY

On 7 December 1736, Franklin and nineteen neighbors, "reposing special Confidence in each others Friendship," formed the Union Fire Company. Franklin had drawn up the ten articles. "Our Articles of Agreement oblig'd every Member to keep always in good Order and fit for Use, a certain Number of Leather Buckets, with strong Bags and Baskets (for packing and transporting of Goods), which were to be brought to every Fire" (A 102). The second article provided that if anyone failed "to provide and keep his Buckets and Baggs," he would pay the company five shillings for every bucket and bag wanting. Third, if any buckets or bags were lost or damaged while fighting a fire, "the same shall be supplyed and repaired at the Charge of the whole Company."

The fourth article spelled out the members' activity at a fire: "THAT we will all of us, upon hearing of Fire breaking out at or near any of our Dwelling Houses, immediately repair to the same with all our Buckets and Baggs, and there employ our best Endeavours to preserve the Goods and Effects of such of us as shall be in Danger by Packing the same into our Baggs: And if more than one of us shall be in Danger at the same time, we will divide our selves as near as may be to be equally helpful." To prevent looting, two members were directed to "attend at the Doors until all the Goods and Effects that can be saved shall be secured in our Baggs, and carryed to some safe Place, to be appointed by such of our Company as shall be present, Where one or more of us shall attend them 'till they can be conveniently delivered to, or secured for, the Owner."

The remaining articles dealt with running the company. Fifth, the members agreed to meet the last Monday of every month "to consider of what may be further useful." Members who missed a meeting had to pay a shilling. The sixth article set forth the company's administration. Each member would serve in turn as the clerk for a month. The clerk was the executive. He would inspect the buckets and bags and report on them at every meeting; collect all the fines; notify every member of the meeting at least six hours beforehand; inform every member of the forthcoming election of new members; read over a copy of the rules and a list of all the members at every meeting; and be accountable to the

Figure 24. *Firefighters and fire-fighting equipment in the mid-eighteenth century. Top half of the meeting notice of the Hand-in-Hand Fire Company, New York. When Franklin and his friends started the Union Fire Company in 1736, the members agreed to each keep two buckets and a bag; in 1739 they agreed to each keep four buckets; and in 1741, they agreed to keep also a fire hook. In 1742, the company voted to buy a fire engine. In 1743, the members agreed that each would keep six buckets, four cloth bags, one basket, and one fire hook—all ready, in good condition, in case of a fire. In 1746, the company bought six ladders.*

A card of about 1750 announcing a meeting of New York's Hand-in-Hand Fire Company shows firefighters with their equipment, which was similar to that kept by the Union Fire Company members.

At the top, a house is on fire. In the left center, men have formed two lines from the pump to the fire engine, one line passing the full buckets of water for the fire engine, which is shooting a stream of water into the burning building, and the other line returning the empty buckets back to the pump. In the lower left, two men with fire hooks are running to the fire. In the lower middle, men are bringing up ladders. On the right side, middle and lower, men with their bags are carrying off goods from the burning building. Two men in the middle are carrying a basket full of goods. Courtesy, New York Public Library.

company for, and turn over to the next succeeding clerk, all the company's money. Any member who refused to serve as clerk would forfeit five shillings.

The seventh article set the membership at twenty-five and specified that no new member could be admitted, nor any alteration made in the articles, until the meeting after the proposal. Further, the entire company had to be acquainted with any proposed changes by the clerk. Whereas normal business could be approved by three-fourths of the members present, revisions of the articles had to be approved by three-fourths of the total number of members. The eighth article called for each member to keep two lists of all the members, one fixed in open view near the buckets and bags, and the other to be produced at every meeting if required, with a fine of six pence for noncompliance. Ninth, all fines would be paid to the clerk for the use of the company. If any member refused to pay, he would be excluded. Finally, upon the death of a member, the others would aid his widow, just as if her husband had been living; she only keeping buckets and bags. Twenty persons signed the agreement.

Members

Four founding members were among Franklin's close friends: William Parsons (1701–57), William Plumsted (1708–65), Hugh Roberts (1706–86), and Philip Syng, Jr. (1703–89). Parsons, Roberts, and Syng were all members of the Junto and the Library Company. Plumsted, merchant, joined Franklin in St. John's Lodge and the Library Company, and later became a trustee of the Academy of Philadelphia. One Union Fire Company member, James Morris (1707–51), a leading pacifist, baker, and merchant, served in the Pennsylvania Assembly. Five members served on the Philadelphia Common Council: John Dillwyn (1693–1748); George House (d. 1754), the Quaker shoemaker who sent Franklin and Meredith their first customer; Joseph Paschall (1699–1741); Edward Roberts (1680–1741), merchant and mayor of Philadelphia (1739–41), the father of Franklin's good friend Hugh Roberts; and Benjamin Shoemaker (1704–67), a distiller. Two others were also members of the Library Company: Samuel Coates (1711–48), merchant; and William Rawle (d. 1741), a director of the Library Company in 1733 and 1734 who ran a ferry between Philadelphia and New Jersey.

In addition, the following persons joined: John Armitt (1702–62), merchant, older brother of Stephen; Stephen Armitt (1705–51), joiner; William Cooper, presumably the Philadelphia merchant who guaranteed the New Castle paper money in 1742 and served as executor of William Rawle's estate; Thomas Hatton (1718?–72), sea captain and merchant, who dropped out when he went on a voyage and was later readmitted; Richard Sewell, attorney and later sheriff; Edward Shippen (1703–81), a merchant, partner of James Logan, and older brother of William Shippen; and Lloyd Zachary (1701–56), physician, later a trustee of the Academy of Philadelphia, whose obituary in the *Pennsylvania Gazette* on 16 December 1756 Franklin probably wrote..

On 30 May 1737 the Union Fire Company elected four additional members. Three were Philadelphia Common Councilmen: George Emlen (1694–1764), brewer; Samuel Powel, Jr. (1705–59), merchant; and Charles Willing (1710–54), merchant, mayor in 1748 and 1754, a captain in the Associators' company no. 1, 1748, and a trustee of the Academy of Philadelphia. Thomas Lloyd (d. 1754), merchant, was the fourth. All these men lived near Franklin, who, from 1728 to 1757, lived at various addresses on Market Street between Front and Fourth

Streets, except from 1748 to 1750, when the Franklins lived two blocks farther west, at the northeast corner of Second and Sassafras (Race) Streets.

FIRES AND BUSINESS

The Union Fire Company began meeting on 27 December 1736, but no minutes were regularly kept until 30 May 1737. Hugh Roberts, the sixth person to serve as clerk, brought a record book to the meeting and kept the first minutes. He noted that "the foregoing Articles were not till now fully compleated and agreed on"; therefore regular minutes had not hitherto been kept. "This Evening the Company (which at present consists of Twenty Persons) met at the House of John Roberts. Absent only William Rawle, William Parsons, & Edward Shippen. Several Persons being nominated as desirous of joining with the Company, the four following were by Ballot unanimously chosen, to wit, Samuel Powel, junr., Thomas Lloyd, George Emlen, & Charles Willing. Hugh Roberts officiated as Clerk, and at the Conclusion of the Meeting deliver'd to his Successor B. Franklin the Company's Book, and 17/6 in cash, which is the Company's present Stock." Noted and signed, "I received it, B. Franklin."

Franklin continued publicizing the dangers of fire. The 26 May 1737 *Gazette* reprinted a news note about the destruction of Panama City. A woman smoking a cigar at night failed to put it entirely out as she went to bed. It started a fire and destroyed the house, "nay the Fire was so contagious that it consumed the City . . . in less than three Hours Time." Three thousand houses, "with all their Riches and Furniture," burned "all to Ashes."

A proposal to increase membership to thirty was made on 28 November 1737, nominating as possible members Thomas Lawrence, Joseph Turner, William Bell, Thomas Hopkinson, Andrew Bradford, and Samuel Rhoads. That night, Joseph Turner's stable and hay burned, and the company fought and extinguished the fire. The following month, the company took no action concerning the proposed new members. Perhaps the members disagreed about the company's ideal size. Franklin wrote in the *Autobiography* that "The Utility of this Institution soon appear'd, and many more desiring to be admitted than we thought convenient for one Company, they were advised to form another; which was accordingly done" (A 102–3).[3]

Not until a year later, 25 December 1738, did three-fourths of the company vote to raise their number to thirty. Then they admitted William Bell (d. 1745), formerly a sea captain, now a merchant; Thomas Lawrence (1689–1754), merchant, partner of James Logan and later of Edward Shippen, Pennsylvania councillor, lieutenant colonel of the militia Association (1748), trustee of the Academy of Philadelphia, and mayor in 1727, 1728, 1734, 1749, and 1754; and Joseph Turner (1701–83), formerly a sea captain, now a merchant and partner of William Allen. All three were among those who had applied to join over a year earlier. One wonders if there were some objection to Thomas Hopkinson or Samuel Rhoads. Perhaps they lived at some distance from the other members or were no longer interested in joining. Andrew Bradford had by then become a charter member of the Fellowship Fire Company, organized 1 March 1738. Thomas Hopkinson became a member of the Hand-in-Hand Fire Company, which was not organized until 1741.[4] The accounts show that Franklin charged Hopkinson's company for a quire book (probably for its minutes) on 28 February 1741/2 and printed its articles of agreement and list of members in March 1741/2.

In 1736 the Union Fire Company met at 6 p.m. from October through February and at 7 p.m. from March through September. At first it met at John Roberts's tavern on High (later Market) Street near the Market, but when Roberts moved to Second Street, the company instead met (30 April 1739) at David Evans's at the sign of the Crown on the south side of Market Street between Second and Third Streets. It last met there on 30 August 1742. Beginning 27 September 1742, it met at Henry Pratt's tavern, at the sign of the Ship a Ground at the northeast corner of High (Market) and Water Streets. When Pratt moved (14 August 1746) two blocks north to the Royal Standard on the north side of Market Street between Second and Third Streets, the company moved with him, continuing to meet at the Widow Pratt's after Henry Pratt's death in April 1749.

At the beginning, Franklin attended the Union Fire Company meetings regularly. He was present at all seven recorded 1737 meetings, and he missed only two in 1738. But once the fire company was successfully operating, Franklin frequently found other use for his time. In 1739 he missed half the monthly meetings. Though each absence cost him a shilling, he attended only twice in 1740. Though Franklin rarely missed a meeting of the Library Company directors, he often absented himself from the Union Fire Company meetings. Its meetings were routine, usually with no business. Ordinarily, the members probably had a social drink and dinner and some gossip about fires.

Parson Weems's Creation

Mason Locke Weems followed his enormously successful *Life of George Washington* (1800; the fifth edition, 1806, first carried the cherry-tree episode) with a *Life of Benjamin Franklin* (1817). For his *Life of Franklin*, Weems made up a story in the form of a letter from "J. Clymer" to Franklin, thanking him for saving Philadelphia from a potentially disastrous fire. As Clymer was going to bed on New Year's Eve 1739, he heard the cry of "FIRE, FIRE, FIRE!" Shortly thereafter, he heard "a most tremendous noise in the streets." Fire engines, "attended by the shouting firemen and crowds of citizens," came up "rattling like thunder." Clymer rushed to the fire, where he saw "the whizzing torrents mounting above the raging flames, and then, arching, come down upon them in drenching showers. Other engines again, leveled direct at the burning buildings, would dash their furious floods against them with astonishing force, bursting in the windows, knocking off the shingles, and scattering their streams around like drowning rains." The next day, 1 January, Clymer wrote Franklin, addressing him as "my revered Sir . . . my great and good Sir . . . my honoured Sir," and thanking him for the machines, which the "public spirited" Franklin "first introduced . . . into this city."

No record of a Philadelphia fire exists for New Year's Eve 1739; no one in 1740 addressed Franklin in such hyperbolic terms; no fire engines in Philadelphia in 1739 or 1740 were capable of shooting up such high water; and only the Philadelphia Corporation, not Franklin's Union Fire Company, had purchased the few small fire engines present in Philadelphia in 1740—though the Union Fire Company would shortly add to them. It's a dramatic story. Not as good as George Washington and the cherry tree—but just as apocryphal.

Another legend concerning Franklin and the Union Fire Company is that he first introduced suspenders, or galluses, as a normal part of a fireman's clothes,[5] but no evidence supports the statement. No reference to any uniform or special fire-fighting clothes turns up in the Union Fire Company minutes to 1776, after which Franklin was no longer active in the company. One authority says that Philadelphia's firemen had no distinguishing apparel until a hat was generally adopted in 1788.[6] When summoned by the cry of "Fire!" the members of the Union Fire Company no doubt wore whatever they happened to have on if it was daytime, and whatever practical clothes happened to be handiest at night.

Equipment

After Franklin's numerous absences from the Union Fire Company meetings in 1740, he evidently resolved to do better. He was present for nine of the twelve monthly meetings in 1741. In 1742, he missed only two. In 1743, he missed half. In 1744, he missed five. Other members also attended sporadically. At the beginning of 1743, the members voted to charge a fine of five shillings for missing three consecutive meetings. For the next several years, Franklin rarely missed three in a row. In 1745, Franklin attended all but two meetings. In 1746, he missed seven, and in 1747 he missed four.

When Franklin organized it, the Union Fire Company could not afford to buy all the desirable equipment. Gradually, however, through small fines, the company built up a treasury for purchasing equipment, and it occasionally received gifts of fire-fighting tools. Thomas Say gave Stephen Armitt a fire hook, which he in turn presented to the company on 24 April 1738. Armitt and Hugh Roberts were asked to procure a chain and rope for the hook and to pay for them from the company stock. The company voted on 26 March 1739 to double the number of buckets so that every member would have four buckets, each purchased at the member's expense. On 25 August 1740 the company voted to buy 54 additional fire buckets from Obadiah Eldridge, paying ten shillings each. On 28 December 1741 the members agreed "that a small Fire Hook might be Necessary to Every member," and Hugh Roberts was requested to procure and pay for them from the company's funds. He gave an accounting on 27 September 1742. Roberts had paid £2.15.6 to Anthony Nicholas (whose fire engine failed to satisfy) for 24 fire hooks; 12 shillings to Joshua Ash for 24 poles at 6d; 1 shilling to Ash for hauling the poles; 6d to Charles Brockden for shaving the poles and fixing the fire hooks; 10 shillings to Samuel Johnson for painting the poles; and 3s 6d to John Rouse for stamping the hooks; in all, £4.10.

The company voted on 29 November 1742 to purchase a fire engine of £12 sterling value from London. Since the company's funds were insufficient, Franklin, John Armitt, John Dillwyn, Syng, Stephen Armitt, James Morris, Samuel Coates, and William Bell each lent five shillings. The company evidently bought it from Richard Newsham of Cloth-Fair, London.[7] After acquiring the pump in the summer of 1743, the members voted to attach wheels to it and asked Franklin on 29 August 1743 to have it done. He did so, presenting John Jones's charge of 11s 5d on 24 September 1744. On 29 July 1745 Joseph Turner submitted his bill for the fire engine itself: "15.6.0; plus Commission and Insurance, 19.11 & 1/4," for a total in sterling of £16.5.11 and 1/4 pence. At the exchange of 60 percent, that amounted to £26.1.5 and 3/4 in Pennsylvania currency, or about half a year's salary for a good artisan.[8]

On 30 December 1745 the company reimbursed Franklin 13s 4d, which he had paid "to the Smith for an Improvement to the Company's Fire Engine." Did the ingenious Franklin devise the unidentified improvement? He was regarded as mechanically talented by his peers, who placed him in charge (26 August 1751) of repairing the fire engine. On 27 January 1745/6 the company voted to purchase and install a pump "to be fixed at the end of the Wharff," appointing Franklin, Hugh Roberts, and Richard Sewall a committee for the purpose. Further, the company decided to buy six ladders. At the same meeting, the members determined that, rather than continuing to rotate the funds monthly, a member should be appointed treasurer. The clerk, however, remained the executive. Two months later, 31 March 1746, the company chose Benjamin Shoemaker treasurer.

THE ARTICLES OF 1743

Franklin combined practicality and idealism in the Union Fire Company's new articles, signed on 31 January 1742/3.[9] They contained the necessary practical matters, but they also stated the Union Fire Company's basic philosophy: "As this Association is intended for a general Benefit, we do further agree, that when a Fire breaks out in any part of this City, though none of our Houses Goods or Effects may be in any apparent Danger, we will nevertheless repair thither with our Buckets, Bags and Fire Hooks, and give our utmost Assistance to such of our Fellow Citizens as may stand in need of it, in the same Manner as if they belonged to this Company."

"A general Benefit"—how like Franklin!

Article one reflected the change from two buckets, four cloth bags, and one basket to the new requirements: six buckets (four had been agreed upon on 26 February 1739), four bags, and one fire hook (as agreed upon 28 December 1741).

Article four had major changes. Experience had taught the members more about fire fighting, and the article spelled out in greater detail what they should do. "Upon our first hearing the Cry of Fire in the Night-time we will immediately cause two or more Lights to be set up in our Windows; and such of our Company whose Houses may be thought in Danger shall likewise place Candles in every Room, to prevent Confusion, and that their Friends may be able to give them the more speedy and effectual Assistance." Article four added a two-shilling fine for members who neglected to help, "unless they can assign some reasonable Cause to the Satisfaction of the Company."

Article five attempted to counter the frequent absences by reinstating the old fine of one shilling for missing a meeting and increasing the fine to five shillings if one missed three meetings in a row. Franklin, Thomas Lawrence, and Edward Shippen each paid five shillings on 27 June 1743 for missing the previous three meetings. Article six raised the fine for refusing to serve as clerk from five to ten shillings. And article seven reflected the change in membership from twenty-five to thirty, and declared that a simple majority, rather than three-fourths, could enact the company's business. Franklin printed the articles, charging £3.5 on 31 October 1743.

Of the original members, Joseph Paschall, William Rawle, and Edward Roberts had died. Thomas Hatton, a sea captain and merchant, had gone to sea. George House had dropped out, as had the later member Charles Willing. The company therefore elected nine new members when adopting the new articles: John Bard (1716–79) was a physician. Peter Bard (1714–69), merchant, owned the Mt. Holly Iron Works. Charles Jones was an original Schuylkill Fishing Company member. William Logan (1718–76), son of James Logan, was a merchant, Philadelphia Common Councillor, and a Pennsylvania provincial councillor. Reese Meredith (1708–78), Oxford-educated, was a merchant. Luke Morris (1717–93), owner of a ropewalk, was a Junto member who became a director of the Philadelphia Contributionship. Samuel Morris (1711–79), merchant, tanner, and Common Councillor of Philadelphia, belonged to the Library Company and became a manager of the Pennsylvania Hospital and a trustee of the Academy of Philadelphia. Samuel Neave (1707?–74), merchant, was also an original member of the Schuylkill Fishing Company. Charles Norris (1712–66), merchant, later became a manager of the Pennsylvania Hospital.[10]

BUSINESS, 1743–1747

The nozzles of most Philadelphia water pumps were mischievously removed on Saturday night, 24 November 1744, and the Union Fire Company members decided that the prank threatened their fire-fighting ability. They offered a £5 reward to whoever "shall discover any of the Persons concern'd in removing the said Nossels or doing any other Damage to the Pumps in the Streets whereby they may be render'd incapable of discharging Water." Franklin printed the notice in the *Gazette* beginning 29 November 1744 and continuing, with lapses, through 26 March 1745. On 25 March, the company paid him ten shillings for the ad. On 29 April 1745, Thomas Hatton, the sea captain and an original member (no. 13), was readmitted in the place of the deceased William Bell. Samuel Preston Moore (1710–85), physician, who became a treasurer of the Pennsylvania Hospital in 1768, was chosen a member on 27 January 1746 in place of Dr. John Bard. On 30 November 1747, the company admitted John Mifflin (1715–59), merchant, later director of the Philadelphia Contributionship and an assemblyman in 1762; and Thomas Stretch (1695–1765), a Quaker clockmaker, original member and first governor of the Schuylkill Fishing Company, a neighbor on Second Street, and son of Peter Stretch, a Philadelphia city councilman.

FIRE FIGHTING

Fire fighting by the Union Fire Company members is not mentioned in the minutes, though they record payment for equipment lost at fires. Some information can be gathered from the newspaper reports on the fires. The earliest note in the minutes is Thomas Lloyd's loss of a bucket at Joseph Turner's fire (26 November 1737). The next year, the *Gazette* reported a fire in a store near William Fishbourne's wharf (15 February 1738), and in the fall, a fire occurred at Mr. Clark's near Black-Horse-Alley (30 November *Gazette*). On 6 February 1739, "A Fire broke out at the upper End of Front-street, & burnt down three or four Houses in a short Time." We know the Union Fire Company members turned out, for Edward Roberts lost a bucket "at the fire by John Norris's" (26 February minutes). In 1740, the only fire reported in the *Gazette* was "Mr. Hamilton's fire" (3 April 1740). Early on Sunday morning, 17 May 1741, "a Fire broke out in a House at the Upper End of Front Street, near the Ship yards . . . the People sav'd their Goods, and it was extinguished before it got to the second Floor." At this fire, William Plumsted and Charles Willing each lost a bag, and Philip Syng had a bucket damaged.

Along with other members of the Union Fire Company, Franklin fought a major conflagration at about 2 a.m. on Wednesday, 5 January 1742/3. The fire

broke out in *Water-Street*, at the Blockmaker's Shop, near the *Rose and Crown*; and the Chief Buildings thereabouts being Wood, it presently got to such a Head, that tho' no Industry was wanting, it could not be mastered till 6 or 7 Dwelling Houses, besides Stores, &c. were reduced to Ashes. *William Clymer*, Blockmaker, *John Ryan*, Merchant, *Thomas Say*, Sadler, *Thomas Ingram*, Tavern-keeper, *Robert Hopkins*, Baker, & others, were burnt out, and the Fire was so sudden, that some of them sav'd but very little, and others none of their Goods, (except Mr. *Say* who sav'd almost everything by the Diligence of the Fire-Company, of which he was a member.) The Engines and leather Buckets were of vast Service; a strong Party Wall, with a Battlement above the Roof, contributed very much to the Saving of Mr. *Till*'s new House, and consequently the rest of the Row towards Market-Street, the Wind, tho' there was not much, being that

Way.—-Collections are making for the Sufferers, which we hear amount already to 7 or 8 hundred Pounds; one Gentleman having given 100 Pistoles, and others very considerable Sums.

Franklin's account of the fire (which echoes his earlier appreciation of fire walls, 4 February 1734/5) appeared in the 13 January 1742/3 *Gazette*. It noted the "vast Service" of engines and leather buckets, and stressed the advantage of belonging to a fire company. Thomas Say belonged to the Fellowship Fire Company.[11] Franklin added, "We hear there are several New Companies erecting in Town for mutual Assistance in Case of Fire." In effect, he urged the reader, "Join!"[12]

Advertisements in the 27 January 1742/3 paper show that Franklin, along with numerous others, fought the 5 January fire: "Lost at the late Fire in Water-Street, two Leather Buckets, marked B. FRANKLIN & Co. Whoever brings them to the Printer hereof, shall be satisfied for their Trouble." The next week, 2 February, another ad for fire-fighting equipment appeared: "Lost at the late Fire, two leather Buckets, marked W. PLUMSTED & Co., one Ditto, marked E. SHIPPEN & Co., one ozenbrigs Bag, marked E. SHIPPEN & Co., one ozenbrigs Bag, marked AR & Co., one Ditto, marked WP & Co., two ditto, marked SA & Co, one ditto, marked RS & Co. Whoever brings them or any of them to John Armitt, in Front Street, shall be satisfied for their Trouble." Judging from the marks on the equipment lost, at least John and Stephen Armitt, William Plumsted, Edward Shippen, Richard Sewall, and "AR" (perhaps he belonged to another fire company) fought the fire with Franklin.

In a 2 February 1743 note, Franklin editorialized, "The Town has been twice alarm'd by Fire within this Week past. The first was occasion'd by a foul Chimney which set Fire to the Roof of a Kitchen. The other by boiling or burning Oil for Painting, which flowing over upon the Floor endanger'd the House. Boiling Oil is a wild ungovernable Thing: such Business should never be done within Doors." As for Franklin's buckets, either they were not returned or he lost two more in another fire later that year, for on 31 October 1743 he charged the company £1 for two buckets.

The *Pennsylvania Gazette* reported a fire on Second Street (11 January 1744); on Chestnut Street (29 January 1745); and on Seventh Street, near the statehouse (3 April 1746). It did not, however, report the fire in December or January 1745/6 where Hugh Roberts lost a bucket (27 January minutes). Nor did it report the fire in March or April 1747 where Franklin lost a bag (27 April minutes). From 1736 through 1757, we can be sure that Franklin and the other members of the Union Fire Company rushed out to help in every Philadelphia fire.

At the December 1747 meeting, Franklin proposed an extraordinary meeting of the company for 4 January 1748, "to consider investing their present cash in the Association lottery." Franklin described that meeting in the *Autobiography*, and I will discuss it in the first chapter of Volume 3, devoted to Franklin's voluntary militia association. He also started a fire insurance company in 1751 within the Union Fire Company, but that story will also be told in Volume 3. Until 1757, when he knew he was shortly going to go to England at the behest of the Pennsylvania Assembly, he remained a member of the company.

It may have been Franklin or Syng who proposed on 30 July 1750 that the company purchase a fire bell. On 27 August the company voted £25 toward the cost and asked Syng and Franklin to apply to the other fire companies to see what they would contribute. The only other company with sufficient funds to help was the Hand-in-Hand Company. On 30 September 1751 the Union Fire Company ordered that Daniel Benezet be paid the £50 and send for a fire bell. After it arrived, the Union Fire Company noted on 24 February 1751/2 that Benezet was owed an additional £16.2. The next month, 30 March 1752, the company appointed Franklin and Syng a committee to consult with the Hand-in-Hand Company on where to place the bell and suggested the new Academy of Philadelphia as a location. The 27 April minutes show that the Hand-in-Hand Fire Company agreed and further said that it would pay one-half of the additional charge. Philadelphia's first fire alarm was placed at the academy.

By the mid-1750s Franklin was increasingly out of town or so busy that he rarely attended Union Fire Company meetings. In 1756 he was present only for the May and September meetings. The latter was the last meeting he attended before he left on his first English agency. In 1757 he paid fines for nonattendance through March. On 25 April 1757, the Union Fire Company minutes noted that Franklin was "Excused his Quarterly fine being gon for England." Throughout his first English agency (1757–62), the Union Fire Company continued to list Franklin as absent every meeting and to waive his fines until late 1762, after he returned to Philadelphia.

By 1762, the company met only every other month, at William Whitebread's, the King Arms on Second Street. Franklin attended on 29 November 1762. In 1763 he was present only on 31 January and the special meeting on 14 February. In 1764 he never attended but evidently paid fines for absence until 26 November, when the minutes noted that he would be excused further fines until his return. Franklin arrived back in Philadelphia from his second English agency (1764–75) on 5 May 1775, and the Union Fire Company fined him 2 shillings for absence on 31 July 1775. He attended a meeting on 25 September 1775 for the first time since 1763. The company now met at the George Inn, at the corner of Second and Arch Streets. Franklin continued to pay fines, but this is the only meeting that the minutes record he attended during this Philadelphia stay (1775–77). In the back of the minute book, however, an account of absences from March 1775 through March 1776 lists Franklin as absent in May and July but present in September (as confirmed by the minutes) and November 1775, and then absent in January and March 1776. So he presumably also attended the November 1775 meeting.

The 1775 members included a few people who had belonged to the company in the 1730s and 1740s, but most were new. Three former members were Samuel Morris, Luke Morris, and Samuel P. Moore. Two members had signed the articles of 31 January 1743: William Fishbourne and Israel Pemberton. Three more were among those who signed before Franklin left Philadelphia in 1757: Philip Benezet, Thomas Wharton, and Joshua Howell. Those who were probably new[13] to Franklin in the Union Fire Company were Joseph Wharton, Jr., Samuel Purviance, Samuel Hudson, William Wishart, Thomas Foxcraft, Enoch Story, Charles Moore, Josh. Pemberton, Peter Stretch, William Forbes, Samuel Howell, Jr., John Lownes, Joseph Paschall, Joel Evans, Samuel Wheeler, and Robert Hopkins, Jr.

When he returned to Philadelphia in 1785, Franklin was no longer considered a member. By that time, the seventy-nine-year-old Franklin was too frail to be a fire fighter.[14] He may have helped, however, by keeping fire-fighting equipment and contributing advice and funds, as he had called on old people to do in his essays "Brave Men at Fires" (1733) and "Hints on the Subject of Fires" (1735).

Conclusion

By 1747 Philadelphia had six fire companies.[15] At the December 1747 meeting, the Union Fire Company ordered John Mifflin and Hugh Roberts to be a committee "to request the other Fire Companys of this City to Appoint Committees from their several Companys to Join with them to Enquire into the Condition of all the Fire Engines in this City and make Report thereof at the next meeting." That initiated the movement toward cooperation of the various fire companies. Nearly four years later, 30 September 1751, Franklin and Philip Syng reported that they had met with the representatives of seven other fire companies who had agreed to have a quarterly meeting where all the fire engines would be brought together and tried out. With that resolve, fire fighting came of age in Philadelphia. Thereafter, the fire companies met together quarterly to practice with their engines and equipment—and probably to compete with one another. The Union Fire Company and Franklin had set the pattern for fire fighting. The merger of the personnel and machinery of the various fire companies and the Philadelphia City Council's equipment had together created an efficient citywide fire-fighting organization. Another of Franklin's ideas and his sustained effort had improved the lives of Philadelphia's citizens—and, perhaps, saved lives.

FIFTEEN

Earning a Living: Printer, Publisher, Merchant, Bookseller, and Postmaster

I accepted it [the Philadelphia postmastership] readily, and found it of great Advantage; for tho' the Salary was small, it facilitated the Correspondence that improv'd my Newspaper, encreas'd the Number demanded, as well as the Advertisements to be inserted, so that it came to afford me a very considerable Income.—A 101

DESPITE INITIATING SEVERAL CIVIC PROJECTS and fulfilling numerous responsibilities, Franklin devoted most of his time from 1736 through 1747 to earning a living. He was primarily a printer and publisher, but peripheral aspects of printing and shopkeeping developed into major businesses. The small retail shop accompanying most printing presses developed into a profitable retail store. The few common books sold by most printers were constantly augmented until Franklin's shop became an important new and secondhand bookstore. The necessity for constant quantities of paper motivated Franklin to become the most important wholesale paper merchant in the colonies. And the newspaper editor's desire for news and for the distribution of the papers made Franklin anxious to become Philadelphia's postmaster.

PRINTER AND PUBLISHER

Job printing (i.e., handbills, advertisements, blank forms, posters, and other small pieces) was the bread and butter of every colonial printer. Surviving job printings were not generally collected or valued before 1974, when C. William Miller initiated the bibliographical study of such items in *Benjamin Franklin's Philadelphia Printing*.[1] Most printers, including Franklin, published hundreds of job printings every year. Though the amount of money charged for printing such items was small, the total was profitable. For a handbill printed on a half sheet, Franklin charged one penny apiece if the order was for 300 or more. At one cent, 300 would cost 15 shillings or £1.3. Most persons purchased only one copy of a form: a bill of sale sold for three pence, a power of attorney or a bond cost four pence, and an apprentice's indenture cost eight pence a pair (both parties wanted a copy).

The second mainstay of Franklin's printing business was government printing. For Pennsylvania (1730–66); the Three Lower Counties (1730–52); and New Jersey (1740–48),[2] Franklin printed the official documents. These usually consisted of the *Votes and Proceedings* of the House (none from Delaware is known), the laws and acts passed, and the governor's proclamations. He also printed Pennsylvania's Indian treaties. As with most government jobs, he printed additional copies that he could sell to the public. In some cases, after printing the hundred or so copies paid for by the government, he printed hundreds more if he thought they might sell (e.g., the Lancanster Indian treaty, 1744). In addition, Franklin printed paper currency for these colonies—perhaps the most profitable single employment for a colonial printer. Franklin received £394.5 for Pennsylvania's £80,000 paper currency issue (the largest he ever printed) of 10 August 1739; and £185.8.4 for its £10,000 issue of 1 August 1744. Before his retirement at the beginning of 1748, Franklin had printed eleven paper currency issues: four for Pennsylvania, four for New Jersey, and three for Delaware, plus a small private issue for a merchant. Earlier, with Samuel Keimer he printed the New Jersey paper money of 25 March 1728, and he probably printed the Delaware money of 1729.[3]

The trustees of Pennsylvania's Loan Office lent out the paper currency, so every new currency issue necessitated the printing of Loan Office mortgage bonds.[4] These were among the more profitable blank forms. In 1737 Franklin printed the mortgage bonds for the 16 August 1733 New Jersey bill. (Since currency bills had to be approved in England before the bills could be circulated and bonds could be issued, the actual printing is later than the date the colony passed the money bill.) The borrower received one copy of the form, and the Loan Office trustees kept a copy. Franklin supplied the Loan Office of each county with a bound copy of blank mortgage bonds. Showing his inclination to try to organize and systematize, he added at the front of each book a set of narrow rubricated folio leaves to index the mortgagers' names. No one seems to have done so previously.[5]

To show something of Franklin's business in various legal forms, I will itemize the major orders for forms printed on credit in 1739. Franklin twice printed mortgages and associated items for Charles Brockden, clerk of the Pennsylvania Loan Office. In March he printed 50 mortgages, counterparts, bonds, and bonds & warrants. On 10 December 1739, he charged for printing Pennsylvania's mortgage bonds for the 1739 reemission and further striking of £11,110. Brockden paid him 5 shillings for printing 600 mortgages; another 5 shillings for 600 counterparts; another 5 shillings for 600 bonds and warrants; and finally, another 5 shillings for 600 records. For binding the records, Franklin charged 12 shillings, and for covering the records, another 12 shillings. In all, the December 10 charge to Brockden was £2.12.[6] These are only the major orders for forms he printed on credit and represent a small portion of the total number that he sold. From printing thousands of such forms, Franklin made a profitable business.

At least as important financially as job printing and government printing were two recurring imprints: the *Pennsylvania Gazette*, published weekly; and the annual almanac *Poor Richard*. A subscription to the *Pennsylvania Gazette* cost ten shillings a year. The sale of single issues was not uncommon, and the usual charge was three pence. Franklin had over a thousand newspaper subscribers throughout the period 1736–47. He also printed a broadside carrier's address annually, delivered by the newsboy for a tip on New Year's Day. *Poor Richard* sold for 5 pence; shop owners and others who bought a dozen or slightly more paid 3½ pence per pamphlet; wholesalers who bought in quantity paid 3 pence (i.e., £1.5 per hundred), and partners like James Parker paid £1 per hundred. By 1736 Franklin was selling nearly ten thousand copies annually. Less important financially was the sheet or pocket almanac (to be used as a calendar, without the preface and sayings that accompanied *Poor Richard*). A sheet almanac sold for 1 penny retail; wholesalers paid 8 pence a dozen. Franklin also published almanacs by others, who simply hired him as a printer.

Like other colonial American printers, Franklin brought out pamphlets and books that organizations or individuals paid for. Before the end of the seventeenth century, the Boston booksellers acted as publishers, hiring local printers to typeset works that had a ready market, but no other American town during the colonial period had a similar network of publishers. Colonial printers generally did not publish pamphlets or books except those that were commissioned. Being hired as a printer guaranteed some small profit; publishing was a gamble. The typical colonial printer might take a chance on a broadside, almanac, or small pamphlet but rarely on anything longer. What distinguished Franklin as a printer was the number of items he printed at his own risk. He published more pamphlets and books on his own initiative than any other American printer of his day. Each one was a gamble. If it sold well, Franklin made a profit; if it did not, he lost. He was the primary publisher (though Boston had larger printing shops) in America from the start of his business in 1729 until he retired early in 1748.

In 1736, before becoming clerk of the Pennsylvania Assembly on 14 October, he published three imprints at his own risk: an edition of the Reverend Jonathan Dickinson's captivity narrative, *God's Protecting Providence Man's Surest Help*; another edition of *Every Man His Own Doctor* (he had printed one in 1734); and James Logan's *Charge to the Grand Inquest* of 13 April. Since Logan's *Charge* did not sell, the wealthy Quaker bought a number from Franklin and gave them away. Authors hired Franklin to print three items: The leader of the Ephrata religious community, Conrad Beissel, paid for a supplement to his *Hymns*; Governor Lewis Morris of New Jersey paid for a political tract; and the poet and schoolteacher William Satterthwaite paid for his poem *Mysterious Nothing*, remitting the outstanding ten shilling charge on 16 August 1737. No copies of Dickinson's narrative or of Satterthwaite's poem survive.

Franklin thought Indian treaties were an important political and literary genre. The most interesting government printing of 1737 was *A Treaty of Friend-*

ship Held with the Chiefs of the Six Nations at Philadelphia, in September and October, 1736, advertised on 22 September 1737. Franklin printed it as a folio. Few short publications appeared in large paper format, broadsides being the obvious exception. Generally only long and important publications claimed that distinction. To print a pamphlet in that format allied it with the most important and distinguished books of the times. Franklin also used a large type, generous leading between the lines, and large blank borders. Franklin (and later, Franklin and Hall) subsequently printed numerous Indian treaties, each as a folio. As a group, they are the most aesthetically pleasing products of his press. Thomas Penn, however, judged Franklin foolish for printing them as folios because it made "them look larger than they are."[7]

Richard Peters, the Anglican minister who became secretary to the council and to the proprietors, probably paid Franklin to print his *Two Last Sermons* (15 September), setting forth his differences with the Reverend Archibald Cummings of Christ Church. The Philadelphia Yearly Meeting of Quakers paid for printing two thousand copies of *Instructions for Right Spelling* by George Fox (September). Other than the usual serial publications, the only 1737 imprint Franklin printed at his own risk was Isaac Watts's *Divine Songs Attempted in Easy Language for the Use of Children* (24 March).

The year 1738 was unusual in Franklin's history as a printer: he evidently published nothing at his own risk except the usual serial publications (the newspaper and almanac, the carrier's address and sheet almanac). He had added new duties as a postmaster to his already extraordinarily busy schedule, and, as we have seen, he was also engaged early that year in refuting the false charge that he was involved in a mock Masonic initiation resulting in the death of Daniel Rees.

Franklin's most interesting printing of 1738 was for the eighteenth-century abolitionist Benjamin Lay (1681?–1759), "the singular Pythagorean, cynical, Christian philosopher," who lived in a cave and bought pieces of fine china in order to break them in the public market as symbols of vanity. It was his third abolitionist pamphlet. For the Quaker merchant Ralph Sandiford, he had printed *A Brief Examination of the Practice of the Times* in 1729 and reprinted it under a new title, *The Mystery of Iniquity*, in 1730.[8] Franklin printed Lay's antislavery pamphlet, *All Slave-Keepers That Keep the Innocent in Bondage, Apostates* (though dated 1737, it was published a day or two before 24 August 1738). Authorities have said that Franklin published the book anonymously "for fear of earning the wrath of Philadelphia's elite,"[9] but, like other printers, Franklin often did not put his name on pieces that he printed for pay. It was certainly no secret that he printed it. Franklin advertised the book in his *Gazette* and sold it in his shop.

Lay was ahead of his time and ahead of other Pennsylvania Quakers, who censured the book and disowned Lay on 16 November 1738. Recalling the book forty years later, Franklin said to Benjamin Rush on 3 May 1787 that though the style and organization were "confused," the book "contained just thoughts and good sense but in bad order." Writing a sketch of Lay, Rush later recalled that Franklin told him that when Lay brought him the book to publish, he looked it over and told him that there seemed to be "no order or arrangement in it. 'It is no matter said Mr. Lay—print any part thou pleasest first.'"[10]

Franklin must have had two presses working in his printing shop for most of the 1730s, and he probably added a third press about the time that he bought several new fonts of type in late 1737 or early 1738. He first used the new Caslon type in the *Pennsylvania Gazette* on 4 May 1738. We know that when he turned over his printing shop to David Hall at the beginning of 1748, it included three presses.[11] Of course, he had purchased presses for his partners, beginning with Thomas Whitmarsh on 9 September 1731 and including one for his nephew James Franklin on 27 October 1753. When he ordered the presses, Franklin asked, as we will see in Chapter 18, that they include his own technological improvement.

Mailman

As the editor of a newspaper, it was natural for Franklin to want to become postmaster. A reciprocal relationship existed between postmasters and the colonial American newspaper publishers. The local postmasters often owned the newspapers, which were generally published the day after the post arrived. The postmaster was in the best position to know the latest news. He not only received and gave out letters but also allowed newspapers to be carried post free. Andrew Bradford was the Philadelphia postmaster in 1729 when Franklin purchased the *Pennsylvania Gazette*. Franklin noted that since Bradford "kept the Post Office, it was imagined he had better Opportunities of obtaining News," and consequently "his Paper was thought a better Distributer of Advertisements than mine, and therefore had many more, which was a profitable thing to him and a Disadvantage to me" (A 69).

At first Bradford followed the prevailing practice and allowed Franklin to send the *Gazette* through the mail, but about 1733, as Franklin's paper became successful, Bradford forbade the post riders to carry it. So Franklin bribed them, and the carriers took the papers. Nevertheless, the situation was unsatisfactory. Late in 1734, Franklin appealed to the American postmaster general, Alexander Spotswood of Virginia. Perhaps because Spotswood was unhappy with Bradford, who was delinquent with his payments and accounts, Spotswood granted Franklin's request to have the newspapers carried by the post riders. Franklin promptly advertised in the *Gazette* on 23 January 1734/5 that "By the Indulgence" of Spotswood, he was "allow'd to send the *Gazettes* by the Post, Postage free, to all Parts of the Post-Road from Virginia to New England: So that all Gentlemen and others, living on the Post Roads, may have this Paper sent them by every Post, as usual before the late Obstruction" (A 101).

Bradford lagged further and further behind in accounts and payments to

Spotswood, who grew disgusted with him and offered Franklin the position: "I accepted it readily, and found it of great Advantage; for tho' the Salary was small, it facilitated the Correspondence that improv'd my Newspaper, increas'd the Number demanded, as well as the Advertisements to be inserted, so that it came to afford me a very considerable Income" (A 101).

Franklin began his duties on 5 October 1737. For the publication of his newspaper the next day, Franklin added to his imprint the word *Post-Master*: "PHIL-ADELPHIA: Printed by B. FRANKLIN, Post-Master, at the New Printing Office near the Market. *Price* 10 s. a Year. Where Advertisements are taken in, and Book-Binding done reasonably, in the best Manner." Franklin's advertisements increased dramatically. That day, 6 October, the advertisements took up just over one page, but on 13 October, a week after Franklin announced he had been appointed postmaster, the advertisements occupied more than two pages. For the two years before Franklin became postmaster, the advertisements did not quite average one page; for the two years after, they averaged a page and a half. Franklin recalled in the *Autobiography*: "My old Competitor's Newspaper declin'd proportionably, and I was satisfy'd without retaliating his Refusal, while Postmaster, to permit my Papers being carried by the Riders." Franklin later did retaliate, though at the express command of Spotswood. Franklin noted that Bradford "suffer'd greatly from his Neglect in due Accounting" and drew the moral that businesses "should always render Accounts and make Remittances with great Clearness and Punctuality." Persons known for doing so thereby acquired "the most powerful of all Recommendations to new Employments and Increase of Business" (A 101).

Franklin noted on 3 November "that the Post-Office of *Philadelphia*, is now kept at *B. Franklin*'s in *Market-Street*. And that *Henry Pratt* is appointed RIDING POST MASTER for all the Stages between *Philadelphia* and *Newport* in *Virginia*, who sets out about the Beginning of each Month, and returns in 24 Days, by whom Gentlemen, Merchants and others, may have their Letters, &c. carefully convey'd, and Business faithfully transacted, he having given good Security for the same to the Hon. Col. Spotswood, Post-Master General of all his Majesty's Dominions in *America*."[12]

When Franklin became the Philadelphia postmaster, mail service within the colonies extended from Piscataway (Portsmouth, New Hampshire) to Newport, Virginia. Horses were at great risk on ferries and could not cross when waters were turbulent. Spotswood improved the southern postal service in 1738 by having the post rider from Philadelphia go no further south than the Susquehanna ferry, where he exchanged letters with the Maryland post rider, who went no further south than the Potomac ferry, where he exchanged letters with the Virginia post rider. Spotswood announced in the *Virginia Gazette* on 28 April 1738 that "Riders are engaged so conveniently, that no Post Horse is to cross Patowmack or Susquehanna, by which means the Mail will pass much more certain than usual, it having been often retarded before, by bad weather when it was impossible for a horse to pass these wide Ferries." At the same time, Spotswood announced that postal service now continued as far south as Edenton, North Carolina. On 25 May 1739 he announced that the service extended to Charleston, South Carolina. Rather than increasing Franklin's Philadelphia post office business, the establishment of overland delivery to Charleston may have diminished it. Before 1739, persons in Virginia and Maryland sending mail to the West Indies often directed it to Philadelphia, "from whence Vessels are almost always going to one or other of the Islands" (28 April 1738 *Virginia Gazette*). After May 1739, Virginians probably sent their West Indies letters via Charleston.

The post office was the intelligence center of every colonial town. Not only did the post riders carry the latest news between the larger colonial towns, but law required the ship captains to deliver "Letters and Pacquets on board to the Post-Master, or his Deputy, under the Penalty of *Five Pounds, British Money,* for every several Offence" (*Pennsylvania Gazette*, 15 July 1731). In times of crisis, whenever the post rider was due in or a ship arrived, persons crowded the post office for the latest information. When the New England troops were attacking Cape Breton in the spring of 1745, Franklin mentioned that the Philadelphia post office "was filled with thirty inquiries at the coming in of every post" (3:26). And, of course, discussions of the significance of the latest intelligence took place at the post office.

In the winter, postal service was cut back. Fewer ships sailed, and in the coldest weather the Delaware River froze. Franklin notified the public on 3 January 1738 that the "Northern Post . . . will continue to go once a Fortnight during the Winter Season." Weekly service resumed on 21 March.

Organizing the Post Office

Like every postmaster before him, Franklin tried to put the post office on a cash basis. He advertised, "To prevent the unnecessary Trouble of keeping Accounts, and the Loss that attended delivering Letters on Trust; *No Letters will be delivered hereafter to any Person whatever, without the Money immediately paid.* Which it's hoped will not be taken amiss" (3 January 1738). Bradford had attempted to do the same in the fall of 1736, when he advertised that "for the Future, there will be no Accounts kept for Postage, nor any Letters delivered without Postage paid" (*Mercury*, 21 October 1736). Despite Franklin's resolve, he kept numerous accounts with various individuals, some of whom gradually came to owe him dozens of pounds. By 1753 he was owed over £800 on post office accounts (2:180). Unlike Bradford, however, Franklin promptly accounted to and paid the postmaster general; perhaps, when he did so, he moved the post office debts to those owed him personally.

As Philadelphia postmaster, Franklin improved the postal service, twice showing his organizational ability. He designed and printed a postmaster's waybill, with the heading "From the Post-Office at [blank] to the Post-Office at [blank]." The form had separate categories for "Unpaid Letters," "Paid Letters,"

From the Post-Office at _____ to the Post-Office at _____																			
	Rates.		Unpaid Letters.				Sums due		Paid Letters.				Sums paid		Free Letters.				
	Dwt.	Gr.	S.	D.	T.	P.	Dwt.	Gr.	S.	D.	T.	P.	Dwt.	Gr.	S.	D.	T.	P.	
At	7	16	15				105		1 wanting											
At	7	16	2				15	8												
At	14			1			14													
At	14	16		1			14	16												
At							149													
At																				
At	7			1	2		7													
At																				
At							156													

Figure 25. *Postmaster's waybill, designed by Franklin to organize postmasters' accounts. Like his numbering of the items in the Charter of Pennsylvania, the waybill shows Franklin's efforts to organize and systematize procedures and data.*

The form is headed "From the Post-Office at [Franklin filled in "Philad"] to the Post-Office at" [Boston]. The three categories of letters are the "Unpaid," "Paid," and "Free." Under the first two categories, the form notes: "S. D. T. P.," which stands for a Single sheet, a Double sheet, a Triple sheet, and a Packet. Roughly, the charge between the two cities for a pennyweight (Dwt) letter was one shilling, and the charge for each additional grain (Gr.) was one pence. Reading across the first line, 15 single sheet letters were charged at 7 shillings, for a total of 105 shillings. A note under the "Paid Letters" says "1 wanting," probably referring to one of the 15 single sheet letters. Reading across the second line, there were two single sheet letters which weighed slightly more, 7 pennyweights and 16 grains, for a total of 15 shillings and 8 pence. At the bottom, the total for all the sums due was 156 shillings or £7.16s. The form is signed "June 13, 1745. B. Franklin."

Other colonial postmasters adopted Franklin's form. By 6 January 1746, the deputy postmaster general for North America, Eliot Benger, was purchasing copies for other postmasters and probably requiring them to use the form in reporting their accounts. Courtesy, American Philosophical Society, Philadelphia.

and "Free Letters." Under "Unpaid Letters" the form had columns for the weights (pennyweights and grains) of the various sizes (single sheet, double sheet, treble sheet, or parcel) of letters, then the total weight per category. The little form was sent along with the mail from one post office to another. Just over three inches high and slightly less than eight and a half inches wide, it organized and simplified postal record keeping.

Once other postmasters saw Franklin's form, they purchased copies. After Elliott Benger became postmaster general of North America, he evidently required postmasters to use the form. On 6 January 1746, Franklin billed Benger for 500 copies that he sent to John Nicholls, New York postmaster. Copies of Franklin's form have been found in a number of repositories.[13] Franklin also initiated a major step in improving mail delivery: he began printing in the *Pennsylvania Gazette* lists of persons who had uncalled-for letters at the post office.

In 1738 he printed such lists on 21 March, 11 May, 20 July, and 2 November. He thereby enlisted the public in helping him deliver the mail, for a person's friends or acquaintances would tell him or her that a letter was waiting in the post office.

On 12 October 1739, Alexander Spotswood directed Franklin to commence suit against Andrew Bradford for not settling his accounts for the past four years. Bradford had continually pled with Spotswood that he was sick, but Spotswood had learned that he was well. At the same time, Spotswood forbade Franklin to allow Bradford free use of the post for his letters and papers. Franklin had no alternative and employed John Webbe in the suit. Thereafter, Bradford bribed the carriers, as Franklin had been forced to do earlier. Franklin ignored the bribery.

ALEXANDER SPOTSWOOD

Franklin's relationship with Alexander Spotswood may have influenced the printer's opinions. Spotswood was among the few English officials who became Americanized. After his years as governor (1710–22), Spotswood returned to Virginia to run his iron foundry, the largest in colonial America. In the *New-England Courant* on 31 December 1722, James Franklin had implicitly contrasted the triumphant welcoming procession of Virginia's former governor Spotswood with the surprise departure of the unpopular Massachusetts Governor Samuel Shute. Franklin's known affiliation with Spotswood began with post office business, but Franklin may have known him before appealing to him in 1734. Spotswood no doubt corresponded with Franklin before asking him to assume the position of Philadelphia postmaster in 1737. Thereafter, the two must have corresponded frequently on post office business, though no letters between them are extant. If the former Virginia governor visited Philadelphia after 1737, he would have called on Franklin, and Franklin on him. Records, however, of Spotswood's activities during the 1730s and 1740s are few. Nevertheless, the accounts of the Philadelphia shoemaker William Meade suggest that Spotswood visited Philadelphia, that Franklin and Spotswood became friends, and that Franklin performed helpful chores for him. Meade charged Franklin on 18 April and on 16 and 17 May 1740 for shoes for "thy friend spotswood." After Spotswood appointed Franklin postmaster in 1737, Spotswood probably relied on Franklin to carry out any business he had in Philadelphia.

If Spotswood and Franklin spent time together, they probably discussed British-American relations. In Virginia, Spotswood remained in touch with English political thinking and revealed to William Byrd of Westover (30 September 1732) scorn for the Board of Trade and sympathy for America. He told Byrd that if the Massachusetts Assembly would stand firm in its opposition to a fixed salary for its governor, "he did not see how they could be forced to raise money against their will." Further, if an act of Parliament directed Massachusetts to do so, "though it be against the right of Englishmen to be taxed but by their representatives," the British authorities "would find it no easy matter to put such an act in execution."[14] Franklin, who began the *Pennsylvania Gazette* in 1729 with an editorial on the Massachusetts issue, agreed with Spotswood. If the two ever talked about British-American relations, Franklin would have found Spotswood's analyses of Great Britain's positions fascinating. Perhaps, rather than Spotswood influencing Franklin, Franklin influenced Spotswood. As postmaster general, Spotswood no doubt received all the colonial papers. He probably read Franklin's 1729 editorial.

Spotswood was an enthusiast for a future American empire; so was Franklin. He had been so impressed with James Logan's 1732 manuscript on the future of America that he copied it.[15] Spotswood had led a fabled 1716 trip of the Knights of the Golden Horseshoe to the Shenandoah Valley, where he claimed all of America as far west as the Mississippi River for the British. Franklin no doubt knew of the expedition. The topic of America's future must have been a favorite with Spotswood; it became a favorite with Franklin. Along with Logan, Spotswood may well have influenced Franklin's thinking about an American empire.

The Mail System

After Spotswood's death in 1740, Head Lynch, another Virginian, served as postmaster general for North America until his death in 1743, when he was succeeded by Elliott Benger on 18 August. Benger had been in charge of the General Post Office on Spotswood's land at New Post, Virginia.[16] Franklin, as the Philadelphia postmaster, filled out a £500 bond for Benger on 25 April 1744, with Robert Grace as his cosigner. The bond was recorded on 4 June. Franklin's accounts reveal that on 12 November 1744, he began handling gold, pistoles, and notes of exchange for Benger. He had earlier, after becoming postmaster in 1737, occasionally received paper currency from his customers in other colonies (especially Maryland, New Jersey, and New York) and exchanged it for Pennsylvania paper currency. The historian Ruth Lapham Butler believed that Franklin served as comptroller "during the last few years of Postmaster Benger's administration,"[17] but Franklin's accounts with Benger remain essentially the same from Benger's appointment as deputy postmaster general in 1744 to his death in 1752. Perhaps Benger appointed Franklin comptroller in 1744, shortly after receiving Franklin's bond.

The overland post riders were bonded and supervised, but the post office system simply did not work with mail delivered by sea. Only the captains of the annual packet faithfully delivered the mail to the post office. Other shipmasters were importuned upon arrival by persons asking for their mail. If the ship was owned locally, the captain took the owner's mail to him. Persons who expected mail commonly came aboard the ship upon its docking and went through the mail, taking whatever letters were addressed to them or to their friends. Sometimes ship captains took the mail bag to a favorite inn, where various persons went through it. Peter Kalm described what happened when he arrived in Philadelphia on 15 September 1748: "As soon as we had come to town and cast anchor many of the inhabitants came on board to inquire for letters. They took all those which they could carry, either for themselves or for their friends. Those which remained the captain ordered to be carried on shore and to be brought to a coffee-house, where everybody could make inquiry for them." In this case, like many others, the postmaster—and, consequently, the crown—received no payment for the mail. Though persons who broke the post office law seem never to have been prosecuted, its violation sometimes had serious consequences. Letters occasionally did not reach their destinations; some fell into the hands of thieves. Most ship captains only delivered the mail to the post office after a number of people had gone through it. The postmaster received what no one else wanted.

Franklin tried to have all the letters and packages brought to the post office. It would have ended the confusion concerning the delivery of letters and prevented thievery. "Evil-minded Persons have made use of such Opportunities to pocket and embezle Letters of consequence, and either destroy them or delay the Delivery a long time, to the great Damage and Injury of those to whom they were directed" (2:377). But he found the merchants and ship owners would not change, for it would cost them. Indeed, since major merchants and ship owners like William Allen ran up postal bills totaling dozens of pounds with Franklin, they must have saved dozens more by having their shipmasters and friends deliver letters to them. Franklin's attempted reform failed.

Because the Philadelphia merchant John Clifton suffered a loss, he advertised in the *Gazette* on 7 February 1748/9 that a letter addressed to him containing a bill of lading and a bill of exchange for £15 sterling from Peter Furnell of Jamaica was brought by Captain Thomas Stamper to Philadelphia. Captain Stamper brought the letter onshore "amongst the general letters" and allowed various persons to go through the bag. The letter addressed to Clifton was taken. "As that letter and bill of exchange can be of no service to any one but the subscriber, unless it is to satisfy an impertinent curiosity; The Person possessed of it, is desired to convey the same to the Post-Office, and no questions shall be ask'd." Clifton concluded, "All masters of vessels, and others, are desired, as a favour, not to deliver any letters directed to me, to any person, except such as I shall send for them, or to the Post-master of this place, as I shall chearfully pay postage for the same." Even in an advertisement complaining of the system's failure, the victim intended to continue violating it.

Franklin allowed his friends and family to use the post gratis, partly to save them money (the addressee paid the postage, but mail addressed to the postmaster was free) and partly because letters to postmasters were generally more secure. His father, Josiah, writing to a relative in Blenheim, England, on 11 January 1744, said that he could be best reached by directing to Benjamin Franklin, postmaster at Philadelphia. When Dr. John Mitchell in Virginia wrote Cadwallader Colden in New York on 10 September 1745, Mitchell sent the letter to Franklin, who sent it on to Colden. When John Bartram wrote Colden in December 1745, the letter was sent "Free B. Franklin." Mitchell, Colden, and Bartram were all part of colonial America's scientific establishment. Franklin was not only helping his friends, he was also subsidizing American science. He was also depriving the post office of funds and himself of a 20 percent commission.

Official correspondence between the London authorities and the colonial governments demanded special treatment. When Franklin was temporarily absent in the spring of 1748 and the mail from London contained letters for Governor Jonathan Belcher of New Jersey, Franklin's responsible helpmate, Deborah, Franklin, hired a special courier and immediately sent them on to Belcher on 16 March 1748. Franklin made only a few improvements in the postal system while postmaster of Philadelphia and, later, comptroller, but he improved the system dramatically (as we will see in Volume 3) after becoming joint deputy postmaster general of North America in 1753.

Printing the Great Awakening

Though Franklin risked more and lost more often than any other colonial printer, he often succeeded. Every year during the 1730s, Franklin published one or two religious imprints, but that changed with the coming of George Whitefield and the Great Awakening. The year 1738 was typical. Franklin printed two religious imprints and twelve nonreligious ones. In 1739 he published at his own risk Elizabeth's Rowe's religious poem *The History of Joseph* and also *The Art of Preaching*, a poem imitating Horace's *Art of Poetry*, containing parallel passages of Horace's Latin and the English imitation. Both failed. In 1743 he was still trying to remainder *The History of Joseph* to the Boston booksellers.

Before any other American printer, Franklin thought that publishing the amazingly effective itinerant revivalist George Whitefield might be profitable. Soon after Whitefield's arrival in America in the fall of 1739, Franklin asked for and received permission to publish his journals and sermons by subscription. From William Parks in Williamsburg to John Franklin in Boston, Franklin's agents collected funds for the edition. Most volumes published by subscription were prestigious items that would have comparatively few sales, like Richard Lewis's *Muscipula* (Annapolis: William Parks, 1728) or Thomas Godfrey's *Juvenile Poems* (Philadelphia: Henry Miller, 1765). Perhaps Franklin used subscriptions because he was at first uncertain whether Whitefield's journals and sermons would sell. In fact, they became best-sellers, with the first journal going through two editions. The venture turned out to be the best-selling subscription publishing in colonial America. Franklin probably employed two of his three presses on Whitefield's journals and sermons from fall 1739 to late summer 1740. He commented in the *Pennsylvania Gazette*: "No books are in Request but those of Piety and Devotion; and instead of idle Songs and Ballads, the People are every where entertaining themselves with Psalms, Hymns and Spiritual Songs" (12 June 1740). Earlier, he had lost money on an edition of Isaac Watts's *Psalms of David*; and he had remarked that a Robin Hood songbook sold from his shelves quickly while Watts's *Psalms* languished. Now, however, he believed it would sell and brought out another edition (1740), a large book, and thus a major investment.[18] Indeed, he printed an enormous amount of religious literature in 1740. Among other religious tracts, Franklin gambled on Gilbert Tennent's *The Danger of an Unconverted Ministry*, which enjoyed two editions.

Other than the *Pennsylvania Gazette* and *Poor Richard*, the volumes of journals and collected sermons of Whitefield were probably Franklin's most successful publishing venture. He advertised on 22 May 1740 that the first volumes were ready. Since many persons had sent in their names to subscribe without sending in money, and since the number of copies printed was less (or so he said) than the total number of names, the persons who had paid or those who first brought money "in their hands" would have the preference. One wonders if the advertisement was merely a way for Franklin to sell the volumes quickly, but, given Whitefield's enormous popularity in 1740, Franklin may have been truthful. He gambled on these religious works, partly because he judged that they would now sell, partly because he could now afford to lose money (though he did not intend to do so), and partly because he now had a network of printers and booksellers from Charleston, South Carolina, through New England who would take his products—knowing that they could return them to Franklin if the books remained on their shelves. He also printed in 1740 a school text, *A New and Complete Guide to the English Tongue*, at his own risk. Late that year, Franklin announced his plan for the first American magazine (see Chapter 12). By 1740, he had become colonial America's dominant printer.

His official printing included the invaluable *Collection of Charters . . . of Pennsylvania* (1740). In it, Franklin again revealed a desire to order and systematize material. The original charter and all previous printings had no divisions. It was one long paragraph, making it difficult to find or cite a particular passage. Franklin divided it into twenty-three numbered sections. The sections have been followed in almost all subsequent printings, and legal opinions to the present generally cite these divisions.[19] One aberrant imprint, dated 1740 but evidently not completed before 1741, was printed at the "New Printing Office." It was not, however, printed by Franklin, nor was he paid to print it, nor did he bring it out at his own risk. He allowed his apprentice, Joseph Rose, to use his press and types to bring out a collection of the poems of his father, Aquila Rose, *Poems on Several Occasions* (advertised on 13 August 1741). Franklin no doubt remembered that the London printer Samuel Palmer allowed him to make a similar arrangement to print his early philosophical tract, *A Dissertation on Liberty and Necessity* (1725).

In 1741 Franklin again gambled on a number of religious works, including another edition of *The Art of Preaching* and another of Isaac Watts's *Psalms of David*. Franklin ventured into eighteenth-century sensational publication (dying speeches of criminals) when he printed John Ury's speech at his execution in New York for "being concerned in the late Negro-conspiracy." The speech was made on 29 August, and Franklin published it in Philadelphia on 4 September—a record time. Though Franklin attempted to publish the Library Company *Catalogue* before the annual meeting (4 May), he simply did not have the time. The *Catalogue* actually appeared sometime after 13 July 1741. During the first half of the year, he was also publishing monthly issues of the *General Magazine and Historical Chronicle*.

The war with Spain (1739–42) occasioned several 1741 publications. A broadside "Extract of a Letter [dated 3 April] from one of the Officers, before Cartegena" appeared in the late spring. Governor George Thomas's proclamation "concerning Recruits for the Expedition against Havana" appeared on 28 September 1741. Naturally the *Pennsylvania Gazette* carried the war news. Franklin printed two pamphlets by Quakers supporting defensive warfare: James Logan's address, *To Robert Jordan, and Others the Friends of the Yearly Meeting* (22 September), in which Logan said that civil government is founded upon force and that Friends "who for conscience-sake cannot join in any law for self-defense [should] decline standing as candidates at the ensuing election"; and Samuel Chew's *Speech Delivered to the Grand-Jury, New-Castle*, which argued that defensive war was not against Quaker principles (after 21 November). For Conrad Weiser and James Logan, he printed a piece of political propaganda (20 September) exhorting the German electorate to support the proprietary candidate. As usual, however, on 1 October 1741 the Quaker candidates prevailed.

Franklin printed more German imprints in 1742 than in any other year. For the United Brethren, he printed eight German titles, and for the Moravian minister and missionary Count Zinzendorf (1700–1760), he brought out nine German imprints, plus two in English. In addition, Franklin printed eight other religious pamphlets, several at his own risk, most notably an edition of Jonathan Edwards's *Distinguishing Marks of a Work of the Spirit of God*. He also published volume 1 of Samuel Richardson's *Pamela*, the first novel to be printed in America. Franklin was so swamped with religious imprints that he could not bring out the second volume until 1744. The novel was a failure. English and Irish publishers could print more copies with cheaper labor and materials than their American competitors.

As Franklin's printing business grew, Andrew Bradford's declined. Bradford died at age fifty-six on 24 November 1742, a decade before his father. Bradford's *American Weekly Mercury* continued under his widow, Cornelia, to 1 March 1743 and then with her partner, Isaiah Warner, to 18 October 1744, after which she took it over until 22 May 1746, when its last known issue appeared. The end of 1742, however, saw the start of another Philadelphia newspaper, the *Pennsylvania Journal* (established 2 December), edited by William Bradford (1721/2–1791), the nephew of Andrew Bradford. After Franklin's retirement in 1748, the *Pennsylvania Journal* became an important Philadelphia paper.

In 1743, Franklin printed at least twenty-seven imprints, including five government publications, fourteen pieces for private individuals or organizations, and six ventures at his own risk. Four imprints reflected his special interests. Reform of the police and of taxation, which he had advocated in his Junto proposal of about 1735, was proposed in *A Bill for the Better Regulating the Night Watch*. On 14 May, just before setting out on a trip to New England, he printed *A Proposal for Promoting Useful Knowledge among the British Plantations in America*, the founding document of the American Philosophical Society. The *Articles of the Union Fire-Company* revised and expanded the company's first set of guiding principles, affirming its purpose to be of general service to the community. His second Indian treaty (the first appeared in 1737), *The Treaty Held with the Indians of the Six Nations. At Philadelphia, in July, 1742*, which was first advertised on 10 March 1742/3, described a ceremony he witnessed. The talented Onondago Indian chief Canasatego, who impressed Franklin, was the orator for the Six Nations.

The demand for religious books tapered off during the decade. In 1747, at the end of the Great Awakening, he printed thirteen nonreligious pieces and three religious ones—nearly the same proportion as a decade earlier.[20]

AMERICAN PAPER

Printers used enormous amounts of paper. When Franklin started printing in 1728, he bought all his paper from merchants in Philadelphia or England. During the period 1736–48, Franklin gradually emerged as a dealer in American paper and a sponsor of American papermakers. Partially because of Franklin, the Philadelphia area became the center of American papermaking. He did business with all the established Pennsylvania papermakers and encouraged new ones. William Dewees, Sr., William Dewees, Jr., Henry Dewees, Matthias Meuris, Anthony Newhouse, and Thomas Wilcox all turn up frequently in Franklin's accounts. Franklin supplied them with rags and bought paper from them. By 1743 he was buying large amounts of paper that he sold to others, thus becoming the major paper merchant not only in Philadelphia but throughout colonial America. The Philadelphia area had eleven paper mills, and the rest of America had only three more.[21] One wonders if Franklin recalled from his Boston youth that the hero of Massachusetts's Old Charter Party, John Wise, had in 1721 advocated making paper as one possible way to help the American economy.

Franklin became friends with the various papermakers, especially William Dewees, Jr., and Thomas Wilcox. They charged materials on credit with him, and he visited their printing mills and experimented with them in making special kinds of paper.[22] In the spring of 1743 Franklin acquired a large amount of Spanish paper, and for the next four years he sold quantities of it to other American printers. Since Great Britain was at war with Spain from 1739 to 1748, Franklin probably bought the paper from an American privateer that took a Spanish ship as a prize. Even after Franklin retired as a printer, he remained the principal wholesale merchant for American paper until he left Philadelphia in 1757. Fourteen years later, when he received a letter from Humphrey Marshall, who lived in Chester County outside Philadelphia, Franklin recognized that it was written on a superior American-made paper. Franklin wrote back on 22 April 1771 that he was the more pleased to see it, "having had a principal Share in establishing that Manufactory among us many Years ago, by the Encouragement I gave it." Brissot de Warville said that Franklin told him in 1788 that he had established eighteen paper mills. That seems exaggerated, though Franklin's accounts reveal that he did business during 1736–47 with at least twelve.[23] He wrote most of parts 3 and 4 of his *Autobiography* on paper made by George Christopher Helmbold at Lower Merion, Montgomery County, Pennsylvania, and by Joshua and Thomas Gilpin at Brandywine, New Castle County, Delaware. Even at the end of his life, he promoted the Gilpins and other Philadelphia-area papermakers and lent them the latest treatises on papermaking.[24]

THE VIRGINIA PAPER MILL

Franklin's dealings with Virginia's William Parks illustrate his role in colonial papermaking. In the early fall of 1742, Parks came to Philadelphia and consulted Franklin about building a paper mill. Franklin advertised in the *Pennsylvania Gazette* on 16 and 23 September 1742 that a carpenter "capable of building a good Paper-Mill" and another person who "understands the Making of Paper, are wanted to undertake and carry on that Business in a neighbouring Colony." Franklin asked them to appear at his shop on 25 September. Evidently William Parks and Franklin interviewed them. Parks returned to Williamsburg, leaving Franklin as his agent. On 8 October, Franklin noted that Parks had left £11.10 with him, and he recorded that on Parks's verbal order he had advanced £5 to papermaker Johan Conrad Shütz (generally spelled "Sheets" in Franklin's early accounts). On 23 October, Franklin advanced another £8 to "Sheets" and £5 to the carpenters. In the fall and winter of 1742 on Archer's Hope Creek near Williamsburg, Shütz built Virginia's first paper mill.

Franklin advanced Shütz's wife five shillings on 25 December 1742, and a few weeks later (17 January) Franklin recorded that he had paid the carpenters who were building the mill an unspecified amount. On 26 January, he received £11.13.6 from Parks, "Cash by the Post," and gave "Sheets the Paper maker's Wife" £1. On 29 March Franklin recorded that he had advanced Shütz, his wife, and the carpenter a total of £33.10. The following day, Franklin recorded sending Parks 915 pounds of rags at one and a half pence per pound. The paper mill was in operation by the spring of 1743, and Franklin was selling Parks rags. In his dealings with Parks, Franklin was too generous (perhaps partially because of his desire to sponsor American industry): when Parks died in 1751, he owed Franklin £113.10.8½.

BOOKSELLER

Franklin was among colonial America's preeminent book men. Besides being a voracious reader and a major collector, he was a bookseller. Most printers sold the commonest books, and Franklin began by doing so. The first issue of the *Pennsylvania Gazette* printed by Franklin (2 October 1729) advertised "Bibles, Testaments, Psalters, PsalmBooks," and legal forms. Nearly every year through the 1730s and 1740s Franklin increased his stock of new and secondhand books, frequently advertising them in the *Gazette*. A long advertisement on 25 May 1738 noted that the price was marked in each book. The list included such popular classics of the day as Addison's *Works*, Butler's *Hudibras*, Milton's *Paradise Lost*, the *Spectator*, and *Telemachus*. Setting in type an advertisement for several hundred books in the *Gazette* on 7 February 1739/40, Franklin amused himself by juxtaposing titles that clashed with one another. He transformed the dry list into something diverting and somewhat irreligious. (Professor Kevin Hayes assured me that all the titles were actual books.) Here is a selection from the list: "Arraignment of lewd Women, Parismus and Parismenus, Art of Money-Catching, Duty of Prayer, Cynthia a Novel, Republick of Letters, Life of our blessed Saviour, Garden of Love, Ladies' Delight, Man's great Interest, History of Dr. John Faustus, London Jests, and Cambridge Jests, Travels of our blessed Saviour, Lives of the Apostles, Fair Rosamond, Book of Knowledge, Life and Death of Moll Flanders, Oxford Jests, Histories of England and Ireland, Ladies Religion, Argalus and Parthenia, Pure Love, England's Compleat Jester." Franklin inserted a bit of sardonic whimsy in the list of books for sale on 21 May 1741: "Every Man his own Lawyer, Every Man his own Doctor, (Note, in a short time will be published, *Every Man his own Priest*)."

Few books survive with the notation that they were purchased from Franklin, but the American Philosophical Society has four volumes of *Reports and Cases of Law . . . Collected by . . . William Leonard*, which Isaac Norris II noted that he bought from him.[25] As we would expect of the patriotic American and book man, Franklin owned a personal copy of the fundamental Americana bibliography of the day, White Kennett, *Bibliotheca Americanae primordia; an attempt towards laying the foundation of an American Library* (London: Churchill, 1713).[26] Franklin's book selling business took a step forward with a separately-printed *Catalogue of Choice and Valuable Books*, which he sold at auction in his shop, beginning on 11 April 1744, with the lowest acceptable price marked in each book. The bibliographer James N. Green commented that Franklin found himself "overstocked and resorted to an inventory clearance sale." The books were generally "expensive, pedantic, Latin and Greek, used or otherwise unsalable."[27] One could not accumulate so many volumes quickly. The catalogue demonstrates that Franklin had been for some time Philadelphia's primary bookbuyer and bookseller.

A book auction held in the spring of 1745 has been a mystery. Because the bookbinder Joseph Goodwin gave away the sale catalogue, he has been assumed to be the bookseller. Though a published *Catalogue* and, later, a supplement were advertised, neither is extant. Franklin's bibliographer C. William Miller therefore questioned whether Franklin printed them.[28] The auction, "at the large

Room over Mr. *Vidal*'s School in *Second Street*," was advertised in the *Gazette* on 5, 12, and 19 March 1745. The sale began on Monday evening, 11 March, and continued every evening until all the books were sold. The supplement to the auction catalogue was advertised as "Just Published" on 19 March, with the sale of its titles to commence the following Monday evening, 25 March. Franklin's financial accounts suggest that he, rather than Goodwin, actually owned these books. A series of entries in his ledgers dated 28 March records debts from various persons for books, with five of them specifying "For Books bought at Auction," and one, William Bingham's, has the annotation, "Posted from Auction Memorandum." Evidently Joseph Goodwin conducted the sale as Franklin's agent and kept a separate memorandum (probably an annotated catalogue) for Franklin.

Three further bits of evidence tend to support the hypothesis that these were from Franklin's stock. First, Franklin is known to have been a bookseller; the bookbinder Goodwin is not. Second, Goodwin appears regularly in Franklin's accounts from 1742 to his death in 1747. During the year of the auction, 1745, "Mr. Gooding, bookbinder" (i.e., Joseph Goodwin) turns up eight times in Franklin's accounts, none of the charges being for advertisements in the *Gazette*, for separate advertisements, or for the catalogues. Had the auction advertisements in the *Pennsylvania Gazette* or the catalogues been printed for Goodwin, he probably would have charged them, as he did for his other business dealings with Franklin. Third, Franklin lent Goodwin 20.6 on 9 February and paid him for "work done" £1.0.6 on 4 March and 8.6 on 20 March. The pay could have been for binding books or for conducting the auction.

The evidence strongly suggests that Goodwin distributed the catalogues and kept track of the sales for Franklin. If the *Catalogue* and the supplement were of Franklin's books, he surely printed them, thus confirming Miller's guess that he did. Franklin gave up the bookselling business when he gave up printing at the beginning of 1748. His partner, David Hall, took over the bookselling as well as the printing. Franklin wrote Cadwallader Colden on 29 September 1748 that he had "absolutely left off Bookselling."

KING GEORGE'S WAR, 1744–1748

Great Britain's war with Spain and France occasioned several 1744 printings: for Pennsylvania Franklin published Governor George Thomas's *Proclamation* declaring war with France (11 June); for New Jersey he brought out Governor Lewis Morris's *Proclamation* of war and his *Proclamation* exhorting citizens to be ready; and for his friend and patron James Logan Franklin published one of his most beautiful and prized imprints, Logan's translation of Cicero's *Cato Major* (1744). As he wrote Cadwallader Colden on 28 November 1745, he did not always look to make money by his printing: "If I can be a Means of Communicating anything valuable to the World, I do not always think of Gaining, nor even of Saving by my Business." One job printing of 1744 that surely interested

Franklin was an advertisement to see "The Solar Camera Obscura Microscope" and "Musical Clock, made by that great Master of Machinery David Lockwood." Though Dr. Archibald Spencer included the solar camera in his lectures, Lockwood probably had a better instrument. Franklin may have attended the lecture, given through July and August, perhaps with admission in exchange for printing the bill. Finally, in 1744 Franklin printed two religious works at his own risk: the first known Philadelphia edition of *The New-England Psalter* and Isaac Watts's *Preservative from Sins and Follies*, a popular work using a question-and-answer format.

A Treaty Held at . . . Lancaster . . . June, 1744 demonstrates how Franklin ventured as a businessman/printer/publisher even when he was hired simply as a printer. The Pennsylvania Assembly paid Franklin to print about one hundred copies. (Since Franklin's pay for printing was listed as a lump sum, one cannot tell the exact amount the assembly paid Franklin to print a specific item.) The treaty would have been given to thirty assemblymen, one clerk, the members of the council and its clerk, the governor and other Pennsylvania officials, the proprietors and their officers in England, and the British chain of command. Franklin, however, printed hundreds more. Though he did not have to pay for setting the type, he paid for the additional paper, ink, and labor. The large number of additional copies was a publishing gamble. European authors frequently praised Indian oratory, so Franklin supposed the English public would be interested and sent three hundred copies to William Strahan in London (18 September 1744). It was listed for sale in the *Gentleman's Magazine* and *London Magazine* for May 1745, where the price was given as 1s 6d (sterling), but the treaty did not sell. Europeans would rather praise Indian oratory than read it.

Franklin advertised it for sale in the *Pennsylvania Gazette* on 6 September 1744 at eighteen pence (1s 6d), Pennsylvania currency—about one-third cheaper than the English price. He sent 25 copies to the Annapolis printer Jonas Green (14 September), 50 more copies to Green (6 October), an additional 50 to Green (16 October), and he sold one copy to Robert Strettel (25 September). In 1745, he sent 25 copies to his partner James Parker (27 June), 6 more to Jonas Green (2 September), 1 to Thomas Lawrence (20 September), and 6 to Israel Pemberton, Jr. (12 November). William Parks in Williamsburg reprinted the treaty, so he must have purchased at least one copy, and he would not have reprinted it unless it was selling well in Virginia. It seems extremely unlikely that Franklin did not send Parker any copies for over nine months. No sales are recorded for New England, but the treaty must have sold throughout the area. He probably simply gave his sister-in-law Anne Franklin in Rhode Island 50 or so free copies, but he must have shipped off some to Connecticut and a hundred or more to the Boston market. In addition to the 464 copies itemized in the extant accounts, I believe that he issued at least 300 more to sell. Altogether, he probably printed close to 1,000 copies of the treaty.[29]

Though Franklin sold individual copies for 1.6, he sold to distributors for one shilling, and, surprisingly, sold the last 50 copies to Green on 16 October 1744 for ten pence apiece. Since Pennsylvania currency was worth only about 60 percent of English sterling, and since Franklin would not have charged Strahan more than ten pence per copy in Pennsylvania currency plus handling and shipping, the price the English booksellers charged was surprisingly high. No doubt that was part of the reason for its poor sale there.

In 1745, Franklin published three books on his own venture. For an original and long-awaited medical treatise, Dr. Thomas Cadwalader's *Essay on the West-India Dry-Gripes*, Franklin revised the preface. He gambled and lost by publishing an edition of the New Testament. Franklin still had 51 copies when he sold the printing business to David Hall in 1748. English printers could print and sell a much larger edition (thousands rather than hundreds of copies), and therefore they could undersell American publishers on such popular items as Bibles. Franklin also reprinted a children's book, *The Friendly Instructor* (or *Familiar Dialogues*).

The following year, Franklin printed Governor Thomas's *Proclamation* "to raise troops for the immediate reduction of Canada" (9 June 1746); and his *Proclamation* of 14 July "declaring a Day of Public Thanksgiving" for the duke of Cumberland's victory over the Stuart Pretender (Bonnie Prince Charlie) at Cullenden Moor. For the use of various militia in the continuing war, he gambled on selling *The New Manual Exercise* by William Blakeney and Humphrey Bland (it sold well and was reprinted in 1747). He published America's first secular courtesy book, *Reflections on Courtship and Marriage* (1746), which I discuss among Franklin's writings (Chapter 19). He also printed *The Charter, Laws, and Catalogue of Books* for the Library Company. Though the Great Awakening was trailing off, Franklin thought George Whitefield's recent sermons would sell and brought out *Five Sermons*. Franklin also printed a fourth Indian treaty, *An Account of the Treaty Held at Albany, October 1745*.

Besides selling copies of James Parker's New Jersey *Bill in the Chancery*, Franklin printed 22 items in 1747, his last year as a printer: three government printings, two private ones, and a whopping 17 ventures at his own risk. Seven of Franklin's gambles were issued for his brainchild, the Militia Association. Among the other ten, perhaps the most interesting was Thomas Dilworth's instruction book, *A New Guide to the English Tongue*, a reprint of "the most popular speller of the eighteenth century."[30] Franklin's edition contains the first American illustrations of Aesop's fables. Franklin either cut them himself or had a Philadelphia engraver do them under his direction. Normally the woodcuts would simply copy the English or European ones. It took extra thought and work to Americanize them. Franklin did so. One woodcut shows that unique American adaptation, the Conestoga wagon, and another features Franklin's distinctive Pennsylvania stove in the fireplace.[31]

Franklin started a publicity campaign for his voluntary militia association in 1747 (named simply the "Association") and gave away publications supporting

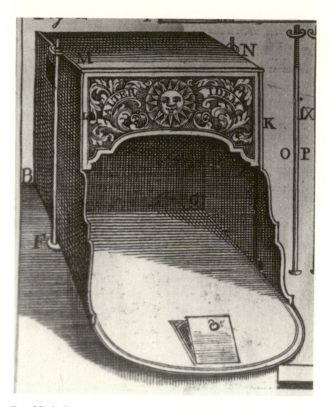

Figure 26a. Franklin's "New-Invented Pennsylvania Fireplace" with its distinctive front plate, 1744. Compare this front plate of Franklin's Pennsylvania Fireplace with that in the woodcut illustrating Aesop's fable. From Benjamin Franklin, An Account of the New Invented Pennsylvania Fire-Places *(Philadelphia: B. Franklin, 1744). Courtesy, Library Company of Philadelphia.*

it. He published two editions of the pamphlet he wrote to inaugurate the Association, *Plain Truth* (17 November and 3 December). It was a local best-seller, and Franklin could have made a considerable sum by charging for it. He published a broadside *Form of Association*, which he circulated for signing at a series of citizens' meetings beginning 24 November. At that assembly, he urged the formation of a volunteer militia and the raising of funds for batteries along the Delaware. Desiring Quaker support, he published Matthew Green's *Copy of Verses wrote by a Gentleman, Lately Deceased, Occasioned by His Reading Robert Barclay's Apology* (ca. November), arguing that Quakers need not oppose defensive war. To benefit the Association, Franklin organized a lottery and published tickets for it. At the end of the year, he brought out a letter in the *Gazette* (a supplement to the 29 December issue) urging that Philadelphia's citizens defend themselves against French and Spanish ships raiding along the Delaware River.

Figure 26b. An Americanized version of a woodcut illustrating Aesop's fable, showing a Franklin stove in the fireplace, 1747. When he printed the first American illustrations for Aesop's fables, Franklin gave them American characteristics. Thus, in the woodcut illustrating "Of the Good Natur'd Man and the Adder," from Thomas Dilworth, New Guide to the English Tongue *(Philadelphia: B. Franklin, 1747), the stove in the background has the device of the glowing sun on it, the same found in Franklin's "New-Invented Pennsylvania Fireplace." In another cut, Franklin portrayed a Conestoga wagon. The woodcuts were unique and valuable. Franklin's partner James Parker used them when he reprinted Dilworth in New York in 1754. When the Franklin and Hall partnership ended in 1766, Parker valued the twelve cuts at three pounds, an expensive price (13:63). Courtesy, Rare Book and Manuscript Library, Columbia University.*

EMPLOYEES AND PARTNERS

Franklin's first partners and his early employees before 1736 have been discussed above. His apprentices during these years included Joseph Rose, who worked for Franklin in the years at least from 1739 to 1741. James Chattin, who lived with the Franklins in 1747, served at first as an apprentice. Chattin set up in Lancaster in 1751 and moved his printing shop to Philadelphia in 1752. When Franklin journeyed to New England in the early summer of 1753, he evidently left a pamphlet with Chattin which he, following Franklin's directions, printed anonymously. William Franklin and others attributed it to Franklin, but it does not survive (4:513).

Edward Lewis, who moved in with the Franklins on 14 August 1737, is a puzzle. He received £9 a year, plus "Accomodations, of Meat, Drink, Washing and Lodging." That was too little for Lewis to have been a journeyman printer (on 28 July 1755, Daniel Fisher was offered £25 a year to act as Franklin's clerk), but Lewis was not officially an apprentice. Franklin added, "He is to go away when anything offers more to his Advantage." Perhaps he was an older person who wanted to learn printing. He may be the "old Lewes" in Franklin's accounts (19 April 1736).

The journeyman printers Franklin employed included Olaf Malander, a Swedish schoolmaster, who worked for him from at least 1739 to 1744. That year, Franklin sent him to Rhode Island, probably to work for Anne Franklin. Franklin sponsored his journeyman James Parker as his printing partner in New York (20 February 1742). Before then, Parker lived with the Franklins for several years. Like most of his other partnerships, it continued for six years. Samuel Johnston, identified in the accounts as formerly a Boston printer, may have worked for Franklin in 1742 and 1743. Among other printers, the mapmaker Lewis Evans worked for Franklin from 1736 to 1747 and then, for various special chores, until the early 1750s. Henry Miller also turns up in the 1742 accounts. Samuel Holland appears repeatedly in the accounts as a journeyman printer in 1746 and 1747 before going to Lancaster. Miller and Holland later worked with Franklin's press and types in Lancaster, printing the *Lancastersche Zeitung* in 1752 and 1753. After they dissolved their partnership, Holland rented the press from Franklin (14 June 1753). Thomas Smith worked as a journeyman printer for Franklin for at least two years before being sponsored as a partner in Antigua. By 16 April 1748, Franklin identified Smith as of Antigua in his accounts.

Besides Timothy, Malander, Miller, and Holland, Franklin sometimes employed other printers who could speak German. Joseph Crellius, who translated Franklin's *Plain Truth* into German, worked for him in 1747. Gotthard Armbrüster appears in the 1745 accounts. His imprint occurs on a number of pieces in 1747 and 1748, including the German translation of *Plain Truth* by Crellius. Johann Böhm (d. July 1751) printed at least eight pieces with Franklin's German types from 1749 to 1751, using Franklin's name as co-printer. And Anton Armbrüster (d. 1796) used Franklin's name for two imprints in 1756.

The bookbinders were not generally Franklin employees (Stephen Potts was an exception) but instead they were often allied with printers. Most books in England and Europe were sold unbound, but since labor was more expensive in America, English books sent to America were commonly bound. Franklin had numerous accounts with bookbinders, beginning with Samuel Potts, his fellow employee with Samuel Keimer and a charter member of the Junto. The ledgers contain more accounts with the happy but improvident Potts (generally loaning him money) than any other person. Though bookbinder William Davies worked for Franklin as early as 1729,[32] his name only appears in the surviving accounts from 25 October 1739 to 8 January 1741. Davies owed him £4.1. when Franklin retired as a printer. Franklin had two other extensive accounts with bookbinders. Charles Harrison, the Boston bookbinder and bookseller, appears in the accounts from 10 July 1740 to 9 July 1745. Last, Philadelphia bookbinder Joseph Goodwin did business with Franklin from at least 30 August 1742 to 10 December 1746 and owed him £2.6 in 1748.

There were minor accounts with other bookbinders: John Hyndshaw (23 November 1730 to 28 November 1731); Mr. Hill, "the Book Binder" (20 December 1735 to 31 August 1736, though he still owed Franklin five shillings in 1748); Mr. Saits, the Dutch bookbinder on Chestnut Street (14 April to 7 October 1742); John Balthezer Schuppius (just two entries, 21 July 1743 and another from 1743); Adolph Young (just one entry, 31 August 1745); and Nathaniel Holland (several between 7 May and 6 November 1747). Finally, Francis Skinner, bookbinder, may have been the person who bought skins from Franklin on 30 and 31 August 1736.

WILLIAM STRAHAN AND DAVID HALL

On 14 January 1742/3, William Strahan, a successful London printer, wrote James Read (Franklin's neighbor), asking if he knew of a possible opportunity for his foreman, the printer David Hall. Franklin thus became acquainted not only with Strahan, who became Franklin's closest friend during his first agency in England (1757–62), but also with David Hall, who became Franklin's Philadelphia partner and successor in 1748. Franklin replied to Strahan on 10 July 1743 that he had three printing-houses in three different colonies and that he planned to set up a fourth "if I can meet with a proper Person to manage it, having all Materials ready for that purpose." Franklin proposed that Hall come to Philadelphia "that I may see and be acquainted with him." He added that if he and Hall did not agree, he would employ him for twelve months and pay his passage back to England if he wanted to return there. Journeyman printer Hall arrived in Philadelphia on 20 June 1744 and lodged and boarded with the Franklins.

Franklin hit it off with William Strahan. He wrote Strahan on 4 July 1744 that he had long wanted "a Friend in London whose Judgment I could depend on, to send me from time to time such new Pamphlets as are worth Reading on any Subject (Religious Controversy excepted) for there is no depending on Titles and Advertisements." Accordingly, he sent Strahan funds to purchase the pamphlets. He continued, "We have seldom any News on our Side the Globe that can be entertaining to you on yours. All our Affairs are *petit*. They have a miniature Resemblance only, of the grand Things of Europe. Our Governments, Parliaments, Wars, Treaties, Expeditions, Factions, &c. tho' Matters of great and Serious Consequence to us, can seem but Trifles to you." Franklin gave his proof: "Four Days since our Naval Force receiv'd a terrible Blow. Fifty Sail of the Line destroy'd would scarce be a greater Loss to Britain than that to us: And yet 'twas only a new 20 Gun Ship sunk, and about 100 Men drowned, just as she was going out to Sea on a privateering Voyage against the King's Enemies"

(2:411). As usual, Franklin kept the audience of his letter in mind: he knew what Strahan would be likely to think, and he played up to Strahan's expectations. Though Strahan would not have known it, Franklin was recalling a sentiment that Cotton Mather expressed in *Magnalia Christi Americana*: Describing frontier conflicts with the Indians and knowing that the small numbers of persons involved might seem insignificant to a European audience, Mather apologized that "a war between us and a handful of Indians" might "appear no more than a *Batrachomyomachia* to the world abroad."[33]

Franklin wrote Strahan again at the end of the month (31 July 1744), ordering "about 300 lb. weight of good new English Letter, which I shall want to compleat a little Printing house for our common Friend Mr. Hall." He also sent along copies of James Logan's translation of Cicero's *Cato Major*, saying that he would accept books from Strahan in exchange. Franklin observed, "This kind of Commerce may be advantageous to us both, and to Mr. Hall; since if [we] have a reasonable Sale where we live for such Things as we print, what we do over and above, and can get dispos'd of at a foreign Market, is almost so much clear Gain" (2:413).

Thanking Strahan on 12 February 1744/5 for sending some London pamphlets, Franklin said, "I would not have you be too nice in the Choice of Pamphlets you send me. Let me have everything, good or bad, that makes a Noise and has a Run: for I have Friends here of Different Tastes to oblige with the Sight of them. If Mr. Warburton publishes a new Edition of Pope's works, please to send me as soon as 'tis out, 6 Setts. That Poet has many Admirers here, and the Reflection he somewhere casts on the Plantations as if they had a Relish for such Writers as Ward only, is injurious." Franklin referred to a couplet concerning Edward Ward and America in the *Dunciad*: "Not sail, with Ward, to Ape-and-monkey Climes, / Where vile Mundungus trucks for viler rhymes" (3:13).

With sentiments anticipating his letter to George Washington of 5 March 1780, Franklin wrote of the reputation of contemporary English authors: "Your authors know but little of the Fame they have on this Side the Ocean. We are a kind of Posterity in respect to them. We read their Works with perfect Impartiality, being at too great a Distance to be byassed by the Fashions, Parties and Prejudices that prevail among you. We know nothing of their personal Failings; the Blemishes in their character never reach us, and therefore the bright and amiable part strikes us with its full Force. They have never offended us or any of our Friends, and we have no Competitions with them, and therefore we praise and admire them without Restraint." Then Franklin commended the poetry of James Thomson's *Seasons*. In closing, Franklin showed that he and Strahan, though they had never met personally, were becoming friends: "I cannot return your Compliments in kind; this Quaker plain Country producing none. All I can do is, to demonstrate, by a hearty Readiness in serving you when I have an Opportunity, or any Friend you recommend, that I do truly esteem and love you, being, Sir, Your obliged humble Servant B Franklin" (3:13–14).

Within a year of coming to America, Hall was impatient about his future and wrote Strahan for advice. On 9 March 1745 Strahan replied, "As to your terms with Mr. F. I again tell you I think they are very fair. . . . Trust to his Generosity; and I dare say he will deal honourably by you."[34] On 16 November 1746 Franklin intended to send him to the West Indies as his printing partner, but voyages were dangerous during the war. Instead, Franklin made him foreman of his shop. By 1 June 1747 Franklin had decided to retire and make Hall his partner and successor as printer in Philadelphia. The partnership was signed on 1 January 1748 and was to take effect on 21 January. Unlike Franklin's earlier partnerships, the one with Hall gave the partner a thriving business and an existing contract as printer to the assembly, so the term of partnership was eighteen years. On 21 January 1748, Franklin, age forty-two (fifteen days after his forty-second birthday), retired as a printer and a bookseller. Nevertheless, he continued until 1757, as we shall see, to write often for the *Pennsylvania Gazette*, to provide the copy for *Poor Richard*, to guide the choice of pamphlets and books issued by the partnership, and to remain active as a paper merchant and postmaster.

SIXTEEN

Concerned Citizen

In Prudence they [the tanners] ought not to have triumph'd before the Victory; and in Justice they should not have call'd that a Daring Attempt on the Liberties of the Tradesmen of Philadelphia, which was only a modest Attempt to deliver a great Number of Tradesmen from being poisoned by a few, and restore to them the Liberty of Breathing freely in their own Houses.—Franklin, on the environment, Pennsylvania Gazette, *30 August 1739*

FRANKLIN WAS THE MOST CIVIC-MINDED colonial American. All his life he lived in cities (though the largest ones in colonial America would be considered small towns today) and cared about their healthiness, safety, and beauty. His major projects are well-known: the Library Company of Philadelphia (1731), the Union Fire Company (1736), the Academy and College of Philadelphia (1748), the Philadelphia Contributionship for Insuring Homes from Loss by Fire (1751), and, with Dr. Thomas Bond, the Pennsylvania Hospital (1751). They were all successful and, transformed, all exist today. The first two have been discussed above, and the others will appear in Volume 3. Besides these, he mentioned other projects in the *Autobiography*: police (the night watch), street cleaning, paving, and lighting (A 85–86, 104–5). He attempted three others. On two, he spent comparatively little time: fairs and sidewalks. To the third, the public dock, he devoted hundreds of hours—and met with, at best, limited success.

PHILADELPHIA'S FAIRS

In the *Gazette* on 27 November 1731, Franklin published a brief anonymous letter against Philadelphia's fairs, which were held twice a year, in mid-May and mid-November. He attempted to give the letter authority by saying, "*A Gentleman desired me to publish This.*" The gentleman (i.e., Franklin) claimed that all "disinterested sober People, tho' of different Persuasions," thought that "our Fairs, as they are used and manag'd," did not help the "Commerce" of Philadelphia, and they were "manifest Nuisances . . . greatly destructive to the Morality, Sobriety, and Good Manners of the People." It was "almost scandalous for" persons to be seen there. "Trifling Commodities," toys, and cakes made up the insignificant mart. Many people behaved rudely at the fairs, and prostitutes frequented them, attempting to seduce youths. A licentious and unbounded liberty was taken at these times to attract people into the numerous booths in the streets and highways. Drinking was common, and drunken louts filled the streets. Excited by a few bad companions and becoming intoxicated, servants ran away during fairs more frequently than at other times. If "Masters prudently deny their going, they become sowre and untractable, begrutching or failing in their due Labour." Appealing to the prejudices of his readers (and perhaps to his own), he wrote, "the insolent dangerous, and scandalous Collection of Negroes, mixing with low white Servants and Boys in their paltry and noisy Games, not only in vast Crowds in the place of the Fair, but in many parts of the Streets . . . [makes it] hard for People to go along without Abuse, or being rudely jostled." And at night, after the business of the fairs was over, unruly crowds disturbed the city's inhabitants.

The "gentleman" persona hoped that "the discreet and sober Inhabitants" would petition the assembly to abolish fairs or at least to regulate them. Franklin followed up the article by drafting a petition to the House of Representatives, paraphrasing the faults listed in the article and asking that the fairs "either be thoroughly regulated . . . or else totally abolished" (1:211–12). But the Pennsylvania legislature ignored the request, and nothing was done about Philadelphia's fairs until after the Revolution. Perhaps Franklin never presented the petition. One problem with the newspaper essay is that the speaker, a "gentleman," seems scornful (as most "gentlemen" were) of the lower classes. That makes him a less than sympathetic speaker—not someone with whom the audience (largely artisans and farmers) would identify. It was also a surprising persona for Franklin, who evidently thought the posture suitable for condemning a popular entertainment. Franklin's objections seem similar to those of a busybody killjoy. Did his attitude reflect his New England background?

Slippery Sidewalks

An essay on icy, slippery sidewalks appeared in the 11 January 1732/3 *Gazette*. The persona was a good-natured, elderly man, afraid of falling. He said that "Walking the Street on one of these late slippery Mornings, I caught two terrible Falls, which made me . . . get my Shoes frosted" (i.e., affixed with metal tips to prevent slipping on ice). "I am a stiff old Fellow, and my Joints none of the most pliant. At the Door before which I fell last, stood a Gentleman-like Looby, with a couple of Damsels, who all made themselves wonderful merry with my Misfortune: And had not a good Woman, whose Door I had just passed, come and helped me up, I might for ought I know, have given them an Hour's Diversion before I found my Legs again. This good Woman, Heaven bless her, had sprinkled Ashes before her Door: I wish her long Life and better Neighbours."

The elderly man (twenty-seven-year-old Franklin) condemned the "merry People" who deliberately enjoyed "such Entertainments as I afforded them. . . . Strange Perverseness of Disposition! to delight in the Mishaps which befall People who have no way disoblig'd us." But now that his shoes were "frosted," he planned the next icy day to tour the town, "and take a general List of all the

Housekeepers, whom I will divide into three Classes." The usual basis for division into three classes of people in colonial America was socioeconomic: the "better sort," "common sort," and "lower sort." (Franklin later satirized those persons who referred to themselves as the "better sort" in two essays signed "Obadiah Plainman," 5 and 29 May 1740.) The essay on slippery sidewalks replaced the usual categories with ones based on social responsibility and feelings for others. He used both biblical and classical comparisons[1] to praise responsible citizens: "The humane, kind, compassionate, benevolent Class, I shall easily distinguish by the Ashes at their Doors, as God's People were distinguish'd in AEgypt by the Sprinkling of their Door-posts. The malicious and ill-natured Class I shall know by their Mirth at every Fall or accidental Slip of the Passengers in the Street. The indifferent, thoughtless Class, are the rest. As every Man that walks upon uneven Ice, hazards at each Step his Limbs; methinks some Honours ought to be decreed those of my first Class, proportionate to what the Romans gave him that sav'd the Life of a Fellow Citizen: They shall, however, be sure of my Respect and Friendship." The old gentleman resolved to be as "cross-grain'd" toward the malicious and thoughtless "as 'tis possible for a good-natur'd old Man to be; who is Your Friend and Reader, N. N."

The sympathetic persona immediately wins the compassion of the audience. We admire and respect him. The problem of slippery sidewalks remains today, though many communities legislate sidewalk clearance. For once, Franklin proposed no remedy—he evidently just meant to encourage responsible citizens to scatter ashes.

POLICE

With exceptions, the police in colonial towns were an assorted rabble of roustabouts. Philadelphia was growing rapidly in population, wealth, and problems. As it added thousands more persons every decade and was transformed from a pleasant village on a large river into a major port city, safety became a concern. In the fall of 1735, Franklin suggested reforming the system of paid night watchmen. The existing system was inefficient and unfair to the poor. He described the city watch, pointing out its faults: "It was managed by the Constables of the respective Wards in Turn. The Constable warn'd a Number of Housekeepers to attend him for the Night. Those who chose never to attend paid him Six Shillings a Year to be excus'd, which was suppos'd to be for hiring Substitutes; but was in Reality much more than was necessary for that purpose, and made the Constableship a Place of Profit. And the Constable for a little Drink often got such Ragamuffins about him as a Watch, that reputable Housekeepers did not chuse to mix with. Walking the Rounds too was often neglected, and most of the Night spent in Tippling."

Franklin wrote a paper for the Junto "representing these Irregularities, but insisting more particularly on the Inequality of this Six Shilling Tax of the Constables, respecting the Circumstances of those who paid it, since a poor Widow

Housekeeper, all whose Property to be guarded by the Watch did not perhaps exceed the Value of Fifty Pounds, paid as much as the wealthiest Merchant who had Thousands of Pounds-worth of Goods in his Stores" (A 101–2). Franklin carefully chose the persons to compare—a poor widow housekeeper (not an impecunious retailer) compared to the wealthiest merchant. Walter Isaacson noted that it was "one of the first arguments in America for progressive taxation."[2] Franklin made his early innovative argument for progressive taxation seem like common sense. Franklin "proposed as a more effectual Watch, the Hiring of proper Men to serve constantly in that Business; and as a more equitable Way of Supporting the Charge, the levying a Tax that should be proportion'd to Property." The "Idea being approv'd by the Junto, was communicated to the other Clubs, but as arising in each of them. And tho' the Plan was not immediately carried into Execution, yet by preparing the Minds of People for the Change, it paved the Way for the Law obtain'd a few Years after, when the Members of our Clubs were grown into more Influence" (A 102).

Eight years later, 6 January 1742/3, a Philadelphia grand jury cited the same abuses Franklin had detailed (only the foreman's name is known—the ironmonger William Branson, who had been selling Franklin sheets of iron for his experiments on stoves), and so the Philadelphia Common Council took up the issue on 28 January and appointed a committee "to draw up a proper scheme for the better regulation of the Watch, who are to Lay the Same before the next Council." At that time (1743), four Common Council members were also Junto members: William Coleman and William Plumsted, who were founding members, and Thomas Hopkinson and Samuel Rhoads, who had joined slightly later.

The Philadelphia Corporation discussed the report on 7 and 14 February and asked the Pennsylvania Assembly to act. The legislators deliberated on the watch (2 and 11 August), deciding on the latter date that since the bill proposed taxing the citizens of Philadelphia, they should be acquainted with it. Two days later, the assembly of 1742–43 wound up the legislative year (its last day was 13 August). It merely ordered Franklin to print *A Bill for the Better Regulating the Nightly Watch* and distribute it with the *Pennsylvania Gazette*, thereby putting off any action until the next assembly, which would be elected on 1 October. The twelve-page pamphlet is an attractive Franklin imprint; he distributed it with the 18 or 25 August 1743 issue of the *Pennsylvania Gazette*.[3] The assembly of 1743–44, however, ignored the city watch. On 9 January 1744/5, a number of Philadelphia citizens (organized by Franklin?) petitioned the assembly to consider it, but that assembly adjourned the following summer without doing so. Evidently the Philadelphia representatives, Israel Pemberton (who represented Philadelphia from 1731 through 1749) and Oswald Peele (from 1741 through 1747) did not push the measure. Nothing was done for the next several years, no doubt partly because of the crises during King George's War, 1744–48.

Franklin was elected to the Philadelphia Common Council on 4 October 1748. On 6 November 1749, the council again considered the problem of the city

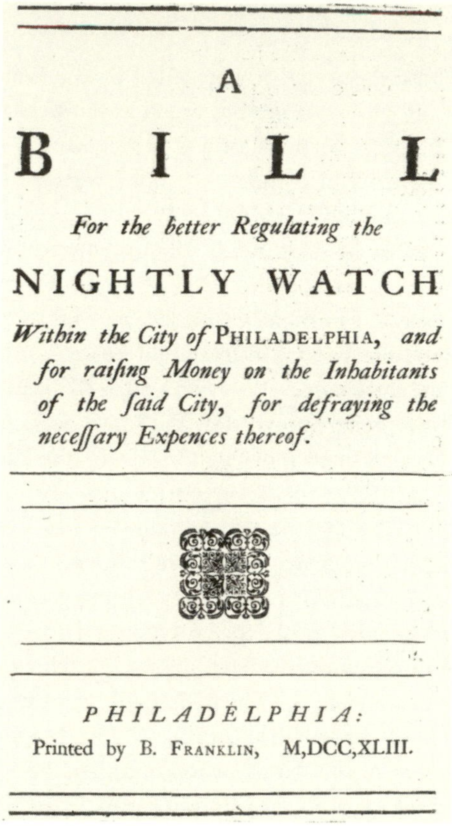

A
B I L L

For the better Regulating the

NIGHTLY WATCH

Within the City of PHILADELPHIA, *and for raiſing Money on the Inhabitants of the ſaid City, for defraying the neceſſary Expences thereof.*

PHILADELPHIA:
Printed by B. FRANKLIN,   M,DCC,XLIII.

Figure 27. Crusading for a more equitable tax and better police: the title page of A Bill for the Better Regulating the Nightly Watch *(1743). In the fall of 1735 Franklin wrote a paper for the Junto on the inadequacies of the Philadelphia police. The nightly watch usually consisted of a group of ragamuffins who were of little use. The taxes charged for the watch were the same for everybody: the old widow with no possessions paid as much as the great merchants. Franklin proposed that the tax assessment be proportionable to the property one owned. The Junto approved the plan.*

Eight years later, the Philadelphia Grand Jury (with the ironmonger William Branson, a friend of Franklin, as its foreman) complained of the same faults of the nightly watch. The Philadelphia Corporation took it up and recommended that the General Assembly pass a bill making the changes Franklin had originally recommended. Franklin's friends and fellow Junto members William Coleman, Thomas Hopkinson, and Samuel Rhoads were among the councilmen who presented the bill to the assembly on 3 May 1743. But the assembly did not enact it. It merely referred the bill to the "next Assembly; and in the mean Time it is ordered to be printed, and dispersed by the Clerk with his Newspapers." The 1743 bill, like the final one of 1751, contained Franklin's reforms.

After Franklin was elected to the Philadelphia Common Council in 1748, it petitioned the assembly again to enact a bill on the nightly watch. Finally, 9 February 1750/1, the bill containing Franklin's recommendations of 1735 passed. That did not quite end his project. He was elected to the assembly shortly thereafter (April 1751) and as an assemblyman drafted regulations for the constables and watchmen on 7 July 1752. Courtesy, Historical Society of Pennsylvania, Philadelphia.

watch, observed that it would require time to have the assembly act, and asked each constable to report every morning to the mayor any disturbance of the previous night. Franklin served (8 January 1749/50) on the Philadelphia Council committee to petition the assembly.

On 11, 12, 24, and 25 January 1749/50, the assembly considered the petition and drew up a bill, which, on 27 January, was returned to the committee to be revised and printed. No printed copy is extant; it languished.[4] A year later, 15 January 1750/1, the assembly appointed a committee to draw up a bill for regulating the watch. The Philadelphia members of the legislature were now Joseph Fox and William Clymer (who died in April 1751). They must have supported the bill. When the committee reported seven days later (22 January 1751), it had transformed the bill to include lighting "the Streets, Lanes, and Alleys of the said City." The act was superior to Franklin's original plan, for it included lighting the streets. Franklin said in the *Autobiography* that the honor of placing the first light before his house had been mistakenly ascribed to him but was really done by John Clifton, and he merely followed Clifton's example. Does that mean that Franklin had the second street light in Philadelphia?

Like several of the city's civic improvements, lighting began with a group of private citizens. They had organized on 21 December 1749. Each agreed to pay three shillings and nine pence per month for lighting the lamps nightly in front of their houses. Franklin no doubt signed, along with Clifton, John Smith, William Logan, Isaac Greenleafe, and others. When the legislative committee presented the act on 22 January 1751, the committee members had consulted with the private group organized over a year earlier.

The revised act was read in the assembly on 22, 23, and 24 January and passed on 26 January. The *Pennsylvania Gazette* reported that on Monday night, 30 September 1751, "the Streets of this City began to be illuminated with Lamps, in Pursuance of a late Act of Assembly." On 1 February, however, Governor James Hamilton found fault with the bill; the House nevertheless urged him to sign it on 2 February; and on 6 February he sent an amended version to the House. The assembly accepted some of the amendments on 7 February and rejected others. Finally, Gov. Hamilton agreed on 8 February and signed the bill on 9 February 1750/1. The act specified that the mayor, recorder, and aldermen would draw up regulations for the constables and watchmen. Section 9 said the wardens and city assessors would determine and judge what sum of money "shall be necessary to be raised and levied," and section 10 empowered the wardens and assessors to tax the inhabitants proportionally to the wealth of their property.[5]

Franklin, who was elected a member of the legislature in April 1751 and who was also an alderman in the Philadelphia Council, drafted regulations for the constables and watchmen on 7 July 1752 (4:327–32). Seventeen years after Franklin proposed reforming the policing of Philadelphia and making the system of taxation more equitable, he succeeded.[6]

Franklin found the globe lamps purchased from London inefficient: "they admitted no Air below, the Smoke did not readily go out above, but circulated in the Globe, lodg'd on its Inside, and soon obstructed the Light they were intended to afford; giving, besides, the daily Trouble of wiping them clean: and an accidental Stroke on one of them would demolish it, & render it totally useless." Franklin studied the lamp and probably experimented with different designs. He came up with a better lamp. It had four flat planes with a long funnel above to draw up the smoke and apertures below to aid the smoke's ascent. The resulting lamps were "kept clean, and did not grow dark in a few Hours as the London Lamps do, but continu'd bright till Morning; and an accidental Stroke would generally break but a single Pane, easily repair'd" (A 126).

STREET CLEANING AND PAVING

Franklin told in the *Autobiography* of his admiration for Philadelphia, where the streets were "laid out with a beautifull Regularity." They were "large, strait," and crossed "each other at right Angles." But they were unpaved. "In wet Weather the Wheels of heavy Carriages plough'd them into a Quagmire," making them difficult to cross. In dry weather "the Dust was offensive." Franklin lived near the large Jersey Market in Market Street and "saw with Pain the Inhabitants wading in Mud while purchasing their Provisions." In the 1730s, a strip of "Ground down the middle of the Market was at length pav'd with Brick, so that being once in the Market" persons "had firm Footing, but were often over Shoes in Dirt to get there." Franklin no doubt brought up the subject in the Junto and presented the problem with the solution. He said that "By talking and writing on the Subject, I was at length instrumental in getting the Street pav'd with Stone between the Market and the brick'd Foot-Pavement that was on each Side next the Houses."

That was a major improvement, but "the rest of the Street not being pav'd, whenever a Carriage came out of the Mud upon this Pavement, it shook off and left its Dirt upon it, and it was soon cover'd with Mire, which was not remov'd." A street cleaner should be hired. Franklin thought that the job could be done if each property owner on the street paid six pence a month. But perhaps not all householders would pay unless they saw the advantage of a clean street. Franklin alone hired "a poor industrious Man" to clean the street twice a week and carry "off the Dirt from before all the Neighbours Doors" (A 124–25).

A few weeks later, Franklin "wrote and printed a Paper, setting forth the Advantages to the Neighbourhood that might be obtain'd by this small Expence; the greater Ease in keeping our Houses clean, so much Dirt not being brought in by People's Feet; the Benefit to the Shops by more Custom, as Buyers could more easily get at them, and by not having in windy Weather the Dust blown in upon their Goods." He "sent one of these Papers to each House, and in a Day or two went round to see who would subscribe an Agreement to pay" six pence a week to have the streets cleaned. "It was unanimously sign'd, and for a time well executed. All the Inhabitants of the City were delighted with the Cleanliness of the Pavement that surrounded the Market, it being a Convenience to all" (A 125).

No copy of the printed paper (probably a small broadside) is extant; the date of Franklin's first attempt to clean Philadelphia's streets is unknown, but it was probably in the 1730s. The example of Market Street had a good effect: it "rais'd a general Desire to have all the Streets paved; and made the People more willing to submit to a Tax for that purpose." The tax was passed more than a decade later. And when Franklin wrote about it in the *Autobiography* in 1788, he misremembered: he "drew a Bill for Paving the City, and brought it into the Assembly. It was just before I went to England in 1757 and did not pass till I was gone, and then with an Alteration in the Mode of Assessment, which I thought not for the better, but with an additional Provision for lighting as well as Paving the Streets, which was a great Improvement" (A 125). But the additional provision for lighting the streets was added, as we have seen, to a bill on the police, not to one on paving the city. Further, no bill on paving the streets turns up in legislative records before Franklin left for London in 1757. Franklin may have drawn up such a bill and left it with a fellow member of the assembly. His long interest in the project and the fact that the later bill was for both paving and cleaning the streets suggest that it was based on Franklin's draft.

When the Pennsylvania Assembly appointed a committee on 3 February 1762 to draw up an act for paving the streets, five of the eight members were friends of Franklin: Thomas Leech, John Hughes, Joseph Galloway, John Baynton, and Samuel Rhoads. Leech, who chaired the committee, had been closely associated with Franklin for twenty years. An act for paving and cleaning the streets passed in the Pennsylvania Assembly on 26 March 1762, while Franklin was in London. He arrived back in Philadelphia on 1 November and took his seat in the legislature on 11 January 1763. Just over two weeks later, 28 January 1763, he was assigned to a committee to draft a supplemental bill for paving and cleaning the streets of Philadelphia, which passed on 22 February.

ENVIRONMENTALIST: THE PUBLIC DOCK

In 1739 Franklin initiated a drive to clean up the area around the public dock and to rid the city of the nuisance arising from "Slaughter-Houses, Tan-Yards, Skinner Lime-Pits, &c. erected on the publick Dock, and Streets, adjacent." The area stank, and Franklin thought it was unhealthy. On 15 May 1739, "a great Number" of citizens petitioned the Pennsylvania Assembly asking that "for the Convenience and Reputation of the City, and the Health of the Inhabitants, the Erecting of new Tan-Yards, &c. within the City, may be restrained, and that those already made, may be removed within such Term of Years as shall be judged reasonable." Since Franklin led the movement, he probably wrote, organized, and signed the environmental protest.[7] The legislature took up the matter on 17 May, commanding "that Notice be given to the Tanners of the said City, that they may attend this House To-morrow Morning, and shew Reason, if any they have, why the Prayer of the Petition should not be granted." After the tanners petitioned for further time, the assembly gave them until the next legislative session but ordered that "in the mean time no Person presume to erect, plant or dig any Tan-pits, Lime-holes, or Slaughter-houses, within the City of *Philadelphia*, on Pain of incurring the Displeasure of this House."

At the next session of the 1738–39 assembly, 8 August, the tanners asked that they "not be obliged to leave the City, but laid under such Regulations and Restrictions as may effectually remove the Mischiefs complained of." The legislators requested that both the tanners and some of those who petitioned against them "attend this House To-morrow Morning, at Nine a Clock, in order to be heard in Support of their several Petitions." They did so. In the postscript to the 18 October 1739 *Gazette*, an anonymous author (Franklin) wrote that "Young [Samuel] M[orri]s" appeared for the tanners (his father belonged to the Union Fire Company): "He assumed a Military Air and Strut, placed himself at the Front of the Tanners, putting one Leg foremost; he drew his Handkerchief, rowled it up in his Hand, gave it a few elegant Flirts and Toffes, and having gained a proper Posture, he look'd on the Spectators, with an Air of Grandeur, Self-sufficiency, and Contempt." ("Military Air and Strut . . . Flirts and Toffes"—what a wonderful put-down!) Although Speaker Andrew Hamilton "with great Civility (pursuant to the Practice and good Order of the House) would have let him" and the tanners "know the Reasons why they were admitted to appear—But the Young man had no Patience, he soon interrupted and began his Speech—This occasioned a small Complaint, and at last he was with some Difficulty prevailed with to be silent until a proper Time."

During his denial of any problem, Morris "said much about the Sweetness and Cleanliness of their Trade, and said he could smell no Stink. That their Trade was sweet, and affirmed it was untrue to say otherwise. That what some People called a Stink from the Pits, was a sweet Smell. That the Tanners were as healthy as other Men, adding, Are not we healthy Men?" Of course the tanners agreed, but evidently they realized that many persons wanted action on the petition.

The next Friday morning, 10 August 1739, the tanners proposed to ameliorate the environmental nuisance: "A convenient Method for the better regulating of Tan-yards, submitted by the Tanners to the Honourable House of Representatives of the Freemen of the Province of Pennsylvania." The tanners recommended that "the Tan-yards be well paved between all the Pits, and wash'd once every Day; let the Watering-pools and Masterings (which are the only Parts that afford offensive Smells) be inclosed on every side, and roofed over, within which Inclosure may be a subterranean Passage to receive the Washings and Filth of the Yard into the Dock or River at High-Water; Let the whole Yard be likewise inclosed on all Sides with some strong close Fence, at least seven or eight Feet high, and every Tanner be obliged every Week to cart off his Tan, Horns, and such offensive Offals." Tanners William Hudson, Jun., Samuel Morris, John Ogden, John Howell, William Smith, and, for John Snowden (who was out of town), the testimony of Samuel Morris and John Howell all guaranteed the action. Discussing the affair, Professor Michal McMahon noted that the tanners were among Philadelphia's elite citizens and commented that Franklin was "politically courageous" in opposing them.[8]

The assembly dodged the environmental issue, saying it concerned only Philadelphia. Since "the Tanners, Skinners, &c. have planted their Fatts, Limepits, &c." in the city, "the Inconveniences arising from those Yards and Pits must be best known there." The assembly therefore requested the Philadelphia Common Council "to make such Provision for the Relief of the Petitioners, against the Tanners, Skinners, Butchers, &c. as they shall find to be necessary and consistent with the Powers of their Corporation." If the Philadelphia Council needed the legislature's help, it should apply to the assembly. When the Philadelphia Council met two days later on 12 August it ignored the environmental question, perhaps partly because of the tanners' personal influence. William Hudson, Sr. (d. 1742), was a member of the corporation and had been mayor in 1725; Samuel Morris's father, brother, and other relatives were members, and he himself was elected to the corporation in 1755.[9] The city government did nothing.

"The Account of the Tanners"

With the Pennsylvania Assembly's inaction, the tanners considered themselves vindicated. Because Franklin and the *Pennsylvania Gazette* supported the ecological measure, the tanners took their writings to the *American Weekly Mercury*, where, as usual, Andrew Bradford opposed the younger printer and his newspaper. The tanners celebrated the inaction as a victory and scorned Franklin and the other environmentalists in the *Mercury* on 16 August 1739. After describing the petition, the *Mercury*'s "Account of the Tanners" (which was probably written primarily by Samuel Morris, Jr.) reported that the testimony before the Pennsylvania Assembly against them was "without Foundation," for the complaint really ought to be charged to the "present disorderly Condition of the Dock, which was a Receptacle for all kinds of filth from a very great part of the Town, and in the upper Parts of it without water sufficient to carry it off." The tanners' apologist further claimed that the "abundance of Necessary-Houses on the Dock," not the tanyards, caused the smell and unpleasant appearance of the lower dock.

Though the petition had argued that the dock area bred disease, the *Mercury* article contended that the tanners proved, "by clear Instances, that it was not truly asserted in that Petition, that the Health of the Inhabitants was affected by Tanyards, and especially it appeared that they did not promote contagious Distempers among us, because that when such Distemper ranged with great violence in this City, the Inhabitants who were in the Neighbourhood of the Tanyards were preserved from it more than in other Parts of the Town." The tanners' spokesman said that they showed that the practice in Philadelphia was the same as in London and in other densely populated parts of Great Britain. Though Franklin and the petitioners had cited the precedent of New York, the tanners claimed that in New York, butchers, "a Trade that of necessity was much more offensive than Tanning," were allowed because the location was convenient for the citizens. The *Mercury* advocate said that the petitioners had gone too far in giving as reasons for removing the tanners—"the Tann, Horns, Dead Dogs, Country People losing their Dogs, Tanners Dogs biting People, a Dog mangled, an other rescu'd from a Slaughterhouse." Such allegations were "impertinent to the Point." The tanners were applying "to the Mayor and Recorder for a Regulation of the Dock and Dock-Street" and would abide by that regulation. The *Mercury* author claimed that the Pennsylvania Assembly agreed with the tanners.

"The Account of the Tanners" celebrated that "the Petition was Rejected, [and] the Tanners' right to follow their Trades within the City, according to their own Proposals, asserted." Their spokesman concluded with the popular Whiggish political clichés: "For this happy Conclusion of an Affair that was Prosecuted with such Violence, and so immediately threatned the Tanners with the Loss of their Properties, they, no doubt, will ever gratefully express their Acknowledgements to those Worthy Members who stood so firmly for their Liberties, and next them to their Fellow Citizens who Petitioned on their Behalf, and to those too who having sign'd the other Petition, saw at last the Consequences of it, and how far such a Precedent might be made use of to the Destruction of many other Tradesmen, or almost any others, they saw it and generously renouncing an Inadvertant Error, strove with much earnestness to frustrate such a daring attempt on the LIBERTIES OF THE TRADESMEN OF PHILADELPHIA."[10]

Public Domain

Franklin was disgusted. The tanners' advocate lied about some facts, misrepresented others, and concluded by applying popular clichés to their selfish cause. On 30 August he replied with an anonymous *Gazette* letter addressed to "Mr. Franklin." The tanners had published a "partial" account of the hearing before the assembly, "magnifying what was said on their own side, and stifling every thing that was urged by the Petitioners." He recounted the petition's request, declared "that many offensive and unwholesome Smells do arise from Tan-Yards, to the great Annoyance of the Neighbourhood," and noted that the pollution lessened the value of the surrounding real estate. Dock Street and the dock were intended "for publick Service," but the tanners had "taken up and encumber'd the Street with their Pits, &c. and had choaked the Dock (which was formerly navigable as high as *Third Street*) with their Tan, Forms, &c." The petitioners had noted that the dock should be of use in case of fire, but it was now just "a grievous Nuisance."

What was at stake? In Franklin's view it was a question of public domain and public rights versus the selfish interests of a few powerful persons: "As the Tanners who own Land on the Dock are very few, and the People whose Interest is affected by their Remaining there, are a very great Number, the Damage they would suffer in removing, would be but a Trifle, in Comparison to the Damage done to others, and to the City, by their Continuing where they are."

Franklin's position remained consistent throughout his life: he believed in the principles underlying what we now call the right of eminent domain. All wealth over and above that necessary for the basic requirements of subsistence, clothing, and shelter was created by arbitrary conventions of society—and thus such wealth was at the disposal of society.[11] Franklin quoted the proposal of the tanners themselves to prove that they recognized the nuisance. He then quoted the *Mercury*'s false report and refuted it with the words used in the assembly in what was later to be the exact published form. (The minutes that were not yet published and thus were available only from the clerk, Franklin.) Then he asserted: "It is hard to imagine what could induce the Tanners to publish a Relation, so partial and so false; Did they imagine the Mayor and Commonalty would never hear of the Resolve of the House? or that the long-injured Petitioners would forget to prosecute their Petition, according to the Direction of that Resolve?" The angry Franklin said, "In Prudence they ought not to have triumph'd before the Victory; and in Justice they should not have call'd that a *Daring Attempt on the Liberties of the Tradesmen of Philadelphia*, which was only a modest Attempt to deliver a *great Number* of Tradesmen from being poisoned by *a few*, and restore to them the *Liberty* of Breathing freely in their own Houses." He tried to finish on a reasonable note, saying that some tanners would hardly thank the "Hot-Heads which produc'd that Paper, and call'd it *The Account of the Tanners*."

The Tanners' "Just" Cause

Two weeks later, Thursday, 13 September 1739, the *Mercury* writer replied. He said that "the Affair of the Tanners had made a great deal of Noise in this City," claimed that the attempt to regulate the tanners and butchers "was highly Iniquitous," and boasted that he had avoided "all personal Reflections." He indirectly confessed his misrepresentations by saying that he omitted some arguments "partly because they cou'd not be fully recollected and partly to avoid enlarging the paper to a tiresome length." He avowed that the person principally responsible for the petition made arguments that rendered "the Relators veracity Questionable." Therefore he chose "not to relate" the arguments.

Though the author's style is awkward, and his meaning is murky, the *Mercury* author's condescending attitude is clear. He implied that he was being kind to the principal opponent (Franklin) in not giving more of his opinions. "This

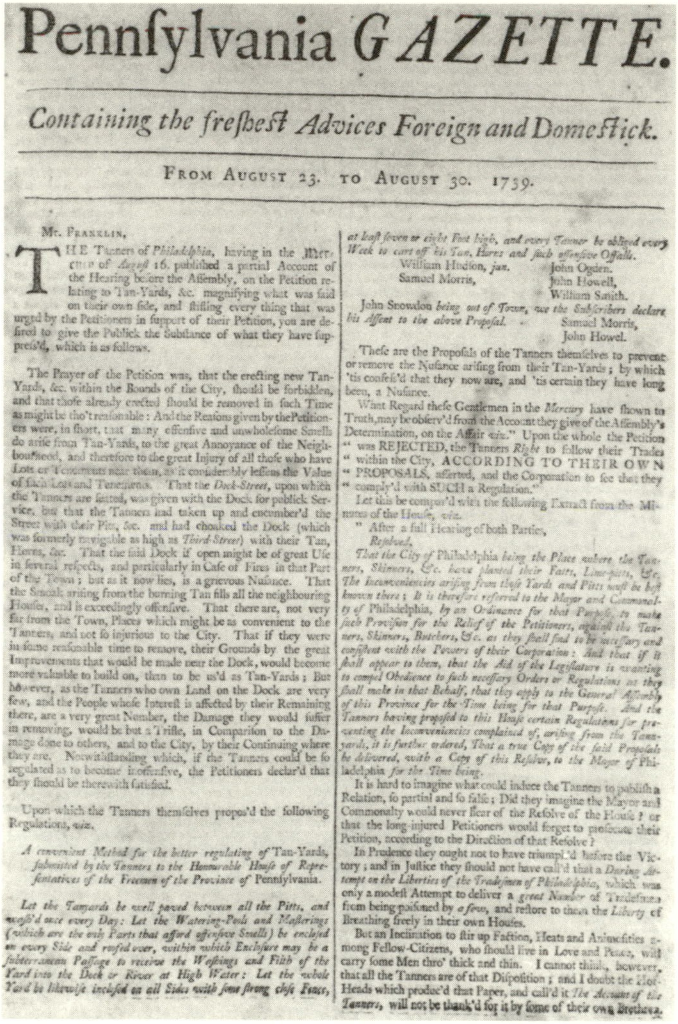

Figure 28. A failed environmental campaign, "The Tanners of Philadelphia," Pennsylvania Gazette, 30 August 1739. By 1739, the creek that flowed into the Delaware River between Spruce and Walnut streets had become a public nuisance, with necessary houses on it and with persons throwing trash into it. The tanners who lived by the creek were the greatest offenders. Not only did the tanyards stink, but the tanners disposed of unused animal parts in the creek.

In the spring of 1739, Franklin petitioned the assembly to clean up the former creek and to have the tanyards moved out of town. The tanners replied that they would clean up their yards and improve the creek. The assembly decided it was a Philadelphia matter and referred it to the Philadelphia Corporation. The tanners considered themselves vindicated and celebrated in Andrew Bradford's American Weekly Mercury, 16 August 1739. Franklin replied with this essay, attacking the tanners as selfish spoilers of the environment. But nothing was done about the nuisance until after Franklin's first English agency, when he was back in Philadelphia and serving in the assembly. Then, 4 March 1763, he finally managed to have two bills passed that ameliorated the problem. Courtesy, Library Company of Philadelphia.

the Writer of that Paper experienced in those few Instances he gave of the Gentlemen's Candor and Management on the other Side, and therefore, had he remembered the rest, it wou'd have been prudent to have left them to be related by the authors." He "wou'd not by any means Insinuate a want of Capacity in the Gentleman who principally had the management of the Affair before the Assembly," he would just note it "as an instance of the aukward Figure that Men of the most capable Cunning may make in the Espousal of a bad Cause." Attributing "cunning" to Franklin became a frequent criticism.

A brilliant writer and an adroit politician, Franklin was nevertheless no orator. When he led the opposition to the tanners and spoke on the floor of the House, it was, so far as I know, the first time that he did so. He was no doubt awkward. Later, after spending more than thirty years in public bodies, he wrote of himself that he was "a bad Speaker. Never eloquent, subject to much Hesitation in my choice of Words, [and] hardly correct in Language" (A 90).

The *Mercury* writer thought the property rights of the tanners were more important than the health of the many: He wrote, "If it was true, as asserted, *That a very great Number suffer for the Interest of a few*, yet it shou'd have been consider'd, whether it wou'd not have been more Just and Human to have prevented the ruin of the few and their Families, (who are intirely Innocent of the Transgression of any Law) tho' it were with some small Disadvantage to each particular of a great Number." In a rambling sentence, he also claimed that "it is not the Interest of a few Tanners against a great Number of others [because] almost all the Ground between *Walnut Street Bridge* and *Third Street*, on both sides the Dock, is in Possession of the Tanners, and letting alone the burning of the Tann, it is almost impossible that any ones Interest below the Bridge shou'd be affected by the Yards, so that whatever offensive Smells there may be among them, is of Disadvantage to themselves." The apologist would have his audience believe that the smell did not spread outside the area where the tanners lived and had their businesses. But Dock Creek, even at Front Street, was merely three and a half blocks from Market Street; at Third Street, Dock Creek was only a block and a half from Market Street.

Arguing before the assembly, Franklin had claimed that the tanners and butchers were "a hindrance to the Improvement of the City" and blamed the sickness and deaths of some persons on Dock Street's unhealthy conditions. The *Mercury* apologist attempted to refute the arguments. He said the tanners were poor but loving family members, struggling to make a living. He appealed to the reader: because the tanners "do not Improve their own Grounds in a way that they think will not be so Advantagious to them as the Present, it shall be call'd a hindrance to the Improvement of the City, and for that and the Imaginary loss of two or three Men, they shall be depriv'd of the Liberty of following their Trades in it, and Banish'd from it, and the greatest Pleasure that the World affords, the Society of their Relations and Friends, to sit down where-ever their little means can cheapest furnish them with Ground and Conveniencies."

After his sentimental appeal, the tanners' defender charged that it was "hard to imagine with what Design the Gentlemen [petitioners] appear'd before the Assembly, unless it was to show their Talent at Invective and Scandal." They found, however, "themselves incapable of supporting so bad a Cause" and finally joined the tanners in promoting regulations for Dock Creek. The spokesman again insisted that "since no Part" of the petition "was Granted . . . we rejoyce in having escaped the Danger and call it *VICTORY*." He claimed that "after the House Adjourn'd," most members "express'd themselves well satisfied with the Method."

The tanners' apologist continued that all "impartial Men" would judge that "the Assembly's granting the Tanners continuance in the City, and their liking so well the Proposals " were reasons to conclude "that the Petition was Rejected and the Tanners right to follow their Trades in the City according to their own Proposals asserted." After adding that "Two of the Tanners on the lower Part of the Dock" were beginning to abide by the self-imposed restrictions, he said that if those "above the Bridge" did the same, "there is no doubt but the Gentlemen of the Corporation will think it Sufficient."

The *Mercury* author charged that his *Gazette* antagonist (though everyone knew it was Franklin, he was not named), like all persons "who oppose the Cause of Truth and Liberty," could not reply "with any substantial Arguments" and therefore attempted by "low Arts and mean Cavils" to claim "Partiality and Falshood." According to the *Mercury* writer, the *Gazette* author had threatened the tanners with another petition "to remove them out of Town, and this he tells them they will do according to the Resolve of Assembly." (I reread Franklin's 30 August indictment and failed to find the *Mercury* author's reference; perhaps Franklin said it orally.) The tanners' apologist continued, "But the Gentleman must be more Cunning than any one else if he can find any such Resolve, and outwit the whole Assembly if he can find any such Meaning in the Resolve he hath Quoted." He concluded his 13 September piece saying "that the Justice of the Cause he has been Engag'd in the Defence of, gives him an entire Satisfaction as to what is done, but knowing that Writing is not his Business, and especially that a good Cause needs little Vindication, he declines the Controversy for the Future and thinks it his Duty to employ his thought on Matters that are his more Immediate Concern." Again he hinted that Franklin was his opponent, for writing was Franklin's business.

Pestilence

Franklin replied in a supplement to the *Pennsylvania Gazette* of 18 October 1739. A prefatory note, addressed to "Mr. Franklin," stated that the piece had not been sent in sooner because of the usual political agitations attending the annual 1 October election. Franklin cited the votes of the House of Representatives as evidence that the writer in the *Mercury* of 16 August and 13 September boldly lied. Franklin said that the tanners "asserted that Tan-Yards were allowed in the principal Towns of *Britain*, particularly in *London, Bristol,* and *York.*" The petitioners, however, pointed out that there was "not one Tanyard in the City of *London.*" But then young Morris claimed "That it is plain they are allowed in the City of *London*; for they are settled in *Southwark.*" Franklin commented, "And this all Men know is without the City, and not on the same side of the River."

Franklin argued that though the tanners denied it, the case of New York was "a Precedent exactly parallel to the Case in Debate." He rebutted the claim that the tanners were healthier than other persons. The last major distemper in Philadelphia was in 1699, "which swept off great Numbers. . . . At that Time there were but Two Tanyards on the *Dockstreet*, or even in the City, *viz. Hud-son*'s and *Lambert*'s, and but few Houses in the Neighbourhood—*Lambert* was seized with the Distemper in a very violent and uncommon Manner, he sickened, died, and was buried, in less than two Days—Thus one Tanner died out of two—And from the Houses nighest the *Dock* a great many died, whose Names and Places of Abode were well known to some now living." Franklin added that "the Experience of our Neighbours at *New-York* and their Proceedings thereon, amount to . . . full Proof" of the possible pestilential effects of tanning houses.

In closing, Franklin objected again to the tanners' claim that the petition was a precedent "that may be made use of to the Destruction of other Tradesmen, and a daring Attempt on the Liberties of the Tradesmen of Philadelphia." He rejoined, "If those Writers can perswade the Tradesmen of this City to believe their several Callings to be as offensive, infectious and injurious to their Neighbours, as that of the Tanners—this very mean Artifice might serve the Turn—But until then, they have no Right to make such Inferences—they are very unjust, and no modest Man would rank those Callings, which are clean, wholesome, and agreeable, with the Tanners Imployment, which is at best but a necessary Nuisance, and so esteemed, and therefore prohibited in most well regulated Towns and Cities." (Franklin had instances such as the tanners' appeal to the clichés of Whiggism in mind when he later wrote, "Such is the Imperfection of our Language, and perhaps of all other Languages, that notwithstanding we are furnish'd with Dictionaries innumerable, we cannot precisely know the import of Words, unless we know of what Party the Man is that uses them" [11:277].)

Failure

The Philadelphia Corporation did nothing, and Franklin lost his environmental battle. Franklin's alienation of the tanners was among the reasons that he suffered a temporary loss of popularity at the next election of Library Company directors.[12] The tanyards and the stench remained.

Resurrection

Eight years later the death of several persons who lived in the dock area raised anew the issue of the dock's unhealthiness. Richard Peters wrote Thomas Penn on 4 September 1747 that yellow fever and other fevers appeared first in the houses around the dock and therefore the council thought the "quantity of Filth & Mudd breeds or at least very much contributes to the Malignancy of Distempers." Peters asked that Penn suggest a scheme to remedy the situation. Penn replied on 30 March 1748 that the fevers evidently came from the West Indies. Nearly five months before Penn replied, the Philadelphia City Council discussed the dock (19 October 1747) and judged the area to be "a very great nuisance, and injurious to the Health of the Inhabitants . . . living near it." Though Franklin was not yet a member of the council (he was elected the following year, 4 October 1748), the City Council appointed him with Samuel Powel, John Stamper, Samuel Rhoads, Edward Warner, and William Logan to be a committee to recommend action. As Michal McMahon has noted, these members of the Common Council were builders and technologists.[13]

Franklin inserted an allusion to the unhealthiness of the Dock Street area in the "Proclamation for a General Fast" (9 December 1747), which he wrote for the governor and council. Though the purpose of the proclamation was to gain support for the Militia Association, Franklin mentioned that the inhabitants "have been sorely visited with mortal Sickness in the Summer past." On 24 February 1748 the committee to consider Dock Street recommended that a dock and a landing place should be built, the dock dug out and cleansed so that the bottom would be covered with water, and that the channel above the dock deepened and walled. It was an ambitious plan. Since the committee realized the expense would be considerable, it had approached the adjacent property owners who had agreed "to digg, wall, and clense, their several and respective Shares of the said Dock" provided that they were granted the profit arising from the landing of wood and other goods on the new dock and landing place. That was unacceptable because the dock had been and still was public. The committee proposed a special tax to clean up the dock, giving two reasons for its necessity. First, if the dock remained an eyesore and greeted arriving persons with a stench, the nuisance might prevent the future growth of the city by discouraging immigrants. Second, it filled "our own Inhabitants with Fears and perpetual Apprehensions, while it is suspected to propagate infectious Distempers." The City Council, however, decided to consult with city assessors, and the proposal again languished.

A Small Success

Fifteen years later, Franklin was back in Philadelphia after his first English agency (1757–62). He was sworn in as a member of the Pennsylvania Assembly on 11 January 1763. On the twenty-fourth, the Pennsylvania Assembly received a remonstrance and petition complaining about the dock. The next day, it received another petition saying that the dock should be cleaned. On 28 January, a committee including Franklin brought in a bill for paving and cleaning Philadelphia's streets. On 3 February, the House appointed a committee including

Franklin (and six of the eight members serving on the 28 January committee) to consider the dock. The committee reported on 9 February that it was "necessary" that the dock "be cleansed, and properly walled." The resulting act authorized purchasing lots for public landing places and directed the Philadelphia street commissioners to clean, repair, and make the dock navigable. It further required the owners of land bordering the dock to wall with stone their portions of the dock's banks at their own expense. When it became law on 4 March, another act was passed that day: "An Act to prevent and remove certain Nuisances in . . . Philadelphia," which forbade throwing any dirt, rubbish, "carcase, carrion or filth" into the water by Dock Street.[14] Two years later, a supplement to the bill for paving the city (15 February 1765) conceded that the attempts to clean the upper parts of Dock Creek had failed and ordered Dock Creek north of Walnut Street to be walled over as a public street.[15]

CONCLUSION

When Franklin discussed his civic projects in the *Autobiography*, he also recalled his suggestions for keeping the streets of London clean, noting such practical matters as the advantage of having one gutter rather than two. He apologized for devoting "Attention to Affairs of this seemingly low Nature" and observed that "Human Felicity is produc'd not so much by great Pieces of good Fortune that seldom happen, as by little Advantages that occur every Day" (A 129). He devoted considerable attention to civic affairs in the *Autobiography* because he wanted more persons to become better citizens. Franklin made "Public Spirit" a virtue to be inculcated in the Academy of Philadelphia, wanting "to fix in the Minds of Youth deep Impressions of the Beauty and Usefulness of . . . Public Spirit" (3:412).

Franklin invested hundreds of hours in improving the city's safety, its intellectual potential, and its environment. Twenty-four years after starting the campaign to clean up the docks, he succeeded—temporarily. Keeping the streets clean and well paved, keeping them lighted at night, keeping the cities safe, keeping the taxes equitable, and keeping the environment healthy will always require new answers to new and old problems by concerned citizens. After years of effort, Franklin finally had some partial success. In his day, he was the most concerned citizen. A visitor in Philadelphia recorded on 24 February 1750/1 that "few Towns if any in England . . . are better Illumined with Lamps & those of the best Sort, nor their watch better regulated."[16]

SEVENTEEN

George Whitefield and the Great Awakening

He that shall discover that [how to make people virtuous] will, in my opinion, deserve more, ten thousand times, than the inventor of the longitude.—Franklin to Whitefield, 6 August 1749

THE MOST FAMOUS MINISTER of the mid-eighteenth century and the most famous scientist of the day became frequent collaborators and good friends. George Whitefield and Franklin came together at first through reciprocal business interests and later joined together and attempted to help one another in their efforts to do good. It was a successful collaboration. Whitefield could be considered the first media sensation of the modern world, and Franklin, as publisher of the *Pennsylvania Gazette*, helped make him so. Whitefield gave Franklin his sermons and journals to print (these became Franklin's most successful large book imprints); Franklin celebrated Whitefield's orphanage, defended it from critics, and contributed funds to it; and Whitefield raised money for Franklin's projects, the Academy of Philadelphia and the Pennsylvania Hospital. Their friendship transcended these collaborations. Though each had theological reservations about the other, they respected, admired, and liked one another. Their friendship was a tribute to each.

The religious fervor called the Great Awakening (ca. 1740–48) was America's first and perhaps most intense large-scale religious revival.[1] Growing out of the European pietistic movement and English humanitarianism, it answered American needs. A revival supplied the conversions that New England's covenant theology demanded, and it furnished an outlet for the emotional and spiritual life of an isolated population living in tiny communities, on remote farms, and on the frontier. Evangelicalism was popular and successful in the cities (though Boston, New York, and Philadelphia were all small towns by today's standards).

A harbinger of the Great Awakening arrived in New Jersey in 1720, when the Reverend Theodorus J. Frelinghuysen, a Dutch Reformed minister, settled there. His impassioned preaching and emphasis on inner religion and rebirth were popular with many of his parishioners, but some resisted.[2] The quarrels from 1720 to 1726 in the Dutch Reformed churches to which Frelinghuysen ministered prefigured the widespread church schisms and feuds from 1740 to 1744. By 1726, however, Frelinghuysen had established himself and his revivalistic preaching in New Jersey.[3]

In 1726, the Reverend William Tennent, Jr., became the Presbyterian minister at Neshaminy, Pennsylvania, started the "Log College," and began training revivalist ministers, including his four sons and Samuel Blair. They gradually became friends with and were influenced by Frelinghuysen. The following year, 1727, Jonathan Edwards was appointed minister of the church in Northampton, Massachusetts, where his grandfather, Solomon Stoddard, had enjoyed a series of minor revivals between 1675 and 1725. In 1728 William Law's best-selling *Serious Call to a Devout and Holy Life*, which was to influence the Wesleys and Whitefield, appeared in England.

At the end of 1734, Jonathan Edwards excited the members of his Northampton parish to a state of religious fervor with a series of sermons on justification by faith alone. Edwards's account of the revival, *A Faithful Narrative* (1737), became the model and inspiration for revivals throughout New England. Franklin read *A Faithful Narrative* and praised it (28 July 1743). During the 1730s, the graduates of William Tennent's Log College were becoming prominent Presbyterian evangelical ministers. Gilbert Tennent's revivalistic sermon, *Solemn Warning to the Secure World from the God of Terrible Majesty* (1735), illustrated the new fervor of Presbyterian sermons. Later in the decade, minor revivals frequently took place in New Jersey. When the Anglican George Whitefield returned to America in 1739, he found allies among the Tennents and many New England ministers. He also befriended and was befriended by the German pietists in Pennsylvania, though these alliances splintered after Whitefield left Pennsylvania.

GEORGE WHITEFIELD

In the mid-1730s, the English Anglican minister George Whitefield decided to go to Georgia to join John and Charles Wesley, who had arrived in Savannah on 6 February 1735/6. John Wesley compiled and wrote his first collection of hymns while in Charleston, South Carolina. Franklin's partner Lewis Timothy printed his *Collection of Psalms and Hymns* (1737), which the literary historian Richard Beale Davis described as "the first real Anglican hymnal published in the world and the first hymnal of colonial America." Davis said it marked "the beginning of a great hymn-singing tradition in both Anglican and Methodist churches."[4] Charles Wesley left Savannah for England on 26 July 1736, and John Wesley left Charleston on 22 December 1737, with neither effecting any significant religious changes.

Whitefield, not disheartened by their comparative failure, arrived in Georgia in the spring of 1738. He found that numerous immigrants died shortly after coming to Georgia, leaving infants and children. Though seasoning killed immigrants in every colony, it did so especially in the South, partly because of the climate and diseases in the Georgia low country and partly because the debtors and other poor people who were brought to Georgia were not as healthy as those who immigrated to the other colonies. Pitying the situation of the orphans, Whitefield resolved to raise funds for them. He sailed back to England that fall, took orders as an Anglican priest, secured a grant of 500 acres ten miles from Savannah, and raised £1,000 for the orphanage.

Before 1739, Whitefield was mentioned only once in the *Pennsylvania Gazette* (30 June 1737), for remitting to the trustees of Georgia £80 for erecting a church at Frederika, Georgia. After he returned to Great Britain, English newspapers throughout 1739 celebrated the astonishing success of his outdoor preaching to thousands. Franklin reprinted two of these reports (5 and 12 July 1739) and subsequently featured two accounts of his forthcoming voyage to America (23 August and 11 October).

Whitefield's second American visit began in the fall of 1739. He was a surprising figure. Like many Anglican ministers, he wore a black gown and a bushy, white wig, and his bright blue eyes were especially striking because he was extremely cross-eyed.[5] He landed at Lewes (Delaware) in the evening (30 October). He preached there the next afternoon and then set out for Philadelphia, arriving shortly before 11 p.m. on 2 November. He remained in America until 16 January 1741. He visited Philadelphia five times during the period. During the fourteen plus months in America, he inspired a great religious revival.

Earlier than other newspaper editors, Franklin appreciated Whitefield's attempts to do good and his celebrity status. His sermons were news. During 1740, Franklin's *Pennsylvania Gazette* published more material by and about Whitefield, mainly favorable, than any other newspaper.[6] Isaiah Thomas, the early historian of American printing, wrote in 1810: "This celebrated itinerant preacher, when he visited America, like a comet drew the attention of all classes of people. The blaze of his ministration was extended through the continent, and he became the common topic of conversation from Georgia to New Hampshire. All the newspapers were filled with paragraphs of information respecting him, or with pieces of animated disputation pro or con; and the press groaned with pamphlets written in favor of, or against, his person and ministry. In short, his early visits to America excited a great and general agitation throughout the country, which did not wholly subside when he returned to Europe. Each succeeding visit occasioned a renewal of zeal and ardor in his advocates and opponents; and, it has been said, that from his example American preachers became more animated in their manner."[7]

Philadelphia

Whitefield arrived in Philadelphia late on Friday night, 2 November, immediately calling upon the Reverend Archibald Cummings, minister of the Anglican Christ Church. Cummings invited him to preach. On Saturday afternoon, 3 November, and "every Day since" he preached in Christ Church. But it could not contain the multitude who gathered to hear him, so on 8 November, he preached on the courthouse stairs. Whitefield noted in his *Journal*: "The inhabitants were very solicitous for me to preach in another place besides the church; for it is quite different here from what it is in England. There, the generality of people think a sermon cannot be preached well without; here, they do not like it so well if delivered within the church walls."[8] In Philadelphia the Presbyterians, Baptists, Quakers, and other members of different religions did not like to go into the Anglican church, whereas in England, most people were Anglicans. Preaching in the open encouraged members of all religions to hear Whitefield. The decision was momentous. If America's Great Awakening had a particular starting date, it was not 30 October 1739, when Whitefield arrived, but 8 November, when he started preaching outdoors.

The *Gazette*'s next issue, 15 November 1739, reported, "On Thursday last [8 November], the Rev. Mr. Whitefield began to preach from the Court-House-Gallery [where votes were cast in the elections] in this City, about six at Night, to near 6000 People before him in the Street, who stood in an awful Silence to hear him; and this continued every Night, 'till Sunday." Whitefield also estimated the crowd at about six thousand. The next day, 9 November, he wrote: "I . . . preached again at six in the evening, from the Court House steps. I believe there were nearly two thousand more present to-night than last night. Even in London, I never observed so profound a silence." On Monday, 12 November 1739, he set out for New York, where, Franklin reported, he was "to preach at Burlington in his Way going, and in Bucks County coming back. Before he returns to England he designs (God willing) to preach the Gospel in every Province in America, belonging to the English. On Monday the 26th he intends to set out for Annapolis."

Such announcements, which later gave specific places, dates, and times for Whitefield's sermons, were essential in attracting the large crowds that attended his sermons. When Franklin and, later, other newspaper editors announced Whitefield's agenda, they became, in effect, his publicity agents. They would not have done so, however, unless they believed that numerous customers wanted the information.

In New Jersey on 14 November, Whitefield heard the Presbyterian minister Gilbert Tennent preach. Whitefield recorded in his *Journal* that he "never before heard such a searching sermon. He convinced me more and more that we can preach the Gospel of Christ no further than we have experienced the power of it in our own hearts." The next day in New York, Whitefield called upon the Reverend William Vesey (1674–1746), the bishop's commissary, but the old Anglican minister had heard that he made "a disturbance in Philadelphia" and that he caused "divisions in other places." Vesey refused to allow him to preach in New York's Anglican churches. So Whitefield preached in the open and in the Presbyterian, Congregational, and other churches where he was offered a pulpit. On his way back to Pennsylvania, Whitefield met the Reverend Theodorus J. Frelinghuysen in New Brunswick, New Jersey, on 20 November. Whitefield called the Dutch Reformed minister "a worthy old soldier of Jesus Christ" and saluted him as "the beginner of the great work which I trust the Lord is carrying on in these parts."[9]

Thinking that printing Whitefield's sermons and journals might be profitable, Franklin proposed publishing them by subscription, advertising in the 15 November 1739 *Gazette*. The subscription was successful. Whitefield recorded on 28 November, "one of the Printers" (Franklin) told him he had already received two hundred subscriptions for his journals and sermons. On 22 May 1740, Franklin advertised that the first two volumes of Whitefield's works, one of his sermons and one of his journals, would be ready the following Monday: Since "many People, during the Printing of the Books, have sent in their Names, or subscribed, without paying the first Subscription Money; and as the whole Number of Names far exceeds the Number of Books printed; those Subscribers who have paid, or who bring the money in their hands, will have the preference." As a consequence of the Whitefield contract and Philadelphia's religious fervor, Franklin published more imprints more successfully in 1740 than in any other year.[10]

Whitefield's second Philadelphia visit began on Friday, 23 November 1739, and continued to Thursday, 29 November. On Sunday, 25 November, Richard Peters, an Anglican clergyman who had been the assistant minister at Christ Church (1735–37), publicly criticized Whitefield, who replied with a sermon. The revivalist recorded in his *Journal* that Peters was "very dark in all the fundamentals of Christianity" and "an entire stranger to inward feelings." Whitefield nevertheless continued to have Christ Church available as a possible venue for his preaching. When Whitefield preached his Philadelphia farewell sermon on 28 November, Christ Church could not contain one-half the crowd, "whereupon they withdrew to Society-Hill, where he preach'd from a Balcony to a Multitude, computed at not less than 10,000 People."[11] The 6 December *Gazette* published his itinerary. Franklin's first polemical Whitefield piece appeared on 13 December 1739: "The Conduct and Doctrine of the Rev. Mr. Whitefield vindicated from the Aspersions and malicious Invectives of his Enemies." In the 27 December paper Franklin reprinted an anonymous poem praising Whitefield.

Whitefield's ecumenicalism appealed to Franklin and allowed the minister to preach to the widest possible range of religions persons. Though some ministers and laymen objected to his emotionalism, he was wonderfully successful with numerous varieties of religious persons—Anglicans, Presbyterians, Baptists, Moravians, Congregationalists, and others. "In one sermon Whitefield asked Father Abraham how many Presbyterians lived in heaven. 'None,' came the answer. How many Quakers were there? 'None!' How many Baptists?' 'None!' Who then lived in heaven? 'Only good Christians,' said Father Abraham."[12]

Just before Whitefield returned to Philadelphia, Franklin began printing a series of Whitefield's letters (10 and 24 April, 1 May 1740), vindicating his state-

ment that "Archbishop *Tillotson* knew no more of Christianity than *Mahomet.*"
Franklin subsequently published them together as a pamphlet titled *Three Letters.* Whitefield's third Philadelphia visit began on Monday evening, 14 April,
and lasted until Tuesday, 22 April. He sought out the Reverend Archibald Cummings on 15 April, who told him "that he could lend me his church no more,
because I had not treated the Bishop of London well, in my Answer to his late
Pastoral Letter; and also, because I had misquoted and misrepresented Archbishop Tillotson, in a letter published in the last week's *Gazette.* I told him he
had best shew that in public. He replied, the printers would not publish anything for them, and that the press was shut against them. I answered, it was
without my knowledge." The rumor that Whitefield "had engag'd all the Printers not to print any Thing against him" was widely reported. Franklin contradicted it on 8 May and 24 July 1740.

The *Pennsylvania Gazette* reported on 24 April 1740 that Whitefield preached
on 15 April "to about 8000 on Society Hill." He remained in the Philadelphia
area until Sunday, 20 April, when he "preached two Sermons on Society Hill,
and collected for the Orphans in *Georgia,* in the Morning £150 10s. and in the
Evening, when it's computed there were 15,000 Auditors, 83£, in all 233£ 10s
Currency, which is about 150£ Sterling." Persons flocked in from the countryside to hear him. The audience was half again as large as Philadelphia's population.

In the *Autobiography,* Franklin testified to Whitefield's effective preaching.
Perhaps the sermon he described was the one Whitefield delivered on Sunday
morning, 20 April. Franklin wrote that he had resolved not to contribute to the
Georgia orphanage because he believed that the orphans should be brought to
Philadelphia or to some other urban center, rather than transport all the workmen, materials, schoolmasters, and orphans to the Georgia wilderness. Then
Franklin described how Whitefield gradually softened his resolve so that the
humanitarian skeptic decided first to give the copper coins that he was carrying,
then the silver, and finally, at the end of the sermon, gave everything he had
with him, gold and all (A 88). It's a wonderful tribute to the power of Whitefield's preaching, but it seems quite unlikely that Franklin would be carrying
that much money, especially in different coins. Most likely, he often carried a
few coins and some Pennsylvania paper currency.

Franklin, however, no doubt often contributed after Whitefield's sermons,
for many of them were raising money for deserving charities. This sermon undoubtedly concerned the miserable plight of the Georgia orphans, not the religious truths of Christianity. Franklin also used a favorite device to support the
truthfulness of the case he was making. He supposedly escaped his own limited
point of view when testifying to Whitefield's spellbinding appeal: "At this Sermon there was also one of our Club, who being of my Sentiments respecting
the Building in Georgia, and suspecting a Collection might be intended, had by
Precaution emptied his Pockets before he came from home; towards the Con-

clusion of the Discourse however, he felt a strong Desire to give, and apply'd to a Neighbor who stood near him to borrow some Money for the Purpose. The Application was unfortunately to perhaps the only Man in the Company who had the firmness not to be affected by the Preacher. His Answer was, *At any other time, Friend Hopkinson, I would lend to thee freely; but not now; for thee seems to be out of thy right Senses*" (A 105). Franklin implied that the inner spirit, which affected him and the Anglican Thomas Hopkinson, did not affect the cool, calculating mind of one Philadelphia Quaker.

WHITEFIELD AND SLAVERY

Franklin interrupted Whitefield's letters criticizing Tillotson to publish in the *Gazette* on 17 April 1740 Whitefield's antislavery letter dated Savannah, 23 January 1739/40, addressed to the inhabitants of Maryland, Virginia, and North and South Carolina. It was bold of Whitefield to write the antislavery letter and bold of Franklin to print it. Not only did Franklin have numerous southern customers for his *Gazette*, but the Middle Colonies had numerous slaveowners. Though Franklin had published three antislavery pamphlets, Whitefield's letter marked the first essay in the *Pennsylvania Gazette* condemning slavery. Indeed, it was only the second editorial against slavery published in an American newspaper. John Campbell had published an essay against slavery (though it was strongly racist) in the 10 June 1706 *Boston News-Letter*. Whitefield bravely wrote: "As I lately passed through your Provinces, in my Way hither, I was sensibly touched with a Fellow-feeling of the Miseries of the poor Negroes. . . . Whatever be the Event, I must inform you, in the Meekness and Gentleness of Christ, that I think God has a Quarrel with you for your Abuse and Cruelty to the poor Negroes. Whether it be lawful for Christians to buy Slaves, and thereby encourage the Nations from whence they are brought, to be at perpetual War with each other, I shall not take upon me to determine."

Alas, too bad that Whitefield did not "determine" the issue then, for he might have become an abolitionist. He continued, "Sure I am, it is sinful, when bought, to use them as bad nay worse than as though they were Brutes; and whatever particular Exceptions there may be (as I would charitably hope there are some) I fear the Generality of you that own Negroes, are liable to such a Charge; for your Slaves, I believe, work as hard if not harder than the Horses whereon you ride. . . . God . . . does not reject the Prayer of the poor and destitute, nor disregard the Cry of the meanest Negroes! The Blood of them spilt for these many Years in your respective Provinces, will ascend up to Heaven against you."

Franklin respected and admired Whitefield's stand. Franklin republished the essay with *Three Letters from the Reverend Mr. G. Whitefield* (1740). Only one other newspaper printed the essay, the 29 April *New England Weekly Journal*.[13] Though sympathizing with Whitefield's point of view, Franklin may have owned a slave at the time—and definitely did so by 1745. Not until 1772 (19:187–88) did he himself write against slavery.

Whitefield intended to help slaves. On the last day (22 April) of his early spring visit to Philadelphia, Whitefield bought "five thousand acres of land on the forks of the Delaware, and ordered a large house to be built thereon, for the instruction of" African Americans. Back in Philadelphia, the minister recorded (9 May 1740), that he had agreed "to build my Negro Schools on the land which I have lately purchased." He never did so. His funds proved insufficient to support both the Georgia orphanage and the Pennsylvania school. In 1741, Count Zinzendorf, a leader of the Moravian Church, bought Whitefield's Pennsylvania land from his assistant, William Seward. Six years later, Whitefield purchased a plantation and slaves in South Carolina to support the orphanage. Though committed to the Christian education and humane treatment of slaves, he nevertheless defended the institution of slavery on biblical grounds. A recent historian has argued that one source of the slaveholders' nineteenth-century paternalism descends from the attempts of George Whitefield and southern evangelicals to ameliorate (but not abolish) the institution of slavery in the Great Awakening.[14]

The Dancers

On 16 April 1740, the Reverend William Seward, Whitefield's assistant and publicist, took away the keys of Robert Bolton's assembly room, where the dancing school, the weekly Dancing Assembly, and concerts were held. Upon Seward's promise "to pay for any Damage he should sustain thereby," Bolton gave him the keys to the assembly room. Seward noted in his journal: "May the Lord strengthen me to carry on this Battle against one of Satan's strongest Holds in this City,—supported in Part too by the *Proprietor*, whose Father bore a noble Testimony against those Devilish Diversions." Furious at being locked out, the gentlemen in the Dancing Assembly broke open the door and threatened to cane Seward. He nevertheless gave Franklin a brief news note for the 1 May *Gazette*: "Since Mr. *Whitefield*'s Preaching here, the Dancing School, Assembly and Concert Room have been shut up, as inconsistent with the Doctrine of the Gospel: And though the Gentlemen concern'd caus'd the Door to be broke open again, we are inform'd that no Company came the last Assembly Night."

The next day, 2 May, Seward called on Franklin, where he found several gentlemen of the Dancing Assembly. Seward recorded in his journal that they "accosted me very *roughly*, concerning a *Paragraph* I had put in the Papers, alledging it to be false. . . . They much insisted that my Paragraph insinuated" that Whitefield had convinced them of the evil of dancing. The gentleman said they abhorred his preaching. Seward answered that few persons would interpret the paragraph in that way and that if they did, it only honored the gentlemen. He added that he himself "was formerly as fond of" dancing and frivolity as they, "but, blessed be the Lord, that I was convinced to the contrary."

Reply

Offended by Seward's note of 1 May, the Dancing Assembly gentlemen published a note the following week saying that Seward had "on the 16th of *April*
shut up the Door of the Concert Room without any previous Application to, or
consent had of any of the Members." When informed that his act made him
liable to prosecution, Seward went (Wednesday, 30 April), and asked "Pardon of
some of the principal Gentlemen of that Society for his Indiscretion, repeatedly
assuring them, that he knew nothing of any Gentlemen's having hired the
Rooms, and that if he had the least Intimation of it, he would not have caused
them to be shut up." Though Seward apologized, the dancers said that he had
time to retract the notice but did not. Further, Seward lied "in order to have an
Apology for his Conduct; for Mr. *Bolton*, of whom the Rooms were taken, had
before *Seward*'s shutting them up, inform'd him, that they were hired by some
of the chief Persons in Town, for a Term then unexpired." They also told their
version of their chance meeting with Seward at Franklin's shop on 2 May. They
had come to ask who gave the printer that notice. Franklin told them it was
William Seward, who happened, just at that time, to come into the printing
shop. According to the dancers, Seward confessed that Bolton had told him that
the assembly rooms had been rented by gentlemen, "tho' he had so lately pretended and affirmed the Contrary, when he ask'd Pardon."

The Dancing Assembly gentlemen contradicted Seward's statement that no
members came at the last Dancing Assembly. They had ordered the door to be
unsealed on 16 April, the very night it was closed. The next night they met
"according to Custom," and Tuesday, 22 April, the last appointed date. "But
the Assembly being only for the Winter Season, is now discontinued of course,
and the Concert being for the whole Year, still goes on as usual." The Dancing
Assembly members then censured Seward: "After this Account of *Seward*'s Behaviour, no one can wonder at his low Craft, in getting this Paragraph foisted
into the News Papers just before his Departure for *England*, in order to carry it
along with him, and spread his Master's Fame, as tho' he had met with great
Success among the *better Sort* [emphasis mine] of People in *Pennsylvania*, when
at the same Time, to his great Mortification, he can't but be sensible that he has
been neglected by them."

Irritated by the gentlemen's calling themselves the "better sort," Franklin
prefaced their 8 May reply by noting that their vindication approached invective. The editor also remarked, "as the publishing of this, will obviate a groundless Report . . . that Mr. Whitefield had engag'd all the Printers not to print any
Thing against him. . . . I shall therefore print it as I received it." But Franklin in
effect announced that he planned to reply to the letter, for he added, "And
when the Publick has heard what may possibly be said in Reply, they will then
judge for themselves."[15]

Obadiah Plainman, a.k.a. Franklin

The following week, 15 May 1740, Franklin, writing as "Obadiah Plainman," responded to the "better Sort." Plainman said that he could not discover in the news report of 1 May "the least injurious Reflection on the Characters of the Gentlemen concerned." He also failed to understand the cause of the gentlemen's outrage after reading their letter of 8 May: "You tell us *the Paragraph manifestly carries in it an Insinuation*, that *the Persons concerned in the Concert declin'd meeting, as thinking it inconsistent with the Doctrine of the Christian Religion*. But, with Submission, I think the Paragraph manifestly insinuates the quite contrary. It mentions, that the Gentlemen concerned in the Concert, *&c.* caused the Door to be *broke open*, which was the strongest Evidence that could be given of their Dislike to the Principles on which it had been shut up. Therefore, tho' it immediately follows, that no Company came the last Assembly Night, it was *most unnatural* to suppose they should so *suddenly* have changed their Sentiments, and declined their Diversions on any religious Consideration."

Plainman defended the news report: "Let us admit for Argument's Sake (which, otherwise, can by no Means be admitted) that the Words are guilty of the Insinuation. . . . Yet, how does it appear that the Characters of the Gentlemen are injured by it? You tell us, *They think so*. But, is that a Reason to induce *Us* to believe it is *really* so? Since you have appealed to the *Mob* as *Judges* of this IMPORTANT Controversy, I must inform you, that the Assertion (and much less, *the Belief*) of any Man, never passes for Argument at *Our* impartial Tribunal. For my own Part (I speak with an humble Deference to the rest of my Brethren) I cannot conceive how any Person's Reputation can be prejudiced, tho' it should be reported, that he has left off making of Legs, or cutting of Capers."

Franklin's slur on dancing reminds us that he never joined the Dancing Assembly or any purely social club—unless the Freemasons be considered such. Most of his Junto friends belonged to the Schuylkill Fishing Company or to another social Philadelphia club. A 1748 list of Dancing Assembly members reveals that his good friends Thomas Hopkinson and William Plumsted belonged. His son, William, joined, but Franklin never did.[16] One wonders if Franklin knew how to dance. He seems prejudiced against it. If he learned to dance, it was not in his Boston home. Perhaps a prejudice against dancing (and inability to dance?) is one of the unremarked Boston (Puritan?) influences on Franklin. But dancing was so common in the eighteenth century that it seems hardly possible that Franklin did not attend some dances. Deborah, brought up an Anglican in Philadelphia, surely danced. Maybe she taught Franklin.

Plainman said, "Perhaps you will object, *that it is not the Fact, but the Motive, which is controverted*. . . . If this be the true State of the Question, *we* unanimously pronounce the Accusation to be groundless. In Matters of such a Nature, no Man can judge of your Thoughts but yourself." No one knows another's motives—or thoughts. As Franklin wrote earlier, "we can judge by nothing but Appearances, and they are very apt to deceive us" (1:67–68). Obadiah Plainman continued, "But you were not contented to stop here, but must needs tell *us* incoherent Stories of Mr. *Whitefield* and Mr. *Seward*, and, under Pretence of a Vindication, foist into the NewsPaper Invectives against those two Gentlemen. You might with equal Propriety have entertained *Us* with the History of *Romulus* and *Remus*, and entituled it 'an Argument to prove, that you did not *think* Dancing, or *idle* Capering an unchristian Diversion.'"

Franklin believed in the basic equality of human beings.[17] Plainman was especially irritated by the gentlemen's assumption of superiority. "I am to reprimand you, Sir, for your disrespectful Behaviour to *Us*, whom you had chosen for your Judges. *We* take Notice, that you have ranked yourself under the Denomination of the BETTER SORT of People, which is an Expression always made use of in Contradistinction to the *meaner Sort, i.e.* the Mob, or the Rabble. Tho' *We* are not displeased with such Appellations when bestowed on *Us* by our Friends, yet *We* have ever regarded them as Terms of outrageous Reproach, when applied to *Us* by our Enemies; for in this (and so it is in many other Cases) the Words are to receive their Construction from the *known* Mind of the Speaker." Franklin's epistemological skepticism concerning meaning and diction has already been manifested several times[18] and will be again in his essay "What is True?" (see Chapter 19).

Plainman continued, "Your *Demosthenes'* and *Ciceroes*, your *Sidneys* and *Trenchards* never approached *Us* but with Reverence: *The High and Mighty Mob, The Majesty of the Rabble, The Honour and Dignity of the Populace, or* such *like* Terms of Respect, were frequent in their Orations; and what a high Opinion they entertained of the Accuracy of *Our* Judgment, appears from those elaborate Compositions they addressed to *Us*." Surprisingly, Franklin included John Trenchard in the litany of great writers. The author of the *Independent Whig* and *Cato's Letters* was among the greatest commonwealth men of the preceding age, but few persons, even in at the peak of Trenchard's renown, would have ranked him with Demosthenes, Cicero, or even Algernon Sidney.

According to Plainman, the former great writers

> never took upon them to make a Difference of Persons, but as they were distinguished by their Virtues or their Vices. But now our present Scribblers expect our Applause for reviling us to our Faces. They consider us as a stupid Herd, in whom the Light of Reason is extinguished. Hence every impertinent Babbler thinks himself qualified to harangue us, without Style, Argument or Justness of Sentiment. Your gross Deficiency in the two latter Particulars I have already given Instances of; and as to your Skill in Language you have furnished *Us* with the following notable Example: You affirm *That Mr.* Whitefield's *Tenets are mischievous*: Therefore, on that Supposition, it is impossible they should be con-

temptible; yet, with the same Breath *you assure Us, that you have them in the utmost Contempt.* This is the merriest Gibberish I ever met with. Surely, you have not published it as a Sample of the Stile of those polite Folks, who by their own Authority, *'contrary to Law and Justice, without any previous Application to or Consent first had'* of their Fellow-Citizens, have usurped the Title of the BETTER SORT.

Franklin signed, "*I am, On Behalf of myself and the Rest of my Brethren of the* Meaner Sort, Yours, *&c.* OBADIAH PLAINMAN." The essay was, for Franklin, surprisingly strident. He must have been angry. Though his writings in the Hemphill affair gradually became strident and vituperative, they had begun with a comparatively reasonable tone. Plainman/Franklin became even more shrill in his second essay.

Richard Peters

Two rejoinders appeared the following week, one in the 22 May *Mercury* signed "Tom Trueman" and an anonymous letter in the *Gazette*. Richard Peters, secretary of the provincial land office (1737–60), a proprietary supporter and secretary of the council, probably wrote both.[19] The *Gazette* letter was obviously by the author of the 8 May essay that Plainman found objectionable. The anonymous writer recognized Franklin as Obadiah Plainman and gave four hints concerning his identity. First, he labeled Plainman as "the Prince and Leader of a Set of People" called the "meaner sort." Franklin's contemporaries widely recognized his egalitarianism. He had become known as a leader of the popular faction with his writings on paper money in 1729. The *Mercury* had criticized him on 6 January 1735/6 for "running violently on the side of the Populace." And Thomas Penn later said (1748) that Franklin was "a sort of Tribune of the People" (3:186).[20]

Second, the anonymous *Gazette* author accused Plainman of being "only a temporizing Convert, drawn in with Regard to your Worldly Gain." Tom Trueman's essay against Plainman similarly charged, "I shall never get one Farthing" by defending Whitefield "which is what you know Somebody can't say." All contemporaries knew that Franklin was Whitefield's primary American publisher and that his sermons and journals were selling well. Trueman, like the *Gazette* writer, remarked on Plainman/Franklin's impiety: "It cannot be said with any Truth that I ever sneer'd either at the Man [Whitefield] or his Doctrine, as the worthy Author of the Letter I am answering has done more than once where he thought it wou'd not hurt his Interest." Franklin made no secret of finding "some of the Dogmas" of Protestantism "unintelligible, others doubtful" (A 76).

Third, the anonymous *Gazette* author defended his use of the "better Sort" by supposing "that a curious Stranger, hearing we had a Library Company in Town, should ask of what People the Society was composed?" He replied, "A better answer could not be given, than that they were of the *better Sort*." Everyone who belonged to the Library Company knew that Franklin was its founder and guiding spirit. Franklin's gentleman opponent made it clear that the young, successful businessman Franklin was not just a mechanic. Though artisans founded the Library Company, the membership was gradually changing. By 1740 the new members were mainly merchants and professional men. Franklin nevertheless liked to think that the members were "common Tradesmen and Farmers" (A 72). When he composed a dedication for the Library Company building in 1789, he said that it was founded by a group of Philadelphia youths, "then chiefly Artisans."

Fourth, the *Gazette* correspondent identified Plainman as the editor of the *Pennsylvania Gazette*. "I shall dismiss you with this Piece of Advice, that the next Time you make Extracts out of other Men's Works, *viz.* those of the Party-Writers in *England*, introduce them a little more *a propo*, for at present your Paper is but a miserable Piece of Patch-Work." The personal and irrelevant attack closed the anonymous letter.

Plainman Again

On 29 May 1740 Obadiah Plainman wrote that the two articles replying to him were evidently by the same person, "*Or*, if by different Persons, that they communicated their Thoughts to one another, and then club'd them together for the Service of the *Public*." The author, or joint authors, Plainman called Tommy Trueman. "You tell me you have found out by my Letter, that I imagine myself the Prince and Leader of a mighty People. I wonder how a Genius so penetrating as yours could be led into so gross an Error: For, alas! I am but a poor ordinary Mechanick of this City, obligated to work hard for the Maintenance of myself, my Wife, and several small Children." Franklin's persona was a fictional creation, adopted for the occasion. In fact, Franklin had only one child in 1740, William; Francis had died of smallpox in 1736 and Sarah was not born until 1743. Further, though Franklin was an artisan, he had nevertheless achieved a position by 1740 as a leading Philadelphia citizen—hardly a "poor ordinary Mechanick." He continued, "When my daily Labour is over, instead of going to the Alehouse, I amuse myself with the Books of the Library Company, of which I am an *unworthy* Member." That characterization anticipates Franklin's self-portrait in the *Autobiography*: "In order to secure my Credit and Character as a Tradesman, I took care not only to be in *Reality* Industrious and frugal, but to avoid all *Appearances* of the Contrary. . . . I was seen at no Places of idle Diversion . . . a Book, indeed, sometimes debauch'd me from my Work; but that was seldom, snug, and gave no Scandal" (68).

Plainman repeated Tommy's question, "*What does the Author mean by informing the World that no Company came the*, then, *last Assembly Night? Ay*, what does he mean? This is the 'plaguy' Difficulty that has so *strangely puzzled*, and which still seems to *continue* to puzzle the *Better Sort*. . . . You desire I would show the World the Interpretation the Words will bear. Your Request, my dear Child, is contrary to all Laws of Argument, and therefore (tho' I am heartily sorry it should happen so) I cannot comply with your Desire. If you advance an Assertion, it is at your own Peril to support it with Proofs, which if you fail in, every one has a Right to *reject it as false*." Franklin's study of rhetoric appears in the reference to the "Laws of Argument" just above, as well as in the "allowed Figure of Speech" below.

Plainman replied to Tommy's defense that he did not call the gentlemen the "better sort." Franklin said that if the person were changed from the third to the first, the statement would read, "*We think our Characters injured by the Paragraph, as tho' Mr.* Whitefield *had met with great Success among us the* BETTER SORT *of People of Pennsilvania.*" The use of

> *Better Sort* in your first Letter . . . is evidently engrossed by Those who, with such a commendable Modesty, bestowed it on themselves. Now when private Persons publickly stile themselves, exclusively of all others, the BETTER SORT of People of the Province, can it be doubted but that they look on the Rest of their Fellow Subjects in the same Government with Contempt, and consequently regard them as Mob and Rabble. For so gross an Insult on the People in general, I endeavoured (but without respecting any Party in particular, as you ground-lessly insinuate) to turn the Writer into Ridicule; and therefore made Use of the Words Mob and Rabble, to expose him more effectually; but with very different Ideas annexed to them in my Mind (of which I was careful to give Notice) from those they receive, when deduced from that extraordinary Epistle. In my Animadversions on it I personated the Public, which you charge as a Crime, tho' it is an allowed Figure in Speech, frequently used, and particularly by those great Assertors of *Public Liberty*, whose Names I mentioned at the Time.

Plainman criticized Tommy's "Unskillfulness in Language." "You have not, by your Answer, mended the Blunder I remarked in your first: Your saying, that the same Person may be both mischievous and contemptible, is nothing to the Purpose; for you must regard him in different Views before you can properly affirm so differently of him: But Mr. *Whitefield's* Doctrine you represented simply as mischievous, and, under that Appearance only, you pronounced it the Object of your Contempt. It seems as if you would rather have it believed a Fault in Sentiment than Language: So you admit you understood the Word, but charge the wrong Application of it, to the Defect of your Judgment. In my poor Opinion, you gain nothing by the Change, to furnish Matter of Triumph."

Plainman next took up Trueman's charge that his reply was filled with Extracts out of other Men's Works, viz. *those of the Party-Writers in* England." Writing now as the *Gazette* editor, Franklin replied, "I have, more than once, told you, that no Man has a Right to bring an Accusation before the Publick, without bringing his *Proofs* along with it. You have confined your Evidence, which is to support this Charge, to the Party-Writers of *Great Britain*. I will not limit you to them, but shall admit, that there is a *Possibility* of its being true, if you can produce any Author, of any Age or Country, that ever was engaged in a Controversy *of the like Nature* with Ours. The Paragraph in Dispute contains but five Lines. The Insinuation, deduced from it in your first, is also comprized within five; in your second it takes up fifteen; I *hope* I shall live to see the Day, when It shall have swelled to a large Volume in Folio: For so useful and edifying a Work, as that is likely to be, must redound to the immortal Honour of that IMPORTANT Article of News, in the Reputation and Defense of which I am so *deeply* interested."

Plainman concluded, "As to the PERSONAL SCANDAL, in both your Letters, it is a Commodity I never deal in; and therefore, cannot make you any Return for those *flagrant* UNMERITED *Civilities*, which I have received from your *polite* Hand. However, if you think that such delicate *genteel* Touches of Raillery will be of any Service to you, in the farther Prosecution of this *worthy* Argument, I shall be far from objecting against your Use of them."

An anonymous versifier wrote a twelve-line poem in the 5 June *Mercury*, asking that the participants end the "thin debate" and their public display of impotence. The poem concluded the exchange. As we saw in the Library Company's 1740 election, Franklin suffered a temporary loss of popularity, no doubt partly because of the anger of some Dancing Assembly members. Certainly their spokesman, whom Franklin burlesqued, had special reason to be irate. According to William Seward, "the chief Speaker" for the Dancing Assembly was "Mr. P——," a "Person who opposed Mr. *Whitefield* in the Pulpit, and was formerly a Clergyman, but cast off the Gown for Secular Employment."[21] Richard Peters had already debated Whitefield in public (and been bested, thought the impartial Quaker John Smith), so his opposition to Whitefield may have been one reason for him to defend the Dancing Assembly. He was the primary author (and perhaps the only one) opposing Franklin.

It seems surprising that the thirty-four-year-old Franklin created a controversy concerning what might seem to be a comparatively minor difference of opinion. Perhaps it reveals the depths of his resentment against the class system and the assumption of superiority by "gentlemen"—a trait that characterized eighteenth-century society, even in America. The egalitarian resented the hierarchical class system, though his diction in the sentence just quoted (*inferiors . . . superiors*) discloses its permeation throughout eighteenth-century thought. Franklin's grandson William Temple Franklin recorded in 1818 an anecdote that his grandfather had told concerning the beginning of the Dancing Assembly: "In Philadelphia, where there are no noblesse, but the inhabitants are all either merchants or mechanics, the merchants, many years since, set up an assembly for dancing, and desiring to make a distinction, and to assume a rank above the mechanics, they at first proposed this among the rules for regulating the assembly, 'that no mechanic or mechanic's wife or daughter should be admitted on any terms.' These rules being shown by a manager to Dr. Franklin for his opinion, he remarked, that one of them excluded *God Almighty*. 'How so?' said the manager. 'Because,' replied the Doctor, 'he is notoriously the greatest mechanic in the universe; having, as the Scripture testifies, made all things, and that by weight and measure.' The intended new gentlemen became ashamed of their rule, and struck it out."[22]

Whether or not Franklin made the comment when the Dancing Assembly started in 1740, I believe he related the anecdote to his grandson, for it reflected both Franklin's egalitarianism and the Obadiah Plainman exchange. Perhaps in his egalitarian attitudes, as well as in his prose style, Franklin had been influenced not only by the Reverend John Wise (Volume 1, Chapter 17) but also by Nathaniel Gardner: in "Another Dialogue between the Clergyman and Layman" (22 January 1721/2), the *New-England Courant*'s Gardner had mocked a clergyman for his contempt for "the vulgar Sort of People."

THE NEW BUILDING

Whitefield wrought a major change in Philadelphia: "it seem'd as if all the World were growing Religious; so that one could not walk thro' the Town in an Evening without Hearing Psalms sung in different Families of every Street" (A 103). Whitefield's fourth Philadelphia visit began on Wednesday, 7 May 1740, and lasted four days. Since the Philadelphia Anglican church was closed to him and since meeting in the open air was threatened by rain and other inclement conditions, Whitefield's supporters projected building a large new structure. Franklin recalled in the *Autobiography* that Whitefield "was at first permitted to preach in some of our Churches; but the Clergy taking a Dislike to him, soon refus'd him their Pulpits and he was oblig'd to preach in the Fields. The Multitudes of all Sects and Denominations that attended his Sermons were enormous and it was matter of Speculation to me who was one of the Number, to observe the extraordinary Influence of his Oratory on his Hearers, and how much they admir'd and respected him, notwithstanding his common Abuse of them, by assuring them they were naturally *half Beasts and half Devils*" (A 103).

Before June 1740, Whitefield's adherents found a suitable vacant piece of land at Fourth and Arch Streets. The owners were willing to rent it for £15 a year, and they agreed to sell it to Whitefield's committee within ten years for £300. On behalf of Whitefield, four Philadelphia artisans became the trustees for the building: Edmund Wooley, the builder of Independence Hall; John Coats, a Philadelphia brick maker; John Howell, a tanner who opposed Franklin's 1739 environmental crusade; and William Price, a carpenter. A different and larger group of trustees agreed to be responsible for seeing that the original purposes of a free school and a public place for Protestant evangelical ministers to preach were carried out. They were Whitefield himself; his assistant William Seward; the Presbyterian merchant Samuel Hazard; a blacksmith, Robert Easthouse; the scrivener Charles Brockden; Franklin's neighbor James Read; the Moravian New York merchant Thomas Noble; the cordwainer Edward Evans; and John Stephen

Benezet, the merchant with whom Whitefield stayed while in Philadelphia until Benezet moved to Germantown in 1743.

The deed of trust for Whitefield's New Building specified that it could be used by "such Protestant ministers to preach the Gospel in the said Houses as they [the trustees for Uses] shall judge to be sound in their Principles Zealous and faithful in the Discharge of their Duty and acquainted with the Religion of the Heart and Experimental Piety."[23] Franklin knew the conditions at the time, but he either forgot or wanted to impose his own cosmopolitanism upon the intended use of the New Building. He said it was built "expressly for the Use of any Preacher of any religious Persuasion who might desire to say something to the People of Philadelphia, the Design in building not being to accommodate any particular Sect, but the Inhabitants in general, so that even if the Mufti of Constantinople were to send a Missionary to preach Mahometanism to us, he would find a Pulpit at his Service" (A 103–4). Here he echoed a passage in his "Dialogue" defending Samuel Hemphill in 1735 where "S" asked, if the Turks "should . . . send a Missionary to preach Mahometanism to us, ought we not . . . to give him free Liberty of preaching his Doctrine?" (2:32). No! answered the Presbyterians in the Hemphill affair, and No!, Whitefield's supporters would have answered. Not even all Protestant ministers could use the building— certainly not Catholics or non-Christians.

By June 1740, "Sufficient Sums were soon receiv'd to procure the Ground and erect the Building which was 100 feet long and 70 broad, about the Size of Westminster-Hall. . . . Both House and Ground were vested in Trustees" (A 104). The building was larger than any other in Philadelphia. When Whitefield returned in November, it was almost ready. Whitefield noted in his *Journals*, "The roof is not yet up; but the people raised a convenient pulpit, and boarded the bottom."[24] On Sunday, 9 November, Whitefield preached for the first time in the "New Building." Franklin's *Pennsylvania Gazette* reported, "The Roof is ready to put on, and the Whole in a short Time, we hope, will be finish'd." The following Friday, 14 November, the various trustees entered into a legal agreement concerning its purposes.[25] On 4 December Franklin published Whitefield's letter to a friend in New York describing the New Building and asking the friend to raise funds for it. The last Philadelphia notice of Whitefield in 1740 was a poem "On Hearing George Whitefield at the New Building," which appeared in both the *Gazette* and the *American Weekly Mercury*. By then, Whitefield had sailed for England.

Though Whitefield preached in the New Building when in Philadelphia during his third American circuit (1744–48), it was otherwise generally vacant, except for occasional use by Gilbert Tennent and William Tennent, Jr. Meanwhile, the building's debt rose, and no funds were available to start the intended charity school. After the vacant building was vandalized, the merchant Thomas Bourne (who had been elected a trustee, probably in place of William Seward, who died in 1741) and Samuel Hazard advertised on 5 February 1744/5 that they would pay £10 reward for information leading to the conviction of the guilty party. The debt on the building and ground continued to rise. Finally, on 8 May 1747 the four trustees responsible for the building were ready to give it up. They were the persons financially responsible, the persons to whom the building had been sold. Edmund Wooley and John Coats petitioned the Pennsylvania Assembly for "Leave to bring in a Bill for the Sale of a certain piece of Ground, with the House thereon erected, commonly called the *New-Building*, in order to the Payment of the Debts due therefrom; the same having been originally intended for a Charity School for the Instructing of poor Children gratis in the Knowledge of the Christian Religion, and in useful Literature, with other pious Purposes, none of which have been complied with or carried into Execution by the Trustees for that Purpose appointed." The petition was "read; and ordered to lie on the Table."

The next day, 9 May, the assembly ordered that Wooley and Coats "serve the Parties complained against with a Copy of the said Petition." At the Pennsylvania Assembly meeting of 21 August 1747, Charles Brockden and James Read, as trustees for the use of the New Building, promised to answer Wooley and Coats but asked for more time since some of those trustees were out of town. The assembly adjourned without taking any action. Franklin used the New Building on Tuesday evening, 24 November 1747, when over five hundred men signed the form of militia association that he circulated. And on Thursday, 24 December, Gilbert Tennent preached there "on the Lawfulness of War, and on the Usefulness of the Association." But occasional uses were no solution to the financial problem. Franklin reported to Whitefield on 6 July 1749, "The affair of the building remains in *statu quo*, there having been no new application to the Assembly about it, nor any thing done in consequence of the former." Unless the trustees for the use of the building, who had fallen out among one another, could come up with almost £400 (approximately eight years' earnings for an average artisan),[26] the New Building and its ground would be sold to the highest bidder.

What happened? As readers of the *Autobiography* know, Franklin solved the problem. Sometime after the death of the Moravian member Thomas Noble on 15 March 1746, the other trustees elected Franklin in his place. Franklin said of his election, "Care was taken in the Nomination of Trustees, in whom the Building was to be vested, that Predominancy should not be given to any Sect, lest in time that Predominancy might be a means of appropriating the whole to the Use of such Sect, contrary to the original Intention; it was therefore that one of each Sect was appointed, viz. one Church-of England-man, one Presbyterian, one Baptist, one Moravian, &c. Those in case of Vacancy by Death were to fill it by Election from among the Contributors. The Moravian happen'd not to please his Colleagues, and on his Death, they resolved to have no other of that Sect. The Difficulty then was, how to avoid having two of some other Sect, by means of the new Choice. Several Persons were named and for that Reason not agreed to. At length one mention'd me, with the Observation that I was merely an honest Man, and of no Sect at all; which prevail'd with them to chuse me" (A 118).

Franklin's lack of a formal religion may have been part of the reason, but the other trustees would not have elected him if he had not been considered a good friend of Whitefield's. Indeed, since Whitefield was in Philadelphia during the summer of 1746, he may have suggested electing Franklin; the date, however, of the election is unknown. Further, the trustees were in a quandary concerning the building. The expenses were mounting, and they did not know what to do. They probably hoped that the extraordinarily resourceful and energetic Franklin would come up with a solution. As we will see in the discussion of the founding of the Academy of Philadelphia (Volume 3), he did.[27]

THE KINNERSLEY AFFAIR

During the Great Awakening, Franklin reported the change in religious behavior like a dispassionate anthropologist, but one friend, the Baptist Ebenezer Kinnersley, was disgusted with the revivalists. On Thursday evening, 3 July 1740, the Reverend John Rowland preached at the Baptist church: "The audience was sadly overcome by his description of their wholly-ruined condition as sinners; and the distress rose to such a pitch that Gilbert Tennent went to the pulpit stairs and cried out, 'Oh, brother Rowland, is there no balm in Gilead?' "[28] Rowland changed his message and joyfully proclaimed the way to salvation.

The following Sunday, 6 July, Kinnersley preached. He condemned the evangelicals: "Such whining, roaring Harangues, big with affected Nonsense, have no other Tendency, but to operate upon the foster Passions and work them up to a warm Pitch of Enthusiasm." He castigated Rowland and others. Numerous members of the congregation resented his words and ran out of the church. Subsequently, Kinnersley was tried at a church meeting (12 July) and found guilty of opposing "the powerful Doctrine of *Jesus Christ.*" Asked to apologize, he refused. He wrote a letter defending himself and gave it to Franklin to publish, probably on 15 July, the date he finished it. Franklin put him off, hoping Kinnersley would cool down. But he only became more upset, repeating the popular charge that Philadelphia's printers would not publish anything opposing Whitefield and his followers.

Franklin was ambivalent. Kinnersley condemned emotional excesses that Franklin himself found contemptible. He agreed with Kinnersley that some emotional preaching was cant, but he knew that Whitefield and many evangelical ministers were attempting to help people. The printer also may have realized that the attacks by the revivalistic ministers on the other ministers were weakening the traditional religious institutions and thus providing for greater religious diversity.[29] Finally, Franklin published Kinnersley's letter as a postscript to the 24 July *Pennsylvania Gazette.* He justified doing so in a policy statement, which, like the first part of his "Apology for Printers," took the high ground by arguing for freedom of the press: "It is a Principle among Printers, that when Truth has fair Play, it will always prevail over Falshood; therefore, though they have an undoubted Property in their own Press, yet they willingly allow, that any one is entitled to the Use of it, who thinks it necessary to offer his Sentiments on disputable Points to the Publick, and will be at the Expence of it. If what is thus publish'd be good, Mankind has the Benefit of it: If it be bad (I speak now in general without any design'd Application to any particular Piece whatever) the more 'tis made publick, the more its Weakness is expos'd, and the greater Disgrace falls upon the Author, whoever he be; who is at the same Time depriv'd of an Advantage he would otherwise without fail make use of, viz. of Complaining, *that Truth is suppress'd, and that he could say* MIGHTY MATTERS, *had he but the Opportunity of being heard.*"

Franklin said that the Philadelphia printers had been unjustly criticized for refusing to print anything opposing Whitefield. The printer claimed that the charge was "entirely false and groundless, and without the least Colour of Fact to support it; which all will be convinc'd of when they see the following Piece from one Press, and the Rev. Mr. Cummings's Sermons against the Doctrines themselves, from the other." (Like Richard Peters, Reverend Archibald Cummings, the minister of the Anglican Philadelphia church, preached against Whitefield.) Alluding to Milton's *Areopagitica*, Franklin condemned the attempts to license the press in England and then concluded: "'Tis true, where Invectives are contain'd in any Piece, there is no good-natur'd Printer but had much rather be employ'd in Work of another kind: However, tho' many personal Reflections be interwoven in the following Performance, yet as the Author (*who has subscrib'd his Name*) thought them necessary, to vindicate his own Conduct and Character, it is therefore hoped, on that Consideration, the Reader will excuse the Printer for publishing them." Five subsequent pamphlets appeared in the controversy, two by the Reverend Jenkin Jones with a committee of the Baptist church, supporting the use of emotionalism in religion, and three by Kinnersley, condemning what he considered to be excessive emotionalism and a restriction of viewpoints in religious doctrines. Franklin, however, did not publish them and took no further role in the dispute.[30]

Whitefield's Last 1740 Visit to Philadelphia

Whitefield's fifth visit to Philadelphia began on Saturday evening, 8 November 1740, and lasted nine days, with his sermons again drawing amazing numbers of people. After he left, he wrote Franklin on 26 November: "Adieu. I do not despair of your seeing the reasonableness of Christianity. Apply to God; be willing to do the divine will, and you shall know it." The next day Franklin announced Whitefield's purchase of five thousand acres of land on the forks of the Delaware, "in order to erect a Negroe School there, and to settle a Town thereon with his Friends." Franklin was among the persons appointed to collect money for the purpose, though, as noted above, the project failed. By late 1740, rumor suggested that Whitefield used some money intended for charity for his own purposes. When such charges were made public, Franklin printed Whitefield's account of his finances (22 May 1746), and later printed Josiah Smith's evaluation testifying to Whitefield's financial integrity (23 April 1747). Decades later, Franklin wrote in the *Autobiography*, "Some of Mr. Whitefield's Enemies affected to suppose that he would apply these Collections to his own private Emolument; but I, who was intimately acquainted with him, (being employ'd in printing his Sermons and Journals, etc.) never had the least Suspicion of his Integrity, but am to this day decidedly of Opinion that he was in all his Conduct, a perfectly *honest Man*. And methinks my Testimony in his Favor ought to have the more Weight, as we had no religious Connection. He us'd indeed sometimes to pray for my Conversion, but never had the Satisfaction of believing that his Prayers were heard. Ours was a mere civil Friendship, sincere on both Sides, and lasted to his Death" (A 105–6).

Whitefield's Influence

Religion in American society was more divided by the mid-1740s than at any previous time during its existence. The groups supporting Whitefield drifted apart during his absence between 1741 and 1744. Not only did his Anglican, Presbyterian, Baptist, and Moravian disciples all come to disagree with one another, but his main supporters, the Presbyterians, split into "Old Side" and "New Side" partisans. The Maryland physician and litterateur Dr. Alexander Hamilton recorded in his 1744 travel journal from Maryland to Maine that religion was the common topic of conversation, that he could tell a "New Light" revivalist by his canting tone of voice, and that arguments concerning religion occurred in the taverns and inns.[31]

Disagreements abounded, but no one could doubt that Whitefield had made the colonies more conscious of religion. The Presbyterian ministers, meeting at a Philadelphia Synod in late May 1740, enjoyed a major revival. Franklin reported their activities in the 12 June *Gazette*:

> During the Session of the Presbyterian Synod . . . there were no less than 14
> Sermons preached on Society Hill to large Audiences, by the Rev. Messrs. the
> Tennents, Mr. [John] Davenport, Mr. [John] Rowland and Mr. [Samuel] Blair,
> besides what were deliver'd at the Presbyterian and Baptist Meetings, and Ex-
> poundings and Exhortations in private Houses. The Alteration in the Face of
> Religion here is altogether surprizing. Never did the People show so great a
> Willingness to attend Sermons, nor the Preachers greater Zeal and Diligence in
> performing the Duties of their Function. Religion is become the Subject of most
> Conversations. No Books are in Request but those of Piety and Devotion; and
> instead of idle Songs and Ballads, the People are every where entertaining them-
> selves with Psalms, Hymns and Spiritual Songs. All which, under God, is owing
> to the successful Labours of the Reverend Mr. Whitefield.

Franklin continued, "On Sunday last, the Reverend Mr. *Gilbert Tennent*, preached four Times, viz. at Seven in the Morning on Society Hill, at 10 in the *Presbyterian* Meeting House, and 3 [in the] Afternoon in the *Baptist* Meeting House, and at Seven in the Evening on Society Hill again; at which last Sermon 'tis thought there were near 8000 People." Though Franklin knew such revivals had previously occurred, he was amazed at the transformation. When he wrote the pamphlets defending Hemphill, he had thought religious awakenings were over. Instead he found himself living through a greater revival than any in American history.

Robert Bolton, the Philadelphia merchant who kept a Dancing School, Ball, Assembly, and Concert Room, was among the numerous individuals changed by Whitefield. He opened a school that would also teach African Americans, and fifty-three "Black Scholars" were soon enrolled. "For this he was sent for and arraign'd in Court, as a Breaker of the Negro Law, but on making his Defence was dismiss'd. And the next Day order'd by the Foreman of the Grand Jury to continue his School without Interruption."[32] Since nothing more is known of his attempt to keep a school where African Americans could be taught, it probably soon failed.

Whitefield's five visits to Philadelphia from November 1739 to November 1740 made revivalistic and emotional religion common in Pennsylvania and in America. The Great Awakening changed the lives of many persons and created bonds between the pietistic German and English Protestant religions. In America, religion became more evangelical, more important, and more diverse than ever before. As the deist Dr. Alexander Hamilton testified, religion was the most widespread topic of conversation and of disputes in America during 1744. The Great Awakening was also significant for nonreligious reasons. It revealed the power of the press, not only in the making of a celebrity but in creating a great intercolony movement. The Great Awakening was the first in a series of events that unified the American colonies before 1776.

WHITEFIELD'S THIRD AMERICAN CIRCUIT, 1744–1748

Whitefield's third American tour lasted from 26 August 1744, when he landed in York (now Maine), to the spring of 1748. During that period he visited Philadelphia more than five times. Whitefield wrote Franklin from Boston in the summer of 1745. Franklin recorded in the *Autobiography*: "The following Instance will show something of the Terms on which we stood. Upon one of his Arrivals from England at Boston, he wrote to me that he should come soon to Philadelphia, but knew not where he could lodge when there, as he understood his old kind Host Mr. [John Stephen] Benezet was remov'd to Germantown." (Benezet had moved in 1743, after becoming a Moravian.) Franklin's reply makes it clear that Whitefield had visited his home, no doubt on business but perhaps also socially. "My Answer was; You know my House, if you can make shift with its scanty Accommodations you will be most heartily welcome." According to Franklin, Whitefield replied, "if I made that kind Offer for Christ's sake, I should not miss of a Reward.—And I return'd, *Don't let me be mistaken; it was not for Christ's sake, but for your sake.*" Franklin's anecdote may be true, but the following "jocose" remark was no doubt his own, though he thought that an attribution to someone else would be better. "One of our common Acquaintance jocosely remark'd, that knowing it to be the Custom of the Saints, when they receiv'd any favour, to shift the Burthen of the Obligation from off their own Shoulders, and place it in Heaven, I had contriv'd to fix it on Earth" (A 106).

Whitefield arrived in Philadelphia on Thursday night, 5 September 1745, and, with two brief visits to nearby towns, stayed until 20 September, presumably at Franklin's home. The 12 September *Gazette* reported, "He was met and conducted into Town by about 50 Horse. The Evening following he preach'd at the New-Building, and twice or thrice every Day since to large Audiences." His final sermon on this visit was in the New Building on 19 September. The next morning he left for Maryland.

Whitefield returned on 17 May 1746, spent the summer in the Philadelphia area, preaching often in the New Building, and left in mid-September. During this 1746 visit, Whitefield may again have stayed with the Franklins. The appreciation of Whitefield that appeared in the 25 July *Pennsylvania Journal* and the 31 July *Pennsylvania Gazette* revealed an intimate knowledge of his health and an appreciation of his oratory that dovetails with Franklin's. Because he was accused of partiality to Whitefield, Franklin may have circulated the note before publishing it himself; it was unlike him to reprint something that had appeared in another Philadelphia newspaper: "On Sunday the 20th Instant, the Rev. Mr. Whitefield preach'd twice, tho' apparently much indispos'd, to large Congregations in the New Building in this City and the next Day set out for New York. When we seriously consider how incessantly this faithful Servant (not yet 32 Years old) has, for about 10 Years past, laboured in his great Master's Vineyard, with an Alacrity and fervent Zeal, which an infirm Constitution, still daily declining, cannot abate; and which have triumphed over the most vigorous Opposition from whole Armies of invidious Preachers and Pamphleteers; under whose Performances, the Pulpits and Presses, of *Great-Britain* and *America*, have groaned; We may reasonably think with the learned Dr. WATTS, 'That he is a Man raised up by Providence in an uncommon Way, to awaken a stupid and ungodly World, to a Sense of the important Affairs of Religion and Eternity.'"

The notice continued with an appreciation of Whitefield's oratory: "His sermons here this Summer have given general Satisfaction, and plainly proved the great Ability of the Preacher. His rich Fancy, sound and ripening Judgment, and extensive Acquaintance with Men and Books of useful Literature, have been acknowledg'd by every unprejudiced Person. Purity of Language, Perspicuity of Method, a ready Elocution, an engaging Address, and an apt Gesture, Peculiar to this accomplish'd Orator, consider'd with his unspotted Character in private

Life, have added Force to the plain strong Arguments, and pathetick Expostulations, wherewith his Discourses abounded."

On Saturday, 16 August 1746, Whitefield returned to Philadelphia from New York, perhaps again staying with the Franklins. "He preached twice on Sunday, and once every Day since, in the New-Building, to crowded Auditories." Whitefield had not been in Philadelphia for the public thanksgiving day, 24 July, celebrating the duke of Cumberland's victory over Charles Stuart at Culloden Moor, which concluded the last Jacobite rebellion. Whitefield celebrated the triumph a month later on 24 August. The *Gazette* reported, "Last Sunday Evening the Rev. Mr. Whitefield preach'd to a very large Auditory (among whom were many of the principal Persons of this City) a most excellent Sermon on Occasion of the late Victory over the Rebels; in which he set the Mischiefs of Popery and arbitrary Power, and the Happiness the Nation has enjoy'd under the present Royal Family, in the strongest Lights; and pathetically exhorted to Repentance and Amendment of Life in Gratitude for that Signal Deliverance. No Discourse of his among us has given more general Satisfaction; nor has the Preacher ever met with a more universal Applause; having demonstrated himself to be as sound and zealous a Protestant and as truly a loyal Subject, as he is a grand and masterly Orator." Since Franklin puffed the sermon, since he was Whitefield's main publisher, and since Whitefield may have been staying with him, it seems surprising that Whitefield gave Bradford the sermon to print.[33]

The minister remained in Philadelphia until 1 September, then toured the Jerseys for nine days. He returned on Wednesday, 10 September, and stayed until Thursday, 18 September 1746, when he left for Georgia. Commenting on his last visit, Franklin wrote that the minister was never so "well esteemed by Persons of all Ranks among us" (25 September). The next month, Franklin mentioned Whitefield when writing a letter to Thomas Hopkinson (16 October 1746), refuting Andrew Baxter's *Enquiry into the Nature of the Human Soul*, which concluded by opposing a *theist* to an *atheist*. In doing so, Franklin alluded to Whitefield's journal for 9 November 1740, where the minister wrote that Charles Brockden "has been very zealous to propagate his deistical, I could almost say atheistical, principles."[34] Franklin wrote: "I think they are diametrically opposite and not near of kin, as Mr. Whitefield seems to suppose where (in his Journal) he tells us, *Mr. B[rockden] was a Deist, I had almost said an Atheist*. That is, *Chalk*, I had almost said *Charcoal*."

Back in Philadelphia on 29 May 1747, Whitefield remained in the area until late June. He was not now staying with the Franklins. On 23 June Whitefield wrote Franklin (was Franklin out of town for a few days?), thanking him for writing a preamble to a subscription for the Bethesda Orphan-House but objecting to making the subscription public. Since no copy of Franklin's preamble survives, he evidently followed Whitefield's wishes. Whitefield left for New England about the end of June. When Franklin wrote his brother John in Boston on 6 August 1747, he said, "I am glad to hear that Mr. Whitefield is safe arriv'd, and recover'd his Health. He is a good Man and I love him." The minister again visited Philadelphia early in September. The *Gazette* recorded on 17 September that "he preached frequently at the New-Building to very large and attentive Auditories." He left for Georgia on Monday, 14 September 1747. The revivalist wrote Franklin from Bermuda on 27 May 1748, sending him a letter to print for the ship captains sailing to Bermuda. Franklin had Hall do so, and on 21 July the *Pennsylvania Gazette* advertised Whitefield's *Letter to a Reverend Divine in Boston Recounting His Visit to Bermuda.*

CONTACTS, 1749–1763

When Franklin wrote Whitefield on 6 July 1749, he cited the example, not of Christ, but of Confucius. He told the great revivalist that if he could reform the nobility, "wonderful changes will follow in the manners of the lower ranks." When Confucius saw "his country sunk in vice, and wickedness of all kinds triumphant, he applied himself first to the grandees; and having by his doctrine won them to the cause of virtue, the commons followed in multitudes." Then the skeptic created another of his wonderful *sententiae*: "The mode has a wonderful influence on mankind; and there are numbers that perhaps fear less the being in Hell, than out of the fashion."

Writing Franklin on 26 February 1750, Whitefield generously praised the idea of the Academy of Philadelphia. "I have often thought such an institution was wanted exceedingly; and if well-conducted, am persuaded it will be of public service. Your plan I have read over, and do not wonder at its meeting with general approbation." But naturally Whitefield wanted it to emphasize Christianity more. "I think there wants *aliquid Christi* in it, to make it so useful as I would desire it might be. It is true, you say, 'The youth are to be taught some public religion, and the excellency of the christian religion in particular:' but methinks this is mentioned too late, and too soon passed over. As we are all creatures of a day; as our whole life is but one small point between two eternities, it is reasonable to suppose, that the grand end of every christian institution for forming tender minds, should be to convince them of their natural depravity, of the means of recovering out of it, and of the necessity of preparing for the enjoyment of the supreme Being in a future state." Franklin disagreed but was silent.

Franklin, though, certainly agreed with Whitefield's observation concerning the possible rise of poor persons in the world: "And if a fund could be raised, for the free education of the poorer sort, who should appear to have promising abilities, I think it would greatly answer the design proposed. It hath been often found, that some of our brightest men in church and state, have arisen from such an obscure condition." Whitefield, like Franklin, was such a person, though the minister had the advantage of a formal education. Whitefield concluded by saying that the ultimate success of the institution would depend "on the integrity, disinterestedness, and piety of the gentlemen concerned." Except for piety, Franklin no doubt concurred, though he might have added energy and ability to the other desirable qualities. As Poor Richard said, "There are lazy minds as well as lazy bodies" (May 1740, April 1751).

Whitefield wrote Franklin again on 17 August 1752 after proof of his theory that lightning was caused by atmospheric electricity appeared in the periodicals. As usual, the minister expressed his concern for Franklin's spiritual state, but he was also considerate of the skeptic: "I find that you grow more and more famous in the learned world. As you have made a pretty considerable progress in the mysteries of electricity, I would now humbly recommend to your diligent unprejudiced pursuit and study the mystery of the new-birth. . . . You will excuse this freedom. I must have *aliquid Christi* in all my letters."

THE FOURTH AND FIFTH AMERICAN TOURS

Whitefield's fourth American tour, October 1751 to May 1752, was limited to the South. The fifth American visit lasted from 27 May 1754 to March 1755. He landed in Georgia, came to Philadelphia in early August, and left on 20 August 1754. Deborah Franklin wrote John Franklin's wife an account of Whitefield's visit (5:429). Though what Deborah wrote is unknown, the fact that she was in a position to write a long letter about Whitefield may suggest that the revivalist stayed with the Franklins. Whitefield was back in Philadelphia from 14 to 16 September, Saturday to Monday, but Franklin had left for the northern colonies early in September 1754 on post office business. The friends saw one another in Boston in October. When Whitefield next visited Philadelphia, 18 to 24 December 1754, Franklin had not yet returned. Whitefield wrote him from Virginia on 17 January 1755, mentioning that he had seen Franklin's epitaph, which, though circulating in manuscript copies, had not yet been printed:[35] "Believe on Jesus, and get a feeling possession of God in your heart, and you cannot possibly be disappointed of your expected second edition, finely corrected, and infinitely amended." He expected Franklin and his co-postmaster general, William Hunter, to come to Georgia on post office business, and told Franklin he would be glad to wait on him at the orphanage.

On 2 July 1756, while Franklin was in New York to confer about express mail service with Lord Loudoun, the British commander of the colonial war effort, he wrote Whitefield that he had received and immediately reprinted Whitefield's sermon, *A Short Address to Persons of All Denominations*, on the impending war with France. Whitefield condemned those who "through a fatal scrupulosity against bearing Arms, even in a defensive War" left open to attack "that large, extensive, and that lately most flourishing Province of *Pennsylvania*, the very Centre and Garden of all *North-America*." Naturally Franklin was glad to have Whitefield's support for a Pennsylvania militia. Since the fall of 1748, when William Franklin brought back an account of the beautiful land he had seen north-west of present-day Pittsburgh, Franklin had been interested in the possible English colonization of the land over the Allegheny Mountains. In the same letter, he wrote Whitefield, "I sometimes wish, that you and I were jointly employ'd by the Crown to settle a Colony on the Ohio. I imagine we could do it effectually, and without putting the Nation to much Expence. But I fear we shall never be call'd upon for such a Service. What a glorious Thing it would be, to settle in that fine Country a large Strong Body of Religious and Industrious People! What a Security to the other Colonies; and Advantage to Britain, by Increasing her People, Territory, Strength and Commerce."

Franklin appealed to Whitefield: "Might it not greatly facilitate the Introduction of pure Religion among the Heathen, if we could, by such a Colony, show them a better Sample of Christians than they commonly see in our Indian Traders, the most vicious and abandoned Wretches of our Nation?" Franklin thought of the course of his life (he was now fifty) and wrote, "Life, like a dramatic Piece, should not only be conducted with Regularity, but methinks it should finish handsomely. Being now in the last Act, I begin to cast about for something fit to end with. Or if mine be more properly compar'd to an Epigram, as some of its few Lines are but barely tolerable, I am very desirous of concluding with a bright Point. In such an Enterprize I could spend the Remainder of Life with Pleasure; and I firmly believe God would bless us with Success, if we undertook it with a sincere Regard to his Honour, the Service of our gracious King, and (which is the same thing) the Publick Good." Franklin did not say in this letter that "Serving God . . . is doing Good to Man," though it was a favorite belief.

LAST CONTACTS, 1763–1770

Whitefield's sixth American tour (1763–65) coincided with a period of Franklin's return to Philadelphia (1762–64). In late August 1763, an extremely ill Whitefield landed in Virginia and reached Philadelphia on 22 September. He remained several weeks, recuperating. Franklin's letter to him of 28 November 1763 makes it clear that he did not stay with the Franklins on this visit, for Franklin reported that he was mortified that he had "so long omit[ted] waiting on you here, as to be at length finally depriv'd of the Pleasure of seeing you." Franklin wrote again on 19 June 1764, while Whitefield was in New York. He thanked Whitefield for his "frequently repeated Wishes and Prayers for my Eternal as well as temporal Happiness," offering him "mine in return."

But then Franklin said a little about his own beliefs: "I have my self no Doubts that I shall enjoy as much of both as is proper for me. That Being who gave me Existence, and thro' almost threescore Years has been continually showering his Favours upon me, whose very Chastisements have been Blessings to me, can I doubt that he loves me? And if he loves me, can I doubt that he will go on to take care of me not only here but hereafter?" Franklin knew that his thoughts were heterodox. "This to some may seem Presumption; to me it appears the best grounded Hope; Hope of the Future; built on Experience of the Past." When Franklin wrote his friend William Strahan a week later, 25 June, he repeated the sentiments, then joked about Strahan's skepticism: "Thank me for giving you this Hint, by the Help of which you may die as chearfully as you live. If you had Christian Faith, quantum suff[icit], This might not be necessary: But as Matters are, it may be of Use."

Besides humanitarianism, the American and the Englishman both had in common a belief in the American people and in the justness of the American position in the pre-Revolutionary period. Perhaps Franklin had influenced Whitefield, but the Great Awakener knew the various parts of America and its people better than most Americans. William Gordon, of Jamaica Plain, Massachusetts, wrote in his *History of the American Revolution* that when Whitefield was in Portsmouth on 2 April 1764 he sent for Samuel Langdon (later president of Harvard) and Samuel Haven for a private conference and told them: "I can't in conscience leave the town without acquainting you with a secret. My heart bleeds for *America*. O poor *New-England*! There is a deep laid plot against both your civil and religious liberties, and they will be lost. Your golden days are at an end. You have nothing but trouble before you. My information comes from the best authority in *Great Britain*. I was allowed to speak of the affair in general, but enjoined not to mention particulars. Your liberties will be lost." Gordon added that "Mr. Whitefield could not have heard what the commons did in the preceding month [when George Grenville presented an American Revenue Act to Parliament on 9 March 1764]; his information must have been of an earlier date, and might have been communicated before he left Great Britain."[36]

Whitefield arrived in Philadelphia on 14 September 1764. He made overnight excursions out of town but mainly remained there until Monday, 22 October. Franklin was in the midst of a bitterly fought election campaign until 1 October, but he requested Whitefield to preach for two of his special interests, the academy and the hospital. Whitefield obliged, no doubt because he believed in helping these charities, but perhaps also because it was Franklin who asked. On 17 October, "Whitefield preached an excellent Sermon in the College of this City, for the Benefit of the Charity Children educated there, from St. Matthew vi. 10. 'Thy Kingdom come.' He concluded with a most fervent and Christian Exhortation to the Youth of the Institution; and the Collection at the Doors amounted to £105." Whitefield's farewell sermon on Sunday, 21 October, was a benefit for the Pennsylvania Hospital. The sermon raised £170.12.9. Franklin must have attended both. Whitefield returned to Philadelphia on 4 May 1765, remaining until 24 May, but Franklin was then in London.

Franklin and Whitefield were both in London in February 1766 when the House of Commons debated colonial opposition to the Stamp Act and when Franklin testified on 13 February. Whitefield, like Franklin's American friends, knew that the Philadelphian had been criticized by some American enemies as an advocate of the Stamp Act. Whitefield defended him. In letters to America, Whitefield praised Franklin's examination before the House of Commons. A note by an "eminent Clergyman" in the *Pennsylvania Gazette* (1 May 1766), was probably from Whitefield: "Dr. Franklin spoke very heartily and judiciously, in his Country's Behalf, when at the Bar of the House of Commons." Since the "eminent" clergyman's letter is dated 27 February and since Whitefield called on Franklin in Craven Street, London, on 27 February, one wonders if the two collaborated on the letter (13:176).

When Franklin's sister Jane expressed concern about the rumors against Franklin, he reminded her on 2 March 1767 of "what your Friend good Mr. Whitefield said to me once on such an Occasion: 'I read the Libels writ against you, says he, when I was in a remote province, where I could not be inform'd of the Truth of the Facts; but they rather gave me this good Opinion of you *that you continued to be* USEFUL *to the Publick*: For when I am on the Road, and see Boys in a Field at a Distance, pelting a Tree, though I am too far off to know what Tree it is, I conclude it has FRUIT on it.' "

During late 1767, Whitefield interviewed Franklin about adding a college to the orphanage. On 21 January 1768, Whitefield wrote, asking for another meeting. They probably met, though Whitefield's supplementary plan failed. Perhaps it was concerning this meeting in 1768 that Franklin wrote in his *Autobiography*, "The last time I saw Mr. Whitefield was in London, when he consulted me about his Orphan House Concern, and his Purpose of appropriating it to the Establishment of a College" (A 106). They collaborated one later time, successfully—securing a doctorate of divinity from the University of Edinburgh for New York's Reverend John Rodgers (6 December 1768).

Franklin's last letter to Whitefield was written before 2 September 1769. The American ridiculed the ministry for sending troops to Boston. "It seems like setting up a smith's forge in a magazine of gunpowder." The sixty-three-year-old Franklin revealed his disbelief in God's providence to the great revivalist. His position was similar to that expressed in the "First Principles" of his "Articles of Belief and Acts of Religion," written in 1728 at age twenty-two: "I *see* with you that our affairs are not well managed by our rulers here below; I wish I could *believe* with you, that they are well attended to by those above; I rather suspect, from certain circumstances, that though the general government of the universe is well administered, our particular little affairs are perhaps below notice, and left to take the chance of human prudence or imprudence, as either may happen to be uppermost. It is, however, an uncomfortable thought, and I leave it." Whitefield annotated the letter: "*Uncomfortable* indeed! and, blessed be God, *unscriptural*, for we are fully assured that 'the Lord reigneth,' and are directed to cast *all* our own care on him, because he careth for us" (16:192).

Whitefield made his seventh and last American tour in 1769 and 1770, leaving London for Charleston on 2 September 1769. Franklin was in London. A week before Whitefield died, he wrote a letter from Portsmouth, New Hampshire (23 September 1770), again identifying with the Americans in the pre-Revolutionary difficulties: "Poor *New England* is much to be pitied. *Boston* people most of all.

How falsely misrepresented!"[37] Whitefield died in Newburyport, Massachusetts, on 30 September 1770.

When Franklin wrote his sister Jane on 7 November 1770, he added a postscript, "I condole with you on the Death of my dear old Friend Mr. Whitefield which I have just heard of." To Noble Wimberly Jones of Georgia, Franklin said of Whitefield (5 March 1771): "I knew him intimately upwards of 30 Years: His Integrity, Disinterestedness, and indefatigable Zeal in prosecuting every good Work, I have never seen equaled, I shall never see exceeded." Franklin had written what could have served as Whitefield's epitaph in *Poor Richard* for 1742: "The painful Preacher, like a candle bright, / Consumes himself in giving others light."

WHITEFIELD IN THE *AUTOBIOGRAPHY*

Though Franklin left a classic account of the effectiveness of Whitefield's preaching and though he defended the minister's honesty, integrity, and nobility, he also undercut him. On one occasion when Franklin heard Whitefield, instead of being affected, he mathematically figured out how far Whitefield could be heard. "Imagining then a Semicircle, of which my Distance should be the Radius, and that it were fill'd with Auditors, to each of whom I allow'd two square feet, I computed that he might well be heard by more than Thirty-Thousand. This reconcil'd me to the Newspaper Accounts of his having preach'd to 25,000 People in the Fields, and to the ancient Histories of Generals haranguing whole Armies, of which I had sometimes doubted" (A 106–7).

Franklin's comparison of Whitefield with the Greek and Roman generals in order to test the truth of the classic historians was not original. The *Gentleman's Magazine* for August 1739 published a similar calculation, which estimated that at nine persons per square yard, Whitefield preached to 25,444 persons on 29 July 1739 in Moorfields, England. The *Gentleman's Magazine* editor noted, however, that soldiers in close order stand but four in a square yard, so that would allow but 11,388 auditors. Franklin may have forgotten the *Gentleman's Magazine* note by 1788, when he wrote this part of the *Autobiography*, but he had made a similar calculation of the number in *Poor Richard* for 1749 (3:336), when he surely recalled the earlier article. Ironically, though Franklin's subjects are belief and doubt, his faith in historical accounts is reassured—not his doubts about Christianity's eternal truths. Further, his doubts concerning history are not overcome by Whitefield but by Franklin's applying mathematics to the power of Whitefield's voice. The doubting persona did not verbalize his opinions about Whitefield's theological message: it was so far from concerning him that he did not mention it.

The wonderfully archetypal confrontation of science with religion, of modernity with the supernatural, symbolizes not the defeat of the old Calvinistic theology but its irrelevance to Franklin. Franklin does not tell and did not care what Whitefield's actual message was; it had no place in Franklin's mental world. An anecdote near the end of the *Autobiography* discloses the same trait. Franklin told of nearly being shipwrecked in 1757. The boat was saved at the last moment. Franklin's reaction was not to thank God but to thank the technology that saved the ship: "This *Deliverance* [emphasis mine] impress'd me strongly with the Utility of Lighthouses, and made me resolve to encourage the building more of them in America, if I should live to return there" (A 165). The word *deliverance* has strong religious connotations, thus emphasizing the deliberate irony of Franklin's resolve.

Franklin undermined George Whitefield when he asserted that he could "distinguish easily between Sermons newly compos'd, and those which he had often preach'd. . . . His Delivery of the latter was so improv'd by frequent Repetitions, that every Accent, every Emphasis, every Modulation of Voice, was so perfectly well turn'd and well plac'd, that without being interested in the Subject, one could not help being pleas'd with the Discourse, a Pleasure of much the same kind with that receiv'd from an excellent Piece of Musick." Notice that Franklin does not make the most logical comparison: he refrains from comparing the minister to a well-rehearsed actor and from equating his performance to a play. Such comparisons would be too obviously satirical. But Franklin's comment makes the same criticism (i.e., Whitefield's sermons were carefully rehearsed entertainments—not extemporaneous outpourings of the spirit) while seemingly paying him a compliment on the musical quality of his voice.

Franklin's criticism is all the greater for comparing Whitefield's voice to a musical instrument. Franklin implies that the substance, the content, is as meaningless as a musical note. Whitefield's performance was an aesthetic pleasure—if one could simply listen to the beautiful sounds and cadences and disregard the message. William Faulkner appreciated Franklin's satire of Whitefield and took aspects of the Great Awakener for his character Pastor Whitfield in *As I Lay Dying*, where Vernon Tull says of the minister, "His voice is bigger than him."[38]

Like Franklin, Olaudah Equiano, a former slave whose narrative is a classic in the genre, recorded his own appreciation of Whitefield. Equiano saw a churchyard in Georgia overflowing with people, some of whom had ascended ladders to look in the church's windows. Inquiring as to the reason for the extraordinary crowd, Equiano learned that Whitefield was preaching. Equiano "pressed in amidst the multitude. When I got into the church I saw this pious man exhorting the people with the greatest fervor and earnestness, and sweating as much as I ever did while in slavery on Montserrat beach. I was very much struck and impressed with this; I thought it strange I had never seen divines exert themselves in this manner before, and was no longer at a loss to account for the thin congregations they preached to."[39] Whitefield's "pious" quality, "fervor and earnestness," and copious "sweating" impressed Equiano. Like Franklin, Equiano is more taken by the exterior appearance of Whitefield than by the content of his sermon.

Franklin's primary satire is reserved for Whitefield's content. Whitefield was the greatest revivalistic orator of the eighteenth century and among the major revivalists of modern times, but by 1788, when Franklin was writing the third part of the *Autobiography*, Whitefield's enormous reputation had begun to decline. "His Writing and Printing from time to time gave great Advantage to his Enemies. Unguarded Expressions and even erroneous Opinions delivered in Preaching might have been afterwards explain'd, or qualify'd by supposing others that might have accompany'd them; or they might have been deny'd; but *litera scripta manet*. Critics attack'd his Writings violently, and with so much Appearance of Reason as to diminish the Number of his Votaries, and prevent their Encrease: So that I am of Opinion, if he had never written any thing he would have left behind him a much more numerous and important Sect. And his Reputation might in that case have been still growing, even after his Death; as there being nothing of his Writing on which to found a Censure; and give him a lower Character, his Proselites would be left at Liberty to feign for him as great a Variety of Excellencies, as their enthusiastic Admiration might wish him to have possessed" (A 107).

Perhaps Franklin's underlying satire is reserved for all prophets who lived before the age of print, for their actual words could never be known, and their "Proselites" were and are "at Liberty to feign for" the prophet "as great a Variety of Excellencies, as their enthusiastic Admiration might wish him to have possessed." Franklin may have thought those days were over and that in an age of print, when words would be subjected to thoughtful analysis, no new great prophets would emerge. On the other hand, he knew that most people believed whatever they wanted to believe. Poor Richard said, "It's the easiest thing in the world for a man to deceive himself" (April 1746). Perhaps Franklin wanted to think that modern technology had abolished superstition. Most persons, however, will hope for some supernatural belief in times of danger and crisis. In September 1776, Benedict Arnold's brigade that was to invade Canada and attack Quebec stopped at Newburyport, New Hampshire, where George Whitefield was buried. There, a group of officers with chaplain Samuel Spring entered the church crypt, broke open Whitefield's coffin, took his collar and wristbands, and cut them into little pieces. Like pieces of the true cross, they were passed out to the men.[40] Despite the sacred fetishes, the invasion failed.

The friendship between Whitefield and Franklin complemented both. The great revivalist was devoutly Christian, a firm believer in God, but he also was, like Franklin, fiercely independent. More important, though Whitefield believed that faith, not works, was essential to religion, he devoted his life to good works. He raised more money for various charities than anyone else in his time. Franklin never doubted Whitefield's sincerity and integrity, though he sometimes expressed amazement at the minister's religious beliefs. Both men strenuously dedicated themselves to doing good for humanity, and they respected each other for attempting to do good and for the good each did.

EIGHTEEN

Natural Philosophy

In the founding document of the American Philosophical Society, Franklin wrote that its subjects should be "all philosophical Experiments that let Light into the Nature of Things, tend to increase the Power of Man over Matter, and multiply the Conveniencies or Pleasures of Life."—2:382

NATURAL PHILOSOPHY (the eighteenth-century name for science) gradually replaced theology and moral philosophy as the primary subject of Franklin's writings and intellectual life.[1] But just as those subjects remained crucial to him throughout the second half of his life, so natural philosophy was vital to his intellectual life during his first forty-two years. He read the major influential scientific works of his day (though he probably did not have sufficient mathematics for Sir Isaac Newton's *Principia*), took the scientific courses offered by the itinerant lecturers such as Isaac Greenwood and Dr. Archibald Spencer, shared the interests of the major American natural philosophers like John Bartram, Cadwallader Colden, Dr. John Mitchell, and John Winthrop, studied the natural phenomena around him, frequently hypothesized about the causes of mysterious phenomena, and conducted experiments in natural philosophy.

Franklin's writings on weather and the course of hurricanes, his contributions to the study of lead poisoning and other medical topics, and his project of an American scientific society all contributed to science, but he first became celebrated in what we would today call mechanical engineering. He designed the best stove in the world. Franklin's fireplace warmed an entire room, eliminated most drafts, provided a constant supply of good air, conserved fuel, was safer than existing stoves, and was easier to control. In the mid-1740s, the "Pennsylvania fire-place" made him well-known internationally.

Curiosity inspired Franklin's concern with natural philosophy. An example exists in his first extant journal, kept at age twenty, while sailing from London to Philadelphia. In the afternoon of 28 September 1726, he collected seaweed. He focused on a stalk: "In common with the rest it had a leaf about three quarters of an inch long, indented like a saw, and a small yellow berry filled with nothing but wind; besides which it bore a fruit of the animal kind, very surprising to see. It was a small shell-fish like a heart, the stalk by which it proceeded from the branch being partly of a gristly kind. Upon this one branch of the weed there were near forty of these vegetable animals; the smallest of them near the end contained a substance somewhat like an oyster, but the larger were visibly animated, opening their shells every moment, and thrusting out a set of unformed claws, not unlike those of a crab; but the inner part was still a kind of soft jelly" (1:93).

Fascinated by a bit of seaweed! Whenever he had spare time during an extraordinarily busy life, he turned his attention to science. Everything interested him. "Observing the weed more narrowly, I spied a very small crab crawling among it, about as big as the head of a ten-penny nail, and of a yellowish colour, like the weed itself. This gave me some reason to think that he was a native of the branch, that he had not long since been in the same condition with the rest of those little embrios that appeared in the shells, this being the method of their generation; and that consequently all the rest of this odd kind of fruit might be crabs in due time." In Boston and London, he had learned the scientific method of hypothesizing and testing from the popular scientific classics of the day. They included Francis Bacon's *Advancement of Learning*, Dr. John Keill's *Examination of Dr. Burnet's Theory* (1698), and especially Sir Isaac Newton's *Optics* (1704). He tested his conjecture: "I have resolved to keep the weed in salt water, renewing it every day till we come on shore, by this experiment to see whether any more crabs will be produced or not in this manner. I remember that the last calm we had, we took notice of a large crab upon the surface of the sea, swimming from one branch of weed to another, which he seemed to prey upon; and I likewise recollect that at Boston, in New England, I have often seen small crabs with a shell like a snail's upon their backs, crawling about in the salt water; and likewise at Portsmouth in England" (1:93–94). The ever-curious and observant Franklin had a store of close observations pertinent to tiny crabs to recall.

He hypothesized why the tiny crabs used a shell. "It is likely nature has provided this hard shell to secure them till their own proper shell has acquired a sufficient hardness, which once perfected, they quit their old habitation and venture abroad safe in their own strength. The various changes that silk-worms, butterflies, and several other insects go through, make such alterations and metamorphoses not improbable." The following day, Thursday, 29 September 1726: "Upon shifting the water in which I had put the weed yesterday, I found another crab, much smaller than the former, who seemed to have newly left his habitation." So he thought his theory might be correct. Since "the weed begins to wither, and the rest of the embrios are dead," he could not continue the observations. But "This new comer fully convinces me, that at least this sort of crabs are generated in this manner" (1:94).

Franklin returned to the pelagic crabs the following day, 30 September: "I took in some more gulf-weed to-day with the boat-hook, with shells upon it like that before mentioned, and three living perfect crabs, each less than the nail of my little finger. One of them had something particularly observable, to wit, a thin piece of the white shell which I before noticed as their covering while they remained in the condition of embrios, sticking close to his natural shell upon his back. This sufficiently confirms me in my opinion of the manner of their generation. I have put this remarkable crab with a piece of the gulf-weed, shells, &c. into a glass phial filled with salt water, (for want of spirits of wine) in hopes to preserve the curiosity till I come on shore" (1:95).

The observations on the tiny crabs are a good example not only of Franklin's curiosity but also of his procedure. Describing the crabs, Franklin at first gave his erroneous thoughts about the "fruit of the animal kind" that the weed bore, then narrated the sequence of his observations, proceeded to the hypothesis that these fruits were embryo crabs, attempted to keep the weed to test his hypothesis, and after collecting another sample of seaweed with crabs on it the following day, finally found some evidence that his hypothesis was correct. Why did he investigate the seaweed, with its forty tiny crabs? Curiosity—and a hope to understand and to explain for his own satisfaction.

His observations of the minute sea crabs were not Franklin's first experiments. In Volume 1, Chapter 2, I discussed the swim palettes he designed for his hands and feet, as well as his body sailing by means of a kite—efforts that prefigured sustained adult scientific pursuits. In the above notes on the crab, Franklin used the common sailor's term, "gulf-weed," for a sea grass found in the gulf stream. Unstudied at the time, the gulf stream later became a major subject of his scientific investigations, but he gave no indication of puzzling about the significance of the term "gulf-weed" in 1726.

Medicine

Even if Franklin had not been curious about almost all matters, he would have been interested in medicine. Every well-educated person in the seventeenth and eighteenth centuries had an interest, and often some relative expertise, in medicine. Most ministers in small towns in the seventeenth century acted as physicians. Eighteenth-century planters like William Byrd of Virginia practiced medicine not only on their slaves but also on their friends, families, and themselves. Franklin was not at all exceptional in his interest in medicine—or in his practicing it. He wrote his parents on 6 February 1744 that he feared he was "too busy in prescribing, and meddling in the Dr's Sphere, when any of you complain of Ails in your Letters." He said that he himself always employed a physician when ill and that they should regard his advice "only as a Mark of my good Will, and put no more of it in Practice than happens to agree with what your Dr. directs." His father evidently suffered from a kidney stone, and Franklin gave advice on the effects of soap, salt, honey, and molasses as treatments (2:413–14). He designed a flexible catheter for his brother John. Typically, Franklin wanted it done right, so he explained what he wanted to a Philadelphia silversmith (Philip Syng?) and supervised its production. The tube, Franklin wrote, "is also a kind of Scrue, and may be both withdrawn and introduc'd by turning. Experience is necessary for the right using of all new Tools or Instruments, and that will perhaps suggest some Improvements to this Instrument as well as better direct the Manner of Using it" (4:386).

In his theories concerning the common cold, Franklin was prescient. Those theories, as well as his writings on gout, will be discussed in later volumes.

Smallpox Inoculation

Franklin's first medical subject was inoculation for smallpox. Scholars generally assume that Franklin and his older brother James agreed with Dr. William Douglass and other *New-England Courant* writers in 1721 who opposed inoculation. James Franklin, however, twice announced (4 September and 4 December 1721) that the *Courant* would print pieces either for or against inoculation. No supporters of inoculation sent him anything favoring it. Why should they? After Dr. William Douglass opposed inoculation in the *Boston News-Letter* for 24 July 1721, the editors of the *Boston News-Letter* and the *Boston Gazette* refused to print anything against it. One reason James Franklin started the *Courant* was to allow Dr. William Douglass and others who opposed inoculation an organ to make their opposition public. Inoculation's primary proponent was Cotton Mather. He came to believe, with some justice, that James Franklin and the *New-England Courant* personally opposed him. Neither he nor the Boston authorities would publish in the *Courant*. The only good reason to think that the young Franklin and his brother James may have opposed the practice is that, so far as we know, neither was inoculated. Perhaps they both had smallpox before 1721.

On the other hand, several factors would have impressed the brothers. The primary one was, of course, the success of inoculation. Zabdiel Boylston inoculated 241 people in 1721, of whom six died and of those six, four had smallpox when inoculated. Second, Boylston was well regarded by them: he was James Franklin's personal physician. Third, the best scientist of the day in Massachusetts, Harvard's Thomas Robie, favored inoculation. Both James and Benjamin Franklin probably personally believed in inoculation.[2]

Another smallpox epidemic struck New England in the spring of 1730. Franklin wrote about it in his 14 May *Pennsylvania Gazette*, advocating inoculation. "There is an Account published of the Number of Persons inoculated in Boston in the Month of March, amounting to Seventy-two; of which two only died, and the rest have recovered perfect Health. Of those who had it in the common Way, 'tis computed that one in four died. Several Hundreds have been inoculated, and but about four in the Hundred have died under Inoculation; and even those are supposed to have first taken the Infection in the common Way." Franklin used mathematical probabilities to urge the safety of inoculation. In the 28 May paper, he reprinted an account of the method and use of inoculation from Chambers's *Dictionary*. On 11 June and 6 August, he featured news of the smallpox's prevalence and decrease in Boston, noting on 11 June that 510 persons had been inoculated, 11 of whom died.

During the spring of 1731 Philadelphia experienced a smallpox epidemic.

Franklin announced in the 4 March *Pennsylvania Gazette*: "The Practice of Inoculation for the Small-Pox, begins to grow among us. *J. Growdon*, Esq; the first
Patient of Note that led the Way, is now upon the Recovery, having had none
but the most favourable Symptoms during the whole Course of the Distemper;
which is mentioned to show how groundless all those extravagant Reports are,
that have been spread through the Province to the contrary. *For an Account of
the Method and Usefulness of Inoculation, see our* Gazette, *#80*" (28 May 1730).

Quoting the note, medical historian John Duffy commented that Franklin
was among the "first to support" inoculation in Philadelphia.[3] Franklin reprinted an article on smallpox inoculation in the 11 March *Gazette* from the
Philosophical Transactions of the Royal Society. He wrote an editorial on 25 March
1731 urging "Compassion and Regard for the Sick." On 8 July Franklin noted,
"The Small-pox has now quite left this City. The Number of those that died
here of that Distemper, is exactly 288, and no more. 64 of the Number were
Negroes; If these may be valued one with another at £30 per Head, the Loss to
the City in that Article is near £2000." The abstract intellectual appraisal of the
value of humans is chilling. A recent historian observed, "The actual total from
his own weekly accounts of mortality was 308, including 65, not 64, Negro
deaths." Perhaps, however, the weekly mortality accounts included all deaths,
not just those from smallpox.[4]

When another outbreak of smallpox occurred in the fall of 1736, Franklin
published verses in favor of inoculation in *Poor Richard* for 1737, which appeared
before 11 November. One fatality in that epidemic was four-year-old Francis
Folger Franklin, the love and joy of Deborah and Franklin. He died on 21 November, "aged 4 Years, 1 Mon. & 1 Day," according to his tombstone. Rumor
that he had died after being inoculated caused Franklin to publish the following
notice: "Understanding 'tis a current Report, that my Son Francis, who died
lately of the Small Pox, had it by Inoculation; and being desired to satisfy the
Publick in that Particular; inasmuch as some People are, by that Report (join'd
with others of the like kind, and perhaps equally groundless) deter'd from having that Operation perform'd on their Children, I do hereby sincerely declare,
that he was not inoculated, but receiv'd the Distemper in the common Way of
Infection: And I suppose the Report could only arise from its being my known
Opinion, that Inoculation was a safe and beneficial Practice; and from my having said among my Acquaintance, that I intended to have my Child inoculated,
as soon as he should have recovered sufficient Strength from a Flux with which
he had been long afflicted" (30 December 1736).

Franklin continued to endorse inoculation. The *Gazette* reported on 13 April
1738, "We hear from *Barbadoes*, that there are upwards of 3000 Persons down
with the Small-Pox, where Inoculation is very much practised and proves very
successful." In the spring of 1746 a mild smallpox epidemic occurred in Philadelphia and New Brunswick, with few deaths. Franklin wrote on 29 May 1746
that since 10 April, 160 persons (mainly children) in Philadelphia had been inoc-

ulated. He did not mention to his correspondent that one was his daughter Sarah, aged two and a half, inoculated on 18 April (3:74).

Poor Richard Improved for 1750 commended the spread of inoculation in England: "and tho' at first it was reckoned by many to be a *rash* and almost *impious* Action, to give a Distemper to a Person in Health; so changeable are the Opinions of Men, that it now begins to be thought *rash* to hazard taking it in the common Way, by which one in seven is generally lost; and *impious* to reject a Method discovered to Mankind by God's good Providence, whereby 99 in 100 are saved" (3:445). Franklin cited statistical probabilities to defend inoculation and collected statistics on inoculation and sent them to his correspondents (4:340). In addition to printing numerous notices favoring inoculation,[5] he encouraged new developments in treating smallpox. The Scots physician and poet Dr. Adam Thomson developed a regimen of mercury, antimony, and quinine for preparing patients for inoculation. He came from Maryland in late 1748 to Philadelphia to practice. Franklin publicized his method by having him lecture at the Academy of Philadelphia on 21 November 1750, and he published Thomson's *Discourse on the Preparation of the Body for the Small-Pox*. When an anonymous author in the *Pennsylvania Journal* attacked Thomson for implying that the trustees of the academy were his patrons, he asked Franklin to testify that he had permission to deliver the lecture before the trustees. Consequently, Franklin wrote for the *Pennsylvania Gazette* on 17 December 1750: "I do certify, that the Fact, as he has stated it in his Preface, relating to his being allow'd by the Trustees to deliver a publick Oration on the Small-Pox in the Academy, is right, to the best of my Remembrance." Later, Franklin published Dr. John Kearsley's *Letter to a Friend* (5 March 1751), replying to Thomson. Though they differed over the preparation, both Thomson and Kearsley favored inoculation.

Franklin's major contribution to inoculation came in 1759, when he wrote a preface for Dr. William Heberden's *Some Account of the Success of Inoculation*, briefly tracing the history of inoculation in Europe and the colonies. Franklin mentioned that many persons had "*scruples of conscience*" concerning the "*lawfulness* of the practice." He said that he hoped that "a *sensible Clergy*" might in time remove such scruples and concluded, "On the whole, if the chance were only as *two* to *one* in favour of the practice among children, would it not be sufficient to induce a tender parent to lay hold of the advantage? But when it is so much greater, as it appears to be by these accounts (in some even as *thirty* to *one*) surely parents will no longer refuse to accept and thankfully use a discovery God in his mercy has been pleased to bless mankind with; whereby some check may now be put to the ravages that cruel disease has been accustomed to make, and the human species be again suffered to increase as it did before the Smallpox made its appearance. This increase has indeed been more obstructed by that distemper than is usually imagin'd: For the loss of one in ten thereby is not merely the loss of so many persons, but the accumulated loss of all the children and childrens children the deceased might have had, multiplied by successive generations" (8:286). Franklin paid for printing the pamphlet and sent fifteen hundred copies to his partner David Hall on 12 July 1759 "to be given away." During the Boston smallpox epidemic of 1764, the *Boston Evening Post* of 26 March 1764 quoted Franklin's conclusion from the pamphlet, and both the *Massachusetts Gazette* of 29 March 1764 and the *Boston Evening Post* of 2 April 1764 quoted his statement that the clergy might in time remove the popular prejudice against inoculation.

Lead Poisoning

Like his interest in smallpox inoculation, Franklin's concern with lead poisoning began while he was a teenager in Boston. In a letter of 31 July 1786 to Benjamin Vaughan, the eighty-year-old Franklin wrote out the information he had gathered on lead poisoning throughout his life. He began in Boston. In 1723, North Carolina's officials complained to the Massachusetts authorities that the New England rum "poisoned their People, giving them the Dry Bellyach, with a Loss of the Use of their Limbs." The complaint caused "a general Discourse in Boston." Upon examining the distilleries, "it was found that several of them used leaden Still-heads and Worms, and the Physicians were of Opinion, that the Mischief was occasioned by that Use of Lead." The House appointed a committee on 10 June 1723 to investigate the effects of using lead in distilling rum. The report concluded lead was pernicious. The House debated the report on 20 June and asked that a bill be drawn up. It was read on 8 and 10 August and passed with amendments on 30 August. The engrossed bill was brought down the next day. "An Act for Preventing Abuses in Distilling of Rum and other Strong Liquors, with Leaden Heads or Pipes" became law on 3 September 1723, three weeks before Franklin ran away to Philadelphia.

Working for Samuel Palmer in London (1725), Franklin dried the types by placing the sloping case before the fire. In the damp London winters, warming the types had an additional "Advantage, when the Types were not only dry'd but heated, of being comfortable to the Hands working over them in cold weather. I therefore sometimes heated my Case when the Types did not want drying. But an old Workman, observing it, advis'd me not to do so, telling me I might lose the Use of my Hands by it, as two of our Companions had nearly done, one of whom that us'd to earn his Guinea a Week, could not then make more than ten Shillings, and the other, who had the Dangles, but seven and sixpence. This, with a kind of obscure Pain, that I had sometimes felt, as it were in the Bones of my Hand when working over the Types made very hot, induced me to omit the Practice."

The type foundry of John James (d. 1772) was downstairs in the same building as Palmer's printing house. When Franklin had an opportunity, he asked James "if his People, who work'd over the little Furnaces of melted Metal, were not subject to that Disorder." James "made light of any danger from the effluvia, but ascribed it to Particles of the Metal swallow'd with their Food by slovenly Workmen, who went to their Meals after handling the Metal, without well washing their Fingers, so that some of the metalline Particles were taken off by their Bread and eaten with it" (S 9:531–32). The explanation sounded plausible, but the pain Franklin had felt in his own hands made him suspect that lead could be absorbed through the skin.

In Philadelphia over two decades later, Dr. Thomas Cadwalader drafted an essay on how lead poisoning caused the "West India Dry Gripes" but lost the manuscript. Franklin advertised (24 November 1738) for it to be returned. It was, or Cadwalader rewrote it. At Franklin's repeated request, Cadwalader gave the manuscript to him. Franklin revised the rambling introduction and published it at his own risk on 2 May 1745. *An Essay on the West-India Dry-Gripes* was Philadelphia's first locally composed medical publication. Financially, the pamphlet failed; Franklin probably thought it would, but he published it as a contribution to knowledge. As he wrote Cadwallader Colden six months later, "If I can be a Means of Communication anything valuable to the World, I do not always think of Gaining, nor even of Saving by my Business" (3:46). As in Boston, lead poisoning in Philadelphia was caused by using lead pipes in the distilling process.

A London acquaintance, Dr. George Baker, wrote an essay in 1767 on the causes of colic, particularly the "Drybellyach." Franklin informed him that pewter pipes (which had a high lead content) were known in New England to cause the sickness and said that he believed that the "Drybellyach" always proceeded from a metallic cause. He had observed, he told Baker, that the sickness affected tradesmen who used lead in their work (14:214, 15:51).

In his 1786 letter to Vaughan, Franklin recalled visiting furnaces for smelting lead ore in Derbyshire, England, in August 1759.[6] He was told then that the smoke from the furnaces was pernicious to the neighboring grass and other vegetables, "but I do not recollect to have heard any thing of the Effect of such Vegetables eaten by Animals. It may be well to make the Enquiry." When he made this suggestion in 1786, the environmentalist probably hoped that others would make the inquiry. In America, he had often observed that on the roofs of shingled houses, "where Moss is apt to grow in northern Exposures, if there be any thing on the Roof painted with white Lead, such as Balusters, or Frames of dormant Windows, &c., there is constantly a Streak on the Shingles from such Paint down to the Eaves, on which no Moss will grow, but the wood remains constantly clean and free from it" (W 1165).

Though that seemed like praise for the white lead paint, Franklin wondered about the possibility of its poisoning people. "We seldom drink RainWater that falls on our Houses; and if we did, perhaps the small Quantity of Lead, descending from such Paint, might not be sufficient to produce any sensible ill Effect on our Bodies." But he had heard of a case in Europe where an entire family was afflicted "with what we call the Dry Bellyach, or *Colica Pictonum*, by drinking

RainWater. It was at a Country-Seat, which, being situated too high to have the Advantage of a Well, was supply'd with Water from a Tank, which received the Water from the leaded Roofs. This had been drunk several Years without Mischief; but some young Trees planted near the House growing up above the Roof, and shedding their Leaves upon it, it was suppos'd that an Acid in those Leaves had corroded the Lead they cover'd, and furnish'd the Water of that Year with its baneful Particles and Qualities" (W 1165).

Visiting Paris in 1767, Franklin and his traveling companion, Sir John Pringle, went to La Charité, a hospital famous for treating *Colica Pictonum*. Franklin "brought from thence a Pamphlet containing a List of the Names of Persons, specifying their Professions or Trades, who had been cured there. I had the Curiosity to examine that List, and found that all the Patients were of Trades, that, some way or other, use or work in Lead; such as Plumbers, Glaziers, Painters, &c. excepting only two kinds, Stonecutters and Soldiers. These I could not reconcile to my Notion, that Lead was the cause of that Disorder. But on my mentioning this Difficulty to a Physician of that Hospital, he inform'd me that the Stonecutters are continually using melted Lead to fix the Ends of Iron Balustrades in Stone; and that the Soldiers had been employ'd by Painters, as Labourers, in Grinding of Colours."

On 20 February 1768 Franklin wrote to the Philadelphia physician Dr. Cadwalader Evans that he had long been of the opinion that the dry bellyache "proceeds always from a metallic Cause," for he had observed "that it affects among Tradesmen those that use Lead, however different their Trades, as Glazers, Type-Founders, Plumbers, Potters, White Lead-makers and Painters." After summarizing what he knew and hypothesized about lead poisoning, he concluded the letter to Vaughan (31 July 1786), by remarking that the knowledge of the "mischievous Effect from Lead is at least above Sixty Years old; and you will observe with Concern how long a useful Truth may be known and exist, before it is generally receiv'd and practis'd on" (W 1166). Franklin's reflection was not only just—it was prophetic. In the United States, lead continued to be used in paint until 1978.

Perspiration

Writing the New York intellectual and politician Dr. Cadwallader Colden (1688–1776) on 15 August 1745, Franklin set forth a series of thoughts and observations on perspiration and fever. Colden had theorized that the human body not only perspired but also absorbed fluids. He supposed that the absorbing channels communicated with the veins and that the perspiring channels communicated with the arteries. Franklin, however, observed that all fluids "by the hydrostatical Law press equally in all Directions." Therefore, it was questionable whether the direction of one of the minute vessels where it joined with a vein or artery "*with* or *against* the Stream of Blood" would be sufficient to produce such contrary effects as perspiring and absorbing. Franklin suggested that the same vessel could carry either an absorbing fluid or a perspiring fluid. "Yet I cannot say, I am certain the mere Direction of the Vessels will have no Effect; I only suspect it, and am making a little Machine to try an Experiment with for Satisfaction."

A "little Machine." What could it have been? Franklin's theories were wrong, but they were closer to the truth than those of the Edinburgh-trained physician, Colden, though he knew the current studies of the body. My friend Marguerite D. Thew, M.D., tells me that some absorption occurs through the sweat ducts, but most goes through the submicroscopic openings in the skin cells themselves by diffusion. Franklin also suggested that the heart acts as a suction cup as well as a pump. Blood flows along a pressure gradient that is highest when the ventricles pump by contracting and lowest when the ventricles dilate, the latter creating a negative pressure. Since the dilation is a passive process of relaxation, it requires no suction.[7]

Other Medical Topics

Franklin published works concerning medicine in his newspaper, almanac, and separate publications. He wrote an afterword for Dr. John Tennent's *Every Man His Own Doctor* (1734 and 1736), warning that the Pennsylvania ipecacuanha, or Indian physic, was much stronger than the Virginia variety. In the *Pennsylvania Gazette* for 5 February 1735/6, Franklin reprinted an article on diphtheria from the *Boston Gazette*, and he put in the 1737 *Poor Richard* an Indian cure for a rattlesnake bite.

When his friend the Philadelphia botanist John Bartram discovered ginseng, a supposed medical panacea, growing near the Susquehanna, Franklin publicized the find in the 27 July 1738 *Gazette*. The next week, 3 August, he advertised Dr. John Tennent's proposals for printing by subscription, "A Treatise on the Diseases of Virginia"; and in the next *Gazette* he published the method of using salt to draw out the poison of a rattlesnake bite. Tennent's account of how to use the Seneca rattlesnake root to treat pleurisy appeared in the *Gazette* on 19 and 26 July 1739, and Franklin advertised the root for sale at the post office on 3 July 1740. *Poor Richard* for 1741 published John Bartram's account of "the true Indian Physick," the plant ipecacuanha (2:298–99). The 1742 almanac contained "Rules of Health and Long life" and "Rules to find out a fit Measure of Meat and Drink."

On 1 September 1743, while Boston was experiencing a diphtheria epidemic, Franklin sent an anonymous letter, dated from Philadelphia, to the (Boston) *American Magazine and Historical Chronicle*, suggesting that the symptoms for the epidemic were the same as those described by Joseph Pitton de Tournefort in *A Voyage to the Levant*. Franklin closed the letter with three queries: "I should be glad to learn of some of your Physicians, whether the Throat Distemper, (which, if I mistake not, was thought to be a new Disease, arising originally in *New-England*) be not described in this Account of the Child's Plague in the Levant? Whether from the Circumstances and Place of its first Appearance there is any Reason to suppose it was imported? And whether Experience in *New-England* justifies any Method of treating it, like that here directed?" The author's most valuable suggestion is that the remedy the Greeks used on Iona might also be successful in Boston.

Since Franklin was the Philadelphia agent for the *American Magazine and Historical Chronicle* and must have been frequently in contact with its Boston editors (John Rogers and Daniel Fowle), since Franklin commonly used the signature "F. B.,"[8] and since the Library Company of Philadelphia possessed a copy of Tournefort's *Voyage into the Levant*,[9] I agree with Francisco Guerra and Whitfield J. Bell, Jr., that Franklin wrote the letter to the editor of the *American Magazine*.[10] He no doubt recalled that Cotton Mather had initiated smallpox inoculations in Boston after reading about inoculations in the Middle East. The letter might be regarded as another indirect influence of the great American Puritan on Franklin.

In the *Pennsylvania Gazette* for 11 and 26 January and 2 February 1744, Franklin reprinted Cadwallader Colden's essay on the New York yellow fever epidemics of 1741 and 1742. Colden recommended keeping the environment (especially the water, sewers, drains, and docks) clean as an effective way to prevent fevers during the late summer and fall. Franklin probably reprinted the essay partially because it indirectly supported his environmental arguments against the Philadelphia tanners in 1739. A year before Franklin retired as a printer, the 6 January 1746/7 *Gazette* published Drs. Thomas and Phineas Bond's request for information concerning the healing power of the "new discovered Wells in Virginia."

TECHNOLOGY

Franklin's interest in technology began when he was a boy, possibly when his father took him to see various craftsmen such as joiners, bricklayers, turners, braziers, and others: "It has ever since been a Pleasure to me to see good Workmen handle their Tools." He found, too, that his rudimentary ability in various crafts was useful for doing minor repairs around the house and for constructing "little Machines for my Experiments while the Intention of making the Experiment was fresh and warm in my Mind" (A 10). While an apprentice, he no doubt watched his brother James make woodcuts for his publications. At age nineteen and twenty, he saw the London type founders make letters, and the next year, when working for Samuel Keimer in Philadelphia, he made types and cuts when they were needed. Working for Keimer in the spring of 1728, Franklin contrived copperplate engravings for the New Jersey paper money. Franklin was interested in technology and what we would today call mechanical engineering throughout his life. A voracious and attentive reader, he knew the popular books on mechanics and on engines and machines used in war.[11] When he watched workmen doing tasks, he focused with intensity.

Printing

The technology that Franklin knew best was printing. Many colonial American printers produced books and other printed items of beauty, as did Franklin, but no other colonial printer contributed so much to printing technology. The printer and book man indulged himself by buying the expensive classic, Joseph Moxon's *Mechanick Exercises . . . the Art of Printing* (London, 1683).[12] In the early 1730s, Franklin and his friend Joseph Breintnall experimented with impressions of the leaves of American trees and plants. Nature printing (i.e., inking a leaf and making a copy of it) was an old technique.[13] With the help of John Bartram, Breintnall made a complete collection of the American leaves found around Philadelphia. When Breintnall lost a "Sheet and a half of Prints of Leaves," he advertised for them in the 26 April 1733 *Pennsylvania Gazette*, saying that they were "Part of a compleat Set. Whoever brings them to the Printer hereof, shall be well rewarded." Breintnall's nature printing inspired Franklin.

Perhaps Franklin began experimenting with applying nature printing to the technology of the printing press simply to see if it could be done. As Eric P. Newman, the primary authority on early American paper money, wrote me, Franklin must have begun with either a mold of wet papier mâché or soft plaster. He placed a leaf on it, then pressed the leaf into the wet plaster or papier mâché with a flat board, and left the mold to dry and harden. Then he washed away the leaf, oiled the plaster/papier mâché, and made a plaster negative (strengthened with some material like ground asbestos or powdered brick) of the impression. After the plaster negative hardened, a thin layer of hot lead or type metal could be poured over it to produce a positive lead cut. The thin lead cut could then be nailed to a wood board and fitted into the printing frame along with the set type.[14]

While devising a method of printing copies of the same leaf, Franklin realized that the technique might be extremely useful—and profitable. A lucrative income for an ingenious colonial printer was printing paper currency. The paper currency of colonial America was, however, often counterfeited. Franklin realized that the printed impressions of leaves in paper currency would be practically impossible to counterfeit.

When New Jersey received permission in the early summer of 1735 to issue £50,000 in paper currency, Franklin told some key assembly members that he had a new secret technique that would make counterfeiting extremely difficult. He said that he would print the currency for £160—an expensive price, but it would be cheaper in the long run because the paper money could not be counterfeited. The forging of paper money created two expensive problems: first, it lowered the value of paper money; second and more important, the money that was imitated had to be recalled and reemitted with new designs—an expensive proposition.

Franklin got the contract. The New York printer William Bradford had com-

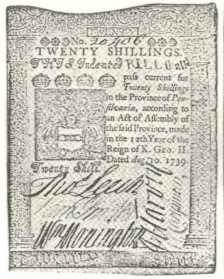

Figure 29. Nature printing, a new technique to prevent counterfeiting. Counterfeiting of colonial paper currency was common. Franklin used complex variations of spelling and type to make counterfeiting more difficult. He also devised a way to print images of leaves on paper currency, thus making it extraordinarily difficult to counterfeit. For some time, other printers did not understand how he did it. Franklin first used the technique in printing New Jersey's paper currency for 1735, but no examples of that issue of £50,000 are extant. When William Bradford learned that Franklin had been awarded the contract, he complained that Franklin was paid £160 for it, whereas he would have done it for £100 "or less." Bradford's product, however, would soon have been counterfeited.

The earliest extant example of Franklin's nature printing is in Poor Richard *for 1737, accompanying an article on the Indian "Rattle-snake Herb," which he illustrated with a species of a golden-rod leaf. The earliest extant nature printing on paper currency is Franklin's Pennsylvania paper money of 1740. Courtesy, Eric P. Newman Numismatic Education Society, St. Louis, Missouri.*

peted for the job and lost, occasioning the first intercolonial criticism of Franklin as a businessman. The 21 June 1736 *New York Gazette* complained that "the Persons appointed by the [New Jersey] Assembly" who were supposed "to get the said Bills Printed in the best and cheapest manner . . . agreed to have said Bills printed for the Sum of £160 Proclamation Money, whereas another Person would have done it for £100 or less. But such is the effect of Party, Faction and Prejudice. Its no matter, its the Country's Money, and if the Publick cannot afford to pay well, who can? Its proper to serve a Friend when there is an Opportunity." Bradford did not know at the time that Franklin proposed an entirely new technique to the committee; instead he attributed Franklin's winning the contract to "Party, Faction and Prejudice." In fact, Franklin's mechanical inge-niousness won the contract. Franklin went to Burlington, New Jersey, in mid-July 1736 to print the New Jersey money under the inspection of an assembly committee. A notice in the 2 August 1736 *Pennsylvania Gazette* noted that he was "at Burlington with the Press, laboring for the publick Good to make Money more plentiful." Since the *Pennsylvania Gazette* was coming out regu-larly in Philadelphia, he must have had two presses by this time.

In 1736, Joseph Breintnall wrote a description of the "Rattle-snake Herb" that Indians used supposedly to cure poisonous snakebites. Franklin published the description in *Poor Richard* for 1737, which, as usual, came out in November of the prior year. To illustrate which plant was the correct one, Franklin printed a leaf of it. Because of that nature printing, we can be sure that the plant was the common goldenrod. He continued to use nature printing for later issues of paper money from Delaware, New Jersey, and Pennsylvania, but he slightly improved the technique. Instead of placing the leaf directly against the oiled, wet plaster of paris, he placed a loosely woven piece of cloth like fine burlap or cheesecloth on the surface before laying the leaf on it and pressing the design into the plaster of paris. After the plaster had hardened, the cloth made it easier to remove the leaf. Then the hardened plaster could be oiled and a plaster nega-tive made. Impressions of the cloth, as well as the leaf, are visible on the later printed currency.

When Cadwallader Colden wrote William Strahan on 3 December 1743, he mentioned that the previous summer he had met a printer "the most ingenious in his way without question of any in America," to whom Colden told his idea for a kind of stereotyping process. Franklin acquainted him with "the Method which had been used in Holland . . . but he thought the method by types *en creuse* to be an improvement." Franklin evidently informed him about the cum-bersome method tried out by the Dutch printer Johann Muller (fl. 1701–18), who had soldered types together, and said that Colden's suggested intaglio proc-ess would be better.[15] Colden continued, "as he is a man very lucky in improving every hint he has done something on this foundation & which I have seen which has puzzled all the printers in this country to conceive by what method it is done." The printers must have had in mind either the goldenrod print from the 1737 *Poor Richard* or the New Jersey paper money. In both, Franklin had used a version of an intaglio process to make molds from leaves of plants.

Strahan's reply on 9 May 1744 showed that he recognized the unnamed American printer from Colden's assessment: "From the Character you give of him, I am sure it must be Mr. Franklin you mean, whose Fame has long ago reached this Part of the World, for a most ingenious Man in his Way." Strahan, like Franklin, thought that Colden's stereotyping would not be an improvement (2:386–87). Was there a note of condescension in Strahan's assessment of Frank-lin as "a most ingenious Man in his Way"? Though they became close friends in the late 1750s and early 1760s, they drifted apart in the pre-Revolutionary period because Strahan had the typical English/British (he was a Scot) prejudice against America and Americans.

Another major problem with the colonial paper currency was that the paper itself often wore out before the time that it was due to be "sunk" or burned. As it wore out, the bills had to be replaced, an expensive process calling for a reemission act. Franklin tried to produce an especially strong paper for use in the currency. He succeeded, collecting special rags for the "Money paper," as Franklin called it in his accounts.[16] The rags for "Money paper" and the resulting product were more expensive than the normal best quality writing paper. Franklin also experimented with various additives to produce stronger paper. Among other substantives, Franklin tried to strengthen paper with mica. Mica was common, cheap, and easy to add in the papermaking process. It became a normal ingredient in Franklin's later "money paper." Since the stronger paper money lasted longer, Franklin was actually cutting down his business by devising a stronger paper.

He also experimented with paper made from asbestos. He wrote Peter Collinson on 26 June 1755, sending along a sample and apologizing that it was so "tender," adding that he "made some formerly that was much stronger." Franklin inspired William Dewees, Jr., and John Gorgas, papermakers, to try making paper from asbestos. The two papermakers finally produced a successful imitation of asses' skin paper from asbestos for memorandum books. It was cleaned after being "sullied by wear or defaced by writing" by putting it in the fire, "from whence it was taken out perfectly cleaned, and its texture uninjured."[17]

Seven years before the letter to Collinson, Franklin told the Swedish scientist Peter Kalm of a trick that he had played on one of his journeymen printers. Having had some paper made of asbestos, he told a susceptible journeyman that "he would see a miracle, a sheet of paper which did not burn." Of course the journeyman insisted it would, whereupon Franklin threw it in the fire. It remained unburned. The man was terrified. (As we will see later, Franklin loved to play wizard.) "Mr. Franklin then explained to him . . . the peculiar qualities of the paper. As soon as he was gone, some of his acquaintances came in, who immediately recognized the paper. The journeyman thought he would show them a great curiosity and astonish them. He accordingly told them that he had curiously made a sheet of paper which would not burn, though it were thrown into the fire. They pretended to think it impossible, and he as strenuously maintained his assertion. At last they laid a wager about it, but while he was busy with stirring up the fire the others slyly besmeared the paper with fat. Unaware they had done so, the journeyman threw it into the fire and that moment it was all in flames. This astonished him so much that he was almost speechless, upon which they could not help laughing, and so disclosed the whole artifice" (4:58–59).

Did Franklin actually play such a prank or did he simply make it up to put on the Swedish scientist? John Bartram, Gustavus Hesselius, and Franklin all told the greenhorn Kalm tall tales. Franklin, for example, told him a variation of the old story of an Indian selling Manhattan for $24.00: the English bought Rhode Island from the Indians for a pair of spectacles.[18] Whether he played the prank or simply put on the scientist, Franklin was indulging in typical American humor.

Another technical printing innovation occurred to Franklin. He admired the hand-painted Dutch Delftware tiles common in Pennsylvania, even though they were chiefly "Scripture Histories, wretchedly scrawled."[19] He thought that the plates about moral virtues in Marin le Roy de Gomberville's *Moral Virtue Delineated* (London, 1726)[20] would be better aesthetically and more useful. "I wished to have those moral Prints, (which were originally taken from Horace's poetical Figures) introduced on Tiles, which being about our Chimneys, and constantly in the Eyes of Children when by the Fire-side, might give Parents an Opportunity, in explaining them, to impress moral Sentiments" (20:459).

Franklin wrote Dr. John Mitchell, a Virginia physician and mapmaker who was then in England, proposing printing tiles for ornamenting chimneys and describing how it could be done from copper plates—perhaps the earliest proposal for printing copperplate engravings on earthenware.[21] Mitchell suggested it to "several of the principal Artists in the Earthen Way about London, who rejected it as impracticable." Over twenty years later, his English friend Peter Burdett sent Franklin examples of Burdett's process for transferring aquatint engravings to pottery. In reply, Franklin recalled his correspondence with Mitchell, and wrote Burdett on 3 November 1773: "I know not who (now we speak of Inventions) pretends to that of Copper-Plate Engravings for Earthen-Ware, and am not disposed to contest the Honor of it with any body, as the Improvement in taking Impressions not directly from the Plate but from printed Paper, applicable by that means to other than flat Forms, [is] far beyond my first Idea. But I have reason to apprehend I might have given the Hint on which that Improvement was made" (20:459).

Franklin suggested an improvement to the standard eighteenth-century press, either when he bought a third press about 1738 or perhaps earlier. Ordering it, Franklin asked that the press maker introduce a change in the usual design. He repeated the request when he wrote William Strahan on 27 October 1753 for a press: "If you can persuade your Pressmaker to go out of his old Road a little, I would have the Ribs made not with the Face rounding outwards, as usual, but a little hollow or rounding inwards from end to end: And the Cramps made of hard cast Brass, fix'd not across the Ribs, but longways so as to slide in the hollow Face of the Ribs. The Reason is, that Brass and Iron work better together than Iron and Iron; Such a Press never gravels; the hollow Face of the Ribs keeps the Oil better, and the Cramps bearing on a larger Surface do not wear as in the common Method. Of this I have had many Years Experience." The printing historian Lawrence C. Wroth pointed out that Franklin had corrected a "fundamental mechanical error" in the operation of the press—and that his improvement was ignored.²² Franklin, however, probably got the press he wanted, but, if not, he would have made the change himself—or had it made.

THE FRANKLIN STOVE

The experimenter tested iron not only in the printing press but also in stoves. Franklin bartered for a stove from Thomas Hart as early as 1730, but no evidence suggests he was devising heating devices so early. Franklin's accounts with William Branson, however, reveal that Franklin was testing plans for stoves by the winter of 1737–38. Branson, a Philadelphia Baptist and leading merchant, was an investor in and agent for the Reading Furnace. On 14 January 1737/8, Franklin bought a stove from Branson, and on 27 January, the inventor purchased twenty-eight and three-quarters pounds of steel from him. On 12 June, Franklin purchased an additional ten and a half pounds of London steel, and then on 15 November 1738, he bought another stove. After he fashioned a design that improved the existing stoves and began selling them to his friends, he had his friend Robert Grace make the steel plates. Though Branson's account with Franklin continues through 1747, the last stove or steel Franklin purchased from him was on 15 November 1738. Once Franklin realized that his mechanical tinkering might result in better stoves and be profitable for the ironmonger, he switched to buying steel and stoves from his good friend Grace, who had helped him buy out his former partner Hugh Meredith in 1730. Grace probably began making versions of Franklin's plates in the winter of 1739–40.

Three years after he started experimenting with stoves, Franklin advertised iron fireplaces for sale on 5 February 1741. It seems surprising that his first advertisement of stoves for sale appeared near the end of the winter. Perhaps he was not satisfied until then, or perhaps Grace produced only a few stoves in the fall of 1740, all of which sold privately. Hugh Roberts, Philip Syng, and other friends purchased early versions of the stove. It did not have the ornament of the sun on the front panel and did not have an air box in the back (12:386)—features present when the pamphlet on the stove was published in 1744.

The experimenter continued to tinker with the fireplace, and in the following winter on 3 December 1741 he advertised: "To be Sold at the Post-Office in Philadelphia, *THE NEW INVENTED IRON FIRE-PLACES*; where any Person may see some of them that are now in Use, and have the Nature and Advantages of them explain'd." Evidently they sold out within a few weeks, for on 20 January 1742, he advertised: "*JUST* came down from the Furnace, a fresh Parcel of *IRON FIRE-PLACES*; to be sold at the Post-Office." By the following winter, he and Grace were making the stoves in two sizes (11 November 1742). No advertisements for the fireplaces appeared in the winter of 1743–44: perhaps all that Grace manufactured were selling well; or perhaps Franklin was then designing what he believed to be an improvement and so did not want to sell the old version. The 1744 version had an air box. The smoke had to go over the air box, back down on the other side and through a passage in the floor, and then up the chimney. With that improvement, Franklin was carried away by theory and harmed the stove's operation.

Franklin wrote *An Account of the New Invented Pennsylvanian Fire-Places* in the fall of 1744 to promote the stove. He advertised the pamphlet on 15 November 1744. It discussed the different kinds of fireplaces, their advantages and disadvantages, and the theory underlying the "New Invented Fire-Place." Robert Grace, who manufactured and sold the plates at his Warwick Furnace in Chester County, Pennsylvania, paid for the pamphlet. Franklin's accounts record that on 17 December 1744 Grace paid £19.11 "For Sundries Printing &c. & paying the Boston Engraver for work for the new invented Fire Place." Lewis Evans, the cartographer, made the drawings of the stove and James Turner of Boston engraved them.

Environmentalist Franklin said that because less wood would be consumed by the new stove, it would be much cheaper to operate—and he emphasized that wood, the common American fuel, was growing scarcer and that the new stove would conserve a dwindling natural resource.[23] He said that for the past three winters many families in Pennsylvania had experienced the benefit of the new stoves (thus confirming that the initial public sales of the stove occurred in the winter of 1740–41).

The fire expert began by explaining the theory underlying the stove, offering five observations concerning the properties of air, heat, and fire. First, "Air is rarified by *Heat*, and condens'd by *Cold*." Second, "Air rarified and distended by Heat, is specifically lighter than it was before, and will rise in other Air of greater Density." Consequently, the air over the fire becomes lighter and rises. Third, "Fire throws out Light, Heat, and Smoke." Light and heat move in right lines with great swiftness. Smoke moves only as it is carried up by "the Stream of rarified Air. And without a continual Accession and Recession of Air to carry off the Smoaky Fumes, they would remain crouded about the Fire, and stifle it." Fourth, heat may be separated from both the smoke and the light by an iron plate, which allows heat to pass through it without the others. Fifth, though fire sends out its heat and light in every direction, "the greatest sensible Heat is over the Fire, where there is, besides the Rays of Heat shot upwards, a continual rising Stream of hot Air, heated by the Rays shot round on every Side" (2:422–23).

Franklin analyzed the six heating methods in use, noting the national origin of each. This section, like his description of heat exchange, showed that he knew all the scholarship. "The large open Fire-places used in the Days of our Fathers, and still generally in the Country, and in Kitchens" had many disadvantages. They consumed enormous quantities of wood, required that a door be kept open to admit fresh air to carry off the smoke, and did not warm the room. The drafts caused sicknesses and ruined good looks. Women especially suffered: large open fireplaces caused colds "which fall into their Jaws and Gums, and have destroy'd early many a fine Set of Teeth in these Northern Colonies. Great and bright Fires do also very much contribute to damage the Eyes, dry and shrivel the Skin, and bring on early the Appearances of Old-Age" (2:424–25). Franklin, a shrewd advertiser, implied that his new stove kept women looking young and beautiful. (Did advertisers before Franklin commonly make such appeals?)

The second stove was "the newer-fashion'd Fire-places, with low Breasts, and narrow Hearths." They required a large quantity of air, which rushed "in at every Crevice so strongly, as to make a continual Whistling or Howling; and 'tis very uncomfortable as well as dangerous to sit against any such Crevice." In this as well as the large open fireplace, most heat was lost: "For as Fire naturally darts Heat every way, the Back, the two Jambs, and the Hearth, drink up almost all that's given them, very little being reflected from Bodies so dark, porous and unpolish'd; and the upright Heat, which is by far the greatest, flies directly up the Chimney. Thus Five Sixths at least of the Heat (and consequently of the Fewel) is wasted" (2:427).

The third category was the French fireplaces "with hollow Backs, Hearths and Jams of Iron . . . for warming the Air as it comes into the Room." These stoves, designed by the French inventor Nicolas Gauger, were major improvements because they heated a room with considerably less fuel. But the intricate design, the large initial expense, and the difficulty of installing them in existing chimneys all prohibited their being commonly used. In addition, most of the heat went up and was lost, as in the common English fireplaces.

Fourth, the Holland iron stove, with a flue at the top and an iron door opening into the room, was an iron box of six metal sides fastened together and raised off the floor on short legs. The hinged door in front allowed fuel to be inserted, and a hole in the top carried off the smoke through a pipe. Franklin praised this stove, though it had two defects: "There is no Sight of the Fire, which is in itself a pleasant Thing." And one could not easily use it for cooking: "One cannot conveniently make any other Use of the Fire but that of warming the Room" (2:428).

Fifth, he discussed the German stove, a box lacking one side. "'Tis compos'd of Five Iron Plates scru'd together; and fix'd so as that you may put the Fuel into it from another Room, or from the Outside of the House." Though it provided heat, "People have not even so much Sight or Use of the Fire as in the Holland Stoves, and are moreover oblig'd to breathe the same unchang'd Air continually, mix'd with the Breath and Perspiration from one anothers Bodies, which is very disagreeable to those who have not been accustomed to it."

The sixth and final method of heating was iron pots, with open charcoal fires. Though Franklin wrote before oxygen, much less carbon dioxide, was discovered, he appreciated their roles. The iron pots provided efficient warming, but the fumes from the coals gradually made the air "disagreeable, hurtful to some Constitutions, and sometimes, when the Door is long kept shut, produce fatal Consequences" (2:429).

Franklin's Pennsylvania fireplace avoided the inconveniences of other fireplaces and retained their advantages. His iron fireplace could be set inside a regular open fireplace in which a false back was added to the chimney, making an enclosed flue. The front had a shutter (the damper was among the new improvements, one that would be further refined after he went to England in 1757)[24] that could be raised and lowered. Franklin advised that after the fire was started, the shutter be lowered, "and the Opening being by that Means contracted, the Air rushes in briskly and presently blows up the Flames." After the fire was well started, the shutter was raised to allow a view of the fire. Behind the fire, an enclosed air box rose nearly to the top of the fireplace. The smoke rose from the fire, over the top of the air box, down behind it to the floor where it entered the flue. Fresh air entered the air box through holes in the bottom plate, was heated by the fire, and released into the room by shutters in the upper parts of the two side plates. A register controlled the flow of air into the flue, and by use of the front shutter and register, a fire could be stifled and secured at any time (2:432–35).

Good ventilation appealed to Franklin. A nonsmoker, he found that the smell of tobacco could be disagreeable. He suggested that in rooms "where much Smoking of Tobacco is used," a hole of five or six inches square be cut into the stove funnel near the ceiling. The hole should have a shutter, so that it could be conveniently opened or closed. When open, the hole would cause a strong air current to rise through it which would quickly carry off tobacco smoke. "By this means . . . the Tobacco-Smoke does not descend among the Heads of the Company near the Fire, as it must do before it can get into common Chimneys" (2:433). (Did anyone before Franklin try to accommodate non-smokers in an environment where people smoked?)

In the Pennsylvania fireplace, the greatest part of the heat was not lost up a chimney but instead warmed the room. Franklin wrote, "My common Room, I know, is made twice as warm as it used to be, with a quarter of the Wood I formerly consum'd." Since wood was "one of the most expensive articles of housekeeping," the saving was considerable. Another advantage of the Pennsylvania fireplace was that a fire could speedily be made by the help of the shutter and could be extinguished easily by closing the shutter before and the register behind. With the fire extinguished, the coals and heated iron continued to give warmth most of the night. Further, the sparks could not escape to set the house ablaze. "With all these Conveniencies, you do not lose the pleasant Sight nor Use of the Fire, as in the Dutch Stoves, but may boil the Tea-Kettle, warm the Flat Irons, heat Heaters, keep warm a Dish of Victuals by setting it on the Top, & c." (2:438).

Franklin concluded the pamphlet by returning to the environmental and economic advantages of conserving wood. With the Pennsylvania fireplace, "our Wood may grow as fast as we consume it, and our Posterity may warm themselves at a moderate Rate, without being oblig'd to fetch their Fuel over the Atlantick. . . . We leave it to the *Political Arithmetician* to compute, how much

Money will be sav'd to a Country, by its spending two thirds less of Fuel; how much Labour sav'd in Cutting and Carriage of it; how much more Land may be clear'd for Cultivation; how great the Profit by the additional Quantity of Work done, in those Trades particularly that do not exercise the Body so much, but that the Workfolks are oblig'd to run frequently to the Fire to warm themselves." Probably recalling his days in the London winters of 1724–25 and 1725–26, he left it to physicians to say "how much healthier thick-built Towns and Cities will be, [which are] now half suffocated with sulphury Smoke, when so much less of that Smoke shall be made, and the Air breath'd by the Inhabitants be consequently so much purer" (2:441).

RECEPTION

The stove and the pamphlet caused American intellectuals to appreciate Franklin. James Alexander wrote Cadwallader Colden on 12 November 1744 that Franklin's "piece about his new invented Stove chimneys is very much approved of here & Shows him to be a man of Sense and of a good Stile." The next month, Colden wrote John Frederick Gronovius: "I send with this a curious and new Invention for warming a room with a small fire more effectually than can be done by a large fire in the common method and is free of the inconveniencies which attend the Dutch & German Stoves; because by this contrivance there is a continual supply of fresh warm air. It may be particularly usefull to you & Dr. Linneus, by preserving your health while it keeps you warm at you[r] studies. It is the Invention of Mr. Benjamin Franklin of Philadelphia the Printer of it, a very Ingenious man. Experience confirms the benefit of it."[25]

The Swedish naturalist Peter Kalm, who spent the winter of 1748–49 in Philadelphia, talked to Franklin several times about the new stoves, and Franklin lent him one that Kalm found efficient. Kalm recorded two contrivances that Franklin made in his own fireplace. The first involved cleaning the chimney: "If the stove is narrow it is not so easy to sweep the chimney, after everything is closed up by masonry; but Mr. Franklin had a brick removed beside the stove, let a man pass down through the chimney, clean it, and when he reached the bottom near the stove had him force the soot through the hole made by the removal of the brick. When this was done the brick was replaced." The second concerned the flow of fresh air: "To get fresh air into the stove of a house with no cellar, and where no outside air is wanted, Mr. Franklin this year had had the stove in his own room set on a rim of masonry six inches from the floor, with an opening through the bricks on one side to let the cold air near the floor enter, pass through the air-box, where it was heated, and then pass through the holes on the iron sides of the stove into the room, etc. This brought about a constant circulation of air" (4:62).

A contemporary celebrated the stove on 8 September 1746, in Thomas Fleet's *Boston Evening Post*.[26] The anonymous writer, possibly Fleet, noted that several letters to the editor had recently appeared recommending frugality. He called attention to the possibility of saving the scarce and expensive commodity of firewood by using "the *New-invented Philadelphia Fire Places*, or as they ought to be called, both in Justice and Gratitude, Mr. Franklin's *Stoves*." He said that experiment proved that one cord to possibly as much as a cord and a half of walnut wood would suffice for an entire winter for an ordinary family using a Franklin stove. "Every Body can calculate what a Saving this must be in one of the most necessary Articles of House-keeping; and I believe all who have experienced the Comfort and Benefit of them, will join with me, that the *Author* of this happy Invention, merits a *Statue* from his Countrymen."

The author quoted four lines of verse presenting the euhemeristic theory that the classical gods were actually persons who originally made great advances for mankind:

> Of *old* who to the common Good apply'd
> Or Mind or Means for it were deify'd.
> But chiefly such, who *new Inventions* found,
> *Bacchus* for Wine, *Ceres* that Till'd the Ground.

Though Franklin had been mentioned as a Freemason, editor, printer, and postmaster outside the Philadelphia area, this article first celebrated him for a technical contribution and as a friend to humanity. Franklin modestly called the stove the "New Invented Pennsylvanian Fire-Place," but the *Evening Post* writer called it the "Franklin stove." Franklin did not use the *Pennsylvania Gazette* to spread his reputation; he did not reprint the article.

Franklin idealistically refused to make money from the stove. He recorded in the *Autobiography* that Governor George Thomas (deputy governor of Pennsylvania from 1738 to 1747) "was so pleas'd with the Construction of this Stove . . . that he offer'd to give me a Patent for the sole Vending of them for a Term of Years; but I declin'd it from a Principle which has ever weigh'd with me on such Occasions, viz. *That as we enjoy great Advantages from the Inventions of others, we should be glad of an Opportunity to serve others by any Invention of ours, and this we should do freely and generously*" (A 116). Could the governor actually give Franklin a patent? Perhaps Governor Thomas said that he would support a bill from the legislature giving Franklin exclusive rights to the stove in Pennsylvania. Alternatively, Governor Thomas could have been suggesting that he would write to the London authorities for a patent on behalf of Franklin and that the patent would then be good for Great Britain, including the colonies.[27] Evidently Franklin made nothing from selling the stoves, but his friend Robert Grace, to whom Franklin felt grateful for helping him start the printing business, profited.

After noting that he turned down the patent, Franklin added that a London ironmonger made a few changes in the stove, "which rather hurt its Operation," and got a patent for it "and made as I was told a little Fortune by it.—And this is not the only Instance of Patents taken out for my Inventions by others, tho not always with the same Success, which I never contested, as having no Desire of profiting by Patents my self, and hating Disputes."[28] Franklin concluded the *Autobiography*'s account of stoves by returning to conservation: "The Use of these Fireplaces in very many Houses both of this and the neighbouring Colonies, has been and is a great Saving of Wood to the Inhabitants" (A 116–17). He gave his parents a Pennsylvania fireplace, which was advertised in the sale of their household articles on 1 November 1752.

Despite its improvement over previous stoves, the Pennsylvania fireplace had a major defect. When the smoke reached the brick passage of the flue, it would only draw if the brick walls were hot. Unless the fire were constantly fueled, the brick passage would tend to cool. As it cooled, the draft would diminish and the smoke would spill back into the room. Franklin let the scientific theory of heat exchange overcome the practical and useful. What the ordinary housekeeper did was to eliminate the air box, seal the bottom plate, cut a hole in the back plate for the smoke to go up the chimney, and seal the back of the stove inside the fireplace.[29] Franklin's stove fell out of favor, but it was not entirely superseded until after Sir Henry Bessemer discovered how to make malleable cast iron in 1855.

COLOR AND HEAT ABSORPTION

Heat, not only from burning fuel but from solar power, interested Franklin. About 1732, Franklin repeated an experiment suggested by the Dutch physician Hermann Boerhaave. He had read about the different degrees to which black, scarlet, and white cloths took and held heat. Boerhaave noted that a glass prism focusing the sun's rays would set afire black paper more easily than white. Later, he made the practical suggestion that white garments better preserved the body from the blistering sun.[30] Franklin designed a more complex experiment. He described it to Mary Stevenson about November 1760. He chose "a number of little Square Pieces of Broad Cloth from a Taylor's Pattern Card, of various Colours. They were Black, deep Blue, lighter Blue, Green, Purple, Red, Yellow, White, and other Colours or Shades of Colours. I laid them all out upon the Snow in a bright Sunshiny Morning. In a few Hours (I cannot now be exact as to the Time) the Black being warm'd most by the Sun was sunk so low as to be below the Stroke of the Sun's Rays; the dark Blue almost as low, the lighter Blue not quite so much as the dark, the other Colours less as they were lighter; and the quite White remain'd on the Surface of the Snow, not having entred it at all" (9:251). The experiment roughly ascertained the order in which colors absorbed heat. He interested his Junto friend Joseph Breintnall in the experiment, no doubt hoping that Breintnall would come up with something new. Breintnall made the tests on 25 January 1736/7, with similar results.[31]

COMMUNICATION AMONG ANTS

One summer day about 1745 or 1746, Franklin devised an experiment to test his theory that ants communicated. He told Peter Kalm about his reasons for thinking so: "When an ant finds some sugar, it runs immediately under the floor to its hole, where having stayed a little while a whole army comes out, unites and marches to the place where the sugar is, and carries it off by pieces. If an ant meets with a dead fly, which it cannot carry alone, it immediately hastens home, and soon after some more come out, creep to the fly and carry it away." On one occasion, Franklin "put a little earthen pot with treacle in it into a closet. A number of ants got into the pot and devoured the treacle very quickly."

Franklin devised a test for his theory that ants communicated. He "tied the pot with a thin string to a nail which he had fastened in the ceiling, so that the pot hung down by the string." He filled the pot with the sweet treacle and put a single ant in it. The "ant ate till it was satisfied; but when it wanted to get away it was under great concern to find its way out. It ran about the bottom of the pot, but in vain. At last it found after many attempts the way to get to the ceiling by the string. After it had come there, it ran first to the wall and then to the floor. It had hardly been away for half an hour, when a great swarm of ants came out, climbed up to the ceiling, crept along the string to the pot, and began to eat again. This they continued till the treacle was all eaten. In the meantime one swarm kept running down the string and the other up all day long" (4:59).

MATHEMATICS

Though Franklin did well in the South Grammar School, he had not applied himself when in George Brownell's school and said that he had "twice fail'd" mathematics. But when an apprentice with his brother James, he found himself "made asham'd of my Ignorance in Figures" and "took Cocker's Book of Arithmetick, and went thro' the whole by my self with great Ease.—I also read Seller's and Sturmy's Books of Navigation, and became acquainted with the little Geometry they contain, but never proceeded far in that Science" (A 15).

Franklin never studied higher mathematics. Most biographers fault him for the omission, and they usually neglect to note that he was a genius with numbers. Franklin modestly claimed he knew no mathematics. He wrote Cadwallader Colden, "Your Skill and Expertness in Mathematical Computations, will afford you an Advantage in these Disquisitions, that I lament the want of, who am like a Man searching for something in a dark Room, where I can only grope and guess; while you proceed with a Candle in your Hand" (4:448). As we have seen, however, he used statistics in his news reporting, in writing on paper currency, in supporting smallpox vaccination, and in investigating demography. John Adams wrote, "He had abilities for investigating statistical questions."[32]

When working as clerk of the assembly, he sometimes found the debates (and the periods of silence that uniquely characterized Pennsylvania's assembly) so boring that he made doodles of magic squares (A 120). One day in the country, James Logan "shewed me a folio French book, filled with magic squares, wrote, if I forget not, by one M. Frenicle, in which he said the author had discovered great ingeniuty and dexterity in the management of numbers; and, though several other foreigners had distinguished themselves in the same way, he did not recollect that any one Englishman had done any thing of the kind remarkable." Franklin replied that "it was, perhaps, a mark of the good sense of our English mathematicians, that they would not spend their time in things that were merely *difficiles nugae*, incapable of any useful application." Franklin confessed that sometimes when he was bored as clerk of the assembly, he "amused myself in making these kind of magic squares, and, at length, had acquired such a knack at it, that I could fill the cells of any magic square, of reasonable size, with a series of numbers as fast as I could write them, disposed in such a manner, as that the sums of every row, horizontal, perpendicular, or diagonal, should be equal; but not being satisfied with these, which I looked on as common and easy things, I had imposed on myself more difficult tasks, and succeeded in making other magic squares, with a variety of properties, and much more curious" (4:393).

Logan showed him the most complex magic squares in the book, but Franklin thought none was equal to some he had made. Logan asked to see them. The next time Franklin visited him, he took along a square of 8. Logan, however, brought out "an old arithmetical book, in quarto, wrote, I think, by one Stifelius, which contained a square of 16, that he said he should imagine must have been a work of great labour; but if I forget not, it had only the common properties of making the same sum, viz. 2056, in every row, horizontal, vertical, and diagonal." Challenged by someone having made a larger square, Franklin went home

> and made, that evening, the following magical square of 16, which, besides having all the properties of the foregoing square of 8, i.e. it would make the 2056 in all the same rows and diagonals, had this added, that a four square hole being cut in a piece of paper of such a size as to take in and shew through it, just 16 of the little squares, when laid on the greater square, the sum of the 16 numbers so appearing through the hole, wherever it was placed on the greater square, should likewise make 2056. This I sent to our friend the next morning, who, after some days, sent it back in a letter, with these words: 'I return to thee thy astonishing or most stupendous piece of the magical square, in which—but the compliment is too extravagant, and therefore, for his sake, as well as my own, I ought not to repeat it. Nor is it necessary; for I make no question but you will readily allow this square of 16 to be the most magically magical of any magic square ever made by any magician. (4:396)

James Logan, though amazed by Franklin's ability with numbers, was a thorough master of advanced mathematics and annotated and corrected mathematical printing errors in his copies of Isaac Newton's books, including three editions of the *Principia*.[33]

Inspired by Logan's praise, Franklin applied the principles of a magic square to a magic circle: "consisting of 8 concentric circles, and 8 radial rows, filled with

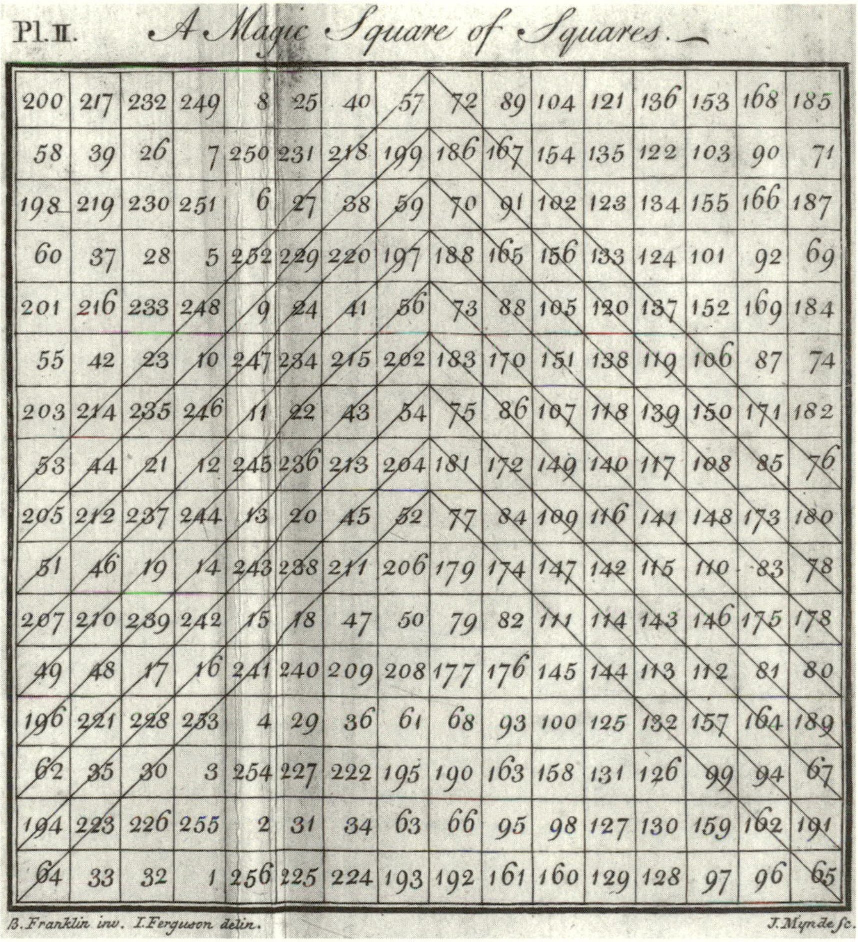

Pl. II. A Magic Square of Squares.

200	217	232	249	8	25	40	57	72	89	104	121	136	153	168	185
58	39	26	7	250	231	218	199	186	167	154	135	122	103	90	71
198	219	230	251	6	27	38	59	70	91	102	123	134	155	166	187
60	37	28	5	252	229	220	197	188	165	156	133	124	101	92	69
201	216	233	248	9	24	41	56	73	88	105	120	137	152	169	184
55	42	23	10	247	234	215	202	183	170	151	138	119	106	87	74
203	214	235	246	11	22	43	54	75	86	107	118	139	150	171	182
53	44	21	12	245	236	213	204	181	172	149	140	117	108	85	76
205	212	237	244	13	20	45	52	77	84	109	116	141	148	173	180
51	46	19	14	243	238	211	206	179	174	147	142	115	110	83	78
207	210	239	242	15	18	47	50	79	82	111	114	143	146	175	178
49	48	17	16	241	240	209	208	177	176	145	144	113	112	81	80
196	221	228	253	4	29	36	61	68	93	100	125	132	157	164	189
62	35	30	3	254	227	222	195	190	163	158	131	126	99	94	67
194	223	226	255	2	31	34	63	66	95	98	127	130	159	162	191
64	33	32	1	256	225	224	193	192	161	160	129	128	97	96	65

B. Franklin inv. I. Ferguson delin. J. Mynde sc.

Figure 30. A magic square of 16. While listening to debates (and, in Quaker style, silences) in the Pennsylvania Assembly, the bored Franklin sometimes doodled, making magic squares. When James Logan learned this, he asked to see one, and Franklin brought him a magic square of 8. Logan then showed Franklin a book containing a magic square of 16. "Not willing to be out-done by Mr. Stifelius, even in the size of my square," Franklin "went home, and made, that evening the following magical square of 16." Logan found it astonishing and stupendous; Franklin joked that it was "the most magically magical of any magic square ever made by any magician." The London astronomer and mathematician James Ferguson said it went "far beyond anything of the kind I ever saw before." From James Ferguson, Tables and Tracts, relative to Several Arts and Sciences *(London, 1767), plate 2. Courtesy, American Philosophical Society, Philadelphia.*

a series of numbers, from 12 to 75, inclusive, so disposed as that the numbers of each circle, or each radial row, being added to the central number 12, they made exactly 360, the number of degrees in a circle; and this circle had, moreover, all the properties of the square of 8." Of Franklin's magic square, the English astronomer James Ferguson (1710–1776) wrote that it went "far beyond any thing of the kind I ever saw before; and the magic circle (which is the first of the kind I ever heard of, or perhaps any one besides) is still more surprising." Three descriptions of the circle exist. One is Franklin's letter to Collinson of about 1752, printed as Letter XXVII in *Experiments and Observations* (1769); a second is in James Ferguson's *Tables and Tracts* (London, 1767); the third survives as a draft in the American Philosophical Society and, revised and expanded, in a letter to John Canton, a fellow member of the Royal Society, on 29 May 1765.

It is compos'd of a Series of Numbers from 12 to 75 inclusive, divided in 8 concentric Circles of Numbers, and rang'd in 8 Radii of Numbers, with the Number 12 in the Center, which Number, like the Center, is common to all the Circles and to all the Radii.

The Numbers are so dispos'd, as that all the Numbers in any one of the Circles, added together, make, with the central Number, just 360, the Number of Degrees in a Circle.

The Numbers in each Radius also, with the central Number, make just 360.

Also Half of any of the said 8 Circles, taken above or under the horizontal double Line with Half the Central Number, make 180, or half the Degrees in a Circle. So likewise do the Numbers in each Half Radius, with half the Central Number.

There are moreover included 4 other Sets of concentric Circles, 5 in each Set, the several Sets distinguish'd by Green, Yellow, Red, and Blue Ink, and each Set drawn round a Center of the same Colour. These Sets of Circles intersect the first 8 and each other; and the Numbers contain'd in each of these 20 Circles, do also, with the Central Number, make 360. Their Halves also, taken above or under the horizontal Line, do, with half the central Number, make 180.

Observe, That there is no one of the Numbers but what belongs to at least two different Circles, some to three, some to four, and some to five; and yet all so plac'd (with the central Number which belongs to all) as never to break the requir'd Number 360 in any one of the 28 Circles. (12:148–49)

ASTRONOMY, INCLUDING COMETS AND ECLIPSES

The astronomical parts of almanacs depended on mathematics not only for such information as the time of the rising and setting of the sun but also for information regarding comets and eclipses. When fourteen years old in Boston, Franklin probably read the Harvard scientist Thomas Robie's 1720 *Almanack*, which included "an account of the Solar System, according to Copernicus and the Mod-

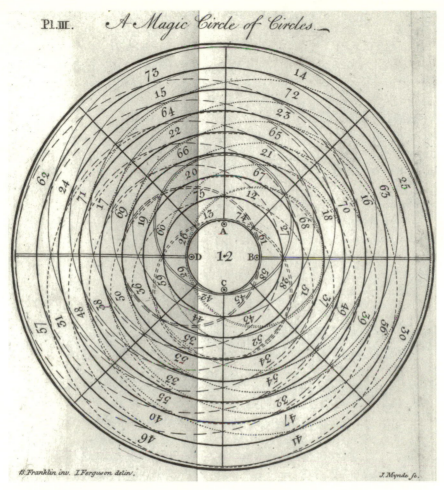

Figure 31. A magic circle, the first ever devised. James Ferguson thought it "still more surprising" than the magic square of 16. In addition to the regular black concentric circles, Franklin used green, red, yellow and blue colors to mark the paths of the other concentric circles, each centered around a small dot in the center of the circle, and each dot lettered A, B, C, or D. To represent Franklin's circles of colors, Ferguson had the engraver use lines of small dots, double small dots, dashes, and double small dashes. He advised the reader that the pattern would be clearer if the reader colored in the lines of dots and dashes. From James Ferguson, Tables and Tracts, relative to Several Arts and Sciences (London, 1767), plate 3. Courtesy, American Philosophical Society, Philadelphia.

ern Astronomers," with tables of "The Middle Distances of the Planets from the Sun," and of "The Diameter of the Sun and Planets with the Moon," all "calculated from the latest Observations by Sir Isaac Newton's Rules." Perhaps the first eclipse of the sun that Franklin carefully observed occurred 27 November 1722, for on 12 November 1722 Robie published in the *New England Courant* directions for observing the eclipse.

Franklin systematically surveyed forthcoming eclipses when he started *Poor Richard*. For 1733, Franklin included brief notes on the four eclipses, two of the sun and two of the moon, even though only two of them would be visible in Philadelphia. After describing the eclipses for 1736, Franklin explained the difference between solar and lunar eclipses: "All Lunar Eclipses are universal, *i.e.* visible in all Parts of the Globe which have the Moon above their Horizon, and are every where of the same Magnitude: But Eclipses of the Sun do not appear the same in all Parts of the Earth where they are seen; being when total in some Places, only partial in others; and in other Places not seen at all, tho' neither Clouds nor Horizon prevent the Sight of the Sun it self."

The 1736 *Poor Richard* also contained a passage of astrology that only the credulous could take seriously. The astrologer Poor Richard said:

> As to the Effects of these two great Eclipses, suffer me to observe, that whoever studies the Eclipses of former Ages, and compares them with the great Events in the History of the Times and Years in which they happened (as every true Astrologer ought to do) shall find, that the Fall of the *Assyrian*, *Persian*, *Grecian* and *Roman* Monarchies, each of them, was remarkably preceded by great and total Eclipses of the Heavenly Bodies. Observations of this kind, join'd with the ancient and long-tryed Rules of our Art, (too tedious to repeat here) make me tremble for an Empire now in being. O *Christendom!* why art thou so fatally divided against thy self? O *Poland!* formerly the Bulwark of the Christian Faith, wilt thou become the Flood-gate to let in an Inundation of Infidelity? O mischievous *Crescent!* when shall we see thee at the Full, and rejoice at thy future Waning? May Heaven avert these presag'd Misfortunes, and confound the Designs of all wicked and impious Men!

More typical of Franklin were the "Enigmatical Prophecies" for the year 1736. He punningly predicted, "Not long after [the middle of the year], a visible Army of 20000 *Musketers* will land, some in *Virginia* and *Maryland*, and some in the lower Counties on both sides of *Delaware*, who will over-run the Country, and sorely annoy the Inhabitants: But the Air in this Climate will agree with them so ill towards Winter, that they will die in the beginning of cold Weather like rotten Sheep, and by Christmas the Inhabitants will get the better of them."

Franklin's interest in astronomy continued, as he also reported phenomena in the newspaper. When a comet was seen in Philadelphia, Franklin printed a detailed news article about it on 3 March 1742, with quotations from William Whiston's *New Theory of the Earth* and Dr. John Keill's *Astronomical Lectures*.[34]

Of the five 1743 eclipses, four were to be invisible, but the eclipse of the moon on 21 October was to be visible and total. It would begin at 8:29 p.m., with total darkness starting at 9:27; the middle of the eclipse would occur at 10:16; the end of total darkness at 11:05; and the end of the eclipse at 12:03. The whole duration was to be 3 hours and 34 minutes; and the total darkness was to last an hour and 38 minutes. Franklin supplied an illustration of this eclipse, as he did for ones in 1746 and 1747, but a storm obscured the 1743 eclipse in Philadelphia.[35]

METEOROLOGIST

The inability of Philadelphians to see the 1743 eclipse led Franklin to a theory concerning northeast storms. Franklin had been curious about the direction of storms since at least 1734. He reported on a fierce thunderstorm on 25 September 1734 and gave the different times of the day that it struck Philadelphia, Conestoga, and the mouth of the Delaware Bay. His interest in the great nor'easters or hurricanes enabled him to theorize about their path—and to recheck their course. Franklin intended to observe the lunar eclipse predicted for 21 October 1743, but Philadelphia experienced a hurricane, and the disappointed observer could not see the eclipse. To his surprise, however, he found that despite the fact that during the hurricane the wind blew from the northeast, the eclipse had been observed in Boston and other places to the northeast. He read in the *Boston Evening Post* (24 October): "Last Friday night, soon after a total and visible eclipse of the Moon (which began about nine and ended past one o'clock) came on a storm of wind and rain, which continued all the following day with great violence, and the wind being at N.E., the tide was raised as high within a few inches as that remarkable one about 20 years ago." Franklin surely recalled that storm, for on 4 March 1722/3 he had satirized Cotton Mather's comments on it.

He gathered data on the paths of various hurricanes and found that they moved up from the southeast. He first mentioned his "singular opinion" concerning the path of hurricanes to his Connecticut friend Reverend Jared Eliot on 16 July 1747: "though the course of the wind is from northeast to southwest, yet the course of the storm is from southwest to northeast; the air is in violent motion in Virginia before it moves in Connecticut, and in Connecticut before it moves at Cape Sable." Only when he was sure of the truth of his hypothesis did he publish the information—and then in a curious place. The *Pennsylvania Gazette* for 13 October 1748 announced that "The Map of *Pennsilvania, New Jersey* and *New York* Provinces, by Mr. *Lewis Evans*, is now engraving here, and in great Forwardness." Lewis Evans (ca. 1700–1756), mapmaker, was his friend and longtime employee. The map was completed before 21 February 1749. In an empty space on the map, Franklin's meteorological theory was engraved, along with several of Franklin's speculations on weather, atmospheric electricity, geology, and paleontology. The Evans map published Franklin's theory of the movement of hurricanes: "All our great Storms begin to Leeward: thus a NE Storm shall be a Day sooner in Virginia than Boston" (3:392n.).

Professor William Morris Davis, perhaps the best-known nineteenth-century meteorologist, expressed his surprise that Franklin showed himself generous "to the point of indifference," in publishing this information where another, the mapmaker, would naturally be given credit for it. But, Davis said, "to give credit where credit is due," Franklin was the first American meteorologist, and with his theory of the movement of hurricanes "the science of weather prediction" began in America.[36]

In the Lewis Evans map, Franklin gave a condensed summary of his observations on Philadelphia-area weather: "Land Winds passing over a large shaded (and very often frozen) Continent (on both sides of the Mountains) are always dry and cold and the Sea Winds wet and warm. NE is a settled high Wind, and most often wet. & SW Squawly & unsettled. The hottest Weather is with a S Wind and Calms, and the coldest with NW. Snow comes from N to NE. Rainy Storms from NE to E; and high dry Wind from the W. The Land Winds blow above 3/4 of the Year" (3:393n).

A year later, in reply to Jared Eliot's request (perhaps because of Franklin's earlier letter to him or perhaps he saw the information on the Evans map), Franklin wrote him on 13 February 1749/50, amplifying the earlier account of 16 July 1747. In Philadelphia, the hurricane of 21 October 1743 began before 8 p.m.: it "continued violent all Night and all next Day, the Sky being thick clouded, dark and rainy, so that neither Moon nor Stars could be seen. The Storm did a great deal of Damage all along the Coast, for we had Accounts of it in the News Papers from Boston, Newport, New York, Maryland and Virginia. But what surpriz'd me, was to find in the Boston Newspapers an Account of an Observation of that Eclipse made there: For I thought, as the Storm came from the NE, it must have begun sooner at Boston than with us, and consequently have prevented such Observation. I wrote to my Brother about it, and he inform'd me, that the Eclipse was over there, an hour before the Storm began."

Since 1743, Franklin had "made Enquiries from time to time of Travellers, and of my Correspondents N Eastward and S. Westward, and observ'd the Accounts in the Newspapers from N England, N York, Maryland, Virginia and South Carolina." He found it to be "a constant Fact, that N East Storms begin to Leeward; and are often more violent there than farther to Windward." He attempted to explain why. If the air in the South were "heated by the Sun" and became "exceedingly rarified," it would rise, and suppose the air to the north, covered with clouds, was cold and condensed. Then, "the rarified Air being lighter must rise, and the Dense Air next to it will press into its Place; that will be follow'd by the next denser Air, that by the next, and so on" (3:464). Walter Isaacson observed that thus Franklin first expressed the theory that "rising air heated in the south created low-pressure systems that drew winds from the north."[37]

In the Evans map, Franklin also considered the effect of the weather on shipping and made his first comment on light (a subject about which, he wrote,

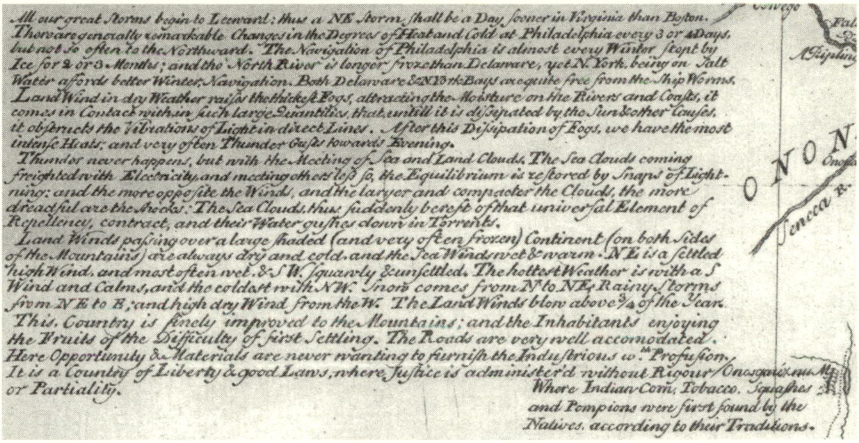

All our great Storms begin to Leeward: thus a NE Storm shall be a Day sooner in Virginia than Boston. There are generally remarkable Changes in the Degrees of Heat and Cold at Philadelphia every 3 or 4 Days, but not so often to the Northward. The Navigation of Philadelphia is almost every Winter stopt by Ice for 2 or 3 Months; and the North River is longer frozen than Delaware, yet N. York, being on Salt Water affords better Winter Navigation. Both Delaware & N. York Bays are quite free from the Ship Worms. Land Wind in dry Weather raises the thick & Fogs, attracting the Moisture on the Rivers and Coasts, it comes in Contact within such large Quantities, that until it is dissipated by the Sun & other Causes, it obstructs the Vibrations of Light in direct Lines. After this Dissipation of Fogs, we have the most intense Heats; and very often Thunder Gusts towards Evening.

Thunder never happens, but with the Meeting of Sea and Land Clouds. The Sea Clouds coming freighted with Electricity, and meeting others less so, the Equilibrium is restored by Snaps of Lightning: and the more opposite the Winds, and the larger and compacter the Clouds, the more dreadful are the shocks. The Sea Clouds thus suddenly bereft of that universal Element of Repellency, contract, and their Water gushes down in Torrents.

Land Winds passing over a large shaded (and very often frozen) Continent (on both Sides of the Mountains) are always dry and cold, and the Sea Winds wet & warm. NE is a settled high Wind, and most often wet. &c S W squarely & unsettled. The hottest Weather is with a S Wind and Calms, and the coldest with NW. Snow comes from N to NE, Rainy Storms from NE to E, and high dry Wind from the W. The Land Winds blow above ¾ of the Year.

This Country is finely improved to the Mountains; and the Inhabitants enjoying the Fruits of the Difficulty of first Settling. The Roads are very well accommodated. Here Opportunity & Materials are never wanting to furnish the Industrious w. Profusion. It is a Country of Liberty & good Laws, where Justice is administer'd without Rigour or Partiality.

Where Indian Corn, Tobacco, Squashes, and Pompions were first found by the Natives, according to their Traditions.

Figure 32. New meteorological and electrical theories, engraved in Lewis Evans, Map of Pennsylvania, New-Jersey, New-York, and the Three Delaware Counties (1749). In empty spaces in the map, James Turner engraved Franklin's speculations on the movement of hurricanes, on atmospheric electricity, geology, and paleontology. The first publication of Franklin's theory of the direction of nor'easters is at the top left of the map: "All our great Storms begin to Leeward: thus a NE Storm shall be a Day sooner in Virginia than Boston." The earliest publication of Franklin's speculation on atmospheric electricity follows: "Thunder never happens, but with the Meeting of Sea and Land Clouds. The Sea Clouds coming freighted with Electricity, and meeting others less so, the Equilibrium is restored by Snaps of Lightning: and the more opposite the Winds, and the larger and compacter the Clouds, the more dreadful are the shocks."

At the bottom right of the illustration, Evans marked the site of an Iroquois agricultural myth: "Onwgaréxnu M[ountain]. Where Indian Corn, Tobacco, Squashes, and Pompions were first found by the Natives, according to their traditions." Franklin heard the Indian tradition from Conrad Weiser and from Evans and incorporated it into two later works: a mock captivity narrative, "The Captivity of William Henry" (1768) and "Remaks Concerning the Savages of North America" (1784). Franklin also told the myth to Gottfried Achenwall in 1766, who published it in "Observations on North America," which had several editions and translations. James R. Masterson identified Onwgaréxnu Mountain as the modern Toppin Mountain, just west of Green Lake, which is southwest of exit 14 on I 81, between Binghamton and Syracuse, New York.

In the Pennsylvania Gazette, 13 October 1748, Franklin noted that the map was "now engraving here, and in great Forwardness," and he announced in the paper for 21 February 1748/9 that Evans's map was for sale. Courtesy, American Philosophical Society, Philadelphia.

he was much in the dark): "There are generally remarkable Changes in the Degrees of Heat and Cold in Philadelphia every 3 or 4 Days, but not so often to the Northward. The Navigation of Philadelphia is almost every winter stopt by Ice for 2 or 3 Months, and the North River is longer froze than Delaware, yet N. York being on Salt Water affords better Winter Navigation. Both Delaware and N. York the Bays are quite free from the Ship Worms. Land Wind in dry Weather raises the thickest Fogs, attracting the Moisture on the Rivers and Coasts, it comes in contact with, in such large Quantities, that, untill it is dissipated by the Sun and other Causes, it obstructs the Vibrations of Light in direct Lines. After this dissipation of Fogs, we have the most intense Heats; and very often Thunder Gusts towards Evening" (3:392n.).

Franklin also published in the Evans map his earliest thoughts on atmospheric electricity, on the cause of lightning, and on the reasons for fierce thunderstorms. To that date (the winter of 1748–49), these were the most valuable scientific theories made in America. Amazingly, Franklin not only published them anonymously but in a place where it would be natural for those who did not know of the Franklin-Evans relationship to assume that the theories were by Evans.

Almost anyone else would have been content to state the new fact, but Franklin tried to understand why northeast storms moved up the coast from the south. In the 13 February 1749/50 letter to Jared Eliot, he theorized, "Suppose a great Tract of Country, Land and Sea, to wit Florida and the Bay of Mexico, to have clear Weather for several Days, and to be heated by the Sun and its Air thereby exceedingly rarified; Suppose the Country North Eastward, as Pensilvania, New England, Nova Scotia, Newfoundland, &c. to be at the same time cover'd with Clouds, and its Air chill'd and condens'd. The rarified Air being lighter must rise, and the Dense Air next to it will press into its place; that will be follow'd by the next denser Air, that by the next, and so on."

Franklin made two analogies: "Thus when I have a Fire in my Chimney, there is a Current of Air constantly flowing from the Door to the Chimney: but the beginning of the Motion was at the Chimney, where the Air being rarified by the Fire, rising, its Place was supply'd by the cooler Air that was next to it, and the Place of that by the next, and so on to the Door." The second concerned water in a long sluice: "So the Water in a long Sluice or Mill Race, being stop'd by a Gate, is at Rest like the Air in a Calm; but as soon as you open the Gate at one End to let it out, the Water next the Gate begins first to move, that which is next to it follows; and so tho' the Water proceeds forward to the Gate, the Motion which began there runs backwards, if one may so speak, to the upper End of the Race, where the Water is last in Motion." Franklin then applied the analogies: "We have on this Continent a long Ridge of Mountains running from N East to S. West; and the Coast runs the same Course. These may, perhaps, contribute towards the Direction of the winds or at least influence them in some

Degree." He was imagining how the ocean, the coast, and the mountains might serve to influence the weather conditions along the east coast of North America.

GEOLOGY AND PALEONTOLOGY

Franklin's interest in geology and paleontology appeared in his subscription paper for John Bartram and in his plan for an American Philosophical Society. Franklin had featured the question of the age of the earth on the front page of *Poor Richard* from 1733 to 1747. Franklin gave its age from various religious sources and from the standard Christian sources and also the best-known "scientific" sources of the times: "The Eastern Church," "the Latin Church," "the Computation of W[illiam] W[histon]," "the Roman Chronology," and "the Jewish Rabbies." He dropped the age of the earth and its different answers when he expanded the almanac in 1748.

He had probably heard as an adolescent of the enormous fossils (supposed at the time to be the bones of giants but now thought to be mastodons) discovered at Claverack, New York, in 1705. Cotton Mather described them in a letter to Dr. John Woodward, which was published in the *Philosophical Transactions of the Royal Society* for 1714. Other New England intellectuals, including the poet Edward Taylor in remote Westfield, were fascinated by them.[38] In the *New-England Courant* of 4 March 1723, Franklin had ridiculed Cotton Mather's explanation of an extraordinarily high tide in Boston and had burlesqued Mather's unusual word *hypothesimania*. Franklin evidently had read Mather's letter in the Royal Society's *Transactions*. Franklin may have recalled the giant bones when considering Bartram's explorations. Bartram collected fossil seashells and impressions of shellfish high in the mountains. He donated some to the Library Company of Philadelphia on 13 December 1742.

Some time after 1742 (and probably before 1749, when Lewis Evans's map was published), Bartram drew for Franklin a rough map of the Allegheny Mountains and the river system east of them, from South Carolina to New York (the Santee River to the Hudson). It attempted to be a geological map, locating the areas where Bartram had found seashells in the mountains. At the head of the Susquehanna Bartram noted "sea shels in stone," and at the head of the Delaware he wrote, "limestone & sea shels in it." He probably made the map at Franklin's request and gave it to him after presenting him with fossils collected on the locations. Franklin docketed the map on the back, "Mr. Bartram's Map very curious."[39]

After absorbing Bartram's information, Franklin wrote Jared Eliot on 16 July 1747 about the changes in the surface of the earth and the evident different levels that the sea had attained in past times: "Now I mention Mountains it occurs to tell you, that the great Apalachian Mountains, which run from York River back of these Colonies to the Bay of Mexico, show in many Places near the highest Parts of them, Strata of Sea Shells, in some Places the Marks of them are in the solid Rocks. 'Tis certainly the *Wreck* of a World we live on! We have Specimens

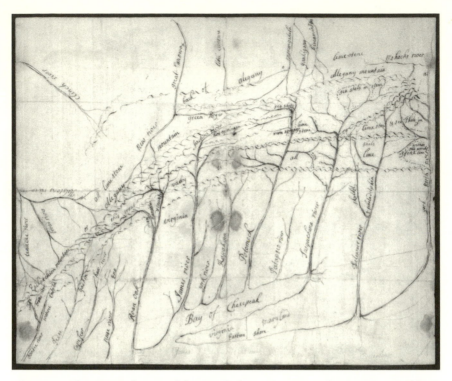

Figure 33. John Bartram's map of the Appalachian Mountains, showing rivers and locations of seashells on mountains. On the back, Franklin wrote, "Mr. Bartram's Map very curious." Bartram drew the map primarily to indicate where he had found fossil seashells in limestone in the Allegheny Mountains. The map testifies to Bartram's extensive travels in colonial America. Along the bottom, it indicates the major rivers along the Atlantic from the Santee (about halfway between Myrtle Beach and Charleston) in South Carolina to the Hudson or North River. Along the south edge, the map extends as far west as Holston's and Clinch rivers. (Further west, they join to form the Tennessee River.) Along the top or west of the map, the Kanawha River flows into the Ohio. The Youghiogeny River flows into the Monongahela River south of Pittsburgh. And the Kiskiminetas River flows into the Allegheny River north of Pittsburgh. Along the north, the map extends as far west as the Mohawk River, which winds around Schenectady and flows into the Hudson above Albany, at Troy, New York. Courtesy, American Philosophical Society, Philadelphia.

of those Sea shell Rocks broken off near the Tops of those Mountains, brought and deposited in our Library as Curiosities."

Lewis Evans used Franklin's geological speculations in a commentary on the "Endless Mountains" engraved in his 1749 map. The engraved writing also echoes Franklin's 1747 letter to Eliot. Evans superimposed his observations on Franklin's and suggested that the biblical deluge (and perhaps another before or since) was the source of the sea fossils found high in the mountains. Franklin had reservations about the biblical deluge, for he mentioned in 1788 the "old difficulty" of how to dispose of its water" after the deluge was over.[40]

Evans had journeyed west, explored the mountains, and described what he saw. He commented, "These Mountains are about 900 Miles in Length and back of Pensilvania from 70 to 100 Miles right across; scarce an Acre of 10 of which is capable of Culture. They are not confusedly scatter'd, & here and there in lofty Peaks over topping one another, but stretch in long uniform Ridges, scarce half a Mile Perpendicular in any Place I saw them." Evans's next sentences echo Franklin's fascination with sea fossils found on mountaintops and elsewhere, his creation of theories to explain the fossils, and his suggestion that we live on the "ruins" of the world. Evans (echoing Franklin?) had engraved on the map: the fossils "furnish endless Funds for Systems and Theories of the World." The engraving continued, "this Earth was made of the Ruins of another."

Evans found that in New Jersey, "the Land is made by an accumulation of Sand from the Ocean: Digging there about 18 foot thro white worn Sand, you come to a Stratum, of Sea Mud mixt with Shells and other Drift Trash; and in some Places vast Beds of Shells of all Sorts, in Pairs, entire, 30 Miles from the Sea." Like Franklin, Evans cited Dr. John Woodward, who theorized "from infinite Examples discover'd, that this World had been in a State of Dissolution." And, probably following Franklin, Evans continued, "But the Power he ascribes to the Water of Deluge is too much a Miracle to obtain Belief. We have here glaring Marks of a Deluge of far more recent Date, which the Compass of Britain might not perhaps have furnish'd the Dr. with." I suspect that Evans based the entire passage on Franklin's theories. The sentiments in the last sentence, with its implicit pride in the large size of America compared to England, often occur in Franklin's later writings. At about this time, Franklin coached Evans in natural philosophy and at least partially designed for him a set of lectures on the subject.[41] Like Evans, Peter Kalm also printed information from Franklin or from John Bartram (Franklin's main source) concerning seashells found in the rocks on mountaintops (4:55). As we will see, Franklin continued his interests in the age of the world, geology, and fossils.

BOTANY

According to the Philadelphia historian John F. Watson, Franklin introduced the osier willow, *Salix viminalis*, to America.[42] He noticed a discarded willow basket sprouting in Dock Creek, took the shoots, and planted them in the garden of Isaac Norris, where they flourished. The tree became a popular ornamental and later supplied the material for basket-making. Elizabeth Graeme Fergusson, who was once engaged to William Franklin and knew Benjamin Franklin well, recorded another version of the anecdote in a footnote to stanza three of her poem, "A Tribute to American Genius and Friendship." She wrote, "About thirty years past a Basket made of Willow . . . came from England and lay a Winter in a damp Cellar belonging to Dr. Franklin; And in the spring swelld and Budded Showing strong Marks of Vegetation. Dr. Franklin gave it to Miss Deborah Norris, a lady who had a particular taste for Gardening. She had it planted in her Garden near the State House in Philadelphia. It was by her Cherishd and with what Success all in that City know. But perhaps they don't know that by much the great part of the Willows which now are so plentifully planted over the State of Pennsylvania took Rise from this Emigration."[43] A third version says that Franklin chanced to observe a twig of the willow sprouting in a basket just brought on shore from the hold of a ship, which he gave to Deborah Norris, who cultivated it at the Norris garden at Fair Hill.[44]

GREENWOOD AND SPENCER

In addition to introducing valuable new plant species to America (and from America to Europe), Franklin attempted to aid individual natural philosophers as well as the study of natural philosophy in America. When Isaac Greenwood, who had been Hollis Professor of Mathematics and Natural Philosophy at Harvard until he was dismissed in 1738, came to Philadelphia to lecture in 1740, he called on Franklin. They had been acquainted during Franklin's youth in Boston where Greenwood, four years older, had written a tract defending Cotton Mather and attacking the New England Couranteer Dr. William Douglass. Greenwood's *Friendly Debate* (1722) had provoked Nathaniel Gardner's similarly titled *Friendly Debate* (1722), the immediate inspiration for Franklin's Silence Dogood essay series. Franklin no doubt called on Greenwood in London in 1725, where he was assisting the Royal Society's experimenter, John Theophilus Desaguliers, and occasionally performing experiments for the society. Greenwood studied and lived with Desaguliers throughout the year and a half that Franklin spent in London.[45] *Pennsylvania Gazette* readers knew of Isaac Greenwood's course of experiments from the long poem Franklin reprinted on 4 February 1734/5 celebrating Greenwood's Boston lectures.

Public lectures and demonstrations were usually held in the large rooms of coffeehouses or taverns, which meant the lecturer rented the space and thus paid out part of his profit from the fee charged for attendance. Franklin suggested to Greenwood that he might be able both to use a room in the statehouse, adjacent to the Library Company's collection, and to borrow the Library Company's air pump. Greenwood accepted the suggestion. Franklin called a special meeting of the Library Company directors on 28 May 1740, and "The Directors willing to encourage so useful a Design, agreed to grant the said Request for such a Time as will be sufficient for going thro' one Course of Experiments and Lectures." Despite knowing that Greenwood had fled creditors in England in 1726 and that he had been dismissed from Harvard for excessive drinking in 1738, Franklin loaned him £20 on 21 May 1740.

Franklin advertised Greenwood's course in the 5 June 1740 *Pennsylvania Gazette* and collected subscriptions for it at the post office. In effect, he acted as

Greenwood's agent. Perhaps Franklin repaid Greenwood's debt to him from the funds that he collected, though probably not, for the debt is not cancelled in his accounts. The course was an updated version of Greenwood's Boston lectures. He had published an outline of them as *An Experimental Course of Mechanical Philosophy* (Boston, 1726). In the twelve-page pamphlet, the third lecture consisted of an introduction to electricity: "various Experiments concerning Electrical Attraction and Repulsion; wherein the chief Circumstances, and Properties of that remarkable Phaenomenon are shewn." Since Franklin had an omnivorous interest in science, he must already have known the bits of electrical knowledge that Greenwood explained.

In 1743 Franklin met Dr. Archibald Spencer in Boston, where he attended his series of lectures. In the *Autobiography*, Franklin credited Spencer with awakening his interest in electricity. When Spencer came to Philadelphia in the spring of 1744, Franklin performed the same favors that he had for Greenwood: obtaining the room in the statehouse next to the library for him, advertising his lecture series, distributing a catalogue of the experiments, and collecting funds for the course at the post office. He acted as Spencer's agent, too, evidently gratis, and continued to function as his agent for the approximately six months that Spencer spent in Philadelphia.

Franklin said in the *Autobiography* that he purchased all Dr. Spencer's apparatus (119), but that would not have been in 1744. After leaving Philadelphia, Spencer lectured elsewhere, including Williamsburg in 1746. He returned to England in 1747 or 1748, where he remained until 1750.[46] He must have kept his apparatus until after his Williamsburg lectures in 1746. Franklin probably bought Spencer's apparatus shortly before Spencer returned to England, perhaps as early as the fall of 1746. By that time, Spencer's electrical apparatus was out of date (due primarily to the invention of the Leyden Jar in 1746), but Franklin was interested in other aspects of the lectures. We know that Spencer lectured on the circulation of the blood. Perhaps the "glass machine for exhibiting the circulation of the blood in the arteries and veins of the human body," which Franklin showed Manasseh Cutler and other guests on Friday, 13 July 1787, was from Spencer's apparatus. Franklin had probably first seen such glass anatomical figures depicting circulation of blood when he was in London in 1725.[47]

Another scientific lecturer came to Philadelphia in the summer of 1744. He first advertised in the *Pennsylvania Gazette* for 12 July: "Just Arrived from London, The Solar or Camera Obscura Microscope." The advertisement, which was repeated occasionally in the *Gazette* through 30 August, said: "The Animalculae in several Sorts of Fluids, with many other living and dead Objects, too tedious to mention, will be shewn most incredibly magnified, at the same time distinct." Franklin may not have bothered to see this operator's solar microscope, for we know from notes on Spencer's lectures (5 June 1744) that he, too, had demonstrated a solar microscope. Franklin twice revealed that he had seen a solar microscope. In describing the wonders of the microscope (*Poor Richard* for

1751), he included a number of observations typical of the solar microscope: "The Circulation of the Blood is to be seen very distinctly in the Tail of a small Fish, the Web of the Foot of a Frog," etc. (4:90). And he wrote to James Bowdoin on 13 December 1753 that he remembered seeing in "a Drop of Kennel Water magnify'd by the Solar Microscope to the Bigness of a Cart Wheel . . . Numbers of visible Animalculae of various Sizes swimming about; but I was sure there were likewise some which I could not see, even with that Magnifier; for the Wake they made in Swimming to and fro was very visible, tho' the Body that made it was not so." Similarly, though elementary particles cannot be seen, physicists in the twenty-first century can detect them by their trails of condensed water when they pass through a cloud chamber or by trails of bubbles when they pass through a bubble chamber.[48]

JOHN BARTRAM

Franklin tried to organize support for the brilliant, self-taught Quaker farmer and botanist John Bartram. Bartram attained an international reputation in natural history during the 1730s. When he could spare time from farming, he collected rare plants and insects. He went up the Schuylkill River in 1736, searched the Eastern Shore of Maryland and Virginia in 1737, journeyed to mainland Virginia in 1738, and made several trips to New Jersey. His frequent discovery of new plant and insect species astounded the international natural history circle. By 1741 Bartram thought that he might be able to raise a subscription among his friends to allow him to spend several years "in searching and observing natural production of the mountains plains lakes rivers springs and grottoes in our four northern governments of york jersey pensilvania and maryland." He told the Antigua physician J. Slingsby Cressy of the scheme on 29 March 1741. Cressy replied on 20 August that he would add his "Mite." The London Quaker merchant Peter Collinson encouraged the subscription on 3 February 1741/2, and later mentioned it to Thomas Penn.[49] Bartram also consulted Franklin, who attempted to organize the subscription for him. The 10 March 1742 *Pennsylvania Gazette* announced that "a Subscription is on foot for the Encouragement of Mr. John Bartram, Botanist, to travel thro' the Province of New-York, Pennsylvania, New-Jersey and Maryland, in Search of curious Vegetables, Fossils, &c. of all kinds; which 'tis hop'd will meet with Success, he being a Person exceedingly well qualified, for such an Employment."

The following week Franklin wrote and published a subscription paper for Bartram. "A Copy of the Subscription Paper, for the Encouragement of Mr. John Bartram promised in our last." Franklin organized the paper as a resolution, though without naming the "preamble," the "whereas" clauses, and the "resolution." The introduction (or preamble) emphasized the usefulness of the study of botany, which had furnished "Cures for many Diseases, and their Gardens, Groves and Fields with rare and pleasant Fruits, Flowers, Aromaticks, Shades and Hedges." Then followed three points comparable to the "whereas" clauses in a resolution. First, the American wilderness had numerous unknown plants and trees "whose Virtues and proper Uses are yet unknown to Physicians and curious Persons." The second unstated "whereas" introduced Bartram, assuring the potential patrons that he was ideally qualified for the endeavor. The third implied "whereas" clause proposed "an annual Contribution for his Encouragement." It noted that Bartram had promised to carry through the project if he received sufficient payment to "maintain himself and Family."

Franklin concluded with the resolution: "We the Subscribers, do therefore severally promise, for Us, our Heirs, Executors and Administrators, to pay him yearly the Sums annex'd to our Names for three Years next ensuing, he for so long time industriously employing himself in the Premises." At the end Franklin said, "*Subscriptions are taken in at the Post-Office in Philadelphia*," and, lest the scheme seem utopian, he added the information that "*Near £20 a Year is already subscribed.*" Perhaps the subscription had some slight success, for Bartram journeyed to the Catskills that summer,[50] but the three-year subscription failed. Bartram's English patron and customer, Lord Petre, died at age twenty-nine on 2 July 1742. Had he lived, he probably would have subscribed and secured subscriptions from his friends.[51] The project would have succeeded. Bartram's other patrons were neither as wealthy nor as well connected. Further, James Logan, among the wealthiest Pennsylvanians of the day and Philadelphia's intellectual leader, refused to help. For some time Bartram continued to hope that Thomas Penn might contribute, but eventually that dream faded.[52] A surprising aspect of both Franklin's report of Bartram's project and his subscription form was the emphasis on fossils. Though Bartram collected fossils and donated some to the Library Company of Philadelphia, he was primarily known as an authority on plants and insects. Perhaps the emphasis on fossils revealed Franklin's influence.

THE AMERICAN PHILOSOPHICAL SOCIETY

John Bartram had thought as early as the fall of 1737 of founding an American scientific society for the exchange of plants, knowledge, and ideas.[53] He wrote Peter Collinson about a possible "academy or society" for the discovery of "natural secrets arts and syences." Collinson discouraged him on 10 July 1738: "Had you a Sett of Learned Well Qualified Members to Sett out with It might Draw your Neighbours to correspond with you." Collinson supposed, however, that Bartram had an academy in mind. He continued, "to teach Sciences" would require "Salaries and good Encouragement—and this will require publick as well as proprietary assistance—which can't be att present complyed with Considering the Infancy of your Colony."[54] Temporarily, Bartram let the matter drop.

Proposal for Promoting Useful Knowledge

Bartram must have talked to Franklin about an American scientific society. When Franklin visited New England in the spring of 1743, he took along a brochure promoting it. On 14 May he published for his own use and for private distribution a broadside, *A Proposal for Promoting Useful Knowledge among the British Plantations in America*. Franklin again used a modified resolution structure. The first section of the *Proposal* contained four paragraphs: the first three paragraphs contained implied "whereas" clauses and the fourth a conclusion, suggesting the formula, "Therefore, Be it Resolved." Franklin began, "The English are possess'd of a long Tract of Continent, from Nova Scotia to Georgia, extending North and South thro' different Climates, having different Soils, producing different Plants, Mines and Minerals, and capable of different Improvements, Manufactures, etc." No one could disagree with that. The second paragraph (like Franklin's letter of 16 May 1733 to Thomas Penn on behalf of the Library Company) echoed Francis Bacon's theories on the development of colonies and countries:[55] "The first Drudgery of Settling new Colonies, which confines the Attention of People to mere Necessaries, is now pretty well over; and there are many in every Province in Circumstances that set them at Ease, and afford Leisure to cultivate the finer Arts, and improve the common Stock of Knowledge. To such of these who are Men of Speculation, many Hints must from time to time arise, many Observations occur, which if well-examined, Plantations, or to the Benefit of Mankind in general." Though the "first Drudgery" continued in Georgia and on the frontiers, by 1743 Boston, New York, Philadelphia, Charleston, and smaller towns, as well as some plantations and farms, had a number of ingenious and wealthy Americans.

A third paragraph explained why comparatively little progress had been made even though some colonists now had time for philosophical investigation. The reasons included "the Extent of the Country," which meant that like-minded persons could seldom see and converse with one another, "so that many useful Particulars remain uncommunicated, die with the Discoverers, and are lost to Mankind." The solution, contained in the implicit "Resolved" clause, followed in the fourth paragraph: "That One Society be formed of Virtuosi or ingenious Men residing in the several Colonies, to be called *The American Philosophical Society*; who are to maintain a constant Correspondence." All the natural philosophers in the colonies knew of the existence of the Royal Society of London and similar European societies. This was to be the American scientific society.

Franklin next listed a series of practical details concerning the future society's location, structure, and business. He proposed that Philadelphia be its headquarters,[56] where there should be always "at least seven Members, viz. a Physician, a Botanist, a Mathematician, a Chemist, a Mechanician, a Geographer, and a general Natural Philosopher, besides a President, Treasurer and Secretary." Except for the secretary (Franklin), the members were not listed in the proposal. He specified the frequency of meetings and the normal business of communicating "to each other their Observations, Experiments, etc."

The first area of science that Franklin mentioned was natural history. From the discovery of America, its new plants and animals had been of great interest to European naturalists. The most active circle of "natural philosophers" in America was the natural history circle, and among them, most were especially interested in botany. As Franklin knew, John Bartram had an international correspondence with a European circle, first introduced to him by James Logan. But one correspondent led to another, and by 1743 Bartram communicated regularly not only with such American savants as Cadwallader Colden in New York and William Byrd, Mark Catesby, John Custis, and Isham Randolph in Virginia, but also with English and European naturalists, including Peter Collinson and Sir Hans Sloane in England, John James Dillenius, Carl von Linné and John Frederick Gronovius in Europe, as well as J. Slingsby Cressy in Antigua. So Franklin's first subject was: "All new-discovered Plants, Herbs, Trees, Roots, etc. their Virtues, Uses, etc. Methods of Propagating them, and making such as are useful, but particular to some Plantations, more general. Improvements of vegetable Juices, as Cyders, Wines, etc."

The second area was medicine: "New Methods of Curing or Preventing Diseases." Perhaps Franklin recalled the extraordinary historic importance of Boston's inoculation for smallpox. He had a circle of physician friends and was himself interested in medicine. And he knew that the brilliant young Dr. Thomas Bond, fresh from his medical studies in Paris, hoped to make future medical contributions.

Franklin also enumerated paleontology and geology: "All new-discovered Fossils in different Countries, as Mines, Minerals, Quarries, etc." Franklin had heard stories of (what proved to be) mastodon fossils,[57] had seen the fossils collected by John Bartram, and he had himself sold Sir Hans Sloane in 1725 an American mineralogical curiosity, a purse made of asbestos (see frontispiece to Volume 1).

Next came "New and useful Improvements in any Branch of Mathematicks." Franklin's neighbors Thomas Godfrey and Theophilus Grew were both mathematicians. Perhaps Franklin knew that Godfrey was trying to create a new and better quadrant. Within the next two years he printed in the *Pennsylvania Gazette* a "Method for the Longitude briefly sum'd up" (30 May 1745) and further thoughts on longitude (7 August 1746) by the ingenious Reverend Joseph Morgan (1671–1745?), whose publications James Franklin brought out in Boston when Franklin was an apprentice and whose later works Franklin published in Philadelphia. Franklin had already toyed with magic squares and circles, and though he did not see a use for them, he knew they improved his mathematical facility. Perhaps he intended to communicate them to the American scientific circle, but later he sent them along to Collinson.

Another topic, "New Discoveries in Chemistry, such as Improvements in Distillation, Brewing, Assaying of Ores, etc.," appears to be pure Franklin, though he had perhaps heard of making whiskey from Indian corn (some Americans already made a liquor later called bourbon) and he learned in the

1750s of the experiments made by the Reverend Jared Eliot of Connecticut, who extracted iron ore from sea sand.[58]

The penultimate category was mechanical engineering: "New Mechanical Inventions for saving Labour; as Mills, Carriages, etc. and for Raising and Conveying of Water, Draining of Meadows, etc." The Reverend Joseph Morgan projected such devices, including locks in rivers, side dams, and fish ladders. Franklin had published Morgan's ideas in the *Pennsylvania Gazette* (18 and 25 May, 8 June 1732). As we have seen, someone (perhaps Franklin) had suggested an improvement in 1745 to the fire engine purchased by the Union Fire Company. Franklin had probably heard of Colonel John Schuyler's copper mine on the Passaic River, which he kept free of water by employing pumps. Franklin visited it at the end of August 1749 (3:465).

Franklin's list of projects concluded with a grand summary: "All new Arts, Trades, Manufactures, etc. that may be proposed or thought of. Surveys, Maps and Charts of particular Parts of the Sea-coasts, or Inland Countries; Course and Junction of Rivers and great Roads, Situation of Lakes and Mountains, Nature of the Soil and Productions, etc. New Methods of Improving the Breed of useful Animals, Introducing other Sorts from foreign Countries. New Improvements in Planting, Gardening, Clearing Land, etc. And all philosophical Experiments that let Light into the Nature of Things, tend to increase the Power of Man over Matter, and multiply the Conveniencies or Pleasures of Life."

He proposed communications with other scientific societies, naming the Royal Society of London and the Dublin Society. The "intended Members" already corresponding with the Royal Society included John Bartram, James Logan, and Cadwallader Colden. Every American Philosophical Society member would receive quarterly abstracts "of every Thing valuable communicated to the Society's Secretary at Philadelphia; free of all Charge except the Yearly Payment" of a piece of eight per member. An account of all disbursements would be kept and sent to members annually. Postmaster Franklin said that communications between "the Secretary of the Society" and the members were to be "Postage-free." Carl Van Doren commented that the free postage "was more important than is now commonly realized." For a single sheet, the postage for a letter from Philadelphia to New York was 9d (the pay for about an hour's work for a good artisan), from Philadelphia to Boston was 1s. 9d. Most scientific communications were longer than a sheet.[59]

Franklin also said that an annual collection "of such Experiments, Discoveries, Improvements, etc. as may be thought of publick Advantage" would be published. He made himself the secretary and specified the duties: "That the Business and Duty of the Secretary be, To receive all Letters intended for the Society, and lay them before the President and Members at their Meetings; to abstract, correct and methodize such Papers, etc. as require it, and as he shall be directed to do by the President, after they have been considered, debated and digested in the Society; to enter Copies thereof in the Society's Books, and make out Copies for distant Members; to answer their Letters by Direction of the President, and keep Records of all material Transactions of the Society, etc." He concluded, "Benjamin Franklin, the Writer of this Proposal, offers himself to serve the Society as their Secretary, 'till they shall be provided with one more capable." When he wrote that, he knew it ended on an ironic note; but he also knew that by putting himself in the laboring position of secretary, rather than the leading position of president, he thereby made his leadership acceptable. He had begun to avoid presenting himself "as the Proposer of any useful Project that might be suppos'd to raise one's Reputation in the smallest degree above that of one's Neighbors" (A 74).

First Members

Surprisingly, no evidence exists that Franklin circulated copies of the *Proposal* during his New England trip; perhaps he had second thoughts about revealing himself as its author. He did, however, tell others about the proposed society. Franklin chanced to meet the New York intellectual Cadwallader Colden in Connecticut during the early summer of 1743 and told him of the planned society. Colden was enthusiastic. He wrote Franklin in October saying he wanted "very much to hear what you have done in your scheme of erecting a society at Philadelphia for promoting of usefull Arts and Sciences in America." Franklin replied on 4 November that he had been "in a continual Hurry ever since my Return, and had no Leisure to forward the Scheme of the Society: But that Hurry being now near over, I purpose to proceed in the Affair very soon, your Approbation being no small Encouragement to me." The following spring on 27 March 1744, Bartram sent Colden "one of our proposals for forming A Philosophical Society." Bartram wrote his letter on the back of Franklin's printed folio *Proposal*, and Franklin franked the sheet for mailing. Presumably Franklin had not previously given Colden a copy of the *Proposal*. Bartram wrote, "We have already had three meetings & several Learned & curious persons from our neibouring Colonies hath allready Joyned membership with us & we hope thee will pleas to do us the honor to be involved in our number."[60]

A week later, 5 April, Franklin informed Colden that the American Philosophical Society, "as far as relates to Philadelphia, is actually formed, and has had several Meetings." The Philadelphia members were Dr. Thomas Bond (1713–84), physician; John Bartram (1699–1777), botanist; Thomas Godfrey (1704–49), mathematician; Samuel Rhoads (1711–84), mechanician; William Parsons (1701–57), geographer; Dr. Phineas Bond (1717–73), general natural philosopher; Thomas Hopkinson (1709–51), president; William Coleman (1705?–69), treasurer; and Franklin, secretary.[61] Franklin also reported in the same letter that the society had added a number of members from other colonies: James Alexander (1691–1756) of New York, attorney general of New Jersey and an intellectual; Robert Hunter Morris (1700?–64), chief justice of New Jersey and later governor of Pennsylvania; Archibald Home (1705?–44), secretary of New Jersey, a poet and litterateur; John Coxe (1708–53) of Trenton, a member of the New Jersey Council; David Martin (1696–1751) of Hunterdon County, New Jersey, first rector of the Academy of Philadelphia; and Richard Nicholls (?–1775), postmaster of New York.[62]

On 29 April 1744, Bartram informed Colden that "Our Philosophick Society increaseth finely. I think we had 7 members initiated last meeting of which thee was one by unanimous consent." Bartram also explained the absence of James Logan. The aging intellectual Quaker had decided to have nothing to do with the project. Bartram explained that he and Franklin had "resolved that his not favouring the designh should not hinder our attempt and if he would not go along with us we would Jog along without him." Joseph Breintnall also would have been a logical member. Maybe he simply felt too financially strapped to join. In the same letter, Bartram wrote, "the next fifth night [3 May] we are to have another meeting where Doctor spence will accompany us. he exhibits Phylosophical lectures now at Philadelphia and approves of our design: offers to take our proposals with him to the west indies with A favourable acount of our proceedings."[63] Perhaps the most important information in Bartram's letter is an actual date of an American Philosophical Society meeting—Thursday, 3 May 1744. Since Franklin's other organizations (Junto, Freemasons, Library Company, Union Fire Company) all met on a regular schedule, I suspect that the American Philosophical Society did, too. If so, it met the first Thursday night of every month. In that case, the three earlier meetings would have taken place on 2 February, 1 March, and 5 April.

In June 1744, Colden wrote Collinson that the Philadelphians have "done me the honour to take me into their Society, tho I be not in any manner acquainted with any of them except Mr. Bartram who has undertaken the Botanical part." Actually, since Colden had met Franklin the preceding summer and corresponded with him since, his statement wasn't accurate. Colden's neighbor, Dr. Evan Jones, sent him on 17 July 1744 a paper on a rattlesnake bite, indirectly revealing that Jones, too, had heard of the founding of the American Philosophical Society: "thee may freely put it into what other Dress thee pleases & then Communicate the same for the aprobation of them Gentlemen in Philadelphia who have formed themselves into a societie for the propagation of useful knowledge please to make my kind regard acceptable to Doctor Thomas Bond also to our honest Friend James the Botanist & to all the Gentlemen of your societie tho am personially unacquainted."[64]

Spreading the Word

Colden wrote of the project in June to Collinson, who immediately and enthusiastically replied (23 August 1744): "I can't enough commend the Authors & promoters of a Society for Improvement of Natural knowledge Because it will be a Means of uniteing Ingenious Men of all Societies together and a Mutual

Harmony be got which will be Dayly produceing Acts of Love & Friendship and will ware away by Degrees any Harsh opinions, parties may have Conceived of Each other . . . I Shall wait with Some Impatience for their Memoirs I expect Something New from your New World, our Old World as it were Exhausted."[65]

On 12 September, the Virginia naturalist and physician Dr. John Mitchell (1711–68)[66] called at John Bartram's and spent the night. The next day, Bartram took him to town where he introduced him to Franklin. Franklin interrupted his work and spent all day with Mitchell. That evening, Franklin wrote Colden that he and Mitchell were going to James Logan's the next day. Though Franklin was practical and shrewd in business, he was, after achieving a modicum of financial security, always eager to put intellectual interests and civic projects ahead of his printing and other businesses. Altogether, Mitchell spent nearly three weeks in Philadelphia, no doubt much of that time with Franklin. He allowed Franklin to have his manuscript on yellow fever transcribed. Franklin sent it to Colden on 25 October 1744, asking that it be returned. Years later, Franklin gave the manuscript, with Colden's letter, to Benjamin Rush, who followed some of its suggestions during the 1793 yellow fever epidemic in Philadelphia—and believed it helped him save thousands of lives. It was twice printed in the beginning of the nineteenth century.[67] Mitchell also gave Bartram a manuscript on the pines in Virginia. When Mitchell asked for its return, Bartram asked Lewis Evans to make a copy for Colden; Evans did so and Bartram returned the original.[68] The Philadelphians elected Mitchell to the American Philosophical Society in 1744. He went to England in 1746. Franklin had his partner David Hall reprint Mitchell's article on potash from the *Philosophical Transactions* in the *Pennsylvania Gazette* (18 and 25 December 1750). In England, Mitchell made his great contribution, *Map of the British and French Dominions in North America* (1755). When Franklin went to London in 1757, Mitchell introduced him to a group of influential Scotsmen and Englishmen, including the earl of Bute, for whose uncle, Archibald Campbell (1682–1761), third Duke of Argyll, Mitchell had earlier secured a "Pennsylvanian Fire-Place."[69]

James Alexander wrote Colden on 12 November 1744, "I am much of your mind that Mr. Franklins proposeal of a Society will prove very usefull—at our last Court Mr Chief justice [James De Lancy], Mr [Daniel] Horsmanden, Mr [Joseph] Murray, Mr [William] Smith, & Several others sent their names as members of the [American Philosophical] Society. . . . I shall be very glad to See him here at New York, & shall give him all the Encouragement in my power to proceed in the affairs of the [American Philosophical] Society & other useful undertakings."[70] Colden proposed to Franklin in December 1744[71] that he publish a philosophical miscellany. Franklin liked the idea, which was similar to the compilation he suggested in the *Proposal*, and asked Dr. Mitchell's permission to publish his essay on yellow fever. Mitchell, however, replied on 12 September 1745 that it was too imperfect to print.

Flagging Interest

Answering Colden's inquiry about the progress of the American Philosophical Society, Bartram wrote on 7 April 1745, "we make at present but a poor progress in our Phylosophick Society: the tumultuous reports of wars Invasions and reprisals exercises most of our thoughts and discourses and many is under apprehensions of being more sensibly touched with these Calamities." Bartram also explained the lack of progress by saying that the "major part of our inhabitants may be ranked in three Classes: the first Class are those whose thought and study is intirely upon geting and laying up large estates and any other attainment that dont turn immediately upon that hinge thay think it not worth thair notice. the second Class are those that are for spending in Luxury all thay can come at and are often the children of avaritious Parents." Bartram probably had himself, Franklin, and Joseph Breintnall in mind when he described the third class: "those that necessity obliges to hard labour and Cares for A moderat and happy maintainance of thair family and these are many times the most curious tho deprived mostly of time and material to pursue thair natural inclinations."

Bartram wrote Colden on 4 October 1745 that his European correspondents had been informed of their scientific society and had "great expectation of fine accounts therefrom." Bartram himself had never mentioned it "for fear it should turn out but poorly; but I find the[e] mentioned [it] to Collinson, hee to Catesby, and hee to Gronovius." Bartram showed the letters to Franklin, "and he layeth the blame on us; and Dr. Bond Saith Ben. Franklin is in fault; however wee three talks of carrying it on with more diligence then ever which we may very easily do if we could but exchange the time that is spent in the Club, Chess and Coffee House for the Curious amusements of natural observations." Colden replied on 7 November that "as it is certain that some have been too lazy, so others may have been too officious; which makes the more prudent afraid of them." Gronovius asked on 2 June 1746 how it went with the society, "and what improvements they have made."[72]

But the members had done little. Even Franklin was discouraged. He wrote Colden on 15 August 1745, "The Members of our Society here are very idle Gentlemen; they will take no Pains." He still intended, however, to publish a scientific miscellany. But then a long session of the assembly (which filled his days with note-taking and his nights with socializing when not supervising his shop) from 6 January to 5 February 1745/6 "has hitherto hinder'd me from beginning the Miscellany" (3:67). He told Colden on 16 October 1746 that he intended to publish a piece on wooden cannon in the miscellany, and he said, "It will not be long after my Return from Boston before you will see the first Number of the Miscellany. I have now Materials by me for 5 or 6." That was, however, Franklin's last mention of the philosophical miscellany.

Why the Failure?

Franklin devoted more effort, time, and money to a dozen other interests than to the American Philosophical Society. He started several, such as the Academy of Philadelphia, after he abandoned the American Philosophical Society. He could have made it a reality in late 1746 or early 1747 by publishing the first philosophical miscellany. He chose not to. Ironically, the American Philosophical Society probably failed because of Franklin's scientific success.

By 1746, Franklin was "immersed in electrical experiments" (10:310). Had he started the American scientific miscellany in 1743 or 1744, he might have published his electrical experiments in it. But it did not yet exist in 1746, and by then he knew he was making original and important experiments and drawing original and important conclusions concerning the nature of electricity. Because of the Pennsylvania fire place, he already had some international reputation as a natural philosopher. If he started an American Philosophical Society miscellany, he should publish the electrical experiments there. But if he sent them on as letters to Peter Collinson, and if the experiments were as original as he thought them, they would appear in the world's most prestigious scientific journal, the *Philosophical Transactions of the Royal Society of London*. Publication in the *Transactions* would draw the attention of the world.

I believe the first American Philosophical Society failed because of Franklin's ambition. If he wanted his work to appear in the *Philosophical Transactions*, it would be foolish to continue with plans for a miscellany publication for the American Philosophical Society. If a miscellany existed, Franklin should publish his research there. Franklin's friends in the American Philosophical Society, however, especially John Bartram and Dr. Thomas Bond, kept it in mind. In 1768, while Franklin was in England, they revived the society.

CONCLUSION

On 22 October 1730 Franklin saw a "very bright Appearance of the *Aurora Borealis*." Reporting it in the 29 October *Pennsylvania Gazette*, Franklin wrote, "But a sufficient Number of Observations have not yet been made by the Curious, to enable them to assign the Cause of this Phaenomenon with any Certainty." Naturally he followed it up with other reports of the phenomenon from other papers (12 November). Later he came to believe that the display was electrical in nature and supplied his own theories concerning it. His interest in the aurora borealis is typical. He had an intense curiosity about nearly all phenomena. When a teenager he was "extreamly ambitious" to become a man of letters (A 14). As he grew older, he added a desire to make contributions to humanity as a natural philosopher. When he performed his early experiments in electricity, he began to think that he might be able to do so. That hope was a major reason he signed an agreement to retire as a printer on 1 January 1747/8, five days before turning forty-two.

NINETEEN

Satires and Other Writings
1736–1747

The Speech of Miss Polly Baker, before a Court of Judicature, at Connecticut in New England, where she was prosecuted the fifth Time for having a Bastard Child; which influenced the Court to dispense with her Punishment, and induced one of her Judges to marry her the next Day.—Franklin's hoax and satire in The Maryland Gazette, *11 August 1747*

THAT SCIENCE AND TECHNOLOGY CONSTITUTE not a national but an international world is true today, but in the eighteenth century, the primary constituency of the Third Realm (i.e. the existence of an international order in addition to the state and the church) was the entire world of learning, especially literature. The leading members of the Republic of Letters were such writers as Milton, Pierre Bayle, Voltaire, and, after 1752, Franklin.[1] They were well-known not only in their own countries but throughout the Western world. Most members of the Republic of Letters were identified with either literature or science, but Franklin became the preeminent representative of the Third Realm in the middle and late eighteenth century by attaining international renown in both. The incredible variety of the subjects and genres of Franklin's writings includes satires, hoaxes, bagatelles, treatises on currency and economy, technical philosophical disquisitions, essays on moral philosophy, grotesque poems, ribald mock letters, and much more. There hardly seems to be a subject about which Franklin did not write. Though his songs are discussed in Chapter 12 and his political pieces in Chapter 13, the following survey examines his notable compositions from this period, which include his most ribald writings.

MANUSCRIPT AND PRINT

The bagatelle as a literary genre is a short writing especially intended, at least initially, for a small circle. It is the classic genre of salon society. Usually such writings were not printed. A number of Franklin's bagatelles, skits, satires, hoaxes, essays in letter form, and actual letters exist in multiple eighteenth-century manuscript copies, and even some of the ostensibly public pieces were not printed in his lifetime. Sending a private copy of a well-crafted writing was a flattering attention to a friend or an acquaintance. The copies often differ, for

Franklin, like most other authors, revised the piece as he copied it, sometimes in accordance with the particular person or audience who would receive the copy, sometimes simply to improve it.[2] Thus, the two primary texts of "The Speech of Miss Polly Baker," neither printed by Franklin, were intended for two different audiences, one English, one American. Differences in texts can indicate that the author has revised it, for others generally simply copied a piece, and printers rarely changed a manuscript—except to correct or to make mistakes or to impose a "house style" upon it.

Like many other litterateurs, Franklin frequently wrote for a group of acquaintances, who copied his writings and circulated them.[3] They were read by contemporaries in New England, the Middle Colonies, and the South—and in England, long before Franklin went there in 1757. Others often published his writings, usually without his permission. Naturally the rival Philadelphia printer Andrew Bradford was delighted to publish Franklin's manuscripts. Not only did these make Bradford's periodicals more interesting, but Bradford also had the private pleasure of scooping the young and successful printer with his own writings. Perhaps Bradford first did so on 8 February 1732 when he printed Franklin's translation from German to English of the mistreatment of Palatine immigrants by the ship captain who brought them to America. Though Franklin meant to publish that article, he wrote numerous items that he did not intend to publish for years—if ever. One example of a piece that circulated in manuscript for years before being published is the biblical imitation "A Parable against Persecution." Numerous manuscript copies exist, most differing in some details. The earliest known reference to the "Parable" is in Ezra Stiles's letter on 2 August 1755, in which he enclosed a copy to an unnamed correspondent (6:155). We know that Franklin gave copies to various friends, but he was chagrined to find it published by William Strahan in the *London Chronicle* on 17 April 1764. Franklin said the publication "depriv'd him of the Pleasure I often had in amusing People with it." Of course the person most amused was Franklin himself, for he pretended it was a chapter from Genesis, and some persons to whom he read it said they remembered it from the Bible.

Other writings that he circulated in manuscript include his epitaph (1:109–11); the skit "The Morals of Chess," written early in the 1730s and finally published in France in June 1779; the three songs discussed in Chapter 12; "The Speech of Miss Polly Baker" (3:120–25); the essay in letter form of 6 June 1753 on faith versus works (4:503–6); and the essay in letter form of 13 December 1757 against mocking religion (7:293–95). He learned of their publication when he saw them in print, most without attribution. Many of his writings pretend to be letters. Even his *Autobiography* maintains that fiction, complete with a dateline and an addressee. The letter format makes the writing seem informal and immediate, yet it ostensibly explains why the author might later have a copy on hand. Merchants and others commonly kept bound volumes in which they drafted their letters. Though the actual letter sent usually differed in minor ways, the letterbook draft served as the retained copy.

Franklin wrote numerous pieces for publication, usually in one of his periodicals—the *Pennsylvania Gazette, Poor Richard,* or the *General Magazine.* He thought the letter form could be—and, coming from an excellent writer, often was—artful.[4] His private letters also circulated in manuscript. The Reverend Mather Byles, a well-known Boston poet and wit, wrote him late in 1765 that he had just been reading a letter of Franklin's written to his sister Elizabeth Hubbart a decade before "on the Death of your Brother, which is handed about among us in Manuscript Copies. . . . The Superstition with which we seize and preserve little accidental Touches of your Pen, puts one in mind of the Care of the Virtuosi to collect the Jugs and Galiposts with the Paintings of Raphael."[5] Franklin's letter of 22 February 1756 on John Franklin's death was addressed to his sister Elizabeth but intended for others as well, especially family members. Franklin knew that copies would probably be made and circulated, though the letter was personal. So even Franklin's personal letters, especially after he became an international scientific celebrity in 1752, were regarded as literary documents, prized, copied, and circulated by others. The letters, like his other writings, had more interests (in literature as well as science), more tones (adapted for such different audiences as children, young ladies, devout ministers, and skeptics), and more personae than any other writer I know.

We moderns tend to think that print assures a degree of permanency, but it did not in the eighteenth century. Few issues of the *Maryland Gazette* printed by William Parks survive. Few issues of the *Virginia Gazette*(s) from the 1750s and 1760s are extant. Many pieces that he himself wrote survive in unique copies. Most of Franklin's writings appeared in obscure publications anonymously or pseudonymously. Some newspapers and magazines in which his publications are known to have appeared no longer exist. Few of his writings before 1748 were known or, if known (e.g., *Poor Richard*), were not valued by his contemporaries. Not even Franklin collected them all, though he kept manuscript copies of many. Certainly no library did. (There were no public libraries.) Few writers imagined (some probably hoped) that what they wrote would be preserved and would endure. Franklin evidently did not write for fame—until, possibly, after he became famous. He wrote to explore topics that interested him; he wrote to challenge himself in comparison to other writers, especially Jonathan Swift; he wrote to amuse others and himself; and sometimes, early in his career, he wrote filler for his newspaper and almanac. When Franklin's sister Jane asked him for copies of all his writings, he replied on 24 December 1767 that he could as easily gather "all the past Parings of my Nails."

"THE DRINKER'S DICTIONARY"

Language fascinated Franklin. The rich colloquial vocabulary used to describe drunks had been a subject of Silence Dogood No. 12, where he theorized that shame for inebriation inspired drunks to invent and repeat the euphemisms for drunkenness. "They are seldom known to be *drunk*, tho' they are very often *boozey, cogey, tipsey, fox'd, merry, mellow, fuddl'd, groatable, Confoundedly cut, See two Moons*, are *Among the Philistines, In a very good Humour, See the Sun*, or, *The Sun has shone upon them*; they *Clip the King's English*, are *Almost froze, Feavourish, In their Altitudes, Pretty well enter'd*, etc." Franklin returned to the vocabulary of drunks in "The Drinker's Dictionary" (13 January 1736/7), quoting *Poor Richard* for his epigraph: "Nothing more like a Fool than a drunken Man" (November 1733). In this first citation of *Poor Richard*, Franklin no doubt enjoyed the irony both of quoting himself as an authority and of quoting an almanac maker, a figure generally scorned in the literary world. He opened "The Drinker's Dictionary" with an echo of Silence Dogood No. 12: "'Tis an old Remark, that Vice always endeavours to assume the Appearance of Virtue: Thus Covetousness calls itself *Prudence*; *Prodigality* would be thought *Generosity*." Franklin speculated that people created so many circumlocutions because humans "naturally and universally approve Virtue in their Hearts, and detest Vice; and therefore, whenever thro' Temptation they fall into a Practice of the latter, they would if possible conceal it from themselves as well as others, under some other Name than that which properly belongs to it. But DRUNKENNESS is a very unfortunate Vice in this respect. It bears no kind of Similitude with any sort of Virtue, from which it might possibly borrow a Name; and is therefore reduc'd to the wretched Necessity of being express'd by distant round-about Phrases, and of perpetually varying those Phrases, as often as they come to be well understood to signify plainly that A MAN IS DRUNK."

Though it has been thought for over half a century that the list of synonyms for being drunk was Franklin's original compilation, Joel S. Berson recently found the source in a nearly identical list in the *Boston New England Weekly Journal* for 6 July 1736. There it is attributed to "An ingenious Gentleman, whom the Publick have already celebrated." The high praise, and even the title "Gentleman," would hardly apply to the thirty-year-old Franklin. The internal evidence of the sayings, especially the reference to Boston and to "Sir Richard" (alluding to the popular Boston chapbook *The Indictment and Trial of Sir Richard Rum*), suggests that the list was indeed compiled by a New England writer, interested in language, but whose identity is unknown. To venture a guess, I suggest that it might be by the Bostonian John Colman (1670–1763) if he is, as Robert D. Arner speculated, the author of the chapbook.[6] In reprinting the piece, Franklin revised a number of the sayings and omitted a few, but otherwise the list of synonyms is the same as that published in Boston six months earlier. Franklin called it "a new Piece, lately communicated to me."

Like the introduction, the conclusion is Franklin's. He mockingly contrasted collecting words for the "Drinker's Dictionary" with the usual methods of compiling dictionaries: "The Phrases in this Dictionary are not (like most of our

Terms of Art) borrow'd from Foreign Languages, neither are they collected from
the Writings of the Learned in our own, but gather'd wholly from the modern
Tavern-Conversation of Tiplers." Then he ended with an echo of the preface to
the *New England Weekly Journal* list: it said that nothing so divests a person "of
his Humanity and puts on him the Brute, nay't throws him below their Level"
as drunkenness. Echoing that thought in his conclusion, Franklin wrote that he
did not doubt that there were many more synonyms for being drunk, "and I
was even tempted to add a new one my self under the Letter B, to wit, *Brutify'd*:
But upon Consideration, I fear'd being guilty of Injustice to the Brute Creation,
if I represented Drunkenness as a beastly Vice, since, 'tis well-known, that the
Brutes are in general a very sober sort of People." Franklin's ending reverses the
usual order of the great chain of being. In so doing, he may have thought of
Swift, who in *Gulliver's Travels* had made Houyhnhnms, horses with reason,
superior to humans. Franklin made all beasts superior.

Ghostwriter

Beginning with George Washington, presidents of the United States have often
been too busy to write their own speeches. In colonial America, the secretaries
of some colonial governors no doubt drafted parts of their speeches, but, with
the one exception I shall now present, I know of no evidence for any ghostwrit-
ten address from a legislature. Every colonial assembly had numerous occasions
to write speeches, and committees of the talented authors among the members
were appointed to draft them. The compositions by colonial legislators created
the tradition responsible for the great political writings of the Revolutionary
period, including the Declaration of Independence, the Constitution, and the
Federalist Papers. After being elected a representative in the Pennsylvania House
in 1751, Franklin became the primary writer of its speeches to the governor. But
evidence shows that he wrote one speech—for another colony—earlier.

In the "Outline"for his *Autobiography*, Franklin jotted down "Writing for
Jersey Assembly" (205). Nothing about the topic appears in the book. Franklin
mentioned the episode in a conversation with John Jay on 19 July 1783: "Dr.
Franklin told me that not long after the elder Lewis Morris . . . came to the
Government of New Jersey, he involved himself in a Dispute with the assembly
of that Province. The Doctor (who was then a printer in Philadelphia) went to
Burlington while the Assembly was sitting there, and were engaged in the Dispute with their Governor. The House had referred his message to a Committee,
consisting of some of their principal Members. Jos. Cooper was one of them.
But tho they were Men of good understanding and respectable, yet there was
not one among them capable of writing a proper answer to the Message, and
Cooper who was acquainted with the Doctor prevailed upon him to undertake
it. He did and went thro the Business much to their Satisfaction. In Consider-

ation of the Aid he gave them in that way and afterwards, they made him their Printer."[7]

John Jay's information allows us to narrow down the possible speeches. During Lewis Morris's governorship, the assembly met alternatively at Perth Amboy (near New York) and at Burlington (near Philadelphia). The first session of the New Jersey Assembly after Morris became governor in 1738 met at Perth Amboy, beginning on 27 October 1738. No speeches by the House to the governor were interesting or remarkable; Joseph Cooper was not on any committee to reply to the governor's address;[8] and the New York printer, John Peter Zenger, was voted the printer by the House of Representatives and mentioned (in preference to other printers) later in the New Jersey *Votes and Proceedings*.[9] There is no reason to think that Franklin was present in Perth Amboy during this session or that he wrote an address from the House to the governor.

The second session of the New Jersey Assembly after Lewis Morris became governor met in Burlington on Thursday, 10 April 1740. On 16 April, Governor Morris attacked the representatives in a blistering speech. On Friday, 18 April 1740, the House appointed a committee consisting of "Mr. [Mahlon] Stacy, Col. [Thomas] Farmar, Mr. Richard Smith of Burlington, Mr. [Joseph] Cooper, Mr. [Aaron] Leaming, and Mr. [John] Low" to draw up the reply. On the same day, the House "Ordered, That Benjamin Franklin do print his Excellency's Speech, and the Minutes and Votes of This House."[10] The reply to the governor's speech was not presented until 25 April. The sequence suggests that Franklin was asked to print the *Votes and Proceedings* of that New Jersey Assembly session before writing a speech for the assembly, rather than, as his anecdote suggested, as a reward for doing so. Franklin probably journeyed to Burlington a day or two before the legislative session started in an effort to secure the New Jersey printing; but if he had not, he would have gone there after being elected printer on 18 April in order to make arrangements with the Speaker of the New Jersey Assembly, Colonel Andrew Johnston, for the prompt and safe transferral back and forth every week of the manuscripts and printed votes. The bibliographer C. W. Miller commented that the *Votes and Proceedings* for the 1740 spring and summer sessions of the New Jersey Assembly "appear to have been printed weekly."[11]

On Friday, 25 April 1740, "Mr. [Mahlon] Stacy Reported from the Committee appointed to draw up an Address to his Excellency, That they had drawn up an Address, which he presented to the House, and the same was read. Ordered to be engrossed." Though nearly all committee addresses were revised and amended in the House (acting as a committee of the whole) before being engrossed (i.e., before the official, fair copy was prepared), this address won the instant approval of the entire House. In diction, logic, and especially in tone, it is the one superior speech prepared by a committee of the New Jersey legislature during the administration of Governor Morris. By adopting phrases and clauses from the speech that Morris delivered on 16 April, it turned the tables on Morris—thoroughly ridiculing his speech and using all its arguments against him. Individuals and committees of colonial New Jersey produced many notable speeches,[12] but no other that I have read is as humorous (if one knows Morris's angry speech), as devastating, or as well-written as this one. It required a master hand.

Governor Lewis Morris had opened the assembly on 16 April 1740 by lamenting that the last assembly session had not made a body of laws that "would have rendred any Difference with future Governors almost impracticable, and the Work of future Assemblies short and easy." The assembly/Franklin replied on 28 April by agreeing: "We His Majesty's dutiful and loyal Subjects, the Representatives of the Province of New-Jersey, in General Assembly conven'd, beg Leave sincerely to sympathize with your Excellency, and the good People of this Province, on their Disappointment; who were in Expectation of such a Body of Laws, for the Benefit of the Inhabitants and their Posterity, and the Security of the Government, as would have rendered any Difference with future Governors almost unpracticable, and the Work of Subsequent Assemblies short and easy."

Morris had said that the members of the house had "Time Sufficient to have gone far in this great Work, their Session being, I think, as long as any *New Jersey* ever knew, as expensive to the Publick, and without being delay'd by any Adjournments but what themselves desir'd." The House seemingly conceded and presented a humble posture: "It appears, by the Minutes of the last House of Representatives, that they sat a considerable Time, without any Adjournment but what themselves desired." Then the reply began to suggest that someone other than the members of the House might share part of the blame for the lack of accomplishment. "But when we consider the Difficulties they met with, our Charity leads us to hope, they were not negligent in their Stations, nor answerable for all the Delays of that Session."

Franklin continued for the members: "They made a considerable Progress in preparing a Number of such Bills as (of their Several Titles) we conceive the Country have very much at Heart: For what Reasons they were not pass'd into Laws, this House do not take upon them to determine." Since the only bill that passed during the previous legislative session was the support bill for the government, Franklin was ironically reminding Morris that the representatives had done more than the governor. Morris had accused the representatives of quarreling among themselves and with the council, thereby not doing their duty. He had said, "Most Men are too unwilling to own themselves in the Wrong, when they are so; But few Men, when they give themselves Leave to think, and seriously reflect upon their past Conduct, can well avoid discovering their Mistakes. Good men will readily own them, and wise Men will endeavour not to fall into the like a second Time. Tho' we are not all half so good or wise in every Respect as we should be, I am willing to hope that we are all good and wise enough (if not to own our Mistakes) yet not to commit the like, when with

a serious Attention we have discovered them to be so; and to endeavour all that
we can, to shun every Thing that may prevent or obstruct the Publick Good,
which it is so much the Duty of every one of us to promote."

Franklin's reply repeated Morris's sentiments. Morris had arrogated to himself the cause of moderation and justice; using Morris's own words, Franklin
took it back for the assembly. "We are of Your Excellency's Opinion, that most
Men are too unwilling to own themselves in the Wrong, when they are so; and
that but few Men, when they give themselves Leave to think, and seriously reflect upon their past Conduct, can well avoid discovering their Mistakes: Good
Men will readily own them, and wise Men will endeavour, not to fall into the
Like a Second Time. And though we are not all half so good, or wise, in every
Respect, as we should be; yet willing to hope that we are all good or wise enough
(if not to own our Mistakes) yet not to commit the Like again, when, with a
serious Attention, we have discovered them to be so; and shall endeavour all
that we can, to shun every Thing, that may prevent or obstruct the Publick
Good, which it is so much the Duty of every one of us to promote and secure."

Morris's charges against the members of the assembly were turned into
charges against the council and against Morris himself. Morris had said, "Let
every Man that has been concern'd in the Debates of the last Assembly, look
into himself, examine his own Breast, and see whether in many of the Disputes
that then happened, the Gratification of his own Resentments, or his Friends,
or the Support and Uniting of a Party he was engag'd with, had not a greater
Influence upon his Conduct, than any Regard for the Publick Good? If it had,
let him resolve to do so no more, and heartily endeavour to keep those Resolutions." Franklin paraphrased and repeated Morris: "We would willingly hope,
that no Man concern'd in the Debates of the last Assembly, had more Regard
to the Gratification of his own Resentments, and Uniting a Party prejudicial to
the Publick Good, than to support with Zeal what they conceived to be a Duty
incumbent on them, for the Benefit of their Country: If there be such, let him
repent, and resolve to do so no more." Just as Morris had called for the legislature to repent, the members called to Morris—repent.

Morris called together the legislature to give the members a second opportunity of doing "all the Good you can for your Country." Franklin replied, "We
thank your Excellency for giving us this Opportunity of doing all the Good we
can for our Country, by making such Laws, as are fit for us to have, and your
Excellency to consent unto. No others, knowingly, will be proposed by us."
Again, the assembly took over the noble and superior position that Morris had
assumed.

Appealing to the members' sympathies, Morris had told them, "By the
Course of Nature I cannot be long among you, and perhaps this may be the last
in my Power to give you; It will therefore be prudent in you to make the proper
Use of it." Then the governor returned to lecturing the members on their proper
conduct: "Avoid unnecessary Jangles, which can only tend to defeat the good

Purposes of your Meeting: Hear with Patience; argue with Calmness and Temper, for Truth and not for Victory, on Subjects worthy of and fit for your Consideration; and then, by the Blessing of God, there may be a happy Issue of your
Consultations and Debates. I say, fit for your Consultation." Morris sounded
like an aged minister, commenting on how short a time he had left to do good
among his flock. Franklin echoed him: "Your Excellency's prudent Consideration, that by the Course of Nature you cannot be long amongst us; altho' it
gives us a real Concern, yet we hope this will not be the last Opportunity in
your Power to give us, of acting in Conjunction with you, for the Advantage
and Prosperity of this Province. Notwithstanding it ought to excite every one of
us, to make the proper Use of the present; avoiding unnecessary Tangles, which
can only tend to defeat the good Purposes of our Meeting." Franklin again
reversed Morris's arguments and, in echoing him, lectured him.

Secret instructions to the governors were a constant source of friction in the
colonial period. Governors never wanted (and often were forbidden) to reveal
their instructions—and the legislators always wanted to know and publicize
them. The governor said that there were "many Things perhaps in your Desires"
that he could not grant, "consistent with that Trust His Majesty has been gra-
ciously pleas'd to repose in me." He must veto any laws that he thought not fit
and convenient for them, as well as any laws that violated his instructions.
Franklin seemingly agreed while really accusing Morris of wasting the representatives' time by not allowing them to know his instructions. "If there should be
any Thing in our Desires, which may not be fit for Your Excellency to grant,
consistent with that Trust His Majesty hath reposed in you; when Your Excellency shall observe any Thing of that Nature on our Minutes, it would be very
acceptable, if you would be pleased to signifie the same to us, and thereby prevent our giving Your Excellency any further Trouble, or spending our Time
unnecessarily about them."

Franklin defended the members' actions as consistent with the constitution
and implicitly accused Morris of capriciously rejecting good laws. Morris told
the representatives that they should not attempt to force him to assent to a law
by denying him funds. Franklin observed, "We like our present Constitution
too well, to be uneasy at Your Excellency's having a Negative Voice to any Law
we shall propose for your Assent; and were never tempted to believe, that because the Council and Assembly pass'd a Bill, that by their doing so, you were
under Obligation to pass it into a Law; unless you were satisfied it is reasonable
and fit for you so to do; But if when the Copy of any Bill be sent to Your
Excellency, you should discover a Defect in any Part thereof, you would be
pleased to point out the same, to this or the Upper House, it might then be re-
considered, and amended; and the Country not be deprived of the Benefit of a
good Law, for the Sake of a Defect or Imperfection contain'd in some Part of
the Bill only." Franklin deliberately omitted any reply to Morris's reference to
the assembly's power to withhold the governor's salary. Mentioning it would, at

best, have been impolitic and given the governor reason to reply and would, at worst, make the assembly seem to be boasting about their command of the finances, including the governor's salary.

The governor had lectured the assembly on making good laws. Franklin's reply echoed him: "Your Excellency's Observation is very just, That the Making suitable Laws for the Well-governing of a Country, is far from being an easy Undertaking; and what Your Excellency has said to us on that Head, we hope will have its proper Weight with us, and induce us the more to take such Care in the Drawing our Bills, as will be most likely to be attended with the Success desired; and are persuaded, that the Method recommended by Your Excellency (if truly followed) will go far to render our Laws more perspicuous than they have hitherto been; and consequently more intelligible, more likely of obtaining Approbation both there and at Home, and more effectual for the Ends intended by them."

The entire assembly reply echoed Morris's speech. After its humble opening, Franklin gradually adopted the instructive, superior, and condescending tone of Morris's speech, using all of his arguments, and adding that he had wasted their time. Just as Franklin omitted Morris's warning against denying him money, so Franklin strategically added an underlying assembly complaint—against the governor's secret instructions. The speech's rhetorical effect is devastating. Lurking behind the serious and uplifting moral phrases and high intentions of the representatives' speech, behind its superior and condescending tone, a parodic voice lampoons Morris for his moralistic harangue, implying that he fools nobody—except perhaps himself. The speech mimicked, mocked, and ridiculed Morris. Further, though overshadowed by the parodic voice, the content of the speech is remarkable. It expresses the proto-American sentiments of the American legislatures. The underlying message was that the elected representatives are the conscientious servants of the people and guard their rights and privileges, while the governor and Prerogative Party, together with the English authorities, oppose the mass of the people with hypocritical selfishness.

The facts concerning this speech dovetail with the reminiscence recorded by John Jay in 1783. It was early in Governor Lewis Morris's administration (he was appointed in 1738 and died in 1746). The assembly met in Burlington. Joseph Cooper was a member of the committee appointed to prepare the address; in fact, it was the only time he was on the committee to reply to the governor.[13] For several years thereafter, Franklin printed for the New Jersey legislature. Franklin previously printed occasional imprints for New Jersey,[14] but only beginning with this session did his imprint read "Printer to the King's Most Excellent Majesty for the Province of New Jersey."[15] Among his other firsts, perhaps we can add that Franklin was America's first ghostwriter for a legislature.

"THE RELIGION OF THE INDIAN NATIVES"

The most popular Indian speech before Thomas Jefferson praised "Logan's Speech" extravagantly in *Notes on the State of Virginia* was Franklin's deistic satire, *A Speech Deliver'd by an Indian Chief, in Reply to a Sermon Preached by a Swedish Missionary, in Order to Convert the Indians to the Christian Religion.* Since deism held that true religion was a series of fundamental principles found among all peoples, some deists attributed a version of deism to the American Indians. Robert Beverley did so in his *History of Virginia* (1705), and John Lawson's *New Voyage to Carolina* (1709), which portrayed the American Indians as noble savages, inspired the English freethinker John Toland to write an account of deistic American Indians, "Account of the Indians at Carolina."[16] Franklin knew these earlier works and wrote a series of deistic Indian satires, the first of which, *An Indian Speech*, has not previously been attributed to him.[17] The speech adapted an actual Indian speech that replied to a Swedish minister's sermon to a group of Indians near Lancaster, Pennsylvania.

The Reverend Jonas Aurén (d. 1713), a Lutheran minister, preached that the Indians must be converted to Christianity in order to be saved. An Indian, probably a Susquehanna chief, answered him. Aurén reported the Indian's speech in a letter dated 13 January 1699/1700[18] to the Reverend Erick Björck, the head of the Swedish ministry in America, who was living in what is now Wilmington, Delaware. When Björck returned to Sweden in 1714, he took his manuscripts with him. In 1731 his son, Tobias Erik Björck, published a graduation dissertation in Latin at the University of Uppsala. Tobias Björck used his father's materials in writing *De Plantatione Ecclesia Svecanae in America* ("The history of the planting of the Swedish church in America").[19] The last chapter of the thesis discussed "the causes why the heathen are not easily converted" and printed Jonas Aurén's letter in Latin.

Tobias Björck's dissertation came to the attention of the litterateurs in the Delaware Valley, the site of New Sweden. Franklin's friend and neighbor, the artist Gustavus Hesselius (1682–1755), was among the persons who knew it. Hesselius had emigrated to America in 1712 with his older brother Andreas, who succeeded Eric Björck as the head of the Swedish ministers in the Delaware Valley. Andreas Hesselius wrote a prefatory letter in English for the publication of Björck's dissertation.[20] Gustavus Hesselius, who turns up dozens of times in Franklin's accounts from 1733 to 1747, must have known the Björcks as well as most of the Swedes in the Delaware Valley. He probably knew the Reverend Jonas Aurén, who had married Lydia, daughter of Hance Justis on 16 November 1710. Aurén died in 1713. Gustavus Hesselius's biographers speculate that his second wife, Lydia, was Jonas Aurén's widow.[21] Franklin read the pamphlet, found Aurén's letter fascinating, and rewrote the Indian speech in English as a deistic satire.

Coming from the theological quarrels in the Hemphill affair (1735), Franklin found the Indian speech a compelling document. In the Hemphill controversy, Franklin argued that good works were more important than faith and that persons merited happiness in an afterlife if they lived good lives here on earth. He maintained it was not necessary to believe in a particular religious creed in order to live virtuously and be rewarded by God. As he wrote in the first Hemphill tract, "A Dialogue between Two Presbyterians": "A virtuous Heretick shall be saved before a wicked Christian" (2:33). Franklin's defense of the Reverend Samuel Hemphill failed, and a commission of the Presbyterian Synod censured the minister and suspended him. Despite Franklin's additional pamphlets vindicating Hemphill, the Presbyterian Synod unanimously declared Hemphill unorthodox and permanently dismissed him on 22 September 1735. Franklin's intemperate last two pamphlets in the controversy prove that he was furious about Hemphill's trial and expulsion. Smarting over his defeat, he may have translated and revised *An Indian Speech* as an argument that he had been right in the Hemphill controversy.

Franklin's English adaptation of the Indian speech circulated in manuscript. A copy came into the hands of John Webbe, a lawyer and litterateur with whom Franklin had various dealings in the late 1730s. In 1740, Franklin suggested to Webbe that he edit a magazine that Franklin would publish. As we have seen, Franklin and Webbe had different conceptions of the magazine. Webbe took the idea to Franklin's printing competitor, Andrew Bradford. Consequently, Franklin and Webbe quarreled and edited rival magazines. In the third and last issue of the failing *American Magazine* (March 1741), John Webbe published "The Religion of the *Indian* Natives of *America*, explained, in an Argument held by one of them at *Connestogoe* in *Pennsylvania*, with a *Swedish* minister, in the Year 1690. *Translated from the Latin.*"[22]

Though Franklin had published news of deists and a number of deistic essays and satires,[23] Bradford printed nothing previously that might be interpreted as a religious satire. The temptation to publish Franklin's manuscript, however, overcame Bradford's scruples. Besides, who would complain about the impiety of the Indian speech? Not Franklin, its author, and not Pennsylvania's government officials, for Andrew Hamilton, the former attorney general of Pennsylvania, who was also the just-retired Speaker of the Pennsylvania Assembly and the best lawyer in Pennsylvania, was a deist and good friend of Franklin. Hamilton would have been willing to defend Franklin in court. If Bradford had been charged by the authorities with printing an irreligious piece, he no doubt would immediately and happily turn over Franklin as the author. Indeed, perhaps only Franklin's authorship of the piece gave Bradford the courage to print it. Webbe and Bradford must have found it delicious irony to publish Franklin's composition in the *American Magazine*.

When Franklin's partner James Parker reprinted a version of *An Indian Speech* in his *New York Gazette* on 27 April 1752, the local authorities prosecuted him.[24] Parker asked Franklin to intercede for him. Franklin did so, writing his scientific friend and lieutenant governor of New York, Cadwallader Colden, that the piece was an "old" thing and had been printed previously "here" in Philadelphia and in London. Franklin said that since no notice had been taken of it, the speech had caused no controversy and been forgotten. The New York authorities dropped the prosecution.

The speech has no introduction in Björck's dissertation. Franklin added one. It begins with four premises: God exists; there is an afterlife; one's happiness or misery there depends on one's behavior in this world; and man is by nature more prone to vice than virtue. The method and the first three propositions are similar to Franklin's *Dissertation on Liberty and Necessity* and to his Junto speech, "On the Providence of God in the Government of the World" (1:264–70). Though Franklin gave brief proofs for the first three premises, he gave none for the fourth. Presumably, everyone's experience confirmed the evil nature of mankind. The premise is old-fashioned Protestantism, Anglican as well as Calvinist. Deism, as well as the recent trends in late seventeenth-century and early eighteenth-century Christianity (Arianism, Socianism, and liberal Anglicanism) generally held that man was inherently benevolent.[25] It was extraordinary for a deistic satire to posit the evil nature of mankind. Franklin, however, unlike most deists, found humans more prone to vice than virtue.[26]

From these four propositions, Franklin inferred a chain of consequences. Humans feared the punishment awaiting them in an afterlife and wanted to escape both the fear and the punishment. Cunning persons established priestcraft to comfort them. Like the evil nature of mankind, a psychological explanation (guilt and fear of punishment) for the existence of priestcraft is rare among deists. Usually it is simply said that cunning persons imposed on the majority. Continuing the ordinary deistic argument, the preface said that various fraudulent schemes replaced the religion of nature. Consequently, God sent Christ to earth to reestablish Christianity or the religion of nature, with its fundamental principle, "Love your Neighbor as yourself." But since human nature remained the same, various further schemes of priestcraft arose, even concerning Christianity, accompanied by "infinite Wrangles on the Meaning of Sounds." (The epistemological skepticism is typical of Franklin.)[27] Some persons, however, attempted to restore Christianity's original purity. The few were opposed by persons who made "monstrous Representations" of Christianity. According to the preface, one such false doctrine was eternal punishment for persons like the pre-Christian pagans and the American Indians who did not worship Jesus Christ, though it was impossible for them ever to have heard of his name.

Reprints omitted the introduction. Franklin did not include it in a copy he later sent to the press.[28] The title commonly used was *A Speech Deliver'd by an Indian Chief, in Reply to a Sermon Preached by a Swedish Missionary, in Order to Convert the Indians to the Christian Religion*. The later editions only contained a prefatory note saying that the missionary preached the sermon in or about 1710[29] at an Indian treaty in Conestoga, in which the missionary set forth the "Necessity of a Mediator" and attempted to convince the Indians to embrace Christianity.

The speech itself began with the Indian orator saying that before he explained to the missionary why the Indians would not adopt Christianity, he would tell the missionary something about the Indian religion. The Indian chief said that Indians and their ancestors believed in an afterlife where they will be rewarded or punished in accordance with their lives on earth. They imitated their forefathers in believing in good works. Their belief had stood the test of time and could not have arisen from fable, for false doctrines can never last long where free inquiry exists. Indians had always thought it was "the sacred, inviolable, natural Right of every Man to examine and judge for himself." The idea of rewards or punishments in an afterlife must either have been "revealed immediately from Heaven" to ancestors or "implanted in each of us, at our Creation." Whatever method God used, "it is still in our Sense a divine Revelation."

Franklin added most of these ideas to the Latin original. (It contained no reference to faith versus works, to the benefit of free inquiry, to the right of every person to judge for himself, or to the various ways of receiving a "divine Revelation.") All these opinions also appeared in Franklin's writings during the Hemphill affair (above, Chapter 10).

The Indian then quizzed the missionary. Did he believe that the Indians' virtuous ancestors were all eternally condemned? Did he think that all the virtuous living Indians "are in a State of Damnation?" If so, his belief was "impious." If the missionary admits no other revelation but the Bible, he denies the basis of the Indians' belief, the doctrine of future rewards or punishments for our deeds in this life. If the minister says that God has revealed himself to Indians but insufficiently for their salvation, such a situation is no better than no revelation at all. God would not show them the goal (an eternal happy life) to be achieved without showing them how to achieve it. Could the missionary really believe that Indians are damned for not doing "Things, which he himself acknowledges were impossible" for them to do?

Indians believed "that every Man is possessed of sufficient Knowledge for his own Salvation." For all we know, God "may have communicated himself to different Races of People in a different Manner." The Indian's suggestion that different races of people may have received revelation in different ways implied that not all mankind was descended from Adam and Eve. The suggestion of polygenesis in *An Indian Speech* shocked some readers.[30] The Indian granted that some persons may have received the word of God in writing. If so, "their Revelation has no advantage over ours, since both must be equally sufficient to save, or the End of a Revelation would be frustrated." If both are true, they are the same in substance, and the only difference lies in the mode of communication. The precepts in the written revelation could only be designed for those who have the commands in writing. They cannot be intended for others who never had the writing. Had God thought the writing necessary for the Indians' salvation, he would have given it to them. To say that God could not have equally revealed himself to all mankind at the same time is "Nothing less than an absolute Denial of his Omnipotence." God can make his will manifest without the help of any book or of any "Bookish-Man." Here *An Indian Speech*, like much deistic propaganda, attacked the idea of ministers and/or priests or any mediators between humans and God.

Consider the nature of God. If we are God's creation, then "we are under the Care and Protection of God." It cannot be imagined that God would abandon his own creatures. To say that God has condemned the Indians to live "in a damnable Error thro' so many Ages, is not only a Denial of his Providence, but represents him as a Tyrant." How can a just God be thought to have given immortality to beings only to condemn them eternally for not having knowledge that he has withheld from them? The Indians' conception of our "gracious God" would not allow them to believe the missionary's doctrine. "God has cared for us from the beginning of time until the present, when we now enjoy our lives and have everything necessary for our existence. Since God has looked after us in all these matters of comparatively little importance, it is absurd to think that he has neglected us in the matter of eternal salvation." The last sentiment is another opinion not in the Latin text but it is in Franklin's writings (e.g., 11:231–32).

The Indian continued, "If God does abandon us, he would only do so with just cause. If an ancestor committed a crime, God would punish the criminal either here or hereafter but would never punish the innocent for the criminal's guilt. Those who teach otherwise paint the Almighty, as a very whimsical ill natured Being." The implied satire of the idea of original sin was much stronger than in the Latin text. Franklin derided the idea of original sin earlier in the Hemphill writings and later in his *Remarks Concerning the Savages of North America* (2:114; W 969–74).

In concluding, the Indian said that Christians are "much more vicious than we." How could they be favored by God and the Indians be condemned? Does God confer favor with partiality for no reason? To judge the Christian doctrines by the bad behavior of most Christians, Indians must conclude that the Indians' revelation is not "inferior."

In translating and revising the Indian speech, Franklin added a number of ideas that were not in the original, omitted some, and gave it a stronger ending. It caused controversy in various publications, with a flurry of pieces in the *London Magazine* after it appeared there in 1760. A modern authority on eighteenth-century religion, who did not know of the speech's numerous other printings or suspect Franklin wrote it, cited a 1753 edition as a "fascinating" document of the "Deist controversy."[31] As we will see later in the biography, Franklin used elements of the speech in composing both "The Captivity of William Henry" (1768) and *Remarks Concerning the Savages of North America* (1783).

Essay on Paper Currency

Though the rival *American Magazine* scooped him with his own writing, Franklin contributed two pieces to the *General Magazine*. In the January issue, he reprinted an English government report on the paper money of the colonies and followed it up in the February issue with his reply, "Essay on Paper-Currency, Proposing a New Method for Fixing its Value."[32] In order to fix the price of colonial currencies and to regulate the money supply, Franklin proposed an adumbration of the Federal Reserve Board. Despite being ignored by previous scholars, the essay contributes to economic theory. It also affirms Franklin's Americanism and his early interest in a British American empire. In order to state the complicated essay as clearly as possible, to emphasize the sequential structure, and to make the different theses convenient to refer to, Franklin adopted the method of numbering each point, many of which were only one sentence. This method anticipated the technique he used in his electrical experiments and in "Observations Concerning the Increase of Mankind" (1751).

In the "Essay on Paper-Currency," Franklin used an impartial observer persona who was also a humble projector: the anonymous author opened by observing that "the Honourable the House of Commons of *Great Britain*" believed that American paper money "hath been prejudicial to the Trade of *Great Britain*, by causing 'a Confusion in Dealings, and lessening of Credit in those Parts.'" The author feared that Great Britain would take measures to hinder or prohibit any future emissions. But if a scheme for fixing and ascertaining the value of paper currency were adapted, then there would be no need for any restraints on the colonial currencies, "as the Confusion complained of in Dealings would thereby be avoided." Before setting forth the scheme, the persona adopted the pose of a monetary authority: "I shall first set down a few plain Remarks touching the Fluctuation of Exchange, and the Value of Gold and Silver in the Colonies; with some Observations on the Ballance of Trade; in order to render what follows the more clear and intelligible." The method was that recommended by the Port Royalists, echoing Descartes.

Franklin gave ten seemingly commonsense observations, with occasional deductions.

1) Everyone concerned in trade must "either *draw* Bills of Exchange on other Countries, or *buy* Bills to send abroad to ballance his Accounts."

2) Since exports and imports in any colony are often managed by different persons, and those chiefly employed in importing may exceed those employed in exporting, "there may sometimes be many Buyers and few Sellers of Bills of Exchange, even whilst the Exports may exceed in Value the Imports: And it is easy to conceive, that in this Case, Exchange may rise."

3) He pointed out that the British merchants who were trading to the colonies were often unacquainted with the advantages of building ships in the colonies or exporting commodities of the American colonies to the West Indies or other foreign markets. Therefore the British merchants "frequently order all their Remittances in Bills of Exchange," even though the bills may be less advantageous than building ships or exporting goods. The practice of asking for bills of exchange increases the demand for bills and enhances their price.

4) Conversely, "A great Demand in *Europe* for any of the Commodities of the Colonies, and large Orders for those Commodities from the *British* Merchants to their Factors here, with Directions to draw for the Value, may occasion Exchange to fall for a Time, even tho' the Imports should be greater than the Exports."

5) The effect will be "that a sudden great Demand for Bills in the Colonies, may, at any time, advance the Exchange; and a sudden great Demand abroad for their Commodities may fall the Exchange." The usage of *fall*, while perfectly understandable in context, is unusual, an example of Franklin's penchant for understandable, though unusual, diction.[33]

6) Gold and silver will rise and fall in value, "very near in Proportion as Exchange rises and falls; being only wanted, in those Colonies that have a Paper Currency, for the same Use as Bills of Exchange, *viz.* for Remittances to *England*."

7) When few People can draw on England or furnish those who want remittances with gold or silver, paper currency may fall in value compared to sterling money and gold and silver, yet keep its original value in respect to all commodities.

8) "From all these Considerations, I think, it appears that the Rising or Falling of the Exchange can be no sure Rule for Discovering on which Side the Ballance of Trade lies; because that Exchange may be affected by various Accidents independent thereof."

To determine the balance of trade more certainly, Franklin advanced two further considerations.

9) Whatever is imported must be paid for in the produce or manufactures of the country. If the exports in one year are insufficient to pay for what is imported, the deficiency must be made up by exporting more in the future; otherwise the colony becomes debtor for the deficiency, which at last must be discharged (if it is ever discharged) by land.

10) If the debt of any colony to Great Britain has been increasing for several years, it demonstrates that the balance of trade is against that colony. On the other hand, if the debt to Great Britain is lessening yearly, or if it is not increasing, then the balance of trade is not against that colony. Nevertheless, the currency of that colony may be gradually declining in value in comparison to sterling.

After these ten observations, Franklin turned to his proposal, a scheme "for fixing the Value of a Paper Currency." In the manuscript draft, this began a second series of six numbered points, but in the published version, he continued the former numbering.

11) "Let it be supposed, that in some one of the Colonies the Sum of 110,000 in Bills of Credit was proposed to be struck, and all other Currencies to be

called in and destroyed." He suggested that the value of these bills be fixed "at the Rates settled by the Act of Parliament made in the Sixth Year of Queen Anne."

12) Franklin proposed that 100,000 of the 110,000 pounds "be emitted on Loan, upon good Securities, either in Land or Plate, according to the Method used in *Pensylvania*, the Borrowers to pay *Five per Cent per Annum* Interest, together with a *Twentieth* Part of the Principal, which would give the Government an Opportunity of sinking it by Degrees, if any Alteration in the Circumstances of the Province should make it necessary: But if no such Necessity appeared, so much of the Principal as should be paid in, might be reemitted on the same Terms as before." This was the standard Pennsylvania practice.

The next proposal, however, was entirely new:

13) "The other *Ten Thousand* Pounds to be laid out in such Commodities as should be most likely to yield a Profit at Foreign Markets, to be ship'd off on Account of the Colony, in order to raise a Fund or Bank in *England*: Which Sum, so laid out, would in two Years time, be returned into the Office again by the Interest Money." That is, the 5 percent interest per year on 100,000 pounds would be 10,000 pounds in two years, and that 10,000 would be in the colonial loan office.

14) A colonial bank (or a special fund in an English bank) would be established in England. The main trustees or managers of the colonial bank (or funds) in England would be located in America. They would be "impowered and directed to supply all Persons that should apply to them, with Bills of Exchange, to be drawn on the Colony's Banker in *London*, at the aforesaid" standard rate of exchange established under Queen Anne. "The Monies thus brought in, to be laid out again as before [as in #12 above] and replaced in *England* in the said Bank with all convenient Speed: And as these provincial Bills would have, at least, as good a Credit as those of any private Person; every Man, who had occasion to draw, would, of Course, be obliged to dispose of his Bills at the same Rate." Thus Franklin would fix the rate of exchange.

Here he added a consideration that had not been in his original draft.

15) "By Means of this Bank," he proposed "to regulate the Rate of Exchange; and therefore it would be necessary to make it so large, or procure the Trustees such a Credit in *London*, as should discourage and prevent any mischievous Combinations for draining it and rendering the Design useless. I know of no Inconvenience that could arise by allotting double the proposed Sum for that Service [that is, 20,000 rather than 10,000 for foreign investments], but that the annual Interest [on the 100,000, amounting to 5,000] would be lessen'd; which [the annual interest of 5,000] in some Governments has been

found a useful Engine for defraying the publick Expence." As Franklin knew, the interest on its paper money was the chief way that Pennsylvania financed the government. "But if only a Credit should be thought needful, over and above the said Sum, and upon some Emergency Recourse should be had to it, the Interest-Money would soon afford sufficient Means for answering that Credit."

The following two points and the conclusion also appeared in the draft.

16) The trustees should be empowered and directed to take in foreign coins at the rates prescribed by Parliament from persons who wanted to change them for paper currency and to exchange gold and silver for them. Franklin thought that such exchange might reduce those coins again to a currency that was only bought and sold as a commodity. Alternatively, part of the proceeds of what could be sent abroad might be returned to the province in gold and silver for creating a fund in the colony.

17) "I hope it will appear upon examining into the Circumstances of the Paper-Money-Colonies, by the Rule proposed above, that the Ballance of Trade has not been so much against them as is commonly imagined; but that the Fall of their Currencies, with Respect to Sterling, and to Gold and Silver, has been chiefly occasioned either by some such Accidents as are above shewed to influence it; which by this Scheme will be all prevented: Or to their being issued without any good Foundation for supporting their Credit, such as a Land Security, etc. However that be, I think, there can be no room, upon our Plan, to fear, that the Credit of the Paper-Currency can be injur'd, even though the Ballance of Trade were against the Colony, while their Bank in *London* can be duely supported."

Near the conclusion, Franklin added to the draft a few summary thoughts: when a colony finds itself in a disadvantageous trade position, it should "think timely of all proper Means for preventing it; such as encouraging Iron-Works, Ship-building, raising and manufacturing of Hemp and Flax, and all other Manufactures not prohibited by their Mother Country. They might likewise save considerable Sums, which are now sent to *England*, by setting up and establishing an Insurance-Office." The proposal for a colonial insurance office, like that for a colonial bank, was a new idea. "This, I think, might effectually be done by an Act of Assembly for impowering the Trustees of the Loan-Office to subscribe all Policies that should be brought to them, on such Terms as should be settled by the said Trustees jointly with a Committee of Assembly, at a Meeting for that Purpose, once a Month, or oftner if necessary. Besides the saving to the Country in the Article of Trade, it would probably yield a considerable yearly Income towards the Support of Government; it being evident, that most prudent Insurers are great Gainers upon the Whole of their Insurances, after all Losses are deducted."

The scheme would have two very great advantages: exports would be increased, and consequently bring the balance of trade more in favor of the colonies, and the rate of exchange would be fixed and ascertained. The latter should "remove the Prejudices which the Merchants in *England* seem to have conceived against a Paper Currency in the Colonies."

Franklin was not ready to admit that the authorities in Great Britain wanted only to benefit England—not Great Britain as a whole. If they thought that such a plan would improve the trade of the colonies and detract from England's advantages, they would veto it, even though the rate of exchange would be fixed. Franklin was also naive concerning the great American merchants. In effect, Franklin advocated that the colonial government compete with the wealthy private merchants in international trade and insurance. The greatest colonial merchants (like William Allen) were usually members of the governor's councils or of the colonial assemblies. They would not want the state to compete with them, even if it were for the general good. The idealistic Franklin ignored the selfishness of nations and of individuals. Like his later Albany Plan of Union, the essay on paper currency was universally ignored.

"The Divine Prescience"

Franklin's second essay in the *General Magazine* returned to a favorite topic, theology. A "Letter from Theophilus, Relating to the divine Prescience" appeared in the March issue and asked, *"Whether God concurs with all human Actions or not?* That is, Whether he be the principal efficient Cause of every Action we produce?" Theophilus/Franklin said that some theologians discriminate between the "principal efficient Cause" and the "second Causes" of actions. The discrimination follows the distinction between primary and secondary qualities of matter, which was suggested by the Greek philosophers, espoused by Robert Boyle, given its greatest statement by John Locke, and refined by Berkeley.[34] But *"if God did not concur with every Action that's produc'd, then there would be an Action, and consequently some Being, independent of God, which is absurd."* The statement was the same as the first of four propositions regarding free will that Franklin had discussed and rejected in "On the Providence of God in the Government of the World." In the 1730 essay he claimed the argument meant that God "is now no more a God" (W 165). He also declared that if the position were true, there would be no possible reason for prayers (W 166). In reconsidering the question, the argument of Theophilus seems inconclusive—and perhaps atheistic.

Theophilus affirmed that unless all acts have been decreed from eternity, "there is no Possibility . . . of defending the Doctrine of the Divine Prescience." He concluded: "So that whoever denies God's immediate Concourse with every Action we produce, must of Consequence deny God's Foreknowledge." Theophilus/Franklin asked that in a future *General Magazine* someone remark on what he had said. Perhaps Franklin meant to reply to Theophilus in a future magazine with a revision of his unpublished Junto speech of 1730. He did not, but his old acquaintance, the Reverend Joseph Morgan (who presumably did not know that Franklin was Theophilus), replied that he dreaded the consequences of any future writing on the subject, for such arguments often favored "*Blasphemy*."[35] Morgan was right. The consequences of the argument are twofold: first, it denies all freedom of the will; and second, it makes God immediately responsible for all evil.

The Theophilus letter rephrased the arguments in Franklin's early philosophical work, *A Dissertation on Liberty and Necessity* (1725). Most Franklin scholars claim that he progressed beyond his early materialism and Pyrrhonism.[36] But I see little evidence that he did so. I am not suggesting that his ideas on theology and metaphysics were fixed—they were not—but he remained unsatisfied with the justifications for the existence of suffering, evil, and death. In his *Dissertation* he wrote, "*if a Creature is made by God, it must depend upon God, and receive all its Power from Him; with which Power the Creature can do nothing contrary to the Will of God, because God is Almighty*" (1:60). Further, "*if the Creature is thus limited in his Actions, being able to do only such Things as God would have him to do, and not being able to refuse doing what God would have done; then he can have no such Thing as Liberty, Free-will or Power to do or refrain an Action*" (1:61–62).

Like his *Dissertation* and his Junto lecture "On the Providence of God," the Theophilus letter both burlesqued the standard definitions of the attributes of God and satirized the nature of the God that followed from those definitions. Though Franklin not infrequently wrote on opposite sides of the same question, he returned in his theological writings to the same fundamental question of theodicy—*Unde Malum?* Franklin reiterated in the Theophilus letter that the existence of evil contradicted the basic Christian belief that a God existed who is both all-powerful and all-good.

"What is True?"

On 24 February 1742/3, when publishing an account of the Pennsylvania Moravians, Franklin wrote on the nature of truth, which some persons have thought philosophy's ultimate question. The article gave two extracts describing the Moravians' discipline and their constitution. At the end, Franklin added a comment, supposedly from a Moravian, revealing Franklin's own profound skepticism concerning theology, reality, and epistemology: "The Questions, Accounts and Testimonys falling under the Consideration of Magistrates, go upon that Point; *what is true*? But Posterity likes very often, and that justly, to hear *how a Thing is true*, especially in Matters of Religion, where the Appearance of a Thing, (which however with Men exceeding often goes for the *verum physicum* and *metaphysicum*) infinitely differs from the *verum morale*." At least these four orders of reality—the appearance, the physical reality, the metaphysical structure of thought, and the moral truth—may all be brought to bear on how something is true. In short, the world has different and sometimes conflicting realities. The different realities may all be true, but what is true within one reality or system of thought need not be true of another.

Franklin echoed the traditional Aristotelian distinction between physics and metaphysics, to which classical authors had later added morals. They were followed by Saint Augustine and by John Locke, whose *Essay Concerning Human Understanding* is probably Franklin's primary source.[37] He no doubt also was struck by Pascal's belief that "things appear true or false, according to the Face one sees them with," and may echo Pascal's statement that one must consider "how and in what Sense" something is true.[38] Franklin's observation also anticipates Melville's dramatic presentations of various world systems in his novels, especially *Billy Budd*. When Franklin used the conventional discrimination between *right* (which can be identified with truth in the following quotation) and *might* in a letter to his son-in-law, Richard Bache, on 13 September 1781, he added a difference concerning *right*: "moral and political Right sometimes differ; and sometimes are both subdued by Might."

The supposed Moravian continued, "It is therefore much the best, considering human Imperfection, that each Party describes itself as good, and as bad, as sincerely and as insincerely as they can and will, and leave it to such as are capable, to gather as much as is possible of what is true and solid, from Peoples Stile and Expressions." Style as the test of truth! Reflecting the Port Royal *Logic*, Franklin had claimed in Silence Dogood No. 14 that because writers meant different things by such words as *the church*, it was necessary to define the words one used. After he started the *Pennsylvania Gazette*, he pointed out that a political point of view had to be considered in determining the truth of newspaper reports (23 October 1729); he noted that a newspaper's political point of view affected its reports of victory or defeat in battle—as well as the body counts of the slain (19 December 1734); he had recently been disgusted with the Philadelphia tanners for appropriating the language of Whiggism in their selfish cause (16 and 30 August 1739); and he later recorded (early August 1764) that different political parties in Pennsylvania used exactly the same words to support opposite facts (P 11:277). The statement of the "Moravian" is Franklin's most direct assertion of epistemological skepticism.[39]

Franklin next referred to the accounts of Christ by Matthew, Mark, Luke, and John: "But when they are described by others, a 1700 Years Experience teaches us, that even when they are described during their Period of Time (for after that all Accounts are of no Value), the *Apologetes* do praise very often the meanest Things, and the *Satyrics* very often criticize on the best Things, either for Want of Sincerity or Capacity." At the end of Franklin's brief exploration of metaphysics and epistemology, written in the guise of an explication of Moravian doctrines, we are left with an unknowable world. As he later said, "Nothing in life is certain."

"An Apology for the Young Man in Gaol"

Franklin's most salacious poem concerned an aborted crime. The persona Franklin chose was surprising, a godlike *censor morum*, disgusted with the animality and bestiality of human beings. Crime reporter Franklin noted on 25 August 1743, "Last Sunday a young Fellow about 20 Years of Age was brought to Town from Whitemarsh and committed to Prison, being charg'd with Ravishing a poor old Woman upwards of Eighty, and injuring her so that her Life is tho't to be in Danger." Andrew Bradford's *American Weekly Mercury* did not contain this news note. Gradually more information and rumors came in about the old lady and the lascivious young man. The thirty-seven-year-old Franklin found the reports concerning the actions of both the young man and the older woman repulsive and disgusting. Evidently the old woman had encouraged the man's sexual advances. Franklin expressed his reaction in a grotesque poem, "*An* Apology *for the young Man in Gaol, and in Shackles, for ravishing an old Woman of 85 at* Whitemarsh, *who had only one eye, and that a red one.*"[40]

The title itself goes on too long for an entirely serious piece, and the two last dependent clauses cause disbelief and rejection. The title also heightens the crime's disgusting elements, making the old woman eighty-five (as the events unfolded, it was more likely that she was in her fifties rather than in her mid-eighties) and making her especially repulsive by giving her "only one eye, and that a red one." In their various news notes, neither the *Pennsylvania Gazette* nor the *American Weekly Mercury* mentioned her eyes. Presumably she had two comparatively unremarkable ones. Ralph Ellison used a similar description as a touchstone for the comic grotesque in *Invisible Man*: "Why . . . it would be worse than if I had accused him of raping an old woman of ninety-nine years, weighing ninety pounds . . . blind in one eye and lame in the hip."[41]

Franklin's authorial voice begins by scorning the animality of the youth who attempted to ravish the old woman and then, adopting a tone of condescending cynicism, imagines how his miserable crime could possibly have been more outrageous. The superior posture is perfectly embodied in the verse form Franklin chose—the heroic couplet, itself a replication of the finely balanced cadences of eighteenth-century formal decorum. It is as if the outrageous words were set to the music of a precise, stately, and elaborate minuet. The godlike speaker disdains mankind's carnality. As usual with his bagatelles, Franklin did not print this one. He wrote the poem for private circulation in manuscript copies, though he may have printed a few on a small broadside instead of writing out duplicates. (That was his later practice with the French bagatelles.) A copy fell into the hands of Andrew Bradford, who printed it as an anonymous poem in the *American Weekly Mercury* on 15 September 1743.

The Olympian speaker opened by declaring that necrophilia would have been preferable to the youth's action:

> Unhappy Youth, that could not longer stay,
> Till by old Age thy Choice had dy'd away;

> A few Days more had given to thy Arms,
> Free from the Laws, her aged Lump of Charms,
> Which, tho' defunct, might feel not less alive
> Than we imagine Maids of Eighty-five; (ll. 1–6)

The narrator posed another grotesque possibility: if only the youth had waited until the old woman had become completely blind:

> Or hadst thou staid till t'other Eye was gone,
> Thou mightst have lov'd and jogg'd securely on. (ll. 7–8)

The poet then transformed himself into a condescending apologist for the criminal scum. The subject and tone shift from disgust at the salaciousness of the young man and of mankind to a lawyer's imagined mock apology for the crime. The persona asks, given the lascivious animality of mankind, is this degenerate so different from us? In a world where bestiality and the rape of young girls exist, should not this poor sod be pardoned?

> Yet may thy Council urge this prudent Plea,
> That by one Crime, thou has avoided three;
> For had a Mare or Sow att[r]ack'd thy Love,
> No human Form to save thy Life would move;
> Or had thy Lust been offer'd to a Male,
> All Vindications would and ought to fail;
> Or hadst thou sought a blooming Virgin's Rape,
> Thou shouldst not from the Penalty escape: (ll. 9–16)

Finally, the other person involved, the old German woman, is considered and scorned by the speaker:

> But when the Object is long past her Flow'r,
> And brings no County-Charge, and wants no Dow'r;
> Who, slighted all her Life, would fain be ravish'd,
> Thou shouldst be pit'd for thy Love so lavish'd. (ll. 17–20)

Franklin's speaker, like that of Jonathan Swift and many great satirists, ends by disdaining the animality of mankind, including himself. One is reminded that John Adams wrote Thomas Jefferson an anecdote wherein Franklin scoffed about humans, even philosophers, as supposedly rational persons: they would happily abandon their abstruse thoughts in favor of gnawing "a morsel of damn'd Hogs arse."[42]

Though it may at first seem surprising that Franklin also scorned the victim of the crime, evidently rumors had reached him that the old German woman enticed the youth. Both the *Mercury* and the *Gazette* reported the trial's outcome. The 29 September *Gazette* said: "Yesterday William Coulter, a likely young Fellow of about 22 Years of Age, was tried at a Court of Oyer and Terminer, on an Indictment for ravishing a miserable old Dutch Woman of fourscore. The Jury acquitted him of the Rape, but found him guilty of an Assault." The *Mercury* did not give the "fourscore" age, but said the young man was found "guilty of an Assault with Intent to ravish." Fifteen months later, the 18 December 1744 *Gazette* reported: "We hear that the old Dutch Woman, that prosecuted the young Fellow for a Rape, some time since, is lately married." Franklin added no comment.

"Old Mistresses Apologue"

Another bawdy piece also reveals a strange fictive world. Franklin's "Old Mistresses Apologue" or "Advice to a Young Man on the Choice of a Mistress" (25 June 1745) circulated among a group of literary friends. No printed copy survives from the eighteenth century, but several eighteenth-century manuscript copies are extant. The bagatelle begins as a letter addressed to "My dear Friend," supposedly in reply to a request for a medicine to diminish the friend's "violent natural Inclinations" (i.e., his sexual lust). Adopting the pose of a fatherly sage, Franklin responded that "Marriage is the proper Remedy." He celebrated matrimony, saying that a husband and wife are "more likely to succeed in the World. A single Man has not nearly the Value he would have in that State of Union. He is an incomplete Animal. He resembles the odd Half of a Pair of Scissars. If you get a prudent healthy Wife, your Industry in your Profession, with her good OEconomy, will be a Fortune sufficient." Thus ends the utilitarian and prudential argument of the wise, old persona.

At the new paragraph, the speaker becomes an experienced roué. "I repeat my former Advice, that in all your Amours you should *prefer old Women to young ones.*" He then gives eight reasons. The first reason partially continues the speaker's initial pose as an elderly sage with utilitarian and complaisant social values: "Because as they have more Knowledge of the World and their Minds are better stor'd with Observations, their Conversation is more improving and more lastingly agreable." Second, an older woman will do numerous favors for the hedonistic and somewhat sybaritic young man: "They learn to do a 1000 Services small and great, and are the most tender and useful of all Friends when you are sick."

The third reason begins the direct sexual references while continuing utilitarian considerations: "Because there is no hazard of Children, which irregularly produc'd may be attended with much Inconvenience." The fourth reason confirms the speaker's persona as a seasoned roué, the master of a double life, a clever deceiver: "Because thro' more Experience, they are more prudent and discreet in conducting an Intrigue to prevent Suspicion." It also suggests that the speaker is a trickster—which indeed becomes one of the dominant impressions at the end of the piece.

With the next reason, the shape-shifter transformed himself into a satyr, an embodiment of lecherousness, covered with a skein of rationality—a satyr hid-

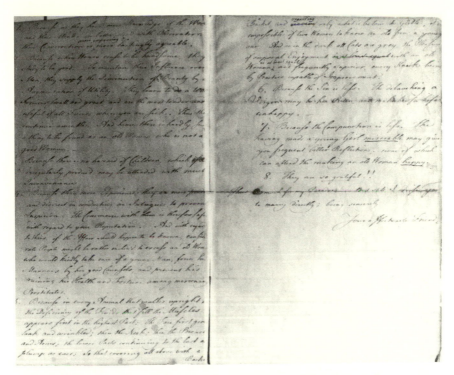

Figure 34. Franklin's manuscript containing eight reasons for preferring an old mistress to a young one, from "Old Mistresses Apologue," 25 June 1745. The most ribald of Franklin's essays did not appear in any collection of his works until 1961, when it was published in The Papers of Benjamin Franklin *(3:30–31).*

The few revisions may be of interest. In reason #3, the cancelled last word in the first line is probably "if." The cancelled word on the top of the second page is probably "viewing." In line 4, after "Enjoyment," the cancelled words are "is least equal," which is inserted in the following line. Courtesy, Rosenbach Museum and Library, Philadelphia.

ing under the rational diction of science: "Because in every Animal that walks upright, the Deficiency of the Fluids that fill the Muscles appears first in the highest Part: The Face first grows lank and wrinkled; then the Neck; then the Breast and Arms; the lower Parts continuing to the last as plump as ever: So that covering all above with a Basket, and regarding only what is below the Girdle, it is impossible of two Women to know an old from a young one. And as in the dark all Cats are grey, the Pleasure of corporal Enjoyment with an old Woman is at least equal, and frequently superior, every Knack being by Practice capable of Improvement." The metamorphosis is complete. The kindly elder sage has become the connoisseur of lechery and animality, "every Knack being by Practice capable of Improvement." That statement reflects back on the "1000 Services small and great" and makes one think that they include "Knacks" of sexual feats. The denial of individuality and of mind ("regarding only what is below the Girdle") reduces humans to sexual machines.

But "Old Mistresses Apologue" is not a satire of humanity. The tone and voice are light. It is a hoax and a joke, though with some overtones of the disdain for humanity revealed by "An Apology for the Young Man in Gaol" and by the great satires of the Revolutionary period, like "The Sale of the Hessians" (1777) and the "Supplement to the *Boston Independent Chronicle*" (1782). The speaker, however, is not superior, and the persona is comfortable in his shape-shifting role. Further, Franklin would have expected his contemporaries to recognize that his fifth reason echoed popular folklore. He knew the sentiments not only from popular culture, but also from his favorite book of proverbs, Thomas Fuller's *Gnomologia* (1732), no. 5396: "Regarding only what is below the girdle, it is impossible of two Women to know an old one from a young one. In the dark all Cats are grey." Franklin used Fuller more than any other single source in compiling *Poor Richard*.[43]

In the sixth and seventh reasons, the satyr shifts back to posing as an old expert on affairs of the heart: "Because the Sin is less" and "because the Compunction is less. The having made a young Girl *miserable* may give you frequent bitter Reflections; none of which can attend the making an old Woman *happy*." The last statement leads naturally into a celebration of sexuality and a blow against the double standard. Old women as well as old men are lustful animals: "8thly and Lastly, They are *so grateful!!*" The sage ends abruptly, "But still I advise you to marry directly; being sincerely Your affectionate Friend."

"Old Mistresses Apologue" reflects eighteenth-century literary modes and attitudes. It has at least two sources. The first is popular folklore as reflected in the saying from Fuller noted above. The second is a pamphlet titled *A Young Man's Reasons for Marrying an Old Woman in a Letter to His Friend*.[44] The London pamphlet was listed among the new books in the *Gentleman's Magazine* for May 1745. Since the *Gentleman's Magazine* for May would have been published in London in June, Franklin could hardly have heard of it in Philadelphia by 25 June. Perhaps Franklin saw an earlier unrecorded printing or heard of the piece before its publication. Or perhaps Franklin wrote "Old Mistresses Apologue" at a date later than 25 June 1745, though that date appears in Franklin's hand on the key manuscript. Or perhaps both the pamphlet and Franklin's bagatelle derive from another source. Franklin shows no indebtedness whatever to the formal and dreary style or to the pedagogical persona of the boring, forty-five-page London pamphlet. If the pamphlet's title inspired him, Franklin changed the argument from marrying an old woman to choosing an old mistress. Whether or not Franklin knew the pamphlet, its existence shows that such works as "Advice to a Young Man on the Choice of a Mistress" existed in the eighteenth century. Unlike its possible, dreary inspiration, Franklin's "Old Mistresses Apologue" is a small masterpiece of eighteenth-century bawdry.

Reflections on Courtship and Marriage

Franklin returned to a favorite subject, a defense of marriage, in an anonymous conduct book titled *Reflections on Courtship and Marriage* (1746).[45] Battle-of-the-sexes essays and poems in the periodicals often satirized and condemned courtship and marriage. Franklin, however, praised marriage repeatedly. In addition to the periodical literature, two previous manuals influenced him, Cotton Mather's *Ornaments for the Daughters of Zion* (republished in 1741 at the urging of George Whitefield), and Jonathan Swift's *Letter to a Very Young Lady on Her Marriage*. Franklin reacted against both. Mather's roles for women were based on the Bible. Swift's advice was directed to wealthy persons and were not pertinent to Franklin's American audience. Both were comparatively condescending to women. Franklin emphasized friendship, ethics, and middle-class values, and he considered the role of men as well as women in marriage. He nevertheless reprinted Swift at the end of *Reflections*, perhaps partly so the curious reader could compare the differences between the two authors. Though Franklin has passages of typical eighteenth-century sexism, his conduct book is more modern and less misogynist than those of Mather, Swift, or Franklin's slightly later contemporaries.[46]

After an advertisement from the publisher (i.e., Franklin), *Reflections on Courtship and Marriage* contained two letters, the first on courtship, the second on marriage. The persona of the anonymous speaker in both letters is the same. The speaker describes a dispute concerning the advantages and disadvantages of marriage and then agrees with the person who defended the benefits of marriage. The speaker, however, granted his opponent's position that the usual education for women was inferior. Then he took up five topics for a proper courtship. First, do not marry for money. It leads to a flat and insipid relationship. Second, do not marry simply for sexual passion. Infatuation soon is gratified, and thereafter the attraction dwindles. Third, courtship should be sincere and honest. Fourth, flattery and bombast, so common not only in novels but also in descriptions of courtship in courtesy books, are false and should be avoided. Last, friendship and companionship were the bases for a lasting and loving relationship, and they were founded on reason, good sense, mutual respect, and empathy. In a postscript, the author noted that he had said nothing of the role of parents in courtship. The courting couple should be considerate of the parents' wishes, but finally the persons who were courting should, if adults, do what they think best.

In the second section of the above letter, Franklin, the anonymous author, portrayed the infatuated suitor's condition:

> An amorous Complexion, a lively Imagination, and a generous Temper, are so
> apt to be charm'd with an agreeable Person, the insinuating Accomplishments
> of Musick and Dancing, *un bon Grace*, and a *Gaieté de Coeur*, that it is instantly
> transported, sighs, languishes, dies for Possession. In this *distempered* Condition,

and *amorous Fit* of Madness, his sanguine and heated Imagination paints her out to him, in all the romantick Lights of an *Arcadian Princess*, an *Angel Form*, and a *heavenly Mind*, the *Pride of Nature*, and the *Joy of Man*, a *Source* of *immortal Pleasures*, *Raptures* that will *never satiate*, *Bliss uninterrupted*, and *Transports too big for Expression.*————Bloated with all these nonsensical Ideas or *Chimeras*, worked up to a raging Fit of Enthusiasm, he falls down and worships this *Idol* of his own intoxicated Brain, runs to her, talks Fustian and Tragedy by wholesale. Miss blushes, looks down, admires his Eloquence, pities the dying Swain, catches the Infection, and *consents*, if *Papa* and *Mamma* will give *theirs*." (11–12)

The paragraph is a tour de force. The diction, with its two French phrases, reinforces and mocks the overblown emotionality being portrayed; then, following the dash, the straightforward criticism of the excessive sentiments ("—Bloated") confirms the ridicule; and finally, the homely, colloquial diction of "Papa" and "Mamma" serves to undercut the earlier inflated style, highfalutin' phrases, and French diction. Franklin's attitude, though not his persona's, was that the high-blown style and the French words were as feigned as the emotions being satirized. The writer burlesques the "bloated" style and foreign phrases. In that paragraph, Franklin expressed his commonsense attitudes through style as well as substance.

The second letter considered the marriage relationship, also in five parts. First, the author warned against attempting prerogative and dominion in marriage. Second, quarrels should be avoided. Third, marriage partners should cultivate the reciprocal care and pleasure of one another. Fourth, the married couple should be modest and decent in public and private. And fifth, both husband and wife should manage their respective business with prudence and discretion, consulting one another and sharing burdens and pleasures. In conclusion, the author celebrated marriage but reminded the reader that flaws and limitations were synonymous with the human condition.

In the first section of the second letter, Franklin said that though the law of a country may give the man "*tyrannick* and *arbitrary Power* . . . over his Wife" (or "the reverse"), such power is not "derived from *Reason* or *Nature*." Marriage is a "voluntary and mutual Contract between the Sexes, the End or Design of which is, or should be, their joint Happiness." It was "absurd and ridiculous to suppose or conclude" that by marrying either party consented to bind themselves over "to an *imperious* or *tyrannical Sway*." Franklin asserted that "a tyrannick and arbitrary Power . . . is contrary to the Will and Happiness of any rational Being; and must in consequence render a matrimonial Life uncomfortable and miserable" (30–31). As he wrote Emma Thompson on 8 February 1777, "you, with all other Women who smart or have smarted under the Tyranny of a bad Husband, ought to be fix'd in *Revolution* Principles" (23:297). Men and women were equal partners in marriage.

In the fourth section of the second letter, Franklin used the "argument by contrast" and condemned uncleanness in dress and person. The passage has been the one in the pamphlet most frequently quoted:

> This Negligence and Dirtiness of Person, (if we expect or desire a Man to love us at the same Time) is taxing him with the Want of his Senses, with the Taste and Appetite of a Hog, whose Joy is Filth. Let us survey the Morning Dress of some Women. Down Stairs they come, pulling up their ungarter'd, dirty Stockings—Slip-shod, with naked Heels peeping out—No Stays or other decent Conveniency, but all *Flip Flop*—A Sort of a Clout thrown about the Neck, without Form or Decency—A tumbled, discoloured Mob, or Night Cap, half on, and half off, with the frowsy Hair, hanging in sweaty Ringlets, staring like *Medusa* with her Serpents—Shrugging up her Petticoats, that are sweeping the Ground, and scarce ty'd on,—Hands unwashed—Teeth furr'd—and Eyes crusted:—But I beg your Pardon, I'll go no farther with this sluttish Picture, which I am afraid has already turned your Stomach. If the *Copy*, and but an Imperfect one it is, be so shocking to us, what think you must the *Original* be to the poor Wretch her Husband, who, perhaps, for some Hours every Day in the Week, has the comfortable Sight and Odour of this Tatterdemalion. God help his Stomach! (40–41)[47]

From the declamatory style, Franklin returned to a dispassionate presentation: "A Wife that is desirous of maintaining herself in the Affections of a Man of Sense and Spirit, should take as much Care of the Neatness of her Person, as if she was to be every Day a Bride; and whoever neglects this Conduct, must blame themselves, if their Husbands grow cool and indifferent; for it has a natural Tendency to make a Man so. It debases the Character of a Wife, and renders her cheap and unlovely" (41–42).

The final section recommended that both parties manage their respective business with discretion. The subject that hardly seems to belong in *Reflections on Courtship and Marriage* is the long passage on how a man should conduct his business (44–46). Though an unusual subject for a conduct book, it is characteristic of Franklin's attention to the practicalities of life.

Franklin's advocacy of cleanliness above is typical of conduct books, used by Swift—and by John Adams in letter of advice (a draft of an essay) written to his "nieces." When Franklin took up the old topic, he enlivened it in the vivid presentation of the "tatterdemalion" above. But then, as so often, Franklin thought of what the opposite entailed and wrote an ironic and humorous skit on two kinds of compulsive behavior of some good housekeepers. The first concerned orderliness. One "Fault is that *Bigotry* and *Passion* for Neatness, which makes a Woman fretful and uneasy at every accidental or unavoidable Speck of Dirt, or the least Disordering of her Furniture: You must rub your Shoes till the Bottoms of your Feet are almost sore, before you are permitted to enter a Room. Then so many nonsensical Exhortations and impertinent Questions are propos'd, that one might enter a Garrison Town in War-time with less ado. Such as, *Pray don't meddle with that*, and *Pray don't put this out of its Place*, that one would think there was a Spell on all the Furniture, or a Man was going to run away with Part of it" (48). The comparisons to garrisons in wartime and magic spells are extravagant and amusing. Did anyone complain of the excesses of middle-class household virtues earlier? Perhaps so, but I haven't read them.

Franklin moved on to the topic of cleanliness—and of overdoing it: another inconvenience "is the *ill timing* of *Cleanliness*, and the carrying it to such *Extreams*, that a Man's House is made an uneasy, and almost *useless*, Habitation to him. Some Women have such amphibious Dispositions, that one would think they chose to be half of their Lives in Water; there's such a Clatter of Pails and Brushes, such Inundations in every Room, that a Man can't find a dry Place for the Sole of his Foot; so that what should tend to make a Man's House an agreeable and wholesome Dwelling, becomes so *dangerous* and *unpleasant*, that the *Desire* of *Health* and *Peace* drives him out of it. And these Overflowings of Neatness are often so *ill timed*, that a Man's Business is interrupted, and his Meals made uncomfortable by 'em" (47–48). Moderation and good sense were more important than a painstaking fastidiousness concerning a virtue.

In concluding, Franklin celebrated marriage and praised a good wife: "a Wife thus *wisely* and *discreetly* filling her Sphere of Action. What *Veneration!* What *Praise!* What *Love* and *Esteem*, can sufficiently equal her *Merit!* The Character of a Wife, can scarcely shine in a more exalted Point of Light, nor do a more publick Honour to herself and her Husband. Whoever possesses such a One, *Joy* will *sparkle* in his Eye, and *Pleasure* fill his Breast" (51). The celebration is generous—and rare in courtesy literature. Few writers celebrated marriage and women with such high praise. Franklin did. And having done so, he characteristically recalled the normal realities. "'Tis a Truth as universally experienced as owned, that no State of Life is exempt from the Alternatives of Pleasure and Pain, the bitter and sweet; and that a Perfection of Happiness is not the Lot of Humanity" (52). As Poor Richard said, "The Golden Age never was the present Age" (November 1750).

Franklin's *Reflections on Courtship and Marriage* became a popular conduct book, with sixteen editions to 1807. John Adams read it in January 1759, the year that a sixth edition was published. It may have influenced Adams's draft of an essay on the topic, though Adams was generally more old-fashioned in his suggestions for the conduct of young ladies—except for his surprising advocacy of bundling—but then, when Adams drafted the essay, he was an unmarried young man of twenty-five and probably yearned for a little bundling. Having suggested bundling, however, he broke off, perhaps alarmed at what he had written.[48]

REBUTTAL OF ANDREW BAXTER

Franklin took up technical questions in philosophy and theology again after Thomas Hopkinson praised Andrew Baxter's *Enquiry into the Nature of the*

Human Soul in the Junto one night early in October 1746. Baxter attempted to prove the existence of God and the human soul from Newtonian physics. Hopkinson judged it "the plainest and clearest Thing that ever was wrote on such a dark Subject." Franklin read part of it and gave it up. "The Author lays down the Vis Inertiae of Matter as a Foundation on which all Philosophy and even Religion are to be built" (3:91). But Franklin doubted that the *vis inertiae* existed. Examining several of Baxter's arguments, he thought that Baxter failed to distinguish between a *great* Force apply'd *at once*, and a *small* one *continually* applied. Franklin attempted to prove mathematically that "the greatest assignable Mass of Matter will give way to [or be moved by] the least assignable Force." Where then, "is the mighty *Vis Inertiae?*" Franklin also said that if two globes, each as large as the sun were "exactly equiposed in Jove's Ballance," and if a mosquito landed on one, would it "not give Motion to" both suns, "causing one to descend and the other to rise?" If such a motion could be produced by a mosquito, where is the "Vis Inertiae?" (3:85–86). A. Owen Aldridge has noted that Franklin did not "recognize the difference between velocity and acceleration," and that he later came to accept the *vis inertiae*, which was a principle of Newtonian physics.[49]

Baxter had concluded God and the soul existed, and claimed "the *Atheist* hath a desperate Cause in Hand." Franklin quoted Baxter's sentence, changing only *Atheist* to *Deist*: "if the Doctrine of the Immateriality of the Soul, and the Existence of God, and of Divine Providence are demonstrable from *no plainer* Principles, the *Deist* hath a desperate Cause in Hand." That is, if this argument were the best that could be adduced to prove the existence of God, the believer had "a desperate Cause in Hand."

Franklin added a brief paragraph on cosmology or creation. "If God was before all Things, and fill'd all Space; then, when he form'd what we call Matter, he must have done it out of his own Thinking immaterial Substance. The same, tho' he had not fill'd all Space; if it be true that *Ex nihilo nihil fit*. From hence may we not draw this Conclusion, That if any Part of Matter does not at present act and think, 'tis not from an Incapacity in its Nature but from a positive Restraint" (3:88).

Earlier, in the "Philoclerus" letter of 1730, Franklin had anticipated this position when he suggested that "Spirit can act upon Matter." And later in life, Franklin often stated that "mind would one day become *omnipotent* [emphasis mine] over matter." Though the English philosopher and novelist William Godwin believed that Franklin meant that undreamed-of labor-saving devices would be invented, Franklin may have been suggesting that the mind and matter were synonymous and that mind governed matter.[50] Franklin's use of the word *omnipotent* rather than a word like *control* seems more suitable diction for theology than for mechanics.

Franklin wrote in the *Autobiography* that he began to doubt of revelation itself after reading "Some Books against Deism . . . preached at Boyle's Lectures"

(A 58). Among the most famous of Boyle's lectures was Samuel Clarke's *Discourse Concerning . . . Natural Religion and . . . Christian Revelation* (1706), which quoted the arguments of four kinds of deists in order to refute them. Franklin no doubt read Clark, if not in his father's library then later. The minister's first proposition was, "It is absolutely and undeniably certain that something has existed from all eternity." Clark quoted, of course, the commonplace that something could not come from nothing: *Ex nihilo nihil fit.* The dictum was fundamental in Atomistic or Epicurean philosophy, cited repeatedly by Lucretius. Franklin read numerous works concerning cosmology, including Lucretius, but Clarke's alone would have been sufficient background for Franklin's argument concerning the sentience of all matter. Franklin concluded his letter to Hopkinson by expressing his reservations concerning metaphysics: "The great Uncertainty I have found in that Science; the wide Contradictions and endless Disputes it affords; and the horrible Errors I led myself into when a young Man, by drawing a Chain of plain Consequences as I thought them, from true Principles, have given me a Disgust to what I was once extreamly fond of" (P 3:88–89). Franklin probably remembered and agreed with Pascal, who scorned "Metaphysical Proofs of God."[51]

Franklin nevertheless continued throughout his life to take up major questions of theology, though in the future he did so mainly in passing. Ironically, James Bowdoin confirmed Franklin's suspicions of the possible "endless Disputes" in metaphysics on 27 January 1755 by sending him several thousand words of carefully reasoned thought concerning Franklin's approximately eighty words on the sentience of matter (P 5:483–89).

"The Speech of Miss Polly Baker"

"The Speech of Miss Polly Baker" is the third of Franklin's ribald compositions during the mid-1740s.[52] Longer, more complex, and more artful than either "An Apology for the Young Man in Gaol" or "Old Mistresses Apologue," "The Speech of Miss Polly Baker" first appeared in a London newspaper, the *General Advertiser*, on 15 April 1747. No one knows how the editor of the newspaper, Henry Woodfall, came by a copy. It must have been circulating in manuscript copies. Ten English newspapers and the three most popular English magazines (the *Gentleman's Magazine*, *London Magazine*, and *Scots Magazine*) all reprinted it within a month. Practically no other eighteenth-century writing achieved such immediate popularity. It also appeared in several American newspapers, first in the *Boston Weekly Post Boy* (20 July 1747). From the late eighteenth century to the present, the speech has occasionally turned up as an actual speech in histories and in collections of legal documents—ostensibly documenting the Puritan morals of colonial New England.

Two texts exist. The second originally appeared in the (Annapolis) *Maryland Gazette* on 11 August 1747. Editor Jonas Green prefaced it with a comment: "The following very famous *SPEECH* has been published in the *London* and

The following very famous SP ECH has been published in the *London* and *Gentleman's Magazines* for *April* past, as well as in some other *British* Papers; but was there printed incorrectly, which I suppose was occasioned by the Mutilation it suffer'd, in passing through the Hands of Transcribers before it reach'd the Press in *London:* And happening to have a correct Copy of it by me, I cannot think it amiss to give it my Readers, not doubting it's favourable Reception.

The SPEECH of Miss Polly Baker, before a Court of Judicature, at Connecticut in New England, where she was prosecuted the fifth Time for having a Bastard Child; which influenced the Court to dispense with her Punishment, and induced one of her Judges to marry her the next Day.

MAY it please the Honourable Bench to indulge me a few Words: I am a poor unhappy Woman; who have no Money to Fee Lawyers to plead for me, being hard put to it to get a tolerable Living. I shall not trouble your Honours with long Speeches; for I have not the presumption to expect, that you may, by any Means, be prevailed on to deviate in your Sentence from the Law, in my Favour. All I humbly hope is, that your Honours wou'd charitably move the Governor's Goodness on my Behalf, that my Fine may be remitted. This is the Fifth Time, Gentlemen, that I have been dragg'd before your Courts on the same Account; twice I have paid heavy Fines, and twice have been brought to public Punishment, for want of Money to pay those Fines. This may have been agreeable to the Laws; I do not dispute it: But since Laws are sometimes unreasonable in themselves, and therefore repealed; and others bear too hard on the Subject in particular Circumstances; and therefore there is left a Power somewhere to dispense with the Execution of them; I take the Liberty to say, that I think this Law, by which I am punished, is both unreasonable in itself, and particularly severe with regard to me, who have always lived an inoffensive Life in the Neighbourhood where I was born, and defy my Enemies (if I have any) to say I ever wrong'd Man, Woman, or Child. Abstracted from the Law, I cannot conceive (may it please your Honour) what the Nature of my Offence is. I have brought five fine Children into the World, at the Risque of my Life: I have maintained them well by my own Industry, without burthening the Township, and could have done it better, if it had not been for the heavy Charges and Fines I have paid. Can it be a Crime (in the Nature of Things I mean) to add to the Number of the King's Subjects, in a new Country that really wants People? I own I should think it rather a Praise worthy, than a Punishable Action. I have debauch'd no other Woman's Husband, nor inticed any innocent Youth: These Things I never was charged with; nor has any one the least cause of Complaint against me, unless, perhaps, the Minister, or the Justice, because I have had Children without being Married, by which they have miss'd a Wedding Fee. But, can even this be a Fault of mine? I appeal to your Honours. You are pleased to allow I don't want Sense; but I must be stupid to the last Degree, not to prefer the honourable State of Wedlock, to the Condition I have lived in. I always was, and still am, willing to enter into it; I doubt not my Behaving well in it, having all the Industry, Frugality, Fertility, and Skill in Oeconomy, appertaining to a good Wife's Character. I defy any Person to say I ever Refused an Offer of that Sort: On the contrary, I readily Consented to the only Proposal of Marriage that ever was made me, which was when I was a Virgin; but too easily confiding in the Person's Sincerity that made it, I unhappily lost my own Honour, by trusting to his; for he got me with Child, and then forsook me. That very Person you all know; he is now become a Magistrate of this County; and I had hopes he would have appeared this Day on the Bench, and have endeavoured to moderate the Court in my Favour; then I should

have scorn'd to have mention'd it; but I must Complain of it as unjust and unequal, that my Betrayer and Undoer, the first Cause of all my Faults and Miscarriages (if they must be deem'd such) should be advanced to Honour and Power, in the same Government that punishes my Misfortunes with Stripes and Infamy. I shall be told, 'tis like, that were there no Act of Assembly in the Case, the Precepts of Religion are violated by my Transgressions. If mine, then, is a religious Offence, leave it, Gentlemen, to religious Punishments. You have already excluded me from all the Comforts of your Church Communion: Is not that sufficient? You believe I have offended Heaven, and must suffer eternal Fire: Will not that be sufficient? What need is there, then, of your additional Fines and Whipping? I own, I do not think as you do; for, if I thought, what you call a Sin, was really such, I would not presumptuously commit it. But how can it be believed, that Heaven is angry at my having Children, when, to the little done by me towards it, God has been pleased to add his divine Skill and admirable Workmanship in the Formation of their Bodies, and crown'd it by furnishing them with rational and immortal Souls? Forgive me Gentlemen, if I talk a little extravagantly on these Matters; I am no Divine: But if you, great Men, * must be making Laws, do not turn natural and useful Actions into Crimes, by your Prohibition. Reflect a little on the horrid Consequences of this Law in particular: What Numbers of procur'd Abortions! and how many distress'd Mothers have been driven, by the Terror of Punishment and public Shame, to imbrue, contrary to Nature, their own trembling Hands in the Blood of their helpless Offspring! Nature would have induc'd them to nurse it up with a Parent's Fondness. 'Tis the Law therefore, 'tis the Law itself that is guilty of all these Barbarities and Murders. Repeal it then, Gentlemen; let it be expung'd for ever from your Books: And on the other hand, take into your wise Consideration, the great and growing Number of Batchelors in the Country, many of whom, from the mean Fear of the Expence of a Family, have never sincerely and honourably Courted a Woman in their Lives; and by their Manner of Living, leave unproduced (which I think is little better than Murder) Hundreds of their Posterity to the Thousandth Generation. Is not theirs a greater Offence against the Public Good, than mine? Compel them then, by a Law, either to Marry, or pay double the Fine of Fornication every Year. What must poor young Women do, whom Custom has forbid to solicit the Men, and who cannot force themselves upon Husbands, when the Laws take no Care to provide them any, and yet severely punish if they do their Duty without them? Yes, Gentlemen, I venture to call it a Duty; 'tis the Duty of the first and great Command of Nature, and of Nature's God, *Increase and multiply;* A Duty, from the steady Performance of which nothing has ever been able to deter me; but for it's Sake, I have hazarded the Loss of the public Esteem, and frequently incurr'd public Disgrace and Punishment; and therefore ought, in my humble Opinion, instead of a Whipping, to have a Statue erected to my Memory.

* *Turning to some Gentlemen of the Assembly, then in Court.*

HAGUE, April 25.

IT is very evident, by the advices which we receive by the way of Venice, of Poland, and even of Vienna itself, that whatever promises or declarations the Turks may make, they seem to be preparing for an irruption into the Hungarian dominions; and some private letters speak of an incursion already made, by direction of the bashaw of Belgrade, under pretence of making reprisals for some money that was seized, belonging to a Greek merchant. We the less wonder at this, because we know that besides other Emissaries, the French court have an ambassador at Constantinople, the most capable of conducting

---

Figure 35. The American text of "The Speech of Miss Polly Baker," Maryland Gazette, 11 August 1747. The speech was Franklin's first international literary success. After appearing in a London newspaper of 15 April 1747, it was immediately reprinted in several other London newspapers before appearing in the two most popular English magazines of the day. Franklin often circulated copies of his writings among friends, sometimes making changes for a particular audience. Both the English and the American texts of the "Speech" satirized the double standard for the rich and the poor, and for men and women, and both also contained covert deistic propaganda.

The American version that editor Jonas Green of the Maryland Gazette published assumed the reader's greater familiarity with colonial America and its institutions. Thus the asterisk and the note in the American text are directed to legislators who make the laws, whereas in the English text it would seem that Polly is addressing the judges. The American text more severely criticized New England's blue laws. If such criticism had appeared in England, Franklin probably thought that English readers would have applied it to all the colonies and that it would have supported English anti-American attitudes. Courtesy, Maryland Hall of Records, Annapolis.

Gentleman's Magazines for *April* past, as well as in some other *British* Papers; but was there printed incorrectly, which I suppose was occasioned by the Mutilation it suffer'd, in passing through the Hands of Transcribers before it reach'd the Press in *London*: And happening to have a correct Copy of it by me, I cannot think it amiss to give it my Readers, not doubting it's favourable Reception." Actually, only one difference between the two texts seems to me an error by a transcriber; the several other differences all result from the piece being intended for different audiences. The version published in London was intended for an English audience; the copy that Jonas Green published was written for an American audience. The English text contains information that Americans all knew, information superfluous for an American audience; the English text also has errors concerning America—ones that an English reader would not recognize but an American reader would. I cite the American text, for I find it slightly superior for the reasons noted below. In the title, the English text adds after Connecticut, "near Boston," thus reading "at Connecticut near Boston in New England." For Americans, "near Boston" was unnecessary; Franklin dropped it from the American text.[53]

The Speech, Polly's Arguments, and Franklin's Humor

The speech is a humorous hoax. Students laugh aloud when they hear the title. "*The SPEECH of Miss* Polly Baker, *Before a Court of Judicature, at* Connecticut *in* New England, *where she was prosecuted the fifth Time for having a Bastard Child; which influenced the Court to dispense with her Punishment, and induced one of her Judges to marry her the next Day.*" The reversal turns the world turned upside down. Instead of being punished, the five-time offender went free, and one of the judges married her. The outcome is totally unexpected, the readers are relieved, and their curiosity is aroused.

The risqué subject matter (the trial of a prostitute) lends itself to smutty sexual innuendos and puns, and Franklin could be wonderfully bawdy. The speech opens: "May it please the Honourable Bench to indulge me a few Words: I am a poor unhappy Woman; who have no Money to Fee Lawyers to plead for me, being hard put to it to get a tolerable Living." I believe that the Franklin who at age sixteen wrote that "Women are prime Causes of a great many Male Enormities" (P 1:19) would also subtly pun on the prostitute's way of earning a living: she has it "hard put" to her "to get a tolerable Living." At the same time Franklin is establishing her ethos: She is hardworking, respectful, and humble. The persona, Polly, is entirely serious; Franklin's underlying voice is comic and makes the sexual jokes. Polly Baker and Franklin usually agree, but Franklin finally satirizes Polly.

Polly said: "I shall not trouble your Honours with long Speeches; for I have not the presumption to expect, that you may, by any Means, be prevailed on to deviate in your Sentence from the Law, in my Favour. All I humbly hope is, that your Honours would charitably move the Governor's Goodness on my Behalf, that my Fine may be remitted. This is the Fifth Time, Gentlemen, that I have been dragg'd before your Courts on the same Account; twice I have paid heavy Fines, and twice have been brought to public Punishment, for want of Money to pay those Fines." Franklin may pun on the source of her income: twice she lacked "want of"/wanton money to pay. He is also establishing her pathos: she is poor, ostracized, and punished. Franklin implicitly criticizes the double standard of the judicial system for having one law for the poor and another for the rich.

Polly Baker continued, "This may have been agreeable to the Laws; I do not dispute it: But since Laws are sometimes unreasonable in themselves, and therefore repealed; and others bear too hard on the Subject in particular Circumstances; and therefore there is left a Power somewhere to dispense with the Execution of them; I take the Liberty to say, that I think this Law, by which I am punished, is both unreasonable in itself, and particularly severe with regard to me, who have always lived an inoffensive Life in the Neighbourhood where I was born, and defy my Enemies (if I have any) to say I ever wrong'd Man, Woman, or Child." She has continued to establish her ethos (though it violates the stereotypical prostitute that Polly should have such a good character— another example of the world turned upside down): she is "inoffensive" and never wrong'd "Man, Woman, or Child." A possible smutty implication is that every man has gotten at least his money's worth.

Franklin continued with an obvious pun, accentuated by having a rhetorical stop (the opening of a parenthesis) after it: "Abstracted from the Law, I cannot conceive (may it please your Honours) what the Nature of my Offence is. I have brought Five fine Children into the World, at the Risque of my Life: I have maintained them well by my own Industry, without burthening the Township, and could have done it better, if it had not been for the heavy Charges and Fines I have paid." The diction, "Risque," suggests that she has brought those five fine children into the world by her risqué life.

Polly defended her actions: "Can it be a Crime (in the Nature of Things I mean) to add to the Number of the King's Subjects, in a new Country that really wants People? I own I should think it rather a Praise worthy, than a Punishable Action." Polly, like Franklin, believes in philoprogenitiveness and questions the law that punishes her. Both defend prostitution. Franklin had no doubt read Bernard de Mandeville's defense of prostitution, *A Modest Defense of the Public Stews* (1724), which had appeared the year before Franklin arrived in London. Franklin knew Mandeville (in fact, his description of Mandeville at his favorite tavern is the only private view of him) and was influenced by him.

Polly defended herself: "I have debauch'd no other Woman's Husband, nor inticed any innocent Youth: These Things I never was charged with; nor has any one the least cause of Complaint against me, unless, perhaps the Minister, or the Justice, because I have had Children without being Married, by which they have miss'd a Wedding Fee." Thus she amplified her earlier statement that she always gave good money's worth and never wronged man, woman, or child. (The American text inserted "innocent" before "Youth," thereby making the text somewhat more realistic; naturally prostitutes occasionally had youthful customers.) Franklin had also subtly introduced a critical note about ministers and justices, suggesting they actually performed their duties for money. Similarly, Silence Dogood No. 4 had criticized Harvard students who supposedly became ministers for the money.

Claiming she was innocent, Polly asked, "But, can even[54] this be a Fault of mine? I appeal to your Honours. You are pleased to allow I don't want Sense; but I must be stupid to the last Degree, not to prefer the honourable State of Wedlock, to the Condition I have lived in. I always was, and still am, willing to enter into it; I doubt not my Behaving well in it, having all the Industry, Frugality, Fertility, and Skill in Oeconomy, appertaining to a good Wife's Character." Polly's praise of herself is becoming stronger, and Franklin repeated his joke about her "Industry" in her profession. Moreover, including "Fertility" in the catalogue of otherwise prudential wifely virtues ("Industry, Frugality, and Skill in Oeconomy") humorously clashes with the rest of the catalogue.

Waxing more eloquent, Polly asserted: "I defy any Person to say I ever Refused an Offer of that Sort: On the contrary, I readily Consented to the only Proposal of Marriage that ever was made me, which was when I was a Virgin; but too easily confiding in the Person's Sincerity that made it, I unhappily lost my own Honour, by trusting to his; for he got me with Child, and then forsook me." When Polly argues that she never "Refused an Offer of that Sort," one at first thinks she is saying that she never refused a sexual liaison. Franklin meant the joke. He also, like Polly, protested against the double standard for men and women, which penalized and punished Polly but ignored the man's participation. Franklin had, long ago, assumed complete responsibility for William Franklin—an unusual example of the father, rather than the mother, caring for the illegitimate infant.

Polly Baker inveighed, "That very Person you all know; he is now become a Magistrate of this County; and I had hopes he would have appeared this Day on the Bench, and have endeavoured to moderate the Court in my Favour; then I should have scorn'd to have mention'd it; but I must Complain of it as unjust and unequal, that my Betrayer and Undoer, the first Cause of all my Faults and Miscarriages (if they must be deemed such) should be advanced to Honour and Power, in the same Government that punishes my Misfortunes with Stripes and Infamy." Franklin again followed a pun with a rhetorical pause (opening a parenthesis) to emphasize it. The change in the English text of "County" to "Country" may suggest that the person who first seduced her and who is "now a Magistrate of this Country" (we recall Hamlet, in Ophelia's lap, also punning on "Country matters") is indeed the judge and ruler of her sexual part. But for Americans, familiar with the government structure, "county" is better because more accurate. Franklin and his persona Polly both have continued the satire on the double standard for men and women. Polly has been censured, fined, and punished, while her betrayer and undoer has been advanced to honor and power.

Becoming passionate, Polly declared: "I shall be told, 'tis like, that were there no Act of Assembly in the Case, the Precepts of Religion are violated by my Transgressions; If mine, then, is a religious Offence, leave it, Gentlemen, to religious Punishments. You have already excluded me from all the Comforts of your Church Communion: Is not that sufficient? You believe I have offended Heaven, and must suffer eternal Fire: Will not that be sufficient? What need is there, then, of your additional Fines and Whippings?" Polly Baker and Franklin both argue for the separation of church and state. Morality and law should be separate.

Polly Baker defended her actions: "I own, I do not think as you do; for, if I thought, what you call a Sin, was really such, I would not presumptuously commit it. But how can it be believed, that Heaven is angry at my having Children, when, to the little done by me towards it, God has been pleased to add his divine Skill and admirable Workmanship in the Formation of their Bodies, and crown'd it by furnishing them with rational and immortal Souls?" The fictional Polly is serious and, though in part an obtuse narrator, she shows (as such narrators often do in the foreign observer tradition)[55] overtones of a true moral vision, calling into question the traditional mores and standards of society. She echoes the popular belief in scientific deism, claiming that God is responsible for the creation of infants and for giving them souls.

Now impassioned in her defense, Polly said, "Forgive me Gentlemen, if I talk a little extravagantly on these Matters; I am no Divine: But if you, great Men, [Turning to some Gentlemen of the Assembly, then in Court] must be making Laws, do not turn natural and useful Actions into Crimes, by your Prohibitions. Reflect a little on the horrid Consequences of this Law in particular: What Numbers of procur'd Abortions! And how many distress'd Mothers have been driven, by the Terror of Punishment and public Shame, to imbrue, contrary to Nature, their own trembling Hands in the Blood of their helpless Offspring! Nature would have induc'd them to nurse it up with a Parent's Fondness. 'Tis the Law therefore, 'tis the Law itself that is guilty of all these Barbarities and Murders. Repeal it then, Gentlemen; let it be expung'd for ever from your Books."

Polly has continued her argument that prostitution is no sin unless someone is hurt. Further, both Polly and Franklin contend that the law is responsible for numerous abortions and for distraught mothers killing their infant bastards. Foolish and severe laws have caused terrible crimes. Polly and Franklin both castigate the law's arbitrariness and rigidity. The marginal note in brackets above is unique to the American text. Americans all knew that elected political representatives, not the judges, made the laws. The longish passage beginning "Reflect a little" is also unique to the American text. I suspect that Franklin did not want to include it in a text that would circulate in England because it might add to the English prejudices against America. Franklin enjoyed making fun of New England's blue laws, but he resented the English doing so.

Polly Baker went on: "And on the other hand, take into your wise Consideration, the great and growing Number of Batchelors in the Country, many of whom, from the mean Fear of the Expence of a Family, have never sincerely and honourably Courted a Woman in their Lives; and by their Manner of Living, leave unproduced (which I think is little better than Murder) Hundreds of their Posterity to the Thousandth Generation. Is not theirs a greater Offence against the Public Good, than mine? Compel them then, by a Law, either to Marry, or pay double the Fine of Fornication every Year." Again, Polly and Franklin both object to the double standard. And though they both celebrate the idea of more people, Polly has become carried away with her argument. Franklin undercut her by saying she would create her own arbitrary and harsh laws.

A peroration concluded Polly's speech: "What must poor young Women do, whom Custom have forbid to solicit the Men, and who cannot force themselves upon Husbands, when the Laws take no Care to provide them any; and yet severely punish if they do their Duty without them; Yes, Gentlemen, I venture to call it a Duty; 'tis the Duty of the first and great Command of Nature, and of Nature's God, *Increase and multiply*: A Duty, from the steady Performance of which nothing has ever been able to deter me; but for it's Sake, I have hazarded the Loss of the public Esteem, and frequently incurr'd public Disgrace and Punishment; and therefore ought, in my humble Opinion, instead of a Whipping, to have a Statue erected to my Memory."[56]

Franklin again joked about Polly's attractions and profession. "Custom has forbid" women to solicit the men—but we are reminded that Polly Baker, like other prostitutes, did so. Franklin's speaker Polly thought it was foolish that women could not, like men, court their favorites, and I suspect that Franklin agreed with Polly. Yet there is also the joke—prostitutes do solicit men. When this voluptuous fertility symbol maintains that she should have a "statue erected to my Memory," we think that Franklin may pun about phalluses "erected" in her memory. The passage, "Yes, Gentlemen, I venture to call it a Duty; 'tis the Duty" is unique to the American text and makes the conclusion resounding.

Polly Baker: Classical Rhetoric

"The Speech of Miss Polly Baker" is a mock classical oration, beginning with an *exordium* and a *narratio*, progressing through secondary and primary *partitios*, containing *amplificatios*, *refutatios*, and *digressios*, and concluding with a *peroration*.[57] Jonathan Swift's *Modest Proposal*, like several of his other works, used the oration as a structural mode.[58] Why? And why did Franklin use the form in his Speech of Polly Baker? The oration was a formula that all educated eighteenth-century persons knew. A writer could—as Franklin and Swift did—increase the reader's pleasure by playing with (and against) the audience's expectations of the form. In addition, the order of the arguments and their logic may either burlesque the oration (as Swift and especially Franklin do) or reinforce it. In either case, using the form asks the reader to apply his rhetorical skills (practiced upon classical orations and commencement debates throughout his school years) and thus invites a critical reading. Sophisticated eighteenth-century readers would have recognized "The Speech of Miss Polly Baker" as a mock oration and would have delighted in the ethical arguments (the whore has all the virtues except chastity), the long digressions, the false logic, and the other uses and burlesques of the classical form. For Franklin's educated contemporaries, it added to the fun that an unlearned prostitute delivered in her own defense a classical oration. It, too, exampled the world upside down.

The rhetorical handbooks studied by educated persons from the sixteenth to the nineteenth centuries contained a section on the proofs, which consisted of *ethos*, or establishing the speaker's good character and credibility; *pathos*, or arousing the feelings of the audience; and *logos*, or using arguments, generally syllogistic reasoning, to make a point. Every sentence in the speech contains at least one rhetorical proof. The ethical proof is predominates.

The Speech opens with Polly Baker's establishing her respectful attitude and humble posture: "*MAY* it please the Honourable Bench to indulge me a few Words." She has "not the presumption to expect" that the magistrates will "deviate" from the law in her behalf. She has never done anyone any injury: I "defy my Enemies (if I have any) to say I ever wrong'd Man, Woman or Child." She is hardworking and frugal, a husbandless mother who has "maintained" her children "well" by her "own Industry." She has done a public service by adding "to the Number of the King's Subjects, in a new Country that really wants People." She would make a good wife and has all the skills (and more) "appertaining to a good Wife's Character." She owes her downfall to her too honest and trusting nature: "I unhappily lost my own Honour, by trusting to his." The lover who abandoned her is someone "you all know; he is now become a Magistrate of this County; and I had hopes he would have appeared this Day on the Bench, and have endeavoured to moderate the Court in my Favour; then I should have scorn'd to have mention'd it." She is not a presumptuous sinner, but a partner with God (!) in the production of children. She modestly apologizes for her extravagances in talking about religion: "I am no Divine." And she perseveres in her duty despite overwhelming odds. She is respectful, humble, harmless, industrious, frugal, public-spirited, motherly, trusting, forbearing, enduring, loving, Christian, and dutiful—all of which fully establish Polly Baker's ethical position.

The proof of pathos, that is, of appealing to the sympathies of the audience, is essential. Polly Baker claimed that she is "a poor unhappy Woman" with "no Money to Fee Lawyers to plead for me." She said that she has been "dragg'd before your Courts" five times, fined twice, and was twice "brought to public

Punishment, for want of Money to pay those Fines." The law, she argued, is "particularly severe with regard to me." She risked her life in having children. Moreover, she was a wronged virgin, the victim of a conscienceless magistrate. She has, paradoxically, lost her honor because she is a woman of honor. She is socially ostracized, excluded "from all the Comforts" of "Church Communion." In the conclusion, she asks what "poor young Women" must do, when the laws do not provide them with husbands. She maintains that she has done her Christian duty, enjoined by the Bible, despite fines and whippings. Many of the ethical arguments also appeal to the sympathies of the audience, especially Polly's portrayal of herself as a husbandless mother, striving against overwhelming odds to rear her five children.

The third and final kind of "inartificial proof" open to a classical orator was *logos*, or proving the case by reasoning. Franklin was, of course, a believer in the inductive method of scientific proof. In his scientific writings, he constructed theories and designed proofs to test them. As he wrote at the end of his argument concerning his best-known single hypothesis, the electrical nature of lightning—"Let the experiment be made." At the same time, Franklin delighted in false arguments to undercut a point. He had learned from the Port Royal *Logic* and from Nathaniel Gardner's burlesques of the syllogistic reasoning of Increase and Cotton Mather to be suspicious of such reasoning.[59] Franklin often used false logic to suggest that a position opposite to that being urged by an obtuse persona was correct.

Polly Baker's arguments are based on syllogistic reasoning. She used a double syllogism in the argument: "But since Laws are sometimes unreasonable in themselves, and therefore repealed; and others bear too hard on the Subject in particular Circumstances . . ." The major premise of the first syllogism is that "Laws are sometimes unreasonable in themselves and therefore repealed"; the minor premise asserts (without proof) that this law is unreasonable in itself; and the conclusion, of course, is that the law should be repealed. The major premise of the other syllogism is that laws sometime "bear too hard on the Subject in particular circumstances—and therefore their execution may be ameliorated"; the minor premise is that this law is "particularly severe with regard to me"; and the implied conclusion (stated at the end of the speech) is that no punishment should be exacted in her (or, it is implied, in any similar) case.

Polly Baker uses a well-known logical fallacy, a petitio principii, that is, assuming one of the premises, in her argument. Her major premise is that any woman of sense would rather be married than single; her minor premise is "You are pleased to allow I don't want Sense"; and the conclusion, of course, is that she would prefer to be married. But insofar as we know, the magistrates have not said that she doesn't "want sense."[60] Even if the magistrates granted it, the whole point is irrelevant. The argument is an ignoratio elenchi, a red herring, for the argument changes the subject and dodges the issue.

So, too, does Polly Baker's argument that she has not committed a religious offense. Besides, if put as a syllogism, the major premise is a petitio principii. Major premise: God does not create people and give them souls if he does not approve of their origin; minor premise: her children have souls; conclusion: God approves of her having children. (The same argument could be used to justify rape if children resulted.) This argument examples both *argumentum ad verecundiam* (the appeal to traditional values) and another well-known topic in the invention of arguments, the argument from consequences. Polly Baker's argument for philoprogenitiveness also illustrates the argument from consequences: "Can it be a Crime . . . to add to the Number of the King's Subjects, in a new Country that really wants People?" Although Aristotle admits the argument from consequences as one of the twenty-eight valid topics, the argument in this case is another irrelevance. Polly Baker also turns the argument against the accuser or judges (the sixth of Aristotle's valid topics), thus undercutting their implied moral superiority. But a crime is not right merely because a judge has committed it.

Franklin's favorite ruse is the most glaring logical fallacy—the reductio ad absurdum. When Polly Baker maintains that she cannot conceive what the nature of her offense is, maintains that she gave birth to her children "at the Risque" of her life, brought them up "by my own Industry," and proclaims that she thinks it "rather a Praise worthy, than a Punishable Action"—the entire sequence is a reductio ad absurdum. The readers know that, for prostitutes, children are an undesired by-product of the profession. Polly inverts the normal feeling and carries it to a ridiculous conclusion. A more concise reductio is Polly Baker's reducing the only possible "Cause of Complaint against" herself to one made by "the Minister or the Justice, because I had Children without being Married, by which they have miss'd a Wedding Fee." This venal sin is not her fault, for she is and always has been willing to marry. Even more obviously absurd is the charge against bachelors: "by their Manner of Living," bachelors "leave unproduced . . . Hundreds of their Posterity to the Thousandth Generation," which is, Polly assures us "little better than murder." The masterpiece of drawing out a far-fetched argument to its logical and absurd end is found in the conclusion of the speech, where Polly argues that she has been religiously following the duty enjoined on her by the Bible, "A Duty, from the steady performance of which, nothing could deter me."

The whole speech is an example of false logic, for Polly Baker blurs the essential question (did she commit fornication?) and addresses only a possible consequence of fornication (having bastards). The law is not against illegitimate children—but against prostitution and fornication outside of wedlock; bastards are simply a proof of fornication. Nothing said by Polly Baker replies to the actual law. Thus, the entire speech is a logical irrelevance, an ignoratio elenchi. But the false logic is suitable, for Franklin has deliberately created an obtuse persona in Polly Baker. And the persona, like the logic, is another aspect of Franklin's rhetorical strategy in the speech.

Polly Baker: Sources

In his delightful book on Polly Baker, Max Hall devoted a chapter to "Polly's origins," suggesting that one source may have been the actual career of Eleonor Kellog, who was tried in Worcester, Massachusetts, on 5 November 1745 for the fifth time for the crime of fornication as proven by her having a fifth bastard child.[61] Though nothing about the trial appeared in the newspapers, Franklin could have heard about her. A minor source Franklin certainly knew echoed an essay in the *New-England Courant*. Addressing Samuel Sewall on 4 February 1722/3, Franklin cited the proverb, "Where there is no law, there is no transgression."[62]

Franklin may also reflect John Trenchard and Thomas Gordon, who wrote, "The Violation therefore of Law does not constitute a Crime where the Law is bad; but the Violation of what ought to be Law, is a Crime even where there is no Law. The Essence of Right and Wrong, does not depend upon Words and Clauses inserted in a Code, or a Statute Book, much less upon the Conclusions and Explications of Lawyers; but upon the Reason and Nature of Things, antecedent to all Laws." Franklin read this in *Cato's Letters* and also saw it quoted in the *New-England Courant* (14 May 1723). The *Courant*'s editor, James Franklin, may have intended the quotation to be an indirect comment on a news note in the same issue on the murder of bastard children: "We hear from the Eastward, that two Women have lately murder'd their Bastard Children, one at Salem, the other at Hampton." In the context of the quotation from Trenchard and Gordon, Franklin probably found the law itself partially responsible for the crime.

Three more important sources exist. Franklin's childhood acquaintance, the poet and businessman Joseph Green (1706–80), was Boston's best-known wit and poet of the 1730s and 1740s. Born in the same month and year as Franklin, Green graduated from Harvard in 1726. He frequently satirized his childhood friend Mather Byles, lampooned the Boston Masons' processions, and travestied the speeches of Governor Jonathan Belcher.[63] Some of Green's poetic satires appeared in the Boston newspapers and pamphlets, but more circulated in manuscript. As the best-known litterateur of the Middle Colonies and a person with numerous Boston connections, Franklin no doubt read Green's manuscript travesties, though no extant evidence proves it. Green's burlesques circulated widely, and several manuscripts that were not printed exist in eighteenth-century copies. Like Franklin's bagatelles, Green's satires privately amused colonial America's litterateurs.

In a letter of 7 June 1733 to his friend Captain Benjamin Pollard of Portsmouth, New Hampshire, Green gave the latest Boston news, burlesquing the style of newspaper reports. One paragraph reported the death of a well-known

Boston prostitute. Green imitated the *Boston News-Letter*'s obituaries of famous citizens:

> Sometime before last Lords Day, Mrs. *Mary Godfrey* (the Relict of Mr. *Thomas Godfrey*, Mariner of this Town, first Daughter to Mr. James Pitts, late of Boston, deceased, and Sister to the present Mrs. *Lydia Mackeune* of the said Boston) yielded up her Spirit (which was meek and quiet) to God who gave it; leaving behind her an Infant Train, being several in Number, which were not begotten without her Maternal Co-operation.—Touching her Character, which deserves a Place in a gilded *Volume* (having in her life time been very instrumental to the large Consumption of *Gilding*) she was a voluptuous Woman, whose Price was not above half a Crown, the Heart of her Husband did safely trust in her; her Children rose up & call'd her, pray forsooth Mother, her husband also & he—
> —ed her. Again she was a strict observer of the first Commandment, vizt. To increase and multiply: And as her Piety & Vigour recommended her to the Gay & Wanton, so did her Civilities to the Vulgar for her deportment was ever humble, & when she open'd her—it was with Wideness, by which she acquired so universal an Acquaintance & Esteem, as perhaps has hardly been exceeded by any person of her Age, Orb & Opportunity. It might have been added that she was a person of comely proportions, good Features (before the Small Pox), a genteel Mien & handsome Behaviour, but these are things of small Note; for, as Favour is deceitful, so Beauty is vain, but a Woman that pleaseth the Men, she shall be praised.[64]

Among the similarities between Franklin's speech and Green's mock obituary are the subject (praise for a famous prostitute), the prostitute's personality (her fine character), her numerous children (Polly Baker's five and Mary Godfrey's "Infant Train"), punning, and satire (a burlesque of the religious diction). But perhaps the most convincing bit of evidence suggesting that Franklin knew Green's travesty is the seemingly verbal echo: Green refers to "the first Commandment, vizt. To increase and multiply"; Franklin to "the first and great Command of Nature, and of Nature's God, *Increase and multiply*." The similarities could all be accidental, but that seems unlikely.

Two other sources are from a favorite Franklin author, Jonathan Swift. Franklin is indebted for the basic idea and echoes some subjects in Swift's contemporaneously famous poem, "To their Excellencies the Lords Justices of Ireland. The humble petition of Frances Harris, Who must starve, and die a maid if it miscarries."[65] Mistress Frances Harris was a maid whose savings have been stolen. She thought it "as safe as my maidenhead" because she kept it "tied about my middle, next my smock." She asks her friend the parson, whom she has considered a possible suitor, if he can "cast a nativity, when a body's plundered." He is insulted to be taken for a conjuror. The poem presents her circumstances and concludes by requesting the Lords Justices to order for her "a share in next Sunday's collection" and to direct the chaplain, "or instead of him, a better," to marry her.

The form or genre of "The Speech of Miss Polly Baker" is like Swift's poem: a speech by an uneducated person to a group of justices. Swift imitates the usual form of a petition, beginning with "Humbly showeth" and concluding with "shall ever pray"; Franklin imitates the form of the classical oration. Like Swift, Franklin uses sexual suggestions, asks that bachelors be compelled to marry, and concludes by exposing the preposterous vanity of the speaker. There are more differences than similarities between Swift's poem and Franklin's mock speech, but he no doubt knew the poem and was influenced by it.

Franklin also alludes twice to Swift's great satire, *A Modest Proposal*. Swift wrote of a projector's concern for mothers who murder their children: "*There is likewise another great Advantage in my Scheme, that it will prevent those voluntary Abortions*, and that *horrid practice of Women murdering their Bastard Children*; alas! too frequent among us, sacrificing the *poor innocent* Babes, I doubt, more to avoid the Expense than the Shame, which would move Tears and Pity in the most Savage and inhuman Breast." Swift's sentiment is echoed in the passage on the murder of bastard infants unique to the *Maryland Gazette* text.

The second allusion to *A Modest Proposal* is found in the conclusion of "The Speech of Polly Baker." She proposes that she "ought, in my humble Opinion, instead of a Whipping, to have a Statue erected to my Memory." The outrageousness of Polly Baker's proposal echoes that of Swift's projector (the impractical visionary idealist) who claimed that "whoever could find out a fair, cheap, and easy Method of making these Children sound and useful Members of the Commonwealth, would deserve so well of the Public *as to have his Statue set up* for a Preserver of the Nation" (emphasis mine). I believe that Swift's influence on Franklin was probably more important than that of any other author, excepting the little-known but prolific writer for the *New-England Courant*, Nathaniel Gardner. Every "very knowing American" would have recognized the allusion at the end of the speech. The use of two of Swift's writings reinforces the humor of the speech, placing it in a tradition of hoaxes and satires. At the same time, by associating Polly Baker with the absurdly vain Frances Harris and the inhuman projector of the *Modest Proposal*, the allusions tend to undercut and satirize Polly.

Franklin's Underlying Satire

Franklin argued for the separation of church and state, of purely moral judgments from criminal judgments. He also implied that New England's blue laws were ridiculous. Americans frequently told and wrote anecdotes concerning them. In a letter of 11 December 1762, Franklin joked with his Connecticut friend Jared Ingersoll about Connecticut's blue laws, especially that colony's "excessively strict Observation of Sunday." In Flanders, "there was plenty of Singing,

Fiddling, and Dancing" on Sundays. Franklin ironically commented, "I look'd round for God's Judgments but saw no Signs of them," and concluded the paragraph by remarking that it "would almost make one suspect, that the Deity is not so angry at that Offence as a New England Justice." At least one 1747 writer tried to carry further the American humor contained in "The Speech of Miss Polly Baker." In the *Gentleman's Magazine*, a pseudonymous "William Smith" identified Polly Baker as the wife of Paul Dudley (a most incongruous choice, though a family name infamous in New England oral satire)[66] and burlesqued the rural practice of "bundling" (my use of the word, like my use of "blue laws" is anachronistic). Like New's England blue laws, bundling later became a standard object of American satire.

"Custom has forbid" women to solicit the men—but we are reminded that Polly Baker, like other prostitutes, did so. Franklin, though, thinks it foolish that women were not supposed to be attracted to certain men and were not supposed to indicate their attraction. Although the fictive Polly Baker doesn't know that her real crime is fornication, Benjamin Franklin knew what she would have been charged with—and we know that he thought fornication, though treated by most people and by the law as shameful, was not. (We recall Franklin's satire on the human race in his letter of 7 June 1782 to Joseph Priestley: "for without a Blush they assemble in great armies at NoonDay to destroy, and when they have kill'd as many as they can, they exaggerate the Number to augment the fancied Glory; but they creep into Corners, or cover themselves with the Darkness of night, when they mean to beget, as being asham'd of a virtuous Action.") While the naive and obtuse Polly Baker argues that there should be no law against having bastard children, Franklin implicitly argues that there should be no law against fornication, so long as one is not betraying one's partner in marriage or enticing innocent youths. To a degree, Franklin's aims are identical to those of Polly Baker. On legalized prostitution, women's rights, the double standard, blue laws, the separation of church and state, the arbitrariness and rigidity of the law, and on the law itself creating certain crimes—on all of these, Franklin agreed with Polly Baker. But in some ways Franklin goes beyond his persona, and in others he ridicules her.

When the fictive Polly Baker brings up the double standard for men and women, Franklin also touches on the double standard for the rich and the poor. Polly Baker innocently pleads for herself because she has "no money to fee the lawyers" to plead for her. She complains that it is "unjust and unequal" that her influential first lover "should be advanced to Honour and Power" while she is punished. Franklin, like his readers, knew that the poor were commonly unable to make effective pleas for themselves, while the rich and influential would often not be brought to trial—or if brought to trial, frequently escaped justice by hiring the best legal talent. As he wrote in *Poor Richard* for September 1734, "*Laws* like to *Cobwebs* catch small Flies, / Great ones break thro' before your eyes."

Triumphantly concluding that she has done the duty "of the first and great Command of Nature, and of Nature's God, *Increase and multiply*," Polly Baker argues for a philoprogenitiveness that Franklin believed in. But Franklin (if not Polly Baker) also mocked biblical proofs and ridiculed those persons who apply the Bible to every action. Polly, like Franklin's later persona Father Abraham in "The Way to Wealth" (the common name for the preface to *Poor Richard* for 1758), is absurdly literal. Franklin is partially satirizing biblical fundamentalism. He also slyly satirizes ministers when Polly equates them with magistrates ("Minister, or the Justice"), when she suggests that the loss of a paltry fee would make the ministers (and justices) angry with her, and when she apologizes for her ridiculous essay into theology by saying "I am no Divine." The arguments of the ministers, Franklin insinuates, are no better than Polly's in their absurd logic and proofs.

Franklin, but not his persona Polly Baker, satirizes the most popular eighteenth-century proof for the existence of God—the design argument. According to this argument, the regularity and order of nature demonstrate that it was created by a supremely intelligent being. Polly Baker uses the argument when she asks, "But how can it be believed that Heaven is angry at my having Children, when, to the little done by me towards it, God has been pleased to add his divine skill and admirable Workmanship in the Formation of their Bodies, and crown'd it by furnishing them with rational and immortal Souls?" If one believes the argument from design, then Franklin has cleverly trapped the reader. Logically, he must concede that Polly Baker is right. But, as noted above, the same argument would justify rape that resulted in pregnancy. Franklin's use of the design argument burlesques it, and he must have slyly enjoyed the clever diction in the opening clause, "But how can it be believed?" He later ridiculed the design argument in "On Drinking" (1779?), and he earlier burlesqued it in his essay "The Death of Infants" (20 June 1734) in which God, the great clockmaker, has gone mad.[67]

In passing, Franklin lampooned the first cause argument for the existence of God when he has Polly say that the absent magistrate who originally seduced her is the "first Cause" from which all her misfortunes followed. One major version of the first cause argument maintains that if the causes of any event or any existing thing are explored back through their numerous possible removes, the reasoner will finally come to an ultimate cause, God. A second version, the design or cosmological argument, provides the basis for scientific deism: manifestations of order or apparent design in the world demonstrate the existence of a divine designer. Franklin's use of the diction "first Cause" alludes to and (in this humorous satire) mocks these concepts. But Franklin's major religious satire in the speech is based not on either the cause or design arguments but on theodicy. Franklin ridiculed the ideas of God's goodness and omnipotence in conjunction with the existence of evil in the world. As he testified in a letter of 27 June 1763, Franklin considered unanswerable the question asked by

Robinson Crusoe's man Friday: "*Why God No kill the Devil?*" Polly Baker complained of the injustice in the fact that the "first Cause . . . should be advanced to Honor and Power, in the same Government that punishes my Misfortunes with Stripes and Infamy." Literally, the "first Cause" is her former fiancé who impregnated and jilted her. But Franklin, for whom religion was always a favorite subject of satire, also meant the perceptive reader to think of the standard "first Cause"—God.

Franklin's complaint—though not Polly's—says that if God is all-powerful and all-knowing—if God is either directly, or indirectly but ultimately, responsible for everything that happens—then it is God, the "first Cause," that is the "Betrayer and Undoer" of man. God is therefore the cause of "all" man's faults. Franklin implicitly argues that it is "unjust and unequal" that God "should be advanced to Honor and Power" in the opinion of anyone who finds evil in the world. The ultimate religious satire maintains that if humans really believe in an all-powerful God, then God should be regarded by men as the cause of evil and of their sinful nature.

The train of thought replicates the first part of his *Dissertation on Liberty and Necessity*; Franklin had not changed his opinion. But Franklin knew that men believe what they want to believe and that they use logic to reinforce their wishful desires. As he wrote in the *Autobiography*, "So convenient a thing it is to be a *reasonable Creature*, since it enables one to find or make a Reason for everything one has a mind to do" (A 35). Franklin even introduced a situational joke into the religious satire. Although he uses the archetypal image of God as the Judge of mankind, God is a delinquent judge (like Polly's first lover)—absent from court. And, of course, by implication, God is absent from the world.

The most fundamental satire, apart from the pride of humans, is that on reason. Human beings will indeed "find or make a Reason for everything" they have a mind to do. Reason is merely the tool of the passions, the emotions, the desires of mankind. Polly's reasoning, which makes the prostitute the hero of society, is but one more beautiful example of the ability of humans to lie to themselves—and to believe the lie, because they are convinced it is true by their reason. Franklin often satirized reason, often noted how humans managed to lie to themselves, but he did so nowhere more artfully than in "The Speech of Miss Polly Baker."

Parallel to the satire on religion and reason is Franklin's ridicule of the notions of natural law and of "following nature." As the above paragraphs imply, reason, nature, and natural law (like the "first Cause" and like the "designs" of God) are also the "Betrayer and Undoer" of man and cause man's faults. Belief in reason, nature, and natural law is as foolish as belief in an omnipotent and omniscient God. The learned naturalist Franklin knew that nature abundantly justified cannibalism (it was the cod's eating smaller cod that called forth his rejection of vegetarianism and his self-satire on his reasons for abandoning it) and infanticide. Although his later public writings sometimes echo the cosmic optimism expressed by Pope in "whatever is, is right," Franklin's private writings often testify to his disgust for the existing state of affairs, even for the nature of human beings. Further, as we have seen, the epigraph for his *Dissertation on Liberty and Necessity* satirized the best-known existing expression of that optimism before Pope—Dryden's "whatever is, is in its causes just."

Polly Baker: Persona

Polly Baker is a naïf. She does not understand what her crime is. She seems to think that she is in court for having children, though she has been fined and punished four times previously for prostitution. Having children was simply evidence of her prostitution. The only time she alludes to the actual law is toward the end of her speech in her digression on bachelors, who should be compelled to marry or to "pay double the Fine of Fornication every year." When Polly says that she cannot "conceive" what the nature of her crime is, she combines the quality of a naïf with those of an obtuse speaker. But it is a particular kind of obtuseness, having overtones of true moral vision. The combination of seeming obtuseness and of true superior morality is typical of the foreign-observer persona.

Polly Baker exemplifies the literary usefulness as well as the characteristics of this persona. In bringing to her trial not only a lack of knowledge of the technical laws of New England but also an unbelievable ignorance of the common mores and standards of behavior of Western civilization, Polly Baker calls these mores and standards into question. The naive-obtuse-moral point of view is a splendid disguise for the skeptical and relativistic qualities of the mind of her creator, Benjamin Franklin, whom the Marquis de Condorcet, among others, believed to be a Pyrrhonist.[68] Significantly, both the letter to Priestley and Franklin's 1783 "Remarks Concerning the Savages of North-America" echo Montaigne, whose radical skepticism is more akin to the fundamental, private Franklin than is the deistic optimism he so frequently and successfully affected. (Montaigne was considered the epitome of Pyrrhonism in the Port Royal *Logic; or the Art of Thinking*, Franklin's favorite early handbook on logic.)[69]

Polly Baker began the speech with a humble apology in a modest and reasonable tone but soon after became carried away with her own reasoning. As Polly's speech progressed, she changed her goal from a timid desire to have the governor remit her fine to a passionate demand that the law itself be repealed because its underlying principles are wrong. As she talked, she became vehement and proud, revealing that she not only believed herself to be innocent of any crime but also that she thought herself morally superior—even to her judges. The most remarkable characteristic of her tone is that it is wholly serious. Polly Baker's attitude is one of passionate commitment. Polly personifies the foolish vanity of humans that Franklin had partially exposed in his letter on Betty Diligent and the hypocrisy of those engaged in trade (3 December 1730), as well as in his wonderful spoof of five supposed letters from young women, each of whom was certain she was the most beautiful woman in Philadelphia (20 and 27 November 1735).

Polly calls herself the hero of society. The fictive Polly Baker is Franklin's representative human being. Her obtuse blindness to her real situation, her passionate conviction of the justice of her own position, her belief in her absurd and wishful logic, and, especially, her supreme vanity all characterize human nature, as Franklin saw it. It is precisely because Polly Baker is, finally, a laughingstock that she is Franklin's representative human. In reading Polly Baker's "humble Opinion" at the conclusion of her speech, the reader may recall Franklin's observation in the first paragraph of the *Autobiography*, "Indeed I scarce ever heard or saw the introductory Words, *Without Vanity I may say, etc.* but some vain thing immediately followed." When Polly Baker asserts that she "ought, in my humble Opinion, instead of a Whipping, to have a statue erected to my Memory," she reveals her blind, overweening pride. The reader laughs at her last reversal in the piece—but Franklin means for us to laugh not only at her but at all human beings, and thus the reader, like Franklin, is finally laughing at the nature of humanity—and at himself.

The ultimate authorial voice in the speech is cynical, pessimistic, and even despairing. It is allied thematically with the subtle satire on the nature of man, on man's pride in his reason, on the ideas of natural law and the appeal to nature, on the existence of God, and on what mankind's notions of God reveal about the nature of man. But Franklin knew that his eighteenth-century audience (whether English or American) would turn on him for even his relatively acceptable opinions concerning the separation of church and state, unless he masked his ideas within a hoax. Further, to safeguard himself from the possible attacks of some outraged persons, Franklin concealed his authorship. When the older Franklin considered whether or not to make public his religious opinions, he concluded, "He that spits against the Wind, spits in his own Face" (P 7:294). But the cynicism, pessimism, and despair of the underlying authorial voice broke through to the literal, surface level at one place in the speech. One passage directly revealed something other than the cheerful, optimistic Franklin that most readers are conditioned to find. The section on mothers murdering their own infants, unique to the *Maryland Gazette* text, completed the speech thematically as well as structurally. The authorial voice in the passage on the murder of infants is tragic—disgusted with the law that is responsible for the murders, disgusted with mankind for creating and tacitly supporting such laws, disgusted with mothers capable of murdering even their own children, and disgusted with the nature of human beings. It is an amazingly angry and vicious voice that breaks through the mask. Though the passage clashed with the tone and prevailing authorial voice, it is consistent with the more subtle themes of the speech and with its underlying satire.

Franklin's joke is finally an ironic satire on and lament for mankind.

GOVERNOR GOOCH'S SPEECH TRAVESTIED

A fulsome and illogical exchange between Virginia's governor Sir William Gooch and the Virginia legislature aroused Franklin. The smug pride and self-congratulations of the Virginians, the absurd linking of fires with incendiary preachers, and the misplaced attack on itinerant ministers all became subjects for Franklin's burlesque. The immediate occasion for the Virginians' speeches was a fire that broke out in the Virginia capitol building and destroyed it on 30 January 1747. Subsequently, when the Virginia General Court met on 1 April, Governor Gooch addressed its members on the "astonishing Fate of the *Capitol*," suggested that it must have been set deliberately because "a Fire kindled by Accident could not have made so rapid a Progress," said that no Virginian could have done it, and praised the conduct of the clerks in saving the records, "Efforts that would have been vain, had not the Wind, at the bursting out of the Flames, changed from the *East* to the *Northwest*." He added a separate address to the House of Burgesses, apologizing for recalling them, complimented them on their "sincere and zealous Regard to the real Interest of the Community, for which I have so often applauded you," called them the "Fathers of your Country," and asked that they "apply the most effectual Means for restoring the Royal Fabrick to its former Beauty and Magnificence, with the like elegant and capacious Apartments, so well adapted to all the weighty Purposes of Government."

The council fulsomely replied that they were "not a little touched with the Infirmities of your Honour, a great Instrument, under Divine Providence, of conveying many Benefits to the Community." They compared "the hellish Attempts of malicious Incendiaries" with the itinerant ministers traveling in the country, and they praised the Church of England. The governor replied that he would do everything "to oppose the Progress of Heterodoxy and Immorality."

Franklin was already irritated by Gooch's charge to Virginia's grand jury on 18 April 1745, when the Virginia governor encouraged the grand jury to prosecute itinerant ministers who visited Virginia. The Philadelphia Presbyterian Synod had affirmed on 28 May that the itinerants were part of the "New Light" Newcastle Presbytery, not members in good standing of the Philadelphia Synod. In turn, Gooch assured the Presbyterian Synod on 20 June 1745 that he had not believed that their ministers were involved. All three articles were reprinted in Philadelphia.

Franklin ridiculed Gooch and the Virginians. Franklin reprinted the Virginians' exchange in the 14 May 1747 *Pennsylvania Gazette* from the *Virginia Gazette* of 2 April. Then, using hudibrastic rhymes and a deliberately awkward free verse, Franklin travestied the exchange, sending both the original exchange and his burlesque to his partner James Parker, who printed them in a supplement to the 1 June *New York Gazette*. Franklin enclosed an introductory letter, signed "*NED. TYPE*": "*Mr. Printer*, It may entertain the curious and learned Part of your Subscribers, if you give them the following Genuine *Speech* and *Address*, which, for the *Importance* of the *Subject*, *Grandeur* of *Sentiment*, and *Elegance* of *Expression*, perhaps exceed Any they have hitherto seen. For the Benefit of more common Readers, I have turn'd them, with some Paraphrase, into *plain English Verse*. I am told by Friends, that my Performance is excellent: But I claim no other Praise than what regards my *Rhyme*, and my *Perspicuity*. All the other Beauties I acknowledge, are owing to the *Original*, whose true Sense I have every where follow'd with a scrupulous Exactness. If envious Critics should observe, that some of my Lines are *too short* in their Number of Feet, I own it; but then, to make ample Amends, I have given *very good Measure* in most of the others."

Following the original exchange of speeches between Governor Gooch and the Virginia legislature, Parker printed, "*The SPEECH Versyfied*":

> L——d have Mercy on us!—the *CAPITOL*! the *CAPITOL*! is burnt down!
> O astonishing Fate!—which occasions this Meeting in Town.
> And this *Fate* proves a *Loss*, to be deplored the more,
> The said *Fate* being th'*Effect* of Malice and *Design*, to be sure. (ll. 1–4)

Franklin found Gooch's suspicion that the fire had been set ridiculous, made fun of Gooch's supposition that fires burn faster when deliberately planned, and burlesqued the self-importance of the Virginians:

> But when you consider, that the first *Emission of Smoke* was not from below,
> And that Fires kindled by Accident *always burn slow*,
> And not with half the Fury as when they *burn on purpose* you know
> You'll be forced to ascribe it (with Hearts full of Sadness)
> To the horrid Machinations of desperate Villains, instigated by infernal
>   Madness.
>   God forbid I should accuse or excuse any without just Foundation,
> Yet I may venture to assert,—for our own Reputation,
> That such superlative Wickedness never entred the Hearts of *Virginians*, who
>   are the *CREAM* of the *British* Nation. (ll. 7–14)

Franklin also satirized the mutual self-congratulations of Virginia's governor and General Court:

> Our Treasury being low, and my Infirmities great,
> I would have kept you prorogu'd till the Revisal of the Laws was compleat;
> But this Misfortune befalling the *Capitol* of the Capital of our Nation
> Require your immediate Care and Assistance for its *Instauration*.
> To press you in a Point of such Usefulness manifest,
> Would shew a Diffidence of your sincere Zeal for the public Interest
> For which you and I always make such a laudable Pother,
> And for which we've so often *applauded one Another*. (ll. 26–33)

The council's reply was even more nonsensical than the governor's address:

> We the King's *best Subjects*, the Council of this Dominion,
> Are deeply affected (as is every true *Virginian*)
> With the unhappy Occasion of our present Meeting:
> —In Troth we have but a sorry Greeting.
> We are also not a little touch'd (in the Head) with the
> same *Weakness* as your Honour's. (ll. 1–5)

Franklin thought it nonsensical that Virginia's council linked the fire and the Great Awakening. Virginia's established Anglican church had long persecuted Presbyterians. Though Franklin's wife and children belonged to Philadelphia's Christ Church and though his son Francis was buried in its graveyard, Franklin revealed in this satire that he was irritated by Virginia's condescension toward Presbyterians and other dissenters. Connecting the Great Awakening's fire imagery with actual arson was absurd:

> Besides, this *FIRE* puts us in Mind of *NEW-LIGHT*;
> And we think it Heav'n's Judgment on us for tolerating the Presbyterians,
> Whose Forefathers drubb'd ours, about a hundred Year-hence.
> We therefore resolve to abate a little of our Drinking, Gaming, Cursing and
>   Swearing,
> And make up for the rest, by persecuting some itinerant Presbyterian. (ll. 13–17)

Franklin also mocked both Gooch's military career as colonel of the American regiment at Cartagena (for which he was knighted, despite the expedition's miserable failure) and Virginia's lack of support for New England's successful 1745 expedition against Cape Breton:

> We take this Opportunity, that we may not be suspected of Malignity,
> To congratulate you, Sir, on your Promotion to the Baronet's Dignity;
> A fresh Instance of just Regard to your long and faithful Services we say,
> Because from *Carthagena* your Honour came safe away,
> And you lent and sent such **great Assistance* for reducing *CANADA*. (ll. 22–26)
> (*One Whole Company.)

Gooch thanked the council for their address and agreed with them concerning the vile Presbyterians:

> And, (lest here and hereafter we're left in the Lurch)
> To promote *true Religion*, (I mean our own Church)
> I'll heartily concur with you, and lend a few Knocks
> To suppress these confounding New-Light Heterodox.
> Then if from our Sins, we also refrain,
> Perhaps we may have our *CAPITOL!* our dear *CAPITOL!* our glorious *ROYAL
>   CAPITOL* again. (ll. 7–12)

Franklin had three probable sources for his travesty. First, he used the feminine rhymes and some diction from Samuel Butler's *Hudibras*, the most popular long poem of the Restoration and eighteenth century. Of course *Hudibras* was an anti-Presbyterian poem, and Franklin's poem defends an oppressed Presbyterianism against a self-righteous Anglicanism, but Franklin believed that Presbyterianism had as much right to exist as any other Christian religion. Indeed, the travesty takes pride in Cromwell and other Puritans defeating the Royalists. Though one scholar has argued that Franklin was particularly anti-Presbyterian, the argument seems inconsistent and illogical.[70] In the travesty on Gooch and the Virginians, Franklin satirized Anglicanism and implicitly praised Virginia's Presbyterian ministers.

Franklin also recalled the travesties that the Boston poet Joseph Green had written of the speeches of Governor Jonathan Belcher. In the 1730s, Green's hudibrastic travesties of Belcher's speeches circulated widely in manuscript. Just as I believe Franklin was influenced in his "Speech of Miss Polly Baker" by Green's letter to Benjamin Pollard, so, too, do I think that Franklin's satire of Gooch was influenced by Green's various travesties of Belcher's speeches. Though Franklin used some hudibrastic rhymes, his form was essentially free verse.[71] Unlike Walt Whitman's beautiful free verse, Franklin's was deliberately awkward, adding to the satire.

Another possible source was a letter by Hugh Bryan in the *South Carolina Gazette*. Franklin reprinted it in his March 1741 *General Magazine*, with a note stating that Bryan, George Whitefield (who revised the letter), and Lewis Timothy (Franklin's partner) were all bound over to appear at the next session of court "to answer for the same as libellous." Bryan's letter blamed a recent Charleston fire on the people's irreligion. The "New Light" Bryan especially blamed the Charleston fire on Anglicans and other "Old Siders" and antirevivalists. Such assignment of cause was typical of the religious literature of the day, but the fervently religious Bryan went beyond the normal boundaries by criticizing not only the civil and especially the religious leaders of South Carolina but even the king himself for not "being born again of God." Franklin thought such religious declamations foolish. Since Franklin knew Bryan's piece well, he probably was reminded of it when the Virginians blamed the burning of their capitol on the "New Lights" or revivalists.

The Annapolis printer Jonas Green reprinted Franklin's spoof in the *Maryland Gazette* on 16 June 1747. As in his printing of the American text of "The Speech of Miss Polly Baker," Green revealed that he was among the American literati who knew Franklin's private writings. In a 25 July letter to Franklin, Green reported that the travesty "made a deal of Laughter here; and was well approved of by some in that Colony" but tweaked Franklin by adding that he had not heard whether Gooch "himself lik'd it." Dr. Alexander Hamilton of Annapolis alluded to Gooch's speech and Franklin's burlesque of it in his literary history of the *Maryland Gazette* (29 June 1748). Franklin had made Gooch's speech a touchstone of the absurd, an assessment Hamilton repeated in his *History of the Tuesday Club* when he called attention to "that Irrational Creature, of whatever Species it was, multipede, quadrupede or bipede, that but very lately, wickedly desperately and villanously set fire to the Capitol of Williamsburg."[72]

James Parker again printed Franklin's travesty in the *New York Gazette* on 20 May 1751; eighteen years later, the *American Magazine* (March 1769), which Lewis Nicola edited in Philadelphia, reprinted it in the pre-Revolutionary period. Its influence may have been far-reaching. William Livingston probably knew it when he burlesqued Governor Thomas Pownall's speech in Weyman's *New York Gazette* for 26 March 1759.[73] The author of the free-verse travesties of General John Burgoyne's proclamations in 1775 and 1776 probably knew either (or perhaps both) Franklin's or Livingston's parody. The travesties of Burgoyne, in turn, inspired a series of burlesques of British speeches throughout the Revolutionary War.[74]

CONCLUSION

Franklin's interests in theology and philosophy continued to be a dominant aspect of his writing, with the "Speech by an Indian Chief," "On Divine Prescience," "What Is True?" and the "Refutation of Andrew Baxter." Manners and morality were the primary subjects in *Reflections on Courtship and Marriage*. Economics turned up in the "Essay on Paper-Currency." He wrote two satires on the governors of neighboring provinces: one a speech from the New Jersey Assembly to Governor Lewis Morris on 28 April 1740; and the other a travesty of Virginia governor William Gooch's speech. The former anticipated several themes that recur in the speeches Franklin wrote as a Pennsylvania assemblyman in the 1750s (secret instructions to the governor, prerogative power, and the right of the assembly to control taxes), and the latter defended Presbyterianism and religious freedom while satirizing Virginia's established religion. Both show the saucy and intrepid Franklin. Several belletristic writings appeared: the Drinker's Dictionary, the mock "Apology for a Young Man in Goal," "Reasons for Preferring Old Mistresses to Young Ones" ("Old Mistresses Apologue"), and "The Speech of Polly Baker." The last ones, especially "Reasons for Preferring an Old Mistress," are among Franklin's most ribald writings. Of course "The Speech of Polly Baker" is also a social and religious satire.

These writings reveal Franklin's mature prose. He wrote more savagely, philosophically, and with more complexity. Except for a few ministers, Franklin had emerged as the most prolific American writer of his day. His style was more accessible and yet more densely packed with possible meanings than any American contemporary. Not until Edgar Allan Poe did America produce a writer who was both as popular and as subtle as Franklin. By 1748 he had become a major writer, but he was as yet comparatively unknown in the Third Realm except to a select group of Americans. In the international world of eighteenth-century letters, Jonathan Edwards had succeeded Cotton Mather as the best-known living American writer, though his fame was primarily among Protestant ministers and other devout Christians interested in theology. Many of Franklin's writings dating from this period became internationally famous later in the Republic of Letters, none more so than "The Speech of Miss Polly Baker."

TWENTY

Assessing Franklin, Age 30 through 41

The Questions, Accounts and Testimonys falling under the Consideration of Magistrates, go upon that Point; what is true? But Posterity likes very often, and that justly, to hear *how a Thing is true*, especially in Matters of Religion, where the Appearance of a Thing, (which however with Men exceeding often goes for the *verum physicum* and *metaphysicum*) infinitely differs from the *verum morale*.
—*Franklin, "What Is True?" Pennsylvania Gazette, 24 February 1742/3*

WHEN THE PENNSYLVANIA ASSEMBLY ELECTED FRANKLIN its clerk in 1736, he achieved a position as a member of the Pennsylvania establishment. He owed the place to his friend Andrew Hamilton, Speaker of the assembly, but Franklin was recognized as an up-and-coming Philadelphian. As printer to the legislature (1730), founder of the Library Company (1731), grand master of the Masons (1734), and founder of the Union Fire Company (1736), Franklin was becoming Philadelphia's indispensable citizen. As clerk of the assembly, he took the assembly's minutes, and as the printer for the assembly, he published them. The clerk's job helped him maintain his influence with the legislators—and to be awarded most of its printing contracts. The position, as he recognized, was good for his business. So, too, was the position of postmaster of Philadelphia, to which he was appointed the following year, 1737. The postmaster in colonial America typically owned the local newspaper. Franklin recalled that he found the position "of great Advantage; for tho' the Salary was small, it facilitated the Correspondence that improv'd my newspaper, encreas'd the Number demanded, as well as the Advertisements to be inserted, so that it came to afford me a very considerable Income" (A 101). By 1740, the *Pennsylvania Gazette* had become the dominant American newspaper and *Poor Richard's Almanac* the most popular almanac in the Middle Colonies.

Earlier printers like Andrew Bradford attempted to complement their printing establishments by supporting local paper manufacturers, by buying pitch houses to make soot for the manufacture of ink, and by becoming postmasters to help with gathering and distributing their newspapers, but no other colonial printer was also both the clerk of the legislature and the printer of its publications. No printer before Franklin built what might be considered a major vertical business empire. By 1740, he had significant investments and connections in the printing business from the production of paper and ink to the intercolonial distribution of books, pamphlets, and periodicals. No other printer sponsored young printers as partners, except for their immediate relatives. Franklin was generous in doing so, for he wanted to help beginners in business, but the idealist was also practical. He hoped the partnerships would make money; some did. By 1740 Franklin had become a successful businessman and entrepreneur.

Deborah continued to be an essential business partner. By 1736 she commonly had help with the household chores and, after 1743, with their daughter, Sarah. Deborah had long been in charge of the shop; she now was an expert helper with running the post office, collecting rags, and dealing with the papermakers. When Franklin was out of town for brief or extended periods (the visits to Boston in 1743 and 1746), Deborah took charge whenever any crisis occurred in his normal business affairs—including printing, merchandising, and managing the post office. Franklin's father died in 1745, and Franklin's son William (b. ca. 1728) was growing up. Franklin became the pater familias of the extended Franklin family during these years, aiding his brother's widow, Anne, in Newport, Rhode Island, in business affairs; bringing up her son James; helping his sister Jane financially; and sponsoring her son Benjamin in the printing business.

Franklin added new friends to such close associates as Robert Grace, Hugh Roberts, and Thomas Hopkinson from the Junto. They now included the self-taught Quaker botanist John Bartram, the carpenter and builder Samuel Rhoads, the Baptist preacher and fellow electrical experimenter Ebenezer Kinnersley, the Great Awakener George Whitefield, and several members of the Pennsylvania Assembly, especially Thomas Leech of Philadelphia, and the Lancaster County representatives John Wright, his sons John and James Wright, and Samuel Blunston—as well as Wright's daughter Susannna, a fine poet and intellectual whom the Franklins visited at Hempfield, Lancaster County.

Franklin no longer frequently satirized clergymen and religion. He had not changed his religious opinions, as "The Divine Prescience" in his *General Magazine* (1741) demonstrated, but that piece was primarily interrogatory, not a satire or a challenge. Another religious writing, "What Is True?" (1743), revealed his profound skepticism, but it did not directly attack either religion or clergymen. Both pieces caused comment, and both confirmed Franklin's reputation as a skeptic. Though he wrote a refutation of the religious philosopher Andrew Baxter, he was withdrawing from theological and philosophical disputes, seeing little possibility of making a valuable contribution. It would have been easy for him to have become an ostensible Anglican and go to church occasionally. Perhaps one should admire him for his independence, for his toleration of almost all beliefs, and for the courage it took to be independent in a religious society. He had not, however, entirely cured himself of tweaking authority. The reply he wrote for the New Jersey Assembly in 1740 to Governor Lewis Morris lampooned the governor's speech. And in an unprovoked and uncalled-for satire of 1 June 1747, he travestied Governor Gooch's speech on the fire that burned

Virginia's capitol. In his early forties, Franklin still had elements of a young smart aleck.

Franklin had achieved an intercolonial and, indeed, international reputation as an extraordinary printer. The Reverend Gilbert Tennent wrote him on 22 September 1741 that he hoped Franklin "may be kept humble notwithstanding of the gifts of nature and providence with which you are favour, and may be enabled to improve your uncommon genius for Gods glory your own and others benefit." New York's Cadwallader Colden wrote the London printer William Strahan on 3 December 1743 that a certain printer was "the most ingenious in his way without question of any in America." Strahan, the dominant English printer of the day, recognized the unnamed person: "From the Character you give of him, I am sure it must be Mr. Franklin you mean, whose Fame has long ago reached this Part of the World, for a most ingenious Man in his Way" (May 1744).

Designing an improved stove brought Franklin his first widespread recognition among colonial and European intellectuals. James Alexander and Cadwallader Colden, dominant New York savants, praised the stove, and the latter sent copies of Franklin's pamphlet on the subject to the Leyden scholars Drs. John Frederick Gronovius and Carl von Linné. Gronovius had it translated into Dutch. The stove is a good example of Franklin's scientific method. He read all the literature on stoves available, including works in French, experimented with fireplaces for more than six years, produced prototypes of the stove for himself and his friends, published a pamphlet, *An Account of the New Invented Pennsylvanian Fire-Places* (1744), and offered the fireplace for public sale. An anonymous writer celebrated the stove in the *Boston Evening Post* (1746), naming it "Franklin's *Stove*" and claiming that for designing it, Franklin deserved "a *Statue* from his Countrymen." The author claimed that he deserved to be regarded as an *amicus humani generis*, or friend of humanity, an epithet frequently applied to him in his later years.

On the other hand, the controversy with John Webbe and Andrew Bradford about the first American magazine reveals two of Franklin's weaknesses. He played on national stereotypes in ridiculing Webbe in "Teague's Oration" (1741). Though such opinions were common in the eighteenth century and often evident in eighteenth-century humor, Franklin should not have appealed to the prejudice. A second shortcoming was his naiveté concerning nations and persons. His "Essay on Paper-Currency" (1741) did not recognize that England would only sponsor legislation that directly benefitted England, and he did not realize that neither English nor American merchants would want to set up a government office to compete with themselves.

Franklin became more involved with Pennsylvania politics. Besides continuing to support a militia and paper currency, he took an active role in the elections of 1737 and 1741. In 1740, he was accused by some Proprietary Party member of refusing to print Governor Thomas's reasons for rejecting a bill and criticized for not supporting the government even though he held an official position. While Thomas Penn was in Pennsylvania (1732–41), Franklin came to have personal contempt for him. Penn grasped all the Delaware Indian lands he could possibly commandeer in the Walking Purchase (1737), and at the same time he refused to share in Pennsylvania's expenses for Indian relations. These actions must have given Franklin an insight into his avariciousness. Penn's refusal to allow the quitrents to be paid in Pennsylvania currency undercut Pennsylvania's economy and made him hated by many people. When Penn was burned in effigy during the 1741 election, Franklin must have felt that the insult was deserved. Franklin may even, at this early date, have sympathized with the feeling expressed repeatedly from 1740 to 1743 that royal government would be better for the province than the proprietary regime. One reason he published Governor Thomas's private letter as Quaker Party propaganda in 1741 was that the governor called for more Acts of Trade and Navigation—which offended Franklin's Americanism. So, too, did the treatment of and scorn for American soldiers during King George's War and the impressment of Americans by Britain's navy. Franklin revealed his pride in America when he celebrated American privateers and other ships in 1744—they were already as numerous as Britain's navy in Queen Elizabeth's time.

Franklin retired as a printer, publisher, and bookseller in 1748 just after attaining the age of forty-two. He had started experimenting with electricity in the fall of 1745 and wanted to be able to spend more time on his scientific studies. He also wanted to devote time to several public projects. Perhaps the most important reason for his retirement was the warfare on Pennsylvania's borders, with the French and Indians threatening the frontier and with Spanish and French ships raiding up the Delaware Bay. He stopped his research into electricity in late 1747 and the first half of 1748 in order to spend full time organizing the defense of Pennsylvania. He loved his "philosophical Amusements," as he sometimes called his scientific experiments, but human life, civic duties, and morality were all more important to him. His retirement in 1748 from his trade no doubt also fulfilled an ambition to escape from the social system in which a tradesman was naturally subservient to a gentleman. Franklin's social status had been changing during the previous eleven years. He brought up his son William as a gentleman, and when William joined the army he went in as an ensign. The printer bought a wig in 1745 and purchased his own horse by 1747. During that year, he also had a structure built for a carriage. His retirement from printing confirmed the social status that he had achieved. Though Franklin held egalitarian beliefs and satirized those who considered themselves superior, he knew that he lived in a hierarchical society.

Franklin's brother John paid to have a portrait of Benjamin Franklin painted by Robert Feke sometime between 1745 and 1748. John Franklin hung the portrait beside his own in his Boston home. In the portrait, Franklin presented himself as a successful tradesman, wearing a brown wig with tight curls rather than the more expensive and longer white or gray wig, which indicated a gentleman's status. Art historian Wayne Craven contrasted Franklin's portrait with that of James Bowdoin (painted by Feke around the same time), whose "embroidered satin waistcoat, worn under a handsome brown velvet coat" was an obvious symbol of wealth. By 1746, Franklin had evidently begun to put on weight, and though the suit and flowing waistcoat do not reveal the actual contours of his body, he appears to be slightly stout, with a round full face. The Junto members occasionally exercised on the banks of the Schuylkill River, but it seems unlikely that Franklin exercised regularly during his thirties. His little spare time was spent studying.

By 1746 he had begun the electrical experiments that were to make him internationally famous. They were interrupted in late 1747, as we shall see in Volume 3, when Franklin became caught up in solving what had been the irreconcilable political quandary of Pennsylvania. During his thirties, he wrote a number of satires partly directed against the nature of human beings—and against himself. Like Jonathan Swift and other satirists, Franklin observed his own pride, pretensions, and frailities with some scorn. All humanity is the satirical butt of the satires "An Apology for a Young Man in Gaol" and "The Speech of Miss Polly Baker." Polly is Franklin's representative human being. In concluding her speech, the prostitute said (Franklin probably thought the foolish boast especially applicable to his own pride): "Yes, Gentlemen, I venture to call it a Duty; 'tis the Duty of the first and great Command of Nature, and of Nature's God, *Increase and multiply*: A Duty, from the steady Performance of which nothing has ever been able to deter me; but for it's Sake, I have hazarded the Loss of the public Esteem, and frequently incurr'd public Disgrace and Punishment; and therefore ought, in my humble Opinion, instead of a Whipping, to have a Statue erected to my Memory."

APPENDIX 1. *New Attributions*

The attributions to Benjamin Franklin are all in addition to those in the *Canon*.

The following checklist gives the source of the writing and a reference to the chapter where it is discussed in the biography.

BENJAMIN FRANKLIN

1735 *A Letter to a Friend in the Country, Containing the Substance of a Sermon Preach'd at Philadelphia, in the Congregation of the Rev. Mr. Hemphill, Concerning the Terms of Christian and Ministerial Communion* (2:65). Melvin Buxbaum, *Franklin and the Zealous Presbyterians* 234 n. 105, has previously ascribed the whole pamphlet to Franklin, and I agree (Chapter 10).

1737 Anon., "On the forthcoming Election," 29 September 1737, *Pennsylvania Gazette.* Probably by Franklin (Chapter 13).

1741 "A Speech Deliver'd by an Indian Chief, in Reply to a Sermon Preached by a Swedish Missionary," *American Magazine*, March 1741, pp. 90–94, as the "Religion of the Indian Natives" (Chapter 19).

1743 "To the Author of the American Magazine," on the "Throat Distemper" in Boston, dated "Philadelphia, Sept. 1. 1743," by "F. B." *American Magazine and Historical Chronicle* 1 (October 1743): 70–71. Previously suggested by Francisco Guerra and by Whitfield J. Bell, Jr. (Chapter 18).

OTHER AUTHORS

Thomas Bordley: essay in the *American Weekly Mercury*, 14 February 1720/1, protesting the Board of Trade's forbidding duties or other taxes on slaves or convicts shipped to America (Chapter 19).

John Webbe: nine new attributions to Webbe in the *American Weekly Mercury*, 1732 (Chapter 6).

APPENDIX 2. *Franklin's Organizations: Dates and Locations of Meetings, 1727–1747*

1. 1727: Junto. The Junto met every Friday night beginning in the fall of 1727. I speculate that after Franklin was elected clerk of the assembly in 1736, the members usually did not meet when the assembly was in session. They must also have frequently cancelled meetings for social and other occasions. Franklin attended the Junto until he departed for England in 1757. He began attending again in 1762 and continued until he sailed for England in 1764. No minutes of the Junto meetings are extant and its meeting places are unknown.

2. 1731: Freemasons. The freemasons met the first Monday night of every month. Beginning in February 1730/1, Franklin attended the monthly meetings and the annual celebration on St. John the Baptist's Day, 24 June (when that occurred on a Sunday, the Freemasons met on another day). He continued to attend until leaving for England in 1757, then resumed attendance when back in Philadelphia (1762–64). Meeting places: 1) the lodge met at John Hobart's Sun Tavern on Water Street until Hobart moved in 1733; 2) by June 1733, the Masons met at Thomas Mullen's Tun Tavern, also on Water Street (at the corner of Tun Alley, the first alley south of Chestnut Street); 3) from early 1735 until 1749, the Freemasons met at Owen Owen's Indian King Tavern, at the southwest corner of High Street and Biddle Alley.

3. 1731: Library Company of Philadelphia. The Library Company directors met the second Monday night of every month beginning in November 1732 and on the day of the annual election, 1 May. Franklin attended the monthly and numerous special meetings of the directors until the election in May 1757, when he expected to leave for England shortly. He was reelected a director in 1763 and 1764. Meeting places: 1) the directors began meeting in 1731 at Nicholas Scull's Bear Tavern on the southwest corner of Market and Third Streets; 2) after the books arrived in 1732 and were put in the "Library Room" in the house that Louis Timothée was renting from Robert Grace (site of the present 131 Market Street), the directors met there from 14 November 1732 to the spring of 1734; 3) beginning 8 April 1734, they met at John Robert's coffeehouse, which was located "in High Street near the Market" (*PG*, 25 April 1734); 4) In early April 1739, Roberts moved to Second Street; he died later that year, but the directors continued to meet at the Widow Roberts's until 1745; 5) that year Breintnall opened a tavern, the Hen and Chickens, on Fourth Street between Market and Chestnut, and the directors began meeting there; after his death on 16 March 1746, the directors continued meeting at the Widow Breintnall's.

4. 1736: Pennsylvania Assembly. After Franklin was elected clerk of the Pennsylvania Assembly on 15 October 1736, he attended its meetings, which were held sporadically throughout

the year from October to September. He attended all meetings of the Pennsylvnia Assembly as clerk until elected a member of the assembly in 1751. Meeting places: 1) the assembly met at various private dwellings, though often in the court house, which was in the middle of Market Street, just north of Second Street; 2) for a brief period, the assembly met in an old house on the west side of Chestnut Street, between Fourth and Fifth Streets; 3) beginning in September 1735, the assembly met at the State House (now Independence Hall), on the east side of Chestnut Street between Fourth and Fifth Streets.

5. 1736: Union Fire Company. Franklin organized the Union Fire Company on 7 December 1736 and attended its meetings on the last Monday night of every month. He belonged to the company until leaving for England in 1757, and attended meetings again in 1762–64. Meeting places: 1) the Union Fire Company at first met at John Roberts's tavern on High (later Market) Street near the Market; 2) when Roberts moved to Second Street, the company instead met (30 April 1739) at David Evans's at the Sign of the Crown on the south side of Market Street between Second and Third Streets; it met there through 30 August 1742; 3) beginning 27 September 1742, it met at Henry Pratt's tavern, at the sign of the Ship a Ground at the northeast corner of High (Market) and Water Streets; when Pratt moved (14 August 1746) two blocks north to the Royal Standard on the north side of Market Street between Second and Third Streets, the company moved with him.

6. 1744: American Philosophical Society. From at least February to May 1744, the American Philosophical Society held meetings. I hypothesize that it met on the first Thursday night of the month. Its meeting place or places are unknown.

APPENDIX 3. *Pennsylvania Assembly: Pay to Franklin*

Table A.1 records payments to Franklin by the Pennsylvania Assembly. Generally the payment was described "as Clerk and for Printing," but additional payments for printing were sometimes recorded. The references are to the dates when the Pennsylvania Assembly recorded the payment, and full references may be found in the *Documentary History of Benjamin Franklin*. For a brief discussion, see Chapter 13.

Table A.1. Totals by Year, 1736–1747

Year	As Clerk & For Printing	Ref	Other Printing	Ref	For Mail	Ref
1736–37	24.9.6	13 Aug	1.10.0	10 Aug		
1737–38	38.7.6	2 Sept				
1738–39	77.8.0	11 Aug				
1739–40	113.2.0	3 Sept	393.24.12[1]	1 Sept		
1740–41	50.7.0	22 Sept	142.0.4	22 Aug		
1741–42	55.4.6	28 Aug	50.0.0 [2]	28 Aug		
1742–43	154.6.4	13 Aug	211.0.0	13 Aug		
1743–44	62.1.2	11 Aug	11.10.0	11 Aug		
1744–45	31.16.0	7 Sept	24.5.0	7 Sept		
1745–46	111.13.6	23 Aug	57.1.0	23 Aug	25.3.3	23 Aug
1746–47[3]	67.14.4[4]	23 Aug	329.44.23[5]	23 Aug		
Total	782.87.34 = £786.9.10		1218.94.39 = £1222.17.3			

1. 60.18.4 for "Paper, and other Materials for the Paper Money," and 333.6.8 "for printing the Paper Money."
2. A partial payment for printing the laws; the balance of the £261 was to be paid upon delivery of the books.
3. He was also paid £57.15.0 for purchasing the English *Statutes at Large*, for which he evidently charged no commission.
4. The entry was payment "as clerk and for postage" (rather than "for printing").
5. The amount includes 181.17.10 for paper currency; plus 136.16.9, "per order"; and 12.11.4 by "John Kinsey, for Franklin."

Table A.2. Minimum Pay as Clerk and Maximum as Printer

Year	As Clerk & for Printing	Days in Session	Minimum Pay as clerk at 6s (£)	Maximum pay as Printer (£)
1736–37	24.9.6	18	5.8s	19.1.6
1737–38	38.7.6	19	5.14s	32.13.6

1738–39	77.8.0	47	14.2s	63.6.0
1739–40	113.2.0	77	23.2s	90.0.0
1740–41	50.7.0	30	9.0s	41.7.0
1741–42	55.4.6	39	11.14s	43.10.6
1742–43	154.6.4	64	19.4s	135.2.4
1743–44	62.1.2	52	15.12s	46.9.2
1744–45	31.16.0	36	10.16s	21.0.0
1745–46	111.13.6	60	£18	93.13.6
1746–47[1]	67.14.4[2]	28	8.8s	59.6.4
Total	786.9.10	412	143.8.0	645.9.10

1. He was also paid £57.15.0 for purchasing the English *Statutes at Large*, for which he evidently charged no commission.

2. The entry was payment "as clerk and for postage" (rather than "for printing").

APPENDIX 4. *Sample Wages and Prices in Colonial Philadelphia*

Prices varied from year to year, and the information here is intended only to give a rough idea of the approximate amount. In most cases, it should be correct within 10 percent. For more specific data, see the three books listed at the end.

Journeymen printers' wages. In "Prices of Printing Work in Philadelphia, 1754," Franklin wrote: "Small Jobs reckoned by the Hour, at 9 d per hour," but he added that the amount was "too much" if the journeymen had constant work; "but in American Numbers being generally small, they must often stand still, and often make ready." Therefore, the following salary in 1754 would have been generous for a journeyman printer:

> 9d an hour = 72d = 6s a day
> 6s a day = 30s = £1.10 a week
> £1.10 a week = £52.52s = £54.12 a year

Pay for an unskilled worker. Nine pounds a year, plus "Accomodations, of Meat, Drink, Washing and Lodging." Franklin paid Edward Lewis that amount. He moved in with the Franklins on 14 August 1747 and was "to go away when anything offers more to his Advantage."

Pay for a clerk. Twenty-five pounds a year, plus room, board, and washing. Franklin offered Daniel Fisher that amount on 28 July 1755.

Pay for teachers at the Philadelphia Academy, 12 September 1751. Sixty pounds a year for tutors; £125 a year for math professor; £150 a year for English master; £200 a year for the rector (Latin and Greek teacher).

Room and board at an inn or private lodging. On 15 September 1748, Peter Kalm paid 20s a week for "a room [which he evidently shared], candles, beds, attendance and three meals a day. But wood, washing and wine, if required, were extra." Kalm, *Travels* 17–18.

For detailed information on Pennsylvania prices, see Anne Bezanson, Robert D. Gray, and Miriam Hussey, *Prices in Colonial Pennsylvania* (Philadelphia: University of Pennsylvania Press, 1935). For prices in colonial America in general, see John J. McCusker, *Money and Exchange in Europe and America, 1600–1775: A Handbook* (Chapel Hill: University of North Carolina Press, 1978), and U.S. Department of Commerce, Bureau of the Census, *Historical Statistics of the United States, Colonial Times to 1970: Bicentennial Edition* (Washington, D.C.: U.S. GPO, 1976) 2:1197, ser. Z 585.

SOURCES, DOCUMENTATION, DATES

The basis for the biography is the *Documentary History of Benjamin Franklin*, a chronologically arranged calendar of his activities (meetings of the Junto, Library Company directors, Union Fire Company, etc.), writings, whereabouts, and the attacks on him and references to him throughout his life. For the period through 1747 (i.e., to his retirement from printing), I include all the references that I have found, and I quote at length the most important ones that are not in the *Papers of Benjamin Franklin*. Since there are so many more references to Franklin in the latter part of his life, I calendar more and quote less as the volumes progress. The *Documentary History* relieves the biography of numerous footnotes, for the dates in the biography may be consulted in the *Documentary History*, where references to the Franklin texts and the most pertinent scholarship will be found. Of course, for most writings of Franklin, the reader may simply go from the biography directly to the *Papers*, which is chronologically arranged. The source is in the *Documentary History* whether or not it appears in the *Papers*. The *Documentary History* for the period covered in the published biography is available on the Internet. I will always be grateful for any factual material concerning Franklin that is not in the *Documentary History* (lemay-@udel.edu). The *Documentary History* may be found at http://www.english.udel.edu/lemay/franklin.

I have also transcribed into one chronological record Franklin's various financial accounts. Like the *Documentary History*, *The Accounts of Benjamin Franklin* is available on the Internet. Previously, G. S. Eddy published excerpts from Franklin's Ledger A&B; excerpts from his Ledger D; the entire account book kept during his first mission to England, 1757–62; and excerpts from a workbook of the printing house of Franklin and Hall, 1759–66. So far, I have only made available the accounts to his retirement as a printer in 1748. I am greatly indebted to the work of G. S. Eddy, but as the editors of *The Papers of Benjamin Franklin* have noted, Eddy made mistakes and "a substantial number" of omissions (P 7:165). There are few accounts for Volume 1 but many for Volume 2. The name index to the *Accounts* contains biographical notes on the persons I have been able to identify.

DOCUMENTATION

The great edition of Franklin's writings is *The Papers of Benjamin Franklin* (New Haven: Yale University Press, 1959–), 37 volumes through 2004. Since it is arranged chronologically, references to Franklin's writings can easily be found by the dates. In those cases where Franklin's document occupies more than two pages, references to the *Papers* are given in the text by volume and page within parentheses.

In addition to using dates throughout the biography as keys to references in *The Papers of Benjamin Franklin* and in the *Documentary History*, I use both endnotes and parenthetical references (the latter mainly for references to Franklin's writings). Full references for endnotes occur only for those items cited only once or twice; for those works cited frequently, brief citations only are given in the endnotes and full citations appear in the following list of abbreviations.

Franklin's writings are cited from *The Papers of Benjamin Franklin*; if they are not in the *Papers*, then they are from the Library of America edition of the *Writings*; if in neither, then either from Albert H. Smyth's edition of the *Writings* or from the original sources. The text I use of the *Autobiography* is the Lemay and Zall *Genetic Text*, which shows all Franklin's revisions, additions, and cancellations as such and preserves exactly what Franklin wrote, including abbreviations, careless slips of the pen, etc. In quoting from it, I retain Franklin's eighteenth-century spelling, but I silently expand the abbreviations, correct the few careless slips of the pen, and ignore the symbols showing what words or passages have been revised. I also ignore punctuation that has been superseded by subsequent revisions. Since all quotations from the *Autobiography* give the page number of the *Genetic Text*, readers interested in examining the original cancellations, revisions, etc., may conveniently examine it. When a printed source is entirely in italics or uses italics frequently, I quote it in roman type.

DATES

Until September 1752, England used the Julian calendar, in which the new year began on March 25. When Great Britain adopted the Gregorian calendar in 1752, eleven days were dropped (3 through 13 September 1752). I use the Julian calendar through 2 September 1752, and thereafter the Gregorian calendar. Under the Julian calendar, Franklin was born on 6 January 1705, but according to our present Gregorian calendar, he was born on 17 January 1706. For dates between January and March 25, in order to avoid confusion as to which year is meant, I use both dates. Thus I write that Franklin was born 6 January 1705/6, using the Julian calendar for the day and the month, but making it clear what year is actually meant. Starting in 1753, Franklin usually celebrated his birthday on 17 January.

ABBREVIATED REFERENCES

IN THE TEXT

Numbers otherwise unidentified refer to a volume and page of *The Papers of Benjamin Franklin*, ed. Leonard W. Labaree et al. (New Haven, Conn.: Yale University Press, 1959—[37 volumes through 2004]). In cases where there might be some doubt, a "P" precedes the reference.

"A" before a number refers to *The Autobiography of BF: A Genetic Text*. (See below.)

IN THE NOTES

Though some abbreviations (like VD) will be the same for all volumes, some will differ from volume to volume. "Miller" in Volume 2 refers to C. William Miller.

BIBLIOGRAPHY

A	*The Autobiography of BF: A Genetic Text*. Ed. J. A. Leo Lemay and P. M. Zall. Knoxville: University of Tennessee Press, 1981.
AAS	American Antiquarian Society, Worcester, Massachusetts
Aldridge	Alfred Owen Aldridge. *BF: Philosopher and Man*, Philadelphia: Lippincott, 1965.
Aldridge, *Nature's God*	Alfred Owen Aldridge. *BF and Nature's God*. Durham: Duke University Press, 1967.
Amacher	Richard E. Amacher. *BF*. New York: Twayne, 1962.
Amory and Hall	Hugh Amory and David D. Hall. *A History of the Book in America, Volume One: The Colonial Book in the Atlantic World*. Cambridge: Cambridge University Press, 2000.
ANB	*American National Biography*.
Anderson	Douglas Anderson. *The Radical Enlightenments of BF*. Baltimore: Johns Hopkins University Press, 1997.
APS	American Philosophical Society, Philadelphia.
AWM	*American Weekly Mercury*.
BF	Benjamin Franklin.
bk.	book.
Cabanis	Pierre J. G. Cabanis. *Oeuvres Complètes*. 5 v. Paris: Bossange Freres, 1823–25.

Calendar	J. A. Leo Lemay. *A Calendar of American Poetry in the Colonial Newspapers and Magazines through 1765*. Worcester, Mass.: American Antiquarian Society, 1972.
Canon	J. A. Leo Lemay. *The Canon of BF: New Attributions and Reconsiderations*. Newark: University of Delaware Press, 1986.
Catalogue (1741)	*Catalogue of Books Belonging to the Library Company of Philadelphia*. Philadelphia: Franklin, 1741.
ch.	chapter.
Colden	Cadwallader Colden. *Letters and Papers*. 9 v. New York: New York Historical Society, 1918–37.
Cook	Elizabeth C. Cook. *Literary Influences in Colonial Newspapers, 1704–1750*. New York: Columbia University Press, 1912.
Crane	Verner Winslow Crane. *BF and a Rising People*. Boston: Little, Brown, 1954.
DAB	*Dictionary of American Biography*. 11 v. Ed. Dumas Malone. New York: Scribner's, 1958–64.
DeArmond	Anna Janney DeArmond. *Andrew Bradford*. Newark: University of Delaware Press, 1949.
DF	Deborah Franklin.
DH	*Documentary History of BF*.
Diamondstone	Judith M. Diamondstone. "The Philadelphia Corporation, 1701–1776." Ph.D. diss., University of Pennsylvania, 1969.
European Americana	John Alden et al., eds. *European Americana: A Chronological Guide to Works Printed in Europe Relating to the Americas*. 6 v. New Canaan: Readex, 1980–97.
Evans	Charles Evans. *American Bibliography: A Chronological Dictionary to 1800*. 14 v. Chicago: Evans and American Antiquarian Society, 1903–59.
Granger	Bruce I. Granger. *BF: An American Man of Letters*. Ithaca, N.Y.: Cornell University Press, 1964.
Green	James N. Green. *Poor Richard's Books: An Exhibition of Books Owned by BF Now on the Shelves of the Library Company of Philadelphia*. Philadelphia: Library Company, 1990.
Hamilton	Dr. Alexander Hamilton. *The Itinerarium*. Ed. Carl Bridenbaugh. Chapel Hill: University of North Carolina Press, 1948.
Hanna	William S. Hanna. *BF and Pennsylvania Politics*. Stanford, Calif.: Stanford University Press, 1964.

Horle	Craig Horle et al., eds. *Lawmaking and Legislators in Pennsylvania: A Biographical Dictionary, v. 2, 1710–1756*. Philadelphia: University of Pennsylvania Press, 1997.
Hutson	James H. Hutson. *Pennsylvania Politics, 1746–1770*. Princeton, N.J.: Princeton University Press, 1972.
Isaacson	Walter Isaacson. *BF*. New York: Simon & Schuster, 2003.
Lemay, "American Aesthetic"	J. A. Leo Lemay. "The American Aesthetic of BF." *PMHB* 111 (1987): 465–99.
Lemay, "Lockean Realities"	J. A. Leo Lemay. "Lockean Realities and Olympian Perspectives: The Writing of Franklin's *Autobiography*," in *Writing the American Classics*, ed. James Barbour and Tom Quirk (Chapel Hill: University Of North Carolina Press, 1990) 1–24.
Lemay, *Men of Letters*	J. A. Leo Lemay. *Men of Letters in Colonial Maryland*. Knoxville: University of Tennessee Press, 1972.
Lemay, *Renaissance Man*	J. A. Leo Lemay. *Renaissance Man in the Eighteenth Century*. Los Angeles: Clark Memorial Library, 1978.
LCP	Library Company of Philadelphia.
Locke, *Essay*	John Locke. *An Essay Concerning Human Understanding*. Ed. Peter H. Nidditch. Oxford: Clarendon, 1975.
Lopez, *Private*	Claude-Anne Lopez and Eugenia Herbert. *The Private Franklin*. New York: Norton, 1975.
Mandeville	Bernard Mandeville. *The Fable of the Bees*. Ed. F. B. Kaye. 2 v. Oxford: Clarendon Press, 1966.
Mather, *Bonifacius*	Cotton Mather. *Bonifacius* (running title, "Essays to Do Good"). Ed. David Levin. Cambridge, Mass.: Harvard University Press, 1966.
McCulloch	William McCulloch. "Additions to Thomas's History of Printing." *Proceedings of the American Antiquarian Society* n.s., 31 (1921): 89–247.
Miller	C. William Miller. *BF's Philadelphia Printing*. Philadelphia: APS, 1974.
NCE	*The Autobiography of BF: A Norton Critical Edition*. Ed. J. A. Leo Lemay and P. M. Zall. New York: Norton, 1986.
Newcomb	Robert H. Newcomb. "The Sources of Benjamin Franklin's Sayings of Poor Richard." Ph.D. diss., University of Maryland, 1957.
OED	*Oxford English Dictionary*. Ed. James A. H. Murray. 13 v. London: Oxford University Press, 1933.

Oldest Revolutionary	*The Oldest Revolutionary: Essays on BF.* Ed. J. A. Leo Lemay. Philadelphia: University of Pennsylvania Press, 1976.
P	*The Papers of BF.*
PAPS	*Proceedings of the American Philosophical Society.*
Parton	James Parton. *Life and Times of BF.* Boston: Osgood, 1864.
Pascal	Blaise Pascal. [Pensées.] *Monsieur Pascall's Thoughts, Meditations, and Prayers.* Tr. Joseph Walker. London: J. Tonson, 1688.
PG	*Pennsylvania Gazette.*
PMHB	*Pennsylvania Magazine of History and Biography.*
Port Royal *Logic*	Antoine Arnauld and Pierre Nicole. *Logic, or the Art of Thinking.* London: W. Taylor, 1770. BF's copy at LCP.
Reappraising	*Reappraising BF.* Ed. J. A. Leo Lemay. Newark: University of Delaware Press, 1993.
Roach	Hannah B. Roach. "BF Slept Here." *PMHB* 84 (1960): 127–74.
S	Albert Henry Smyth. *Writings of BF.* 10 v. 1907; rpt. New York: Haskell House, 1970.
Sabin	Joseph Sabin, Wiulberforce Eames, and R.W.G. Vail, eds. *Bibliotheca Americana.* 29 v. New York: Sabin, 1868–1936.
Sappenfield	James A. Sappenfield. *A Sweet Instruction: Franklin's Journalism as a Literary Apprenticeship.* Carbondale: Southern Illinois University Press, 1973.
Shaftesbury	Anthoy Ashley Cooper, third earl of Shaftesbury. *Characteristics of Men, Manners, Opinions, Times.* Ed. Lawrence E. Klein. Cambridge: Cambridge University Press, 1999.
Shields, *Civil Tongues*	David S. Shields. *Civil Tongues & Polite Letters in British America.* Chapel Hill: University of North Carolina Press, 1997.
Shields, *Oracles*	David S. Shields. *Oracles of Empire: Poetry, Politics, and Commerce in British America, 1690–1750.* Chicago: University of Chicago Press, 1990.
Shields, "Wits"	David S. Shields. "The Wits and Poets of Pennsylvania: New Light on the Rise of Belles Lettres in Provincial Pennsylvania." *PMHB* 109 (1985): 99–144.
Shipton	Clifford K. Shipton. *Sibley's Harvard Graduates.* Boston: Harvard University Press, 1933–.

Sparks	Jared Sparks. *Works of BF.* 10 v. Boston: Hilliard, 1836–40.
Statutes	James T. Mitchell and Henry Flanders, eds. *The Statutes at Large of Pennsylvania from 1682–1801.* Harrisburg, Pa.: State Printer, 1896–1915.
Swift, ed. Davis	Swift, Jonathan. *Prose Works.* Ed. Herbert Davis. 14 v. Oxford: Blackwell, 1939–68.
Thomas	Isaiah Thomas. *History of Printing in America.* Ed. Marcus A. McCorison. New York: Weathervane Books, 1970.
v.	volume.
VD	Carl Van Doren. *BF.* New York: Viking, 1938.
Votes	*Pennsylvania Archives,* 8th ser.
W	BF. *Writings.* Ed. J. A. Leo Lemay. New York: Library of America, 1987.
Walters	Kerry S. Walters. *BF and His Gods.* Urbana: University of Illinois Press, 1999.
WF	William Franklin.
WMQ	*William and Mary Quarterly,* 3rd ser.
Wood	Gordon S. Wood. *The Americanization of BF.* New York: Penguin Press, 2004.
Wood, *Radicalism*	Gordon S. Wood, *The Radicalism of the American Revolution.* New York: Knopf, 1992.
Wright	Esmond Wright. *Franklin of Philadelphia.* Cambridge, Mass.: Harvard University Press, 1986.
Zall	P[aul] M. Zall. *BF, Laughing.* Berkeley: University of California Press, 1980.

NOTES

Chapter 1. Personal and Business Life

1. The *DAB* account of WF (published in 1928) gives 1731 as his date of birth; and the *ANB* sketches (1999) of WF and of DF say the same. Sheila L. Skemp, *WF* (New York: Oxford University Press, 1990) follows the information in v. 1 of the *Papers* (1:lxii) and writes that he "was born some time between September 1730 and March 1731" (4).

2. VD 91.

3. Parton, 177, dates William's birth "about a year after the date [20 November 1728] of his liturgy."

4. The evidence is inconclusive. Like Skemp, Isaacson does not cite the revised opinion of the editors (P 3:474n.); instead, he writes that before WF was allowed to enlist, he tried to run away to sea, "perhaps sometime early in 1746," and then suggests that WF's running away "indicates that he indeed might have been not any older than 15 or 16 at the time" (76). Perhaps so. But the years that Philadelphia was all agog with the success of its privateers were 1742 and 1743, particularly with the amazing success of Capt. John Sibbald's several voyages. The *PG* reported his extraordinary captures on 8 April and 21 December 1742, the latter recording that the Spanish prizes he took were worth at least £90,000. It seems to me that 1742 was a more likely date than 1746 for a Philadelphia youth to want to run off to sea, but the date is unknown.

5. *DAB* and its sources; VD 91.

6. P 10:146–47n. cites John Adams, *Diary and Autobiography*, ed. L. H. Butterfield et al., 4 v. (Cambridge, Mass.: Harvard University Press, 1962) 4:151, and Thomas Bridges to Jared Ingersoll, 30 September 1762. In addition, see the DH 9 September and 1 December 1762; and 9 October 1763. See also James H. Hutson, "BF and William Smith," *PMHB* 93 (1969): 109–13.

7. Parton 198; Sparks Papers, Harvard University microfilm, APS.

8. E. D. Gillespie, *A Book of Remembrance* (Philadelphia: Lippincott, 1901) 17.

9. "Extracts from the Diary of Daniel Fisher, 1755," *PMHB* 17 (1893): 276ff.

10. George Roberts to Robert Crafton, 9 Oct 1763, in P 11:370n. William H. Mariboe, "The Life of WF" (Ph.D. diss., University of Pennsylvania, 1962) 24, found and published this letter. The information is too vague to be credited. Cf. Isaacson 77–78 and Wood 34.

11. Skemp 4.

12. Brands 110.

13. G. S. Rowe, "Infanticide, Its Judicial Resolution, and Criminal Code Revision in Early Pennsylvania," *PAPS* 135 (1991): 200–232, at 225.

14. The notation is on the inside front cover of "Ledger A&B," APS.

15. Jennifer Reed Fry, " 'Extraordinary Freedom and Great Humility': A Reinterpretation of DF," *PMHB* 127 (2003): 167–96.

16. "I Sing My Plain Country Joan" W 294; Accounts: prior to 28 August, 27 November 1731; 21 July 1735.

17. Charlotte Brown, "Journal," in *Colonial Captivities, Marches, and Journeys*, ed. Isabel M. Carter (New York: Macmillan, 1935) 190–93; Fry, " 'Extraordinary Freedom"; cf. Wood 27, 32–33.

18. Among the persons she entertained were Capt. Isaac All; Capt. Nathaniel Falconer; the Dunkard leader, John Peter Miller; Capt. Lewis Ourry; Richard Peters; and Alexander Small, etc. Almost every index in P, vols. 12–20, contains references to the Franklins' mutual friends visiting Deborah. Cf. Wood 33.

19. Peter Kalm saw a sea hen in the Delaware Bay in 1748. Adolph B. Benson, ed., *Peter Kalm's Travels in North America* (1937; New York: Dover, 1966) 13. Eric Partridge, *Dictionary of the Underworld* (London: Routledge, 1961), s.v. *hen*.

20. Lewis P. Simpson, "The Printer as a Man of Letters," in *Oldest Revolutionary* 17–18; Caroline Robbins, *Eighteenth-Century Commonwealth Man* (Cambridge, Mass.: Harvard University Press, 1959); Bernard Bailyn, *Ideological Origins of the American Revolution* (Cambridge, Mass.: Harvard University Press, 1967) 22–54; Isaacson 66.

21. A version of this fable occurs in *Mery Tales, Wittie Questions and Quick Answers* (London: H. Wykes, 1567), item no. 59. Jonas Green, editor of the *Maryland Gazette*, used Franklin's version in his own printing apology on 7 July 1747.

22. *PMHB* 48 (1924): 383–84; Zall #276; cf. 216 and 283.

23. Thomas 370.

24. Edwin Wolf 2nd speculates that Franklin may have studied French as a teen, then returned to it after learning German. Wolf, *Book Culture of a Colonial American City* (Oxford: Clarendon Press, 1988) 200, and facsimile 201. Green 19.

25. Green 16, 32.

26. Quoted from Marcello Maestro, "BF and the Penal Laws," *Journal of the History of Ideas* 36 (1975): 555. See also Antonio Pace, *BF and Italy* (Philadelphia: APS, 1958) 9, 10, 367.

27. P 34:313, 405, and 531; cf. 24:78 n.1; 34:405 n.1.

28. The Association flags will be discussed in Volume 3, Chapter 1.

29. For Read's love of Kempis, see J. Bennett Nolan, *Printer Strahan's Account Book* (Reading: Bar of Berks County, 1939) 61.

30. Richard M. Gummere, *The American Colonial Mind and the Classical Tradition* (Cambridge, Mass: Harvard University Press, 1963) 129.

31. Charles Coleman Sellers, *BF in Portraiture* (New Haven, Conn.: Yale University Press, 1962) 18–22, 11.

32. Claude-Anne Lopez, "Franklin, Hitler, Mussolini, and the Internet," in *My Life with BF* (New Haven, Conn.: Yale University Press, 2000) 3–16.

33. *PMHB* 3 (1879): 231. Richard Bache, Franklin's son-in-law, paid for half of the three seats by 1775 and probably earlier. Accounts, 14 June 1775.

34. John Adams, *Works*, ed. Charles Francis Adams, 10 v. (Boston: Little, Brown, 1850–56) 1:662.

35. Douglas C. McMurtrie, "First Decade of Printing in . . . South Carolina," *Transactions of the Bibliographical Society*, n.s. 13 (1933): 427–31; also McMurtrie, *History of Printing in the United States: Middle and South Atlantic States* (New York, 1936) 307–14.

36. Hennig Cohen, *South Carolina Gazette* (Columbia: University of South Carolina Press, 1953) 230–33.

37. See Volume 1, Chapter 14.

38. Rosalind Remer Fresca, *Printers and Men of Capital: Philadelphia Book Publishers in the New Republic* (Philadelphia: University of Pennsylvania Press, 1996) 19. James Green, in Amory and Hall 271.

39. James Green, in Amory and Hall 273–76.

40. *South Carolina Historical and Genealogical Magazine* 36 (1935): 18.

41. Cohen, *South Carolina Gazette* 233–37.

42. Ibid. 237.

43. Ibid. 240.

44. *Princetonians 1784–90*, ed. Ruth L. Woodward and Wesley Frank Craven (Princeton, N.J.: Princeton University Press, 1991) 526–29.

45. Miller, 457–74, itemizes the job printings listed in the account books.

CHAPTER 2. THE ART OF VIRTUE

1. For Franklin's progenitors, see Louis I. Bredvold, "The Invention of the Ethical Calculus," in *The Seventeenth Century: Studies in the History of English Thought* by Richard Foster Jones et al. (Stanford, Calif.: Stanford University Press, 1951) 165–80; and Norman S. Fiering, "BF and the Way to Virtue," *American Quarterly* 30 (1978): 199–223. G. P. Brooks and S. K. Aalto, "The Rise and Fall of Moral Algebra: Francis Hutcheson and the Mathematization of Psychology," *Journal of the History of the Behavioral Sciences* 17 (1981): 343–56, is also pertinent.

2. Mather, *Bonifacius* 35.

3. *NCE* 70 n.3, 71 n.9.

4. On the "Art of Virtue" (i.e., part 2 of the *Autobiography*), see Aldridge, *Nature's God* 47–57; Fiering 199–223; Granger 225–26; Hugh J. Dawson, "Franklin's 'Memoirs' in 1784: The Design of the Autobiography, Parts I and II," *Early American Literature* 12 (1978): 286–93; and Lemay, "Lockean Realities" 15–18.

5. Alexis de Toqueville, *Democracy in America* (New York: Doubleday, 1969) 525.

6. See also Volume 1, Chapter 14, the peroration to "On the Providence of God in the Government of the World." Montaigne, *Essays*, tr. Charles Cotton (London: Gilliflower, 1693) 2:481–82. Franklin read Cotton's translation; in the standard modern translation by Donald M. Frame, the quotation is found in bk. 2, ch. 16, "Of Glory" 473.

7. Shaftesbury 50. "Public Spirit" was listed as an aspect of morality that should be taught to youths in Franklin's 1749 *Proposals Relating to the Education of Youth* (3:412).

8. Fiering 218.

9. *Canon* 83–84.

10. Thomas Jefferson, *Works*, ed. Paul. Leicester Ford, 12 v. (New York: Putnam, 1893) 10:142, 185, 188.

11. Melville, in *NCE* ; Becker, *DAB*; and VD 782.

12. Lucretius, *De rerum natura* (Cambridge: Harvard University Press, 1975), bk. 4, ll. 1058, 1059.

13. J. A. Leo Lemay, "The Theme of Vanity in Franklin's *Autobiography*," *Reappraising* 372–87.

14. Port Royal *Logic*. All editions have the same structure. These expressions are found in part 1, sec. 3, at the end; and in part 3, sec. 20, no. 5.

15. Lemay, "Lockean Realities" 15–18.

16. Hugh Dawson, "Franklin's 'Memoirs' in 1784," *Early American Literature* 12 (1978): 290, observed: "Not incidentally, this self-depreciating ending turns upon the same irony with which Franklin gives their point to many of the bagatelles he wrote in these Passy years, and this neatly fashioned closure is a unique mark of division in a book whose other parts break off abruptly." Franklin frequently made ironic turns upon the persona when ending an essay. *Canon* 79.

17. P 26:85–86. For an analysis, see J. A. Leo Lemay, "BF," in *Major Writers of Early American Literature*, ed. Everett Emerson (Madison: University of Wisconsin Press, 1972) 205–43, at 234–38.

18. Jonathan Edwards, *Works*, ed. Sereno E. Dwight, 10 v. (New York: Carvell, 1830) 1:151.

19. Herbert W. Schneider, "The Significance of BF's Moral Philosophy," *Studies in the History of Ideas* 2 (1925): 291–312, first stressed that Franklin's "Art of Virtue" in Part 2 of the *Autobiography* presented an ethics of means (i.e., instrumental values), not of ends.

20. As Wood 206 wrote, "The real message of his story is that one has to keep grinding away and not remain satisfied with a speckled ax." On self-deceiving reason, see Volume 1, Chapter 10.

21. *De Augmentis*, bk. 7, ch. 1, in *Philosophical Works of Francis Bacon*, ed. John M. Robertson (London: Routledge, 1905) 562.

22. Larzer Ziff, *The Career of John Cotton* (Princeton, N.J. : Princeton University Press, 1962) 20–21.

23. Professor Bianca Theisen discusses the change in the chapter "Antiautobiography" (the English title of Thomas Berhard's series of autobiographies) in her forthcoming book on German autobiographies.

24. Lemay, "Franklin's *Autobiography* and the American Dream," *NCE* 349–60. Originally, the essay was the concluding part of Lemay, *Renaissance Man* 21–33, 41–44.

25. Pascal 161; see also 78, 153, 157.

26. Lemay, *Renaissance Man* 41 n.70.

27. Cabanis 5:232.

28. *NCE* 289–90. V. S. Pritchett wrote in 1941: "Before Franklin's irony, urbanity and benevolence, Lawrence cuts an absurd figure, rather like a Sunday School teacher who has gone to a *Social* dressed up as a howling dervish, when fancy dress was *not* requested." Pritchett, *New Statesman and Nation* 22 (27 September 1941): 309, reprinted in Pritchett, *Complete Essays* (London: Chatto, 1991) 133. Robert E. Spiller, 1942, and Robert Freeman Sayre, 1963, made similar points. For bibliographical references to Sayre and Spiller, see *NCE* 375.

29. D. H. Lawrence, *Studies in Classic American Literature* (New York: Viking, 1923) 9, 10.

30. Schneider argued that Franklin's freedom in not enmeshing his virtues "with cosmology, psychology, and epistemology is in itself a philosophic achievement" (298). Pritchett, *Complete Essays* 133.

31. Schneider 299.

32. Kimura Ki, *A History of Japanese-American Culture Relations, 1853–1926*, v. 2: *Japanese Literature; Manners and Customs in the Meiji-Taisho Era* (Tokyo: Obunsha, 1957) 116–18.

33. Ralph Lerner, "Dr. Janus," in *Reappraising* 415–24.

34. The first version, "BF," *English Review* 27 (1918) 397–408, is more obviously anti-American than the second, published in Lawrence's *Studies in Classic American Literature* (London: Secker, 1923).

35. Lemay, "American Aesthetic"; *Spectator* 1:297.

36. John Dennis, *Critical Works*, 2 v., ed. Edward Niles Hooker (Baltimore: Johns Hopkins University Press, 1939–43) 1:32.

37. David Hume, *Essays*, ed. Eugene F. Miller (Indianapolis: Liberty Classics, 1985) 191.

38. For a number of comparisons between this essay and Franklin's writings (only a few of which are pointed out below), see *Canon* 60–62. The text is in W 181–84.

39. A 5; P 1:22, 119, 13:233, 16:118, 209, etc. For the pseudonym, see P 13:7–8, 44–49.

40. *The Journal of John Fontaine*, ed. Edward Porter Alexander (Charlottesville: University Press of Virginia, 1972) 86; J. A. Leo Lemay, "Robert Beverley's *History and Present State of Virginia* and the Emerging American Political Ideology," in *American Letters and the Historical Consciousness: Essays in Honor of Lewis P. Simpson*, ed. J. Gerald Kennedy and Daniel Mark Fogel (Baton Rouge: Louisiana State University Press, 1987) 85–86.

41. Raymond D. Havens, "Simplicity: A Changing Concept," *Journal of the History of Ideas* 14 (1953): 3–32, at 8.

42. Havens, 6–8, cites numerous similar passages.

43. Havens surveys "Simplicity" from the late seventeenth century to the Romantic period, discussing the preface to the *Lyrical Ballads* on p. 27 and Wordsworth on p. 31.

44. See also Lemay, "American Aesthetic," esp. 494–95.

45. Several additional references concerning simplicity are cited in *Canon* 62.

46. I identified the references to Bacon's essays as no. 22, "Of Cunning," and no. 6, "Of Simulation and Dissimulation," in W 1526. Mandeville 1:320.

47. Jonathan Williams manuscripts, Lilly Library, Bloomington, Indiana. Cited in *Canon* 61.

48. Mandeville 1:57.

49. Mandeville 2:346n, and n.1, above.

50. Shaftesbury 177–79.

51. David Hume, *A Treatise of Human Nature* (1739–40), ed. David Fate Norton and Mary J. Norton (Oxford: Oxford University Press, 2000) 4–5, 369; also Hume, *An Enquiry Concerning Human Understanding* (1748), ed. Tom L. Beauchamp (Oxford: Clarendon Press, 2000) 40.

52. Alfred Owen Aldridge, "Franklin's 'Shaftesburian' Dialogues Not Franklin's: A Revision of the Franklin Canon," *American Literature* 21 (1949–50): 151–59; Aldridge, *Nature's God* 60–61.

53. Horace, *Satire, Epistles and Ars Poetica*, tr. H. Rushton Fairclough (Cambridge: Loeb Classical Library, 1929) 288–89 (l. 29) and 352–53 (l. 20); Pascal 140; Locke, *Essay*, bk. 2, ch. 21, sec. 41–43, pp. 258–60.

54. Aldridge, "Franklin's 'Shaftesburian' Dialogues" 157; Shaftesbury 176. See also Aldridge, *Nature's God* 61–62.

55. Mandeville 1:323, 48, respectively.

56. Robert D. Arner, "Politics and Temperance in Boston and Philadelphia," in *Reappraising*, 69, points out Franklin's several verbal echoes of Swift.

57. Norman S. Fiering, "Irresistible Compassion: An Aspect of Eighteenth-Century Sympathy and Humanitarianism," *Journal of the History of Ideas* 37 (1976): 195–218.

58. Mark Twain, *Adventures of Huckleberry Finn*, ch. 13.

59. *Calendar* #1777. Desmond Eyles, *"Good Sir Toby": The Story of Toby Jugs* (London: Doulton, 1955). Eyles, 17, dates Fawkes's poem "about 1761."

60. J. D. McFarland, *Kant's Concept of Teleology* (Edinburgh: University of Edinburgh Press, 1970) 48.

61. Franklin made the same observation in his *Dissertation* (1:66). Locke's version is found in his *Essay*, ed. Nidditch (1975) 281.

62. Aram Vartanian, *La Mettrie's L'Homme Machine: A Study in the Origins of an Idea* (Princeton, N.J.: Princeton University Press, 1960).

63. Pascal 146.

64. See ch. 8, "The Church in Danger: Ridicule Runs Riot," in John Redwood, *Reason, Ridicule and Religion: The Age of Enlightenment in England, 1660–1750* (Cambridge, Mass.: Harvard University Press, 1976) 174–96.

65. Alfred Owen Aldridge, "A Religious Hoax by BF," *American Literature* 36 (1964): 204–9; also Aldridge, *Nature's God* 67–68.

66. Lemay, *BF: Optimist or Pessimist?* (Newark: University of Delaware, 1990).

CHAPTER 3. FREEMASON

1. Douglas Knoop, G. P. Jones, and Douglas Hamer, *The Early Masonic Catechisms* (Manchester: University of Manchester Press, 1963) 152–56.

2. The date is based on St. John's Lodge meeting on the first Monday of the month. Clifford P. McCalla, *Sketch of the Early History of St. John's Lodge, Philadelphia from A.D. 1731 to 1738* (Philadelphia: Masonic Printing Co., 1884) 33.

3. Franklin's account in the St. John's Lodge, "Liber B," Pennsylvania Historical Society, Philadelphia, shows that he paid the monthly dues for five months and the remainder of his initiation fee on June 24. That meant his first monthly dues were for February. P 1:202–4 prints his account.

4. Wayne A. Huss, *The Master Builders: A History of the Grand Lodge of Free and Accepted Masons of Pennsylvania*, 3 v. (Philadelphia: Grand Lodge, 1986–89) 1:16–18.

5. The Masonic lodge that Franklin joined hardly represented "another step up the social ladder." Isaacson 106. It gradually changed, over the next two decades, into a group of middle-class citizens.

6. Roach 142 n.55.

7. P 1:202 mistakenly prints 5 November for 1 November.

8. Julius F. Sachse, *Franklin's Account with the Lodge of Masons, 1731–1737, as Found upon the Pages of His Daily Journal* (Philadelphia: Columbia Lodge, [1899?]) 6. This pamphlet is in the APS library, Philadelphia.

9. P 1:203 mistakenly reports Franklin absent on Monday, 4 December.

10. John Hobart advertised in the *PG* for 11 July 1734 that he now kept an inn at the "sign of the Conestoga Wagon in Market-Street next door to the White-Horse."

11. Miller, no. A 76, p. 459, gives the date. Sachse, *Franklin's Account* 8.

12. Sachse, *Franklin's Account* 8.

13. For comments on the effect of the changing social status of the members and on the different lodges, see Steven C. Bullock, *Revolutionary Brotherhood* (Chapel Hill: University of North Carolina Press, 1996) 85ff.

14. Steven C. Bullock, "The Revolutionary Transformation of American Free-masonry, 1752–1792," *WMQ* 47 (1990): 347–69.

CHAPTER 4. THE LIBRARY COMPANY OF PHILADELPHIA

1. LCP, "Articles of Association," 1 July 1731, in DH.

2. Zachariah Poulson, Jr., librarian, compiled the Shareholders' Book from various earlier records about 1800; it has been kept up-to-date since then.

3. Though I have used the list of shareholders in the LCP, the history of the first eighty-five shares may be found in Dorothy F. Grimm, "A History of the LCP, 1731–1835" (Ph.D. diss., University of Pennsylvania, 1955) 298–312. Two other general studies of the early LCP are Edwin Wolf 2nd, *"At the Instance of Benjamin Franklin": A Brief History of the LCP* (Philadelphia: Library Company, 1976; revised and enlarged [by John C. Van Horne and James Green] in 1995); and George Boudreau, "'Highly Valuable & Entensively Useful': Community and

Readership Among the Eighteenth-Century Philadelphia Middling Sort," *Pennsylvania History* 63 (1996): 302–29.

4. When Francis Hopkinson transcribed the early minutes in the late eighteenth century, he slipped and wrote "William" Logan instead of James Logan.

5. *PG*, 2 November, recorded that Cornock "Entred inwards."

6. Edwin Wolf 2nd, "First Books and Printed Catalogues of the LCP," *PMHB* 78 (1954): 45–70, and Wolf, "Franklin and His Friends Choose Their Books," *PMHB* 80 (1956): 11–36, at 15.

7. Wolf, "First Books" 47. Miller #71. Miller speculated that it was printed late in 1732 or early in 1733, and he listed it under 1733. The LCP minutes for 11 December 1732 may suggest that it was already in print; it definitely was before 19 February 1721/3 (Wolf 47–48).

8. *PG*, 25 April 1734; reprinted in the DH.

9. Richard Lewis, *Carmen Seculare* (Annapolis: Parks, 1732); see Lemay, *Men of Letters* 166–67.

10. For the *translatio* idea in eighteenth-century America, see the subject and genre index to *Calendar*. In Titan Leeds, *The American Almanac for 1730*, George Webb had written, "Europe shall mourn her ancient Fame declin'd / And Philadelphia be the Athens of Mankind." *Calendar* #1151. In addition to the notes in Volume 1, Chapter 3, n. 19 and Chapter 10, n. 15, see Shields, "Wits" 123–33.

11. See the genealogical chart, P 8:140–41, also 14:161 n.7, 18:90 n.8.

12. Francis Hopkinson transcribed all the early minutes, and the "F" was his slip of the pen for "T."

13. Edwin Wolf 2nd, *Book Culture of a Colonial American City* (Oxford: Clarendon Press, 1988) 32, does not include Grotius.

14. Cabanis 5:228.

15. S 10:9.

16. Jack P. Greene, *The Intellectual Heritage of the Constitutional Era: The Delegates' Library* (Philadelphia: LCP, 1986), discusses the reading background of the members of the Constitutional Convention, with emphasis on the Library Company books.

17. Wolf, introduction, *Catalogue* (1741) ix.

18. Edwin Wolf 2nd, *The Library of James Logan* (Philadelphia: LCP, 1974), #1426, 1427, 1428.

19. Actually printed in 1747 and titled *The Charter of the LCP* (Philadelphia: Franklin, 1746); Evans 5853.

20. Described and illustrated in [Darrel Sewell, ed.,] *Philadelphia: Three Centuries of American Art* (Philadelphia: Philadelphia Museum of Art, 1976) 37–39.

21. Edmund Berkeley and Dorothy Smith Berkeley, *Correspondence of John Bartram* (Gainesville: University Press of Florida, 1992) 218.

22. Lemay, "Lockean Realities," 12–15.

23. For an examination of Franklin's uses of flourishes and dashes in composition, see A 252–53.

24. John F. Lynen, *The Design of the Present* (New Haven, Conn: Yale University Press, 1969) 90, has contrasted the usual perspective of Franklin's *Autobiography* ("a view qualified and limited to just that portion of reality which appears within the self's horizon") with that of Jonathan Edwards's "eternal point of view" in his "Personal Narrative."

25. Though early in his life Franklin had assumed that blacks were inferior in intelligence to whites, he had changed his mind by 17 December 1763 (P 10:395–96).

26. *NCE* 219. Jefferson, *Writings*, ed. Merrill D. Peterson (New York: Library of America, 1984) 1304–10. From the Enlightenment's traditions of "natural aristocracy," see the index of James Harrington, *Political Works*, ed. J.G.A. Pocock (Cambridge: Cambridge University Press, 1977), s.v. "Aristocracy, natural."

27. *The Private Life of the Late BF* (London: J. Parsons, 1793) 307.

28. Larzer Ziff, *Writing in the New Nation: Prose, Print, and Politics in the Early United States* (New Haven, Conn.: Yale University Press, 1991) 88.

Chapter 5. Man of Letters

1. Two essays, "Rules and Maxims" and "An Apology for Printers," directly reflected Franklin's personal or business life and are considered in Chapter 1. A number of writings on religion and on values, as well as his "Art of Virtue," are in Chapter 2. Essays concerning Pennsylvania politics and Franklin's rivalry with Andrew Bradford are found in Chapter 6. The writings in *Poor Richard* (except for the preface to the 1758 almanac, later titled "The Way to Wealth" are discussed in Chapters 7 and 8. Franklin's defenses of the Reverend Samuel Hemphill in his orthodoxy trial by the Philadelphia Presbyterian Synod constitute Chapter 9.

2. Shields, *Civil Tongues* 262–66; John W. Ward, "Who Was BF?" *American Scholar* 32 (1963): 541–53; John Griffith, "Franklin's Sanity and the Man behind the Masks," *Oldest Revolutionary* 123–38.

3. Robert Bolling, "A Collection of Diverting Anecdotes, Bon-mots and Other Trifling Pieces, 1764." Manuscript volume, Huntington Library, San Marino, California, accession no. BR[ock] 163, pp. 124–25.

4. Port Royal *Logic* 373.

5. In Chapter 7, "*Poor Richard*'s Prefaces," see "The 1736 Preface."

6. P 3:120–25, 35:491–502; W 1115–16.

7. Verner W. Crane, *BF's Letters to the Press, 1758–1775* (Chapel Hill: University of North Carolina Press, 1950) xxvii–xxx.

8. Ellen Cohn briefly discusses its early composition in "BF, Benjamin Vaughan, and *Political, Miscellaneous and Philosophical Pieces*," in *BF: An American Genius*, ed. Gianfranca Balestra and Luigi Sampietro (Rome: Bulzoni Editore, 1993) 160–61.

9. Antonio Pace, *BF and Italy* (Philadelphia: APS, 1958) 5.

10. Niccolo Machiavelli, *The Prince*, tr. Harvey C. Mansfield, Jr. (Chicago: University of Chicago Press, 1985) 59.

11. Port Royal *Logic* 11, revising Martial, bk. 2, epigram 86. "Turpe est difficiles habere nugas / et stultus labor est ineptiarum": "It's demeaning to make difficulties out of trifles, and labor over frivolities is foolish." Martial, *Epigrams*, ed. D. R. Shackleton Bailey, 3 v. (Cambridge, Mass.: Harvard University Press, 1993) 1:194–95.

12. I have emended *giving* to *getting* in accordance with the other authoritative text.

13. P 29:753.

14. Zall #236, 246, 262.

15. P 25:204, with BF writing in imitation of Mme. Brillon's holograph. Claude-Anne Lopez, *Mon cher papa* (New Haven, Conn.: Yale University Press, 1966) 59.

16. DeArmond, 187, pointed out that "Casettier" in the *AWM* of 25 January 1732/3 "practically admitted his indebtedness to 'Chatterbox.'"

17. Amacher 31–34; Granger 10–11.

18. *Proposal for Correcting . . . the English Tongue* (1712), in Swift, ed. Davis 4:11.

19. Usages of the comparatively uncommon "hath" for "has" is a Franklin characteristic.

20. *A Letter to a Young Gentleman, Lately Enter'd into Holy Orders* (1720), in Swift, ed. Davis 9:65.

21. Irving to Henry Brevoort, in P. M. Irving, *Life of Washington Irving*, 4 v. (New York: Putnam, 1862–64) 2:35.

22. Poe's review of Hawthorne's *Twice-Told Tales*. Poe, *Essays and Reviews*, ed. G. R. Thompson (New York: Library of America, 1984) 586.

23. Amacher 34–35.

24. Henry Knight Miller, "The Paradoxical Encomium with Special Reference to Its Vogue in England, 1600–1800," *Modern Philology* 53 (1956): 145–78.

25. Shields, "The British Empire and the Poetry of Commerce," in *Oracles* 13–92.

26. Lemay, *BF: Optimist or Pessimist?*

27. Miller 342.

28. Granger 47–48; Shields, *Civil Tongues* 114–15.

29. Gary E. Baker surveys the material culture in the Anthony Afterwit letter, "He That Would Trive Must Ask His Wife: Franklin's Anthony Afterwit Letter," *PMHB* 109 (1985): 27–41.

30. See, for example, "Consequences of Extravagance," *American Museum*, June 1787.

31. Isaacson 79; see also Granger 48–49.

32. Cf. Wood 50–51. BF's anecdote may reflect Cotton Mather's monkey fable, which Mather adapted from William Dampier's *Voyage* (1697), see Volume 1, Chapter 6.

33. Shields, *Civil Tongues* 37–38; Waldstreicher 97–98.

34. One can discriminate among these ancient folk customs. For representative literature, see E. P. Thompson, "'Rough Music': Le Charivari Anglais," *Annales: Economies, sociétes, civilizations* 27 (1972): 285–312; and Violet Alford, "Rough Music or Charivari," *Folklore* 70 (1959): 505–18. Samuel Butler, *Hudibras*, part 2,

canto 2, ll. 753ff, gives a classic description. Hogarth illustrated it: Ronald Paulson, *Hogarth's Graphic Works*, rev. ed., 1: Introduction and Catalogue (New Haven, Conn.: Yale University Press, 1970), catalogue no. 79 (7), plate 83; and catalogue no. 94, plate 98.

35. *Canon* #50, part of which I echo below. Robert D. Arner, "Politics and Temperance in Boston and Philadelphia: BF's Journalistic Writings on Drinking and Drunkenness" in *Reappraising* 52–77, surveys the topic in detail.

36. Ronald A. Bosco, "'Scandal, Like Other Virtues, Is in Part Its Own Reward': Franklin Working the Crime Beat," in *Reappraising* 91.

37. "On Wine, from the Abbé Franklin to the Abbé Morellet," W 939–42.

CHAPTER 6. POLITICS, RELIGION, AND THE RIVALRY WITH BRADFORD, 1732

1. DeArmond 213–14.

2. On Webbe, see P 2:145–46, 265; Lemay, *Men of Letters* 236–37; and J. A. Leo Lemay, "Hamilton's Literary History of the *Maryland Gazette*," WMQ 23 (1966): 280 n.25.

3. Lemay, *Men of Letters*. For the motif in *The Sot-Weed Factor*, 85–87, and for the Annapolis editions, 358.

4. Cook 97–98.

5. Port Royal *Logic* 163–64.

6. Ibid. 163–64, 354.

7. Lucretius, *De rerum natura*, bk. 3, ll. 469ff.

8. *Canon* 58–60; see the appreciations by Cook 97–98 and Sappenfield 73.

9. Cook 99.

10. For a seventeenth-century example, see Samuel Bailey, "The College Ferula, Being a Reply to 'The Country-man's Apocrypha,'" in Brom Weber, *An Anthology of American Humor* (New York: T. Y. Crowell Co., 1962) 25–26. For the prigs/pigs comparison, see J. A. Leo Lemay, "The Contexts and Themes of 'The Hasty Pudding,'" *Early American Literature* 17 (1982): 3–23.

11. The editors of *The Papers of Benjamin Franklin* commented: "The writer of the piece here introduced who signed himself 'Prosit,' had formerly presented his thoughts in the *American Weekly Mercury*. 'Marcus' customarily replied in the *PG*. When 'Prosit' sent his defense to BF to publish, 'Marcus' found a channel for his rejoinders in Bradford's paper." P 1:271 n.9. Also Norma Summers, "BF—Printing Entrepreneur" 146.

12. Shaftesbury 177–79.

13. Granger 14–15, 17–18, 37, 49–50.

14. Fifteen additional writings from 1732 are: "Query to the Casuist: The Case of the Missing Horse," 18 January; "From the Casuist: The Case of the Missing Horse," and news-note jeu d'esprit on the death of a lion, 25 January; first version of "The Palatine Appeal," 8 February; second version of "The Palatine Appeal," 15 February; "A Burnt Offering," 15 February (b); "On Simplicity," 13 April; "A Quaker Lady on a Lover's Threat," 25 May; Anthony Afterwit, 10 July; Celia

Single, 24 July; Praise for William Penn, 14 August; "On the Benevolence as Well as Selfishness of Man," 30 November; "On Colds," 30 November; "Death of a Drunk," 7 December; and the first *Poor Richard's Almanack*, 28 December.

Chapter 7. *Poor Richard's* Prefaces, 1733–1747

1. J. A. Leo Lemay, "BF" in *Major Writers of Early American Literature*, ed. Everett H. Emerson (Madison: University of Wisconsin Press, 1972) 212. Sappenfield, 60–61, independently came to the same conclusion.

2. Bernard Stuart Capp, *Astrology and the Popular Press: English Almanacs, 1500–1800* (Ithaca, N.Y.: Cornell University Press, 1979) 378, 339.

3. Samuel Maxwell edited the *Rhode Island Almanac* (by "Poor Robin") for 1731; the others were by James Franklin. Clarence S. Brigham, "James Franklin and the Beginnings of Printing in Rhode Island," *PMHS* 65 (1932–36): 536–44, at 539.

4. See Newcomb, 373, for the sources of the poems.

5. The almanacs are best read in the facsimile edition with an introduction by Whitfield J. Bell, Jr., *The Complete Poor Richard Almanacs*, 2 v. (Barre, Mass.: Imprint Society, 1970). Amacher 51–66; Granger 51–76. For a more recent discussion and references to scholarship, see Cameron C. Nickels, "Franklin's Poor Richard Almanacs: 'The Humblest of His Labors," in *Oldest Revolutionary* 77–90. For its context, see Frank Palmeri, *Satire, History, Novel* (Newark: University of Delaware Press, 2003) 44–76.

6. Swift, ed. Davis 2:145.

7. Ibid. 2:155.

8. Ibid.

9. Cf. John F. Ross, "The Character of 'Poor Richard': Its Source and Alteration," *PMLA* 55 (1940): 785–94.

10. Cf. Miller nos. 52 and 53. For notes on the sales, see C. W. Miller, "Franklin's *Poor Richard Almanacs*: Their Printing and Publication," *Studies in Bibliography* 14 (1961): 97–115, at 111–13.

11. Swift, ed. Davis 2:162–63.

12. Franklin discussed the Leibnitz/Clarke debate in "On the Providence of God in the Government of the World" (1730) (see Volume 1, Chapter 14).

13. Swift, ed. Davis 2:162.

14. Franklin's copy of Swift's Bickerstaff essays survives in the LCP. Green 23.

15. Swift, ed. Davis 2:162–63.

16. Theo Brown, *The Fate of the Dead* (Cambridge: D. S. Brewer, 1979) 66 (Addison), also 33–34, 62, 71, 85.

17. John Leich of Cornwall, Conn., professor of foreign languages and political science, emeritus, at the Louisiana Technological University, commented on the Latin at the request of my friend Professor Edward A. Nickerson.

18. C. William Miller, "Franklin's *Poor Richard Almanacs*," *Studies in Bibliography* 14 (1961): 97–115, at 111.

19. Lewis P. Simpson, "The Printer as a Man of Letters," in *Oldest Revolutionary* 12.

CHAPTER 8. *POOR RICHARD*'S PROVERBS

1. Proverb scholars often distinguish among sententiae, sayings, aphorisms, and proverbs. The best discrimination among short, pithy sayings that I know is David S. Shields's introduction to his *Laconics* (Charleston, S.C.: Shields, 2001). I blandly ignore all such distinctions in my discussion. The best study of Franklin's proverbs is Newcomb. See also Amacher 56–64, 181–82; Granger 64–71; VD 109–14.

2. Lewis Leary, "Joseph Dennie on Benjamin Franklin," *PMHB* 72 (1948): 240–46.

3. In addition to the discussion of Silence Dogood No. 1 (Volume 1, Chapter 7), see the remarks on "On Simplicity" (Chapter 2).

4. *The Letters of Philip Dormer Stanhope, 4th Earl of Chesterfield*, ed. Bonamy Dobree, 6 v. (1932; New York: AMS Press, 1968) 2:461. Bartlett Jere Whiting, *Early American Proverbs and Proverbial Phrases* (Cambridge, Mass.: Harvard University Press, 1977) xv, briefly surveys eighteenth-century contempt for proverbs.

5. James Howell, *Lexicon Tetraglotton* (London, 1659). Newcomb, 50–65, shows that Franklin used Howell extensively.

6. Newcomb 51. Also useful is Frances M. Barbour, *A Concordance to the Sayings in Franklin's Poor Richard* (Detroit: Gale, 1974).

7. The sayings are alphabetically arranged by the first nouns in Newcomb, appendix 1, "A Source-Check List of the Sayings of Poor Richard" 255–371. If the saying contains no nouns (pronouns and proper nouns are ignored), then Newcomb alphabetized them by verbals and finally by verbs. The reader interested in the location of the source can look up the proverb in Newcomb, where he will find it quoted with references. For example, the first proverb I quote below is in Newcomb 258 with the source, which is James Howell's *Lexicon Tetraglotton* (1659).

8. Whitfield J. Bell, Jr., *The Complete Poor Richard Almanacks* (Barre, Mass.: Imprint Society, 1970) 1:xxi.

9. *The Writings of Herman Melville*, ed. Harrison Hayford et al., v. 9, *Piazza Tales* (Evanston: Northwestern University Press, 1987) 243.

10. Newcomb 112–17; Aldridge 60.

11. Newcomb 319.

12. Ibid. 315.

13. P. M. Zall, *Mark Twain Laughing* (Knoxville: University of Tennessee Press, 1985) 71, #178.

14. Newcomb 267.

15. Ibid. 369.

16. Mather, *Bonifacius* 24: "The noblest question in the world: *What good may I do in the world?*"

17. *Letters of . . . Chesterfield*, ed. Dobree 2:461.

18. *Complete Works of Captain John Smith*, 3 v., ed. Philip L. Barbour (Chapel Hill: University Of North Carolina Press, 1986) 1:133.

19. *NCE* 248.

20. Newcomb 350.

21. Ibid. 353; Betty Ring, *American Needlework Treasures* (New York: Dutton, 1987) 4; cf. Esther C. Averill, "Lugubrious Rhymes of Samplers," *Antiquarian* 8, no. 2 (March 1927): 28–34. I thank Amy Moore for calling my attention to the verse in the samplers.

22. Lester Cappon, ed., *Adams-Jefferson Letters*, 2 v. (Chapel Hill: University of North Carolina Press, 1959) 2:399.

CHAPTER 9. FRANKLIN AND POLITICS, 1730–1736

1. William S. Hanna, *BF and Pennsylvania Politics* (Stanford, Calif.: Stanford University Press, 1964) 25–32; Francis Jennings, *BF, Politician* (New York: Norton, 1996) 17.

2. *English Advice to the Freeholders* (Boston: Franklin, 1722), 20 April 1722.

3. George Simson, "Legal Sources for Franklin's 'Edict,'" *American Literature* 32 (1960): 152–57.

4. *PG*: in 1731: 17 June p. 6; 24 June p. 4; 1 July p. 1; 8 July p. 1; 15 July p. 1; 22 July p. 1; 27 Nov. p. 1; in 1732: 27 April p. 4; 11 May p. 4; 8 June p. 3; 31 July p. 1; 28 Dec. p. 1; and in 1733: 12 April p. 2; 10 May p. 2; 28 June p. 4; 12 July p. 3. See *Canon* 55–57.

5. *Royal Instructions to British Colonial Governors, 1670–1776*, ed. Leonard W. Labaree, 2 v. (1935; rpt., New York: Octagon Books, 1967) 2:673–74, #939.

6. My attribution. For the context, see Carroll T. Bond, ed., *Proceedings of the Maryland Court of Appeals, 1695–1729* (Washington, D.C.: American Historical Association, 1933) xli ff.

7. DeArmond 81.

8. Dr. Benjamin Rush's notes on conversations with Franklin, *PMHB* 29 (1905): 23–24.

9. DeArmond 87–90. For more information concerning the deteriorating relations between Hamilton and his opponents, as well as more information on the satiric attacks on him, see Horle 430–32.

10. DeArmond 90.

11. Horle 430–31, 779, 780.

12. In the only recorded reaction of a contemporary, James Logan thought that the last sentence was too vulgar. Horle 446 n.127.

13. DeArmond 97–98; Horle 2:435.

14. Joseph E. J. Johnson, "A Quaker Imperialist's View," *PMHB* 60 (1936) 97–130.

15. Johnson 118.

16. Thomas Jefferson wrote Isaiah Thomas about Virginia's control of its colonial printer because he printed its official business. Thomas 556.

CHAPTER 10. THE HEMPHILL CONTROVERSY

1. William S. Barker, "The Hemphill Case, Franklin, and Subscription to the West-

minster Confession," *American Presbyterians* 69 (1991): 243–57, at 243. Major
discussions are in Merton A. Christensen, "Franklin on the Hemphill Trial:
Deism Versus Presbyterian Orthodoxy," *WMQ* 10 (1953): 422–40; Aldridge, *Nature's God* 86–98; Anderson 79–85; and Melvin H. Buxbaum, *BF and the Zealous
Presbyterians* (University Park: Pennsylvania State University Press, 1975) 76–115.

2. *Minutes of the Presbyterian Church in America, 1706–1788*, ed. Guy S. Klett (Philadelphia: Presbyterian Historical Society, 1976) 121 and 103–4, respectively.

3. William N. Engle, ed., *Records of the Presbyterian Church in the United States . . .
1706–1788*, 2 v. (Philadelphia, 1841) 1:105–6.

4. Shipton 4:222.

5. *Extract of the Minutes of the Commission of the Synod* (Philadelphia: Bradford,
1735). Evans 3951 could not locate a copy, but one is in the Presbyterian Historical
Society, Philadelphia. Cited in the text of this chapter as *E* and page number.

6. Marilyn J. Westerkamp, *Triumph of the Laity: Scots-Irish Piety and the Great
Awakening, 1625–1760* (New York: Oxford University Press, 1988) 160.

7. Franklin's letter to Joseph Huey, 6 June 1753, advocates works, rather than faith,
as essential (P 4:503–6).

8. Aldridge, *Nature's God*, 89–90, pointed out the allusion to Bayle.

9. Crane 24–25; see also Volume 1, Chapter 18, n.6.

10. Shipton 4:222.

11. Ebenezer Pemberton, *A Sermon Preached Before the Commission* (New York:
Zenger, 1735) 10, 19, 12–13, 15, respectively. Evans 3945.

12. Robert Cross, *The Danger of Perverting the Gospel of Christ, Represented in a
Sermon Preach'd Before the Commission of the Synod at Philadelphia, April 20*th,
1735 (New York: Zenger, 1735) 7, 15, 16, 19, 23, and 27, respectively. Not in Evans,
but a copy is in the Presbyterian Historical Society, Philadelphia.

13. Cross 30.

14. Samuel Willard, *Some Miscellany Observations . . . Respecting Witchcrafts, in a
Dialogue between S. & B.* (Philadelphia: Bradford, 1692); Evans 631. Since Willard
was Josiah Franklin's pastor, the work may well have been among the books in
Franklin's father's library.

15. For traditions on the subject of behavior, see Fiering, "BF and the Way to Virtue" 199–223.

16. Richard Webster, *History of the Presbyterian Church in America* (Philadelphia:
Wilson, 1857) 340.

17. Barker, 252, citing an annotated copy at Princeton Theological Seminary.

18. Buxbaum 234 n.105.

19. Martin E. Lodge, "The Crisis of the Churches in the Middle Colonies, 1720–
1750," *PMHB* 95 (1971): 195–220.

20. For one early exception (1705), wherein Robert Beverley pretends, on the one
hand, to be condemning Catholic priests and, on the other, to attack Indian
conjurors, see J.A. Leo Lemay, "The Amerindian in the Early American Enlight-

enment: Deistic Satire in Robert Beverley's *History of Virginia*" in *Deism, Masonry, and the Enlightenment: Essays Honoring Alfred Owen Aldridge* (Newark: University of Delaware Press, 1987) 86–90.

21. Mandeville: see the subheading "Pyrrhonism" in the index under "Ethics."

22. Stephen Foster, *Long Argument* (Chapel Hill: University of North Carolina Press, 1991) 279, citing Willard, *The Peril of the Times Displayed* (Boston: Green and Allan, 1700) 143–47; and E. Brooks Holifield, *Covenant Sealed* (New Haven, Conn.: Yale University Press, 1974) 219–20.

23. Locke, *Essay* 384–94, 657–68.

24. The lot was given to Father Joseph Greaton, S.J., on 15 May 1733. On it, he built a two-story house and a chapel. Joseph L. J. Kirlin, *Catholicity in Philadelphia* (Philadelphia: McVey, 1909) 35.

25. *Minutes of the Presbyterian Church* 129–31.

26. P 2:92–93; allusion noted by Aldridge, *Nature's God* 98.

27. Aldridge, *Nature's God* 52–53, pointed out the Swift allusion. Swift, *A Tale of a Tub . . . Battle of the Books*, ed. A. C. Guthkelch and D. Nichol Smith, 2nd ed. (Oxford: Clarendon Press, 1958) 228–31. At n.4, p. 321, Guthkelch and Smith note resemblances to William Temple and Francis Bacon. See also Brian Vickers, "Swift and the Baconian Idol," in *The World of Jonathan Swift*, ed. Vickers (Cambridge, Mass.: Harvard University Press, 1968) 87–128, at 98–99.

28. In his letter to Joseph Priestley of 21 August 1784, Franklin said "there are several Things in the Old Testament, impossible to be given by *divine* Inspiration; such as the Approbation ascribed to the Angel of the Lord, of that abominably wicked and detestable Action of Jael, the wife of Heber, the Kenite. [Judges 4]. If the rest of the Book were like that, I should rather suppose it given by Inspiration from another Quarter, and renounce the whole" (W 1103).

29. BF, *A Defence of the Reverend Mr. Hemphill's Observations, or an Answer to the Vindication of the Reverend Commission* (Philadelphia: Franklin, 1735), p. [48]. Evans 3901.

30. Barker 249.

31. Shipton 6:535.

CHAPTER 12. PERSONAL LIFE

1. John McVickar, *A Domestic Narrative of the Life of Samuel Bard* (New York: Paul, 1822) 18–19.

2. Cabanis 5:265n. See P 2:352–54. There are six texts: #1, [BF], *Father's Abraham's Speech . . .* (Boston: B. Mecom, [1758]; rpt. in W 293–94); #2, ms at APS in BF's papers though not in his hand, n.d.; rpt. in P 2:352–54; #3, *Monthly Repository of Theology and General Literature* 3 (1808) 214; #4, *Songster's Repository* (New York: Dearborn, 1811) 32; #5, *Songster's Companion* (Brattleboro, Vt., 1815) 282; and #6, McVickar, *Domestic Narrative* 18–19. P 2:352–54 compared texts 2, 3, and 6. Lemay, "Franklin and the *Autobiography*," *Eighteenth-Century Studies* 1 (1967):

185–211, at 189–90, briefly discusses the texts. See also Ellen R. Cohn, "BF and Traditional Music," in *Reappraising* 300–303.

3. The text in W 293–94 is slightly better than that in P 2:352–54; see my discussion in "Franklin and the *Autobiography*"; Cohn published the tune in *Reappraising* 301–2.

4. [BF], *Father Abraham's Speech* (Boston: B. Mecom, [1758]) 24. The pamphlet was reprinted in 1807. For bibliographical notes, see J. A. Leo Lemay, *"New England's Annoyances"* (Newark: University of Delaware Press, 1985) 146–47. Mecom's text is reprinted in W 293–94.

5. Cohn 300.

6. "Extracts from the Diary of Daniel Fisher, 1755," *PMHB* 17 (1893): 263–78, at 272; E[lizabeth] D[uane] Gillespie, *A Book of Remembrance* (Philadelphia: Lippincott, 1901) 17.

7. P 13:329; 3 July 1766.

8. Lopez and Herbert, *Private* 291–302; Gary B. Nash, *Freedom by Degrees: Emancipation in Pennsylvania* (New York: Oxford University Press, 1991); and Waldstreicher.

9. The Charles Moore accounts have been in my on-line DH since 1997. The account is printed in facsimile in Waldstreicher, facing p. 3.

10. VD 299.

11. Franklin's inventory is in the APS. Cohn, 293, has discussed Franklin's musical instruments, finding no evidence that he either owned or played the guitar or violin.

12. BF, Accounts, Ledger A&B 203a; dated only 1731.

13. Leigh Hunt, *Autobiography*, ed. J. E. Morpurgo (New York: Chanticleer Press, 1949) 22, 41.

14. Carleton Sprague Smith, "A Tune for BF's Drinking Song 'Fair Venus Calls,'" *Inter-American Music Review* 10 (1989): 147–55. [David Vinton], *Masonic Minstrel* (Dedham, Mass.: H. Mann, 1816) 40–41.

15. For the *translatio* idea, see Volume 1, Chapter 3, n.19 and Chapter 10, n.15; Chapter 4, n.10 in this volume.

16. Francis Hutcheson, *An Inquiry into the Original of Our Ideas of Beauty and Virtue* (London: Darby, 1725) 77.

17. According to John Bartram, 4 October 1745.

18. For the Rees affair, see DeArmond 138–39; VD 134; James A. Sappenfield, "The Bizarre Death of Daniel Rees," *Early American Literature* 4 (1969): 73–85; Isaacson 106–7; Steven C. Bullock, *Revolutionary Brotherhood* (Chapel Hill: University of North Carolina Press, 1996) 66–67; and Claude-Anne Lopez, "Sin of Commission? Sin of Omission? No Sin at All?" *BF Gazette* 10, no. 4 (2000): 6–7, 9. Cf. Waldstreicher 111–12.

19. Sappenfield, "Bizarre" 78.

20. Julius Friedrich Sachse, *BF as a Freemason* (Philadelphia: Grand Lodge, 1906) 71, the editors of the *Papers* 2:199, and Sappenfield, "Bizarre" 76. The underlying

reason for the error is that Sachse did not reprint the *AWM* report, and the later two authorities evidently used the materials from Sachse, rather than the original printings in the *Mercury*.

21. Pascal 69 (on reason; see also 139–40), 153 (on custom; see also 78, 161), 138 (on certainty; see also 159–60, 217) and 75 (the wager).

22. Pierre Bayle, *A General Dictionary, Historical and Critical*, 2nd ed., 5 v. (London: Bernard, 1735) 2:326. The book was purchased by the Library Company (*Catalogue*, 1741, p. 5) and advertised for sale in the *PG* 17 February 1747. Franklin referred to "Bacon, Locke, Bayle" as "eminent writer[s]" (P 4:74). As we will see below (Chapter 19), Franklin wrote an essay titled "What Is True?" where he distinguished several different kinds of truth.

23. Roach 145–46; P 3:50–51.

24. DeArmond 223–33.

25. C. William Miller, "BF's Philadelphia Type," *Studies in Bibliography* 11 (1958): 179–206, at 187.

26. Franklin advertised on 6 Nov that *Poor Richard* would be for sale on the 21st. Sappenfield 101; Isaacson 116.

27. *Calendar* #850; J. A. Leo Lemay, "Hamilton's Literary History of the *Maryland Gazette*," *WMQ* 23 (1966): 280.

28. Alan Dyer, *A Biography of James Parker, Colonial Printer* (Troy, N.Y.: Whitson, 1982) 4.

29. Spencer's lectures and Franklin's introduction to electricity are discussed in Volume 3, Chapter 2.

30. Hamilton 151.

31. Gillespie, *A Book of Remembrance* 17.

32. DeArmond 214 n.28.

33. He returned to New England in 1724, 1733, 1743, 1746, 1753, 1754–55, 1763, and 1775. On this last trip, Boston was occupied by the British, and Franklin met with George Washington in Cambridge. The trip to Montreal in 1776 was by way of New York and Albany.

34. Gordon S. Wood, *Radicalism* 86; see also Wood 57–58. John Franklin used an armorial bookplate; Franklin did not, though, like all other persons in his position, he used a coat of arms on official documents when minister to France, 1778–85. P 2:xiii, 230.

35. R. Peter Mooz, "Robert Feke," *Philadelphia Painting and Printing to 1776* (Philadelphia: Philadelphia Museum of Art, 1971) 17 (#10); Mooz, "Robert Feke, The Philadelphia Story," in *American Painting to 1776: a Reappraisal*, ed. Ian Quimby (Winterthur, Del.: Winterthur Museum, 1971) 181–216, at 203; Sellers 25–27; Wayne Craven, "American and British Portraits of Benjamin Franklin," in *Reappraising* 249.

36. The Philadelphia tax return of 1756, which is the earliest good estimation of Franklin's wealth after he retired in 1748, placed him around the tenth percentile. It will be discussed in an appendix to Volume 3.

37. Compare Gordon S. Wood 51–60 (also Wood, *Radicalism* 38, 199–200, 291–92), who suggests that Franklin's populist attitudes changed as he became relatively well off.

CHAPTER 13. THE ASSEMBLY CLERK AND PENNSYLVANIA POLITICS

1. Hanna's assertion that before 1751 BF "carefully remained outside the political order" (24) has since been contradicted by several historians, especially Hutson.

2. Horle 2:402.

3. The oaths of allegiance and abjuration are taken from Giles Jacob, *A New Law Dictionary* (London: E. and R. Nutt and R. Gosling, 1729), inserting Franklin's name and changing George I to George II. The oath of supremacy is taken from *PMHB* 9 (1885): 391–92. The versions of these oaths that BF took as a trustee of the College of Philadelphia are printed in P 6:70–72.

4. Sister Joan de Lourdes Leonard, "The Organization and Procedure of the Pennsylvania Assembly," *PMHB* 72 (1948): 235.

5. Ibid. 226.

6. Ibid. 235.

7. John Churchman, *An Account of the Gospel Labours* (Philadelphia: Crukshank, 1779) 71; John Young to his aunt Elizabeth Graeme Ferguson, *PMHB* 2 (1878): 418; P 6:505.

8. DeArmond 213, 231 n.21.

9. Miller 173; Evans 4409.

10. Leonard 234.

11. Votes 3:3617.

12. Ibid. 7:6056.

13. Paul A. W. Wallace, *Conrad Weiser* (Philadelphia: University of Pennsylvania Press, 1945) 96–99, proves that the proprietors did everything that they could to cheat the Indians of as much land in the Walking Purchase as possible. Francis Jennings, *Ambiguous Iroquois Empire* (New York: Norton, 1984) discusses the Walking Purchase, 325–46; and surveys the key documents, 388–97. Jane T. Merritt, *At the Crossroads: Indians and Empires* (Chapel Hill: University of North Carolina Press, 2003) mentions the Walking Purchase numerous times and gives a map of it on p. 48.

14. See Volume 1, Chapter 4; J. R. Pole, *The Gift of Government* (Athens: University of Georgia Press, 1983) 121.

15. Mabel Pauline Wolff, *Colonial Agency of Pennsylvania, 1712–1757* (Philadelphia: n.p., 1933) 100–101.

16. Douglas Edward Leach, *Roots of Conflict* (Chapel Hill: University of North Carolina Press, 1986) 59–60.

17. PA, ser. 1, 1:638–40, 641. Dora Mae Clark, "Impressment of Seamen in the American Colonies," in *Essays in Colonial History Presented to Charles McLean Andrews* (New Haven, Conn.: Yale University Press, 1931) 198–224, at 202–7.

18. Winfred Trexler Root, *Relations of Pennsylvania with the British Government* (1912; rpt., New York: Burt Franklin, 1970) 282.

19. Governor George Thomas, [*A Letter to the Lords of Trade*] [Philadelphia: Franklin, 1741] 1. Evans 4613; Miller 212. Future references are given in the text within parentheses as *Letter* with a page reference. Though Miller attributed the printing to Franklin, he followed Evans in dating the printing 1740, which was impossible, since a copy of the letter was secured in England and returned to Pennsylvania. The first sale of the letter turns up in Franklin's accounts on 31 July 1741.

20. Wolff, 95, cites the Board of Trade Journals, 12 November 1741.

21. Votes 4:2752–63. *A Message to the Governor from the Assembly* (Philadelphia: Franklin, 1742); Evans 5034; Miller 292.

22. "Some Remarks" does not survive. It may have been a manuscript rather than a printed piece.

23. Wolff 103–5; Root 284–86; Votes 3: 2679–80, 2682–86; *Acts, PC* 3:709–10; *Board* 8:25; PA, 1st ser. 1:634.

24. Votes 6:4388–93; P 8:23; 11:167. James H. Hutson, "Benjamin Franklin and Pennsylvania Politics, 1751–1755: A Reappraisal," *PMHB* 93 (1969): 303–71, at 357 and n.141. See also Volume 3, Chapter 1, "The Association."

25. Norman S. Cohen, "The Philadelphia Election Riot of 1742," *PMHB* 92 (1968): 306–19, and William T. Parsons, "The Bloody Election of 1742," *Pennsylvania History* 36 (1969): 290–306, at 298, 299.

26. DH, 8 July 1742.

27. William Robert Shepherd, *History of Proprietary Government in Pennsylvania* (New York: Columbia University, 1896) 551–52; Alan Tully, *William Penn's Legacy: Politics and Social Structure in Provincial Pennsylvania, 1726–1755* (Baltimore: Johns Hopkins University Press, 1977) 32–34.

28. William Black, "Journal," *PMHB* 1 (1877): 43–44; Hamilton 25–26.

29. Paul A. W. Wallace, *Conrad Weiser* (Philadelphia: University of Pennsylvania Press, 1945) 185.

30. *A Treaty Held at . . . Lancaster* (Philadelphia: B. Franklin, 1744) 23, 24; facsimile in Julian T. Boyd, *Indian Treaties Printed by BF* (Philadelphia: Historical Society of Pennsylvania, 1938) 63, 64.

31. *Treaty* 32–33, 36, in Boyd facsimile 72–73, 76.

32. *Treaty* 38, facsimile in Boyd 78. The quotation is a touchstone for the influence of the Iroquois Indians on the union of colonial America. For the controversy, see the July 1996 forum on the topic in *WMQ*.

33. Shipton 4:363; Moody echoed Judges 7:18, 20.

34. J. A. Leo Lemay, "American Origins of Yankee Doodle," *WMQ* 33 (1976): 435–64.

35. Votes 4:3042.

36. Leach 72–73.

37. For BF on Judge Foster and impressment, see P 35:500. John Lax and William Pencak, "Knowles Riot," *Perspectives in American History* 10 (1976): 202–6; Clark, "Impressment," 207, 214.

CHAPTER 14. FIREFIGHTER

1. *The Boston Globe*, 10 December 1999, carried the complete speech; the *New York Times*, 10 December 1999, in an editorial, page A30, called the speech "A Touching Tribute in Worcester."

2. See Franklin's essay "On the Declamatory Style," discussed in Chapter 6.

3. Harold E. Gillingham, "Philadelphia's First Fire Defenses," *PMHB* 56 (1932): 355–77, gives information on the early fire companies.

4. Hopkinson represented it in March 1749. Union Fire Company minutes, p. 105.

5. Lynn E. Schnurnberger, *Let There Be Clothes* (New York: Workman, 1991) 231.

6. J. Thomas Scharf and Thompson Westcott, *History of Philadelphia, 1609–1884*, 3 v. (Philadelphia, 1884) 3:1905.

7. Carl Bridenbaugh, *Cities in Revolt* (New York: Knopf, 1955) 102.

8. See appendix 4.

9. See P 2:375–76, and the facsimile of the printed copy, Miller #340.

10. P 2:376n. There are sixteen later signatures to the articles on p. 45 of the minutes: Israel Pemberton, Jr.; Philip Benezet; Isaac Paschall; Thomas Wharton; W. Grant; Joshua Howell; Joseph Wharton, Jr.; Samuel Purviance; Thomas Hatton; Samuel Preston Moore; John Mifflin; Thomas Stretch; Daniel Benezet; Joseph Stretch; William Fishbourn; and Richard Hockley.

11. The Minutes of the Fellowship Fire Company are at the Historical Society of Pennsylvania, Philadelphia. The members are listed in an appendix to Daniel P. Gilbert, "Patterns of Organization and Membership in Colonial Philadelphia Club Life, 1725–1755" (Ph.D. diss., University of Pennsylvania, 1952).

12. Franklin printed the articles of agreement and a list of names for the Star Fire Company, on 5 July 1743 (Miller no. 339).

13. They joined after the group named in n.10.

14. Isaacson, 105, wrote that after Franklin returned from France in 1785, he would meet with the four remaining members of the company "along with their leather buckets." I have found no evidence for the statement.

15. The Friendship Fire Company was organized 30 July 1747. The firm of Franklin and Hall printed their revised articles of 30 April 1755 about 1761. Miller no. 749.

CHAPTER 15. EARNING A LIVING

1. I rely on Miller throughout all discussions of Franklin's printing.

2. Miller; P 4:7 n.8.

3. See Volume 1, Chapter 13 and Volume 1, Chapter 17. See also appendix 3 for notes on Pennsylvania's pay for paper currency that Franklin printed.

4. See Volume 1, Chapter 15 for Franklin's 1729 Loan Office Register.

5. Keith Arbour, *BF's First Government Printing* (Philadelphia: APS, 1999) #7, pp. 56–57.

6. Arbour speculated that the latter was for the 1739 act for reemitting the money and further striking £11,110.5. Arbour, no. 13, p. 71.

7. Thomas Penn to Richard Peters, 1 March 1745; Miller no. 364.

8. Miller nos. 11 and 31.

9. John F. Watson, *Annals of Philadelphia, and Pennsylvania*, Reverend Willis P. Hazard, 3 v. (Philadelphia: Leary, 1927) 1:552; *ANB* entry for Lay; see also Waldstreicher 80–82.

10. Rush in *PMHB* 29 (1905): 25; also Rush, *Essays, Literary, Moral and Philosophical* (Philadelphia: Bradford, 1806) 299.

11. C. W. Miller, "Franklin's *Poor Richard Almanacs*," *Studies in Bibliography* 14 (1961): 103.

12. DH and Ruth Lapham Butler, *Dr. Franklin, Postmaster General* (Garden City, N.Y.: Doubleday, 1928) 32–34.

13. Miller no. 381.

14. *The Prose Works of William Byrd of Westover*, ed. Louis B. Wright (Cambridge, Mass.: Harvard University Press, 1966) 362.

15. Joseph E. J. Johnson, "A Quaker Imperialist's View of the British Colonies in America: 1732," *PMHB* 60 (1936): 97–130.

16. Fairfax Harrison, "The Colonial Post Office in Virginia," *WMQ*, 2nd ser., 4 (1924): 71–92, at 89–90.

17. Butler 37.

18. James N. Green, "BF as Publisher and Bookseller," in *Reappraising* 98–118. Green lists fifteen "Books of More than Ten Sheets Published at Franklin's Risk and Expense, 1729–1748" 108–10.

19. Hampton L. Carson, "The Genesis of the Charter of Pennsylvania," *PMHB* 43 (1919): 289–331, at 313. Carson thought that Franklin first used divisions in the charter in his 1752 printing of the *Laws*, pp. xviii–xxiv; but the latter follows the same divisions he made in this 1740 printing of the *Collection of Charters* (1–9). For the original without Franklin's divisions, see *The Papers of William Penn* 2:61–77.

20. These numbers are compiled from Miller's bibliography: for 1738, Miller nos. 147–60; for 1740, Miller nos. 186–224; and for 1747, Miller nos. 417–32.

21. Amory and Hall 176.

22. McCulloch 122: "Franklin bought paper principally from Wilcox; and there was an intimacy between them. Franklin often visited Wilcox at his mill."

23. Brissot de Warville, *New Travels in the United States of America, 1788* (Cambridge, Mass.: Harvard University Press, 1964) 188n. Lawrence C. Wroth, "BF: The Printer at Work," in *Typographic Heritage: Selected Essays by Lawrence C. Wroth* (New York: The Typophiles, 1949) 91–134, at 117, suggested that Franklin's word *established* meant that he had "expanded" or encouraged about eighteen paper mills. In either case, Franklin—or, more probably, Warville—exaggerated.

24. A xxx, xxxi–xxxii. Miers Fisher to BF, 5 August 1788.

25. London, Tho. Roycroft for Nath. Elkins, 1658–1675. APS: 346.5/G79r.

26. The APS copy belonged to Franklin.

27. *Reappraising* 106.

28. Miller no. 370; also Robert B. Winans, *A Descriptive Checklist of Book Catalogues* (Worcester, Mass.: American Antiquarian Society, 1981) 16.

29. See the remarks by James N. Green in Sandra M. Gustafson, *Eloquence Is Power: Oratory & Performance in Early America* (Chapel Hill: University of North Carolina Press, 2000) 119n.

30. Clinton Johnson, *Old Time Schools* (New York: Macmillan, 1904) 50.

31. Lemay, "American Aesthetic," 467–71.

32. Arbour 39.

33. Cotton Mather, *Magnalia Christi Americana*, 2 v. (Hartford, Conn.: Andrus, 1853) 2:581.

34. Strahan to Hall, 9 March 1745, Mss, APS.

CHAPTER 16. CONCERNED CITIZEN

1. Exodus 12:7, 13. The Romans placed a crown of oak leaves above the doors of those who had saved a life of a fellow citizen. *Res Gestae Divi Augusti* ("The Acts of Augustus"), 6:34, in Velleius Paterculus, *Compendium of Roman History*, tr. Frederick W. Shipley, Loeb Classical Library no. 251 (1924; Cambridge, Mass.: Harvard University Press, 1979) 398–99.

2. Isaacson 105.

3. *Statutes* 5:514–25 reprinted the pamphlet; Evans 5270, Miller 335.

4. Miller recorded imprints that are not extant but evidently overlooked this bill.

5. *Statutes* 5:117–18.

6. Since the act expired in five years, Franklin brought in a new bill on 5 March 1756. Because the previous bill had prepared the way, the passage of this one was comparatively easy. It was read and debated on 6 and 8 March, passed by the House on 9 March, and delivered to Gov. Robert Hunter Morris the next day. Morris returned it on 6 April, with eleven proposed amendments. The House agreed to some and returned the bill. On 1 and 5 July, the governor said he was ready to pass the bill. On 20 August, William Denny was proclaimed the new governor of Pennsylvania. On 9 September, the House sent up the bill to Gov. Denny saying it had been approved by both the former governor and the House and "lay ready to be enacted into a Law" when he arrived. On 13 September Gov. Denny said he would agree to the bill, and on 15 September 1756, it was enacted. Votes 4207, 4213, 4319, and 4325; *Statutes* 5:224–43.

7. A. Michal McMahon, "'Small Matters': BF, Philadelphia, and the 'Progress of Cities,'" *PMHB* 116 (1992): 157–82. McMahon also considered the controversy in "'Public Service' versus 'Mans Properties': Dock Creek and the Origins of Urban Technology in Eighteenth-Century Philadelphia," in *Early American Technology*, ed. Judith A. McGaw (Chapel Hill: University of North Carolina Press, 1994) 114–47, especially 124–31 (hereafter McMahon, "Dock Creek"). I am grateful to Professor McMahon who called this controversy to my attention in a letter of 12 September 1990 when he asked if I believed Franklin wrote the piece on the tanners in the 30 August 1739 *PG*. DeArmond 114.

8. McMahon, "Dock Creek," 125, 130.

9. Diamondstone 298, 365.

10. Gerard J. Mangone provides an overview of the legal background from the eighteenth century to the present. Mangone, "Private Property Rights: The Development of Takings in the United States," *International Journal of Marine and Coastal Law* 17 (2002): 195–233.

11. *NCE*, 212–23, gives a series of Franklin's quotations on wealth. See especially 222, where he writes: "Private Property . . . is a Creature of Society, and is subject to the Calls of that Society, whenever its Necessities shall require it, even to its last Farthing." See also P 22:533.

12. See Chapter 4.

13. McMahon, "Dock Creek" 134–35.

14. Votes 5413. The bill for paving the city became law, including directions to the street commissioners to clean and repair the dock. *Statutes* 6, ch. 485, pp. 234–46. The bill "To prevent and remove certain nuisances" that forbade throwing any dirt, rubbish, "carcase, carrion or filth" into the dock is *Statutes* 6, ch. 484, pp. 232–34.

15. *Statutes* 6, ch. 524, pp. 409–10.

16. James Birkett, *Some Cursory Remarks . . . 1750–1751* (New Haven, Conn.: Yale University Press, 1916) 67.

CHAPTER 17. GEORGE WHITEFIELD AND THE GREAT AWAKENING

1. For acute thoughts on the Great Awakening, see James H. Hutson, *Religion and the Founding of the American Republic* (Washington, D.C.: Library of Congress, 1998) 24–35.

2. William Warren Sweet, *Religion in Colonial America* (New York: Scribner's, 1949) 275.

3. *ANB*.

4. Richard Beale Davis, *Intellectual Life in the Colonial South*, 3 v. (Knoxville: University of Tennessee Press, 1978) 1272.

5. See the mezzotint by Francis Kyte (1743) and the description of Whitefield in W. J. Bell, ed., "Addenda to Watson's *Annals*," *PMHB* 98 (1974): 159.

6. Lisa Herb Smith, "The First Great Awakening in American Newspapers, 1739–48" (Ph.D. diss., University of Delaware, 1999); cf. Isaacson 113.

7. Thomas 568.

8. *PG*, 8 November 1739; George Whitefield's *Journals* (Edinburgh: Banner of Truth Trust, 1978) 343.

9. Whitefield, *Journals* 347, 348, 352.

10. Whitefield, *Journals* 360; Miller nos. 186–224.

11. Whitefield, *Journals* 356, 359; *PG*, 29 November 1740.

12. David Freeman Hawke, *Franklin* (New York: Harper and Row, 1976) 57.

13. Arnold Dallimore, *George Whitefield* (London: Banner of Truth Trust, 1970), 496, mistakenly wrote that it "was republished by one newspaper after another throughout the Colonies." David A. Copeland, *Colonial American Newspapers*

(Newark: University of Delaware Press, 1997) 142, said that it appeared only in Franklin's *Gazette*. Lisa Herb Smith located the *New England Weekly Journal* reprint.

14. Alan Gallay, "The Origins of Slave Holders' Paternalism: George Whitefield, the Bryan Family, and the Great Awakening in the South," *Journal of Southern History* 53 (1987): 369–94. On Whitefield's plantation and slaves, purchased in January 1747, see Luke Tyerman, *Life of George Whitefield*, 2 v. (London: Hodder, 1876–77) 2:155–58, 169–70.

15. For earlier discussions, see P 2:257–59; and *Canon* 96–102. Cf. Frank Lambert, *"Pedlar in Divinity": George Whitefield and the Transatlantic Revivals, 1737–1770* (Princeton: Princeton University Press, 1994) 119.

16. Scharf and Westcott, 2:864.

17. *Canon* 97–98 documents Franklin's early and continuing egalitarianism.

18. See Volume 1, Chapter 7 (discussing Dogood No. 14); Volume 1, Chapter 8 (discussing *Hoop-Petticoats Arraigned*); and Chapter 16 above (discussing the tanners' "Just" cause).

19. Cf. Isaacson 112.

20. Cf. Wood 47.

21. William Seward, *Journal of a Voyage from London to Philadelphia* (London: Seward, 1740) 22.

22. William Temple Franklin, ed., *Memoirs of the Life and Writings of Benjamin Franklin* 3 v. (London: Henry Colburn, 1817–18) 2:298. Cf. "Information to those who would Remove to America": "The People have a Saying, that God Almighty is himself a Mechanic, the greatest in the Universe" (W 977).

23. Dietmar Rothermund, *Layman's Progress: Religious and Political Experience in Colonial Pennsylvania, 1740–1770* (Philadelphia: University of Pennsylvania Press, 1961) 146.

24. Whitefield's *Journals* 489–90.

25. Rothermund, 145–47, prints the legal deed from the Moravian Archives, Bethlehem, Pa.

26. See Appendix 4, Sample Wages and Prices in Colonial Philadelphia.

27. University of Pennsylvania Archives; Edward Potts Cheyney, *History of the University of Pennsylvania, 1740–1940* (Philadelphia: University of Pennsylvania Press, 1940), 24, found no basis for Franklin's statement that he was a trustee of the New Building. Rothermund, 147, however, citing Moravian Archives, Bethlehem, Pa., box "Pennsylvania Controversies," wrote that Franklin and Henry Antes became trustees as the result of an election after the deaths of William Seward (1740) and Thomas Noble (15 March 1746).

28. Richard Webster, *A History of the Presbyterian Church* (Philadelphia: Wilson, 1857) 471. For a discussion, see J.A. Leo Lemay, *Ebenezer Kinnersley* (Philadelphia: University of Pennsylvania Press, 1964) 18–27.

29. Martin E. Lodge, "The Crisis of the Churches in the Middle Colonies, 1720–1750," *PMHB* 95 (1971): 195–220.

30. For the later pamphlets, see Lemay, *Kinnersley* 27–35.

31. Hamilton, s.v. "religion" in index.

32. *South Carolina Gazette*, 18 July 1740, reporting a private letter from Philadelphia.

33. George Whitefield, *Britain's Mercies* (Philadelphia: Bradford, 1746), Evans 5883.

34. Whitefield's *Journals* 490.

35. First published in 1770. L. H. Butterfield, "BF's Epitaph," *New Colophon* 3 (1950): 9–39, at 23.

36. William Gordon, *History of the American Revolution*, 3rd ed. (New York: Woods for Campbell, 1801) 1:143–48.

37. Tyerman 2:593.

38. William Faulkner, *As I Lay Dying* (New York: Modern Library, 1947) 59.

39. *The Life of Olaudah Equiano or Gustavus Vassa, The African, Written by Himself*, ed. Paul Edwards, 2 v. (London: Dawsons, 1969) 2:5–6.

40. Joel Tyler Headley, *Chaplins and Clergy of the Revolution* (New York: Scribner, 1864) 93.

CHAPTER 18. NATURAL PHILOSOPHY

1. Books frequently cited in this chapter are John Bartram, *Correspondence*, ed. Edmund Berkeley and Dorothy Smith Berkeley (Gainesville: University Press of Florida, 1992); Whitfield J. Bell, Jr., *Patriot-Improvers: Biographical Sketches of Members of the APS*, 2 v. (Philadelphia: APS, 1997–99); I. Bernard Cohen, *BF's Experiments* (Cambridge, Mass.: Harvard University Press, 1941); Cohen, *BF's Science* (Cambridge, Mass.: Harvard University Press, 1990); Cohen, *Franklin and Newton* (Philadelphia: APS, 1956); Colden; Peter Collinson, *Selected Letters*, ed. Alan W. Armstrong (Philadelphia: APS, 2002); Brook Hindle, *The Pursuit of Science in Revolutionary America, 1735–1789* (Chapel Hill: University of North Carolina Press, 1956); Raymond Phineas Stearns, *Science in the British Colonies of America* (Urbana: University of Illinois Press, 1970).

2. See Volume 1, Chapter 4, n.12.

3. John Duffy, *Epidemics in Colonial America* (Baton Rouge: Louisiana State University Press, 1953) 34.

4. Susan E. Klepp, *Swift Progress of Population* (Philadelphia: APS, 1991) 47.

5. Francisco Guerra, *American Medical Bibliography, 1639–1783* (New York: Harper, 1962) 602ff.

6. If it was August 1759, then BF was perhaps with Anthony Tissington. The other good possibility is the spring of 1771 (18:115), or the following November, on his return from Scotland.

7. Dr. Marguerite D. Thew to the author, 28 February 1997. See also P 9:338 n.3.

8. Verner W. Crane, *BF's Letters to the Press*, xxix, xxx, 39, 41, 45, 49, 76, 83, 143, 147, 268, 277.

9. *Catalogue* (1741) 21.

10. Guerra attributed the letter to Franklin, presumably because it was dated from Philadelphia and signed "F. B." Guerra 421 (giving pages 13–15 rather than 70–

71). Whitfield J. Bell, Jr., independently attributed it to Franklin, "BF and the Practice of Medicine," *Bulletin of the Cleveland Medical Library* 9, no. 3 (July 1962): 51–62, at 53.

11. On mechanics, see the variety of books cited in his *Account of the New Invented Pennsylvanian Fireplace* (2:419–45), especially J. T. Desaguliers, "to whose instructive Writings the Contriver of this Machine acknowledges himself much indebted" (2:439). The accounts in history "of the prodigious Force and Effect of Engines and Machines used in War, will naturally introduce a Desire to be instructed in *Mechanics*, and to be inform'd of the Principles of that Art by which weak Men perform such wonders" (P 3:418). And see BF's scientific letters to Polly Stevenson, beginning 1 May 1760.

12. Green 23.

13. For Breintnall and nature printing, see Gordon M. Marshall III in *Philadelphia: Three Centuries of American Art* (Philadelphia: Philadelphia Museum of Art, 1976) 37–39.

14. Eric P. Newman to the author, 26 September 1995. See his early article, "Nature Printing on Colonial and Continental Currency," *Numismatist* 77, no. 2 (February 1964): 147–54.

15. Thanks to James N. Green, Library Company of Philadelphia, for his thoughts by email, 18 June 2002, concerning "types en creuse."

16. Accounts, Anthony Newhouse, 6 November 1746.

17. McCulloch 139.

18. Peter Kalm, *The America of 1750 . . . Travels in North America*, 2 v., ed. Adolph Benson (New York: Dover, 1966) 1:37, 63, 204.

19. For an appreciation, see *Dutch Tiles in the Philadelphia Museum of Art* (Philadelphia: Museum of Art, 1984).

20. Gomberville's first edition was titled *Doctrines of Morality* (London: Bell, 1721).

21. John Sadler of Liverpool seems to have independently invented a similar process in the 1750s, first printing tiles from woodblocks and then from copper plates. Anthony Ray, "Liverpool Printed Tiles," *Transactions of the English Ceramic Circle* 9, pt. 1 (1973): 37–66.

22. Lawrence D. Wroth, *The Colonial Printer* (1938; Charlottesville: University Press of Virginia, 1964) 79.

23. Justin Winsor, *Memorial History of Boston*, 4 v. (Boston: Osgood, 1880–82) 2:465.

24. P 8:194–95.

25. Colden 3:82–83, 91.

26. I am indebted to Dr. Lisa Herb Smith for calling this article to my attention.

27. Bruce W. Bugbee, *Genesis of American Patent and Copyright Law* (Washington, D.C.: Public Affairs Press, 1967), ch. 3, "The Colonial Period in America" 57–84.

28. Franklin perhaps had in mind the London common councillor James Sharp, who took out a patent for a stove in 1781. Others patented his later plans for wheel carriages (11 April 1773), as well as the application of engraving to tiles. NCE 98 nn.4–5.

29. Samuel Y. Edgerton, Jr., "The Franklin Stove," in Cohen, *BF's Science* 199–211.

30. Cohen, *Franklin and Newton* 216–22; and Cohen, *BF's Science* 159–71.

31. Cohen, *BF's Science* 163–64.

32. John Adams, *Works*, ed. Charles Francis Adams, 10 v. (Boston: Little, Brown, 1850–56) 1:664.

33. Edwin Wolf 2nd, *The Library of James Logan* (Philadelphia: Library Company of Philadelphia, 1974), nos. 1417–29.

34. Both volumes were present in the Library Company. *Catalogue* (1741) 45, 24.

35. Illustrations of the eclipses are in *Poor Richard* for 1743, 1746, and 1747, toward the end of the almanac, a page or two after the year's calendar for December.

36. William Morris Davis, "Was Lewis Evans or BF the First to Recognize That our Northeast Storms Come from the Southwest?" *PAPS* 45 (1906): 130. Davis, "Some American Contributions to Meteorology," *Journal of the Franklin Institute* no. 127 (1889): 105. William E. Lingelbach, "Franklin and the Lewis Evans Map of 1749," *APS Yearbook* (1945): 63–73, at 71, wrote that the Evans maps may "be regarded as [the] joint product by Evans, the cartographer, and Franklin, the scientist, patron, and promoter." On the Iroquois agricultural myth and the Evans map, see James R. Masterson, "A Foolish Oneida Tale," *American Literature* 10 (1938–39): 53–65. Masterson 54 located "Onwgaréxnu M[ountain]. Where Indian Corn, Tobacco, Squashes, and Pompions were first found by the Natives, according to their traditions."

37. Isaacson 133.

38. *Philosophical Transactions* 29 (1714): 62–63. Franklin could not have known Edward Taylor's unpublished poem on the subject: Donald E. Stanford, "The Giant Bones of Claverack, New York, 1705," *New York History* 40 (1959): 47–61.

39. Murphy D. Smith, *"Realms of Gold": A Catalogue of Maps in the Library of the APS* (Philadelphia: APS, 1991) 34, no. 32 (3); Edward C. Carter II, "A Passionate Avocation: The Foreshadowing of a Philadelphia Scientific Community, 1682–1769," in *Worldly Goods*, ed. Jack L. Lindsey (Philadelphia: Museum of Art, 1999) 38–39, and figures 57, 58, and no. 501 on pp. 238–39.

40. BF to James Bowdoin, 31 May 1788.

41. See Volume 3, Chapter 2.

42. John F. Watson, *Annals of Philadelphia*, rev. Willis P. Hazard, 3 v. (Philadelphia: Leary, Stuart Co., 1927) 1:408, 2:489.

43. I thank Professor Susan Stabile for the reference.

44. Henry Simpson, *The Lives of Eminent Philadelphians, Now Deceased* (Philadelphia: W. Brotherhead, 1859) 748.

45. Shipton 6:473–75; and David C. Leonard, "Harvard's First Science Professor . . . Isaac Greenwood," *Harvard Library Bulletin* 29 (1981): 135–68, at 144–45.

46. J. A. Leo Lemay, "Franklin's 'Dr. Spence': The Reverend Archibald Spencer," *Maryland Historical Magazine* 59 (1964): 199–216, at 204.

47. *Life, Journals and Correspondence of Manasseh Cutler* (Cincinnati: R. Clarke, 1888) 1:269. For a lecture on the circulation of the blood given while in London, see the *London Daily Post*, 2 January 1725.

48. Thanks to my friend Professor Henry Glyde for supplying the terminology.

49. Bartram, *Correspondence* 153, 166, 173, 182, 216.

50. Ibid. 88–89.

51. Ibid. 194, 198.

52. Ibid. 216, 217.

53. Hindle 64–74, and Carl Van Doren, "The Beginnings of the APS," *PAPS* 87 (1944): 277–89.

54. Bartram, *Correspondence* 66, 93.

55. See Chapter 4, n.9.

56. [John Webbe], in "The Plan of an Intended Magazine," *AWM*, 6 November 1740, called Philadelphia the central city in the colonies.

57. George G. Simpson, "The Beginnings of Vertebrate Paleontology in North America," *PAPS* 86 (1942): 134–35.

58. For Jared Eliot, see the *ANB*.

59. Van Doren, "Beginnings" 280.

60. Bartram, *Correspondence* 237.

61. Biographical sketches are in Bell 10–85.

62. Biographical sketches are in Bell 86–109.

63. Bartram, *Correspondence* 238.

64. Colden 3:65–66.

65. Ibid. 3:69.

66. Bell 138–48; Edmund Berkeley and Dorothy Smith Berkeley, *Dr. John Mitchell* (Chapel Hill: University of North Carolina Press, 1974).

67. Bell, 139, notes that the disease was not yellow fever but probably either Weil's disease or infectious hepatitis.

68. Colden 3:180; Bartram, *Correspondence* 265, 272.

69. Bell 143; Berkeley and Berkeley 131, 147.

70. Colden 3:82–83.

71. Dated December in P 2:446 in accordance with the draft at the New York Historical Society, but the following letter in Colden, *Letters* 3:94 was dated "To Mr. John Bartram at the same Time," and in Bartram, *Correspondence*, 246, that letter is dated 24 October 1744.

72. Bartram, *Correspondence* 261, 278.

CHAPTER 19. SATIRES AND OTHER WRITINGS, 1736–1747

1. Lewis P. Simpson, "The Printer as a Man of Letters: Franklin and the Symbolism of the Third Realm," in *Oldest Revolutionary* 3–20.

2. Francis S. Philbrick, "Notes on Early Editions and Editors of Franklin," *PAPS* 97 (1953): 525–64, at 536, 547, and 562.

3. David S. Shields, "The Manuscript in the British American World of Print," *Proceedings of the American Antiquarian Society* 102 (1992): 403–13. See also Shields, *Civil Tongues*.

4. BF praised the letters of Sir William Temple and Alexander Pope and his friends (4:106).

5. *NCE* 232.

6. Robert D. Arner, "Politics and Temperance," in *Reappraising* 52–77, at 76 n. 39.

7. John Jay, *Papers*, 2 v., ed. Richard B. Morris (New York: Harper, 1980) 2:713.

8. *Votes and Proceedings of the New Jersey Assembly* [27 October 1738–15 March, 1738/9] (New York: Zenger, 1739) 9, 10; Evans 4283. Hereafter *V&PNJ*, plus date.

9. Ibid. (Evans 4283), title page, 10, 45, 55, 56.

10. *V&PNJ*, 10 April 1740 (Philadelphia: Franklin, 1740) 13; Evans 4569; Miller no. 199.

11. Miller no. 199.

12. See the New Jersey House of Representatives address to Governor Lewis Morris, 18 April 1745, *V&PNJ*, 4 April 1745 (Philadelphia: Bradford, 1745) 19–23; Samuel Nevill, "Speech to the House of Representatives of the Colony of New Jersey, on the Second Reading of the Petition from a Number of Persons Styling Themselves Inhabitants Chiefly of the Northern Part of New Jersey, on Saturday the 26th of April, 1746," *New York Post Boy*, 19 and 26 May 1746; and Anthony Nicolosi, "Colonial Particularism and Political Rights: Jacob Spicer II on Aid to Virginia, 1754," *New Jersey History* 87 (1969): 69–88. Richard B. Morris (editor of Jay, *Papers*) thought Franklin wrote the first of these three; cf. *Canon* no. 80.

13. Lewis Morris named Joseph Cooper one of the Quaker demagogues who opposed him. *The Papers of Lewis Morris*, 3 v., ed. Eugene R. Sheridan (Newark: New Jersey Historical Society, 1989–93) 3:179–80.

14. Evans 3693, 3801, 4392.

15. Evans 5014, 5252, 5254, 5818, 5819, 6200.

16. Lemay, "The Amerindian in the Early American Enlightenment" 79–92.

17. I intend to publish an essay titled "*An Indian Speech*: A Deist Satire by Benjamin Franklin," which will give detailed reasons for the attribution.

18. Dated 30 January 1600/1700 in the Latin manuscript by Jesper Swedberg, "Svecia Nova" 242. Copies of Swedberg's manuscript are at the National Archives and the Royal Library, Stockholm, and the Uppsala University Library.

19. Tobias Eric Björck, *De Plantatione Ecclesia Svecanae in America* (Uppsala: J. H. Werner, [1731]). Sabin 5664, 28916; *European Americana* 6:731/24.

20. Olaus Malander, a journeyman printer from Sweden, is another possibility. An entry in Franklin's accounts for 11 June 1739 shows that he was then working for Franklin and boarding with the Franklins. Since Franklin customarily settled his accounts with employees every six months, Malander probably had been working for Franklin at least since December 1738. He last appeared in Franklin's accounts on 31 December 1744.

21. Roland E. Fleischer, *Gustavus Hesselius* (Trenton: New Jersey State Museum, 1987) 19, 29 n.13.

22. DeArmond 237.

23. For the English freethinkers Thomas Woolston and Anthony Collins, and for the deistic "Plain Dealer" essays in the *PG*, see Volume 1, Chapter 18.

24. Leonard W. Levy, *Blasphemy* (New York: Knopf, 1993) 268.

25. J.C.D. Clark, *The Language of Liberty* (Cambridge: Cambridge University Press, 1994) 38–39.

26. Lemay, *B F: Optimist or Pessimist?*.

27. See the discussion below of "What Is True" and the notes cited there.

28. The *PG* text, 31 December 1788, contains unusual and distinctive traits of Franklin's spellings.

29. Though the Latin text dated the speech 1600/1700, the text in the *New York Gazette* (27 April 1752) dated the speech 1710. That date, though not some additions to the *New York Gazette* text, was followed in later printings. A copy, not known to be extant, of the text before 1752 had probably dropped the long introduction found in the *American Magazine* text and given the 1710 date.

30. "R. H.," *London Magazine*, 30 (February 1761), objected to the suggestion that the Indians had "their origin from another source than the rest of mankind."

31. James A. Herrick, *The Radical Rhetoric of the English Deists: The Discourse of Skepticism, 1680–1750* (Columbia: University of South Carolina Press, 1997) 33.

32. *Canon* no. 74, p. 102; printed in Sparks 7:322–24 and in W 286–90. In some aspects, the proposal anticipates his 1765 "Scheme for Supplying the Colonies with a Paper Currency." P 12:47–60.

33. *OED*, s.v. "fall" v, 18. David Yerkes, "Franklin's Vocabulary," in *Reappraising* 396–414. Yerkes corrected and supplemented Lois Margaret MacLaurin, *Franklin's Vocabulary* (New York: Doubleday, 1928). The Packard Humanities Institute's CD-ROM of Franklin's writings, which appeared after Yerkes completed his essay, makes a thorough study of Franklin's vocabulary possible.

34. R. J. Hirst, "Primary and Secondary Qualities," in *The Encyclopedia of Philosophy*, ed. Paul Edwards, 8 v. (New York: Macmillan, 1967) 6:455–57.

35. *General Magazine*, May 1741, p. 340.

36. James Campbell, *Recovering Benjamin Franklin* (Chicago: Open Court Press, 1999) 100–110, and the scholars cited on pp. 106–10.

37. Cicero, *Academica*, 1.5.19, tr. H. Rackham (London: Heinemann, 1933) 429. St. Augustine, *The City of God*, 8.4, tr. David S. Wiesen (London: Heinemann, 1968) 3:19. Locke, *Essay* 578.

38. Pascal 159, 217.

39. As pointed out in Volume 1, Chapter 7, in Silence Dogood No. 14 Franklin echoed the Port Royal *Logic* 70: "If we read in an Historian, that a Prince was

zealous for the true Religion, we cannot tell what he means by it, unless we know what Religion the Historian was of."

40. The *AWM* has "Goal" for "Gaol" in the title; in line 11, it has "attack'd" for "attrack'd"; I have emended both. Bradford was not infrequently a faulty type-setter.

41. Ralph Ellison, *Invisible Man* (New York: Modern Library, 1952) 201.

42. Adams to Jefferson, in *Adams-Jefferson Letters*, 2 v., ed. Lester Cappon (Chapel Hill: University of North Carolina Press, 1959) 2:399.

43. Newcomb 65–80.

44. I am indebted to the Bodleian Library for supplying me with a photocopy.

45. J. A. Leo Lemay, "An Attribution of *Reflections on Courtship and Marriage* (1746) to BF," *Papers of the Bibliographical Society of America* 95 (2001): 59–96.

46. Arthur M. Schlesinger, *Learning How to Behave* (New York: Macmillan, 1947) 8–9.

47. This passage is the favorite among the literary students of Franklin, quoted by VD 158; Francis X. Davy, "BF, Satirist" (Ph.D. diss. Columbia University, 1958), 58; and Amacher 157.

48. John Adams, *Diary and Autobiography*, ed. Lyman H. Butterfield, 4 v. (Boston: Massachusetts Historical Society, 1962) 1:72, 114, 193–96.

49. A. Owen Aldridge, "BF: The Fusion of Science and Letters," in *American Literature and Science*, ed. Robert J. Scholnick (Lexington: University Press of Kentucky, 1992) 39–57, at 46–47.

50. The "Philoclerus" letter is discussed in Volume 1, Chapter 18. William Godwin, *An Inquiry Concerning Political Justice*, in *Political and Philosophical Writings of William Godwin*, ed. Mark Philip (London: W. Pickering, 1993) 3:450–51, 460. Godwin's authority was Franklin's friend Richard Price.

51. Pascal 134. And see Chapter 10.

52. The essential work on Polly Baker is Max Hall, *BF and Polly Baker* (1960; rpt., University of Pittsburgh Press, 1990). See also Alfred Owen Aldridge, *Franklin and His French Contemporaries* (New York: New York University Press, 1957) 95–104. The following discussion revises my essay, "The Text, Rhetorical Strategies, and Themes of 'The Speech of Miss Polly Baker,'" in *Oldest Revolutionary* 91–120 (hereafter Lemay, "Polly Baker").

53. For an examination of all the differences, see Lemay, "Polly Baker" 95–99.

54. The English text contains "ever" instead of "even." Perhaps a copyist misread Franklin's "n" for an "r."

55. A classic in the genre of the foreign observer tradition, Montesquieu's *Persian Letters* (1721; in English, 1722) was among the popular books of the preceding quarter of a century. Franklin surely knew it.

56. Robert Klevay, my research assistant in 2001–02, suggested that in the concluding paragraph Franklin may also allude to Plato's *Apology*. I. Bernard Cohen, *Science and the Founding Fathers* (New York: Norton, 1995) 301–4, has suggested

that Thomas Jefferson's phrase in the Declaration of Independence, "the Laws of Nature and of Nature's God," may come from the conclusion of Polly Baker's speech.

57. Lemay, "Polly Baker" 104–6.

58. Charles Allen Beaumont, *Swift's Classical Rhetoric* (Athens: University of Georgia Press, 1961); George Mayhew, "Swift and the Tripos Tradition," *Philological Quarterly* 45 (1966): 85–101.

59. See Volume 1, Chapter 6, 117–18.

60. In one marginalia jotting, Franklin quarreled with an English author for just this logical failure: "By this word [Dependencies] you assume, what is not granted; and all that follows is therefore unfounded" (P 17:387).

61. A. Owen Aldridge, "Polly Baker and Boccaccio," *Annali dell'Instituto Universitario Orientale, Sezione Romanza* 14 (1972): 5–18, has compared similar themes in Boccaccio's *Decameron* and Franklin's Polly Baker.

62. Lemay, "Polly Baker" 119 n.36.

63. For Green, see Shipton 8:42–53; Kenneth B. Murdock's *DAB* entry; and David M. Robinson's *ANB* sketch. The fullest treatment is Thomas V. Duggan, "Joseph Green—The Boston Butler" (Master's thesis, Columbia University, 1941), which edits most of Green's oeuvre. Supplementing these are *Calendar*; J. A. Leo Lemay, "Joseph Green's Satirical Poem on the Great Awakening," *Resources for American Literary Study* 4 (1974): 173–83; and David S. Shields, "Clio Mocks the Masons: Joseph Green's Anti-Masonic Satires," in *Deism*, ed. Lemay 109–26; and Shields, *Oracles*, esp. 131–36.

64. Duggan, "Joseph Green," 85–86, as corrected from the original in the Massachusetts Historical Society.

65. This short poem (75 lines) is in Pat Rogers, *Jonathan Swift: The Complete Poems* (New York: Penguin, 1983) 85–87.

66. At the time, Paul Dudley was the chief justice of Massachusetts (*ANB*).

67. See Chapter 2, where other Franklin burlesques of the design argument are mentioned.

68. Marie Jean Antoine Nicolas de Caritat, Marquis de Condorcet, *Éloge de M. Franklin* (Paris: Chez Pyre, 1791), in his *Oeuvres complètes* (Brunswick: Chez Vieweg, 1804) 4:117.

69. Robert Newcomb, "BF and Montaigne," *Modern Language Notes* 72 (1957): 489–91; Port Royal *Logic* 8.

70. Melvin H. Buxbaum, *BF and the Zealous Presbyterians* (University Park: Pennsylvania State University Press, 1975); review by J. A. Leo Lemay in *Early American Literature* 10 (1975–76): 222–26.

71. Calling Franklin's or Green's satires "free verse" is anachronistic. In the eighteenth century, these were parodies of verse, somewhat similar to poorly written memorials on monuments.

72. J. A. Leo Lemay, "Hamilton's Literary History of the *Maryland Gazette*," *WMQ* 23 (1966): 279; Dr. Alexander Hamilton, *History of the Tuesday Club*, 3 v., ed. Robert Micklus (Chapel Hill: University of North Carolina Press, 1990) 2:310.

73. Livingston is also credited with the most famous parody of the Revolutionary period: the travesty, which originally appeared in the *Pennsylvania Packet* of 26 August 1777, of General John Burgoyne's proclamation.

74. Francis Hopkinson (1737–91), signer, son of Franklin's close friend Thomas Hopkinson, was one person who wrote such travesties and who probably knew Franklin's earlier one. Beginning in 1765 (P 12:125), he turns up frequently in the Franklin *Papers*.

Index

Priestley, Joseph, 78, 207, 545
Pringle, John, 19, 460
Pringle, William, 87, 88
printing technology, 463–68; and American papermaking, 390–91, 466; asbestos paper, 466; and counterfeiting, 463, 464; improvements to printing presses, 467–68; nature printing, 463–65; printing paper currency, 463–66; printing tiles, 467
Prior, Matthew, 112
Pritchett, V. S., 58
Privy Council, 341
Proprietary Party: and BF's party affiliations, 110, 214, 333; and BF's satire of, 325–26; censure of BF, 110; and Indian affairs, 331; and military defense, 215, 333; opposition to Speaker Hamilton, 219, 223, 322; and paper currency, 215; and T. Penn's agenda, 226; and the 1742 election, 342–45
proprietors of Pennsylvania, insistence that quitrents be paid in sterling, 331–32
prostitution, 6, 534–38
Protestation Presented to the Synod of Philadelphia (Cross), 235
proto-feminism: and BF's LCP *Catalogue* annotations, 112; and BF's mother, 298; and feminine personae, 125–26, 136, 144, 147–48, 166–69, 548–49; and *Poor Richard's* proverbs, 198, 199–200; in *Reflections on Courtship and Marriage*, 528; in "The Speech of Miss Polly Baker," 545. *See also* women
Prouse, James, 68, 202, 359
Provincial Council, 290
public domain, 412–13
Puffendorf, Samuel, 100
Puritanism, New England, 23, 55, 313; influence on Franklin, 39, 429. *See also* Mather, Rev. Cotton

Purviance, Samuel, 375
Pyrrhonism, 238, 295–99, 548; BF ridicules, 156. *See also* skepticism
Pythagoras, 208

Quaker pacifism: and BF's loss of popularity in LCP, 110; and military defense, 110, 215, 229–30
Quaker Party (Delaware), 340–41
Quaker Party (Pennsylvania): and BF's party affiliations, 214, 322; elements oppose Speaker Hamilton, 219, 223, 322; and military defense/military spending, 15, 215, 228–31, 333, 334–36, 340–41, 350–51, 396; and T. Penn's agenda, 226; and Gov. Thomas, 334, 336–39
Quincy, Edmund, 21

Rabelais, François, 186
race, 124, 141–44
Ralph, James, 126, 316
Ramsay, Andrew Michael, *Les voyages de Cyrus*, 18
Randolph, Isham, 493
"Rattle-snake Herb," 461, 464, 465
Rawle, William, 102–5, 366, 367, 371
Ray, Catharine, 19–20
Ray, John, *Wisdom of God Manifested in the Works of the Creation*, 75
Read, Charles, Jr., 97
Read, Deborah, 7. *See also* Franklin, Deborah Read
Read, James, 20, 275–77, 399, 435, 437
Read, John (Deborah's brother), 309
Read, John (merchant), 336
Read, Sarah, 87
reality, 266, 295–99. *See also* Franklin, Benjamin, intellectual life, appearance vs. reality; truth
Reddish, Nicholas, 97
Redman, Thomas, 87
Redwood Library (Rhode Island), 118, 313

ACKNOWLEDGMENTS

A National Endowment for the Humanities grant and a sabbatical leave from the University of Delaware in the academic year 1994–95 allowed me to begin working full time that year on the biography. My research assistants during 1995–2004—Lisa Ray Herb Smith, Donna Lehmann, Amy Moreno, Rob LaRocke, Robert Klevay, Amy Moore, Rachel Mayrer, and Marina Fedosik—have read drafts of this volume for me. Forrest Lehman, my current research assistant, has helped at the final stages, especially with the indexing. My friends Kevin Hayes, Edward A. Nickerson, David S. Shields, Todd Richardson, and Paul M. Zall scrutinized portions of the volume. Professor I. Bernard Cohen read a version of Chapter 18. Professor Carla Mulford read the entire volume. Maggie Hassert has gone over the text with a red pen in hand. I have benefited from the suggestions of each. Jennifer H. Backer has been an excellent copyeditor. At the University of Pennsylvania Press, Erica Ginsburg, Associate Managing Editor, has carefully attended to the manuscript and its production; I am most grateful.

A number of authorities answered questions for me: Barbara Oberg and Ellen Cohn at *The Papers of Benjamin Franklin*; Whitfield J. Bell, Jr., Roy E. Goodman, and Rob Cox at the American Philosophical Society; and John Van Horn and James N. Green at the Library Company of Philadelphia. I am greatly indebted to Susan Brynteson, May Morris Director of Libraries, Linda L. Stein, associate librarian, and a succession of interlibrary loan librarians at the University of Delaware's Morris Library.

My indebtedness to past scholarship, especially to the published volumes of *The Papers of Benjamin Franklin*, is apparent throughout the text and notes.